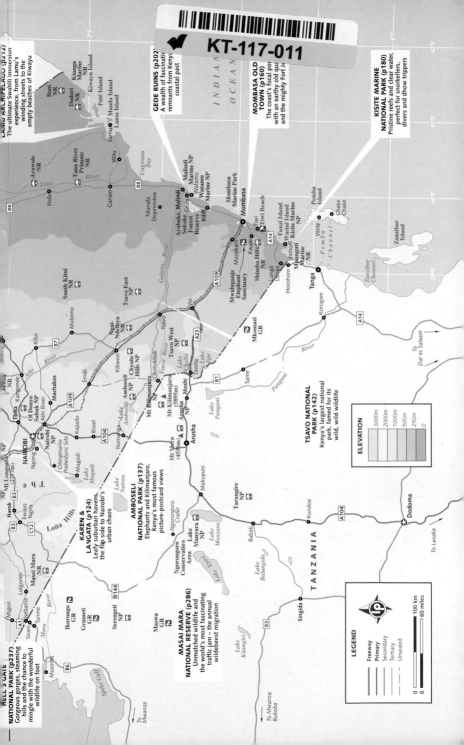

KT-117-011

MELL'S GATE
NATIONAL PARK (p237)
Gorgeous gorges, steaming hills and the chance to mingle with the wonderful wildlife on foot

LAMU ARCHIPELAGO (p212)
The ultimate Swahili immersion experience, from Lamu's winding streets to the empty beaches of Kiwayu

GEDE RUINS (p202)
A wealth of fascinating remnants from Kenya's coastal past

MOMBASA OLD TOWN (p160)
The coast's focal point, with an earthy old quarter and the mighty Fort Je...

KISITE MARINE NATIONAL PARK (p180)
Pristine reefs and clear water, perfect for snorkellers, divers and dhow trippers

KAREN & LANGATA (p124)
Leafy suburban havens, the flip side to Nairobi's urban chaos

AMBOSELI NATIONAL PARK (p137)
Elephants and Kilimanjaro, Kenya's most famous picture-postcard views

MASAI MARA NATIONAL RESERVE (p286)
Unmatched wildlife and the world's most fascinating traffic jam – the annual wildebeest migration

TSAVO NATIONAL PARK (p142)
Kenya's largest national park, famed for its wild, wild wildlife

INDIAN OCEAN

TANZANIA

ELEVATION

	3000m
	2000m
	1000m
	500m
	250m
	0

LEGEND

Freeway
Primary
Secondary
Tertiary
Unsealed

0   100 km
0   60 miles

Destination Kenya

For many people, Kenya is quite simply Africa in microcosm. East Africa's premier tourist destination really does seem to have it all: wildlife and nightlife, cities and beaches, mountains and deserts, traditional cultures and modern arts, all couched in a range of landscapes as staggering in their diversity as they are stunning in their appearance. There are a million different reasons to come here, and picking just one is nigh on impossible.

The classic image of a safari savanna is perhaps the single key selling point for Kenya's tourist industry, and, with all the famous fauna, no keen animal-spotter should go home disappointed. However, clued-up visitors face an infinite choice of alternative settings and activities, from trekking the glacial ridges of Mt Kenya to kitesurfing off the white sands of the Indian Ocean coast, and much more besides.

This sheer diversity is something to be relished, and is by no means limited to the natural surroundings. The people, too, represent a wide cross-section of everything that is contemporary Africa, and everyday life brings together traditional tribes and urban families, ancient customs and modern sensibilities. Setting the world to rights with the locals is just one more small pleasure that comes with the culture.

Finally, sooner or later you'll look up at the starry skies and feel Africa all around you, living, breathing and fuelling a thousand dreams. Whatever your mental image of the continent, Kenya will provide a crucial part of the picture, and it's a microcosm not to be missed.

MITCH REAR

Peoples & Cultures

Encounter the nomadic, pastoral Turkana people (p50) of Loyangalani

Maasai warriors (p47) perform the traditional numba dance, Masai Mara National Reserve

OTHER HIGHLIGHTS

- Take in the atmosphere while riding a matatu through the streets of Nairobi (p95).
- Immerse yourself in the rich culture of the Swahili people (p50).
- Visit the beautifully decorated Hindu and Sikh temples in Mombasa (p154).

A group of young girls attend Sunday School class in Nairobi (p95)

Deserts, Lakes & Mountains

GRANT DIXON

Dawn touches Nelion (5188m) at Mt Kenya National Park (p261)

White pelicans, spoonbills and lesser flamingoes congregate in Lake Nakuru National Park (p243)

MITCH REARDON

OTHER HIGHLIGHTS

▪ Witness the fascinating spectacle of the wildebeest migration at Masai Mara National Reserve (p286).

▪ Be amazed by the vast Shetani lava flows (p142) in southern Kenya.

Experience the desert life of the Gabbra tribe in Kalacha (p338)

ARIADNE VAN ZANDBEF

Islands & Beaches

ARIADNE VAN ZANDBERGEN

Palm trees shade a small mosque on Kipungani beach (p225)

ARIADNE VAN ZANDBERGEN

Explore Lamu Archipelago (p212)
in a traditional dhow

OTHER HIGHLIGHTS

- Discover the imposing Fort Jesus in Mombasa (p157).
- Soak up the captivating architecture and culture at Lamu town (p213).

Be tempted by the beautiful white sand and clear warm waters at Watamu (p198)

ANDERS BLOMQVIST

Activities

Get the blood pumping with a hike around Liki North, Mt Kenya (p261)

KARL LEHMANN

RICHARD M

Go wildlife spotting on safari in Masai Mara National Reserve (p286)

A balloon safari over Masai Mara National Reserve is a breathtaking experience (p286)

CHRISTER FREDRIKS

OTHER HIGHLIGHTS

- Find tranquility as you snorkel among the coral at Kisite Marine National Park (p180).
- Have a close encounter with a giraffe at Langata Giraffe Centre (p128).
- Go rock-climbing in the dramatic Hell's Gate National Park (p237).

Contents

The Authors 12

Getting Started 14

Itineraries 18

Snapshot 24

History 25

The Culture 35

Tribes of Kenya 43

Environment 51

Safaris 59

Wildlife Guide 73

Food & Drink 89

Nairobi 95
History 96
Orientation 96
Information 96
Dangers & Annoyances 101
Sights 104
Activities 106
Tours 107
Festivals & Events 107
Sleeping 107
Eating 111
Drinking 116
Entertainment 117
Shopping 119
Getting There
& Away 119
Getting Around 121

Around Nairobi 123
NAIROBI'S SOUTHERN
OUTSKIRTS 124
Karen & Langata 124
Ngong Hills 130
SOUTH OF NAIROBI 131
Olorgasailie Prehistoric
Site 131
Lake Magadi 131
Athi River 131
Machakos 132
NORTH OF NAIROBI 133
Kiambu 133
Limuru 133

Southern Kenya 135
Bissel 136
Namanga 137
Amboseli National Park 137
Kimana Wildlife Sanctuary 139
Loitokitok 140
Makindu 140
Chyulu Hills National Park 140
Shetani Lava Flow & Caves 142
Tsavo National Park 142
Voi 147
Around Voi 148
Taveta 150
Lake Challa 150

The Coast 151
MOMBASA 154
SOUTH OF MOMBASA 169
Shelly Beach 169
Shimba Hills National
Reserve 169
Mwaluganje Elephant
Sanctuary 170
Tiwi Beach 170
Diani Beach 172
Between Diani Beach
& Funzi Island 179
Funzi Island 179
Shimoni & Wasini Island 179
Lunga Lunga 181
NORTH OF MOMBASA 181
Nyali Beach 182
Bamburi Beach 184
Shanzu Beach 194
Mtwapa 195

Kikambala & Vipingo 195
Kilifi 196
Watamu 198
Arabuko Sokoke
Forest Reserve 201
Gede Ruins 202
Malindi & Around 205
Marafa Depression 212
Tana River 212
LAMU ARCHIPELAGO 212
Lamu 213
Around Lamu 222
Manda Island 225
Paté Island 226
Kiwayu Island 228

Rift Valley 229

Longonot National Park 231
Mt Susua 231
Naivasha 231
Lake Naivasha 233
Hell's Gate National Park 237
Naivasha to Nakuru 238
Nakuru 239
Around Nakuru 242
Lake Nakuru National Park 243
North to Marigat 245
Lake Bogoria National
Reserve 246
Lake Baringo 247

Central Highlands 251

ABERDARES 253
Nyeri & Around 253
Aberdare National Park 256
Nyahururu
(Thomson's Falls) 259
**MT KENYA NATIONAL
PARK** 261
Information 261
Safety 261
Clothing & Equipment 262
Guides, Cooks
& Porters 263
Sleeping 264
Eating 264
Organised Treks 264
The Routes 265
AROUND MT KENYA 269
Naro Moru 270
Nanyuki 272
Around Nanyuki 274
Meru 275
Meru National Park 277

Chogoria 279
Embu 280
Mwea National Reserve 281
Ol Donyo Sabuk
National Park 281
Thika 282

Western Kenya 283

MASAI MARA 285
Narok 285
Masai Mara National
Reserve 286
LAKE VICTORIA 290
Kisumu 290
Lake Victoria's South Shore 296
Ruma National Park 297
Thimlich Ohinga 297
Mbita & Rusinga Island 297
Mfangano Island 298
WESTERN HIGHLANDS 298
Kisii 299
Kericho 300
Kakamega 303
Kakamega Forest
Reserve 304
Eldoret 306
West to Uganda 309
Kabarnet 309
Lake Kamnarok & Kerio
Valley National Reserves 309
Kitale 310
Mt Elgon National Park 312
Saiwa Swamp
National Park 315
Cherangani Hills 315

Northern Kenya 316

ISIOLO TO ETHIOPIA 319
Isiolo 319
Lewa Wildlife
Conservancy 321
Around Lewa Wildlife
Conservancy 322
Archer's Post 323
Samburu, Buffalo
Springs & Shaba
National Reserves 324
Matthews Range 327
Ndoto Mountains 327
Marsabit 327
Marsabit National Park 329
Moyale 330
**MARALAL TO TURKANA'S
EASTERN SHORE** 332
North to Maralal 332

Maralal 332
Around Maralal 335
Baragoi 335
South Horr 335
North to Lake Turkana 336
Loyangalani 336
Sibiloi National Park 338
Kalacha 338
**MARICH TO TURKANA'S
WESTERN SHORE** 338
Marich to Lokichar 339
Lodwar 340
Eliye Springs 342
Ferguson's Gulf 342
Central Island
National Park 343
North to
Lokichoggio 343

Directory 345

Accommodation 345
Activities 348
Business Hours 350
Children 351
Climate Charts 352
Courses 353
Customs 353
Dangers &
Annoyances 353
Disabled Travellers 355
Discount Cards 355
Embassies &
Consulates 355
Festivals & Events 357
Food 357
Gay & Lesbian
Travellers 357
Holidays 358
Insurance 358
Internet Access 359
Legal Matters 359
Maps 359
Money 360
Photography & Video 361
Post 362
Senior Travellers 363
Shopping 363
Solo Travellers 364
Telephone 365
Time 365
Toilets 365
Tourist Information 366
Visas 366
Women Travellers 367
Work 367

Transport   369

GETTING THERE & AWAY   369
Entering the Country   369
Air   369
Land   373
Sea & Lake   375
Tours   375
GETTING AROUND   376
Air   376
Bicycle   376
Boat   377
Bus   377
Car & Motorcycle   378
Hitching   382
Local Transport   382
Safaris   384
Train   384

Health   385

BEFORE YOU GO   385
Insurance   385
Recommended Vaccinations   386
Medical Checklist   386
Internet Resources   386
Further Reading   386
IN TRANSIT   387
Deep Vein Thrombosis (DVT)   387
Jet Lag & Motion Sickness   387
IN AFRICA   387
Availability & Cost of Health Care   387
Infectious Diseases   388
Traveller's Diarrhoea   392

Environmental Hazards   393
Traditional Medicine   393

Language   395

Glossary   400

Behind the Scenes   402

World Time Zones   404

Index   410

Map Legend   416

Regional Map Contents

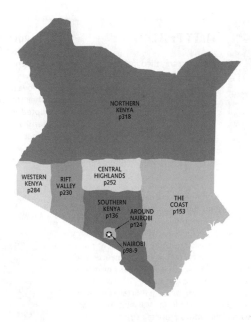

The Authors

TOM PARKINSON
Coordinating Author,
Nairobi, Around Nairobi, Southern Kenya, The Coast

Tom's association with Kenya began just across the border, gazing north from the Serengeti. As co-author on the previous edition of this book he covered 10,000km in the west and north. Second time around, the delights of Nairobi and the coast conspired to give him another perspective on Kenya, from nightclubs and Swahili ruins to barracuda teeth and charity dinners, with a few new scars to show for it. Having worked extensively in North and Central Africa for Lonely Planet, Tom is no stranger to potholes, predators and pit latrines, but finds Kenya keeps giving him reasons to come back.

My Favourite Trip

As alluring as the wilderness always is, Kenya's sheer variety gets me every time. Once I've had my fill of good food in Karen (p129) and late nights in Nairobi (p116), it's time to head down to steamy Mombasa (p154), taking the Namanga border route to pass through the Ngulia Hills in Tsavo West (p143). For pure escapism I'd have to head south to Funzi Island (p179), but otherwise it's a leisurely meander north towards Lamu (p212), my all-time favourite tropical island and Swahili paradise. And if all the dhows, juice and seafood get too much, a short flight and a crowded matatu can take me to Mt Kenya (p261), for glaciers, rainforest and East Africa's best trekking. Spice of life? You betcha!

MATT PHILLIPS
The Rift Valley, Central Highlands,
Western Kenya, Northern Kenya

Matt first travelled in Kenya while on an independent journey that saw him cross 21 African nations en route from Cape Town to Ceuta (that wee Spanish enclave in northern Morocco). He knew he'd love it before his passport's first Kenyan stamp was even dry – moments after stepping over from Uganda, the lone cloud in a dark midnight sky erupted with lightning and flashed like a light bulb for what seemed like an eternity. Since then Matt's done his best to experience all that's supernatural about Kenya, whether crossing the bleak northern deserts, freezing his assets atop Mt Kenya, tracking hyenas in the Mara and, yes, getting soaked while nature puts on light shows.

My Favourite Trip

I'd start in Eliye Springs (p342), beneath the palms on Lake Turkana's gloriously isolated western shore. A long journey south sees me climbing through the lush Cherangani Hills (p315) en route to the heavenly cheese sanctuary of Eldoret (p306). With my tummy full, I head north to Turkana's eastern shore. Stopping at panoramic Lesiolo (p335) is mandatory, before I trade glances with striking Samburu tribespeople in South Horr (p335). I next head across Mt Kulal's unearthly shattered lava fields (p336) before the Jade Sea and Turkana tribes at Loyangalani (p336) take my breath away. From there I head east to climb Mt Marsabit (p327) and then south to trek within the Ndoto Mountains (p327).

CONTRIBUTING AUTHORS

Will Gourlay first fell for Kenya watching a sunset from the Ngong Hills. Subsequent jaunts to Lamu, Lake Turkana and the Western Highlands had him by turns exhausted, dusty and sunburnt, but always exhilarated. A *miraa*-chewing episode with Somali women in taffeta dresses only served to heighten his exhilaration... Will wrote the Snapshot (p24) and updated The Culture (p35), Food & Drink (p89) and Tribes of Kenya (p43) chapters. He is a commissioning editor in Lonely Planet's Melbourne office.

Dr Caroline Evans wrote the Health chapter (p385). Caroline studied medicine at the University of London and completed general practice training in Cambridge. She is the medical adviser to the Nomad Travel clinic, a private travel health clinic in London, and is also a GP specialising in travel medicine. She has been an expedition doctor for Raleigh International and Coral Cay expeditions.

Getting Started

Planning a trip to Kenya is a pleasure in itself: the country is so versatile it's virtually a blank canvas, catering equally for thrill seekers and sun seekers, budget backpackers and high-end high rollers, those who like it tough and those who just want to get going. Whatever you want to do here, you'll discover that it's pretty straightforward to sort yourself out on the ground – in fact, in many cases you'll find that advance planning is often trickier and less reliable than dealing with everything in person once you arrive.

WHEN TO GO

There are a number of factors to take into account when considering what time of year to visit Kenya. The main tourist season is January and February, when the weather is generally considered to be the best – many areas of the country are hot and dry during these months. It's also when you'll find the largest concentrations of birdlife on the Rift Valley lakes. At this time, the animals in the wildlife parks tend to congregate more around the watercourses as other sources dry up, making them easier to spot. However, the parks can get crowded and rates for accommodation generally go through the roof. Make sure you avoid Christmas and Easter unless you want to pay a fortune.

June to October could be called the 'shoulder season' (see p345), as the weather is still dry. During this period the annual wildebeest migration takes place, with thousands of animals streaming into the Masai Mara National Reserve from the Serengeti in July and October.

During the long rains (the low season, spanning from March to the end of May) things are much quieter, and you can get some good deals; this is also the case during the short rains from October to December. The rains generally don't affect your ability to get around unless you're right out in the sticks (although Amboseli National Park can be flooded); it's just that you may get rained on, especially in the Central Highlands and western Kenya.

If you're planning to visit Lamu, you might want to time your visit to coincide with the centuries-old Maulid Festival (see p218).

DON'T LEAVE HOME WITHOUT...

- Sunglasses and hat
- Binoculars
- Answers – on a range of topics, for discussions with inquisitive locals
- Patience – for everyday delays, especially on public transport
- Vaccination card, insect repellent and malaria prophylaxis
- Disposable nappies – if you actually have kids
- Common sense – for avoiding scams (p354)
- Lots of camera film
- Space in your bag – for oversized souvenirs
- Entry visa – if you're feeling organised you could also arrange this before setting out, though they are available on arrival at most airports and land borders. See p366 for full details.

COSTS & MONEY

Travelling in Kenya can cost as much or as little as you like, depending on what kind of standards you're happy with. In general, for the midrange traveller staying in small hotels with a decent level of comfort, eating the occasional Western meal, using matatus and taxis, taking in the odd museum and treating yourself to a beer of an evening should come out in the region of KSh3000 per day. Budget travellers could get this down to as little as KSh800 by foregoing private bathrooms, eating in Kenyan canteens, walking or taking local buses and skipping the booze, while top-end types can find themselves paying anything from KSh8000 upwards for a taste of the high life. Accommodation is the biggest single expense, and staying in Nairobi or on the coast will push costs up sharply (see p345).

On top of this, you'll probably want to allow some extra cash for pricey tourist activities such as trekking, diving and other excursions. The biggest one-off outlay for most visitors will be visiting the national parks, whether on a safari or independently. Basic camping packages cost from US$70 per day (see p64); staying in lodges adds at least another US$50, while using air transport and visiting the country's most exclusive getaways could run over US$500! Package deals from Europe can offer good value out of season, especially if you want to stay around the coast.

TRAVEL LITERATURE

Reading up before you go is a great way to get a feel for Kenya – all kinds of foreign authors have written on the country, and the prospective visitor can choose from a wide range of perspectives on every facet of its culture.

Already a firm favourite among animal lovers and conservationists, *A Primate's Memoir: Love, Death and Baboons in East Africa,* by Robert M. Sapolsky, is an engaging account of a young primatologist's years working in Kenya.

Equally personal and a bit less serious at heart, David Bennun's entertaining *Tick Bite Fever* tells of the author's accident-prone childhood in Africa, complete with suicidal dogs and Kenya Cowboys.

For a more serious look at social and cultural issues, read *No Man's Land: an Investigative Journey Through Kenya and Tanzania,* by George Monbiot, which follows the fortunes of the region's nomadic tribes.

Bill Bryson turns his social conscience and trademark gentle humour on the region in his *African Diary,* concentrating on a seven-day trip to Kenya. All profits (and the author's royalties) go to CARE International.

Londoner Daisy Waugh provides a city girl's take on the thoroughly untouristy town of Isiolo in *A Small Town in Africa,* giving a more modern alternative to the many settlers' tales in print.

Increasingly hard to find but worth the effort, *Journey to the Jade Sea,* by John Hillaby, recounts this prolific travel writer's epic trek to Lake Turkana in the days before the Kenyan tourist boom.

Finally, whether you like her attitude towards the natives or not, *Out of Africa,* by Karen Blixen (Isak Dinesen), remains perhaps the single definitive account of the colonial experience in Africa.

INTERNET RESOURCES

Artmatters (www.artmatters.info) Information on arts and culture from Kenya and East Africa.
Destination Kenya (www.destinationkenya.com) Handy directory of hotels, safari operators and other companies offering tourist activities.
Jambo Kenya (www.jambokenya.com) A broad-based information website with lots of tourist information.

HOW MUCH?

Local matatu ride: KSh20

Plate of stew/
biryani/pilau: KSh120

Large juice: KSh60

Pair of *kangas:* KSh350

Taxi home: KSh400

LONELY PLANET INDEX

Litre of petrol/gas: KSh72

Litre of bottled water: KSh55

Bottle of Tusker: KSh80

Souvenir T-shirt: KSh1000

Sambusa (street snack): KSh10

TOP TENS

Books

Reading about Kenya could take a lifetime, with everything from fiction to memoirs and social analysis covering the country. These favourites encompass the broad spectrum of Kenyan writing and writing on Kenya. See p41 for more on local literature.

- *Mzungu Boy* (2005) Meja Mwangi
- *Petals of Blood* (1977) Ngugi wa Thiong'o
- *Flame Trees of Thika* (2000) Elspeth Huxley
- *I Laugh So I Won't Cry: Kenya's Women Tell the Stories of Their Lives* (2005) ed Helena Halperin
- *A Primate's Memoir* (2004) Robert M Sapolsky
- *The In-Between World of Vikram Lall* (2005) MG Vassanji
- *Tick Bite Fever* (2004) David Bennun
- *The Green Belt Movement: Sharing the Approach and the Experience* (2005) Wangari Maathai
- *Wildlife Wars: My Battle to Save Kenya's Elephants* (2002) Richard Leakey
- *The Tree Where Man Was Born* (1972) Peter Matthiessen

Films

Kenya's spectacular landscapes are a magnet for film-makers, serving as a backdrop for a thousand human stories. This selection highlights fact and fiction, bringing together Hollywood and Nairobi's disparate approaches to the medium. For more on the Kenyan film industry, see p42.

- *Nowhere in Africa* (2002) Director: Caroline Link
- *Enough is Enough* (2005) Director: Kibaara Kaugi
- *Safari ya Jamhuri* (Road to Freedom; 2003) Director: Wanjiru M Njendu
- *Africa, the Serengeti* (1994) Director: George Casey
- *The Constant Gardener* (2005) Director: Fernando Meirelles
- *Babu's Babies* (2003) Director: Christine Bala
- *The Oath* (2004) Director: Nathan Collett
- *14 Million Dreams* (2003) Director: Miles Roston
- *Born Free* (1966) Director: James Hill
- *Out of Africa* (1985) Director: Sydney Pollack

Photo Books

Kenya has provided a fertile field of inspiration for generations of photographers, and in many Nairobi bookshops you can't move for the piles of glossy pictorial tomes showcasing every aspect of the country's geographical and cultural marvels. These are just some of the best examples.

- *Africa Adorned* (1984) Angela Fisher
- *Shootback* (2000) ed Lana Wong
- *African Ark* (1990) Carol Beckwith and Angela Fisher
- *Maasai* (1990) Tepilit Ole Saitoti and Carol Beckwith
- *Turkana: Kenya's Nomads of the Jade Sea* (1997) Nigel Pavitt
- *African Visions: Diary of an African Photographer* (2001) Mirella Ricciardi
- *This Is Kenya* (2005) Jean Hartley
- *Journey Through Kenya* (1994) Mohammed Amin, Duncan Willets and Brian Tetley
- *Through Open Doors: A View of Asian Cultures in Kenya* (1983) Cynthia Salvadori
- *African Ceremonies* (1999) Carol Beckwith and Angela Fisher

Kenya Association of Tour Operators (www.katokenya.org) Contains the full list of KATO-approved member companies.
Kenya Meteorological Office (www.meteo.go.ke) Local and national weather forecasts.
Kenya Wildlife Service (www.kws.org) Up-to-date conservation news and detailed information on national parks and reserves.
Kenyalogy (www.kenyalogy.com) Tourist information and safari guide for visitors, with plenty of practical advice.
Kenyaweb (www.kenyaweb.com) An excellent and varied source of information on everything to do with Kenya.
Lonely Planet (www.lonelyplanet.com) Well, how could we not plug ourselves? Information on travelling to Kenya and elsewhere, travel news and the Thorn Tree bulletin board.
Magical Kenya (www.magicalkenya.com) The official website of the Kenya Tourism Board; has some good information on sights and activities.
National Museums of Kenya (www.museums.or.ke) Information on museums and projects across Kenya.
Nation Newspaper (www.nationmedia.com) Kenya's foremost newspaper has a very good website with news, information and regular features on tourist issues.

Itineraries

CLASSIC ROUTES

SUN, SURF & SWAHILI
Two Weeks/Mombasa to Lamu

The best place to start here is the coastal gateway of Mombasa, where exploring the city's **Old Town** (p160) is a must. You can then choose whether to head north or south; for this itinerary we're starting with the latter, as it makes a nice progression.

The first stop on the way down is quiet **Tiwi Beach** (p170), a tranquil white-sand paradise perfect for self-caterers. Just down the road, you can head on to **Diani Beach** (p172) for a taste of the more full-on resort experience, with all the activities you can handle.

At the far southern end, near the border with Tanzania, **Funzi** (p179) and **Wasini** (p179) Islands provide a dose of real, unspoilt coastal life, and also afford easy access to the excellent **Kisite Marine National Park** (p180).

On the way back north, detour off the main road to visit the densely forested **Shimba Hills National Reserve** (p169), home to the rare sable antelope, and the **Mwaluganje Elephant Sanctuary** (p170).

Once you've passed Mombasa and the northern beach strip, a stop at the charming small town of **Kilifi** (p196) is essential, if only to admire the spectacular creek views from the massive road bridge. From here you can also visit the **Arabuko Sokoke Forest Reserve** (p201) and **Gede ruins** (p202), two real highlights of the coast, en route to the historic town of **Malindi** (p205), now a popular resort centre.

Finally, at the end of the trail awaits the wonderful **Lamu archipelago** (p212), tropical paradise and Swahili heritage gem. As well as exploring the old town and taking the mandatory dhow trip, the much quieter **Paté** (p226) and **Kiwayu** (p228) Islands are well worth two or three days of your time.

This 1500km itinerary takes in all the major spots covered by most safari companies and ends up on the coast for a change of scene. It should take around three weeks, including travelling time, and can easily be broken down into separate sections, such as a five-day trip to the Masai Mara and Lake Nakuru.

Kiwayu Island
Paté Island
Lamu
Malindi
Gede
Arabuko Sokoke Forest Reserve
Kilifi
INDIAN OCEAN
Mwaluganje Elephant Sanctuary
Mombasa
Shimba Hills National Reserve
Tiwi Beach
Diani Beach
Funzi Island
Wasini Island
Kisite Marine National Park

CLASSIC KENYA   **Three Weeks/Nairobi to Mombasa**

For those who want to see the jewels in Kenya's tourist crown, this selection of popular parks brings together a wide variety of landscapes, all within easy reach of the country's two main international airports.

Starting in **Nairobi** (p95), as most people do, the first port of call is the world-renowned **Masai Mara National Reserve** (p286), possibly the definitive slice of safari Africa. It's no coincidence that this is the most popular park in Kenya, and the annual wildebeest migration is truly spectacular.

Take three days or so here, then it's north to **Lake Nakuru National Park** (p243), where one or two days is generally enough to make the most of this flamingo-packed lakeland.

From here the trail leads northeast to the **Samburu National Reserve** (p324), a dusty red contrast to the Mara savanna.

Take a couple of days here, then head to **Mt Kenya** (p261), Africa's second-highest mountain, where a decent trek will take up a good five to six days.

From the giddy heights of the mountains you can head to **Amboseli National Park** (p137), where the even higher peak of Kilimanjaro looms over the open plains.

Then it's a straightforward drive to **Tsavo West National Park** (p143) and on to **Tsavo East National Park** (p145), Kenya's largest and wildest wildlife parks. Together with the private ranches and conservancies around the outside of the parks, these are worth at least four days of your time.

Finally, head down the highway to the ancient Swahili port of **Mombasa** (p154). From here you can fly straight home or start a whole new journey, exploring the Kenyan coast.

The convenient north–south layout of the coastal road system makes this 500km trip very straightforward and completely flexible timewise. You could travel end to end in a few days, but two to three weeks gives you ample time to explore all the major sites.

ROADS LESS TRAVELLED

DESERT FRONTIERS   Three Weeks/Isiolo to Lokichoggio

Heading out into the wild is one of the great Kenyan experiences, and some of the tracks here are very unbeaten indeed – this is one itinerary where the journey is so much more than any single destination. The focal point of the trip is Lake Turkana, the vast lake that dominates the northwest corner of the country.

On the eastern side, the gateway to this region is the small town of **Isiolo** (p319), north of Mt Kenya. There are several good national parks and wildlife reserves in this area, and a side trip out to **Wamba** (p327), in the Matthews Range, is great for walkers.

Alternatively, you can plough straight in to the desert route and head up the rough road to **Marsabit** (p327), the dusty tribal centre of this remote area, which boasts a fine national park.

Assuming you're not tempted to hop over the border to Ethiopia at **Moyale** (p330), a real wild frontier, take the western loop to Turkana via **North Horr** (p337), heading for the tiny lakeside settlement of **Loyangalani** (p336), a base for trips into even more remote parts of the country.

From here the trail leads south again, passing all kinds of scenic zones and the stopover towns of **South Horr** (p335) and **Baragoi** (p335). It's worth stopping for a couple of days in **Maralal** (p332), to replenish supplies and sample the joys of camel trekking.

You could end the trip here, but for the full effect head up to the other side of Turkana, passing through the lush western area around **Marich** (p339) to reach sweltering **Lodwar** (p340) and the lovely lake shore at **Eliye Springs** (p342). The true hard core can even head up to **Lokichoggio** (p343) and gaze longingly towards the Sudanese border.

Depending on the kind of route you take, covering the full scope of this extended wilderness trip could clock up well over 2000km and take anything up to a month with stops.

WESTERN WETLANDS   Two Weeks/Naivasha to Narok

To the west of Nairobi lie some of Kenya's most fertile and scenic spots, characterised by bodies of water and often neglected by visitors in favour of the high-profile national parks.

An excellent place to start is **Lake Naivasha** (p233) in the Rift Valley, a popular freshwater lake with easy access to several national parks and scenic spots. Then it's an easy hop to **Lake Nakuru** (p243) and the smaller lakes **Bogoria** (p246) and **Baringo** (p247), with their wealth of birdlife.

From here, the road west leads past the **Lake Kamnarok** and **Kerio Valley National Reserves** (p309), perfect and little-explored territory for trekkers.

Depending on time, you can take the more direct Eldoret road or the longer Cherangani Hills loop to reach the agricultural town of **Kitale** (p310) and the lovely **Saiwa Swamp National Park** (p315), which is a real wetland treat.

Heading south now, the **Kakamega Forest Reserve** (p304) is an essential stop for walkers and birdlovers alike, and can justify a couple of extra days' stay if you have time. Then continue down the road to the region's main city **Kisumu** (p290), on the shore of Lake Victoria, for a few urban comforts.

Skirting the Winam Gulf, you'll reach the busy service town of **Kisii** (p299), a handy hub for Lake Victoria's small islands, and the tiny **Ruma National Park** (p297), a rarely visited gem.

At the far end of this south road is **Isebania** (p375), where you could cross into Tanzania. Otherwise, if you have a 4WD you can travel the hard way through the **Masai Mara** (p286), ending up in **Narok** (p285). From here you can head back to Nairobi or start the whole circuit again.

This two-week circuit takes in the best of Kenya's temperate western zone, from the Rift Valley to Lake Victoria, in a busy round trip of around 1500km. An extra week can give you more time for the major parks.

TAILORED TRIPS

NATIONAL PARKS: SAVANNA, FOREST & MOUNTAIN

If you have your own transport, it's possible to visit a wide selection of Kenya's parks in a month, starting from Mombasa and ending up in Nairobi (or vice versa).

Just south of Mombasa, **Shimba Hills National Reserve** (p169) is a fine slice of protected forest. As you leave the coast, the road bisects the **Tsavo National Park** (p142), the country's largest, and also skirts the less-established **Chyulu Hills National Park** (p140).

A short detour takes you through **Amboseli National Park** (p137), a perennial favourite, then go via Nairobi to reach the **Masai Mara National Reserve** (p286), the country's most popular safari spot.

North of the Mara, western Kenya holds several excellent parks, including **Kakamega Forest Reserve** (p304) and the **Saiwa Swamp National Park** (p315).

Heading back east you'll find **Lake Bogoria National Reserve** (p246) and the popular **Lake Nakuru National Park** (p243).

Entering the Central Highlands, **Aberdare National Park** (p256) is a good stop before heading north for **Samburu, Buffalo Springs and Shaba National Reserves** (p324) and the **Marsabit National Park** (p329).

Returning to Nairobi, go east round Mt Kenya to visit **Meru National Park** (p277) and the small **Ol Donyo Sabuk National Park** (p281), then finish up with the incongruously urban **Nairobi National Park** (p125).

FOOTSTEPS ACROSS THE LANDSCAPE

Keen walkers and trekkers should never be far from a promising path in Kenya, and a three-week circuit allows intensive exploration of some of the country's best trails.

Starting at the coast, **Arabuko Sokoke Forest Reserve** (p201) is crisscrossed with walking tracks and offers guided bird walks. Off the main Nairobi–Mombasa road, the **Sagala Hills** (p149) and **Taita Hills** (p149) also offer a plethora of possibilities away from the usual tourist routes.

South of Nairobi, the green and pleasant **Ngong Hills** (p130) are a prime rambling destination. Nearby, in the Rift Valley, **Longonot National Park** (p231) offers trekkers the chance to wander up Mt Longonot, while craggy **Hell's Gate National Park** (p237) is great to explore on foot.

Western Kenya has huge potential for serious trekkers, particularly on **Mt Elgon** (p312), by the Ugandan border. The **Cherangani Hills** (p315) are another prime area to get lost in for a couple of days or more.

Heading north, the **Ndoto Mountains** (p327) is a great remote mountain range, while Mt Marsabit provides the exercise in **Marsabit National Park** (p329).

And of course, finally, there's **Mt Kenya** (p261), the grandaddy of them all. Wherever else you walk, this one's essential!

ACTIVITIES: LAND, SEA & SKY

Fans of an active lifestyle are spoilt for choice here, and sampling all the options across the country could easily take up two weeks or more.

Diani Beach (p172), south of Mombasa, is a great place to start, with the full range of water sports plus other pastimes such as quad biking and forest walks.

Seaborne activities are popular along the rest of the coast as well. **Malindi** (p205) is the region's major deep-sea fishing centre, while **Wasini Island** (p179) offers superb diving and **Lamu** (p212) is perfect for dhow trips and windsurfing.

Heading inland, the Taita Discovery Centre, in **Rukinga Wildlife Conservancy** (p149), runs conservation programs for volunteers and visitors alike.

Due south of Nairobi, **Lake Magadi** (p131) makes an interesting detour to investigate the hot springs and picnic in the arid wastes.

Over to the west, **Hell's Gate National Park** (p237) is the best spot in the country for mountain biking, while the **Masai Mara National Reserve** (p286) specialises in balloon safaris.

You can also take to the air in the Central Highlands, at the gliding club in **Nyeri** (p254). Nearby, the **Aberdare National Park** (p256) offers excellent river fishing.

Finally, real adrenaline junkies can hit the rapids for some white-water rafting on the **Ewaso Ngiro River** (p350).

TRIBAL TOUR

If you're interested in meeting Kenya's fascinating tribal peoples, these are some good places to seek them out.

Just outside Nairobi, **Bomas of Kenya** (p124) provides a touristy but interesting overview of various tribal cultures.

Kenya's most famous tribe is the Maasai; you'll see them on a daily basis all over southern Kenya, but their true heartland is of course the **Masai Mara** (p285).

Out west is the domain of the influential Luo, centred in **Kisumu** (p290); little of their traditional culture remains.

The Pokot, found north of Kitale and the **Cherangani Hills** (p315), maintain their age-old pastoral lifestyles, including castle rustling!

On the other side of Lake Turkana, the Samburu are just as distinctive as the Maasai, and **South Horr** (p335) is a good place to encounter them. Further north you'll find the Turkana and Rendille, warrior cultures based around **Marsabit** (p327), and the tiny El-Molo tribe at **Loyangalani** (p336).

Back down in the Central Highlands, the Kikuyu are Kenya's largest tribal group, with their traditional homeland around **Mt Kenya** (p261).

Of the coastal Mijikenda peoples, the Digo, near **Diani Beach** (p172), are the easiest to visit. **Bombolulu Workshops** (p167) and **Ngomongo Villages** (p194), located north of Mombasa, showcase various tribes for tourists, and **Lamu old town** (p213) is the best surviving example of Swahili culture.

Snapshot

Kenya has long been regarded as an island of stability in Africa. That is not to say that things have been uneventful. After much international prodding and internal dissent through the 1990s, Kenya was able to finally embrace multiparty democracy and shrug off Daniel arap Moi's stranglehold on power in late 2002. Somewhat unexpectedly Moi resigned at the end of his term and the Kenyan electorate overwhelmingly rejected his designated successor by voting in Mwai Kibaki and the National Rainbow Coalition (Narc). The pundits heralded a new chapter in the saga of Kenyan politics – but things are not always as they seem.

Kibaki rode to victory as an anti-corruption champion, but little progress was made on that front. In February 2005 the UK High Commissioner to Kenya Sir Edward Clay lamented a familiar litany of ills that still plague the country: abuse of authority, conflict of interest, patronage, nepotism, and favouritism and corruption, both small- and large-scale, in all manner of guises. A corruption inquiry was promptly launched, resulting in several government ministers threatening to resign and the vice president admitting there was 'massive corruption' at senior levels of government.

Bearing this in mind, it is little wonder that long-held dream of economic prosperity has been unforthcoming. Kenya has fallen 20 places on the UN Human Development Index (HDI) over the past three years.

Nonetheless, it seems that the independent spirit of the Kenyan people cannot be repressed. In a blunt rebuke to Mr Kibaki in November 2005 the electorate voted against proposed constitutional changes. These would have been the first constitutional changes in Kenya for 40 years, with some observers claiming they would have handed Kibaki more power and led the country back into shady political territory of earlier times. During the campaign 'Yes' and 'No' camps came to be associated with bananas and oranges respectively in an effort to help illiterate voters. Never before had humble fruit assumed such political significance. The campaign was tense yet orderly, with Mr Kibaki congratulating the electorate for participating in such a historic occasion in a peaceful fashion. He then promptly dismissed his entire cabinet. Kenya watchers are no doubt puzzling over what may transpire from here.

While internal political life remains tumultuous, Kenya is still a regional heavy hitter. It has played a major role in the (thus far fruitless) international attempts to stabilise neighbouring Somalia, and after years of false starts, Kenya has finally joined hands with Tanzania and Uganda in a customs union – paving the way for full revival of the long-defunct East African Community.

Perhaps most indicative of Kenya's sense of self is its recently announced intention to host the 2016 Olympics. No African country has ever hosted the Olympics and Kenya has until to 2009 to prepare its bid. Despite internal ructions and the daily struggle that life entails for many, it seems Kenyans retain an innate self-confidence, a belief that things are on the improve and a desire to see their homeland take a prominent place on the world stage.

FAST FACTS

Population: 31.6 million

Total fertility rate: 3.47 children per woman

Population growth rate: 2.6%

Workforce engaged in agriculture: 75%

Highest point: Mt Kenya 5199m

Land boundaries: 3477km

Number of Kenyan deaths in the Boxing Day 2004 tsunami: one

Oldest town: Lamu (est 15th century)

Number of times Kenya has not won the Olympic steeplechase: none

History

THE BIRTHPLACE OF HUMANITY

Kenya is not just old, it's ancient, and the story of humanity may even have started here, way back through the murky mists of evolution and time. Thanks to some inquisitive poking around by the Leakey family around Lake Turkana, in the north of the country, and at Olduvai Gorge (Tanzania), the Great Rift Valley (p229) has been established as the 'cradle of humanity'. The Leakeys' discoveries of several hominid skulls, one of which is estimated to be 2½ million years old, radically altered the accepted theories on the origin of humans.

Before the East African digs, the generally accepted theory was that there were two species of proto-humans: the 'robust' hominids and the 'gracile' hominids, which eventually gave rise to modern humans. However, the Leakey discoveries suggested that there was a third species, *Homo habilis* (able man), and that it was this group that gave rise to modern humans.

Since then, the human family tree has gained several more branches, with the discovery of new species in central Africa, including *Kenyanthropus platyops* (flat-faced man), discovered in 2002 at Lake Turkana by one of the Leakey clan. Another recent discovery was of bones belonging to a six-million-year-old hominid, nicknamed 'Millennium Man', a strong contender for our oldest ancestor. Prehistory buffs can soak up the atmosphere and check out the myriad of animal fossils left on site at the Sibiloi National Park (p338).

'Prehistory buffs can soak up the atmosphere and check out the myriad of animal fossils left on site at the Sibiloi National Park'

EARLY SETTLEMENT

Over the millennia, this part of East Africa has been populated by peoples from all over the continent, from the Galla of northern Somalia to the San (formerly Bushmen) and Khoikhoi (formerly Hottentots) of South Africa. The first to arrive were the tall, nomadic, Cushitic-speaking people from Ethiopia, who began to move south around 2000 BC, basing themselves first at Lake Turkana and moving south as their livestock stripped the vegetation. A second group of pastoralists, the Eastern Cushitics, followed in around 1000 BC and occupied much of central Kenya.

The ancestors of most of the tribes that occupy Kenya today arrived from all over Africa from around AD 1000. The first immigrants were Bantu-speaking people from West Africa (who gave rise to the Gusii, Kikuyu, Akamba and Meru tribes, among others), occupying much of southern and western Kenya by the end of the 15th century. The Nilotic speakers, who gave rise to the Maasai, Luo, Samburu and Turkana tribes, came from the Nile valley in southern Sudan at the end of the 16th century. Although these were the biggest migrations, tribes continued to move into and out of Kenya right up to the beginning of the 20th century.

ARAB & PERSIAN TRADERS

While tribal migrations were going on in the interior, a non-African force was massing on the coast. Muslims from the Arabian Peninsula and Persia

TIMELINE	2,500,000 BC	2000 BC
	Early hominids inhabit the Rift Valley	The first Cushitic tribes arrive in Kenya

(now Iran) began to visit the coast from the 8th century AD onwards, as part of their annual trade migration around the Indian Ocean. Many set up trading posts along the seaboard, intermarrying with Africans and creating the culture that later became known as Swahili, which is still a distinct influence on the coast today. Slaves and ivory were Africa's primary commodity, but the Arab dhows also exported tortoiseshell, rhino horn and gold.

Before long there were Arab-Swahili city-states all along the coast from Somalia to Mozambique, acting as entrepôts for the trans-Indian Ocean trade; the remains of many of these settlements can be seen on the coast, most notably at Gede (p202). The communities were almost continually at war with each other for supremacy in the region, but these internecine squabbles were generally short-lived.

Arab-Swahili domination on the coast received its first serious challenge with the arrival of the Portuguese in the 16th century.

PORTUGUESE INVADERS

While the Spanish crown was busy backing expeditions to the Americas, the Portuguese were determined to break the Ottoman Turks' grip on trade with the Far East, particularly their dominance in the lucrative spice market. In 1498 Vasco da Gama stopped in at what is now Malindi on his way to India, scouting out the territory and leaving the navigational pillar that can still be seen on the coast (p207). In 1505, Dom Francisco de Almeida's armada staged a full-scale invasion, and they made short work of the city-states of Sofala, Kilwa (in Tanzania) and Mombasa before sailing on to India. The Portuguese then returned to sack Mombasa again in 1528.

Although they came to dominate the coast, the Portuguese experiment was never a great success. Collecting 'tributes' from the Swahili usually required brute force and all attempts to convert the Muslims to Catholicism were a dismal failure. Some states underwent an annual conversion when the Portuguese ships arrived, reverting to Islam as soon as the ships departed for Goa.

The Portuguese had every reason to target the spice trade – weight for weight, spices were more valuable than gold in Europe at the time.

In 1593 the Portuguese constructed Fort Jesus at Mombasa to give them a permanent presence in the region, but the fort changed hands dozens of times in rebellions throughout the 17th century. In response, the Portuguese mounted regular punitive expeditions, which normally involved sailing up the coast and bombarding the least-defended city-state with heavy artillery.

Although the Portuguese are widely blamed for the decline of the Arab-Swahili states from the 17th century onwards, evidence from the abandoned cities along the coast suggests that ultimately it was a combination of failing water supplies, disease and attacks by African tribes that eventually put paid to the Swahili hegemony.

The Portuguese grip on the East African coast was always tenuous and the end came in 1698, when Mombasa fell to Baluchi Arabs from Oman after a 33-month siege. A few token attempts were made to regain power, but by 1729 the Portuguese had left the Kenyan coast for good. Today the mighty Fort Jesus (p157) itself is one of the few surviving signs of their presence.

800	1000
Muslims from the Arabian Peninsula and Persia begin to visit the coast	Bantu peoples arrive from West Africa

OMANI DYNASTIES

The Omani Arabs remained in control of the East African coast until the arrival of the British and Germans in the late 19th century (and, nominally, right up until independence in 1963), and established their main base on Zanzibar, off the Tanzanian coast. Although they shared the same faith, the Swahili regarded them as just as much of a colonising force as the Portuguese, and there were numerous rebellions.

Eventually, Sultan Seyyid Said of Oman decided enough was enough and dispatched the Omani navy to bring the states of Mombasa, Paté and Pemba into line in 1822. As part of his East African empire, the sultan established huge clove plantations on Zanzibar, and the spice business soon became so profitable that he moved his entire court there in 1832. Simultaneously, the slave trade went into overdrive to supply workers for the spice plantations and the French coffee and sugar plantations on Mauritius and Réunion.

By 1800, more than 8000 slaves were passing through the Swahili slave markets every year. Perhaps four times as many died before ever reaching the markets.

Although native Africans stood little chance against the firearms of the Arabs, a handful of tribes waged a resistance war against the slavers. The leaders of these tribes included Manwa Sera, who besieged the Swahili stronghold of Kaze in modern-day Tanzania in the 1860s, and chief Mirambo, who accumulated a massive arsenal of guns and caused so much trouble at Kaze during the 1870s that, at one point, the sultan ceded all claim to the area.

BRITISH EAST AFRICA

While this was happening, Victorian public opinion thousands of miles away in Britain was calling for an end to the East African slave trade. Dr Livingstone's account of the massacre of 400 Bagenya people by slavers at Nyangwe, near Lake Tanganyika, finally forced the British government to play its hand. By using a mixture of knife-edge diplomacy and strong-arm tactics, Sultan Barghash of Zanzibar was forced to sign a treaty banning the slave trade in 1873.

With German expansion into Tanganyika (present-day Tanzania), an agreement was reached between the British and the Germans, granting the sultan a 16km-wide strip of the Kenyan coastline, which would remain under a British Protectorate. The treaty remained in place right up until independence, when the last Sultan of Zanzibar ceded the territory to the new government.

Although control of the coast was largely sewn up, the interior, especially the Rift Valley and the Aberdare highlands, was largely impregnable to outsiders due to the fearsome Maasai and other warlike tribes. A few explorers braved the Maasai heartland – including Gustav Fischer, a German whose party was virtually annihilated at Hell's Gate (p237) in 1882 – but most attempts to enter the Rift Valley were doomed to failure.

The united front of the Maasai began to crack in the late 19th century, following a brutal civil war between the Ilmaasai and Iloikop groups and the simultaneous arrival of rinderpest (a cattle disease), cholera, smallpox and famine. Because of this, the British were able to negotiate a treaty with Olonana (known today as Lenana), the *laibon* (chief or spiritual leader) of the Maasai, allowing them to march the Mombasa–Uganda railway line right through the heart of the Maasai grazing lands. On one

1498	**1505**
The first Portuguese explorers reach Malindi	Dom Francisco de Almeida's armada invades Kenya

level, the Maasai were just accepting the inevitable – their end-of-the-world myth spoke of an 'iron snake' that would one day crawl across their land. Ironically, this once-crucial line now has just two passenger services (p384), a far cry from its conception as the pride of East Africa.

WHITE SETTLEMENT

With the completion of the railway, the headquarters of the colonial administration was moved from Mombasa to the cooler small settlement of Nairobi, and white settlers began to occupy the fertile highlands north of Nairobi. Their interests clashed with those of the Maasai, prompting the colonial authorities to pressure Olonana into restricting the Maasai to two reserves, one on either side of the new railway. However, the white settlers soon wanted the northern reserve as well and, in 1910 and 1911, the Maasai who lived there were forced to trek south, despite Olonana's objections.

Red Strangers: the White Tribe of Kenya (CS Nicholls) has a different, unusually sympathetic perspective on colonialism, examining the history of Kenya's white settler population before and after independence.

Although the Maasai suffered the worst annexations of land, the Kikuyu, a Bantu tribe from the highlands around Mt Kenya and the Aberdares, came to nurse a particular grievance about their alienation from the land. Meanwhile, tribes who lived on poor agricultural land, such as the Luo and Luyha and the tribes of the northeast, were hardly affected at all by British settlement.

White settlement in the early years of the 20th century was led by Lord Delamere, a pugnacious gentleman farmer from Cheshire, England. Since he was not familiar with the land, its pests and its wildlife, his first ventures were disastrous. By 1912, however, Delamere and his followers had shifted to the highlands near Nairobi and established mixed agricultural farms, turning a profit for the colony for the first time and spurring other Europeans to follow suit. These first outposts, Naivasha (p233) and the Ngong Hills (p130), are still heavily white-settled areas today.

The colonial process was interrupted by WWI, when two thirds of the 3000 white settlers in Kenya formed impromptu cavalry units and went off in search of Germans in neighbouring Tanganyika. It resumed after the war, under a scheme where veterans of the European campaign were offered subsidised land in the highlands around Nairobi. The net effect was a huge upsurge in the white Kenyan population, from 9000 in 1920 to 80,000 in the 1950s.

KENYAN NATIONALISM

Meanwhile, the sense of grievance among Africans was growing stronger. The Kikuyu people spearheaded the movement to reclaim Kenya, led from the 1930s by Johnstone Kamau, later known as Jomo Kenyatta, who went on to become Kenya's first president. Kenyatta initially joined the East Africa Association, which was campaigning for land reform, better wages, education and medical facilities for Africans. Although it was official British policy to favour African interests over those of the settlers in the event of conflicts, it was hard for these interests to be heard in the whites-only legislative council. Kenyatta soon joined the more outspoken Kikuyu Central Association, which was subsequently banned for campaigning against white rule.

In 1929, with money supplied by Indian communists, Kenyatta sailed for London to plead the Kikuyu case with the British colonial secretary

1593	1729
The Portuguese construct Fort Jesus in Mombasa	Omani Arabs replace the Portuguese as coastal rulers

who, predictably, declined his invitation to a meeting. While in London, Kenyatta hooked up with a group called the League Against Imperialism, which took him to Moscow and Berlin, back to Nairobi and then back to London, where he stayed for the next 15 years. During this time, he perfected his oratory on the crowds in Trafalgar Square, studied revolutionary tactics in Moscow and built up the Pan-African Federation with Hastings Banda (who later became the president of Malawi) and Kwame Nkrumah (later president of Ghana).

By the time Kenyatta returned to Kenya in 1946, he was the leader of a bona fide Kenyan liberation movement. Using his influence as leader, he quickly assumed the top spot of the Kenya African Union (KAU), a pro-independence group that had considerable support from African war veterans who had been pressured into fighting for the British in WWII.

MAU MAU REBELLION

Although the colonial authorities made some concessions to the KAU, the main agitation for independence was going on underground. Tribal groups of Kikuyu, Maasai and Luo took secret oaths, which bound participants to kill Europeans and their African collaborators. The most famous of these movements was the Mau Mau, formed in 1952 by disenchanted Kikuyu people, which aimed to drive the white settlers from Kenya forever.

The first blow was struck early in 1953 with the killing of a white farmer's entire herd of cattle, followed a few weeks later by the massacre of 21 Kikuyu loyal to the colonial government. The Mau Mau rebellion had started. The government declared a state of emergency and began to gather the tribespeople loyal to them into 'protected villages', surrounded by barbed wire and booby-trapped trenches, primarily to keep the villagers from being recruited to the ranks of the Mau Mau revolutionaries.

Within a month of the rebellion, Kenyatta and several other KAU leaders were put on trial as the alleged leaders of the Mau Mau. Kenyatta was convicted on spurious evidence and sentenced to seven years in jail. The various Mau Mau sects came together under the umbrella of the Kenya Land Freedom Army, led by Dedan Kimathi, and staged frequent attacks against white farms and government outposts, including Treetops Lodge (p258), where Britain's Princess Elizabeth spent her last night before becoming queen.

By the time the rebellion ended in 1956 with the Mau Mau's defeat, the death toll stood at over 13,500 Africans (guerrillas, civilians and troops) and just over 100 Europeans (including 37 settlers) – fairly predictable numbers for the British Empire! Following the end of the rebellion, Dedan Kimathi was publicly hanged by a British colonel named Henderson, who was later deported from Kenya for crimes against humanity.

Upon his release in 1959, Kenyatta resumed his campaign for independence while under house arrest in Lodwar. Soon even white Kenyans began to feel the winds of change, and in 1960 the British government officially announced their plan to transfer power to a democratically elected African government. Independence was scheduled for December 1963, accompanied by grants and loans of US$100 million to enable the Kenyan assembly to buy out European farmers in the highlands and restore the land to the tribes.

The first major Kenyan film to tackle the thorny subject of the Mau Mau rebellion, Kibaara Kaugi's *Enough is Enough* is a fictionalised biopic of Wamuyu wa Gakuru, a Kikuyu woman who became a famed guerrilla fighter and rebel commander in charge of distributing rations.

1873	1887
British pressure ends the Arab slave trade	Work begins on the East African Railway

In the meantime, a division occurred in the ranks of the KAU between those who wanted a unitary form of government with centralised control in Nairobi, and those who favoured *majimbo*, a federal setup. The centralists renamed their party the Kenya African National Union (KANU), while the federalists split off to become the Kenya African Democratic Union (KADU). Kenyatta was released from house arrest in mid-1961 and assumed the presidency of the KANU.

The dark side of the British Empire in Kenya is the subject of not one but two controversial recent books: *Histories of the Hanged: The Dirty War in Kenya and the End of Empire*, by David Anderson, and *Britain's Gulag: The Brutal End of Empire in Kenya*, by Caroline Elkins.

Although some resistance by white settlers was inevitable, the run up to independence was surprisingly smooth. Over subsequent years, a few farms owned by white settlers were bought out by the government and divided up into small subsistence plots supporting 15 to 20 people. The experiment wasn't a great success; Kenyans regarded it as too little, too late, while white farmers feared that the trickle would soon turn into a flood. As Zimbabwe was to discover nearly 40 years later, the immediate effect of land redistribution was a significant decline in agricultural production, from which Kenya has never quite recovered.

The Mau Mau themselves didn't do too well out of their supposed victory either. Once independence had been achieved, Kenyatta declared that the rebellion was a 'disease' and outlawed the group, fearful of Kenyans on either side of the conflict seeking to settle old scores. This 'forgive and forget' policy persisted under Daniel arap Moi, and even today there are no memorials or monuments to mark the guerrillas' struggle, while veterans complain they are forgotten and neglected by the country they fought to save. However, this may change under the new government – President Kibaki is himself a Kikuyu, and one of his first acts on taking power was to repeal the old law banning the Mau Mau, suggesting that now, 50 years on, a reconciliation of this controversial chapter of national history may be possible.

INDEPENDENCE

With independence scheduled for 1963, the political handover began in earnest in 1962. The KANU and KADU formed a coalition government, but the coalition was abandoned after the first Kenyan elections in May 1963. Jomo Kenyatta became Kenya's first president on 12 December 1963, ruling until his death in 1978. Under Kenyatta's presidency, Kenya developed into one of Africa's most stable and prosperous nations. The opposition KADU party was voluntarily dissolved in 1964.

While Kenyatta is still seen as one of the few success stories of Britain's withdrawal from empire, he wasn't without his faults. Biggest among these were his excessive bias in favour of his own tribe and his escalating paranoia about dissent. Opponents of his regime who became too vocal for comfort frequently 'disappeared', and corruption soon became endemic at all levels of the power structure.

At the same time, the British kept a toehold in Kenya in order to provide a training ground for the British Army. Over the next 40 years, huge amounts of ordnance were lobbed around, much of it ending up unexploded in rural areas. In July 2002, the British government finally agreed to pay nearly UK£7 million in compensation to the hundreds of Maasai and Samburu tribespeople injured or killed after accidentally detonating unexploded bombs.

1920	1929
Kenya becomes a British colony	Pro-independence politician Jomo Kenyatta goes to London

THE 1980S

Kenyatta was succeeded in 1978 by his vice president, Daniel arap Moi. A Kalenjin, Moi was regarded by establishment power brokers as a suitable front man for their interests, as his tribe was relatively small and in thrall to the Kikuyu. Moi went on to become one the most enduring 'Big Men' in Africa, ruling in virtual autocracy for nearly 25 years. In the process, he accrued an incredible personal fortune; today many believe him to be the richest man in Africa.

Although Moi's regime was stable compared to the desperate situation in many surrounding countries, it was also characterised by nepotism, corruption, arrests of dissidents, censorship, the disbanding of tribal societies and the closure of universities, as well as the disruptive, sometimes violent activities of KANU Youth, the party's student body. Nyayo House (p101), the main government building and police headquarters in Nairobi, was known and feared throughout the country for the torture cells in its basement, where many opponents of the regime found themselves.

In 1982 KANU publicly banned opposition parties, leading to a military coup by the air force, which was promptly quashed by pro-government forces. In the run-up to the 1987 election, Moi introduced a new voting system and jailed opposition leaders without trial, ensuring that the sole candidate from the sole political party in the country won the election, and there's no prizes for guessing who that was!

After his 'win', Moi expanded the cabinet to fit in more of his cronies and rushed through constitutional reforms allowing him to dismiss senior judges and public servants without any redress. When dissenting politicians were arrested, Christian church leaders took up the call for change, supported by another outspoken critic of government nepotism, Professor Wangari Maathai (see p56), leader of the Green Belt Movement.

Sooner or later, something had to give.

THE 1990S

With the collapse of communism and the break-up of the Soviet Union it was no longer necessary for Western powers to prop up corrupt noncommunist regimes in Africa. Donors who had previously turned a blind eye to civil rights misdemeanours began calling for multiparty elections if economic aid was to be maintained. The multiparty movement gained huge grassroots support in Kenya.

In response, KANU Youth was mobilised to disrupt pro-democracy rallies and harass opposition politicians. Things came to a head on 7 July 1990 when the military and police raided an opposition demonstration in Nairobi, killing 20 and arresting politicians, human-rights activists and journalists.

The rally, known thereafter as Saba Saba ('seven seven' in Swahili), was a pivotal event in the push for a multiparty Kenya. The following year, the Forum for the Restoration of Democracy (FORD) party was formed, led by Jamagori Oginga Odinga, a powerful Luo politician who had been vice-president under Jomo Kenyatta. FORD was initially banned and Odinga was arrested, but the resulting outcry led to his release and, finally, a change in the constitution that allowed opposition parties to register for the first time.

The stories of some of the torture victims held at Nyayo House are told in the haunting 2004 documentary *Walking Shadows*, directed by Ndungi Githuki.

1946	1953
Jomo Kenyatta returns to Kenya	The Mau Mau rebellion starts

Faced with a foreign debt of nearly US$9 billion and blanket suspension of foreign aid, Moi was pressured into holding multiparty elections in early 1992, but independent observers reported a litany of electoral inconsistencies. Just as worrying, about 2000 people were killed during ethnic clashes in the Rift Valley, widely believed to have been triggered by KANU agitation. Nonetheless, Moi was overwhelmingly re-elected.

After the elections, the KANU bowed to some Western demands for economic reforms, but harassment of opposition politicians continued. The 1997 election was also marred by violence and rioting, particularly during the Saba Saba anniversary rally. Again, mysterious provocateurs stirred up ethnic violence, this time on the coast. European and North American tour companies cancelled their bookings and around 60,000 Kenyans lost their jobs. Moi was able to set himself up as peacemaker, calming the warring factions and gaining 50.4% of the seats for KANU, compared to the 49.6% won by the divided opposition parties.

The scene was set for a confrontational parliament, but in a trademark Moi manoeuvre, the KANU immediately entered into a cooperative arrangement with the two biggest opposition parties, the Democratic Party (DP) and the National Development Party (NDP). Other seats were taken by FORD-Kenya and its various splinter groups.

While all this was going on, Kenya was lashed first by torrential El Niño rains and then by a desperate drought that continued right up to 2000, causing terrible hardship in rural areas.

Preoccupied with internal problems, Kenya was quite unprepared for the events of 7 August 1998. Early in the morning, massive blasts simultaneously ripped apart the American embassies in Nairobi and Dar es Salaam in Tanzania, killing more than 200 people. The effect on Kenyan tourism, and the economy as a whole, was devastating. During the next four years, however, coastal businesses slowly moved to rebuild the tourist industry, helped in part by Italian tour operators, who filled the gap left by American, British and German companies.

Further terrorist activity shook the country on 28 November 2002, when suicide bombers slammed an explosives-laden car into the lobby of the Paradise Hotel at Kikambala, near Mombasa. Moments before, missiles were fired at an Israeli passenger plane taking off from Mombasa's airport. Al-Qaeda subsequently claimed responsibility for both acts.

Despite a slump in tourism immediately after the attacks, the impact has been nowhere near as great as in 1998, and visitor numbers on the coast are now as healthy as ever. However, recent worldwide events have reawakened fears of terrorism, and there was widespread controversy when the press reported a shoot-to-kill order for terror suspects supposedly issued by National Security minister John Michuki. In a country with a significant Muslim population, it's small wonder that a jittery atmosphere prevails around these issues.

Just in case he was in any doubt about his popularity by the end of his regime, outgoing president Moi was pelted with mud during his final presidential speech!

AND IT'S GOODBYE FROM MOI

In June 2001, the KANU entered into a formal coalition government with the NDP and DP, creating a formidable power base for the ruling party. However, with Moi's presidency due to end in 2002, many feared that Moi would alter the constitution again. This time, though, he announced his

1963	1978
Kenya gains independence; Kenyatta becomes president	Kenyatta dies; Moi assumes presidency

LEAKEY POLITICS

Of all the famous names in Kenyan public life, one family crops up time and time again: the Leakeys. As if it wasn't enough to discover missing links in humankind's evolutionary chain, publish over 100 books and articles and single-handedly reform the Kenya Wildlife Service, patriarch Richard Leakey has played a pivotal role in national politics for years, despite losing both legs and enduring beatings in the course of his work.

Leakey entered the political arena in 1994 by creating a new opposition party called Safina, which contested the national elections on an anti-corruption ticket. Despite its reformist agenda, Safina was unable to allay the nation's unease about white men being involved in politics and polled just six seats.

After this disappointing performance, Leakey returned to his job as head of the KWS, but in 1999 President Moi unexpectedly appointed his erstwhile opponent – a man he once described as the 'Antichrist' and an 'atheistic colonial' – to the Head of the Civil Service. The appointment was probably a sweetener for the International Monetary Fund (IMF), who refused to lend the government money unless it adopted widespread reforms, but it did allow Leakey to weed out some of the corrupt old guard.

The anti-corruption purge, though, was only able to go so far before it hit an impassable wall. The most prominent corruption case, the Goldenberg Scandal – an incredible KSh20 billion compensation scam – threatened to implicate both the government and the nation's duty-free shops. The anti-corruption unit was wound down in 2001, and Leakey stepped down in March of that year, returning to his old job at KWS. The IMF promptly re-imposed its moratorium on aid to Kenya.

These days Leakey is not so active in national politics, but he still speaks and writes frequently on a whole range of topics, enjoying an unrivalled status as Africa's most prominent palaeontologist, environmentalist, conservationist and political commentator. With his daughter Louise following the academic family path, you can be sure that Kenya hasn't heard the last of the Leakeys just yet.

For more on Kenya's great white dynasty, www.leakey.com charts the fortunes of the family over 100 years in East Africa.

---

intention to retire – on a very generous benefits package – with elections to be held in December 2002.

Moi put his weight firmly behind Uhuru Kenyatta, the son of Jomo Kenyatta, as his successor. He even went as far as to fire vice-president George Saitoti for refusing to support Kenyatta's nomination. Meanwhile, 12 opposition parties (including FORD-Kenya, FORD-Asili, the National Party of Kenya and Saba Saba-Asili) as well as several religious groups united under the umbrella of the National Alliance Party of Kenya (NAK), an organisation that was later known as the National Rainbow Coalition (Narc). Presidential candidate Mwai Kibaki was the former head of the Democratic Party.

Although the party was initially dogged by infighting, within weeks the opposition transformed itself into a dynamic and unified political party. When the election came on 27 December 2002, it was peaceful and fair, and the result was dramatic: a landslide two-thirds majority for Mwai Kibaki and Narc. Despite being injured in a car accident while campaigning, Kibaki was inaugurated as Kenya's third president on 30 December 2002.

President Moi's retirement package, which included several private jets, was eagerly supported by opposition MPs – they were concerned that if it wasn't lavish enough he might stay in power.

1990	1998
Violence at Saba Saba rally forces multiparty elections	Terrorist attacks shake Nairobi and Dar es Salaam

A NEW ERA?

For more on Kenya's
fossil finds look up www
.leakeyfoundation.org.
Members can even sign
up for trips with the
Leakeys themselves.

The optimism that swept Narc into power faded fast, and Kibaki's brave new democracy has been plagued by a constant stream of party infighting, accusations of corruption and economic problems. Even his own wife has had several high-profile brushes with the media. Most Kenyans still support the president himself, but there is a widespread perception that he is too much of a 'quiet man', unwilling to speak up on important issues while his government runs amok around him.

Above all, the path to reform has been slower and more tortuous than many people had hoped, leading to dissatisfaction and an increasing tendency to blame the government for the country's ills. The year 2005 was another uncomfortable one for Kibaki, who faced criticism over his handling of the national housing crisis, the Tom Cholmondeley murder case and the civil service strikes, where thousands of bureaucrats were sacked for taking strike action over pay and conditions.

Some progress has certainly been made since 2002 – you only have to look at the new matatu regulations and omnipresent anti-corruption signs to see the efforts being made. However, security remains a worrying issue, locals complain that the cost of living has almost doubled, and it's feared that some politicians are trying to line their pockets in anticipation of losing their seats in the next election. The new constitution promised for 2003, a highly symbolic component of Narc's election platform, has been bogged down in discussions, disagreements and committees and seems no nearer to fruition, reinforcing the general disillusion.

With elections due to occur once again in 2007 and an energetic Uhuru Kenyatta at the head of the newly regrouped KANU – strengthened by their time in opposition and backed by the increasingly frail Moi – the next few years will be an interesting time in Kenyan politics, and Kibaki certainly has plenty of challenges still to come.

2002	2005
Moi retires; Mwai Kibaki wins national elections	Strikes, shootings, scandals – business as usual?

The Culture

THE NATIONAL PSYCHE

It's fair to say that there is not a great sense of national consciousness in Kenya. Many residents of Kenya are more aware of their tribal affiliation than of being a 'Kenyan' – this is one of the more fascinating aspects of Kenyan life, but the lack of national cohesion undoubtedly holds the country back.

This focus on tribe, however, is usually accompanied by an admirable live-and-let-live attitude, such that only on rare occasions do tribal animosities or rivalries spill over into violence. In fact, Kenyans generally approach life with great exuberance. Be it on a crowded matatu, in a buzzing marketplace or enjoying a drink in a bar, you cannot fail to notice that Kenyans are quick to laugh and are never reluctant to offer a smile. Theirs is a very happy-go-lucky approach to life, despite the fact that many of them live in dire economic circumstances.

Kenyans, too, are extremely gregarious. Rare is the occasion when you will see a lone Kenyan. At the slightest sign of activity a crowd will gather, from the smallest child to the most self-important businessman who happens along. Passers-by become onlookers – events are observed and participated in and, before long, pundits will be offering their version of proceedings and their opinions on all and sundry. This inclusivity often extends to others – any traveller who is willing to be asked to participate in a spontaneous dance or a game of football.

This willingness to participate in life as it happens is perhaps a reflection of the casual approach to time. You will be doing well to press a Kenyan into rushing anything. As is the case for many Africans, Kenyans tend to find that they have a lot of time on their hands so they don't see the need to do anything particularly urgently. The oft-heard maxim 'any time is chai time' is indicative of the Kenyan attitude that few things are so pressing that you needn't sit down and have a chat and a cup of chai before getting on with the job.

Education is of primary concern to Kenyans. Literacy rates are around 85% and are considerably higher than in any of the country's neighbours. Although education isn't compulsory, the motivation to get an education is huge, and you'll see children in school uniform everywhere in Kenya, even in the most impoverished rural communities.

Despite their often exuberant and casual approach, Kenyans are generally quite conservative, and are particularly concerned with modesty in the way they dress. T-shirts and shorts are almost unheard of and while foreign men may *just* be able to pull it off, you may feel like the only person at the wedding who came in casual dress! Shirts are an obsession for Kenyan men and almost everyone wears one, often with a sweater or blazer.

As Kenya undergoes a slow process of modernisation, tradition and modernity are locked in an almighty struggle. This produces some intriguing sights – Samburu nomads in the arid north sporting digital watches alongside their traditional beads, wideboys in traditional Lamu sporting nylon dreads and Rasta caps (amid the *bui-buis* and headscarves) – but inevitably such a process results in the marginalisation of some elements of society. This is particularly the case as urbanisation happens apace. Kenya has its fair share of poverty, alienation and urban overcrowding, but even in the dustiest shanty towns life is lived to the full.

'You cannot fail to notice that Kenyans are quick to laugh and are never reluctant to offer a smile'

LIFESTYLE

Tribe may be important in Kenya, but family is paramount. Particularly as the pace and demands of modern life grow, the role of the extended family has become even more important. It is not unusual to encounter Kenyan children who are living with aunts, uncles or grandparents in a regional town while their parents are working a desk job in Nairobi or working at a resort in Watamu. Nonetheless, filial bonds remain strong – affection is doled out as equally to one's nieces or nephews as to one's own children – and the separation that brings about such circumstances in the first place is without exception a result of a parent's desire to capitalise on opportunities for their family and their children.

The strength of the family in Kenya is mirrored in the community. Life is generally played out in the streets and communal places. There is no such thing as day care for young Kenyans. You will inevitably encounter the archetypal African scene where a range of children of different ages, usually with at least one older sister clutching a younger sibling on her hip, congregate and observe the hustle and bustle of daily life. This happens across Kenya, from coastal communities to villages in the Central Highlands to the shanty towns in Nairobi. And even as urbanisation happens and traditional community structures are fractured, street life remains lively. In any town of any size the afternoon rush hour is always a spectacle – it seems that all the world is afoot as they head home past street stalls and wandering pedlars and the dust rises gently into the coppery African twilight.

For all this, as Kenya gains a foothold in the 21st century it is grappling with ever-increasing poverty. Once categorised as a middle-income country, Kenya fell to be a low-income country, with the standard of living falling drastically from 2002 to 2005. In the UN's 2005 Human Development Report Kenya was ranked at 154 of 177 countries, a drop of 20 places from the previous report in 2002. The Kenyan government said it was not surprised by and indeed 'welcomed' the findings, claiming, rather obtusely, that the report would allow it to now develop policies to address the situation.

POPULATION

Kenya's population in 2001 was estimated at 30,765,900. The population growth rate, currently at around 2.6%, has slowed in the last few years due to the soaring incidence of HIV/AIDS, which now infects 15% of adults.

According to 2001 UN figures, life expectancy in Kenya is 52 years, although some sources place it as low as 47, due to the effects of HIV/AIDS. Only 42% of the population has access to clean drinking water but 87% are now thought to have access to adequate sanitation. The infant-mortality rate is 65 per 1000 births (a marked increase on the 1997 figure) and 51% of the population is aged under 18. A sign of growing poverty in rural regions is migration to urban areas, where 33% of all Kenyans now live, many of them in squalid shanty towns.

SPORT

Football (soccer) is a big deal in Kenya. People are nuts about it, and the big teams draw big crowds. Harambee Stars, AFC Leopards and Mathare United are among the best teams in the Kenyan Premiership. The grounds and pitches are not on a par with those in Europe, but the action is fast, furious and passionate – passion that at times spills out onto the terraces. Tickets to a game cost between KSh300 and KSh600 and it's quite an experience. Check out the *Daily Nation* for fixtures. Kenyans, too, seem

---

Kenya has close to 550,000 AIDS orphans, and an estimated 78,000 children living with HIV/AIDS.

to have a national obsession with the English premiership league. Every Kenyan supports either Arsenal, Man U or Liverpool, even if they can't name a single Kenyan player.

Kenyan long-distance runners are among the world's best, although much of their competitive running takes place outside the country. Even trials and national events in Kenya sometimes fail to attract these stars, despite these events being flagged in the press well in advance. **Moi Stadium** (Thika Rd), outside Nairobi, is a popular venue for events.

The annual **East African Safari Rally** (www.eastafricansafarirally.com) is a rugged 3000km rally – which has been held annually since 1953 – passing through Kenya, Uganda and Tanzania along public roadways, and attracting an international collection of drivers with their vintage (pre-1971) automobiles. If you're here, the spectacle is worth seeking out.

MULTICULTURALISM

Kenya's population is made up almost entirely of Africans, with small (although influential) minorities of Asians (about 80,000), Arabs (about 30,000) and Europeans (about 30,000).

Africans

Kenya is home to over 70 tribal groups. The most important distinguishing feature between the tribes is language. The majority of Kenya's Africans fall into two major language groups: the Bantu and the Nilotic. The Bantu people arrived in East Africa from West Africa after 500 BC, and include the Kikuyu, Meru, Gusii, Embu, Akamba and Luyha, as well as the Mijikenda, who preceded the Swahili in many parts of the coast.

Nilotic speakers migrated into the area from the Nile Valley some time later. This group includes the Maasai, Turkana, Samburu, Pokot, Luo and Kalenjin, which, together with the Bantu speakers, account for more than 90% of Kenya's African population. The Kikuyu and the Luo are by far the most numerous groups, and between them hold practically all the positions of power and influence in the country.

A third language grouping, and in fact the first migrants into the country, are the Cushitic speakers. They occupy the northeast of the country and include such tribes as the El-Molo, Somali, Rendille and Galla.

On the coast, Swahili is the name given to the local people who, although they have various tribal ancestries, have intermarried with Arab settlers over the centuries and now have a predominantly Arabic culture.

See Tribes of Kenya (p43) for more details on the major groups and their diverse cultures.

Since 1968, Kenya has won gold in the Olympic steeplechase in every Games the country has competed in. In the 2004 Olympics Kenya took out gold, silver and bronze medals.

Asians

India's connections with East Africa go back to the days of the spice trade, but the first permanent settlers from the Indian subcontinent were indentured workers, brought here from Gujarat and the Punjab by the British to build the Uganda Railway. After the railway was finished, the British allowed many workers to stay and start up businesses, and hundreds of *dukas* (small shops) were set up across the country.

Asian numbers were augmented after WWII and the Indian community came to control large sectors of the East African economy. However, few gave their active support to the black nationalist movements in the run-up to independence, despite being urged to do so by India's prime minister, and were hesitant to accept local citizenship after independence. This earned the distrust of the African community, who felt the Indians were simply there to exploit African labour.

Although Kenya escaped the anti-Asian pogroms that plagued Uganda during Idi Amin's rule, thousands of shops owned by Asians were confiscated and Asians were forbidden to trade in rural areas. Fortunately, Kenya has learned from the lessons of Uganda's economic collapse and calls for Asians to 'go home' have faded from the political agenda.

RELIGION

Generally speaking, most Kenyans outside the coastal and eastern provinces are Christians, while most of those on the coast and in the east of the country are Muslim. Muslims make up some 10% of the population. In the more remote tribal areas you'll find a mixture of Muslims, Christians and those who follow their ancestral tribal beliefs, although these are definitely a minority.

Christianity

As a result of intense missionary activity from colonial times to the present, just about every Christian denomination is represented in Kenya, from Lutherans and Catholics to Seventh-Day Adventists and Wesleyans. The success enjoyed by all these groups is largely due to their combination of Jesus with education and medicine – getting to the soul through the body, if you will.

As in Central and South America, African Christianity is frequently a combination of traditional and Christian beliefs. There are also many pure, home-grown African Christian groups that do not owe allegiance to any of the major Western groups. Street preachers are common throughout the country, and their fire-and-brimstone sermons normally attract a large crowd.

I Laugh So I Won't Cry: Kenya's Women Tell the Stories of Their Lives, edited by Helena Halperin, offers fascinating glimpses into the lives of Kenyan women.

Hardcore evangelism is making inroads, too. Many TV-style groups, especially from the US, have a strong following here, and if you're channel surfing you will come across televised 'crusades', miracle shows and the like.

It's worth visiting a church to attend a service while you're in Kenya. Even if you can't understand the words, you'll certainly be captivated by what only Africans can do with such beauty and precision – unaccompanied choral singing.

Islam

Most Muslims in Kenya belong to the Sunni branch of the faith and they generally practise a moderate version of Islam, although Wahabi fundamentalism is on the rise due to the numerous *madrassas* (religious schools) built here by Saudi Arabia. Religious demonstrations – usually against America or Israel – are on the increase, and hardline beliefs such as *purdah* (requiring women to cover everything but their eyes) are becoming more and more common along the coast.

Only a small minority of Kenyans belong to the Shiah branch of Islam, and most are found among people from the Indian subcontinent. Within the Asian community are representatives of virtually all Shiite sects, but the most influential are the Ismailis – followers of the Aga Khan. As with all Ismailis, they represent a very liberal version of Islam and are perhaps the only branch of the faith strongly committed to the education of women at all levels as well as their participation in commerce and business.

Hinduism

There are a considerable number of Hindu temples in larger urban areas where people from the Indian subcontinent settled after the completion of the Uganda Railway. Both Mombasa and Nairobi have some grand and ornate temples, most of them used by part of the Swaminarayan sect, who are firm devotees of Vishnu. There are scores of other Hindu sects in Kenya – too numerous to mention here – and many are economically quite influential. Westlands in Nairobi has probably the most influential Hindu population.

Traditional Beliefs

Most people leading a tribal existence in Kenya are animists, and their beliefs and rituals are closely linked to the coming of the rains. God is most commonly manifested in the sun, moon, stars, thunder, lightning and trees, particularly the wild fig tree. Colours are also associated with the manifestations of God – black is considered a 'cool', and therefore good, colour, while red and white are bad, 'hot' colours. Another common belief is in spirit beings, who dwell in powerful places and can be violent and unpredictable. Witchdoctors and soothsayers are employed to act as intermediaries with the spirit world.

Most tribes employ rites of passage for both men and women, marking the boundary between childhood and adulthood. Circumcision is still an important ritual for boys, and groups such as the Bukusu, from near Bungoma, stage mass circumcisions every August. Although female circumcision – or, more correctly, female genital mutilation – is illegal in Kenya, tribal cults such as the Mungiki sect, whose members have carried out forced circumcisions and massacres, have issued frequent edicts that all Kenyan women should be circumcised. See below for more details on this contentious issue. Scarification of men and women is still widely practised and most *morani* (warriors) have distinctive scars on their cheeks.

'Witchdoctors and sooth-sayers are employed to act as inter-mediaries with the spirit world'

WOMEN IN KENYA

To a degree, gender roles remain rigid in Kenya. It is not uncommon to hear conservative views of the a-woman's-place-is-in-the-kitchen variety espoused. That said, women are increasingly gaining more educational opportunities, and, particularly in the cities, are coming to play a more prominent role. Some women are breaking the barriers that are traditionally part of a patriarchal society. Women are visible in Kenyan politics and business.

FEMALE GENITAL MUTILATION

The controversial practice of female genital mutilation (FGM), often euphemistically termed 'female circumcision', is still widespread across Africa, including throughout Kenya. In some parts of tribal Kenya more than 90% of women and girls are subjected to FGM in some form.

The term FGM covers a wide range of procedures from a small, mainly symbolic, cut to the total removal of the clitoris and external genitalia (known as infibulation); the open wound is then stitched up.

The effects of FGM can be fatal. Other side effects, including chronic infections, the spread of HIV, infertility, severe bleeding and lifelong pain during sex, are not uncommon.

Thanks to decades of work by international and local human rights' groups, FGM is now banned in Kenya for girls under 17, but the ritual still has widespread support in parts of the community and continues clandestinely. Despite backing from the World Health Organisation, attempts to stamp out FGM are widely perceived as part of a Western conspiracy to undermine African cultural identity. Many local women's groups, such as the community project Ntanira na Mugambo (Circumcision Through Words), are working towards preserving the rite of passage aspect of FGM without any surgery. It seems likely that it will be African initiatives such as Ntanira na Mugambo, rather than Western criticism, that will finally put an end to FGM.

This isn't to say that Kenyan women have traditionally been pushovers. Far from it! In rural communities women have long been the backbone of society, performing the bulk of farming work and playing a prevalent role in the day-to-day life of the community. Older women have always been accorded respect in tribal societies – many are the tales of matriarchal figures who influence the daily happenings of villages and communities through the judicious use of smiles and bouts of wrath.

ARTS
Music

The Homeboyz Academy (www.africanhiphop .com) in Nairobi aims to give budding artists and producers a head start; it's said you need to crack it in Nairobi if you're going to make it in East Africa!

Although there is an indigenous Kenyan music scene, the overriding musical influences have come from outside, originally from nearby Democratic Republic of Congo. More recently reggae and hip-hop have permeated the Kenyan pop scene.

The live-music scene in Nairobi is quite fluid, but always vibrant, and a variety of clubs cater for traditional and contemporary musical tastes. A good reference is the *Daily Nation,* which publishes weekly top 10 African, international and gospel charts and countrywide gig listings on Saturday. Live-music venues are listed under Entertainment headings throughout this book.

AFRICAN MUSICAL STYLES

The Congolese styles of *rumba* and *soukous,* known collectively as *lingala,* were first introduced into Kenya by artists such as Samba Mapangala (who is still playing) in the 1960s and have come to dominate most of East Africa. This upbeat party music is characterised by clean guitar licks and a driving *cavacha* drum rhythm.

Kenyan bands were also active during the 1960s, producing some of the most popular songs in Africa, including Fadhili William's famous *Malaika* (Angel), and *Jambo Bwana,* Kenya's unofficial anthem, written and recorded by the hugely influential Them Mushrooms.

Music from Tanzania was influential in the early 1970s, when the band Simba Wanyika helped create Swahili *rumba,* which was taken up by bands such as the Maroon Commandos and Les Wanyika.

Benga is the contemporary dance music of Kenya. It originated among Luo people in western Kenya and became very popular from the 1950s onwards. Since then it has spread throughout the country and been taken up by Akamba and Kikuyu musicians. The music is characterised by clear electric guitar licks and a bounding bass rhythm. Some well-known exponents of *benga* include DO Misiani (a Luo) and his group Shirati Jazz, which has been around since the 1960s and is still churning out the hits. You should also look out for Globestyle, Victoria Kings and Ambira Boys.

Contemporary Kikuyu music often borrows from *benga.* Stars include Sam Chege, Francis Rugwati and Daniel 'Councillor' Kamau, who was popular in the 1970s and is still going strong. Joseph Kamaru, the popular musician and notorious nightclub owner of the late 1960s, converted to Christianity in 1993 and now dominates the gospel music scene.

Taarab, the music of the East African coast, originally only played at Swahili weddings and other special occasions, has been given a new lease of life by coastal pop singer Malika.

Popular bands today are heavily influenced by *benga, soukous* and also Western music, with lyrics generally in Swahili. These include bands such as Them Mushrooms (now reinvented as Uyoya) and Safari Sound. For upbeat dance tunes, Ogopa DJs, Nameless, Redsan and Deux Vultures are recommended acts.

RAP, HIP-HOP & OTHER STYLES

Having arrived in Kenya in the 1990s, American-influenced gangster rap and hip-hop are also on the rise, including such acts as Necessary Noize, Poxi Presha and Hardstone. The similarities between the slums of Nairobi and the ghettos of North America may be relatively few, but both have proved cauldrons in which potent rap music has developed. In Nairobi, you're unlikely to miss seeing Snoop Dogg and 50 Cent emblazoned on the side of a matatu, or hearing their music blaring. Admiration for these big names has translated into a home-grown industry. In 2004, Dutch producer Nynke Nauta gathered rappers from the Eastlands slums of Nairobi and formed a collective, Nairobi Yetu. The resultant album, *Kilio Cha Haki (A Cry for Justice)*, featuring raps in Sheng (a street-smart melange of Swahili and English), has been internationally recognised as a poignant fusion of ghetto angst and the joy of making music.

Rapper Emmanuel Jal, a former south-Sudanese child soldier now resident in Nairobi, topped the Kenyan charts in 2005 and later that year performed to great acclaim at Live8 in Britain. He has subsequently recorded an album, *Ceasefire*, with the Sudanese *oud* maestro Abdel Gadir Salim. E-Sir is a popular young singer/rapper who died in a car crash this year and has become something of a hero.

Kenya pioneered the African version of the Reggaeton style (a blend of reggae, hip-hop and traditional music), which is now becoming popular in the US and UK. Dancehall is also huge here – Shaggy has a third home in Kenya and Sean Paul visits regularly.

Other names to keep an eye or ear out for include Prezzo (Kenya's king of bling), Nonini (a controversial women-and-booze rapper), Nazizi (female MC from Necessary Noize) and Mercy Myra (Kenya's biggest female R&B artist).

www.artmatters.info is a fabulous resource covering many aspects of the arts scene throughout Kenya and the rest of East Africa.

Sigana

This is a traditional African performance form. It contains elements of all the major traditional African cultural forms – narration, song, music, dance, chant, ritual, mask, movement, banter and poetry – blending into one long, wonderful storytelling performance. This is not something you'll find very often on the tourist trail, but you have a chance of seeing a show at the **Mzizi Arts Centre** (☎ 574372; Sonalux House, Moi Ave) in Nairobi, which puts on monthly Sigana performances (for more details see p106).

Literature

There are plenty of novels, plays and biographies by contemporary Kenyan authors, but they can be hard to find outside Africa, despite being published by the African branches of major Western publishing companies. The Heinemann's African Writers Series offers a major collection of such works but they are generally only available in Nairobi and Mombasa.

Two of Kenya's best authors are Ngugi wa Thiong'o and Meja Mwangi. Ngugi is uncompromisingly radical, and his harrowing criticism of the neocolonialist politics of the Kenyan establishment landed him in jail for a year (described in his *Detained: A Prison Writer's Diary*), lost him his job at Nairobi University and forced him into exile. Meja Mwangi sticks more to social issues and urban dislocation, but has a mischievous sense of humour that threads its way right through his books.

Titles by Ngugi wa Thiong'o include *Petals of Blood, Matigari, The River Between, A Grain of Wheat* and *Devil on the Cross*. All offer insightful portraits of Kenyan life and will give you an understanding of the daily concerns of modern Kenyans. He has also written extensively in his native

Indian-born Tanzanian writer MG Vassanji's *The In-Between World of Vikram Lall,* set in 1950s Nakuru, explores the twin themes of childhood innocence and the decline of the colonial system.

language, Gikuyu. Notable titles by Meja Mwangi include *The Return of Shaka, Weapon for Hunger* and *The Cockroach Dance.* His most recent title, *Mzungu Boy,* depicts the friendship of white and black Kenyan boys at the time of the Mau Mau uprising. Most of these titles are published by Heinemann, although some have since been reissued.

One of Kenya's rising stars on the literary front is Binyavanga Wainaina, currently resident in South Africa and a writer for the South African *Sunday Times* newspaper, who won the Caine Prize for African Writing in July 2002. The award-winning piece was the short story *Discovering Home,* about a young Kenyan working in Cape Town who returns to his parents' village in Kenya for a year.

For writing by women in Africa try *Unwinding Threads,* a collection of short stories by many authors from all over the continent. An interesting female writer working in Kenya is Marjorie Oludhe Magoye, whose *The Present Moment* follows the life stories of a group of elderly women in a Christian refuge in Kenya. *The Man from Pretoria* is an interesting novel by Kenyan conservationist and journalist Hilary Ngweno.

Dance, Theatre & Performance

Nowhere in Africa won the 2002 Academy Award for Best Foreign Film. One of the indisputable highlights of the film was the interaction of veteran Kenyan actor Sidede Onyulo and five-year-old German actress Lea Kurka, bantering all the while in Swahili.

There are a number of contemporary dance troupes and theatre groups in Kenya, although the majority of performances take place in Nairobi. The Phoenix and Miujiza Players, Mbalamwezi Theatre Group, plus the La Campagnie Gaara and Bakututu dance groups, and Sigana Troupe, are all names to look out for. Other than in purpose-built theatres, plays and performances are often held in the various foreign cultural centres in Nairobi, Mombasa and Kisumu.

For more details on the Kenyan scene contact the **Mzizi Arts Centre** (☎ 574372; Sonalux House, Moi Ave, Nairobi) and check in Saturday's *Daily Nation* to see what's on across the country (see also p106).

The dance troupes of the Bomas of Kenya offer an interesting, if touristy, overview of various tribal dances (for more information see p124).

Cinema

The home-grown film-making industry has long struggled in Kenya, as elsewhere in East Africa. Nonetheless, foreign film makers have often used Kenya as the backdrop for their works. Sydney Pollack's Academy Award–winning 1986 movie *Out of Africa,* starring Meryl Streep and Robert Redford, is perhaps the best-known film shot in Kenya. More recently Caroline Link's *Nowhere in Africa* paints a sympathetic portrait of WWII Kenya seen through the eyes of a refugee Jewish family.

Domestically, a new breed of Kenyan directors is emerging, inspired by the runaway success of the Nigerian video industry and helped along by East African cultural initiatives and forums such as the Zanzibar International Film Festival. One such auteur is Kibaara Kaugi, whose *Enough is Enough* (2004), a brave exploration of the Mau Mau uprising, was shot on a shoestring budget and has garnered critical praise.

Brazilian director Fernando Meirrelles turned his gaze to Kenya to shoot *The Constant Gardener* (2005), the film adaptation of the bestselling John Le Carré novel. Interestingly, the novel was banned in Kenya as it depicted corrupt African officials, but the film's producers were able to charm local authorities into allowing filming to be done in the Kibera slum in Nairobi.

Tribes of Kenya

There are more than 70 tribal groups in Kenya, although distinctions between many of the groups are becoming increasingly blurred, largely as a result of migration to the cities and encroaching Western cultural values. Many smaller tribes have also come in under the umbrella of larger tribal groups to gain protection in intertribal disputes.

Even though many Africans have outwardly drifted away from tribal traditions, the tribe is still the most important aspect of a Kenyan's identity: upon meeting a fellow Kenyan, the first question on anyone's lips is: 'What tribe do you come from?'

Although most Kenyans are nominally Christian, a surprising number still practise traditional religious customs.

AKAMBA

The region east of Nairobi towards Tsavo National Park is the traditional homeland of the Akamba people, which they call Ukambani. Their ancestors were Bantu-speaking, and the Akamba migrated from areas further south several centuries ago. The Akamba became great traders in ivory, beer honey, iron weapons and ornaments, covering the region all the way from the coast to Lake Victoria and up to Lake Turkana. They traded for food stocks from the neighbouring Maasai and Kikuyu, as their own low-altitude land was relatively poor and couldn't sustain their increasing population.

Many Akamba lost their lives during WWI fighting for the British Army.

During colonial times, the Akamba were highly regarded by the British for their aptitude and fighting ability, and were drafted in large numbers into the British Army. After WWI the British tried to limit the number of cattle the Akamba could own (by confiscating them) and also settled more Europeans in Ukambani. In the 1930s the Akamba responded by marching en masse to Nairobi to squat peacefully at Kariokor Market in protest. After three weeks, the administration gave way and the cattle were eventually returned to the people.

All adolescents go through initiation rites to adulthood at about the age of 12. Young parents are known as 'junior elders' (*mwanake* for men, *mwiitu* for women) and are responsible for the maintenance and upkeep of the village, later becoming 'medium elders' (*nthele*) and then 'full elders' (*atumia ma kivalo*), when they take on the responsibility for death ceremonies and administering the law. The last stage of a person's life is that of 'senior elder' (*atumia ma kisuka*), when they are charged with responsibility for maintaining holy places.

The Akamba are famous for their *makonde*-style (ebony) carvings. Subgroups of the Akamba include the Kitui, Masaku and Mumoni.

BORANA

The Borana are one of the cattle-herding Oromo peoples, indigenous to Ethiopia, who migrated south into northern Kenya in the early years of the 20th century. They are now concentrated around Marsabit and Isiolo. Life revolves around a family's animals – traditionally cattle, but also goats, sheep and sometimes camels. The Borana observe strict role segregation between men and women, men being responsible for care of the herds while women are in charge of children and day-to-day life. Borana groups may pack up camp and move up to four times a year, depending on weather conditions and available grazing land. As a nomadic group their reliance on oral history is strong, with many traditions passed on through song.

EL-MOLO

This tiny tribal group has strong links with the Rendille, their close
neighbours on the shores of Lake Turkana. The El-Molo rely on Lake
Turkana for their existence, living on a diet mainly of fish and occasionally
crocodile, turtle and other wildlife. Hippos are hunted from doum-palm
rafts with harpoons, and great social status is given to the warrior who
kills a hippo.

An ill-balanced, protein-rich diet and the effects of too much fluoride
have taken their toll on the tribe which, over the centuries, has become
increasingly vulnerable to disease and attacks from stronger tribes. At
one stage there were just 500 El-Molo, living in two small villages on
islands on the lake.

Intermarriage with other tribes and abandonment of the nomadic
lifestyle has helped to raise their numbers to about 4000, who now live on
the mainland near Loyangalani. Traditional costume is now uncommon
and the traditional dome-shaped huts of the El-Molo are slowly being
replaced by permanent concrete homes.

> Like their neighbours
> the Rendille, the El-Molo
> worship a god called
> Wak and bury their dead
> under stone cairns.

GABBRA

This small pastoral tribe of striking Arabic-looking people lives in the far
north of Kenya, from the eastern shore of Lake Turkana up into Ethiopia.
Many Gabbra converted to Islam during the time of slavery. Traditional
beliefs include the appointment of an *abbra-olla* (father of the village),
who oversees the moral and physical wellbeing of the tribe. Fathers and
sons form strong relationships, and marriage provides a lasting bond
between clans. Polygamy is still practised by the Gabbra, although the
practice is becoming less common as old attitudes to women – as status
symbols and unpaid workers – are being eroded.

> Cattle-rustling is still
> commonplace among the
> Gabbra and Pokot, and
> these days is carried out
> with automatic weapons.

Gabbra men usually wear turbans and white cotton robes, while women
wear *kangas,* thin pieces of brightly coloured cotton. Although *nagaya*
(peace) is a core value of the Gabbra, tribal wars with the Samburu were
once common. The Gabbra are famous for their bravery, hunting lion,
rhino and elephant in preference to 'weak' animals such as antelope.

The Gabbra lost many of their cattle herds to drought and rinderpest
epidemics in the 19th century, and were decimated by malaria and
smallpox before being driven into the Chalbi Desert from their lands in

Ethiopia by the army of Emperor Menelik. Somehow the Gabbra survived this and today continue to live in the harshest environment in Kenya.

GUSII

The Gusii inhabit an area in the western highlands, east of Lake Victoria, forming a small Bantu-speaking island in a mainly Nilotic-speaking area. They were driven from their original territory near Mt Elgon to the Kisii highlands about 200 years ago, as the Luo, Maasai and Kipsigis advanced into their lands. The Gusii strongly resisted the British advance and were later conscripted in large numbers into the British Army.

Among the Gusii, death is considered to be the work of 'witchcraft' rather than a natural occurrence.

The Gusii family typically consists of a man, his wives and their married sons, all of whom live together in a single compound. Initiation ceremonies are performed for both boys and girls, and rituals accompany all important events. Traditionally, the Gusii are primarily cattle herders and crop cultivators, and some also brew millet beer.

As is the case with many of Kenya's tribal groups, medicine men (abanyamorigo) have a highly privileged and respected position. They are responsible for maintaining the physical and mental wellbeing of the group – performing the combined role of doctor and social worker. One of the more bizarre practices was (and still is) trepanning: the removal of sections of the skull or spine to aid maladies such as backache or concussion.

KALENJIN

The term Kalenjin was formulated in the 1950s to describe the group of peoples previously called the Nandi by the British. The Kalenjin comprise the Nandi, Kipsigis, Eleyo, Marakwet, Pokot and Tugen (former president Moi's people) and occupy the western edge of the central Rift Valley area. They first migrated to the area west of Lake Turkana from southern Sudan around 2000 years ago, but gradually filtered south as the climate became harsher.

Although originally pastoralists, most Kalenjin groups took up agriculture. Beekeeping is still a common activity and the honey is used in trade and for brewing beer. The Kipsigis, on the other hand, have a passionate love for cattle and cattle-rustling continues to cause friction between them and neighbouring tribes.

Many Kenyan athletes are Nandi or Kipsigis.

The Nandi, the second-largest of the Kalenjin communities, settled in the Nandi Hills between the 16th and 17th centuries. They had a formidable military reputation and, in the late 19th century, managed to delay the construction of the Uganda railway for more than a decade until Koitalel, their chief, was killed.

As with most tribes, Kalenjin have age-sets into which a man is initiated after circumcision. Polygamy was widely practised in the past. Administration of the law is carried out at the *kok* (an informal court led by the clan's elders). The Kalenjin doctors, who are mostly (and unusually) women, still use herbal remedies in their work. Other specialist doctors still practise trepanning.

KIKUYU

The country's largest tribal group, the Kikuyu make up 20% of the population. Due to this and the influence of Jomo Kenyatta, the first president of Kenya, the Kikuyu remain the most politically influential tribe in Kenya. The original Kikuyu are thought to have migrated to the area from the east and northeast from the 16th century onwards. Their heartland now surrounds Mt Kenya. Famously warlike, the Kikuyu overran the lands of the Athi and Gumba tribes, becoming hugely populous in the process. The Kikuyu also fiercely resisted the British, spearheading the Mau Mau rebellion in the 1950s that was a major catalyst for the end of British rule.

The Kikuyu territory borders that of the Maasai, and intertribal raids on property and cattle were once common. Despite this, intermarriage between them has resulted in many cultural similarities between the tribes today.

The administration of the clans *(mwaki)* – made up of many family groups *(nyumba)* – was originally taken care of by a council of elders, with a good deal of importance being placed on the role of the witch-doctor, the medicine man and the blacksmith. An important tool of the witchdoctor is the *mwano*, a gourd filled with bones and pebbles, used for divination.

The Kikuyu god, Ngai, is believed to reside on Mt Kenya (Kirinyaga – which means either the 'mountain of brightness' or 'black-and-white peak spotted like ostrich feathers'), which accounts for the orientation of Kikuyu homes with the door facing Mt Kenya.

Initiation rites for both boys and girls are important ceremonies and consist of ritual circumcision for boys and female genital mutilation for girls (although the latter is slowly becoming less common). Each group of youths of the same age belongs to a *riikaan* (age-set) and passes through the various stages of life, and their associated rituals, together.

Subgroups of the Kikuyu include the Embu, Ndia and Mbeere.

> The Kikuyu are renowned for their entrepreneurial skills and for popping up everywhere in Kenya (the Kikuyu name Kamau is as common as Smith is in Britain).

LUHYA

The Luhya are of Bantu origin and are made up of 17 different groups. They are the second-largest group after the Kikuyu, but occupy a relatively small area in western Kenya centred on Kakamega, where they settled around the 14th century. Population densities here are incredibly high.

In times past, the Luhya were skilled metal workers, forging knives and tools that were traded with other groups, but today most Luhya are agriculturists, farming groundnuts, sesame and maize. Smallholders also grow large amounts of cash crops such as cotton and sugar cane.

Many Luhya are superstitious and still have a strong belief in witchcraft, although to the passing traveller this is rarely obvious. Traditional costume and rituals are becoming less common, due mostly to the pressures of the soaring Luhya population.

LUO

The Luo people are Kenya's third-largest tribal group, making up about 12% of the population. They live in the west of the country on the shores of Lake Victoria. Along with the Maasai, they migrated south from the Nile region of Sudan around the 15th century.

The Luo's cattle herds suffered terribly from the rinderpest outbreak in the 1890s and most Luo switched to fishing and subsistence agriculture.

During the struggle for *uhuru* (Swahili for 'national independence'), many of the country's leading Kenyan politicians and trade unionists were Luo, including Tom Mboya (assassinated in 1969) and the former vice president Oginga Odinga, who later spearheaded the opposition to President Moi's one-party state.

The Luo are unusual among Kenya's tribal groups in that circumcision is not practised for either sex. The Luo traditionally extract four or six teeth from the bottom jaw, although this is uncommon today. The family group consists of the husband, wife (or wives) and their sons and daughters-in-law. The house compound is enclosed by a fence and includes separate huts for the man and for each wife and son.

> Few Luo today wear traditional costume – they have a reputation for 'flashiness', often carrying two mobile phones.

The family unit is part of a larger grouping of *dhoot* (families), several of which in turn make up an *ogandi* (group of geographically related people), each led by a *ruoth* (chief). As is the case with many tribes, great importance is placed on the role of the medicine man and the spirits.

The Luo, like the Luyha, have two major recreational passions, soccer and music, and there are many distinctive Luo instruments made from gourds and gut or wire strings.

MAASAI

For many, the Maasai are the definitive symbol of 'tribal' Kenya. With a reputation (often exaggerated) as fierce warriors and a proud demeanour, the tribe has largely managed to stay outside the mainstream of development in Kenya and still maintains large cattle herds along the Tanzanian border.

The Maasai first migrated to central Kenya from current-day Sudan, but in the late 19th century they were decimated by famine and disease, and their cattle herds were plagued by rinderpest. The British gazetted the Masai Mara National Reserve in the early 1960s, displacing the Maasai, and they slowly continued to annexe more and more Maasai land. Resettlement programs have met with limited success as the Maasai scorn agriculture and land ownership.

Maasai women are famous for wearing vast plate-like bead necklaces, while men typically wear a red-checked *shuka* (Maasai blanket) and carry a distinctive ball-ended club. Blood and milk are the mainstay of the Maasai diet, supplemented by a drink called *mursik,* made from milk fermented with cow's urine and ashes, which has been shown to lower cholesterol.

At around the age of 14, males become *el-moran* (warriors) and build a small livestock camp *(manyatta)* after their circumcision ceremony, where they live alone for up to eight years, before returning to the village to marry. *Morans* traditionally dye their hair red with ochre and fat. Female genital mutilation is common among the Maasai, despite the best efforts of various human rights groups.

Tourism provides an income to some, either through being guides and camp guards *(askaris),* selling everyday items (gourds, necklaces, clubs

There is a strong Maasai taboo against 'piercing' the soil, and the dead are traditionally left to be consumed by wild animals.

Maasai men dancing.
PHOTO BY JANE SWEENEY

and spears), dancing or simply posing for photographs. However, the benefits are not widespread. In recent years, many Maasai have moved to the cities or coastal resorts, becoming doormen for restaurants and hotels.

MERU

The Meru arrived in the area northeast of Mt Kenya from the coast around the 14th century, following invasions by Somalis from the north. The group was led by a chief *(mogwe)* up until 1974, when the last incumbent converted to Christianity. Justice was administered by a group of tribal elders *(njuuri)*, along with the *mogwe* and witchdoctor, who would often carry out summary executions by giving poison-laced beer to an accused person. Other curious practices included holding a newly born child to face Mt Kenya and then blessing it by spitting on it. Circumcision is also still common.

> The Meru are particularly active in the cultivation of *miraa,* the stems of which contain a stimulant similar to amphetamines and are exported to Somalia and Yemen.

The Meru now live on some of the most fertile farmland in Kenya and grow numerous cash crops. Subgroups of the Meru include the Chuka, Igembe, Igoji, Tharaka, Muthambi, Tigania and Imenti.

POKOT

The Pokot are Kalenjin by language and tradition, but their diet is dominated by meat, supplemented with blood drawn from cattle, milk and honey. Pokot warriors wear distinctive headdresses of painted clay and feathers, similar to those of the Turkana. Flat, aluminium nose ornaments shaped like leaves and lower-lip plugs are common among men. Circumcision is part of the initiation of men and many Pokot women undergo female genital mutilation at around 12 years old.

> After giving birth to their first child, Rendille women adopt a clay head decoration known as a *doko,* which resembles a rooster's comb.

The pastoral Pokot herd their cattle and goats across the waterless scrub north of Lake Baringo and the Cherangani Hills. Cattle-raiding, and the search for water and grazing, has often brought them into conflict with the Turkana, Samburu and the Ugandan Karamojong.

Pokot hill farmers are a separate and distinct group who grow tobacco and keep cattle, sheep and goats in the hills north of Kitale, on the approaches to Marich Pass. These hill farmers have a strong craft tradition, producing pottery and metalwork, as well as snuff boxes from calabashes or horns.

RENDILLE

The Rendille are pastoralists who live in small nomadic communities in the rocky Kaisut Desert in Kenya's northeast. They have strong economic and kinship links with the Samburu and rely heavily on camels for many of their daily needs, including food, milk, clothing, trade and transport. The camels are bled by opening a vein in the neck with a blunt arrow or knife. The blood is then drunk on its own or mixed with milk.

> A woman of the Rendille tribe from Loyangalani. The Rendille are nomadic cattle and camel herders.
> PHOTO BY ABI ARIADNE VAN ZANDBERGEN

The colonial administration in this region found the Rendille to be a thorn in its side, as they managed to avoid taxation and forced labour through indifference and outright hostility. Rendille society is strongly bound by family ties, and these centre around monogamous couples. Mothers have a high status and the eldest son inherits the family wealth. It is dishonourable for a Rendille to refuse a loan, so even the poorest Rendille often has claims to at least a few camels and goats.

Rendille warriors often sport a distinctive visor-like hairstyle, dyed with red ochre, while women may wear several kilos of beads.

SAMBURU

Closely related to the Maasai, and speaking the same language, the Samburu occupy an arid area directly north of Mt Kenya. It seems that when the Maasai migrated to the area from Sudan, some headed east and became the Samburu.

Northern Massai Samburu girl in wedding attire.
PHOTO BY CHRISTER FREDRIKSSON

Like the Rendille, Samburu warriors often paste their hair with red ochre to create a visor to shield their eyes from the sun. Age is an important factor in assigning social status and a man passes through various stages before becoming a powerful elder in his 30s. Circumcision heralds a boy's transition to a *moran*, while female genital mutilation is performed on the day of marriage for girls (usually at around 16 years old). After marriage, women traditionally leave their clan, so their social status is much lower than that of men. Samburu women wear similar colourful bead necklaces to the Maasai.

Samburu families live in a group of huts made of branches, mud and dung, surrounded by a fence made of thorn bushes. Livestock, which are kept inside the fence perimeter at night, are used for their milk rather than for meat.

SOMALI

Nomadic, camel-herding Somali have long lived in the arid deserts of Kenya's northeast. Indeed, the Cushitic-speaking peoples, amongst whom the Somalis are numbered, arrived in Kenya before any of the Bantu-speaking peoples. The northeastern towns where Somalis are in the majority are now largely off limits due to security concerns, but you will also encounter Somalis in most large Kenyan towns, where they often run hotels, general stores and mechanical workshops.

Somali cuisine often features spaghetti, a legacy of the Italian colonisation of southern Somalia.

Somalis are generally tall and thin with fine aquiline features, and all hail from the same tribe, which is divided into nine clans. The clan in particular and genealogy in general is of tremendous importance to Somalis. Most Somalis are adherents of Islam, although their version of Islam is markedly low key and, as a nomadic people, storytelling and poetry are considered highly.

Many Somalis claim to have originated in the Arabian Peninsula, but historical and linguistic evidence disputes this.

SWAHILI PEOPLE

Although the people of the coast do not have a common heritage, they do have a linguistic link: Kiswahili (commonly referred to as Swahili), a Bantu-based language that evolved as a means of communication between Africans and the Arabs, Persians and Portuguese who colonised the East African coast. The word *swahili* is a derivative of the Arabic word for coast – *sawihil*.

The website www .bluegecko.org/kenya/ is a brilliant source of information about the arts and various peoples of Kenya.

The cultural origins of the Swahili come from intermarriage between the Arabs and Persians with African slaves from the 7th century onwards. The Swahili were to become one of the principal slaving forces in Africa. Islam is practised by almost all Swahili, although it usually takes a more liberal form than that practised in the Middle East.

Swahili subgroups include Bajun, Siyu, Pate, Mvita, Fundi, Shela, Ozi, Vumba and Amu (residents of Lamu).

TURKANA

The Turkana are one of Kenya's more colourful (and also most warlike) people. Originally from Karamojong in northeastern Uganda, the Turkana number around 250,000 and live in the virtual desert country of Kenya's northwest.

Like the Samburu and the Maasai (with whom they are linguistically linked), the Turkana are primarily cattle herders, although recently, fishing on the waters of Lake Turkana and small-scale farming is on the increase. The Turkana are one of the few tribes to have voluntarily given up the practice of circumcision.

A surprising number of Turkana men still wear markings on their shoulders to indicate that they have killed another man.

Traditional costume is still commonplace and Turkana men cover part of their hair with mud, which is then painted blue and decorated with ostrich and other feathers. Despite the intense heat of the region, the main garment is a woollen blanket, often with garish checks. Turkana accessories include a pillow-come-stool carved out of a single piece of wood, a wooden fighting staff and a wrist knife. A woman's attire is dictated by her marital and maternal status; the marriage ritual itself is quite unusual and involves the kidnapping of the bride.

Tattooing is also common. Men were traditionally tattooed on the shoulders for killing an enemy – the right shoulder for killing a man, the left for a woman. Witchdoctors and prophets are held in high regard and scars on someone's lower stomach are usually a sign of a witchdoctor's attempt to cast out an undesirable spirit using incisions.

Turkana women in traditional dress.
PHOTO BY ABI CHRISTER FREDRIKSSON

Environment

THE LAND

Kenya straddles the equator and covers an area of some 583,000 sq km, which includes around 13,600 sq km of Lake Victoria. The country is bordered by both land and desert: to the north by the arid bushlands and deserts of Ethiopia and Sudan, to the east by the Indian Ocean and the wastes of Somalia, to the west by Uganda and Lake Victoria, and to the south by Tanzania.

Kenya is dominated by the Rift Valley, a vast range of valleys rather than a single valley, that follows a 5000km-long crack in the earth's crust. Within the Rift Valley are numerous 'swells' (raised escarpments) and 'troughs' (deep valleys, often containing lakes), and there are some huge volcanoes, including Mt Kenya, Mt Elgon and Mt Kilimanjaro (across the border in Tanzania). The floor of the Rift Valley is still dropping, although – at the rate of a few millimetres per year – you are hardly likely to notice!

For an evocative picture of Kenya's physical, environmental and cultural make-up, track down Peter Matthiessen's classic *The Tree Where Man Was Born*, an account of the author's epic journey through East Africa in the 1960s.

The Rift Valley divides the flat plains of the coast from the gentle hills along the lakeshore. Nairobi, the capital, sits in the Central Highlands, which are on the eastern edge of the Rift Valley. The other main population centres are Mombasa, on the coast, and Kisumu, on the shores of Lake Victoria. Kenya can roughly be divided into four zones: the coastal plains, the Rift Valley and Central Highlands, the lakeshore, and the arid wastelands of northern Kenya.

The main rivers in Kenya are the Athi/Galana River, which empties into the Indian Ocean near Malindi, and the Tana River, which hits the coast midway between Malindi and Lamu. Aside from Lake Victoria in the west, Kenya has numerous small volcanic lakes and mighty Lake Turkana, also known as the Jade Sea, which straddles the Ethiopian border in the north.

Within volcanic craters, and on the Rift Valley floor, are several soda lakes, rich in sodium bicarbonate, created by the filtering of water through mineral-rich volcanic rock and subsequent evaporation.

TSUNAMI – THE DISASTER THAT WASN'T

The tsunami that devastated the Asian coast in December 2004 did reach Kenya's Indian Ocean shoreline, 2800km away, but amazingly the area escaped the fatalities suffered by neighbouring Somalia and other affected countries. Just one person died as a result of the wave, fewer even than in Tanzania, which was further away from the epicentre of the earthquake.

This remarkable feat is credited to the swift action of local officials, alerted to the danger by news reports and US authorities, who took immediate steps to get people off the beaches, implementing an evacuation plan originally conceived for emergencies such as oil spills. Police, navy and national media all contributed to the process, an organisational triumph in a country little known for its efficient emergency services.

Of course, the scale of the tsunami's impact was much less than in areas closer to the epicentre, such as Thailand, and only the immediate coastline was affected, with most damage concentrated around Mombasa and Malindi. Fishing communities were worst hit, while the main tourist areas suffered considerable sand erosion but little permanent damage.

Not all communities took the warnings too seriously, however: certain Diani Beach residents even set up deckchairs on the beach to watch the tsunami arrive, claiming disappointment when it was little more than a big swell!

WILDLIFE
Animals

There's such a dazzling array of animals in Kenya that viewing them in the national parks is one of the main reasons for visiting for most people. The Big Five (lion, buffalo, elephant, leopard and rhino) and a huge variety of other less famous but equally impressive animals, from zebras and baboons to elands and mongooses, can be seen in at least two of the major parks. Some of the most interesting are described in the Wildlife Guide in this book, or in much more detail in Lonely Planet's *Watching Wildlife East Africa*.

The bird life is equally varied and includes such interesting species as the ostrich, vulture and marabou stork, whose spooky bill-clacking can be heard in thorn trees across the country. Around bodies of water, you may see flamingos, exotic cranes and storks, and pelicans, while the forests are home to huge hornbills and rare species such as the yellow weaver bird, sunbird and touraco. Superb starlings are a beautiful bronze and turquoise and you'll see them everywhere. There are also dozens of species of weaver bird, which make the distinctive baglike nests seen hanging from acacia trees.

> Having trouble telling your dik-dik from your serval? Try the hand-illustrated *Kingdon Field Guide to African Mammals* (Jonathon Kingdon), widely considered to be the definitive guide to the continent's fauna. It's also available in a pocket edition.

ENDANGERED SPECIES

Many of Kenya's major predators and herbivores have become endangered over the past few decades, because of the continuous destruction of their natural habitat and merciless poaching for ivory, skins, horn and bush meat.

The black rhino is probably Kenya's most endangered species. It is commonly poached for its horn, which is used to make Yemeni and Omani dagger-handles and, to a lesser extent, aphrodisiacs in Asia. Faced with relentless poaching by heavily armed gangs in the 1980s, the wild rhino population plummeted from 20,000 in 1969 to just 458 today. **Rhino Ark** (☎ 020-604246; www.rhinoark.org) raises funds to create rhino sanctuaries in the national parks, complete with electric fencing, and donations are always appreciated. There are currently sanctuaries in Tsavo and Lake Nakuru National Parks, while Aberdare National Park is in the process of being fenced.

While the elephant is not technically endangered, it is still often the target of poachers. A number of elephants are killed every year, especially in the area around Tsavo East National Park. Current numbers are estimated at 28,000.

DUDUS

Because of its lush climate, Kenya has some huge tropical bugs, known as *dudus* in Swahili. Arachnophobes should watch out for the plum-sized golden orb spider, with its famously strong web, and the delightfully named Mombasa golden starburst baboon spider, regarded as a 'small' tarantula since it reaches only 12cm in diameter! There are also several large species of scorpion, often seen after rain.

Perhaps Kenya's most notorious *dudu* is the safari ant. These huge red ants sweep across the countryside in huge columns, consuming everything that lies in their path. Locally they're often known as 'army' or 'crazy' ants for their brutal search-and-destroy tactics. Tribespeople use the pincers of safari ants as improvised stitches for wounds.

An altogether friendlier species is the *jongo* or giant millipede. Although these insect behemoths can reach 20cm in length, they eat only decaying wood and will roll themselves up into a defensive coil if approached.

Plants

Kenya's flora is notably diverse because of the country's wide range of physiographic regions. The vast plains of the south are characterised by distinctive flat-topped acacia trees, interspersed with the equally recognisable baobab trees and savage whistling thorn bushes, which made early exploration of the continent such a tortuous process.

The savanna grassland of the Masai Mara supports a huge variety of animal life. The grass grows tremendously fast after the rains, and provides food for an enormous range of herbivores and insects, which in turn feed a variety of predators. The trampling and grazing of the various herbivores that call the Mara home promotes the growth of grasses, rather than broadleaf plants, which are more vulnerable to damage from grazing, drought and fire.

On the slopes of Mt Elgon and Mt Kenya the flora changes as the altitude increases. Thick evergreen temperate forest grows between 1000m and 2000m, giving way to a belt of bamboo forest that reaches as high as about 3000m. Above this height is mountain moorland, characterised by the amazing groundsel tree and giant lobelias (see p262). In the semidesert plains of the north and northeast the vegetation cover is thorny bush, which can seem to go on forever. In the northern coastal areas mangroves are prolific, and there are still a few small pockets of coastal rainforest.

Kenya's national bird is the lilac-breasted roller, which can be seen in many national parks, including the Masai Mara, Lake Nakuru and Meru National Parks.

NATIONAL PARKS & RESERVES

Kenya's national parks and reserves rate among the best in Africa and around 10% of the country's land area is protected by law. Despite the ravages of human land exploitation and poaching, there is still an incredible variety of birds and mammals in the parks.

Going on safari is an integral part of the Kenyan experience, and more popular parks such as Masai Mara National Reserve and Amboseli National Park can become so overcrowded in the high season (January to February) that you'll struggle to get a wildlife photo without a crowd of Nissan Urvans in the background.

Fortunately, the smaller and more remote parks, such as Saiwa Swamp National Park, see only a handful of visitors at any time of year. In addition to protecting wildlife, some parks have been created to preserve the landscape itself – Mt Kenya, Mt Elgon, Hell's Gate, Mt Longonot and Kakamega Forest are all worth investigating.

Three sites in Kenya are included on the Unesco World Heritage list: Mt Kenya, the Lake Turkana national parks and Lamu's old town.

A number of marine national parks have also been established, providing excellent diving and snorkelling (see p180, p184, p199 and p207).

The most important national parks and reserves are shown in the accompanying table. Smaller parks and reserves include the following:

Central Island National Park (p343) Volcanic island rising out of Lake Turkana.
Longonot National Park (p231) Great Rift Valley views from the crater rim of Mt Longonot.
Marsabit National Park (p329) Featuring large herbivores and dense forest.
Ruma National Park (p297) Home to the country's only population of roan antelope.
Sibiloi National Park (p338) Remote park, home to the remains of *Homo habilis* and *Homo erectus*.

Chyulu Hills National Park (p140) and Tana River National Primate Reserve (p212) are, for the most part, unknown quantities, as the infrastructure for tourism in these parks is not yet really in place.

Entry fees to national parks are controlled by the **KWS** (Kenya Wildlife Service; ☎ 020-600800; www.kws.org; PO Box 40241, Nairobi), while national reserves, such as Masai Mara, are administered by the relevant local council. See p55 for park categories and prices.

NATIONAL PARK & RESERVES

Park/Reserve	Features	Activities	Best Time to Visit
Aberdare National Park (p256)	dramatic highlands, waterfalls and rainforest; elephants, black rhinos, bongo antelope, black leopards	trekking, fishing, gliding	year-round
Amboseli National Park (p137)	dry plains and scrub forest; elephants, buffaloes, lions, antelope	wildlife drives	Jun-Oct
Arabuko Sokoke Forest Reserve (p201)	coastal forest; Sokoke scops owls, Clarke's weavers, elephant shrews, Amani sunbirds, butterflies, elephants	bird tours, walking, running, cycling	year-round
Hell's Gate National Park (p237)	dramatic rocky outcrops and gorges; lammergeyers, eland, giraffes, lions	cycling, walking	year-round
Kakamega Forest Reserve (p304)	virgin tropical rainforest; red-tailed monkeys, flying squirrels, 330 bird species	walking, bird-watching	year-round
Lake Bogoria National Reserve (p246)	scenic soda lake; flamingos, greater kudu, leopards	bird-watching, walking, hot springs	year-round
Lake Nakuru National Park (p243)	hilly grassland and alkaline lakeland; flamingos, black rhinos, lions, warthogs, over 400 bird species	wildlife drives	year-round
Masai Mara National Reserve (p286)	savanna and grassland; Big Five, antelope, cheetahs, hyenas	wildlife drives, ballooning wildebeest migration	Jul-Oct
Meru National Park (p277)	rainforest, swamplands and grasslands; white rhinos, elephants, lions, cheetahs, lesser kudu	wildlife drives, fishing	year-round
Mt Elgon National Park (p312)	extinct volcano and rainforest; elephants	walking, trekking, fishing	Dec-Feb
Mt Kenya National Park (p261)	rainforest, moorland and glacial mountain; elephants, buffaloes, mountain flora	trekking, climbing	Jan-Feb, Aug-Sep
Nairobi National Park (p125)	open plains with urban backdrop; black rhinos, birdlife, rare antelope	wildlife drives, walking	year-round
Saiwa Swamp National Park (p315)	swamplands and riverine forest; sitatunga antelope, crowned cranes, otters, black-and-white colobus	walking, bird-watching	year-round
Samburu, Buffalo Springs & Shaba National Reserves (p324)	semiarid open savanna; elephants, leopards, gerenuks, crocodiles	wildlife drives	year-round
Shimba Hills National Reserve (p169)	densely forested hills; elephants, sable antelope, leopards	walking, forest tours	year-round
Tsavo East & West National Parks (p142)	sweeping plains and ancient volcanic cones; Big Five	wildlife drives, rock climbing, walking	yearround

NATIONAL PARK ENTRY FEES

Admission to parks in Kenya is gradually being converted to a 'smartcard' system, for payment of entry and camping fees. The cards must be charged with credit in advance and can only be topped up at certain locations. Any credit left on the card once you finish your trip cannot be refunded.

At the time of writing the smartcard system was in use at Nairobi, Lake Nakuru, Aberdare, Amboseli, Tsavo East and Tsavo West National Parks. The other parks still work on a cash system. You can purchase and charge smartcards at the KWS headquarters in Nairobi and Mombasa, at the main gates of the participating parks, and at the Malindi Marine National Park office.

There are five categories of parks in Kenya. These are as follows:

Category	Park
A	Aberdare, Amboseli, Lake Nakuru
B	Meru, Tsavo East & West
C	Nairobi, Shimba Hills
D	All other land-based parks, except Arabuko Sokoke and Kakamega
Marine	Kisite, Kiunga, Malindi, Mombasa, Mpunguti, Watamu

The Masai Mara, Samburu, Buffalo Springs & Shaba National Reserves have the same entry fees as category A national parks; entry to Mt Kenya National Park is US$15/8 per adult/child. Arabuko Sokoke and Kakamega Forest Reserves are joint KWS and Forestry Department projects and charge US$10/5 per adult/child.

Entry and camping fees to the parks per person per day are as follows:

Category	Nonresident Adult/child (US$)	Resident Adult/child (KSh)	Camping adult/child Nonresident (US$)/resident (KSh)
A	30/10	500/200	10/300
B	27/10	500/200	10/300
C	23/10	500/200	10/300
D	15/5	500/200	8/200
Marine	5/2	100/50	-

The land-based parks and reserves charge KSh200 for vehicles with fewer than six seats and KSh500 for vehicles seating six to 12. In addition to the public camping areas, special campsites cost US$10 to US$15 per adult nonresident, plus a KSh5000 weekly reservation fee. Guides are available in most parks for KSh500 per day.

All fees cover visitors for a 24-hour period, but a recent change in regulations means that most parks will no longer allow you to leave and re-enter without paying twice.

ENVIRONMENTAL ISSUES

As a country with some of Africa's most spectacular national parks and reserves, and with some of the most amazing animals on earth, it is fortunate that environmental issues have grown in importance over the past few decades.

Wildlife Conservation

KENYA WILDLIFE SERVICE (KWS)

With a total ban on hunting imposed in the country in 1977, the KWS was free to concentrate solely on conserving Kenya's wildlife. This came just in time, as the 1970s and '80s were marred by a shocking amount of poaching linked to the drought in Somalia, when hordes of poachers were driven across the border into Kenya by their lack of success in their

WANGARI MAATHAI, NOBEL LAUREATE

On Earth Day in 1977 Professor Wangari Maathai planted seven trees in her back yard, setting in motion the grass-roots environmental campaign that later came to be known as the Green Belt Movement. Since then, more than 30 million trees have been planted throughout Kenya and the movement has expanded to more than 30 other African countries. The core aim of this campaign is to educate women – who make up some 70% of farmers in Africa – about the link between soil erosion, undernourishment and poor health, and to encourage individuals to protect their immediate environment and guard against soil erosion by planting 'green belts' of trees and establishing tree nurseries.

Maathai, who is now Assistant Minister for the Environment, has worked extensively with various international organisations to exert leverage on the Kenyan government, and was awarded the Nobel Peace Prize in 2004 for her tireless campaigning on environmental issues. However, the Moi regime consistently vilified her as a 'threat to the order and security of the country' and throughout the years she has been the target of repeated acts of violence at the hands of government agents. Maathai's personal views have also attracted controversy in some circles, particularly on the subject of AIDS, which she claims was created by scientists for use in 'biological warfare' against blacks!

Whatever her beliefs, Maathai is certainly a fascinating figure, and the Green Belt Movement is still one of the most significant environmental organisations in Kenya. Maathai's book *The Green Belt Movement* was republished in a new edition in 2005 and is well worth tracking down if you are interested in environmental issues.

own country. A staggering number of Kenya's rhinos and elephants were slaughtered and many KWS officers worked in league with poachers until famous palaeontologist Dr Richard Leakey cleaned up the organisation in the 1980s and '90s. A core part of his policy was arming KWS rangers with modern weapons and high-speed vehicles and allowing them to shoot poachers on sight, which seems to have dramatically reduced the problem.

However, there have been several new raids on elephant and rhino populations since 2001. As a result, there is now open talk of abandoning some of the more remote parks (such as those parks that are close to the Ethiopian or Somali borders) and concentrating resources in the parks where they can achieve the best results and that receive most visitors. At the same time, community conservation projects are being encouraged, and many community-owned ranches are now being opened up as private wildlife reserves, with the backing of both the KWS and international donors.

The East African Wildlife Society (www.eawildlife.org), based in Nairobi, is the most prominent conservation body in the region and a good source of information.

PRIVATE CONSERVATION

It has been claimed that more than 75% of Kenya's wildlife lies outside the country's national parks and reserves, and an increasing number of important wildlife conservation areas now exist on private land. Lewa Wildlife Conservancy (p321), near Isiolo, is a prime example of this trend. Private wildlife reserves often have the resources to work more intensively on specific conservation issues than national parks and preserves can, and it is no accident that some of the largest concentrations of rhinos are within these areas. Supporting these projects is a great way for visitors to contribute to Kenyan communities as well as assist in the preservation of the country's wildlife.

The **Laikipia Wildlife Forum** (☎ 062-31600; www.laikipia.org) is an umbrella organisation that represents many lodges and conservation areas in Laikipia, the large slab of ranch land northwest of Mt Kenya. Ranches in this area are particularly active in wildlife conservation, and the Laikipia Wildlife Forum is a good source of up-to-date information about projects and accommodation in the region. Other private game ranches and conservation areas can be found around Tsavo and Amboseli National Parks.

Deforestation

If we do not protect our remaining forests, Kenya will become progressively thirstier, hungrier, uglier and poorer. The forest excisions are like an axe hanging over the future of our country.
Kenya Forests Working Group

More than half of Africa's forests have been destroyed over the last century, and forest destruction continues on a large scale in parts of Kenya – today, less than 3% of the country's original forest cover remains. Land grabbing, charcoal burning, agricultural encroachment as well as illegal logging have all taken their toll over the years. However, millions of Kenyans still rely on wood and charcoal for cooking fuel, so travellers to the country will almost certainly contribute to this deforestation whether they like it or not.

The degazetting of protected forests is another contentious issue, sparking widespread protests and preservation campaigns. On the flipside, locals in forest areas can find themselves homeless if the government does enforce protection orders, as in the recent Mau Forest controversy (p246).

Despite these problems, some large areas of protected forest remain. The Mt Kenya, Mt Elgon and Aberdare National Parks, Kakamega Forest Reserve and Arabuko Sokoke Forest are all tremendous places to visit, packed with thousands of species of fauna and flora.

Tourism
The tourist industry is the cause of some of Kenya's environmental problems, most notably heavy use of firewood by tourist lodges and erosion caused by safari minibuses, which cut across and between trails and follow wildlife into the bush, creating virtual dustbowls in parks

---

GOOD WOOD

A growing issue in Kenya is the consumption of native hard woods by its woodcarvers. An incredible 80,000 trees are chopped down every year just to provide wood for the carving industry, and trees such as mahogany and ebony (from which the popular black *makonde*-style carvings are made) are increasingly threatened.

In partnership with Kew Gardens in London, WWF-UK and Unesco run a 'Good Wood' campaign to promote the use of common fast-growing trees such as neem, jacaranda, mango and olive. These woods need to be cured before carving, but the end results are almost indistinguishable from carvings made from hard woods. Many handicraft cooperatives now exclusively use wood that is approved by the Forest Stewardship Council, an international body which certifies wood from managed forests.

Visitors buying carvings are strongly encouraged to ask about the source of the materials and to insist that the carver use the above woods. It is hoped that this consumer pressure will help persuade carvers in Kenya to switch over to 'good woods', which will protect the livelihoods of 60,000 carvers as well as Kenya's dwindling hardwood forests. For more information, visit the website www.kenyagatsby.org.

For a list of ecofriendly tour companies, contact the Ecotourism Society of Kenya (www.esok.org).

such as Amboseli, Samburu and Masai Mara. A number of operators were recently banned from the Mara for misdemeanours ranging from non-payment of rent for tented camps to harassment of wildlife, but there are few signs that the ban is being enforced.

The KWS now insists that every new lodge and camp must be designed in an ecofriendly manner. As a result, there are growing numbers of 'ecolodges' in Kenya, which keep their impact on the environment to a minimum through recycling, use of renewable energy resources, and strict controls on dumping of refuse and the types of fuel that are used.

As a visitor, the best way to help combat these problems is to be very selective about who you do business with and very vocal about the kind of standards you expect – see p66 for tips on minimal-impact safaris. The more tourists insist on responsible practices, the more safari operators and hotels will take notice, and while you may end up paying more for an ecofriendly trip, in the long term you'll be investing in a sustainable tourist industry and the preservation of Kenya's delicate environment.

Safaris

'Safari' has to be one of the most evocative words ever to infiltrate the English language. It may just mean 'journey' in Swahili, but to the eager visitors flocking to the Kenyan national parks it means so much more, inspiring visions of wildebeests fording raging rivers, lions stalking their heedless prey through the savanna grass, elephants trundling their way to water, iridescent flamingos lining a salty shore at sunset or the guilty thrill of watching vultures tear flesh and hyenas crunch through bone. For many people, taking that trip into the wild is the sole reason for coming to Africa, and once you've experienced untamed nature first-hand it's hard not to let the bush bug bite. Kenya is not always the cheapest destination for wildlife safaris, but with its huge diversity of habitats, cultures and attractions it's undeniably one of the most appealing. The well-developed travel industry allows access to even the remotest areas with a minimum of effort, though with hundreds of companies vying for the tourist buck, it's worth remembering that not all the predators in this particular game walk on four legs. With a bit of common sense, however, the biggest problem you'll face is choosing a trip, and the hardest thing you'll have to do is return to so-called civilisation afterwards.

PLANNING A SAFARI

It's possible to arrange an entire safari from scratch if you hire your own vehicle, but there are lots of things to sort out (see p72) and it's easier and cheaper to go with an organised group. There are an incredible number of companies out there offering a bewildering array of itineraries, so it's a good idea to shop around and find a company that best fits your requirements. Depending on your tastes, you can travel by minibus, 4WD, truck, camel, bicycle or airplane, or even on foot in some places. More than a few travellers book the first safari that fits their budget and end up feeling that they should have chosen something else; a bit of legwork visiting the various companies may save you a lot of time trying to get a refund if the safari isn't what you thought you had booked.

WARNING

Every year we get dozens of letters from readers complaining about bad experiences on safari and the companies mentioned by far the most are some of Nairobi's budget companies. Incidents reported to us range from mere bad practice, such as dodging park fees and ignoring client requests, to pure rip-offs and outright criminal behaviour, including sexual harassment, threats, abuse and assault. Female travellers in particular bear the brunt of many of the worst cases, even when travelling in pairs or small groups.

With this in mind, we can only reinforce yet again just how important it is to take care when booking a budget safari: do as much research as possible, insist on setting out every detail of your trip in advance, don't let yourself be pressured into anything, don't pay any substantial monies up front and, if in doubt, think seriously about stretching your budget to use a reputable midrange firm. The budget companies listed here are 'reliable' in that they have been operating under the same name for years and will at least attempt to take you out on safari rather than disappearing overnight, but satisfaction is by no means guaranteed whoever you go with. Of course, we do receive plenty of positive feedback as well, so there's no need to let potential problems put you off a safari entirely – just keep your wits about you and make it clear from the start that you won't take any crap from anyone!

Choosing a Safari

There are essentially two types of organised safaris – those where you camp, and those where you stay in lodges or luxury tented camps at night. Some budget companies also have their own lodges on the outskirts of parks, which tend to be cheaper, although you'll often lose quite a bit of time shuttling between the lodge and the parks.

Regular wildlife drives can cause other shifts in animal behaviour patterns – in Tsavo West leopards apparently now lurk in roadside ditches during the day, waiting for dik-dik (small antelopes) scared by cars.

Whatever accommodation you choose, safaris typically start and end in either Nairobi or Mombasa, although there are a few exceptions to this. Most companies use either large Toyota Land Cruiser 4WDs or Nissan Urvans (effectively matatus, or minibuses), which have a hatch in the roof for wildlife viewing. This safe vantage point from which to take photos is something you'll miss out on if you hire your own car. Some bigger companies also use open-sided trucks (see p70), which achieve the same effect. A few companies offer walking or cycling safaris (see p70).

As well as transfers to and from Nairobi or Mombasa and between the parks, safari companies offer two wildlife drives per day. Bear in mind that if you arrange a half-day visit to any park as part of your safari, the chances are you won't be visiting at prime viewing time as you'll spend these periods driving to and from your destination.

WHICH PARKS?

Once you've decided on the type of accommodation and where you want to leave from you'll need to pick your parks. Some travellers choose to maximise their chances of seeing the Big Five (elephant, rhino, leopard, lion and buffalo) by visiting one of the more open but crowded parks such as Amboseli or Masai Mara, and often end up with a lot of 'lions-in-front-of-a-jeep' photos. Others prefer to view wildlife in the less disturbed wilderness of the African bush. While they see less wildlife at many of the other parks due to denser vegetation, nothing can beat the sensation of having a pool of basking hippos all to yourself.

People who are interested in specific pursuits such as bird-watching, fishing or tribal culture will find that some parks (and companies) are better suited to their needs than others (see p67).

We've tried to give an impression of what you can expect to find at the various parks (see p53, and individual park entries), but the wildlife is mobile and does not always want to be seen, so there's no guarantee you'll see every species described in the wildlife books.

You should also give some thought to how far away the various parks are from each other, as it's quite easy to spend half your safari driving between the parks if you're not careful.

When to Go

Wildlife can be seen at all times of year, but the migration patterns of the big herbivores (which in turn attract the big predators) are likely to be a major factor in deciding when to go. From July to October, huge herds of wildebeest and zebras cross from the Serengeti in Tanzania to the Masai Mara, and Amboseli also receives huge herds at this time. This is probably prime viewing time as the land is parched, the vegetation has died back and the animals are obliged to come to drink at the ever-shrinking waterholes. However, most safari companies increase their rates at this time.

The long rains (from March to June) and short rains (from October to November) transform the national parks into a lush carpet of greenery. It's very scenic, but it does provide much more cover for the wildlife to hide behind and the rain can turn the tracks into impassable mush. Safaris may be impossible in the lowland parks during either rainy season.

Booking

Many travellers prefer to get all the planning done before they arrive in the country and book from abroad, either through travel agents or directly with companies. Most safari operators have websites and many will take Internet bookings, but making arrangements with anyone other than a well-established top-end operator this way can be a risky business, and if you're going for a budget option you should certainly wait and do your research on the ground when you arrive.

In the high season, many companies depart daily or every second day for the most popular national parks. To less frequented parks such as Samburu, Buffalo Springs, Shaba and Meru, they generally leave only once or twice per week. In addition, most companies will leave for any of the most popular national parks at any time so long as you have a minimum number of people wanting to go, usually four. If you are on your own, you may have to hang around for a while to be bundled together with a larger group. It obviously makes sense to either book ahead or get a group together yourself rather than just turn up alone and expect to leave the next morning. Advance booking is a good idea for Lake Turkana safaris (p69) and the more exotic options described in this chapter.

The best way to ensure you get what you pay for is to decide exactly what you want, then visit the various companies in person and talk through the kind of package you're looking for. A good starting point is to visit one of the travel agents in Nairobi or Mombasa and pick up as many leaflets as you can get your hands on. You can then make an informed choice about which companies to visit. You can also book through the travel agents, although you'll usually pay a little more than if you negotiate directly with the companies, or check out the offers on www.kenyalastminute.com.

One persistent feature of Kenya's safari scene is the role of the street tout. These people will approach you almost as soon as you step off the plane in Nairobi and try to get you signed up for a safari there and then. They're not all bad guys and the safari you end up with may be fine, but you'll pay a mark-up to cover their commission, while the constant hard sell can be exasperating. At most of the budget companies, it's not even worth trying to enter without a tout as they wait by the door and escort every customer inside. On the plus side, many will take you round several companies, so if you want to do a quick circuit of the budget operators

---

ANIMAL SPOTTING

When you visit Kenya's national parks and reserves you'll be spending a lot of time craning your neck and keeping watchful eyes out for animals and birds. There are a few telltale signs to note, as well as a few things you can do to maximise your chances. Most are just common sense, but it's amazing how many people go belting around noisily expecting everything to come to them.

The best time to see wildlife is between 6.30am and 9.30am, and again from 3.30pm to 6.30pm. Make sure your safari company takes you out during these times. Wildlife drives in the middle of the day are largely pointless, although there are signs that in the popular parks (such as Amboseli and Masai Mara) animals are actually changing their normal hunting habits to avoid the tourists. When the tourists head back to the lodges for lunch, the carnivores go out hunting – in peace.

Drive around slowly and, wherever possible, quietly, and keep your eyes trained on the ground ahead and to the side, and on the branches above. In wooded country, agitated and noisy monkeys or baboons are often a sign that there's a big cat (probably a leopard) around.

Vultures circling are not necessarily an indication of a kill below, but if they are gathering in trees and seem to be watching something, you can reasonably assume they are waiting their turn for a go at a carcass.

they can actually be quite helpful, as long as you're firm about not making a final decision that day.

Bear in mind that once you enter a safari company office, the staff may be reluctant to let you walk out without a firm booking, so you'll often be told that the great price they're offering is only valid on the spot. This is more of a problem in the budget places, so be firm and say no if the proposed safari isn't exactly what you're looking for or if you just want to shop around more. Once you've left you're quite free to come back, in which case it should be easy enough to negotiate back down to the original price.

Costs

With all this competition, prices are remarkably uniform across different companies, but the determining factors are always going to be the type of accommodation, the places you want to visit, the season and the duration of the safari. In general, the longer you go for, the less you pay per day. Whichever type of safari you choose, be aware that you generally get what you pay for. A high degree of personal involvement in camp chores and a willingness to eschew creature comforts usually guarantees a lower price. If you want the opposite, it will cost you more.

When choosing a company, look out for those that give something back to the community or conservation projects. For example, the international Peregrine trekking company recently donated US$11,000 to establish a tree plantation on the edge of the Masai Mara, helping regenerate native woodland and provide an income for local people.

There's a good argument for spending a bit more on your safari and using a reliable vehicle. Too many budget companies are notorious for breakdowns and we get a flood of letters every year from travellers who spent at least one day of their safari waiting for a tow truck or mechanic.

For camping safaris with no frills you are looking at US$70 per day, which should include transport, food (three meals per day), park entry and camping fees, tents and cooking equipment. You'll usually be expected to share a tent even if you're travelling alone, although you can pay a single supplement of around 25% of the daily safari rate and have the tent to yourself. Sleeping-bag hire is typically US$10 per trip on top of the safari price.

The prices for staying in lodges or tented camps are considerably higher on the whole. In high season you're looking at a minimum of US$160 per person per night in the lodges and up to US$350 in the luxury tented camps (these prices will drop in the low season). Again, if you want a room to yourself there's usually a supplement of around 25%, although it can be as high as 50%.

At the end of one of these safaris your driver/guide and cook(s) will expect a reasonable tip. This is only fair since wages are low and they will have put in a lot of effort to make your trip memorable. Remember that other travellers are going to follow you and the last thing anyone wants to find is a disgruntled driver/guide who couldn't care less whether you see wildlife or not. At the time of research, a good tip was around KSh200 per guide/cook per day from each traveller – in other words, what you would spend on a couple of drinks.

Many safaris feature side trips to *manyattas* (tribal villages), which provide an opportunity for displaced villagers to make a bit of income from tourism, either posing for photographs or selling souvenirs. Guides and drivers usually levy a fee of around US$10 per head for this, but often this money goes into the driver's pocket. If you visit a *manyatta*, insist that the driver gives the tribespeople their due.

What to Bring

Any organised safari will provide camping gear or accommodation and all meals. You may have to provide your own drinking water, and alcohol is almost always extra, so bringing your own booze can help keep down costs. Sleeping bags can usually be hired from your safari company or local outfitters. If you're planning to attempt the Mt Kenya trek it's probably worth bringing a decent three-season bag from home.

You'll need enough clothing and footwear for hot days and cold nights, but the amount of baggage you'll be allowed to bring will be limited. Excess gear can usually be stored at the safari company's offices. Don't forget to bring a pocketknife and a torch (flashlight) – the company will provide kerosene lanterns for the camp but it's unlikely they'll be left on all night.

'Luxury' items such as toilet paper and mosquito nets are generally not provided, so you'll need to bring your own. Mosquito nets can often be hired and insect repellent, skin cream and mosquito coils are always a good idea. There are few shops in the bush, so sanitary towels, medicines and other important items should all be brought with you.

Service & Feedback

The service provided by even the best safari companies can vary, depending on the driver, the itinerary, the behaviour of the wildlife, flat tyres and breakdowns and, of course, the attitude of the passengers themselves. It's possible for a good company to provide a bad safari and for bad companies to shine occasionally. It's also a volatile market and a company that has a good reputation one year can go to the dogs the next. We've tried to recommend some of the better companies later in this chapter, but this shouldn't take the place of hands-on research once you arrive in the country.

It's worth getting in touch with the **Kenyan Association of Tour Operators** (KATO; ☎ 020-713348; www.katokenya.org; PO Box 48461, Nairobi) before making a booking. It may not be the most powerful regulatory body in the world, but most reputable safari companies subscribe and going with a KATO member will give you *some* recourse in case of conflict. Accreditation by the **Kenya Professional Safari Guides Association** (KPSGA; ☎ 020-609355; www.safariguides .org; PO Box 24397, Nairobi) is also a good indicator of quality. On the ethical side, the **Ecotourism Society of Kenya** (ESOK; ☎ 020-2724755; www.esok.org; PO Box 10146, Nairobi) also maintains a list of member companies who subscribe to its code of conduct for responsible, sustainable safaris.

One thing to look out for whichever company you book with is client swapping. Quite a few companies shift clients on to other companies if they don't have enough people to justify running the trip themselves. This ensures that trips actually depart on time and saves travellers days of waiting for a safari to fill up, but it does undermine consumer trust. Reputable companies will usually inform you before they transfer you to another company. In any case, it may not be the end of the world if you end up taking your safari with a different company from the one you booked with; just make sure the safari you booked and paid for is what you get.

The brochures for some safari companies may give the impression that they offer every conceivable safari under the sun, but in fact, many companies also advertise trips run by other companies. While it's not the most transparent way to do business, again, it needn't be the end of the world. A reliable company will normally choose reliable partners, and you're only really likely to come unstuck at the budget end of the market. Sadly, the only way some of the shoddier operators can get business is through touts, and these companies employ all sorts of tricks to cut costs, including not maintaining their vehicles, entering national parks through side entrances to avoid fees, and employing glorified matatu drivers with little knowledge of the wildlife as guides.

Be particularly careful of safari companies in Nairobi. Some of these guys don't actually run *any* of their own safaris, and are basically just travel

'A reliable company will normally choose reliable partners, and you're only really likely to come unstuck at the budget end of the market'

agents. If you book with one of these operators and anything goes wrong, or the itinerary is changed without your agreement, you have very little come-back and it'll be virtually impossible to get a refund. Unfortunately, it's often hard to tell which are genuine safari companies and which are agents. If you want to know who you're dealing with throughout, go with one of the more expensive agents and confirm exactly who will be operating which parts of the trip, particularly if you are detouring to Tanzania or Uganda.

We welcome all feedback on your safari experiences and will try to incorporate it into future editions of this book.

TYPES OF SAFARI
Camping Safaris

> A potential problem comes from companies that don't have their own equipment at all and only run out to hire a vehicle *after* they've secured a booking.

Camping safaris cater for budget travellers, the young (or young at heart) and those who are prepared to put up with a little discomfort to get the authentic bush experience. At the bottom of the price range, you'll have to forgo luxuries such as flush toilets, running water and cold drinks, and you'll have to chip in to help with chores such as putting up the tents and helping prepare dinner. Showers are provided at some but not all campsites, although there's usually a tap where you can scrub down with cold water. The price of your safari will include three meals a day cooked by the camp cook(s), although food will be of the plain-but-plenty variety.

There are more comfortable camping options, where there are extra staff to do all the work, but they cost more. A number of companies have also set up permanent campsites in the Masai Mara and Samburu National Reserves where you can just drop into bed at the end of a dusty day's drive. At the top end of this market are some very plush luxury campsites offering hot showers and big permanent tents fitted with mosquito nets, beds and sheets, about as far from real camping as five-star hotels are from youth hostels. See p66 for companies using these kind of sites.

Whatever you pay, you'll end up hot, tired and dusty at the end of the day, but you'll sleep well, and if you're lucky your travelling companions should be like-minded independent souls with a sense of adventure. Few things can match the thrill of waking up in the middle of the African bush with nothing between you and the animals except a sheet of canvas and the dying embers of last night's fire. It's not unusual for elephants or hippos to trundle through the camp at night, or even the occasional lion, and, so far, no-one has been eaten or trampled on – that we know of.

Reliable companies offering camping safaris at the time of writing included the following:

Basecamp Explorer (☎ 020-577490; www.basecampexplorer.com; Ole Odume Rd, Hurlingham, Nairobi) An excellent Scandinavian-owned ecotourism operator offering a nine-day camping itinerary to Samburu, Lake Nakuru and the Masai Mara, with walking at Mt Kenya, Lake Bogoria and Lake Baringo. The firm also has its own luxury site in the Masai Mara (p289) and runs plenty of high-end conservation-based safaris, including trips to Lamu, Tanzania, Mt Kenya and Kilimanjaro.

Best Camping Tours (Map pp102-3; ☎ 020-229667; www.bestcampingkenya.com; I&M Towers, Kenyatta Ave, Nairobi) This company offers budget camping safaris on all the main routes, including Amboseli or Masai Mara (three to four days) and Amboseli and Tsavo West (four days). Longer seven- and eight-day safaris visit various combinations of Amboseli, Tsavo West, the Rift Valley lakes, Masai Mara, Mt Kenya, Samburu and Lake Nakuru. It also runs trips into Tanzania. The average cost is around US$80 per day.

Bushbuck Adventures (☎ 020-7121505; bushbuckadventures.com; Peponi Rd, Westlands, Nairobi) Bushbuck is a small company specialising in personalised safaris. It has a private, semi-permanent camp in the northwest corner of the Masai Mara. As a result, it's relatively expensive, but some company profits are put into conservation projects. Prices range from US$150 per person per day for five people to US$340 for one person. The company is also strong on walking safaris.

Eastern & Southern Safaris (Map pp102–3; ☎ 020-242828; www.essafari.co.ke; Finance House, Loita St, Nairobi) A classy and reliable outfit aiming at the midrange and upper end of the market, with standards to match. The basic three-day Masai Mara package comes in at US$367 per person; five days in the Mara and Lake Nakuru costs US$631. Safaris in Tanzania and Uganda are also available. Rates are based on two people sharing, but are reduced for groups of three or more. Departures are guaranteed with just two people for some itineraries.

Flight Centres (Map pp102–3; ☎ 020-210024; www.flightcentres-kenya.com; Lakhamshi House, Biashara St, Nairobi) This company acts as an informal broker for camping safaris in Kenya. It can shop around for you and is a good barometer of quality. It also runs a few of its own overland safaris (see p70) under the umbrella of its parent company, Africa Travel Co.

Gametrackers (Map pp102–3; ☎ 020-338927; www.gametrackersafaris.com; Nginyo Towers, cnr Koinange & Moktar Daddah Sts, Nairobi) Long established and usually reliable, this company offers a full range of camping and lodge safaris around Kenya, including routes in the remote Lake Turkana (see p69). There are also short excursions to Nairobi National Park, walking treks in Aberdare National Park, Mt Kenya treks and numerous long-haul trips to Tanzania, Uganda and further afield. For shorter safaris, rates are usually around US$75 per day. The longer trips depart on set dates, outlined on its website.

Ketty Tours Mombasa (☎ 041-2315178; ketty@africaonline.co.ke; Ketty Plaza, Moi Ave); Diani Beach (☎ 040-203582; Diani shopping centre) This company specialises in short tours of the coastal region (Wasini, Shimba Hills, Gede etc) and into Tsavo East or West. However, it also offers camping safaris to all the usual parks from two to 10 days. Prices typically start at US$100 per person per day for a camping safari and US$120 to US$150 for a luxury trip.

Let's Go Travel (Map pp102–3; ☎ 020-340331; www.lets-go-travel.net; Caxton House, Standard St, Nairobi) This excellent travel agent runs its own safaris and excursions and also sells on an amazing range of trips from other companies, covering Tanzania, Uganda, Ethiopia and even the Seychelles, as well as plenty of specialist and remote options in Kenya itself. Prices are on the high side for camping but the scope justifies the expense, and it's also a good port of call for unusual lodge safaris and car hire.

Primetime Safaris (Map pp102–3; ☎ 020-215773; www.primetime.co.ke; Contrust House, Moi Ave, Nairobi) A big budget player that's widely touted. We've received several good and a few bad reports, so make sure you know exactly what you're getting. The standard five-day Masai Mara trip will cost around US$65 a day.

Safari Seekers (www.safari-seekerskenya.net) Nairobi (Map pp102–3; ☎ 020-652317; Jubilee Insurance Exchange Bldg, Kaunda St); Mombasa (Map p158; ☎ 041-220122; Diamond Trust Arcade, Moi Ave) This budget company has been operating for some years. It has its own permanent campsites in Amboseli, Samburu and Masai Mara, and runs camping and lodge safaris in both Kenya and Tanzania, plus trips into Uganda. Camping safaris cost US$70 to US$105 per person per day (plus US$10 per person per trip for sleeping-bag hire). Departures are at least once a week, or any time with at least four people. Safari Seekers also offers air safaris to Amboseli and Masai Mara with accommodation at luxury lodges or tented camps.

Saferide Safaris (Map pp102–3; ☎ 020-253129; www.saferidesafaris.com; Ave House, Kenyatta Ave, Nairobi) A relatively new budget operator consistently recommended by readers for its camping excursions.

Sana Highlands Trekking Expeditions (Map pp102–3; ☎ 020-227820; www.sanatrekking kenya.com; Contrust House, Moi Ave, Nairobi) Another of the big budget players and a regular stop on the tout circuit. Its brochure is one of the many identikit ones going around and bears a rather cheeky resemblance to the last edition of Lonely Planet's *Kenya*! However, it has had a good reputation in the past for walking safaris as well as the usual camping and lodge itineraries.

Savuka Tours & Safaris (Map pp102–3; ☎ 020-225108; www.savuka-travels.com; Pan African House, Kenyatta Ave, Nairobi) A big-budget operator with extremely persistent touts. The rates are cheap, but its camp in the Masai Mara is 40 minutes from the nearest gate. On the other hand, we've had many positive reports from customers; just make sure you know how much time you'll actually spend inside the parks. Mara, Amboseli, Lake Nakuru and Samburu itineraries are available.

Special Camping Safaris Ltd (☎ 020-350720; www.camping-safaris.com; Whistling Thorns, sinya/Kiserian Pipeline Rd, Kiserian) This small family-run company offers good trips to Masai Mara

'Few things can match the thrill of waking up in the middle of the African bush with nothing between you and the animals except a sheet of canvas and the dying embers of last night's fire'

MINIMAL-IMPACT SAFARIS

However much you pride yourself on your environmental awareness, there's one wild card on every safari: the driver. The person who controls the car controls the impact your trip makes on the country you're passing through, and with massive professional and financial pressure on them, most drivers will habitually break park rules to get you closer to the action. In the interests of the animals, please observe the following:

■ Never get out of your vehicle, except at designated points where this is permitted. Certain species may look harmless enough, but this is not a zoo – the animals are wild and you should treat them as such.

■ Never get too close to the animals and back off if they are getting edgy or nervous. Stress can alter the animals' natural behaviour patterns and could make the difference between this year's lion cubs surviving or getting killed by other predators.

■ Animals always have the right of way. Slow down if you see animals on the road ahead, and leave them plenty of space.

■ Don't follow predators as they move off – you try stalking something when you've got half a dozen minibuses in tow!

■ Keep to the tracks. One of the biggest dangers in the parks is land degradation from vehicles crisscrossing the countryside. The tyre tracks act as drainage channels for the rain and erode the soil, which affects the grasses that attract the herbivores, which attract the predators. Insist that your driver sticks to the main trails, however good the photo opportunity may seem.

■ Don't light fires except at campsites, and dispose of cigarettes carefully. An old film case is the best place for cigarette butts, which can then be disposed of outside the park.

■ Don't litter the parks and campsites. Unfortunately, the worst offenders are safari drivers and cooks who toss everything and anything out the window. It won't do any harm to point out to them the consequences of what they're doing, or you could just clean it up yourself.

(US$495, four days), or Masai Mara and the Rift Valley lakes (US$625, six days), and a full 10-day safari that takes in Masai Mara, Lakes Naivasha, Nakuru, Bogoria and Baringo, Maralal, Samburu and the Mt Kenya foothills (US$1050). All these rates are based on a group of four people.

Lodge & Tented-Camp Safaris

If you can't do without luxuries, there's another side to the safari business, a world of luxurious lodges with swimming pools and bars overlooking secluded waterholes, and wonderfully remote tented camps that re-create the way wealthy hunters used to travel around Kenya a century ago. Some of the lodges are beautifully conceived and the locations are to die for, perched high above huge sweeps of savanna or water holes teeming with African wildlife. Most are set deep within the national parks, so the safari drives offer maximum wildlife-viewing time. A lot of the environmental bad habits of the 1980s, leopard baiting for example, are falling out of favour.

In the lodges you can expect rooms with bathrooms or cottages with air conditioning, international cuisine, a terrace bar beneath a huge *makuti* (palm-thatched) canopy with wonderful views, a swimming pool, wildlife videos and other entertainments, and plenty of staff on hand to cater for all your requirements. Almost all lodges have a waterhole, and some have a hidden viewing tunnel that leads right to the waterside. Some also put out salt to tempt animals to visit, a dubious habit which shouldn't really be encouraged.

The luxury tented camps tend to offer semipermanent tents with fitted bathrooms (hot showers come as standard), beds with mosquito nets, proper furniture, fans and gourmet meals served alfresco in the bush

The really exclusive ones are even more luxurious than the lodges, and tend to be *very* expensive: many of the guests fly in on charter planes, which should give you some impression of the kind of budget we're talking about.

Some of the companies listed for camping safaris also provide lodge-based safaris, but the following are big, reliable operators that have been around for years. Most are members of KATO. In and around Mombasa, most bookings are done through hotels.

Abercrombie & Kent (Map pp102–3; ☎ 020-6950000; www.abercrombiekent.com; Abercrombie & Kent House, Mombasa Rd, Nairobi)

Micato Safaris (☎ 020-220743; www.micato.com; View Park Towers, Monrovia St, Nairobi)

Pollman's Tours & Safaris (☎ 020-337234; www.pollmans.com; Pollman's House, Mombasa Rd, Nairobi)

Private Safaris (www.privatesafaris.co.ke) Nairobi (☎ 020-554150; Twinstar Tower, Mombasa Rd); Mombasa (☎ 041-476000; Safari House, Kaunda St)

Somak Travel (www.somak-nairobi.com) Nairobi (☎ 020-535508; Somak House, Mombasa Rd); Mombasa (☎ 041-487349; Somak House, Nyerere Ave)

Southern Cross Safaris (www.southerncrosssafaris.com) Nairobi (☎ 020-884712; Symbion House, Karen Rd); Mombasa (Map p155; ☎ 041-475074; Kanstan Centre, Nyali Bridge, Malindi Rd); Malindi (Map p206; ☎ 042-30547; Malindi Complex, Lamu Rd)

United Touring Company (UTC; www.unitedtouring.com) Nairobi (☎ 020-331960; Fedha Towers, Kaunda St); Mombasa (☎ 041-316333; Moi Ave)

Prices are similar across these companies (US$160 to US$350 per day). Abercrombie & Kent uses Land Cruiser 4WDs, while the others tend to use minibuses.

SPECIALIST SAFARIS
Bird-Watching Safaris

Most of the safari companies listed in this chapter offer some kind of bird-watching safaris, but quality varies. For the very best Kenya has to offer, contact **Origins Safaris** (☎ 020-312137; www.originsafaris.info; Fedha Towers, Standard St, Nairobi), originally set up as East African Ornithological Safaris by one of the best ornithologists in Kenya. The company offers 14-day specialist bird-watching extravaganzas that take in Mt Kenya, the Rift Valley lakes, Kakamega Forest Reserve, the Masai Mara National Reserve and Lake Victoria.

Top-class lodges are used throughout this trip and the cost, based on two people sharing, works out at US$4986/5803 per person in the low/high season, coming down to US$3061/3663 per person for groups of six. There are monthly departures throughout the year.

Camel Safaris

This is a superb way of getting right off the beaten track and into areas where vehicle safaris don't or can't go. Most camel safaris go to the Samburu and Turkana tribal areas between Isiolo and Lake Turkana and you'll have a chance to experience nomadic life and mingle with tribal people. Wildlife is also plentiful, although it's the journey itself that is the main attraction.

You have the choice of riding the camels or walking alongside them and most tribes are led by experienced Samburu *moran* (warriors) and accompanied by English-speaking tribal guides who are well versed in bush lore, botany, ornithology and local customs. Most travelling is done as early as possible in the cool of the day and a campsite established around noon. Afternoons are time for relaxing, guided walks and showers before drinks and dinner around a camp fire.

Many safari lodges accumulate their own populations of semi-tame monkeys and other small mammals. The well-fed rock hyraxes at the Voi Safari Lodge in Tsavo East are so relaxed that you may have to shoo them out of your room!

All companies provide a full range of camping equipment (generally including two-person tents) and ablution facilities, but they vary in what they require you to bring. Some even provide alcoholic drinks, although normally you pay extra for this. The typical distance covered each day is 15km to 18km so you don't have to be superfit.

The following companies offer camel safaris of varying lengths:

Bobong Camp (☎ 062-32718; olmaisor@africaonline.co.ke; PO Box 5, Rumuruti) This remote camp offers some of Kenya's cheapest self-catered camel safaris – KSh1000 per day for basic hire of one camel and a handler, no other equipment included. You can create your own package and pretty much roam where you want to. Organised Turkana and Samburu cultural visits can also be arranged (KSh5000 per group).

Desert Rose (☎ 0722-638774; www.desertrosekenya.com; PO Box 44801-00100, Nairobi) These walking camel-train safaris leave from the remote Desert Rose lodge just north of Baragoi in northern Kenya. Simple safaris, with no ice or meat, can be arranged for US$120 per day (minimum six nights), while more luxurious trips, with chilled wine and three-course meals, cost US$220 per day (minimum two people, two nights). All trips are led by experienced guides and you have the Matthews Range, Ndoto Mountains and Ol Doinyo Nyiro (near South Horr) as your playground.

Yare Safaris (Map pp102–3; ☎ 020-214099; yare@africaonline.co.ke; Windsor House, University Way, Nairobi) This well-established independent operator offers seven-day trips to Yare Camel Club & Camp (☎ 065-62295) in Maralal for around US$500, picking up the camels at the Ewaso Ngiro River. Short custom packages are also available from the camp itself – US$20 for a day including lunch or US$35 per day for overnight safaris. All-inclusive packages are US$90 per day.

Cultural Safaris

With ecofriendly lodges now springing up all over Kenya, local tribespeople are becoming increasingly involved with tourism, and there are a growing number of companies offering cultural safaris that allow you to interact with the tribes in a far more personal way than the rushed souvenir stops that the mainstream tours make at Maasai villages. The best of these combine volunteer work with more conventional tour activities and provide accommodation in tents, ecolodges and village houses.

Many of the Lake Turkana safaris covered earlier include a trek to Rendille and Samburu villages and interact with the tribespeople.

Reliable and interesting companies include the following:

Eastern & Southern Safaris (☎ 020-242828; www.essafari.co.ke) Excellent luxury 'Green Safaris' run in conjunction with Kenya's Green Belt Movement, involving visitors in cultural and conservation activities around Nairobi, Amboseli, Lake Nakuru and the Masai Mara. The 13-day package costs US$2028, with optional add-ons to visit the beaches around Mombasa or head into Tanzania.

Eco-Resorts (☎ 042-32191; www.eco-resorts.com; PO Box 120, Watamu) This US-based company offers a variety of activity-based volunteer and cultural packages and customised safaris around Kenya. A proportion of profits go to community and conservation projects.

IntoAfrica (☎ 0114-2555610; www.intoafrica.co.uk; 40 Huntingdon Cres, Sheffield, S11 8AX, UK) Runs seven- and 14-day 'fair-traded' trips providing insights into African life and directly supporting local communities. Its Wild Kenya and Kenya Insights safaris explore cultures *and* offer wildlife viewing. Accommodation is in hotels, bush camps and permanent tented camps. Trips leave on scheduled dates and start at around US$140 per person per day; if you have a group, you can pay more and begin the trip when you want.

Origins Safaris (☎ 020-312137; www.originsafaris.info) Origins also offers a superb range of exclusive cultural safaris around the country, including such rare sights as Samburu circumcision ceremonies and tribal initiation rites in southern Ethiopia.

Fishing Safaris

Kenya offers some wonderful fishing and a local permit should cost you just KSh100, but most organised trips are very much geared towards wealthier visitors.

Cultural interaction can have a surprisingly profound effect on some people – in 2005 one Londoner was so taken with traditional Maasai dress that he started wearing it on the streets back home, causing enough of a stir to make the local press.

Perhaps the grandest option is a flying trip to **Rutundu Log Cabins** (☎ 020-340331; www.letsgosafari.com; cabins US$300) in Mt Kenya National Park, booked through Let's Go Travel. Both Lake Rutundu and Lake Alice, a two-hour drive to the south, are well stocked with rainbow trout, while nearby Kazita Munyi River is stocked with brown trout. Rods, flies, boats and guides are all available. Accommodation is in comfortable and well-equipped self-catering cabins, and return charter flights here from Nanyuki are around US$250. Full board is also available for a considerable extra sum.

Origins Safaris (☎ 020-312137; www.originsafaris.info) also offers flying trips to Lake Rutundu. Trips last four days and cost a whopping US$4222 for a single person, coming down to US$1662 per person for a group of four. Nile perch fishing on Lake Turkana is also a possibility.

For shorter fishing excursions, several top-end lodges in the Masai Mara offer short flying trips to Lake Victoria for Nile perch fishing at around US$425 per person for a half-day. Many can be booked through Let's Go Travel. **Lonrho Hotels Kenya** (☎ 020-216940; www.lonrhohotels.com), recently acquired by Fairmont, also arranges half-day river and lake trout-fishing trips from the Mount Kenya Safari Club (p273) in Nanyuki (US$30 per person).

Deep-sea fishing off the Kenyan coast can be arranged with just about any travel agent or top-end resort in the region; Malindi (p208) is a good place to start.

Flying Safaris

These safaris essentially cater for the well-off who want to fly between remote airstrips in the various national parks and stay in luxury tented camps. If money is no object, you can get around by a mixture of charter and scheduled flights and stay in some of the finest camps in Kenya; arrangements can be made with any of the lodge and tented-camp safari operators. Flying safaris to Lake Turkana and Sibiloi National Park are common, and most safari companies will be able to sort out a countrywide itinerary. Safari Seekers (p65) can arrange reasonably priced flying safaris. Quite a few special-interest safari operators use light aircraft to save time.

Lake Turkana Safaris

There can be few travellers who come to Kenya who do not relish the expedition through the semi-arid wilds of Samburu National Reserve and up to the legendary Lake Turkana (Jade Sea). To get an idea of the country you will pass through, see p332 and p338.

These safaris all use open-sided 4WD trucks that take up to 18 people and two to three staff (cook, driver and courier). You will need to set aside a minimum of seven days to complete the journey.

Bushbuck Adventures (☎ 020-7121505; www.bushbuckadventures.com) This company offers 10-day Lake Turkana safaris on request. Itineraries are tailor-made and tend to keep away from the usual routes. Trips often include guided walks, allowing meetings with Rendille and Samburu tribespeople. The Ndoto Mountains, Matthews Range, Shaba National Reserve and Chalbi Desert can all be included.

Gametrackers (☎ 020-338927; www.gametrackersafaris.com) Gametrackers offers 10- and eight-day options to Lake Turkana and is the only company to include Marsabit National Park. Its 10-day safari takes in Mt Kenya, Samburu National Reserve, Marsabit, Chalbi Desert, Lake Turkana, Maralal and Lake Baringo, and costs US$550 (plus a local payment of US$110 per person in Turkana). The eight-day option visits Lake Baringo, Maralal, Lake Turkana and the Samburu National Reserve, and costs US$440 (plus a local payment of US$75). Both safaris use a powerboat for a short excursion on the lake and traditional Turkana huts make up Gametrackers' camp beside the lake 10km south of Loyangalani. Gametrackers also offers a 10-day combined Lake Turkana and camel safari.

'If money is no object, you can get around by a mixture of charter and scheduled flights and stay in some of the finest camps in Kenya'

Motorcycle Safaris

Operating out of Diani Beach, **Fredlink Tours** (☎ 040-3202647; www.motorbike -safari.com; Diani Plaza, Diani Beach) runs motorcycle safaris to the Taita Hills and the Kilimanjaro foothills, supported by a Land Rover. Large 350cc trail bikes are used and the full six-day trips include a wildlife drive in Tsavo West National Park and two nights' lodge accommodation. The cost is KSh57,800 per rider, including meals, camping, guides, fuel and a support vehicle.

Fredlink also rents out motorcycles and scooters (see p178) and can arrange custom-guided motorcycle tours for around KSh6700 per day. Check its website for more information.

Truck Safaris

Overlanding is a common element of many people's travels through Africa. Although most are bound for elsewhere in Africa – Harare or Cape Town are particularly popular – a few Kenya-only trips are available in converted flat-bed trucks that can carry up to 24 passengers.

Following is a list of popular outfits with tours within Kenya. For more on companies that include Kenya as part of an overland trip, see p375.

Acacia Expeditions (UK ☎ 020-7706 4700; www.acacia-africa.com; 23a Craven Tce, London W2 3QH, UK) As well as overland trips, Acacia runs shorter trips within Kenya, including a four-day Masai Mara package (€295 plus a local payment of US$90), four- and six-day packages to Masai Mara and Lake Nakuru (€275 plus US$170 and €395 plus US$149, respectively), a five-day Mt Kenya trek (€495 plus US$60) and a seven-day Kenyan Wildlife Safari (€445 plus US$179). The company also runs specialist tours for disabled clients.

Flight Centres (☎ 020-210024; www.flightcentres-kenya.com) As well as international overland routes of up to 56 days, this company (under its parent company, Africa Travel Co) has a three-day Masai Mara truck trip for UK£195, plus a US$120 kitty.

Guerba Expeditions UK (☎ 01373-826611; www.guerba.co.uk; Wessex House, 40 Station Rd, Westbury, Wiltshire BA13 3JN); Kenya (☎ 020-553056; guerba@africaonline.co.ke; PO Box 43935, Nairobi) This excellent outfit has deep Kenyan roots. Truck safaris include an eight-day tour covering the Masai Mara and lakes Nakuru and Naivasha for UK£325 (plus US$115 kitty) and a 15-day trip that goes to wildlife parks and the lakes for UK£675 (plus US$180 kitty). Its 14-day Kenya Family Safari & Coast package (from UK£875 plus US$170), covering Masai Mara, Lakes Nakuru and Naivasha, Tsavo West and Diani Beach, takes children over eight years old.

> 'Overlanding is a common element of many people's travels through Africa'

Walking & Cycling Safaris

For the keen walker or cyclist and those who don't want to spend all their time in a safari minibus, there are a number of options. For information on treks in Mt Kenya National Park, see p264.

Bike Treks (☎ 020-446371; www.biketreks.co.ke; Kabete Gardens, Westlands, Nairobi) This company offers walking and cycling as well as combined walking/cycling safaris. Its shortest safari is a three-day Masai Mara combined trip, and there are also six-day walking trips to the Loita Plains and Maasai land west and south of Narok, which include a full-day wildlife viewing drive in the Masai Mara. For cyclists there's a six-day safari through the heart of Maasai land, including a full-day wildlife drive in the Masai Mara. A minimum of three people guarantees departure on any of these safaris. Rates are about US$120 per person per day, including food, accommodation, bicycles and/or guides, but not sleeping-bag hire (around US$15 extra per trip).

IntoAfrica (UK ☎ 0114-2555610; www.intoafrica.co.uk) This environmentally and culturally sensitive company gets more praise from readers than almost any other company we've recommended, emphasising on fair trade. Trips include a variety of routes up Mt Kenya and cultural treks with Maasai people in the Chyulu Hills and Tsavo West National Parks. Prices start at around US$975 for a seven-day trek, leaving on a scheduled departure date. See p68 for more culturally focused safaris.

Ontdek Kenya (☎ 061-2030326; www.ontdekkenya.com; PO Box 2352, Nyeri) This small operator has been recommended by several readers and offers walking trips catered to women, vegetarians and bird-watchers. Destinations include the Rift Valley lakes and Mt Kenya.

Samburu Trails Trekking Safaris (UK ☎ 0131-6256635; www.samburutrails.com; 72 Newhaven Rd, Edinburgh EH6 5QG, UK) A small specialist outfit offering a range of foot excursions in some less-visited parts of the Rift Valley, including easy five-day walks (from US$830 per person) and expedition-standard eight-day mountain treks (from US$992).

Savage Wilderness Safaris (☎ 020-521590; www.whitewaterkenya.com; Sarit Centre, Westlands, Nairobi) Kenya's only white-water rafting company also offers organised and custom walking safaris in the Loita and Chyulu Hills and elsewhere, plus climbing and mountaineering on Mt Kenya.

Sirikwa Safaris (☎ 0733-793524; Kitale) This outfit is run by Jane and Julia Barnley from their farmhouse/guesthouse and campsite about 20km outside Kitale on the Lodwar road. They have considerable knowledge of routes and campsites in the Cherangani Hills and can provide trekking guides (KSh825 per day), porters (KSh412 per day) and expert bird-watching guides (KSh825 per half-day). They can also arrange trips to Kakamega Forest Reserve, Saiwa Swamp National Park, Mt Elgon, Kongelai Escarpment, Tata Falls, Turkwel Gorge and the Cherangani Hills.

ITINERARIES

Whether you take a camping or lodge safari, there's a plethora of options ranging from two to 15 days and, in some cases, up to six weeks, visiting parks in neighbouring countries as well. If possible, it's best to go on a safari for at least five days (preferably longer), otherwise a good deal of your time will be taken up driving to and from the national parks and Nairobi. You'll also see a great deal more on a longer safari and have a much better chance of catching sight of all the major animals. In addition, you may also get a chance to spend some time with local tribespeople on a longer safari. The short trips also make stops in tribal villages, but these are normally just a quick souvenir and photo opportunity, and can be a bit demoralising.

Most itineraries offered by safari companies fall into one of three loosely defined 'circuits', which can all be combined for longer trips. Mt Kenya treks (see p264) are a fourth option, sold separately or as an add-on to any of these basic outlines, and the majority of firms now also offer trips into Tanzania and Uganda. Few organised tours take in the western circuit pushed by the Kenya Tourist Board, which would include places such as Kakamega Forest Reserve (p304) and Mt Elgon (p312).

The Mara Circuit

The standard itineraries pushed on visitors by most companies are three-day and seven-day safaris from Nairobi to the Masai Mara (p286). The shorter version will generally involve two nights in the park and two half-days travelling, while the longer trips will also include stops at Lake Nakuru (p243) and Samburu National Reserve (p324). You also have the option of visiting Lakes Baringo (p247) and Bogoria (p246) while in this region.

The Southern Circuit

Offered as the main alternative to the Mara, southern itineraries make a beeline for Amboseli National Park (p137) and its famous Kilimanjaro backdrop. Anything longer than a three-day trip here should allow you to visit Tsavo West (p143), with a couple more days required to add on Tsavo East (p145) as well. Most companies will give you the option of being dropped in Mombasa at the end of this route rather than heading back to Nairobi, which saves you a bit of travelling and allows you time to explore the marine parks and other attractions of the coast.

The Northern Circuit

The focal point of any northern safari is Lake Turkana (p336), which requires at least seven days to visit effectively due to the long distances involved. Depending on how long you take and which side of the lake

> 'If possible, it's best to go on a safari for at least five days (preferably longer), otherwise a good deal of your time will be taken up driving to and from the national parks and Nairobi'

SAFARI FATIGUE

Taking a longer safari is great, but be warned – endless long days peering out of a sunroof, on bumpy roads, in the heat, eating the same food, stuck with the same people, can take its toll quicker than you might think. And while on the first day any animal you see will be exciting, sooner or later most travellers will experience safari fatigue, that jaded feeling of 'not another zebra, I wanna see a f***ing leopard'... A few cultural activities, an afternoon's relaxation or even just a quick swim can do wonders for keeping things fresh.

---

you visit, possible stops include Lake Bogoria, Lake Baringo, Marsabit National Park (p329), Samburu National Reserve and Maralal (p332); a 14-day safari could even cover all of these.

DO-IT-YOURSELF SAFARIS

This is a viable proposition in Kenya if you have some camping equipment and can get a group together to share the costs of renting a vehicle (see p379). It's not a good idea to go on a do-it-yourself safari by yourself; aside from the everyday risks, if you have to change a tyre in lion country you'll want someone to watch your back!

Doing it yourself has several advantages over organised safaris, primarily total flexibility, independence and being able to choose your travelling companions. However, as far as costs go, it's generally true to say that organising your own safari will cost at least as much, and usually more, than going on a cheap organised safari to the same areas.

Apart from the cost, vehicle breakdowns, accidents, security and a lack of local knowledge are also major issues. Maps are hard to find, particularly for remote areas, and if you do break down in the wild you're well and truly on your own. Not to mention the fact that whoever is driving is going to be too busy concentrating on the road to notice much of the wildlife.

With an appropriate vehicle, all accommodation options are open to you, even out-of-the-way places, and camping and using bandas are two good ways to keep down your costs. **Let's Go Travel** (☎ 020-340331; www.lets-go -travel.net) is the best outfit to contact for this type of accommodation.

If you want to hire camping equipment, the only place to go is **Atul's** (Map pp102-3; ☎ 020-225935; Biashara St, PO Box 43202, Nairobi). Identification, such as a passport, is required and advance booking is recommended and saves time. Expect to pay KSh250 per day for a sleeping bag with liner, KSh500 for a two-person dome tent and KSh120 per day for gas stove (gas canisters are extra). On most items there is a deposit of KSh2000 to KSh3000. For longer trips, it may work out cheaper to buy some things at the big Nakumatt supermarkets in Nairobi, which sell cheap plastic plates, stoves, chairs etc.

It's also possible to hire a vehicle and camping equipment as one package – **Tough Tracks** (☎ 050-2030329; www.toughtracks.com; PO Box 563, Naivasha) offers the rather unusual option of renting a fully fitted 4WD with roof-mounted tent and everything else you might need for a long self-service safari for up to four people, including mobile phone, fridge, gas cooker and cooking utensils. Prices range from UK£85 per day (less than 10 days) to UK£70 per day (25 days or more), with a minimum of five days rental; insurance excess waiver is an additional UK£10 per day (see p379 for more on car-rental insurance). The firm's based in Naivasha but will deliver your vehicle to and pick it up from an agreed point such as an airport.

Wildlife Guide

For many travellers, Africa means animals – and for the wildlife watcher Kenya is one of the prime locations for seeing nature in the raw. Nowhere else on Earth is so great an array of large animals supported by such a range of environmental and climatic variations. All manner of wildlife experience is here: the epic seasonal migrations of huge zebra herds, the excitement of the solitary cheetah bringing down its prey, the skittish avian inhabitants of Arabuko-Sokoke, the protective mother warthog watching over her young.

The East African mosaic of riverine forest, savanna and lake shore was favoured by the earliest humans. For millennia thereafter it was humankind who was the intruder in this domain. Today, only pockets of this once-mighty untouched realm remain, but it is here that the wild-life-watcher is drawn. Whether you hanker after the massed flamingos at Lake Bogoria, the grazing herds of antelope and wildebeest on the savanna, the shrieking monkeys in the forest canopy in Kakamega, or the ponderous elephants and delicately stepping giraffes of Samburu National Reserve, there's no real trick to spotting wildlife in Kenya. If you're in the right place at the right time, wildlife is in abundance, so you need to get out there and put in the time, be it on a safari vehicle, atop a camel or on foot.

Bear in mind, too, that by watching wildlife in Kenya you are help-ing to conserve it. A substantial amount of foreign currency is earned from wildlife tourism in Kenya and other East African countries. The money you spend in visiting national parks and reserves contributes to the long term viability of these sanctuaries where the fabled great cats and innumerable herd animals can continue to carry out their timeless life-and-death drama.

Zebra in motion, Masai Mara National Reserve.
PHOTO BY PHILIP & KAREN SMITH

PRIMATES

BUSHBABY
Greater bushbaby (Otolemur crassicaudatus, pictured); East African lesser bushbaby (Galago senegalensis)

These nocturnal primates have small heads, large rounded ears, bushy tails and enormous eyes. Greater bushbabies are dark brown; tiny lesser bushbabies are light grey with yellow on their legs. They are often in family groups of up to six or seven, but forage alone for sap, fruit, insects and, in the case of greater bushbabies, lizards, nestlings and eggs. Lesser bushbabies make spectacular treetop leaps.

Size: Greater bushbaby length 80cm, including 45cm tail; weight up to 1.5kg. Lesser bushbaby length 40cm; weight 150g to 200g. **Distribution:** Lightly wooded savanna to thickly forested areas; greater and lesser bushbabies occur mostly in southern and central Kenya. **Status:** Common but strictly nocturnal.

The male vervet monkey has a distinctive bright-blue scrotum, an important signal of status in the troop.

PHOTO BY DAVID WALL

VERVET MONKEY
Cercopithecus aethiops

Conspicuous inhabitants of the woodland-savanna, vervet monkeys are easily recognised by their grizzled grey hair and black face fringed with white. Troops may number up to 30. Vervet monkeys have a sophisticated vocal repertoire, with, for example, different calls for different predators. They are diurnal and forage for fruits, seeds, leaves, flowers, invertebrates and the occasional lizard or nestling. They rapidly learn where easy pickings can be found around lodges and campsites, but become pests when they are accustomed to being fed.

Size: Length up to 130cm, including 65cm tail; weight 3kg to 9kg; male larger than female. **Distribution:** All savanna and woodland habitats. **Status:** Very common and easy to see.

The blue monkey's social group may be as large as 30 but generally numbers between four and 12.

PHOTO BY ANDERS BLOMQVIST

BLUE (SAMANGO) MONKEY
Cercopithecus mitis

Similar to vervet monkeys, but slightly larger and much darker, blue monkeys have a grey to black face, black shoulders, limbs and tail, and a reddish-brown or olive-brown back. They are more arboreal than vervet monkeys and generally prefer dense forest and woodland rather than savanna. They feed largely on fruit, bark, gum and leaves. Social groups usually consist of related females and their young, and a single adult male. Their broad diet allows them to occupy relatively small home ranges.

Size: Length 140cm, including 80cm tail; weight normally up to 15kg, but as much as 23kg; male larger than female. **Distribution:** Throughout most evergreen forests and forest patches. **Status:** Locally common; active by day; often difficult to see in foliage.

EASTERN BLACK-AND-WHITE COLOBUS
Colobus guereza

This colobus is glossy black with a white face, bushy white tail and a white fur 'cape'. Newborns are initially white, gaining their adult coat at around six months. The black-and-white colobus spends most of its time in the forest canopy, where it feeds mostly on leaves. The ready availability of its food enables it to survive on quite small home ranges, usually maintained by troops of up to 12 animals, consisting of a dominant male, females and young.

Size: Length 140cm, including 80cm tail; weight 3.5kg to 10kg; male larger than female. **Distribution:** Forests in western Kenya; the similar Angolan black-and-white colobus *(C. angolensis)* can be found in southeast Kenya. **Status:** Locally common; active during the day but often difficult to see among foliage.

The black-and-white colobus' low-energy diet means it is relatively inactive but it makes spectacular leaps when moving through the treetops.

PHOTO BY ARIADNE VAN ZANDBERGEN

BABOON
Papio cynocephalus

Baboons are unmistakable. The yellow baboon *(P. c. cynocephalus)* and the olive baboon *(P. c. anubis;* pictured) are named for their differing hair colour. Baboons live in troops of between eight and 200; contrary to popular belief there is no single dominant male. Social interactions are complex, with males accessing only certain females, males forming alliances to dominate other males, and males caring for unrelated juveniles. Baboons forage in woodland-savanna for grasses, tubers, fruits, invertebrates and occasionally small vertebrates.

Size: Shoulder height 75cm; length 160cm, including 70cm tail; weight up to 45kg; male larger than female, and twice as heavy. **Distribution:** The yellow baboon is common in central and eastern Kenya; the olive baboon is more common in western Kenya. **Status:** Abundant.

Ever opportunistic, baboons often visit campsites and may become (dangerous) pests.

PHOTO BY JASON EDWARDS

CARNIVORES

PANGOLIN
Manis temminckii

Ground pangolins are covered with large rounded scales over the back and tail, and have a sparse covering of hair on the face and underbelly. Pangolins (which are also known as scaly anteaters) walk on the outer edges of their paws with their claws pointed inwards, leaving a distinctive track.

Size: Length 70cm to 100cm; weight 5kg to 15kg. **Distribution:** Throughout Kenya, apart from the northeast, in many habitats except dense forest. **Status:** Relatively uncommon; nocturnal and difficult to see.

Pangolins subsist entirely on ants and termites that they excavate from termite mounds, rotting wood and dung heaps.

PHOTO BY ANDREW VAN SMEERDIJK

JACKAL
Golden jackal (Canis aureus); black-backed jackal (Canis mesomelas, pictured); side-striped jackal (Canis adustus)

Golden jackals are often the most numerous carnivores in open savanna and are very active by day. Black-backed jackals have a mantle of silver-grey hair and black-tipped tails; they are the most common night scavengers. Side-striped jackals are grey with a light stripe along each side and a white-tipped tail. All have a similar social and feeding behaviour. Pairs are long-lasting and defend small territories.

Size: Shoulder height 38cm to 50cm; length 95cm to 120cm, including 25cm to 40cm tail (shortest in the golden jackal); weight up to 15kg. **Distribution:** Throughout Kenya, preferring open plains and woodlands; side-striped jackal most abundant in well-watered wooded areas. **Status:** Abundant in parks and settled areas.

BAT-EARED FOX
Otocyon megalotis

These little foxes eat mainly insects, especially termites, but also wild fruit and small vertebrates. They are monogamous and are often seen in groups comprising a mated pair and offspring. Natural enemies include large birds of prey, spotted hyenas, caracals and larger cats. They will bravely attempt to rescue a family member caught by a predator by using distraction techniques and harassment, which extends to nipping larger enemies on the ankles.

Size: Shoulder height 35cm; length 75cm to 90cm, including 30cm tail; weight 3kg to 5kg. **Distribution:** Throughout Kenya; absent from mountainous habitat and dense forest. **Status:** Common, especially in national parks; mainly nocturnal but often seen in the late afternoon and early morning.

WILD DOG
Lycaon pictus

Wild dogs' blotched black, yellow and white coat, and their large, round ears, are unmistakable. They live in packs of up to 40, though usually 12 to 20. They are widely reviled for eating their prey alive, but this is probably as fast as 'cleaner' methods used by other carnivores. Mid-sized antelopes are their preferred prey, but wild dogs can take animals as large as buffaloes. They require enormous areas of habitat and they are among the most endangered carnivores in Africa.

Size: Shoulder height 65cm to 80cm; length 100cm to 150cm, including 35cm tail; weight 20kg to 35kg. **Distribution:** Much reduced, now restricted to the largest protected areas, including Tsavo National Park. **Status:** Highly threatened: numbers reduced by persecution, disease and habitat loss.

CAPE CLAWLESS OTTER
Aonyx capensis

Similar to European otters, but much larger, Cape clawless otters are a glossy chocolate brown with a white or cream-coloured lower face, throat and neck. Only the hind feet are webbed, and, unlike the front feet of most otters, the front feet of Cape clawless otters end in dexterous, human-like fingers with rudimentary nails. Otters are active during early morning and evening, though they become nocturnal in areas where they are hunted by humans. Their main foods include fish, freshwater crabs and frogs.

Size: Length 105cm to 160cm, including 50cm tail; weight up to 30kg. **Distribution:** Large freshwater bodies and along coastlines across Kenya. **Status:** Locally common; active both day and night but usually seen in the early morning and late afternoon.

Otters are very entertaining to watch, being active and vocal – their repertoire includes whistles, mews and chirps.
PHOTO BY ROGER DE LA HARPE/ GALLO IMAGES

HONEY BADGER (RATEL)
Mellivora capensis

Pugnacious and astonishingly powerful for their size, honey badgers have a fascinating relationship with honey guide birds. Honey guides lead them to bees' nests, which honey badgers rip open for honey, and in doing so provide honey guides access to their favoured food – beeswax. Honey badgers are omnivorous, feeding on small animals, carrion, berries, roots, eggs, honey and social insects (ants, termites and bees) and their larvae. Honey badgers are best viewed in parks, where they sometimes scavenge from bins.

Size: Shoulder height 30cm; length 95cm, including 20cm tail; weight up to 15kg. **Distribution:** Widespread, apart from the northeast, in most habitats. **Status:** Generally occurs in low densities, but populations are sustainable; apparently active by day in parks but nocturnal in areas of human habitation.

The honey badger's thick, loose skin is an excellent defence against predators, bee stings and snake bites.
PHOTO BY LORNA STANTON/ GALLO IMAGES

GENET
Small-spotted genet (Genetta genetta); large-spotted genet (Genetta tigrina, pictured)

Relatives of mongooses, genets resemble slender domestic cats, with foxlike faces. The two species can be differentiated by the tail tips – white in the small-spotted, black in the large-spotted. The former also has a crest along the spine, which it raises when threatened. All-black individuals of both species may occur, particularly in mountainous regions. They hunt on land and in trees, feeding on rodents, birds, reptiles, eggs, insects and fruits. Genets deposit their droppings in latrines, usually in open sites.

Size: Shoulder height 18cm; length 85cm to 110cm, including 45cm tail; weight up to 3kg. **Distribution:** Throughout Kenya. **Status:** Very common but strictly nocturnal; often the most common small carnivore seen at night.

Genets are solitary, sleeping by day in burrows, rock crevices or tree hollows.
PHOTO BY ARIADNE VAN ZANDBERGEN

MONGOOSE

Many of the small animals that dash in front of cars in Africa are mongooses. A few species, such as the dwarf mongoose *(Helogale parvula)* and the banded mongoose *(Mungos mungo)* are intensely social, keeping contact with twittering calls while foraging. Others, such as the slender mongoose *(Galerella sanguinea;* pictured) – with a black-tipped tail that it holds aloft when running – and the white-tailed mongoose *(Ichneumia albicauda)*, are usually solitary. Family groups are better at spotting danger and raising kittens. Invertebrates are their most important prey.

Size: Ranges from the dwarf mongoose at 40cm in length and up to 400g in weight, to the white-tailed mongoose at 120cm and up to 5.5kg. **Distribution:** Throughout Kenya. They prefer open areas to closed woodlands and wooded savanna. **Status:** Common; sociable species are diurnal, while solitary species are generally nocturnal.

AARDWOLF
Proteles cristatus

The smallest of the hyena family, aardwolves subsist almost entirely on harvester termites (which are generally ignored by other termite eaters because they are so noxious), licking more than 200,000 from the ground each night. Unlike other hyaenids, they don't form clans; instead, they forage alone and mates form only loose associations with each other. The male assists the female in raising the cubs, mostly by babysitting at the den while the mother forages. Aardwolves are persecuted in the mistaken belief that they kill stock.

Size: Shoulder height 40cm to 50cm; length 80cm to 100cm, including tail of up to 25cm; weight 8kg to 12kg. **Distribution:** Widespread in savanna and woodland habitats from the south of Kenya into the country's arid north. **Status:** Uncommon; nocturnal but occasionally seen at dawn and dusk.

SPOTTED HYENA
Crocuta crocuta

Widely reviled as scavengers, spotted hyenas are highly efficient predators with a fascinating social system. Females are larger than, and dominant to, males and have male physical characteristics, including an erectile clitoris that renders the sexes virtually indistinguishable. Spotted hyenas are massively built and appear distinctly canine, but they are more closely related to cats than dogs. They can run at a speed of 60km/h and a pack can easily dispatch adult wildebeests and zebras. Their 'ooo-oop' call is one of the most distinctive East African night sounds.

Size: Shoulder height 85cm; length up to 180cm, including up to 30cm tail; weight up to 80kg. **Distribution:** Increasingly restricted to conservation areas. **Status:** Common where there is suitable food, often the most common large predator in protected areas; mainly nocturnal but also seen during the day.

SERVAL
Felis serval

The first impression one gains of servals – tall, slender, long-legged cats – is that they look like small cheetahs. The tawny to russet-yellow coat has large black spots, forming long bars and blotches on the neck and shoulders. All-black individuals do occasionally occur. Other distinguishing features include large upright ears, a long neck and a relatively short tail. Servals are associated with vegetation near water and are most common in flood-plain savanna, wetlands and woodlands near streams. Birds, small reptiles and occasionally the young of small antelopes are also taken.

Servals are rodent specialists, feeding on mice, rats and springhares.
PHOTO BY DAVID WALL

Size: Shoulder height 60cm; length up to 130cm, including tail up to 30cm; weight up to 16kg.
Distribution: Well-watered habitats throughout Kenya. **Status:** Relatively common but mainly nocturnal, sometimes seen in the early morning and late afternoon.

CARACAL
Felis caracal

Sometimes called African lynxes due to their long, tufted ears, caracals are robust, powerful cats that prey on small antelopes, birds and rodents but also take prey much larger than themselves. Caracals are largely solitary, and although male–female pairs may associate more than most other cats, females raise their one to three kittens alone. The sandy body colour is excellent camouflage, but the ears and face are strikingly patterned in black and white and are highly mobile and expressive – features are used for visual signalling.

Caracals' long back legs power prodigious leaps – they even take birds in flight.
PHOTO BY DAVID WALL

Size: Shoulder height 40cm to 50cm; length 95cm to 120cm, including tail up to 30cm; weight 7kg to 18kg; male slightly larger than female. **Distribution:** Throughout Kenya. **Status:** Fairly common but largely nocturnal and difficult to see.

LEOPARD
Panthera pardus

Supreme ambush hunters, leopards stalk close to their prey before attacking in an explosive rush. They eat everything from insects to zebras, but antelopes are their primary prey. Leopards are highly agile and climb well, spending more time in trees than other big cats – they hoist their kills into trees to avoid losing them to lions and hyenas. They are solitary animals, except when a male and female remain in close association for the female's week-long oestrus.

Leopards are heard more often than seen; their rasping territorial call sounds very much like a saw cutting through wood.
PHOTO BY ABI

Size: Shoulder height 50cm to 75cm; length 160cm to 210cm, including 70cm to 110cm tail; weight up to 90kg; male larger than female. **Distribution:** Widely spread throughout Kenya; of all the big cats, the most tolerant of human activity. **Status:** Common but, being mainly nocturnal, they are very difficult to see.

Young male lions are ousted from the pride at the age of two or three, becoming nomadic until around five years old, when they are able to take over their own pride.

PHOTO BY LUKE HUNTER

LION

Panthera leo

Lions spend the night hunting, patrolling territories (of 50 to 400 sq km) and playing. They live in prides of up to about 30, comprising four to 12 related females, which remain in the pride for life, and a coalition of unrelated males, which defend females from foreign males. Lions hunt – certainly as a group, perhaps cooperatively – virtually anything, but wildebeests, zebras and buffaloes are their main targets.

Size: Shoulder height 120cm; length 250cm to 300cm, including tail up to 100cm; weight up to 260kg (male), 180kg (female). **Distribution:** Largely confined to protected areas and present in all savanna and woodland parks in Kenya. **Status:** Common where they occur; mainly nocturnal but easy to see during the day.

Three out of every four hunts fail for cheetahs.

PHOTO BY ANDREW VAN SMEERDIJK

CHEETAH

Acinonyx jubatus

The world's fastest land mammal, cheetahs can reach speeds of over 105km/h but become exhausted after a few hundred metres and therefore usually stalk prey to within 60m before unleashing their tremendous acceleration. Cheetahs prey on antelopes weighing up to 60kg as well as hares and young wildebeests and zebras. Litters may be as large as nine, but in open savanna habitats most cubs are killed by other predators, particularly lions. Young cheetahs disperse from the mother when aged around 18 months. The males form coalitions; females remain solitary for life.

Size: Shoulder height 85cm; length up to 220cm, including tail up to 70cm; weight up to 65kg. **Distribution:** Largely restricted to protected areas and surrounding regions; shuns densely forested areas. **Status:** Uncommon, with individuals moving over large areas; frequently seen in national parks.

Bull elephants live alone or in bachelor groups, joining herds when females are in season.

PHOTO BY ALEX DISSANAYAKE

UNGULATES

AFRICAN ELEPHANT

Loxodonta africana

Elephants usually live in groups of 10 to 20 females and their young, congregating in larger herds at common water and food resources. A cow may mate with many bulls. Vocalisations include a deep rumble felt as a low vibration, and a high-pitched trumpeting given in threat or when frightened. Consuming 250kg of vegetation daily, elephants can decimate woodlands, but this may be part of the savanna's natural cycle. They live for up to 100 years.

Size: Shoulder height up to 4m (male), 3.5m (female); weight 5 to 6.5 tonnes (male), 3 to 3.5 tonnes (female). **Distribution:** Widely distributed in Kenya apart from the north. **Status:** Very common in most of the larger national parks.

HYRAX
Rock Hyrax (Procavia capensis, pictured); Yellow-Spotted Rock Hyrax (Heterohyrax brucei)

Hyraxes (or dassies) occur nearly everywhere there are mountains or rocky outcrops. They are sociable, living in colonies of up to 60. Yellow-spotted hyraxes are distinguished by the presence of a prominent white spot above the eye.

Despite resembling large guinea pigs, hyraxes are actually related to elephants.
PHOTO BY ARIADNE VAN ZANDBERGEN

Hyraxes spend much of the day basking on rocks or chasing other hyraxes. If accustomed to humans they are often approachable, but will dash off if alarmed, uttering shrill screams. Rocks streaked white by hyraxes' urine are often an indicator of a colony's presence.

Size: Rock hyrax length up to 60cm; weight up to 5.5kg. Yellow-spotted hyrax length up to 50cm; weight up to 2.5kg. **Distribution:** Both species are very widely distributed throughout Kenya. **Status:** Common; regularly inhabit areas around lodges, where they become tame.

BURCHELL'S ZEBRA
Equus burchelli

Thousands of Burchell's zebras (one of three zebra species in Africa) join blue wildebeests on their famous mass migration. Larger herds are usually temporary aggregations of smaller groups. Stallions may hold a harem for 15 years, but they often lose single mares to younger males, which gradually build up their own harems. When pursued by predators, zebras close ranks as they run off, making it hard for any individual to be singled out for attack. And yes, it's true – a zebra's stripes are as individual as a human's fingerprints.

The zebra's sociality centres on harems of five to six mares defended by a single stallion.
PHOTO BY MANFRED GOTTSCHALK

Size: Shoulder height 1.4m to 1.6m; length 2.2m to 2.6m; weight up to 390kg; females are slightly smaller than males. **Distribution:** In and around parks throughout Kenya. **Status:** Very common and easily seen.

BLACK (HOOK-LIPPED) RHINOCEROS
Diceros bicornis

In many countries rhinos have been exterminated and the white rhino *(Ceratotherium simum)* is now very rare in East Africa (it remains numerous in southern Africa). The smaller of the two species, black rhinos are more unpredictable and prone to charging when alarmed or uncertain about a possible threat. They use their pointed, prehensile upper lip to feed selectively on branches and foliage. Black rhinos are solitary and aggressively territorial, usually only socialising during the mating season; however, they may form temporary associations.

Poaching for horns has made the rhinoceros Africa's most endangered large mammal.
PHOTO BY JASON EDWARDS

Size: Shoulder height 1.6m; length 3m to 4m; weight 800kg to 1400kg; front horn up to 130cm long. **Distribution:** Restricted to relict populations in a few reserves; black best seen in Nairobi National Park; white best seen in Lake Nakuru National Park. **Status:** Highly endangered but seen in protected areas.

Female warthogs have a pair of distinctive facial warts under the eyes; males have a second set of warts further down the snout.
PHOTO BY ABI

WARTHOG
Phacochoerus aethiopicus

Warthogs grow two sets of tusks: their upper tusks grow as long as 60cm, and their lower tusks are usually less than 15cm long. Sociality varies, but groups usually consist of one to three sows and their young. Males form bachelor groups or are solitary, only associating with females during oestrus. Warthogs feed mainly on grass, but also on fruit and bark. In hard times, they grub for roots and bulbs. They den in abandoned burrows or excavate their own burrows.

Size: Shoulder height 70cm; weight up to more than 100kg, but averages 50kg to 60kg; male larger than female. **Distribution:** Throughout Kenya except in dense rainforest and mountains above 3000m. **Status:** Common, diurnal and easy to see.

Adult bull hippos aggressively defend territories against each other and most males bear the scars of conflicts.
PHOTO BY CHRISTER FREDRIKSSON

HIPPOPOTAMUS
Hippopotamus amphibius

Hippos are found close to fresh water, spending most of the day submerged and emerging at night to graze on land. They can consume about 40kg of vegetation each evening. They live in large herds, tolerating close contact in the water but foraging alone when on land. The scars found on bulls resulting from conflicts are often a convenient indicator of the sex of hippos. Cows with calves are aggressive towards other individuals. Hippos are extremely dangerous when on land and kill many people each year, usually when someone inadvertently blocks the animal's retreat to the water.

Size: Shoulder height 1.5m; weight 1000kg to 2000kg; male larger than female. **Distribution:** Usually found near large areas of fresh water throughout Kenya. **Status:** Common in major water courses and easy to see.

A giraffe's neck has seven cervical vertebrae, the same as all mammals.
PHOTO BY DAVID WALL

GIRAFFE
Giraffa camelopardalis

There are several distinctly patterned subspecies of giraffe, including reticulated giraffes and the more common Masai giraffes. The 'horns' (skin-covered bone) of males have bald tips; females' are covered in hair. Giraffes form ever-changing groups of up to 50; females are rarely seen alone, while males are more solitary. Giraffes exploit foliage out of reach of most herbivores – males usually feed from a higher level than females. Juveniles are prone to predation and lions even take adults; giraffes are most vulnerable when drinking.

Size: Height 4m to 5.5m (male), 3.5m to 4.5m (female); weight 900kg to 1400kg (male), 700kg to 1000kg (female). **Distribution:** Reticulated giraffe occurs in northern Kenya; Masai giraffe is widespread southwest of Nairobi extending into Tanzania; Rothschild's giraffe is restricted to western Kenya near Lake Baringo. **Status:** Relatively common and easy to see.

BUSHBUCK

Tragelaphus scriptus

Shy and solitary animals, bushbucks inhabit thick bush close to permanent water, where they browse on leaves at night. Bushbucks are chestnut to dark brown in colour and have a variable number of white vertical stripes on the body between the neck and rump, as well as a number of white spots on the upper thigh and a white splash on the neck. Normally only males grow horns, which are straight with gentle spirals and average about 30cm in length. When startled, bushbucks bolt and crash loudly through the undergrowth.

Bushbucks can be quite aggressive and even dangerous when cornered.
PHOTO BY MITCH REARDON

Size: Shoulder height 80cm; weight 45kg to 80kg; horns up to 55cm long; male larger than female.
Distribution: Throughout the region, favouring denser habitats. **Status:** Common, but shy and difficult to see.

KUDU

Greater kudu (Tragelaphus strepsiceros, pictured); lesser kudu (Tragelaphus imberbis)

Greater kudus are Africa's second-tallest antelope; males carry massive spiralling horns (the largest of any antelope). They are light grey in colour, with six to 12 white stripes down the sides. Lesser kudus have 11 to 15 stripes; males are blue-grey and females are a bright rust colour. One to three females and their young form groups, and are joined by males during the breeding season. Kudus find their diet in woodland-savanna with fairly dense bush cover.

Strong jumpers, kudus flee with frequent leaping, clearing obstacles more than 2m high.
PHOTO BY LUKE HUNTER

Size: Greater kudu shoulder height 1.2m to 1.5m; weight 190kg to 320kg. Lesser kudu shoulder height 95cm to 110cm; weight 90kg to 110kg. Males larger than females. **Distribution:** Greater kudus can be found throughout Kenya, except in the driest areas; lesser kudus prefer the arid regions of northern Kenya. **Status:** Greater kudus scattered; lesser kudus common.

ELAND

Taurotragus oryx

Africa's largest antelope, elands are massive. The horns of both sexes average 65cm, spiralling at the base then sweeping straight back. The male has a distinctive hairy tuft on the head, and stouter horns. Herds consist of adults, or adults and young, or sometimes just young – group membership and composition change often. The most common large groups consist of 10 to 60 females and young. Males are less gregarious, coming together more sporadically and in smaller numbers, but one or more often join female-and-young herds.

Aggregations up to 1000 elands form where new grass is growing.
PHOTO BY DAVID WALL

Size: Shoulder height 1.5m to 1.8m (male), 1.25m to 1.5m (female); weight 450kg to 950kg (male), 300kg to 500kg (female); horns up to 100cm long. **Distribution:** Patchy distribution in arid zones; best seen in Nairobi and Tsavo National Parks. **Status:** Low density but relatively common and easy to see.

Male buffaloes associate with the females during breeding, and at other times they form male herds or are solitary.

PHOTO BY LUKE HUNTER

AFRICAN BUFFALO
Syncerus caffer

Both sexes of African buffaloes have distinctive curving horns that broaden at the base to meet over the forehead in a massive 'boss' – the female's are usually smaller. Local populations of buffaloes inhabit large home ranges and at times herds of thousands form, but the population's social organisation is fluid: groups of related females and their young coalesce and separate into larger or smaller herds. Although generally docile, buffaloes can be dangerous – especially lone bulls, and females protecting their young.

Size: Shoulder height 1.6m; weight 400kg to 900kg; horns up to 1.25m long; female somewhat smaller than male. **Distribution:** Widespread, but large populations only occur in parks. **Status:** Common and may be approachable where protected.

Duikers are predominantly browsers, often feeding on agricultural crops.

PHOTO BY MITCH REARDON

COMMON (GREY) DUIKER
Sylvicapra grimmia

One of the most common types of small antelope, common duikers are usually solitary, but are sometimes seen in pairs. They are greyish light brown in colour, with a white belly and a dark-brown stripe down the face. Only males have horns, which are straight and pointed and rarely grow longer than 15cm. Their habit of feeding on agricultural crops leads to them being persecuted outside conservation areas, although they are resilient to hunting. Common duikers are capable of going without water for long periods, but they will drink whenever water is available.

Size: Shoulder height 50cm; weight 10kg to 20kg; females slightly larger than males; horns up to 18cm. **Distribution:** Throughout Kenya. **Status:** Common; active day and night, but more nocturnal where disturbance is common.

The waterbuck's oily hair has a strong, musky odour, potent enough for humans to smell.

PHOTO BY DENNIS JONES

WATERBUCK
Kobus ellipsiprymnus

Waterbucks have a shaggy brown coat and white rump, face and throat markings; only males have horns. Females have overlapping ranges, coming and going to form loose associations of normally up to a dozen animals. Young, nonterritorial males behave similarly. Mature males hold territories, onto which females wander (nonterritorial males are also often allowed access). These essentially independent movements sometimes produce herds of 50 to 70. They always stay near water and are good swimmers, readily entering water to escape predators.

Size: Shoulder height 1.3m; weight 200kg to 300kg (male), 150kg to 200kg (female); horns up to 100cm. **Distribution:** Wet areas throughout Kenya. **Status:** Common and easily seen.

REEDBUCK

Common reedbuck (Redunca arundinum); Bohor reedbuck (Redunca reduca, pictured); mountain reedbuck (Redunca fulvorufula)

Brown common reedbucks are found in woodland areas; yellowish bohor reedbucks are prevalent on floodplains; greyer mountain reedbucks inhabit grassy hill country. All have white underparts; males

Reedbucks whistle when advertising territories or when alarmed.
PHOTO BY DENNIS JONES

have forward-curving horns. Common reedbucks form pairs, though mates associate only loosely; female mountain reedbucks form small groups that range over the territories of several males.

Size: Common reedbuck shoulder height 90cm; weight 70kg; horns up to 45cm. Bohor reedbuck 30% smaller; mountain reedbuck 30% smaller again. Males larger than females in common and bohor reedbucks; sexes similar size in mountain reedbucks. **Distribution:** Throughout Kenya wherever suitable well-watered grasslands occur. **Status:** Common.

ROAN ANTELOPE

Hippotragus equinus

Roan antelopes' coats vary from reddish-fawn to dark reddish-brown with white underparts and a mane of stiff, black-tipped hair. Their faces are black and white, their long, pointed ears tipped with a brown tassel. Both sexes have long backward-curving horns. They prefer sites with tall grasses, shade and water. Herds of

Roan antelopes are among Africa's rarest and largest antelopes.
PHOTO BY JASON EDWARDS

normally less than 20 females and young range over the territories of several adult males; other males form bachelor groups. Female herds of up to 50 are common during the dry season when food and water are more localised.

Size: Shoulder height 1.4m; weight 200kg to 300kg; horns up to 100cm. Females smaller than males, with shorter horns. **Distribution:** Mostly at Ruma National Park near Lake Victoria. **Status:** Populations are declining and the species is threatened in Kenya; easily seen where present.

SABLE ANTELOPE

Hippotragus niger

Widely considered to be the most magnificent of Africa's antelopes, sable antelopes are slightly smaller than roan antelopes, but are more thick-set. They have longer horns, often reaching more than 100cm. Sables have a white belly and face markings; females are reddish brown, while mature males are a

Like roan antelopes, sable antelopes are fierce fighters, and are even known to kill attacking lions.
PHOTO BY DENNIS JONES

deep, glossy black. They favour habitats slightly more wooded than that of roan antelopes. Social organisation of the two species is also very similar, but sable female-and-young herds are slightly larger – usually 10 to 30, but up to 70 or so.

Size: Shoulder height 1.35m; weight 180kg to 270kg; horns up to 130cm – the male's are longer and more curved than the female's. **Distribution:** Mostly at Shimba Hills National Reserve. **Status:** Common and easily seen.

To conserve water, oryxes let their body temperature rise to levels that would kill most mammals.
PHOTO BY ANDREW MACCOLL

ORYX
Oryx gazella

Well adapted to aridity, oryxes can survive without drinking. Oryxes are solid and powerful; both sexes carry long, straight horns. Principally grazers, they also browse on thorny shrubs. In areas with abundant water and food, populations are sometimes resident and adopt a social system like that of roan antelopes. More usually, nomadic herds number around a dozen, but can total up to 60. Herds normally contain males and females, but there are strict hierarchies within the sexes. Herds, especially if small, may also be single sex.

Size: Shoulder height 1.2m; weight 170kg to 210kg (male), 120kg to 190kg (female); horns up to 110cm. **Distribution:** Beisa oryx in northern Kenya; fringe-eared oryx in southern Kenya. **Status:** Relatively common and easy to see, but shy.

Hartebeests prefer grassy plains but are also found in sparsely forested savannas and hills.
PHOTO BY ARIADNE VAN ZANDBERGEN

HARTEBEEST
Alcelaphus buselaphus

Hartebeests are red to tan in colour, medium-sized and easily recognised by their long, narrow face and short horns. In both sexes, the distinctively angular and heavily ridged horns form a heart shape, hence their name, which comes from Afrikaans. Dominant males defend territories, which herds of females and their young pass through; other males move in bachelor groups. Herds typically number up to about a dozen (male herds are generally smaller), but aggregations of hundreds and (in the past) thousands also occur.

Size: Shoulder height 1.2m; weight 130kg to 170kg (male), 115kg to 150kg (female); horns up to 85cm. **Distribution:** Wide ranging; Coke's hartebeest, also known as 'Kongoni', is common in Kenya; Jackson's hartebeest is confined to areas near Lake Victoria. **Status:** Common.

Topis' horns, carried by both sexes, curve gently up, out and back.
PHOTO BY ARIADNE VAN ZANDBERGEN

TOPI
Damaliscus lunatus

Topis are reddish brown, with glossy violet patches on the legs and face. Their social system is highly variable. In grassy woodlands, males hold territories with harems of up to 10 females. On floodplains with dense populations, nomadic herds of thousands may form, males establishing temporary territories whenever the herd halts. Elsewhere, males gather on breeding-season display grounds; females visit these 'leks' to select their mates. Both sexes often stand on high vantage points (commonly termite mounds) to view their surroundings and as territorial advertisement.

Size: Shoulder height 1.2m; weight 110kg to 150kg (male), 75kg to 130kg (female); horns up to 45cm. **Distribution:** Widespread throughout medium-length grasslands, common in the Masai Mara National Reserve. **Status:** Common.

BLUE WILDEBEEST
Connochaetes taurinus

Blue wildebeests often form herds in association with zebras and other herbivores. Wildebeests are grazers, and move constantly in search of good pasture and water, preferring to drink daily – this gives rise to the famous mass migration in the Serengeti–Masai Mara ecosystem. Elsewhere, especially where

Blue wildebeests are gregarious, and in some areas form herds of up to tens of thousands.
PHOTO BY LUKE HUNTER

food and water are more permanent, groups of up to 30 are more usual, with larger congregations being less frequent and more temporary. In both situations, males are territorial and attempt to herd groups of females into their territory.

Size: Shoulder height 1.4m; weight 200kg to 300kg (male), 140kg to 230kg (female); horns up to 85cm; male larger than female. **Distribution:** Throughout parks in southern Kenya. **Status:** Very common; 1.5 million occur in the Serengeti–Masai Mara ecosystem.

KLIPSPRINGER
Oreotragus oreotragus

Small, sturdy antelopes, klipspringers are easily recognised by their tip-toe stance – their hooves are adapted for balance and grip on rocky surfaces, enabling them to bound up impossibly rough and steep rockfaces. Klipspringers normally inhabit rocky outcrops; they also sometimes venture into adja-

When disturbed, a pair of klipspringers often gives a duet of trumpet-like alarm calls.
PHOTO BY LUKE HUNTER

cent grasslands, but always retreat to the rocks when alarmed. Klipspringers form long-lasting pair bonds and the pair occupies a territory, nearly always remaining within a couple of metres of each other.

Size: Shoulder height 55cm; weight 9kg to 15kg; horns up to 15cm; female larger than male. **Distribution:** Rocky outcrops and mountainous areas throughout the region. **Status:** Common but wary; often seen standing on high vantage points.

STEENBOK
Raphicerus campestris

Steenboks are pretty and slender antelopes; their back and hindquarters range from light reddish-brown to dark brown with pale underpart markings. The nose bears a black, wedge-shaped stripe. Males have small, straight and widely separated horns. Although usually seen alone, it's likely that

If a predator approaches, steenboks lie flat with neck outstretched, zigzagging away only at the last moment.
PHOTO BY ARIADNE VAN ZANDBERGEN

steenboks share a small territory with a mate, but only occasionally does the pair come together. Steenboks are active in the morning and afternoon and by night; they may become more nocturnal where frequently disturbed.

Size: Shoulder height 50cm; weight up to 16kg; horns up to 19cm; female a little larger than male. **Distribution:** Restricted to central and northern Kenya. **Status:** Relatively common, but easily overlooked.

A dik-dik's territory is marked by up to a dozen large piles of dung placed around the boundary.

PHOTO BY ARIADNE VAN ZANDBERGEN

KIRK'S DIK-DIK
Madoqua kirkii

Dik-diks are identified by their miniature size, the pointed flexible snout and a tuft of hair on the forehead; only the males have horns. Dik-diks are monogamous and pairs are territorial. If one is seen, its mate is usually nearby, as well as that year's young. Both members of the pair, and their young, use dung piles to mark their territory, placing their deposits as part of an elaborate ceremony. Dik-diks feed by browsing on foliage and, being well adapted to their dry environments, don't drink.

Size: Shoulder height 35cm to 45cm; weight 4kg to 7kg; horns up to 12cm. **Distribution:** Throughout Kenya. **Status:** Common but wary and easy to miss; active day and night.

Often dismissed by tourists because they are so abundant, impalas are unique antelopes with no close relatives.

PHOTO BY ABI

IMPALA
Aepyceros melampus

Male impalas have long, lyre-shaped horns averaging 75cm in length. They are gregarious animals, forming resident herds of up to 100 or so. Males defend female herds during the oestrus, but outside the breeding season they congregate in bachelor groups. Impalas are known for their speed and ability to leap – they can spring as far as 10m in one bound, or 3m into the air. They are the common prey of lions, leopards, cheetahs, wild dogs and spotted hyenas.

Size: Shoulder height 85cm; weight 40kg to 80kg; horns up to 90cm; male larger than female. **Distribution:** Savanna regions from central Kenya extending south. **Status:** Very common and easy to see.

Gazelles are often the main prey of predators – so they are very fleet of foot and wary of attack.

PHOTO BY ARIADNE VAN ZANDBERGEN

GAZELLE
Thomson's gazelle (Gazella thomsonii, pictured); Grant's gazelle (Gazella granti)

One of the most common medium-sized antelopes, Thomson's gazelles are smaller and form large aggregations (often of many thousands) on the open plains. They often occur with impala-sized Grant's gazelles, which lack the distinctive black side stripe of the 'tommy'. The social structure is flexible; herds often consist of females and young, with males defending territories around the feeding grounds of females.

Size: Thomson's gazelle shoulder height 65cm; weight 15kg to 30kg; horns up to 45cm. Grant's gazelle shoulder height 85cm; weight 40kg to 80kg; horns up to 80cm. Females of both smaller than males and have much smaller horns. **Distribution:** Thomson's and Grant's gazelle common in savanna and woodland. **Status:** Very common.

Food & Drink

The Kenyan culinary tradition has generally emphasised feeding the masses as efficiently as possible, with little room for flair or innovation. Nonetheless, Kenya is blessed with a cornucopia of natural produce and the 'foodies' scene is definitely on the improve. Kenyan markets are bursting with crisp vegetables, the steamy coast provides abundant tropical fruit and fresh seafood, and throughout the country, meat – be it beef, goat, mutton, or even camel – is consumed with gusto. So, while traditional fare may veer towards the bland and filling, if you are prepared to be adventurous you may well have some memorable or unique gastronomic experiences.

STAPLES & SPECIALITIES

Although there are some interesting Kenyan dishes, travellers mostly encounter simple meat stews and curries with fillers such as rice, potatoes or another high-starch option. These aren't culinary masterpieces – it's just survival food for the locals offering the maximum opportunity to fill up at minimum cost. Vegetarian visitors are likely to struggle; meat features in most meals and many vegetable dishes are cooked in meat stock.

Cooking the East African Way, by Constance Nabwire, is a basic introduction to the food and culinary traditions of the region.

Breakfast in Kenya is generally a simple affair consisting of chai (tea; see p90) accompanied by a *mandazi*, a semi-sweet flat doughnut. *Mandazi* are best in the morning when they're freshly made – they become rubbery and less appetising as the day goes on. Another traditional breakfast dish is *uji*, millet-based porridge similar to *ugali*. *Uji* is best served warm with lashings of milk and brown sugar.

Main Dishes

The true staples of the Kenyan diet are *ugali* and *sukuma wiki*. *Ugali* is maize meal cooked into a thick porridge until it sets hard, then served up in flat slabs. It's incredibly stodgy and tends to sit in the stomach like a brick, but most Kenyans swear by it. It will fill you up after a long day's safari but it won't set your taste buds atingle. Many Kenyan dishes are accompanied by *sukuma wiki* – braised or stewed spinach. *Sukuma wiki* in Swahili means literally 'stretch the week', the implication being that they are so cheap they allow the householder to stretch the budget until

---

KENYA'S NATIONAL DISH

Vegetarians beware – *nyama choma* (literally 'barbecued meat') is Kenya's unofficial national dish and it's a red-blooded, hands-on affair. Most places have their own butchery on site, and *nyama choma* is usually purchased by weight, often as a single hunk of meat. Half a kilogram is usually enough for one person (taking into account bone and gristle), and it'll be brought out to you chopped into small bite-sized bits with vegetable mash and greens. Goat is the most common meat, but you'll see chicken, beef and even antelope and zebra in some of the upmarket places.

Don't expect *nyama choma* to melt in the mouth, though. Its chewiness is probably indicative of the long and eventful life of the animal you are consuming. You'll need a good half hour at the end of the meal to work over your gums with a toothpick. Copious quantities of Tusker beer tend to help it go down. That said, at least one restaurant – Carnivore (p129) in Nairobi – has elevated *nyama choma* into a gourmet experience. It has made it onto at least one list of the 50 best restaurants in the world, so they must be doing something right.

the next weekly pay cheque. Despite its ubiquity, a dish of well-cooked *sukuma wiki* with tomatoes, stock and capsicum makes a refreshing change from the preponderance of meat in other recipes.

Another noteworthy staple, especially in the Central Highlands, is *irio* (*kienyji* in Swahili), made from mashed greens, potatoes and boiled corn or beans. Also common is *mukimo,* a kind of hash made from sweet potatoes, corn, beans and plantains. Vegetarians can find *githeri* – a mix of beans and corn – in most local eateries.

But Kenyan food is all about meat. Kenyans are enthusiastic carnivores; their recognised national dish is *nyama choma* (barbecued meat; see p89), and most other dishes are based around stewed meat, accompanied by a generous portion of carbohydrate. Beef, goat and mutton are the most common, and they tend to be pretty tough. Carbohydrates come in five major forms: *ugali,* potatoes, rice, chapati and *matoke.* The chapati is identical to its Indian predecessor. *Matoke* is mashed green plantains, which when well prepared can taste like buttery, lightly whipped mashed potato.

The most distinctive Kenyan food is found on the coast. Swahili dishes reflect the history of contact with the Arabs and other Indian Ocean traders and incorporate the produce of the region. The results can be excellent. Grilled fish or octopus will be a highlight of any menu, while coconut and spices such as cloves and cinnamon feature prominently. The rice-based dishes, *biriyani* and pilau, are clearly derived from Persia; they should be delicately spiced with saffron and star anise, and liberally sprinkled with carrot and raisins.

You will also encounter Indian food. Most restaurants serve curries and Indian-inspired dishes such as masala chips (ie with a curry sauce) and Indian restaurants on the coast and elsewhere dish up traditional curries and other fare. Western dishes such as roast chicken and steak are staples in more upmarket restaurants found in the bigger towns.

For the lowdown on various Kenyan recipes, including the ubiquitous *ugali* and *sukuma wiki,* check out www.blissites .com/kenya/culture /recipes.html.

Fruit

Because of the country's varied climate, there is often an excellent array of fruits to be found. Depending on the place and the season, you can buy mangoes, papayas, pineapples, passion fruits, guavas, oranges, custard apples, bananas (of many varieties), tree tomatoes and coconuts. Chewing on a piece of sugar cane is also a great way to end a meal. Prices are low and the quality is very high.

DRINKS

Chances are that when you're out in the sun you'll work up quite a thirst. Fortunately Kenya can provide a diverse range of beverages – hot or cold, alcoholic or nonalcoholic – to please all palates.

Nonalcoholic Drinks

TEA & COFFEE

Despite the fact that Kenya grows some excellent tea and coffee, getting a decent cup of either can be difficult, as the best stuff is exported.

Chai is the national obsession and is drunk in large quantities, but it bears little resemblance to what you might be used to. As in India the tea, milk and masses of sugar are boiled together and stewed for ages, and the result is milky and very sweet – it may be too sickly for some, but the brew just might grow on you. Spiced chai masala with cardamom and cinnamon is very pleasant and rejuvenating. For tea without milk ask for chai *kavu.*

As for coffee, the stuff you get served is often sweet and milky and made with a bare minimum of instant coffee. In Nairobi and other larger towns though, there is a steadily increasing number of coffee houses serving very good Kenyan coffee, and you can usually get a good filter coffee at any of the big hotels. With all the Italian tourists who visit the coast, you can now get a decent cappuccino pretty much anywhere between Diani Beach and Lamu.

SOFT DRINKS

All the old favourites are here, including Coke, Sprite and Fanta; they go under the generic term of soda and are available everywhere. As with beer, prices vary depending on where you buy it. In most places you pay around KSh30 per bottle, but in the more exclusive places you can pay up to KSh100. Stoney's ginger ale (known just as Stoney's) is hugely popular, as is Vimto, a fizzy fruity concoction that has a taste that grows on you.

JUICE

With all the fresh fruit that's available in Kenya, fruit juices are a national obsession and the best on offer are breathtakingly good. All rely on modern blenders, however, so there's no point asking for a fruit juice during a power cut. Prices range from KSh30 to KSh150. Although you can get juices made from almost any fruit, the nation's favourite is passion fruit. It is known locally simply as passion, although it seems a little odd asking a waiter or waitress whether they have passion and how much it costs!

Pineapple, orange and mango juices also feature on most menus. If you're worried about hygiene, try to ensure it is blended in front of you and they don't add any tap water. Alternatively, the bottled juices produced by the Picana company are also very good.

The most long-lasting impact that Portuguese explorers had on Kenya was in the culinary field. Portuguese travellers introduced maize, cassava, potatoes and chillies from South America – all of which are now staples of the Kenyan diet.

Alcohol

BEER

Kenya has a thriving local brewing industry and formidable quantities of beer are consumed. You'll usually be given a choice of 'warm' or 'cold' beer. 'Why warm?' you might well ask. Curiously, most Kenyans appear to prefer it that way, despite the fact that room temperature in Kenya is a lot hotter than room temperature in the USA or Europe.

The local beers are Tusker, White Cap and Pilsner, all manufactured by Kenya Breweries and sold in 500ml bottles. Tusker comes in three varieties, Tusker Export, Tusker Malt Lager and just plain Tusker, which are all basically the same product with different labels (although locals swear they can tell the difference). Guinness is also available, but it's nothing like the genuine Irish article. Castle (a South African beer) is made under licence in Kenya by, you've guessed it, Kenya Breweries.

Other local bottled drinks include Hardy's cider, Redd's (a sort of apple alcopop) and Kingfisher (another fruity concoction that's available in several awful flavours).

LETHAL BREW

Kenya has a long tradition of producing its own bootleg liquor, but you should steer well clear of chang'a. In mid-2005, 48 people died near Machakos after drinking a bad batch of chang'a. A further 84 were hospitalised and apparently treated with vodka! Such incidents are not uncommon. The drink, Sorghum Baridi, from Central Province, contains so much methyl alcohol that the bottles are actually cold to the touch! Perhaps the most dangerous chang'a comes from Kisii, and is fermented with marijuana twigs, cactus mash, battery alkaline and formalin. Needless to say these brews can have lethal effects and we don't recommend that you partake.

Beers are cheapest when bought from a supermarket, where a 500ml bottle will cost you around KSh45. If bought from a regular bar, you are looking at KSh80. Bought at a bar in a five-star hotel, though, beer can cost up to KSh200.

WINE

Kenya has a fledgling wine industry and the Lake Naivasha Colombard wines are said to be quite good. This is something that cannot be said about the most commonly encountered Kenyan wine – papaya wine. Quite how anyone came up with the idea of trying to reproduce a drink made from grapes using papaya instead is a mystery, but the result tastes foul and smells unbearable.

On the other hand, you can get cheap imported South African, European and even Australian wine by the glass for around KSh150 in upmarket Nairobi restaurants. In the big supermarket chains such as Nakumatt and Uchumi, you can pay anything from KSh500 to KSh1500 for a bottle of South African wine.

COCKTAILS

The cocktail of the moment is known as *dawa*. Clearly based on the Brazilian *caipirinha*, it's made with vodka, limes and honey. We suggest you enjoy a tipple at a sunset bar overlooking the coast. *Dawa* translates from the Swahili as 'medicine' but we think it may have the opposite effect on you.

LOCAL BREWS

Although it is strictly illegal for the public to brew or distil liquor, this still goes on. *Pombe* is the local beer, usually a fermented brew made with bananas or millet and sugar. It shouldn't do you any harm. The same cannot be said for the distilled drinks known locally as *chang'a*, which are laced with genuine poisons. See p91 for more on the perils of drinking *chang'a*.

WHERE TO EAT & DRINK

The most basic local eateries are usually known as *hotels* or *hotelis* and they often open only during the daytime. You may find yourself having dinner at 5pm if you rely on eating at these places. However, if you have the resources, even in smaller towns it's usually possible to find a

> Pilau flavoured with spices and stock is the signature dish at traditional Swahili weddings. The expression 'going to eat pilau' means to go to a wedding.

KENYA'S TOP FIVE

- Carnivore (p129), Nairobi – how can you argue with a place voted among the world's top 50 gastro experiences? Flush locals enjoy this place as much as the tourists, even though you can't eat zebra here any more.

- Ali Barbour's Cave Restaurant (p177), Diani beach – a truly unique setting for one of the coast's top eateries, peeking out of a coral cave at starry skies and a silky beach. Simply gorgeous.

- Kisumu's lakeside fish-fry shanties (p294) – wade into the smoke, sink into a chair and enjoy fried fish with locals on the shore of Lake Victoria.

- Tamarind Mombasa (p164) – expensive, but totally worth it for the romantic open Swahili-style terrace overlooking the harbour. The seafood's as smart as they come.

- Haandi (p112), Nairobi – undisputed top dog among Kenya's many Indian restaurants, this classy curryhouse provides an authentic taste of the subcontinent.

TRAVEL YOUR TASTEBUDS

If you're lucky (!) and game, you may be able to try various cattle-derived products beloved of the pastoral tribes of Kenya. Samburu, Pokot and Maasai warriors have a taste for cattle blood. Taken straight from the jugular it does no permanent damage to the cattle, but it is certainly an acquired taste. *Mursik* is made from milk fermented with grass ash and is served in smoked gourds. It tastes and smells pungent, to say the least, but it contains compounds that reduce cholesterol, enabling the Maasai to live quite healthily on a diet of red meat, milk and blood. You may be able to sample it at villages in the Masaai Mara.

---

restaurant that offers a more varied menu at a higher price. Often these places are affiliated with the towns' midrange and top-end hotels, and are usually open in the evening. You'll find that many of the big nightclubs also serve food until late into the night.

Menus, where they exist in the cheaper places, are usually just a chalked list on a board. In more upmarket restaurants, they are usually written just in English.

Quick Eats

Eating fast food has taken off in a big way and virtually every town has a place serving greasy but cheap chips, burgers, sausages, pizzas and fried chicken. Lashings of tomato and chilli sauces are present to help lubricate things. A number of South African fast-food chains have taken hold in Nairobi.

Unlike much of Africa, Kenya has no great tradition of street food, although you may encounter roasted corn cobs (costing just a few shillings) and deep-fried yams, eaten hot with a squeeze of lemon juice and a sprinkling of chilli powder. *Sambusas,* deep-fried pastry triangles stuffed with spiced mincemeat, are good for snacking on the run and are obvious descendants of the Indian samosa. The best *sambusas* are crisp and spicy but they tend to become cold and clammy later in the day. Something you don't come across often, but which is an excellent snack, is *mkate mayai* (literally 'bread eggs'), a wheat dough pancake, filled with minced meat and egg and fried on a hotplate. On the coast street food is more common and you will find cassava chips, chapatis and *mishikaki* (grilled kebabs, usually beef, on skewers).

Many of Kenya's staples and specialities are good for quick eats (see p89 for details).

For information on Swahili cuisine and a selection of tangy coastal recipes, go to www .mwambao.com/dishes .htm.

Self-Catering

Preparing your own food is a viable option if you are staying in a place with a kitchen, or if you're camping and carrying cooking gear. Every town has a market, and there's usually an excellent range of fresh produce. Western-style supermarkets are found in major towns.

VEGETARIANS & VEGANS

Vegetarians will have few options, but with a bit of scouting around you will be able to find something. You may find yourself eating a lot of *sukuma wiki* (p89), while other traditional dishes such as *githeri* are hearty, if not particularly inspiring. Beans will also figure prominently in any vegetarian's culinary encounters in Kenya. Many Indian restaurants will provide a vegetarian *thali* (an all-you-can-eat meal) that will certainly fill you up. Buying fresh fruit and vegetables in local markets can help relieve the tedium of trying to order around the meat on restaurant menus.

EAT YOUR WORDS

Want to know *mayai* from *maandazi*? *Samaki* from *sukari*? Make the most of the cuisine scene by getting to know the language. For pronunciation guidelines, see p395.

Useful Phrases

I'm a vegetarian.	*Nakula mboga tu.*
I don't eat meat.	*Mimi sili nyama.*
Is there a restaurant near here?	*Je, kuna hoteli ya chakula hapo jirani?*
Do you serve food here?	*Mnauza chakula hapa?*
I'd like ...	*Ninaomba ...*
Without chilli pepper, please.	*Bila pilipili, tafadhali.*
Please bring me the bill.	*Lete bili tafadhali.*

Menu Decoder

biryani – casserole of rice and spices with meat or seafood
mchuzi – sauce, sometimes with bits of beef and very-well-cooked vegetables
mishikaki – kebab
nyama choma – barbecued meat
pilau – spiced rice cooked in broth with seafood or meat and vegetables
supu – soup; usually somewhat greasy, and served with a piece of beef, pork or meat fat in it
ugali – thick, porridge-like maize- or cassava-based staple, served in a solid form, sold everywhere
wali na kuku/samaki/nyama/maharagwe – cooked white rice with chicken/fish/meat/beans

Food Glossary

BASICS
baridi – cold
joto – hot
kijiko – spoon
kikombe – cup
kisu – knife
kitambaa cha mikono – napkin
sahani – plate
tamu – sweet
uma – fork

STAPLES
chipsi – chips
maharagwe – beans
mkate –bread
matoke – cooked and mashed plantains
ndizi ya kupika – plantains
viazi – potatoes
wali – rice (cooked)

MEAT & SEAFOOD
kaa – crab
kuku – chicken
nyama mbuzi – goat
nyama ng'ombe – beef
nyama nguruwe – pork
pweza – octopus
samaki – fish

FRUITS & VEGETABLES
chungwa – orange
dafu – coconut (green)
embe – mango
kitunguu – onions
mboga – vegetables
nanasi – pineapple
nazi – coconut (ripe)
ndizi – banana
nyanya – tomatoes
papai – papaya
sukuma wiki – spinach (boiled)
tunda – fruit
viazi – potatoes

OTHER DISHES & CONDIMENTS
chumvi – salt
mayai (yaliyochemshwa) – eggs (boiled)
maziwa ganda – yogurt
sukari – sugar

DRINKS
bia (baridi/yamoto) – beer (cold/warm)
maji (ya kuchemsha/ya kunywa/ya
madini) – water (boiled/drinking/mineral)
maji ya machungwa –orange juice

Nairobi

Who's afraid of big bad Nairobi? Quite a lot of people – the city's reputation precedes it, so much so that most visitors dive in and out as quickly as possible. Unsurprising perhaps, as it's true that Kenya's capital requires more big-city common sense than most, and it's hard not to feel a little nervous once the shutters come down and the streets empty after dark.

However, it's easy enough to sidestep the worst dangers here, and there's no reason why a streetwise traveller can't enjoy a stay here. In terms of facilities, the city has more going for it than any other Kenyan conurbation: there's a comprehensive range of shops, the matatus are the funkiest around, most safari companies are based here, the cinemas screen recent movies, the cultural scene is thriving, the nightlife is unbridled and it's virtually the only place in the country where you can get a truly varied diet. Even café culture has reached the downtown area, adding a soupçon of sophistication to the supposed urban badlands.

Even if the inner city does terrify you, it's easy to get out into the suburbs, where you can relax with the large local expat community and make the most of even more top-rank amenities, award-winning restaurants and friendly bars.

In fact, whatever its shortcomings, we actually like Nairobi. Take the time to look beyond the safari offices and supermarkets, throw yourself into the vibrant entertainment scene and, who knows, you might just come to agree.

HIGHLIGHTS

- Broadening your appreciation of all things cultural and environmental at the **National Museum** (p104)
- Surveying the cityscape from the grand heights of the **Kenyatta Conference Centre** (p106)
- Digging in to the country's most varied cuisine scene at any of Nairobi's posh **restaurants** (p111)
- Treating yourself to a **shopping spree** (p119), **feeding frenzy** (p111) or **boozy bender** (p117)
- Acclimatising yourself to Tusker and Kiswahili rap at one of the city's all-night **clubs** (p117)
- The smug feeling of surviving a stay here!

Westlands ★   ★ National Museum
★ Kenyatta Conference Centre;
Restaurants;
Nightclubs

■ TELEPHONE CODE: 020   ■ POPULATION: 2.9 MILLION   ■ AREA: 680 SQ KM

HISTORY

As you might guess from all the tower blocks, Nairobi is a completely modern creation and almost everything here has been built in the last 100 years. Until the 1890s the whole area was just an isolated swamp, but as the rails of the East Africa railway fell into place, a depot was established on the edge of a small stream known to the Maasai as *uaso nairobi* (cold water). Nairobi quickly developed into the administrative nerve-centre of the Uganda Railway, and in 1901 the capital of the British Protectorate was moved here from Mombasa to allow more effective control of the interior.

Even when the first permanent buildings were constructed, Nairobi remained a real frontier town, with rhinos and lions freely roaming the streets, and lines of iron-roofed bungalows stretching ignominiously across the plain. However, once the railway was up and running, wealth began to flow into the city. The colonial government built some grand hotels to accommodate the first tourists to Kenya – big-game hunters, lured by the attraction of shooting the country's almost naïvely tame wildlife. Sadly almost all of the colonial-era buildings were replaced by bland modern office buildings following *uhuru* (independence) in 1963.

As East Africa's largest city and the region's main transport hub, Nairobi is situated firmly at the centre of national life and politics, a position that did the city no favours in 1998, when the US embassy on Moi Ave was blown up by militants linked to Osama bin Laden, killing more than 200 Kenyans. Four suspects were convicted but the lenient sentences and meagre compensation angered many locals, creating a resentment that still lingers in certain quarters.

ORIENTATION

The compact city centre is bounded by Uhuru Hwy, Haile Selassie Ave, Tom Mboya St and University Way. Northeast of the centre, on the eastern side of Tom Mboya St, is the rougher River Rd area, where most cheap hotels and bus offices are found; this district has a bad reputation for robbery, so be careful.

Various suburbs surround the downtown area. Southwest of the centre, beyond Uhuru and Central Parks, are Nairobi Hill, Milimani and Hurlingham, with several hos-

tels, campsites and midrange hotels. Further out are Wilson Airport, Nairobi National Park and the expat enclaves of Langata and Karen (see p124). The country's main airport, Jomo Kenyatta International Airport, is southeast of the centre.

North of the centre you will find the expat-dominated suburbs of Westlands and Parklands, home to large European and Indian communities. The suburbs further out, such as Kibera, Kayole and Githurai, are mainly poverty-stricken slums with terrible reputations for crime, violence and carjacking, and are best avoided.

Maps

For a rudimentary guide to the downtown area, many hotels and travel companies give out free promotional maps. For more detailed coverage, the best option is the *City of Nairobi: Map & Guide* produced by Survey of Kenya. It covers the suburbs and has a detailed map of the central area, but it's difficult to get. Also adequate, with some hotels and places of interest marked, is the 1:15,000 *Map Guide of Nairobi City Centre* (KSh200) published by Interland Maps.

Much better, though bulkier, is *Nairobi AtoZ* (KSh510) by RW Moss. Like the equivalents in other countries, the AtoZ covers the whole city in detail.

INFORMATION

Bookshops

For newspapers and magazines, there are dozens of street vendors and hawkers selling current editions of the daily papers and old editions of Western publications.

Book Villa (Map pp102–3; ☎ 337890; Standard St) New, discounted and second-hand books. Also runs a borrowing scheme.

Bookpoint (Map pp102–3; ☎ 211156; Moi Ave)

Bookstop (☎ 714547; Yaya Centre, Hurlingham)

Text Book Centre Westlands (Map p104; ☎ 3747405; Sarit Centre); Kijabe St (Map pp98–9; ☎ 330340) One of the best bookshops in East Africa. The sister shop on Kijabe St isn't as big or well stocked.

Westland Sundries Bookshop Downtown (Map pp102–3; ☎ 212776; New Stanley Hotel, Kenyatta Ave); Westlands (Map p104; ☎ 446406; Ring Rd Westlands)

Camping Equipment

Atul's (Map pp102–3; ☎ 225935; Biashara St) Hires out everything from sleeping bags to folding toilet seats – see p72.

NAIROBI IN...

Two Days
While most people use Nairobi as a base rather than a destination in its own right, there's still plenty to do if you find yourself with a day or two to kill. Start at the **National Museum** (p104), then head downtown later for **coffee** (p116), some **Chinese** (p113) and a **movie** (p118).

On the second day you can view the city from the **Kenyatta Conference Centre** (p106) and browse contemporary art at the **National Archives** (p105). In the evening, **Carnivore** (p129) in Karen is a must, or you can eat posh at **Alan Bobbé's Bistro** (p114) and dance dirty at **Simmers** (p118) or the infamous **New Florida** (p117).

Four Days
With another two days, you can also venture out towards the suburbs. Westlands has plenty of good eating between the shops at the **Sarit Centre** (p115) and Kenya's best Indian restaurant, **Haandi** (p112), not to mention the friendly **Gypsy's Bar** (p117) and massive club **Pavement** (p117).

For your final 24 hours, breakfast at the **Pasara Café** (p111), take a **swim** (p106), hang at the **Village Market** (p119) and finish at **Casablanca** (p116) for the city's hippest Moroccan food and drinks.

Kenya Canvas Ltd (Map pp102-3; ☎ 343262; Muindi Mbingu St)

X-treme Outdoors (☎ 2722224; www.xtreme-kenya .com; Yaya Centre, Hurlingham)

Clubs & Societies
East African Wildlife Society (☎ 574145; www .eawildlife.org; Riara Rd, Kilimani, PO Box 20110) This society is at the forefront of conservation efforts in East Africa. Annual subscription costs US$65 for overseas members, including subscription to the bimonthly *Swara* magazine.

Friends of Nairobi National Park (Fonnap; ☎ 500622; Kenya Wildlife Service Headquarters, Langata Rd, PO Box 42076) The society aims to protect migration routes between the Masai Mara and the national park. Annual membership is US$30. Meetings are on the first Sunday of every month at the main gate of Nairobi National Park.

Mountain Club of Kenya (MCK; ☎ 602330; www.mck .or.ke; Wilson Airport, PO Box 45741) The club meets at 8pm every Tuesday at the clubhouse at Wilson Airport (Map p126). Members organise frequent climbing and trekking weekends around the country and have a huge pool of technical knowledge about climbing in Kenya. Overseas membership costs US$30.

Nature Kenya (☎ 3749957; www.naturekenya.org; National Museum, PO Box 44486) Located just off Museum Hill Rd, it runs a variety of local outings – see p106. Annual membership is US$25.

Cultural Centres
All the foreign cultural organisations have libraries (p99) open to the public.

Alliance Française (Map pp98-9; ☎ 340054; www .alliancefrnairobi.org; cnr Monrovia & Loita Sts;

(⌚ 8.30am-6.30pm Mon-Fri, to 5pm Sat) Has the best events program of all the centres, showcasing Kenyan and African performing arts.

British Council (Map pp98-9; ☎ 334855; www .britishcouncil.org/kenya; Upper Hill Rd; ⌚ 9.30am-5.30pm Mon-Fri, to 1pm Sat)

Cultural Council of the Islamic Republic of Iran (Map pp98-9; ☎ 214352; Ambank House, Monrovia St; ⌚ 9am-5pm Mon-Fri, 9.30am-4.30pm Sat) Hosts exhibitions and displays on Islam.

Goethe Institute (Map pp98-9; ☎ 224640; www .goethe.de/nairobi; Maendeleo House, cnr Monrovia & Loita Sts; ⌚ 10am-12.30pm Thu-Tue, 2-5pm Mon-Fri)

Japan Information & Culture Centre (Map pp98-9; ☎ 340520; www.ke.emb-japan.go.jp; ICEA Bldg, Kenyatta Ave; ⌚ 8.30am-5pm Mon-Fri) Free video shows and Japanese cinema screenings.

Nairobi Cultural Institute (Map pp98-9; ☎ 569205; Ngong Rd) Holds lectures and other functions of local cultural interest.

Emergency
AAR Health Services (Map pp98-9; ☎ 717376; Fourth Ngong Ave)

Aga Khan Hospital (Map pp98-9; ☎ 3662000; Third Parklands Ave) A reliable hospital with a 24-hour casualty section.

Amref flying-doctor service (☎ 502699)

Emergency services (☎ 999) The national emergency number for to call for fire, police and ambulance assistance. A word of warning, though – don't rely on their prompt arrival.

Police (☎ 240000) For less urgent police business.

St John's Ambulance (☎ 2100000)

NAIROBI

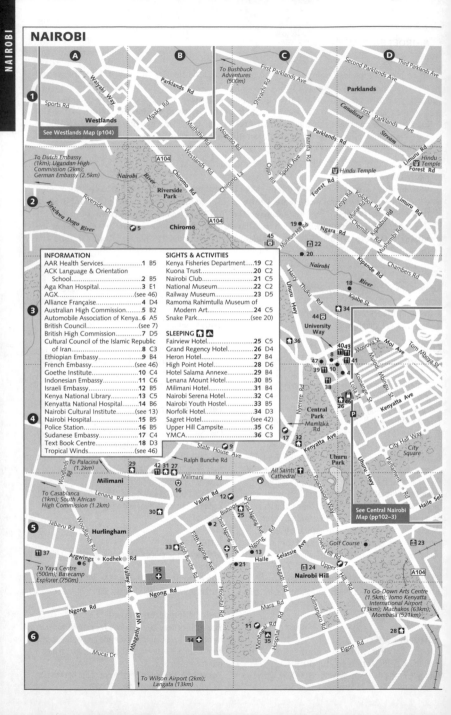

INFORMATION
AAR Health Services..................1 B5
ACK Language & Orientation
School................................2 B5
Aga Khan Hospital...................3 E1
AGX.................................(see 46)
Alliance Française.....................4 D4
Australian High Commission........5 B2
Automobile Association of Kenya..6 A5
British Council.........................(see 7)
British High Commission............7 D5
Cultural Council of the Islamic Republic
of Iran..............................8 C3
Ethiopian Embassy....................9 B4
French Embassy.....................(see 46)
Goethe Institute.....................10 C4
Indonesian Embassy.................11 C6
Israeli Embassy......................12 B5
Kenya National Library..............13 C5
Kenyatta National Hospital.........14 B6
Nairobi Cultural Institute.........(see 13)
Nairobi Hospital.....................15 B5
Police Station.........................16 B5
Sudanese Embassy...................17 C4
Text Book Centre....................18 D3
Tropical Winds.....................(see 46)

SIGHTS & ACTIVITIES
Kenya Fisheries Department.....19 C2
Kuona Trust..........................20 B4
Nairobi Club.........................21 C5
National Museum....................22 C2
Railway Museum.....................23 D5
Ramoma Rahimtulla Museum of
Modern Art.......................24 C5
Snake Park.........................(see 20)

SLEEPING
Fairview Hotel........................25 C5
Grand Regency Hotel...............26 D4
Heron Hotel..........................27 B4
High Point Hotel.....................28 D6
Hotel Salama Annexe................29 B4
Lenana Mount Hotel.................30 B5
Milimani Hotel.......................31 B4
Nairobi Serena Hotel................32 C4
Nairobi Youth Hostel................33 B5
Norfolk Hotel........................34 D3
Sagret Hotel.......................(see 42)
Upper Hill Campsite.................35 C6
YMCA.................................36 C3

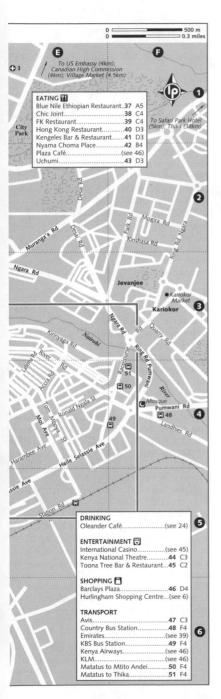

0 — 500 m
0 — 0.3 miles

To US Embassy (4km);
Canadian High Commission
(4km); Village Market (4.5km)

City
Park

EATING 🍴
Blue Nile Ethiopian Restaurant..**37** A5
Chic Joint...............................**38** C4
FK Restaurant.........................**39** C4
Hong Kong Restaurant...........**40** D3
Kengeles Bar & Restaurant......**41** D3
Nyama Choma Place...............**42** B4
Plaza Café...........................(see 46)
Uchumi.................................**43** D3

To Safari Park Hotel
(5km); Thika (38km)

Mogira Rd

Park Rd

Kinshasa Rd

Muranga'a Rd

Desai Rd

Ngara Rd

Kinshasa Rd

Jevanjee

● Kariokor
Market

Kariokor

Ngara Rd

Quarry Rd

Kirinyaga Rd

Nairobi

River

Racecourse Rd

Ring Rd Pumwani

Latema Rd

Accra Rd

Tom Mboya St

Ronald Ngala St

River

Mosque
Pumwani Rd

🚌 51

🚌 50

🚌 48

Mai Ave

Landhies Rd

Harambee Ave

Haile Selassie Ave

...ssie Ave

Station Rd

DRINKING
Oleander Café.....................(see 24)

ENTERTAINMENT 🎭
International Casino...............(see 45)
Kenya National Theatre...........**44** C3
Toona Tree Bar & Restaurant...**45** C2

SHOPPING 🛍
Barclays Plaza.......................**46** D4
Hurlingham Shopping Centre...(see 6)

TRANSPORT
Avis......................................**47** C3
Country Bus Station...............**48** F4
Emirates..............................(see 39)
KBS Bus Station.....................**49** F4
Kenya Airways......................(see 46)
KLM....................................(see 46)
Matatus to Mtito Andei...........**50** F4
Matatus to Thika....................**51** F4

Internet Access

There are literally hundreds of Internet cafés in downtown Nairobi, most of them tucked away in anonymous office buildings in the town centre. Connection speed is usually pretty good, though machine quality varies wildly.

AGX (Map pp98-9; www.agxinternetcafes.com; Barclays Plaza, Loita St; per min KSh1; ⏰ 8am-8pm Mon-Sat) Best connections in town, with a choice of browsers.

Avant Garde e-centre (Map pp102-3; Fedha Towers, Kaunda St; per min KSh1.50; ⏰ 7.30am-9pm Mon-Sat, 11am-6pm Sun)

Capital Realtime (Map pp102-3; ☎ 247900; Lonhro House, Standard St; ⏰ 8.30am-7.30pm Mon-Fri, 10am-4pm Sat)

Dallas Communications (Map pp102-3; ☎ 223655; 20th Century Plaza, Mama Ngina St; per min KSh1)

EasySurf (Map p104; ☎ 3745418; http://easysurfonline .com; Sarit Centre, Westlands; per min KSh4; ⏰ 9am-8pm Mon-Sat, 10am-2pm Sun)

Laundry

Laundries are few and far between in Nairobi. Most people rely on the laundry services offered by the majority of hotels, though these are priced by the item and can work out pretty expensive. The average cost for the following places is around KSh150 per kilogram for a standard overnight service wash.

Lavage Laundrette & Dry Cleaners (Map p104; ☎ 4444111; Mpaka Rd, Westlands) One of the few laundrettes in Nairobi.

White Rose Drycleaners (Map pp102-3; ☎ 227724; Kenyatta Ave)

Libraries

Many of Nairobi's cultural centres (p97) also have libraries available to the public.

Kenya National Library (Map pp98-9; ☎ 2725550; www.knls.or.ke; Ngong Rd; ⏰ 8am-6.30pm Mon-Thu, to 4pm Fri, 9am-5pm Sat)

McMillan Memorial Library (Map pp102-3; ☎ 221844; Banda St; ⏰ 9am-6pm Mon-Fri, 9.30am-4pm Sat) A smaller collection in a lovely colonial-era building.

Medical Services

Nairobi has plenty of healthcare facilities used to dealing with travellers and expats. Avoid the Kenyatta National Hospital (Map pp98–9) because, although it's free, stretched resources mean you may come out with something worse than what you went in with.

AAR Health Services (Map pp98-9; ☎ 715319; Williamson House, Fourth Ngong Ave) Westlands (Map p104; ☎ 446201; Sarit Centre) Probably the best of a number of private ambulance and emergency air-evacuation companies (see p358). It also runs a private clinic in Westlands.

Acacia Medical Centre (Map pp102-3; ☎ 212200; info@acaciamed.co.ke; ICEA Bldg, Kenyatta Ave; ⏰ 7am-7pm Mon-Fri, to 2pm Sat)

Aga Khan Hospital (Map pp98-9; ☎ 740000; Third Parklands Ave; ⏰ 24hr)

KAM Pharmacy (Map pp102-3; ☎ 251700; Executive Tower, IPS Bldg, Kimathi St) A one-stop shop for medical treatment, with a pharmacy, doctor's surgery and laboratory.

Medical Services Surgery (Map pp102-3; ☎ 317625; Bruce House, Standard St; ⏰ 8.30am-4.30pm Mon-Fri)

Nairobi Hospital (Map pp98-9; ☎ 722160; off Argwings Khodek Rd)

Transcom Medical Centre (Map pp102-3; ☎ 217564; Tsavo Rd)

Money

Jomo Kenyatta International Airport has several exchange counters in the baggage reclaim area and a **Barclays Bank** (⏰ 24hr) with ATM outside in the arrivals hall.

There are Barclays branches with guarded ATMs on Mama Ngina St (Map pp102–3), Muindi Mbingu St (Map pp102–3) and on the corner of Kenyatta and Moi Aves (Map pp102–3). There are also branches in the Sarit Centre (Map p104) and on Woodvale Grove (Map p104) in Westlands and the Yaya Centre in Hurlingham.

The other big bank is Standard Chartered Bank, which has numerous downtown branches.

Foreign-exchange bureaus offer slightly better rates for cash. There are dozens of options in the town centre, so it's worth strolling around to see who is currently offering the best deal.

American Express (Map pp102-3; ☎ 222906; Hilton Hotel, Mama Ngina St; ⏰ 8.30am-4.30pm Mon-Fri) Handles travellers cheques and looks after mail for clients (see p362).

Cosmos Forex (Map pp102-3; ☎ 250582; Rehema House, Standard St)

Goldfield Forex (Map pp102-3; ☎ 244554; Fedha Towers, Kaunda St)

Mayfair Forex (Map pp102-3; ☎ 226212; Uganda House, Standard St)

Postbank (Map pp102-3; 13 Kenyatta Ave) For Western Union money transfers.

Travellers Forex Bureau (Map p104; ☎ 447204; The Mall, Westlands)

Photography Equipment

Shops selling and developing film are common across Nairobi (see p361) and most can also do instant passport-size photographs. Processing costs KSh410 to KSh690 for a 36-exposure film, depending on the print size, and digital printing is becoming more common, starting at around KSh30 per picture.

Stocks of film are generally pretty poor outside Nairobi so stock up here before you go on safari. There are plenty more camera shops on Mama Ngina St.

Elite Camera House (Map pp102-3; ☎ 224521; Kimathi St) Reductions for bulk purchases.

Expo Camera Centre Downtown (Map pp102-3; ☎ 226846; info@expo.co.ke; Mama Ngina St); Westlands (Map p104; ☎ 441253; Mpaka Rd) Hires out SLR cameras and lenses.

Fedha Foto Studio (Map pp102-3; ☎ 220515; Fedha Towers, Kaunda St)

Fotoland (Map pp102-3; ☎ 343042; Moi Ave)

Post

The vast **main post office** (Map pp102-3; ☎ 243434; Kenyatta Ave; ⏰ 8am-6pm Mon-Fri, 9am-noon Sat) is a well-organised edifice close to Uhuru Park. There's a very basic poste-restante service in the same office as the parcel desk, where you'll need to bring your parcels so the contents can be examined. Bring a roll of parcel-wrapping paper and parcel tape so you can seal the package once it's been inspected – you can buy these at **Seal Honey** (Map pp102-3; ☎ 216376; 27 Kenyatta Ave). Around the back of the main building is the **EMS office** (⏰ 8am-8pm Mon-Fri, 9am-12.30pm Sat), for courier deliveries (see p362), and there's a Telkom Kenya office upstairs.

If you just want stamps, there are post offices on Haile Selassie Ave (Map pp102–3), Moi Ave (Map pp102–3) and Tom Mboya St (Map pp102–3), and in the Sarit Centre (Map p104) and on Mpaka Rd (Map p104) in Westlands. The Moi Ave office is a good place to send parcels – packing boxes are available for KSh50 to KSh100.

DHL Downtown (Map pp102-3; ☎ 534988; www.dhl.co .ke; International House, Mama Ngina St); Westlands (Map p104; ☎ 6925120; Sarit Centre) Reliable private courier.

Telephone & Fax

Public phones are common in Nairobi but many just don't work. **Telkom Kenya** (Map pp102-3; ☎ 232000; Haile Selassie Ave; ⏰ 8am-6pm Mon-Fri, 9am-noon Sat) has dozens of payphones and you can buy phonecards. Many stands downtown sell Telkom Kenya phonecards and top-up cards for prepaid mobile phones (see p365).

Alternatively, there are numerous private agencies in the centre of town offering international telephone services. Typical charges are KSh150 to KSh200 per minute to almost anywhere in the world.

Lazards (Map pp102-3; Kenya Cinema Plaza, Moi Ave; 7am-10pm;) International phone calls from as little as KSh10 per minute to North America or Europe and international faxes from KSh40 per page. You may need ID to get into the building.

Toilets

It may come as a shock to regular African travellers, but Nairobi now has a handful of manned public toilets around the downtown area offering flush toilets with a base level of hygiene. You'll pay about KSh5 to use them. Some central shopping centres, such as Kenya Cinema Plaza, have free public conveniences.

Tourist Information

Despite the many safari companies with signs saying 'Tourist Information', there is still no official tourist office in Nairobi. For events and other listings you'll have to check the local newspapers or glean what you can from a handful of magazines, which take a bit of effort to hunt down. *Go Places* (free) and the *Going Out Guide* (KSh150) are probably the most widespread, available from travel agents, airline offices and some hotels.

The vast noticeboards found at the **Sarit Centre** (Map p104; Westlands) and **Yaya Centre** (Hurlingham) are good places to look if you're trying to find local information. All sorts of things are advertised here, including language courses, vehicles for sale and houses for rent.

Travel Agencies

Bunson Travel (Map pp102-3; 221992; www .bunsonkenya.com; Pan-African Insurance Bldg, Standard St) A good upmarket operator with offices around Africa and the Indian Ocean islands.

Flight Centres (Map pp102-3; 210024; Lakhamshi House, Biashara St) This company has been doing discounted air tickets for years and is totally switched on to the backpacker market. It also acts as a broker for camping safaris and runs overland trips across Africa.

Let's Go Travel Downtown (Map pp102-3; 340331; www.lets-go-travel.net; Caxton House, Standard St); Westlands (447151; ABC Place, Waiyaki Way); Karen (Map p125; 882505; Karen shopping centre) Also highly recommended, Let's Go is very good for flights, safaris and pretty much anything else you might need. It publishes an excellent price list of hotels, lodges, camps and bandas (huts) in Kenya (also in searchable form on its website), and acts as main booking agent for many off-the-beaten-track and unusual options.

Tropical Winds (Map pp98-9; 341939; www .tropical-winds.com; Barclays Plaza, Loita St) Nairobi's STA Travel representative.

Visa Extensions

Immigration office (Map pp102-3; 222022; Nyayo House, cnr Kenyatta Ave & Uhuru Hwy; 8.30am-12.30pm & 2-3.30pm Mon-Fri) Visa extensions (see p366) can be obtained at this office, round the side of Nairobi's once-feared main administrative building.

DANGERS & ANNOYANCES

Prospective first-time visitors to Nairobi are usually understandably daunted by the city's unenviable reputation – 'Nairobbery', as it is often called by residents, is commonly regarded as the most dangerous city in Africa, beating stiff competition from Johannesburg and Lagos. Carjacking, robbery and violence are daily occurrences, as the warning signs all round town indicate, and the underlying social ills behind them are unlikely to disappear in the near future.

However, the majority of problems happen in the slums, far from the main tourist zones. The downtown area bound by Kenyatta Ave, Moi Ave, Haile Selassie Ave and Uhuru Hwy is unthreatening and comparatively trouble-free as long as you use a bit of common sense, and there are plenty of *askaris* (security guards) around at night. Stay alert and you should encounter nothing worse than a few persistent safari touts and the odd wannabe con artist.

Even around the centre, though, there are places to watch out for: danger zones include the area around Latema and River Rds, a hotspot for petty theft, and Uhuru Park, which tends to accumulate all kinds of dodgy characters.

Once the shops have shut, the streets empty rapidly and the whole city takes on a deserted and slightly sinister air – mugging is a risk anywhere after dark. Take a taxi, even if you're only going a few blocks. This

CENTRAL NAIROBI

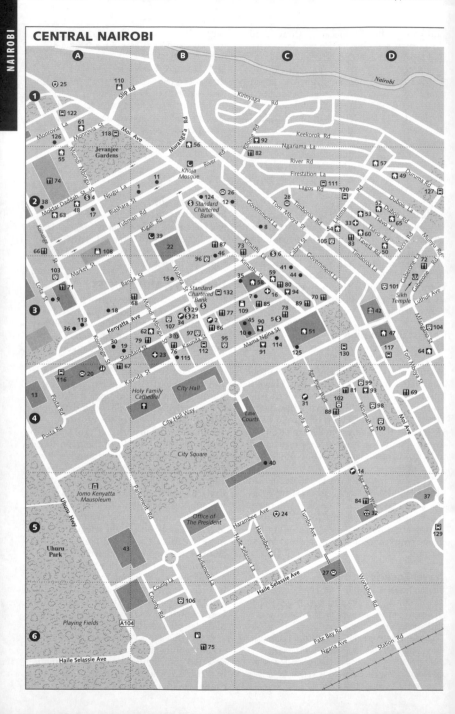

0	200 m
0	0.1 miles

Postbank..............................**29** B3
Seal Honey..........................**30** A3
Spanish Embassy..............(see 114)
Swiss Embassy...................(see 114)
Tanzanian High Commission..**31** C4
Telkom Kenya.....................**32** D5
Telkom Kenya.................(see 20)
Transcom Medical Centre....**33** D2
Ugandan High Commission
  (Consular Section)..........**34** B3
Westland Sundries
  Bookshop.......................**35** C3
White Rose Drycleaners.......**36** A3

SIGHTS & ACTIVITIES
Adventures Aloft...............(see 59)
American Embassy Memorial
  Garden...........................**37** D5
Best Camping Tours..........(see 68)
Gametrackers.......................**38** A2
Jamia Mosque......................**39** B2
Kenyatta Conference Centre.**40** C4
Mzizi Arts Centre.................**41** C3
National Archives..................**42** D3
Origins Safaris...................(see 76)
Parliament House.................**43** A5
Primetime Safaris................**44** C3
Safari Seekers.....................**45** C3
Saferide Safaris...................**46** B2
Sana Highlands Trekking
  Expeditions...................(see 114)
Savuka Tours & Safaris.....(see 132)
Yare Safaris......................(see 122)

SLEEPING
Ambassadeur Hotel............. **47** D3
Down Town Hotel................**48** A2
Eva May Lodge....................**49** D2
Grand Holiday Hotel............**50** D2
Hilton Hotel........................**51** C3
Hotel Africana....................**52** D2
Hotel Greton.......................**53** D2
Iqbal Hotel.........................**54** C2
Kenya Comfort Hotel...........**55** A2
Meridian Court Hotel...........**56** B1
New Kenya Lodge.................**57** D2
New Stanley Hotel................**58** C3
Oakwood Hotel...................**59** C3
Oriental Palace Hotel............**60** D2
Parkside Hotel....................**61** A1
Sixeighty Hotel...................**62** B3
Terminal Hotel.....................**63** A2
Terrace Hotel......................**64** D3
Wilton Gateway Hotel.........**65** D2

EATING
Alan Bobbé's Bistro..............**66** A2
Beneve Coffee House............**67** A4
Café 21..............................**68** B3
California Cookies................**69** D4
Dancing Spoon Café & Wine
  Bar................................(see 95)
Etouch Food Court................**70** C3
Fiesta Restaurant & Bar.......**71** A3
Malindi Dishes....................**72** B3
Nakumatt Downtown............**73** C2
Nakumatt Lifestyle...............**74** A2
Nyama Choma Stalls............**75** B6
Panda Chinese Restaurant......**76** B3
Pasara Café.........................**77** B3
Porterhouse Restaurant........**78** A3
Restaurant Akasaka..............**79** B3
Seasons Restaurant...............**80** C3
Seasons Restaurant............**81** D4

Supreme Restaurant............**82** C2
Taj.....................................**83** D2
Tamarind Restaurant...........**84** D5
Tanager Bar & Restaurant......**85** C3
Thorn Tree Café................(see 58)
Trattoria.............................**86** B3
Tropez................................**87** B2
Uchumi...............................**88** C4
Zeep...................................**89** C3

DRINKING
Dormans Café......................**90** C3
Hornbill Pub.....................(see 47)
Jockey Pub......................(see 51)
Kahawa...........................(see 76)
Nairobi Java House..............**91** C3
Roast House........................**92** C1
Taco Bell...........................**93** D4
Taco's................................**94** C3
Zanze Bar.......................(see 100)

ENTERTAINMENT
20th Century Cinema...........**95** B3
Cameo...............................**96** B3
Club Soundd.......................**97** B3
Florida 2000........................**98** D4
Green Corner Restaurant & Cactus
  Pub................................**99** D4
Kenya Cinema.....................**100** C3
Monte Carlo Club...............**101** D3
Nairobi Cinema...................**102** C4
New Florida.........................**103** A3
Nyanza House Club............**104** D3
Odeon................................**105** C2
Professional Centre............**106** B6
Simmers.............................**107** B3

SHOPPING
City Market........................**108** A2
Gallery Watatu...................**109** C3
Maasai Market....................**110** A1

TRANSPORT
Air India...........................(see 14)
Akamba.............................**111** C2
Akamba Booking Office.......**112** B3
Avenue Car Hire.................**113** A2
British Airways...................**114** C3
Budget..............................**115** B3
Bus & Matatu Stop (for Hurlingham
  & Milimani)...................**116** A4
Bus Stop (for Langata, Karen &
  Airport)..........................**117** D3
Bus Stop (for Westlands)....**118** A1
Buses to Kisii & Migori.......**119** F3
Central Rent-a-Car.............(see 62)
Coastline Safaris Office........**120** D2
Crossland Services..............**121** F2
Davanu Shuttle..................**122** A1
Easy Coach Office...............**123** E5
Ethiopian Airlines..............(see 23)
Glory Car Hire....................**124** B2
Glory Car Hire....................**125** C3
KBS Booking Office............**126** A1
Main Bus & Matatu Area......**127** D2
Matatus to Naivasha, Nakuru,
  Nyahururu & Namanga.**128** F3
Matatus to Wilson Airport, Nairobi
  National Park, Langata &
  Karen..........................**129** D5
Metro Shuttle Bus Stand....**130** D3
Molo Line Services..........(see 131)
Narok Line.......................**131** E2
Riverside Shuttle................**132** B3

INFORMATION
Acacia Medical Centre.......(see 15)
American Express.............(see 51)
Atul's.................................**1** B2
Austrian Embassy................**2** B3
Avant Garde e-centre..........**3** B3
Barclays Bank......................**4** A2
Barclays Bank.....................**5** C3
Barclays Bank.....................**6** C2
Book Villa............................**7** C3
Bookpoint............................**8** C2
Bunson Travel..................(see 77)
Capital Bureau de
  Change.........................(see 112)
Capital Realtime...............(see 77)
Cosmos Forex....................(see 7)
Dallas Communications.....(see 95)
DHL.................................(see 114)
Eastern & Southern Safaris....**9** A3
Elite Camera House...........(see 20)
EMS Office........................(see 20)
Expo Camera Centre...........**10** C3
Fedha Foto Studio.............(see 3)
Flight Centres....................**11** B2
Fotoland............................**12** B3
Goldfield Forex.................(see 76)
Immigration Office............**13** A4
Indian High Commission.....**14** D4
Italian Embassy................(see 114)
Japan Information & Culture
  Centre.........................(see 15)
Japanese Embassy............(see 15)
KAM Pharmacy..................**16** C3
Kenya Canvas Ltd..............**17** A2
Kenya Youth Voluntary
  Development Projects......**18** A3
Lazards............................(see 100)
Let's Go Travel...................**19** A3
Main Post Office.................**20** D2
Mayfair Forex.....................**21** B3
McMillan Memorial Library.**22** B3
Medical Services Surgery....**23** B3
Police Station.....................**24** C5
Police Station......................**25** A1
Post Office.........................**26** B2
Post Office.........................**27** C5
Post Office.........................**28** C2

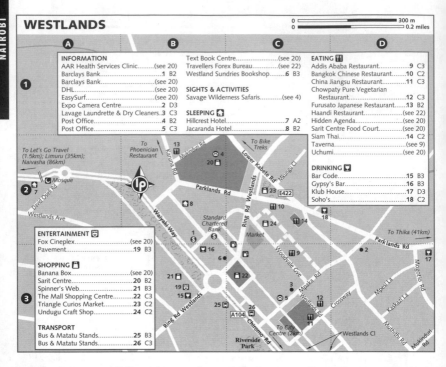

WESTLANDS

0   300 m
0   0.2 miles

INFORMATION
AAR Health Services Clinic........(see 20)
Barclays Bank............................1 B2
Barclays Bank..........................(see 20)
DHL..(see 20)
EasySurf..................................(see 20)
Expo Camera Centre....................2 D3
Lavage Laundrette & Dry Cleaners.3 C3
Post Office................................4 B2
Post Office................................5 C3

Text Book Centre......................(see 20)
Travellers Forex Bureau..............(see 22)
Westland Sundries Bookshop........6 B3

SIGHTS & ACTIVITIES
Savage Wilderness Safaris...........(see 4)

SLEEPING
Hillcrest Hotel............................7 A2
Jacaranda Hotel..........................8 B2

EATING
Addis Ababa Restaurant...............9 C3
Bangkok Chinese Restaurant.......10 C2
China Jiangsu Restaurant............11 C3
Chowpaty Pure Vegetarian
  Restaurant............................12 C3
Furusato Japanese Restaurant.....13 B2
Haandi Restaurant...................(see 22)
Hidden Agenda......................(see 20)
Sarit Centre Food Court............(see 20)
Siam Thai..............................14 C2
Taverna................................(see 9)
Uchumi.................................(see 20)

DRINKING
Bar Code................................15 B3
Gypsy's Bar............................16 B3
Klub House.............................17 D3
Soho's..................................18 C2

ENTERTAINMENT
Fox Cineplex...........................(see 20)
Pavement..............................19 B3

SHOPPING
Banana Box............................(see 20)
Sarit Centre...........................20 B2
Spinner's Web.........................21 B3
The Mall Shopping Centre..........22 C3
Triangle Curios Market..............23 C2
Undugu Craft Shop...................24 C2

TRANSPORT
Bus & Matatu Stands.................25 B3
Bus & Matatu Stands.................26 C3

To Let's Go Travel
(1.5km); Limuru (35km);
Naivasha (86km);

To Phoenician Restaurant

To Bike Treks

Mosque

David Osei Rd

Westlands Ave

Parklands Rd

Lower Kabete Rd

E422

Standard Chartered Bank

Market

Waiyaki Way

Ring Rd Westlands

Mukundun Rd

Karuna Rd

Woodvale Gve

Mpaka Rd

To Thika (41km)

Parklands Rd

Mobotio Rd

Mpesi La

Kaskazi La

Crossway

Muthithi Rd

Mukundun Rd

Westlands Cl

A104

Chiromo Rd

To City Centre (2km)

Riverside Park

will also keep you safe from the attentions of Nairobi's street prostitutes, who flood into town in force after sunset.

Scams

Nairobi's active handful of confidence tricksters seem to have relied on the same old stories for years, and it's generally easy to spot the spiel once you've heard it a couple of times. The usual tactic is to accost you in the street and try and strike up a conversation about current affairs in your country – keep walking; it's probably the most effective way of avoiding the inevitable follow-up.

Apart from the regular safari rip-offs, which can be minimised simply by doing your research, the local speciality is the Sudanese refugee scam (see boxed text opposite).

SIGHTS

There are very few attractions worthy of the name in Nairobi itself, and the most interesting places are out in the suburbs (see p123). That said, the handful of museums and cultural institutions scattered around

the city can easily occupy a spare day, particularly if you're interested in contemporary Kenyan art.

National Museum

A grand alternative to the dozens of poky little local museums around the country, Kenya's **National Museum** (Map pp98-9; ☎ 742131; www .museums.or.ke; Museum Rd; adult/child KSh200/100; ⏰ 9.30am-6pm) is housed in an imposing building amid lush leafy grounds just outside the centre, and has a good range of cultural and natural history exhibits. The gardens are peppered with random sculptures, including a large dinosaur, and the inner courtyard has a life-size fibreglass model of pachyderm celebrity Ahmed, the massive elephant who became a symbol of Kenya at the height of the 1980s poaching crisis and was placed under 24-hour guard by Jomo Kenyatta.

Inside, one of the major attractions is the Peoples of Kenya series of tribal portraits by *Born Free* author Joy Adamson, a fantastic record of the country's cultural diversity. Upstairs are huge galleries of stuffed birds (at least 900 specimens) and animals, and good ethnographical displays on the various Kenyan tribal groups. Downstairs, there are recreations of rock art from Tanzania, an exhibition of hominid fossils from Lake Turkana and various geological displays. The outlying gallery hosts temporary exhibits, covering topics such as Swahili and Asian culture in Kenya and wildlife in the Masai Mara. Volunteer guides offer tours in English, Dutch and French; it's worth booking them in advance. There's no charge for their services, but a donation to the museum is appropriate.

The 1st floor also contains the excellent **Gallery of Contemporary East African Art**, where local artists exhibit their work; as all the items are for sale the displays change regularly, and it's always an interesting cross-section of the contemporary scene. For a look at the artists in action, the **Kuona Trust**, a nonprofit art studio where Kenyan artists can gather and express themselves, is just by the museum. You're welcome to wander around but ask before taking photos.

In the grounds, there's a recreated **Kikuyu homestead** and a **snake park** (adult/child KSh200/ 100; 9.30am-6pm), where you can see black mambas, some sad-looking crocodiles and giant *dudus* (creepy crawlies – see p52). The guided **nature trail** nearby isn't particularly exciting, being so close to two main roads.

National Archives

Right in the bustling heart of Nairobi is the distinctive **National Archives** (Map pp102-3; ☎ 749341; Moi Ave; admission free; 8.30am-5pm Mon-Fri, to 1pm Sat), the 'Memory of the Nation', a vast collection of documents and reference material housed in the fine former Bank of India building. It's mainly used by students and researchers, but the ground-floor atrium and gallery display an eclectic selection of contemporary art, historical photos of Nairobi, cultural artefacts, furniture and tribal objects, giving casual visitors a somewhat scattergun glimpse of East African heritage.

Railway Museum

You don't have to don an anorak to appreciate this interesting little **museum** (Map pp98-9; Station Rd; adult/child/student KSh200/20/100; 8.15am-4.45pm). The main collection is housed in an old railway building, and consists of relics from the East African Railway. There are train and ship models, photographs, tableware and oddities from the history of the railway, such as the Engine Seat that allowed visiting dignitaries like Theodore Roosevelt to take pot shots at unsuspecting wildlife from the front of the train.

In the grounds are dozens of fading locomotives in various states of disrepair, dating from the steam days to independence (which puts the newer trains on a par with those

---

KHARTOUM CHARACTERS

One classic Nairobi con trick that you'll almost certainly be subjected to is the Sudanese refugee story, commonly combined with the equally well-worn university scam. In this gambit it turns out that your interlocutor has totally coincidentally just won a scholarship to a university in your country (if you're British it'll be Reading, or Edmonton for Canadians – the amount of research they do is quite astounding) and would just love to sit down and have a chat with you about life there. Then at some point you'll get the confidential lowering of the voice and the Sudanese portion of the story kicks in with 'You know, I am not from here…', leading into an epic tale of woe that involves them having walked barefoot all the way from Juba to flee the civil war.

Of course once you've shown due sympathy they'll come to the crux of the matter: they have to get to Dar es Salaam to confirm their scholarship and fly out for their studies, and all they need is KSh1700 to get there, not that they could ask you, their new friend, for that much money, just anything you could spare to help them out. Giving money or anything else is likely to result in you being 'arrested' by fake policemen and forced to pay an exorbitant fine. In some cases these accomplices get so into their role that they beat up the original conman for the sake of authenticity, which is obviously quite intimidating!

As with all these type of scams, the best way of avoiding real trouble is to be very choosy in who you talk to and decline any offers or invitations made on the street. After a day or two in Nairobi you'll quickly learn to spot a budding 'refugee', especially the third time the same guy approaches you…

still being used on the Nairobi to Mombasa line). You can walk around the carriages at your leisure. At the back of the compound is the steam train used in the movie *Out of Africa*. It's a fascinating introduction to this important piece of colonial history.

The museum is reached by a long lane beside the train station, or you can cut across the vacant land next to the Shell petrol station on Haile Selassie Ave.

Parliament House

If you fancy a look at how democracy works in Kenya, it's possible to obtain a permit for a seat in the public gallery at **parliament house** (Map pp102-3; ☎ 221291; Parliament Rd) – just remember, applause is strictly forbidden! If parliament is out of session, you can tour the buildings by arrangement with the sergeant-at-arms.

Kenyatta Conference Centre

Towering over City Square, Nairobi's signature building (Map pp102–3) was designed as a fusion of modern and traditional African styles, though the distinctive saucer tower looks a little dated next to some of the city's flashier glass edifices. Staff will accompany you up to the **viewing platform** (adult/child KSh400/200) and helipad on the roof for wonderful views over Nairobi. The sightline goes all the way to the suburbs, and on clear days you can see aircraft coming in to land over the Nairobi National Park. You're allowed to take photographs from the viewing level but not elsewhere in the building. Access may be restricted during events and conferences.

Jamia Mosque

Nairobi's main **mosque** (Map pp102-3; Banda St) is a lovely building in typical Arabic Muslim style, with all the domes, marble and Quranic inscriptions you'd expect from an important Islamic site, and the traditional row of shops down one side to provide rental income for its upkeep. Sadly non-Muslims are very rarely allowed to enter, but you can happily examine the appealing exterior from the street.

American Embassy Memorial Garden

This well-tended walled **garden** (Map pp102-3; Moi Ave; admission KSh20; ⏰ 8am-8pm) occupies the former site of the American Embassy, which was destroyed by the terrorist bombings of 1998 (see p32). It's a lovely little spot despite being right between Moi and Haile Selassie Aves; the entrance fee pays for maintenance and keeps out any undesirables, but also puts it beyond the reach of many ordinary Kenyans, provoking some understandable anger among locals.

Arts Centres

The **Go-Down Arts Centre** (☎ 5552227; Dunga Rd), a converted warehouse in the Industrial Area, contains ten separate art studios and is rapidly becoming a hub for Nairobi's burgeoning arts scene, bringing together visual and performing arts with regular exhibitions, shows, workshops and open cultural nights.

The **Mzizi Arts Centre** (Map pp102-3; ☎ 574372; Sonalux House, Moi Ave), a smaller centre in a central office building, is a good place to view contemporary Kenyan art, craft, dance, literature and performance art. 'Cultural Personality Evenings', when Kenyan cultural stars give lectures, and sigana performances are held here (see p40 for more information on the performing arts).

Art Galleries

There are few public art galleries in Nairobi, but plenty of shops sell work by local artists and they welcome browsers.

In Upper Hill, the impressive-sounding **Ramoma Rahimtulla Museum of Modern Art** (Map pp98-9; ☎ 729181; Rahimtulla Tower, Upper Hill Rd) is actually a small gallery situated in a large skyscraper, promoting and selling work by Kenyan artists.

Of the private galleries, the longest established is the central **Gallery Watatu** (p119), which has regular exhibitions and a good permanent display.

Work by many contemporary Kenyan and African artists is often displayed in the foreign cultural centres (see p97) and in various museums.

ACTIVITIES

Nature Kenya (p97) organises a variety of outings, including half-day **bird walks** (non-members KSh100) from the National Museum at 8.45am every Wednesday.

Most international tourist hotels have **swimming pools** that can be used by non-guests for a daily fee of between KSh200 and KSh500. Hotels with heated pools near the city centre include the Norfolk Hotel (p109), the Grand Regency Hotel (p109) and Milimani Hotel (p111).

A number of private **sports clubs** in the suburbs offer facilities for nonmembers. All are out in the posher suburbs and tend to be rather snooty. Temporary daily membership fees apply.

Impala Club (☎ 565684; Ngong Rd, Karen)

Nairobi Club (Map pp98-9; ☎ 725726; Ngong Rd, Nairobi Hill)

Nairobi Sailing & Sub Aqua Club (Map p126; ☎ 501250; Nairobi Dam, Langata Rd)

TOURS

There's not much to see in downtown Nairobi, but most travel agents and safari operators can take you on a tour of the National and Railway Museums, parliament and the city market for around US$35. Also popular are trips to suburban attractions such as Nairobi National Park (US$55), the Bomas of Kenya (US$40) or the Karen Blixen Museum and Langata Giraffe Sanctuary (US$45) – see p127 and p128 for more on these attractions. Tour companies and details of longer trips can be found on p59.

For an introduction to the world of jua kali, Kenya's open-air manufacturing industry, **People to People Tourism** (☎ 781531; www.people topeopletourism.com) combines tours of the usual tourist sights with visits to jua kali workshops producing crafts and other goods.

FESTIVALS & EVENTS

Kenya Fashion Week (☎ 0733-636300; Sarit Centre, Westlands) An expo-style fashion event held in June, bringing together designers and manufacturers from all over the country.

Tusker Safari Sevens (www.safarisevens.com; Impala Club, Ngong Rd, Karen) A high-profile international seven-a-side rugby tournament held every June. It's always hotly contested and the Kenyan team has a strong record, though in 2005 Samoa took the main cup.

Kenya Music Festival (☎ 2712964; Kenyatta Conference Centre) Held over 10 days in August, the country's longest-running music festival, established almost 80 years ago by the colonial regime. African music now predominates, but Western and expat musicians still take part.

SLEEPING

Nairobi has plenty of accommodation in all categories, but you'll pay more than you would for the same facilities elsewhere in Kenya, especially in the midrange category.

The main budget area is between Tom Mboya St and River Rd, where you'll find dozens of small hotels and guesthouses – they're convenient for transport and the centre, but note that the real rock-bottom cheapies are usually brothels or dosshouses for drunks. The area is a bit rough, so be careful with your belongings when you walk around, and always take taxis at night. Water shortages are a daily occurrence.

Midrange options are strewn all over town. The best ones are predominantly in the main downtown area, around Kenyatta Ave. There are a few top-end hotels found right in the centre, but most are on the outskirts of the downtown area or further out towards the suburbs. Several exclusive little hotels can also be found in Langata and Karen (see p128).

Of the outlying areas, the eastern districts of Nairobi Hill and Milimani have the most promising selection, catering for all budgets.

City Centre

BUDGET

Iqbal Hotel (Map pp102-3; ☎ 220914; Latema Rd; dm KSh300, s/d/tr KSh400/600/960) The Iqbal has been popular for years, and is still possibly the best place in the area to meet fellow budget-conscious travellers. There's supposedly hot water in the morning, but you'd have to be up early – the 7am services at the church next door might help! There's a storeroom where you can leave excess gear for KSh40 per day. It's very secure and the *askari* can arrange taxis at reasonable prices.

New Kenya Lodge (Map pp102-3; ☎ 222202; www.nksafaris.com; River Rd; dm KSh300, r with shared/private bathroom KSh350/650) Another long-standing travellers' haunt, staff here are very friendly and there's a sociable lounge area. Hot water may be available in the evenings. The notice board is well used and the lodge also runs its own safaris, although we've had mixed reports.

Hotel Africana (Map pp102-3; ☎ 220654; Dubois Rd; s/d/tw/tr KSh600/800/1000/1500) The Africana has clean, bright rooms and is better looked after than many places in its class, with a TV room and a roof garden offering a bird's-eye view of the busy streets. The plain but well-catered Coffee House restaurant specialises in Indian vegetarian food. Prices include breakfast, though you can opt out if you really want to save the money.

Wilton Gateway Hotel (Map pp102-3; ☎ 341664; Dubois Rd; s/d KSh600/900) A decent, comfortable hotel popular with Kenyan salesmen. Breakfast is available for KSh100 per person. The Gateway Pub below claims it still sells beer at 1990s prices, which would certainly explain the slight evening noise factor!

Eva May Lodge (Map pp102-3; ☎ 216218; cnr River & Duruma Rds; s/d/tw KSh700/1000/1300) Standards here don't quite do the rather lovely-sounding name justice, but it's a decent guesthouse with small, perfectly reasonable rooms. Breakfast is included, and hot water comes courtesy of an electric shower attachment (when there's any water at all, of course).

Terrace Hotel (Map pp102-3; ☎ 221636; Ronald Ngala St; s/d KSh500/800) One of the better deals you'll get at the budget end, the hotel wears its worn atmosphere like a badge of honour, and compares very favourably to some of the cell-like establishments around it.

YMCA (Map pp98-9; ☎ 2724116; ymca@iconnect .co.ke; State House Rd; s/d KSh940/1480, with shared bathroom KSh690/1180) It might not convince the Village People, but this is an OK place with a range of passable rooms, though these prices only just scrape into the budget category. Rates include the daily membership fee.

MIDRANGE

Kenya Comfort Hotel (Map pp102-3; ☎ 317606; www.kenyacomfort.com; cnr Muindi Mbingu & Monrovia Sts; s US$26-36, d US$32-42, tr US$42-45, q US$52-55) An excellent addition to Nairobi's sleeping scene, this cheerily painted place is kept in top nick, offering a fine selection of modern tiled rooms and a lift for easy access. Breakfast in the popular 24-hour Sokoni bar-restaurant costs an extra US$5 (US$4 if booked in advance).

Down Town Hotel (Map pp102-3; ☎ 310485; Moktar Daddah St; s/d KSh1200/1500) Just down the road from the popular Terminal, Down Town doesn't have quite the personality of its neighbour but provides much the same kind of standards for much the same kind of price. If the Terminal's full, chances are this is where they'll send you for alternative accommodation, and you're unlikely to hold it against them.

Meridian Court Hotel (Map pp102-3; ☎ 313991; meridian@bidii.com; Muranga'a Rd; s/d/tr KSh2950/3650/ 4200; 🖳 🖳) The elaborate lobby here is rather more prepossessing than the grey concrete blocks above it, but it's hardly worth complaining when you're essentially getting a suite for the price of a standard room. There's no great luxury involved but the hotel facilities make it good value.

Parkside Hotel (Map pp102-3; ☎ 333568; parkside@ insightkenya.com; Monrovia St; s/d/tr KSh1300/1700/2200) Just opposite Jevanjee Gardens, Parkside is modest but decent enough value, and manages to keep out a lot of Nairobi's seemingly all-pervading traffic and town noise. Breakfast in the rather nice downstairs restaurant will set you back KSh300 per person.

Ambassadeur Hotel (Map pp102-3; ☎ 246615; Tom Mboya St; s/d/tr US$35/45/65) Believe it or not this big hotel opposite the National Archives once belonged to the posh Sarova chain, and structurally not much has changed, though we suspect room standards were rather more exacting in those days. Breakfast costs US$10 per room, which is obviously a better deal for triples than for singles!

Hotel Greton (Map pp102-3; ☎ 242891; greton@ wananchi.com; Tsavo Rd; s/d/tr incl breakfast KSh950/1200/ 1700) A big block hotel in the heart of the budget district, with a balcony restaurant

---

THE AUTHOR'S CHOICE

Terminal Hotel (Map pp102-3; ☎ 228817; Moktar Daddah St; s/d/tr KSh1200/1500/1800) Sure, there are plenty of bigger, flashier and fancier places to stay in Nairobi, but for our money the Terminal is still one of the only hotels in town where the price actually feels right. The emphasis here is on doing the basics well, with no overblown attempts at tourist frills, and it's an approach that works: staff are relaxed, tolerant and thoroughly amenable, the location's great, the water's hot, the beds are comfortable and most rooms are a decent size. There are a few downsides (street noise, no breakfast, the occasional cockroach) but you could pay over twice as much even in Milimani for shoddier accommodation and impersonal service. As an added plus, the equally personable Dove Cage bar/restaurant (☎ 242194; mains KSh100-380) next door acts as the house eatery and social club. For a reliable haven in fast-paced Nairobi you can't go wrong here, and in the time it takes everybody to learn your name you really will feel like a favoured regular.

overlooking the street. Rooms are spacious and comfortable, there's a salon and gym to keep you looking your best and the whole effect is a lot more inviting than most of the cheap dives nearby.

Grand Holiday Hotel (Map p102-3; ☎ 221244; grandholidaykenya@yahoo.com; Tsavo Rd; s & d KSh1050, tr KSh2000, ste KSh2200) White faces seem to be a bit of a novelty here, judging by the curious whispering among some of the staff, but Kenyan businessmen have latched onto it as a good deal, particularly the suites, which come with huge beds, TVs and spacious red-hued bathrooms.

Oakwood Hotel (Map p102-3; ☎ 218321; www .madahotels.com/oakwood.html; Kimathi St; s/d/tr US$60/ 75/85) It's questionable how they justify these prices, but this very central hotel does at least offer a bit of character, with lots of wood fittings and a lift that's so old-school it could probably draw a pension. The same chain runs several properties around Kenya and Uganda, and also operates balloon safaris in the Masai Mara.

Oriental Palace Hotel (Map p102-3; ☎ 217600; Taveta Rd; s KSh2290-2790, d KSh2790-3260; 🖳) Possibly not what Kubla Khan had in mind – the foyer does at least try and live up to the name, with faux-ivory reliefs and lots of Indian touches, but the rooms opt more for a Western brown retro feel. It's all comfortable enough, albeit with a slight air of neglect in the corridors.

Sixeighty Hotel (Map p102-3; ☎ 332680; www .680-hotel.co.ke; Muindi Mbingu St; s/d/tr KSh4000/5600/ 7200; 🖳) A big, slightly threadbare central hotel aimed squarely at local and international businesspeople. Facilities are good, it's secure and the location's convenient, though there's little inspired about the place. Wi-fi Internet available.

TOP END

It's a big jump even from the upper midrange to Nairobi's real top-end places. All the following rates include breakfast. You may get a better deal if you book through a travel agent, or you *may* be able to talk prices down in the low season. As an added bonus, most places provide access to the VIP lounges in Kenyatta airport for departing guests.

Nairobi Serena Hotel (Map p98-9; ☎ 2822000; nairobi@serena.co.ke; Central Park, Procession Way; s/d US$308/376, ste US$418-736; 🔀 🖳) Consolidating its reputation as one of the best top-flight chains in East Africa, this entry in the Serena canon has a fine sense of individuality, with its international-class facilities displaying a touch of safari style. Given the choice, opt for one of the amazing garden suites, where you can take advantage of your own private patio garden, complete with mini-pergola for eating outside. As it's right opposite Uhuru Park, avoid walking anywhere from here at night.

New Stanley Hotel (Map p98-9; ☎ 316377; www .sarovahotels.com; cnr Kimathi St & Kenyatta Ave; s/d from US$225/250; 🔀 🖳 🏊) A Nairobi classic: the original Stanley Hotel was established in 1902, but the current site has only been in use since 1912 and the latest version is a very smart modern construction, run by Sarova Hotels. Colonial décor prevails inside, with lashings of green leather, chandeliers and old-fashioned fans in the public areas. The various house eateries are well regarded, especially the sophisticated Zen restaurant (international and fusion cuisine), and the poolside terrace on the roof is a fine touch.

Norfolk Hotel (Map p98-9; ☎ 216940; www.lonr hohotels.com; Harry Thuku Rd; s/d US$281/337, ste US$361- 557; 🔀 🖳 🏊) Built in 1904, Nairobi's oldest hotel was *the* place to stay during colonial days, and it still attracts plenty of guests who at least look like they could be old-school settlers. Thanks to the leafy grounds, it has an almost rustic feel that provides an appealing contrast to the modern bent of the more central options. The stylish Ibis Grill Restaurant (mains KSh1300 to KSh3500) is one of the best in Kenya, and the Lord Delamere terrace bar and restaurant is a great place for a drink and snack.

Grand Regency Hotel (Map p98-9; ☎ 211199; www.grandregency.co.ke; Loita St; s/d US$200/240; 🔀 🖳 🏊) Grand Regency is one of Nairobi's classier modern complexes, decked out in stained glass and metal with a huge lofty atrium and great glass elevators. Everything looks brand new, and facilities include four restaurants, a casino and an entire small shopping centre. They add 28% to the bill for VAT and service.

Hilton Hotel (Map p102-3; ☎ 250000; rm.nairobi@ hilton.com; Mama Ngina St; s/d from US$179/209; 🔀 🔀 🖳 🏊) The Hilton dominates the centre of town with its distinctive round tower, occupying virtually an entire block with its rooms, restaurants, shops and other facilities. Executive rooms (s/d US$239/269) include use of an exclusive lounge with complimentary drinks. Prices are exclusive of 26% tax and service charge.

Milimani & Nairobi Hill

BUDGET

Upper Hill Campsite (Map pp98-9; ☎ 2720290; www .upperhillcampsite.com; Menengai Rd, Nairobi Hill; camping KSh300, tents KSh450-1000, dm/r KSh400/1000; 🖳) Off Hospital Rd near the Indonesian embassy, Upper Hill offers a range of accommodation to suit all tastes in a pleasant and secure compound, plus a well-used little restaurant and bar. The core of regular overland clients are supplemented by an international mix of backpackers and budget travellers. Facilities include hot showers and a cosy fireplace with comfortable chairs for those wintry moments. There's a vehicle maintenance bay and the owners can help you find a mechanic. It's a 15-minute walk from the centre, or you can take bus or matatu No 18 from Kenyatta Ave to the Kenyatta National Hospital, which is just around the corner (should you need it).

Nairobi Youth Hostel (Map pp98-9; ☎ 2723012; kyha@africaonline.co.ke; Ralph Bunche Rd, Milimani; dm KSh600-700, d with shared bathroom KSh800, apt KSh2000; 🖳) A well looked-after budget option, Nairobi's Hostelling International (HI) branch is still usually a good place to meet other travellers. The apartments sleep three and have a small kitchenette, but they're often booked up. A year's HI membership costs KSh400, or you can pay a KSh100 surcharge per day. Any matatu or bus going down either Valley or Ngong Rds will drop you off. Many people have been robbed returning to the youth hostel by foot after dark; always take a matatu or taxi at night.

MIDRANGE & TOP END

Heron Hotel (Map pp98-9; ☎ 2720740; www.heronhotel .com; Milimani Rd, Milimani; s/d/tr KSh3295/4490/5780; 🖳 🖳) Anyone who can remember Buffalo Bill's will be astounded at the transformation: management is obviously *very* keen to shake the reputation gleaned in the days not so long ago when the Wild West–themed house bar here was the most notorious brothel in Nairobi. Today it's a model of respectability, changed beyond all recognition, and the kitchenette doubles in particular are an absolute bargain (we actually thought they were suites at first sight!).

High Point Hotel (Map pp98-9; ☎ 2724312; www .highpointcourt.com; Lower Hill Rd, Nairobi Hill; ste KSh4000-5000, apt KSh4000-7000; 🖳 🖳) If you're looking for space and seclusion without laying out a fortune, this World Bank–affiliated suite and apartment complex is an excellent choice and provides ample eye candy for view vultures – you can supposedly see both Mt Kenya and Kilimanjaro from the penthouse balcony, though it would have to be an incredibly clear day. The split-level rooms come with kitchenette and living room, and a range of on-site facilities add to the value.

Palacina (☎ 2715517; www.palacina.com; Kitale Lane, Milimani; ste per person US$190, penthouses US$490; 🖳 🖳) Possibly the first genuine boutique hotel in Kenya, this fabulous collection of impossibly stylish suites must be one of the country's top addresses for those well-heeled sophisticates who still like the personal touch. DVDs and private Jacuzzis help outdo the competition, and there's a separate apartment complex for long-term renters, just in case you don't want to leave.

Fairview Hotel (Map pp98-9; ☎ 2711321; www .fairviewkenya.com; Bishops Rd, Milimani; s/d from KSh5900/8200; 🗶 🖳 🖳 🖧) A good top-end choice nicely removed from the central hubbub. The winding paths and green-filled grounds of this hotel create a refined atmosphere, especially around the courtyard restaurant, and the rooms are helpfully classified like airline seats, ranging from Economy to First. There are also flexible family rooms, charged at KSh8900 basic rate plus KSh2000 to KSh2900 per child (under fives free). It's near the scarily well-guarded Israeli Embassy.

Hotel Salama Annexe (Map pp98-9; ☎ 2729272; Milimani Rd, Milimani; s KSh1500, d KSh2500-3000) The Salama Annexe has a budget feel to it, even in the generously furnished 'deluxe' rooms, and it may be possible to camp here if you're really strapped. Rates include breakfast in the popular but shabby *nyama choma* (barbecued meat) bar-restaurant.

Lenana Mount Hotel (Map pp98-9; ☎ 2717044; Ralph Bunche Rd, Milimani; s/d KSh3000/4500; 🖳 🖳) A quiet three-star hotel with its own health club and sauna. The rooms are a good size, though particularly tall guests might have to duck slightly for the showers, and some have small balconies.

Milimani Hotel (Map pp98-9; ☎ 2722358; www
.hotelmilimani.com; Milimani Rd, Milimani; s/d KSh3500/
5000; ☒) Next door to the Heron, this is a
plain but decent business hotel with a rather
confusing layout, tucked in among the surrounding apartment buildings. Rates are a
bit high for the standards on offer, but it does
have one of the cheaper swimming pools in
town (nonguests KSh200).

Westlands & Parklands
Hillcrest Hotel (Map p104; ☎ 4444883; hillcrest@ africa
online.co.ke; Waiyaki Way, Westlands; s/d KSh1300/1700)
Considering the number of restaurants and
shopping centres in Westlands, it's surprising how little accommodation there is in
the area – this is actually the only mid-
priced option this side of Museum Hill Rd.
It's set in grounds just back from Waiyaki
Way, a short walk from the Sarit Centre.
There's plenty of space, with some nice big
wardrobes, and the general atmosphere is
pleasant and relaxed.

    Safari Park Hotel (☎ 3633000; www.safaripark-hotel
.com; Thika Rd, Parklands; s/d from US$190/220; ☐ ☒)
A huge complex done out in mock traditional décor worthy of a real safari lodge,
perfect if you don't want your luxury experience to end when you leave the national
parks. The boma-style lobby is quite spectacular, particularly the liana chandelier, and
there are so many facilities we won't even
try to list them all (five different restaurants
and the largest swimming pool in Africa,
for starters). A 28% tax and service charge
is added to the room rates.

    Jacaranda Hotel (Map p104; ☎ 4448713; jacaranda
hotel@africaonline.co.ke; Westland Rd; s/d US$120/150;
☐ ☒) Westlands' other convenient tourist
accommodation option is a smart former
Block property, slightly worn around the
edges but generally offering good standards,
with plenty of dark wood, 'tribal' art and
animal prints. There are several restaurants
on site, and free shuttle buses run between
the hotel and downtown three times daily.

EATING
Nairobi is well stocked with places to eat,
particularly in the centre, where you can
choose anything from the cheap workers'
canteens around River Rd to Chinese feasts
and full-on splurges off Kenyatta Ave. For
dinner it's also worth heading out to the
suburbs, which offer dozens of choices of

> ## THE AUTHOR'S CHOICE
> **Pasara Café** (Map pp102-3; ☎ 338247; Lonrho
> Bldg, Standard St; dishes KSh120-350; ☯ from
> 7am Mon-Fri, 8am-6pm Sat) At the forefront
> of Nairobi's burgeoning café culture, this
> stylish modern bar-brasserie never fails to
> impress with its nifty selection of snacks,
> sandwiches, grills and breakfasts, always
> offering something that bit more ambi-
> tious than the usual cafeteria fare. Most
> importantly, it tends to taste pretty damn
> good too. The juices come highly recom-
> mended, and the atmosphere equals that
> of any European coffeehouse, making it a
> fine place to relax with a newspaper away
> from all the stresses of the capital's streets.
> After 5pm it turns into a popular upscale
> bar, with a limited menu of snacks to keep
> your stomach lined and your palate perky.

cuisine from all over the world; Westlands
has the best range, and there are some good
choices in Hurlingham.

    All of the posher places listed here accept
credit cards, and most of them add 17% VAT
to the bill.

Kenyan & Swahili
Like the rest of the country, lunch is the
main meal of the day, and city workers flock
to the dozens of cheap canteens dishing up
simple, classic Kenyan dishes along with
Western staples like chicken and chips.

    Chic Joint (Map pp98-9; ☎ 337119; Utalii House,
Utalii St; mains KSh150-250) One of our favourite
new bar-restaurant discoveries, chic might
not be the first word that springs to mind
but grills, stews and *nyama* by the kilo
should never go out of fashion. Fresh fish
is delivered daily and the tilapia is generally excellent. The patio seating is separated
from Uhuru Hwy by a thick hedge, with
some sizeable speakers providing music in
the evening.

    Malindi Dishes (Map pp102-3; Gaberone Rd; mains
KSh80-200) A great little Swahili canteen. As
the name suggests, this place serves great
food from the coast, including pilau (curried
rice with meat), biryanis and coconut fish,
with side dishes such as *ugali*, naan bread
and rice. You'll get a grand feed here, but
it's a Muslim place, so it's closed for prayer
at lunchtime on Friday.

FK Restaurant (Map pp98-9; ☎ 223448; Hazina Towers, Monrovia St; mains KSh120-200) This immaculate daytime cafeteria at the rear of an office block makes an appealing alternative to the grubbier canteens around it; there's an interior gallery area if you like to look down on your fellow diners. The special breakfast is good value at KSh130.

Dancing Spoon Café & Wine Bar (Map pp102-3; ☎ 227581; 20th Century Plaza, Mama Ngina St; dishes KSh200-350) Next to the 20th Century Cinema, this bright canteen serves good Western and Kenyan food into the evening, and it's a great place for a steak and beer before you take in a movie.

Beneve Coffee House (Map pp102-3; ☎ 217959; cnr Standard & Koinange Sts; dishes KSh20-140; ☒ Mon-Fri) A small self-service chop shop that has locals queuing outside in the mornings waiting for it to open. Food ranges from stews to curries, fish and chips, samosas, pasties and a host of other choices, all at low, low prices.

Tropez (Map pp102-3; Banda St; meals KSh200-290) A handy modern restaurant offering fast grills, curries, chicken and the like. The KSh280 lunchtime buffet is top value, and the KSh200 breakfast isn't bad either. There's another branch of the same chain, with sports bar, at Zeep (Norwich Union Towers, Mama Ngina St).

Seasons Restaurant (Map pp102-3; ☎ 227697; Nairobi Cinema, Uchumi House, Aga Khan Walk; mains KSh240-280, buffets KSh280); Kimathi St (Map pp102-3; ☎ 0720-846276; Mutual Bldg; ☐) Whatever the season, the cafeteria vats here always brim with cheap Kenyan and Western favourites. The Nairobi Cinema outlet has a popular bar and beer garden, and there are a couple of similar branches around the centre. You can bring in your own booze, food or *miraa* (twigs and shoots chewed as a stimulant) for a 'cockage' fee of KSh2500.

NYAMA CHOMA

Kenyans tend to give short shrift to vegetarianism – *nyama choma* (barbecued meat; see p89) is the national dish and just about every pub-restaurant in town will throw a goat leg on the coals for you any time of day.

For a more exotic take on things there are some amazing restaurants where you can really do *nyama* in style. The law now limits what game meat can be served, but should the fancy take you, you can still sample ostrich, camel and even crocodile (like sweet, slightly fishy chicken). These places categorically do not cater to vegetarians.

The two most famous *nyama choma* restaurants here are Carnivore in Langata and Horseman in Karen. For details, see p130.

Nyama Choma Place (Map pp98-9; ☎ 2720933; Sagret Hotel, Milimani Rd; meals KSh400-600) This restaurant at the midrange Sagret Hotel is highly rated by Kenyans. There's a butchery here where you select your meat and then it's tossed on the barbie – any day of the week you'll see clouds of delicious-smelling smoke rising from the restaurant. It's best to come in a group, as meat is sold by weight in the form of whole goat legs or complete racks of ribs. Chips or *ugali* are available with the roast.

Nyama choma stalls (Map pp102-3; Haile Selassie Ave) A definite step down the scale, but worth it for the atmosphere, are the backstreet stalls near the Railway Museum, behind the Shell petrol station. Foreigners are a rare sight, but you'll be warmly welcomed and encouraged to sample other Kenyan dishes such as *matoke* (mashed plantains). A decent lunch should cost no more than KSh200. There are similar stalls near the Kenyatta National Hospital, but you might not want to eat so close to sick people!

Indian

Westlands is the centre of Nairobi's Indian population, but there are a few budget options downtown as well.

Haandi (Map p104; ☎ 4448294; www.haandi-restaurants.com/nairobi_aboutus.htm; The Mall Shopping Centre, Ring Rd Westlands, Westlands; mains KSh600-995; ☒ noon-2.30pm & 7-10.30pm; ☒) An international award-winner widely regarded as the best Indian restaurant in Kenya, Haandi has sister restaurants in Kampala, London and Middlesex and sells its own souvenir T-shirts. The menu reads like a recipe book crossed with a guide to Indian cuisine, and includes wonderful *mughlai* (North Indian) and tandoori dishes and plenty of vegetarian curries.

Chowpaty Pure Vegetarian Restaurant (Map p104; ☎ 3755050; Shimmers Plaza, Westlands Rd, Westlands; mains KSh200-350; ☒ 11am-11pm) A great Indian vegetarian restaurant. The menu is as much a manifesto as a food list, but the food is excellent and includes lots of South Indian dishes such as *dhosa* (lentil pancakes stuffed with vegetable curry).

Supreme Restaurant (Map pp102-3; ☎ 331586; River Rd; meals KSh170-250) Near the junction with Tom Mboya St, this place offers excellent Punjabi vegetarian *thalis* (plate meals) consisting of various curries, rice, dhal, *bhajia* (vegetables fried in lentil flour) and chapatis. It also has superb fruit juices.

Plaza Café (Map pp98-9; ☎ 227612; Barclays Plaza, Loita St; mains KSh300-600; ⏲ 7-9.30am, noon-3.30pm & 6.30-10pm) The Minar chain used to have several branches in the city centre, but now there's just this one, set in the Plaza's basement courtyard. It specialises in *mughlai* dishes but also does standard breakfasts and African dishes, plus good buffet lunches and plenty of vegetarian options.

Taj (Map pp102-3; Taveta Rd; dishes KSh20-100) Basic, ultracheap Indian soul food around the corner from the Iqbal Hotel.

Ethiopian

Blue Nile Ethiopian Restaurant (Map pp98-9; ☎ 0722-898138; bluenile@yahoo.com; Argwings Kodhek Rd, Hurlingham; mains KSh300-450) One of those rare places with a character all its own, Blue Nile's quirky lounge couldn't be mistaken for anywhere else, painted with stories from Ethiopian mythology – if you've ordered one of the many goat dishes, it's best not to read the panels about poison until you've finished your meal! For the full communal African eating experience, order the seven-person *doro wat* (spicy traditional chicken stew, KSh3500) with a few glasses of *tej* (honey wine, KSh125).

Addis Ababa Restaurant (Map p104; ☎ 4447321; Woodvale Grove, Westlands; mains KSh400-500; ⏲ noon-3pm Mon-Sat & from 6pm daily) Unlike the Ethiopian capital itself, this place is easily missed as it's tucked away up some stairs in an otherwise unremarkable block. Locate it and you'll also find good authentic food and occasional live music.

Italian

With Kenya's huge Italian expat population, it's not surprising that there are some good Italian choices here.

Trattoria (Map pp102-3; ☎ 340855; cnr Wabera & Kaunda Sts; mains KSh400-1800; ⏲ 7.30am-midnight) A very popular downtown restaurant swathed in trellises and plants, offering excellent pizzas, pasta, varied mains and a whole page of desserts. The atmosphere and food are excellent and it's packed every night, especially

the upstairs balcony section. Try the penne with vodka and smoked salmon (KSh550). A minimum spend of KSh500 per person applies for dinner, which is seldom a problem.

Taverna (Map p104; ☎ 4445234; Woodvale Grove, Westlands; mains KSh390-800) A quite sophisticated place tricked out in typical checked-tablecloth style, with lots of pasta choices and good seafood – tasty cognac prawns will set you back KSh1500.

Chinese & Thai

Nairobi has plenty of Chinese restaurants but they aren't a cheap option. Almost all offer 'large' (good for two people) and 'small' portions (enough for one). Food is generally excellent, but all these places add 16% VAT to the bill, so prices can soon mount up.

Panda Chinese Restaurant (Map pp102-3; ☎ 213018; Fedha Towers, Kaunda St; mains KSh380-1480; ⏲ noon-2.30pm & 6-10pm) A spacious, very classy Asian restaurant hidden away on Kaunda St. The staff are attentive to the point of overzealousness, especially when it's quiet, and the food is the best Chinese chow we found in Nairobi. Lovers of muzak will also be in their element here.

Hong Kong Restaurant (Map pp98-9; ☎ 228612; rhk@wananchi.com; College House, Koinange St; mains KSh300-600; ⏲ noon-2.30pm & 6-10pm) A bright-red restaurant with good food and not *too* much clichéd décor. It's the cheapest proper Chinese in town and is accordingly popular.

Bangkok Chinese Restaurant (Map p104; ☎ 3751312; Rank Xerox House, Parklands Rd, Westlands; mains KSh290-890; ⏲ 11am-3pm & 6pm-late) The Bangkok has been in business for a number of years but was clearly named by someone with no grasp of geography, as there's virtually nothing Thai on the menu at all. If the disappointment gets too much you can always crack open a bottle of Moët (KSh8990).

Tanager Bar & Restaurant (Map pp102-3; ☎ 221615; Rehema House, Kaunda St; mains KSh280-350; ⏲ 11am-11pm Mon-Sat) A cheap and simple Chinese–African eatery right in the city centre.

China Jiangsu Restaurant (Map p104; ☎ 4446700; Westlands Rd; mains KSh200-600; ⏲ 11.30am-3pm & 6-10.30pm) A stylish rooftop restaurant above the Soin shopping centre. Prices are very reasonable considering the classy balcony setting, and the food's not to be sniffed at either.

NAIROBI

Siam Thai (Map p104; ☎ 3751728; Unga House, Muthithi Rd, Westlands; mains KSh250-680) This attractive restaurant has an extensive menu of actual Thai food (gasp!) and a very good reputation. Unga House can be reached from either Woodvale Grove or Muthithi Rd.

Japanese

Restaurant Akasaka (Map pp102-3; ☎ 220299; Standard St; mains KSh450-800; ☻ noon-2.30pm & 6-10pm Mon-Sat) A wonderful Japanese restaurant next to the Sixeighty Hotel. It's always a little quiet, but this fits the stylish Japanese décor and the food is very authentic. There's even a tatami room (reserve in advance) where you can eat at traditional low tables. Akasaka runs the full gamut of Japanese cuisine including *udon* noodles, sushi sets, tempura, teriyaki and sukiyaki as well as great miso soup. Good-value set lunches are also available.

Furusato Japanese Restaurant (Map p104; ☎ 4442508; Karuna Rd, Westlands; set meals KSh700-1500) Behind the Sarit Centre, this is a very stylish place with seductive set Japanese meals including sushi, *teppanyaki* and tempura. The sushi and sashimi are delicious. Reservations are recommended.

International

Nairobi has plenty of good upmarket restaurants serving mixed cuisine from around the world. For some other sophisticated choices, head to Karen and Langata (p129).

Fiesta Restaurant & Bar (Map pp102-3; ☎ 240326; Koinange St; mains KSh450-1800; ☻ 7am-midnight) Despite the Latin resonances of a Hispanic name and bright adobe-style décor, the brand-new Fiesta doesn't have anything remotely Tex-Mex on offer, concentrating instead on a fine selection of upmarket international dishes. Staff are smiley and almost unnervingly eager to please, and the chefs do themselves particular credit on some very un-Kenyan recipes such as nasi goreng and pork chops with a honey and mustard glaze. The popular bar area occasionally hosts low-key live crooners.

Alan Bobbé's Bistro (Map pp102-3; ☎ 226027; Cianda House, Koinange St; mains KSh987-1850) The talented M Bobbé established this superb French bistro in 1962, and Nairobi gourmets and gourmands alike have been worshipping at his culinary altar ever since. Even reading the chatty handwritten menu is enough to send the palate into raptures.

The interior, doused in red velvet, adds perfectly to the recherché ambience. Reservations and smart dress are encouraged, cigars and pipes are not. Look out for the poodle above Koinange St.

Thorn Tree Café (Map pp102-3; ☎ 228030; New Stanley Hotel, Kimathi St; mains KSh350-1380) The Stanley's legendary café still serves as a popular meeting place for travellers of all persuasions, and caters to most tastes with a good mix of food. If you like a big breakfast the US$15 buffet is worth a go. The original thorn-tree noticeboard in the courtyard gave rise to the general expression and inspired Lonely Planet's own Thorn Tree community; while the café is now on its third acacia and the noticeboard's not the paperfest it once was, a little nostalgia is de rigeur.

Tamarind Restaurant (Map pp102-3; ☎ 251811; www.tamarind.co.ke; Aga Khan Walk; mains KSh900-1800; ☻ 2.30-4.30pm & 8.30pm-midnight) Kenya's most prestigious restaurant chain runs Nairobi's best seafood restaurant, in the National Bank Building between Harambee Ave and City Hall Way. The splendid menu offers all manner of exotic flavours, and the lavish dining room is laid out in a sumptuous modern Arabic-Moorish style. Smart dress is expected and you'll need to budget at least KSh2500 for the full works, particularly if you want wine or cocktails and lobster (KSh330 per 100g).

Porterhouse Restaurant (Map pp102-3; ☎ 221829; Mama Ngina St; mains KSh420-480; ☻ 5-10.30pm) Steak-lovers should make this discreetly swish 1st-floor restaurant their first port of call: apart from a few token dishes such as chicken kiev, the menu here is entirely dedicated to the art of carving chunks of cow, and with a two-person Chateaubriand for just KSh900 it's easy to get into the moo-d (ahem).

Phoenician Restaurant (☎ 3741524; Karuna Rd, Westlands; mains KSh500-800; ☻ Tue-Sun) This new garden restaurant, tucked away behind the Sarit Centre, may well be the first Lebanese restaurant in Kenya. We've heard mixed reports of the food, but there's plenty for veggies and with more starters than main courses, assembling your own mixed mezze offers plenty of scope for a Middle East feast. Live music on Friday.

Kengeles Bar & Restaurant (Map pp98-9; ☎ 344335; Koinange St; mains KSh270-560) Run on the lines of a Western chain restaurant, Kengeles' impressively varied menu encompasses burgers, grills, Mexican, African, Indonesian, Asian and buffet options, and the open-air balcony is a fine place to dine. On a quiet night, though, the service can be truly lousy. The chain was rumoured to be in financial difficulties at time of writing, and had also seemingly fallen out of favour with Nairobi council – see the boxed text on below.

Quick Eats

Traditionally Nairobi's office workers have relied on budget canteens and takeaways for cheap meals; any of the Kenyan and Swahili places listed here (p111) can whip you up a feed in next to no time. There are also innumerable indistinguishable fast-food joints around town following the Western model – Kimathi St and Moi Ave have particularly high concentrations.

FOOD COURTS

Sarit Centre (Map p104; ☎ 3747408; www.saritcentre .com; Parklands Rd, Westlands) This huge food court on the 2nd floor has a variety of small restaurants and fast-food places, including Indian, Chinese, Italian and African food. The Hidden Agenda pub-restaurant (mains KSh360 to KSh800) comes recommended, with Western and Thai menus.

Village Market (☎ 522488; www.villagemarket -kenya.com; Limuru Rd, Gigiri) The open food court here includes Italian, Turkish, German, Thai, Japanese and seafood outlets.

Yaya Centre (Argwings Khodek Rd, Hurlingham) A smaller food court with a reasonable selection of cafés and kiosks. The Saffron restaurant upstairs (mains KSh245 to KSh460) does great Indian eat-in and takeaway food.

Etouch food court (Map pp102-3; Union Towers, cnr Moi Ave & Mama Ngina St) A central collection of cheap'n'easy fast-food joints such as Nando's, Chicken Inn, Creamy Inn, Pizza Inn... you get the idea.

Self-Catering

There are very few places to stay with self-catering facilities, but you can buy supplies for snack lunches, safaris etc as well as cooking ingredients from the many supermarkets downtown and in the suburbs.

Nakumatt Downtown (Map pp102-3; ☎ 335011; Kenyatta Ave); Lifestyle (Map pp102-3; ☎ 340015; Moktar Daddah St); Village (☎ 522508; Village Market, Limuru Rd, Gigiri) The principal supermarket chain in Nairobi and Kenya as a whole, Nakumatt invariably has a huge selection of Kenyan and Western foods and other products. The brand-new Lifestyle store spreads over several floors, with departments stocking all kinds of useful household and outdoor goods.

Uchumi Downtown (Map pp102-3; ☎ 227001; Uchumi House, Aga Khan Way); Comet House (Map pp98-9; Monrovia St); Westlands (Map p104; Sarit Centre, Parklands Rd) Once the main supermarket chain in town, Uchumi has faded fast in Nakumatt's wake

---

SIDEWALK STRIFE

One recent trend in Nairobi has seen all kinds of bars and restaurants extending their seating areas onto the pavement European café–style, often with brightly coloured awnings, plants and other trappings to jazz up the drab street surroundings. A positive development, surely? Apparently not as far as the city council is concerned.

The first sign that all was not well came when an entire vanload of council *askaris* descended on the Kengeles Bar & Restaurant on Koinange St, leaving a startled crowd of punters and passers-by in their wake. The council claimed the owners were warned repeatedly about new regulations banning street extensions and had been told to remove the offending structure; the restaurant, however, said this was the first time they'd heard anything about it at all.

In the wake of the incident other cafés removed their own pavement patios with quite remarkable alacrity, fearful of further action from above. Several nearby rivals have a different take on matters, however – as one competitor suggested to the *Daily Nation* shortly after the event, Kengeles may well have been targeted for personal reasons, as it's rumoured that the proprietors have had wrangles with the council in the past.

Whatever the truth, only a handful of pavement restaurants have dared to hold their ground, and it seems we'll have to wait a while longer before Kenyan café culture finally hits the streets. Until it does, reach for the skies – Nairobi's many 1st-floor balcony restaurants are still the best places in town to catch and shoot the breeze.

and several central branches have closed. Those that remain open still have a good range of items.

California Cookies (Map pp102-3; ☎ 246365; KTDA Bldg, Moi Ave; biscuits KSh35/100g) If your sweet tooth needs pulling, try this busy biscuit bakery for a dose of sugar.

DRINKING
Cafés

Western café culture has hit Nairobi big style, seized on enthusiastically by local expats and residents pining for a decent cup of Kenyan coffee. All these places offer at least some form of food, whether it's a few cakes or a full menu, but none serve alcohol.

Nairobi Java House (Map pp102-3; ☎ 313565; www .nairobijava.com; Mama Ngina St; snacks KSh80-180; ⊙ 7am-8.30pm Mon-Sat) This fantastic coffeehouse is rapidly turning itself into a major brand, and you may see its logo on T-shirts as far afield as London or even beyond. Aficionados say the coffee's some of the best in Kenya, and there are plenty of cakes and other sweet and savoury treats. It's nicely laid out, with art exhibits on the walls, and very popular, so you may have to share a table.

Kahawa (Map pp102-3; ☎ 221900; zulmawani@ ispnbi.com; Fedha Towers, Kaunda St; mains KSh190-410) Also new, Kahawa has an unusual coastal theme – the counter even resembles a traditional dhow, complete with mast. The menu, however, is anything but old-fashioned, proffering an ever-changing cavalcade of unexpected specials to complement the grills and steaks, from frittata to a 'Mexican breakfast'. Speaking of breakfast, this is indeed another good spot to take the most important meal of the day.

Dormans Café (Map pp102-3; ☎ 0724-238976; Mama Ngina St; coffee KSh100-190) Established in the 1960s, this venerable firm has only recently branched out into the café business but has certainly made an aggressive Starbucks-style start, opening a shiny pine outlet right opposite its main rival Nairobi Java. The coffee's good and the selection of teas is impressive, but so far the food just doesn't compete.

Oleander Café (Map pp98-9; Rahimtulla Tower, Upper Hill Rd, Nairobi Hill; drinks KSh40-100) This small elevated café has limited stocks of food and drink, but the terrace is so surrounded by greenery that you barely even notice the busy road below, providing a perfect respite

from town if you happen to be around the Nairobi Hill area.

Café 21 (Map pp102-3; ☎ 341524; I&M Bank Tower, Kenyatta Ave; mains KSh150-380) More of a cafeteria than a purebreed coffeehouse, the neat little 21 does both full meals and snacks or 'bitings'. Sandwiches, grills, pasta and lamb chops all feature, and there's a KSh500 lunch buffet.

Bars

There are plenty of cheap but very rough-and-ready bars around Latema Rd and River Rd. These places aren't recommended for female travellers, and even male drinkers should watch themselves. There are some safer and friendlier watering holes around Tom Mboya St and Moi Ave, and many of the restaurants and hotels listed previously are fine places for a drink. You can also head to Westlands, where the drinking scene brings in a lot more expats.

Even in cosmopolitan Nairobi, foreign women without a man in tow will draw attention virtually everywhere. To avoid this entirely, you can head for the fancier hangouts in the outer suburbs (see p130).

Casablanca (☎ 2723173; Lenana Rd, Hurlingham; ⊙ from 6pm) This hip new Moroccan-style lounge bar has been an instant hit with Nairobi's fastidious expat community, and you don't have to spend much time here to become a convert. Shisha pipes, wines and cocktails conspire to ease you into what's bound to end up as a late night.

Zanze Bar (Map pp102-3; ☎ 222532; Kenya Cinema Plaza, Moi Ave) A lively and friendly top-floor bar with pool tables, a dance floor, cheap beer and reasonable food. During the week things are relatively quiet, but from Friday to Sunday it rocks until the early hours, with a much more relaxed vibe than the big clubs.

Taco Bell (Map pp102-3; Tumaini House, 15 Moi Ave) On the 1st floor, with an open balcony overlooking the street, this popular bar has DJs from Thursday to Sunday. Food is served but there's not a burrito in sight – we suspect the Taco Bell Corporation doesn't know they've borrowed the name...

Taco's (Map pp102-3; Kimathi St) Smaller but otherwise almost identical to Taco Bell, it sells beers by the dozen (!). An over-21s policy applies, for no apparent reason.

Hornbill Pub (Map pp102-3; ☎ 246615; Ambassadeur Hotel, Tom Mboya St) A large, dark but friendly bar stretching the width of the block between Moi Ave and Tom Mboya St, with lashings of cold Tusker and sizzling *nyama choma*.

Jockey Pub (Map pp102-3; Hilton Hotel, Mama Ngina St) The Hilton's house boozer is a cosy English-style hostelry, but nonguests are subject to a hefty minimum-spend requirement. There's a free yard of ale if you can drink it in under three minutes without stopping, a feat possibly not to be attempted on a full stomach.

Roast House (Map pp102-3; Kilome Rd) This split-level green bar-restaurant is one of the better specimens in the River Rd area, with regular DJ nights, but caution is still advised if coming here.

WESTLANDS

Gypsy's Bar (Map p104; ☎ 4440836; Woodvale Grove) Don't be confused by the contradictory signs – this long-running bar is made up of several parts, none of which actually seem to be called Gypsy's! Identity crisis aside, it's probably the most popular bar in Westlands, pulling in a mixed crowd of Kenyans, expats and prostitutes. Snacks are available and there's decent Western and African music, with parties taking over the pavement in summer. This is also as close as you'll get to a gay-friendly venue in Kenya.

Bar Code (Map p104; Westview Centre, Ring Rd) It's nowhere near as cool as it thinks it is, but this very modern late-opening lounge bar does at least have a good range of international spirits and cocktails (KSh300 to KSh550), plus semi-competent DJs spinning R&B and hip-hop for the tiny dance floor. The lurid painted toilets are probably the best bit, in keeping with the vague gangster theme.

Soho's (Map p104; ☎ 3745710; Parklands Rd) A lively and popular place that pulls in a smart Kenyan and expat crowd. As well as the crisp cold beers, there's a good selection of wines and cocktails.

Klub House (Map p104; ☎ 749870; Parklands Rd) Further west, past the large Holiday Inn complex, the Klub House is another old favourite. The spacious bar has more pool tables than anyone else and is a good place to party until late. Music is predominantly Latino, Caribbean and African.

ENTERTAINMENT

For information on all entertainment in Nairobi and for big music venues in the rest of the country, get hold of the *Saturday Nation*, which lists everything from cinema releases to live music venues. There will also be plenty of suggestions run by the magazine *Going Out*.

Nightclubs

There's a good selection of dance clubs in Nairobi's centre and there are no dress codes, although there's an unspoken assumption that males will at least wear a shirt and long trousers. Beer in all these places is reasonably priced at about KSh100, but imported drinks are a lot more expensive.

Due to the high numbers of female prostitutes, men will generally get the bulk of the hassle in all these places, though even women in male company are by no means exempt from approaches by either sex.

Pavement (Map p104; ☎ 4441711; Waiyaki Way, Westlands; admission KSh500) Split between a relaxed ground-level bar and the big, modern basement club where the action happens, Pavement is the dance floor of choice for most resident expats, and isn't as messy as its counterparts in town. Leavening the usual mix of hip-hop and chart pop, weekends here favour the kind of proper jump-up funky house, trance and techno you might get on a night out in Europe. Thursday is Latin night and there are also Sunday jazz sessions.

New Florida (Map pp102-3; ☎ 215014; Koinange St; men/women KSh200/100; ☼ to 6am, later Sat & Sun) The 'Mad House' is a big, rowdy club housed in a bizarre blacked-out saucer building above a petrol station. The music policy ranges from jazz (Monday to Wednesday) to the customary weekend mish-mash of all things naff and Western, with dubious semi-clad floorshows on Friday and Saturday. Whichever night you choose, it's usually mayhem, crammed with bruisers, cruisers, hookers, hustlers and curious tourists, but it's great fun if you're in the right mood (or just very drunk). Entry is usually free before 9pm.

Florida 2000 (Map pp102-3; ☎ 229036; Moi Ave; men/women KSh200/100) The original blueprint for the New Florida, this big dancing den near City Hall Way still works to exactly the same formula of booze, beats and tight-packed bodies. All-hours eats are provided by the Water Margin Chinese restaurant. Monday is salsa-zouk-mamba night, Wednesday is straight-up dance/trance and Sunday is Rasta night.

Club Soundd (Map pp102-3; Kaunda St; admission free-KSh200; ☺ from 3pm) Another central nightspot following much the same pattern, but with a bit more to offer those who take their music seriously: high-profile local posse the HomeBoyz DJs play on Friday, there's salsa on Sunday and a rare trance night on Wednesday. It opens earlier than most similar places, and has a happy hour until 8pm to suck in premature punters.

Two real earthy local hangouts are the **Monte Carlo Club** (Map pp102-3; ☎ 223181; Reata-House, Accra Rd; admission KSh100) and **Nyanza House Club** (Map pp102-3; ☎ 228692; Sheikh Karume Rd; admission KSh100); you'll see posters plastered all over town advertising reggae parties at both. A night out here will be as authentic a modern African experience as you can get, but we couldn't in good conscience suggest that unaccompanied women go anywhere near here.

Live Music

Green Corner Restaurant & Cactus Pub (Map pp102-3; ☎ 335243; Tumaini House, Nkrumah Lane) This very popular after-work bar and restaurant just opposite the Nairobi Cinema has live bands on Thursday and Sunday and DJs the rest of the week. Music is generally modern, East African and enthusiastically received.

Toona Tree Bar & Restaurant (Map pp98-9; ☎ 3740802; toonatree@africaonline.co.ke; International Casino, Museum Hill Rd) Part of the massive International Casino complex by the National Museum, Toona Tree has live bands on Friday and Saturday, playing jazz, blues and 'classic hits'.

At the New Stanley Hotel, the Thorn Tree Café (p114) also has live bands most nights.

Cinemas

Nairobi is a good place to take in a few films at a substantially lower price than back home. The upmarket cinemas show a mix of Western blockbusters and even more popular Bollywood extravaganzas. Tickets range from KSh150 to KSh240, with the best deals available on Tuesdays.

Nu Metro Cinema (☎ 522128; numetro@swiftkenya .com; Village Market, Gigiri; tickets KSh350) The first entry in a chain of modern multiplexes springing up around Nairobi, showing new Western films fairly promptly after their international release. Seats here are pretty

steep, but that's still cheaper than the popcorn at a London picture house.

Fox Cineplex (Map p104; ☎ 227959; Sarit Centre, Westlands) Another good modern cinema in the same price bracket as Nu Metro, located on the 2nd floor of the Sarit Centre.

20th Century Cinema (Map pp102-3; ☎ 210606; 20th Century Plaza, Mama Ngina St), **Kenya Cinema** (Map pp102-3; ☎ 227822; Kenya Cinema Plaza, Moi Ave) and **Nairobi Cinema** (Map pp102-3; ☎ 338058; Uchumi House, Aga Khan Walk) are all owned by the same chain. The first two show mainly Western movies, while the Nairobi Cinema goes through phases of only screening Christian 'message' films.

Odeon (Map pp102-3; Latema Rd) is one of several local cinemas showing a mix of Indian, South African and Western films. Tickets are very cheap but reels are often scratched.

The fleapit **Cameo cinema** (Map pp102-3; Kenyatta Ave) is well placed but appears to show manly sex films.

Theatre

Professional Centre (Map pp102-3; ☎ 225506; www .phoenixplayers.net; Parliament Rd) Local theatre troupe the Phoenix Players put on regular

---

THE AUTHOR'S CHOICE

Simmers (Map pp102-3; ☎ 217659; cnr Kenyatta Ave & Muindi Mbingu St; admission free) If you're tired of having your butt pinched to the strains of limp R&B in darkened discos, Simmers is the place to come to rediscover a bit of true African rhythm. The atmosphere at this open-air bar-restaurant is almost invariably amazing, with the ever-enthusiastic crowds turning out to wind'n'grind the night away to incessant parades of bands playing anything from Congolese rumba to Kenyan *benga* (contemporary dance music). Refreshingly, the women here are more likely to be local girls out for a giggle than working girls out for business, so for once you shouldn't have to worry too much about being hassled, and most people are very friendly should you feel the need to, say, compliment someone on their *lingala* (Congolese) dancing. With free-flowing Tusker, a separate shots bar and plenty of *nyama choma* to keep the lion from the door, it's no wonder the place always feels like a party.

performances at this venue with an unlikely name. Many of the plays are by foreign playwrights but a good proportion are by Kenyans, and new works are well represented. Tickets cost KSh650, though strictly it should be US$20 for nonresidents.

Kenya National Theatre (Map pp98-9; ☎ 225174; Harry Thuku Rd; tickets from KSh200) Opposite the Norfolk Hotel, this is the major theatre venue in Nairobi. As well as contemporary and classic plays, there are special events such as beauty pageants, which are less highbrow but still culturally interesting.

For African theatre, the foreign cultural centres (p97) are often the places to head for. Also, check the *Daily Nation* to see what's on.

SHOPPING

Nairobi is a good place to pick up souvenirs but prices are usually higher than elsewhere in the country. There are loads of souvenir shops downtown and in the area northwest of Kenyatta Ave. Most places sell exactly the same stuff, but there are a few speciality shops with better-than-average crafts. The 'Little India' area around Biashara St is good for fabric, textiles and those all-important souvenir Tusker T-shirts.

If you're interested in buying local music, just wander round the River Rd and Latema Rd area and listen out for the blaring CD kiosks.

City Market (Map pp102-3; Muindi Mbingu St) The city's souvenir business is concentrated in this covered market, which has dozens of stalls selling wood carvings, drums, spears, shields, soapstone, Maasai jewellery and clothing. It's a hectic place and you'll have to bargain hard (and we *mean* hard), but there's plenty of good stuff on offer. It's an interesting place to wander round in its own right, though you generally need to be shopping to make the constant hassle worth the bother.

Gallery Watatu (Map pp102-3; ☎ 228737; Lonhro House, Standard St) If you want fine Kenyan art, this is a good place to check out what's happening prior to investing your hard-earned. There's a permanent display here and many of the items are for sale, but be prepared to part with at least KSh20,000 just for something small.

Spinners Web (Map p104; ☎ 4440882; Viking House, Waiyaki Way, Westlands) Works with workshops and self-help groups around the country. It's

---

SHOPPING IN STYLE

The beautifully conceived **Village Market** (☎ 522488; www.villagemarket-kenya.com; Limuru Rd, Gigiri; 👫) shopping centre has a selection of entertainment activities to while away an afternoon, including the Nu Metro cinema (opposite), a bowling alley, pool hall, water slides, mini golf and a children's playground complete with toy-car rides and a mini-train circuit. You can get here with matatu No 106 (KSh40) from near the train station.

---

a bit like a handicrafts version of Ikea, with goods displayed the way they might look in Western living rooms, but there's some classy stuff on offer, including carpets, wall hangings, ceramics, wooden bowls, baskets and clothing.

Triangle Curios Market (Map p104; Parklands Rd, Westlands) Near the Sarit Centre in Westlands, this is a cheaper collection of stalls at a road junction. There are lots of genuine tribal objects such as Turkana wrist knives and wooden headrests.

Maasai Market Central Nairobi (Map pp102-3; off Slip Rd; 🕐 Tue); Gigiri (Village Market, Limuru Rd; 🕐 Fri) These busy markets are held every Tuesday on the waste ground near Slip Rd in town, and Friday in the rooftop car park at the Village Market shopping complex (above). You can buy beaded jewellery, gourds, baskets and other Maasai crafts, but you'll have to bargain hard. The markets are open from early morning to late afternoon.

Undugu Craft Shop (Map p104; ☎ 4443525; Woodvale Grove, Westlands) Another good charitable venture, this nonprofit organisation supports community projects in Nairobi and has very good-quality crafts.

Banana Box (Map p104; ☎ 3743390; Sarit Centre, Westlands) Among the rather less altruistic commercialism of the Sarit Centre, Banana Box works in conjunction with community projects and refugee groups and offers modern uses for traditional objects.

GETTING THERE & AWAY
Air

Kenya Airways (Map pp98-9; ☎ 32074100; Barclays Plaza, Loita St) operates international and domestic services out of Jomo Kenyatta International Airport, with at least six daily flights to Mombasa plus services to Kisumu (one hour), Lamu (2¼ hours) and Malindi (1¼ hours). Fares come down rapidly if you can book more than a week in advance; if not, it's best to go through a travel agent.

Airkenya (☎ 501601; Wilson Airport, Langata Rd) has daily flights to Lamu (1¾ hours), Kiwayu island (two hours), Malindi and Nanyuki (45 minutes), as well as serving several national parks and Kilimanjaro in Tanzania. **Safarilink** (☎ 600777; Wilson Airport) offers similar services at virtually identical prices.

One-way fares:

destination	fare	frequency (daily)
Amboseli	US$85	2
Eldoret	KSh5700	1
Kisumu	from KSh5605	1
Kiwayu	US$163	2
Lamu	from US$135	3
Lewa Downs	US$115	2
Malindi	from US$85	2
Masai Mara	US$105	3
Mombasa	from KSh6835	6
Nanyuki	US$60-80	2
Samburu	from US$115	3

The check-in time for domestic flights is one hour before departure. The baggage allowance is only 15kg as there isn't much space on the small turboprop aircraft. Reconfirm flights with airlines 72 hours before you depart or you could lose your seat.

Bus

In Nairobi, most long-distance bus company offices are in the River Rd area, clustered around Accra Rd and the surrounding streets. Several companies go to Mombasa, including Akamba, Busscar, Busstar, Mash Express and Mombasa Raha. Most services leave in the early morning or late evening; the trip takes eight to 10 hours with a meal break on the way. Buses leave from outside each company's office. Fares range from KSh400 to KSh700. **Coastline Safaris** (Map pp102-3; ☎ 217592; cnr Latema & Lagos Rds) buses are the most comfortable and expensive.

Akamba (Map pp102-3; ☎ 340430; akamba_prs@ skyweb.co.ke; Lagos Rd) is the biggest private bus company in the country and has an extensive network. It's not the cheapest, but is the safest and most reliable company. It

has buses to Eldoret, Kakamega, Kericho, Kisii, Kisumu, Kitale, Machakos, Mombasa, Kampala (Uganda) and Mwanza, Moshi and Dar es Salaam (Tanzania). Buses leave from Lagos Rd and there's a **booking office** (Map pp102-3; ☎ 222027; Wabera St), near City Hall.

The government-owned **KBS** (Kenya Bus Service; ☎ 229707) is a large, reliable operator, cheaper than Akamba but with slower buses. The main depot is east of the centre on Uyoma St, but there's a downtown **booking office** (Map pp102-3; ☎ 341250; cnr Muindi Mbingu & Monrovia Sts). There are loads of buses to Kisumu and Kakamega and less frequent services to Busia, Eldoret, Kisii, Kitale and Malaba.

Easy Coach (Map pp102-3; ☎ 210711; easycoach@ wananchi.com; Haile Selassie Ave) is a reliable new company serving western Kenyan destinations on the Kisumu/Kakamega route (up to seven daily), with daily buses to Arusha in the other direction.

The **Country Bus Station** (Map pp98-9; Landhies Rd) is a hectic, disorganised place with buses to Machakos, Busia, Eldoret, Kakamega, Kisumu, Nyeri, Nakuru, Nanyuki, Malaba and Meru. Eldoret Express is the biggest operator with plenty of buses to Kisumu and the Ugandan border, while Busscar has very frequent buses to Machakos.

See p377 for details on other bus companies operating out of Nairobi. Typical fares include the following:

destination	fare (Ksh)	duration (hrs)
Arusha	750-800	4 (Tanzania)
Dar es Salaam	1400-1600	12 (Tanzania)
Eldoret	350-500	3
Embu	200	1½
Homa Bay	450	6
Kakamega	400-500	5
Kampala	1000-1350	10-12 (Uganda)
Kisii	350-550	4
Kisumu	400-550	4
Kitale	400-600	5
Machakos	80-120	1
Malindi	800	9-10
Meru	250-350	3
Mombasa	500-1000	6-10
Moshi	700	5 (Tanzania)
Mwanza	1100	12 (Tanzania)
Naivasha	130	1-1½
Nakuru	200-300	2
Nanyuki	200	2
Nyeri	200	1½

Matatu

Most matatus leave from Latema, Accra, River and Cross Rds and fares are similar to the buses. The biggest operator here is **Crossland Services** (Map pp102-3; ☎ 245377; Cross Rd), which serves destinations including Eldoret (KSh350, three hours), Kericho (KSh450, three hours), Kisii (KSh500, five hours), Kisumu (KSh550, four hours), Naivasha (KSh150, one hour), Nakuru (KSh250, two hours) and Nanyuki (KSh250, two hours). On the same road are **Molo Line Services** (Map pp102-3; ☎ 0724-342966) with matatus to Eldoret, Naivasha, Nakuru and Kisumu, and **Narok Line** (Map pp102-3; ☎ 213020), which serves Kisii, Narok (KSh250, three hours) and Kericho.

Other companies are located on the surrounding streets. Head to Accra Rd (Map pp102-3) for matatus to Chogoria (KSh250, 2½ hours), Embu (KSh200, 1½ hours), Meru (KSh300 to KSh350, three hours) and Nanyuki (KSh200, 2½ hours). Matatus leave from Latema Rd for Nyahururu (KSh300, three hours) and Nyeri (KSh200, two hours). There are loads of matatus to Naivasha (KSh130, 1½ hours) and the Tanzanian border at Namanga (KSh250, three hours) from the corner of Ronald Ngala St and River Rd (Map pp102-3). For Thika (KSh70, 40 minutes), go to the Total petrol station on Racecourse Rd (Map pp98-9).

Peugeot (Shared Taxi)

Like matatus, most of the companies offering Peugeot shared taxis have their offices around the Accra, River and Cross Rds area. One reliable company is **Crossland Services** (Map pp102-3; ☎ 245377; Cross Rd), which has cars to Eldoret, Kabarnet, Kericho, Kitale and Nakuru. Other companies serve Isiolo, Kisumu, Meru and Malaba. Fares are about 20% higher than the same journeys by matatu. Most services depart in the morning.

Shuttle Minibus

Shuttle minibuses run from Nairobi to Kampala (Uganda), and to Arusha and Moshi in Tanzania (see p374 for details).

Train

Nairobi train station has a **booking office** (Map pp102-3; ☎ 221211; Station Rd; 9am-noon & 2-6.30pm). Only two useful passenger services currently run from Nairobi (see p384). For Mombasa (1st/2nd class KSh3160/2275, 14 to 16 hours), trains leave Nairobi at 7pm on Monday, Wednesday and Friday; arrive early, as seats are only assigned at the last minute. The return services depart at 7pm on Tuesday, Thursday and Sunday.

For Kisumu (1st/2nd class KSh1415/720, 13 hours), trains depart at 6.30pm on the same days as the Mombasa services. It's advisable to book a few days in advance for either of these routes.

There are also a handful of weekday evening commuter services to Thika, Embakasi and Limuru, but these are of little help to travellers as road transport is far more efficient.

GETTING AROUND

To/From Jomo Kenyatta International Airport

Kenya's main **international airport** (☎ 827638) is 15km out of town, off the road to Mombasa. There's now a dedicated airport bus run by Metro Shuttle (part of KBS), which can drop you off at hotels in the city centre. Going the other way, the main departure point is across from the Hilton Hotel. The journey takes about 40 minutes and costs US$5 per person. Buses run every half-hour from 8am to 8.30pm daily and stop at both air terminals.

A cheaper way to get into town is city bus No 34 (KSh30), but a lot of travellers get ripped off on the bus or when they get off. Always hold onto valuables and have small change ready for the fare. Buses run from 5.45am to 9.30pm weekdays, 6.20am to 9.30pm Saturdays and 7.15am to 9.30pm Sundays, though the last few evening services may not operate. Heading to the airport, buses travel west along Kenyatta Ave.

A much safer method (and also your only option at night) is to take a taxi. The asking price is usually about KSh1200 in either direction, but you should be able to bargain down to KSh800 from town, or even as little as KSh500 from the domestic terminal if you catch a returning or unofficial cab. If you book at one of the 'information' desks at the airport, you'll still end up in a public taxi, but it isn't any more expensive.

To/From Wilson Airport

To get to **Wilson Airport** (Map p126; ☎ 501941), for Airkenya services or charter flights, the cheapest option is to take bus or matatu No 15, 31, 34, 125 or 126 from Moi Ave (KSh20). A taxi from the centre of town will cost you KSh600 to KSh800 depending on the driver. In the other direction, you'll have to fight the driver down from KSh1000. The entrance to the airport is easy to miss; it's just before the large BP petrol station.

Bus

The ordinary city buses are run by **KBS** (☎ 229707) but hopefully you won't need to use them much. Forget about them if you're carrying luggage – you'll never get on, and even if you do, you'll never get off! Most buses pass through downtown, but the main KBS terminus is on Uyoma St, east of the centre.

Useful buses include No 46 from Kenyatta Ave, for the Yaya Centre in Hurlingham (KSh10), and No 23 from Jevanjee Gardens, for Westlands (KSh10). There are services about every 20 minutes from 6am to 8pm Monday to Saturday.

There's also a useful Metro Shuttle service to Ngong Rd and Karen, passing the Karen Blixen Museum. Buses run every 15 minutes from 6am to 8pm Monday to Saturday and 7am to 7.30pm Sunday, departing from Moi Ave. All these services cost KSh20 to KSh40, depending on where you get off.

Car

See p378 for comprehensive information on car hire, road rules and conditions. If you are driving, beware of wheel-clampers: parking in the centre is by permit only (KSh70 per day), available from the parking attendants who roam the streets in bright yellow or red jackets. If you park overnight in the street in front of your hotel, the guard will often keep an eye on your vehicle for a small consideration.

Matatu

Nairobi's horde of matatus follow the same routes as buses and display the same route numbers. For Westlands, you can pick up No 23 on Moi Ave or Latema Rd. No 46 to the Yaya Centre stops in front of the main post office, and Nos 125 and 126 to Langata leave from in front of the train station. As usual, you should keep an eye on your valuables on all matatus.

Taxi

As people are compelled to use them due to Nairobi's endemic street crime, taxis here are overpriced and undermaintained, but you've little choice, particularly at night. Taxis don't cruise for passengers, but you can find them parked on every other street corner in the city centre. At night they're outside restaurants, bars and nightclubs; a fleet of reconditioned old London cabs hangs outside the Hilton Hotel at most times of day.

Fares around town are negotiable but end up pretty standard. Any journey within the downtown area costs KSh200, from downtown to Milimani Rd costs KSh300, and for longer journeys such as Westlands or the Yaya Centre, fares range from KSh400 to KSh500. From the city centre to the Carnivore restaurant is KSh650 one way, or KSh1200 for a return trip with waiting.

You can also find a fewIndonesian-style tuk-tuks operating from Kenyatta Ave. They're cheaper than taxis and good for short hops.

Around Nairobi

For most people, the area around Nairobi is far preferable to the stress of the city itself, and it's no coincidence that the green hills surrounding the capital are home to one of Kenya's largest expat communities. From the secluded suburbs of Karen and Langata to the lush walking trails of the Ngong Hills, a quick matatu ride can whisk you into another world for that much-needed rural escape, and with plenty of upscale restaurants and bars amid the villas there's no need to forego all the creature comforts of urban living. With money and time to spare, staying out this way can also be a special experience to rival even the best city hotels.

And speaking of creatures, taking that short trip out of Nairobi can thrust you firmly into the domain of Kenyan wildlife, whether you're chasing lepidoptera at Butterfly Africa, snogging giraffes at the Langata Giraffe Centre or watching flamingos feed at the raw soda gash of Lake Magadi. You don't even have to go out of sight of the city to feed those safari cravings – Nairobi National Park is literally right outside, with curious fauna peering over the ring road at the heaving metropolis next door.

Elsewhere you can stride the hills of the old Akamba territory around Machakos, brush up your tribal dance steps at the Bomas of Kenya, take in the span of the Rift Valley from the roads near Limuru and chew on succulent *nyama choma* (barbecued meat) at one of Africa's classic restaurants. So don't just sit there moaning about Nairobi: get out of it!

HIGHLIGHTS

- Watching wildlife amid the planes, trains and automobiles in **Nairobi National Park** (p125)
- Tangling tongues with a rubber-necked ungulate at **Langata Giraffe Centre** (p128)
- Making the essential foodie pilgrimage to **Carnivore** (p129) and dancing it off at **Simba Saloon** (p130)
- Striking out for some proper exercise walking the **Ngong Hills** (p130)
- Gawping at the views around **Limuru** (p133) as the road snakes down into the Rift Valley
- Partying the month away with the Langata expats at **Black Cotton** (p130)

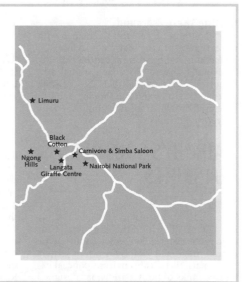

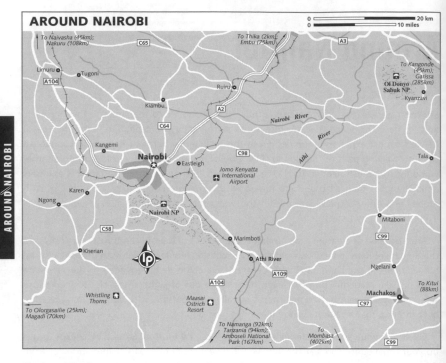

AROUND NAIROBI

0 _____ 20 km
0 _____ 10 miles

To Naivasha (45km);
Nakuru (108km)

To Thika (2km);
Embu (75km)

C65

A3

To Kangonde
(45km);
Garissa
(285km)

Limuru
A104
Tugoni

Ruiru

Ol Donyo
Sabuk NP

Kyanzavi

Kiambu

A2

Nairobi River

River

Kangemi

C64

Nairobi

Eastleigh

C98

Athi

Tala

Karen

Jomo Kenyatta
International
Airport

Ngong

Nairobi NP

C58

Mitaboni

Kiserian

Marimboti

C99

Athi River

A109

Ngelani

A104

To Kitui
(88km)

Whistling
Thorns

Maasai
Ostrich
Resort

Machakos

C97

To Olorgasailie (25km);
Magadi (70km)

To Namanga (92km);
Tanzania (94km);
Amboseli National
Park (167km)

To
Mombasa
(402km)

C99

National Parks

The only national park here is Nairobi National Park (opposite), just south of the city.

Getting There & Around

The whole area covered by this chapter, with the exception of Lake Magadi, is well served by matatus and buses from central Nairobi. Taxis are also readily available; initial asking prices can be as high as KSh1500 when heading into town, but you should be able to bargain them down considerably, especially for return journeys.

NAIROBI'S SOUTHERN OUTSKIRTS

☎ 020

The suburbs to the south of Nairobi, while still technically within the city limits, bear little resemblance to the urban sprawl of the capital. Inhabited mainly by white settlers and expats, these leafy environs conceal extensive ranks of houses and villas designed to recall provincial England, all discreetly set in their own colonial grounds. The genteel atmosphere and a relative wealth of attractions make Karen, Langata and Ngong appealing destinations for a quick and easy escape from city life.

KAREN & LANGATA
Information

Langata Link (Map p125; ☎ 891314; www.langatalink .com; Langata South Rd; 🖳) Aimed mainly at residents, the travel desk here has plenty of information about hotels and restaurants in Langata and Karen as well as further afield.

Bomas of Kenya

The **Bomas of Kenya** (Map p126; ☎ 891801; Langata Rd; nonresident adult/child KSh600/300, resident KSh100/25; ☷ performances 2.30pm Mon-Fri, 3.30pm Sat & Sun) is a cultural centre at Langata, near the main gate to Nairobi National Park. The talented resident artistes perform traditional dances and songs taken from the country's 16 various tribal groups, including Arab-influenced Swahili taarab music, Kalenjin warrior dances, Embu drumming and Kikuyu circumcision ceremonies. It's touristy, of course, but it's still a spectacular afternoon out, and the centre itself has such a high profile that the first meeting of the National Constitutional Conference was held here in 2003, producing the so-called Bomas Draft of the new constitution.

Bus or matatu No 125 or 126 runs here from Nairobi train station (KSh30, 30 minutes). Get off at Magadi Rd, from where it's about a 1km walk, clearly signposted on the right-hand side of the road. Note that if you bring a video camera there's an extra KSh500 charge.

Nairobi National Park
This somewhat underrated **park** (Map p126; nonresident adult/child US$23/10, smartcard required) is the most accessible of all Kenya's wildlife parks, being located only a few kilometres from the city centre. It's possible to visit the park as part of a tour or even by public transport, as the park runs its own wildlife bus (Sunday only).

Founded in 1946, the park's incongruous suburban location makes it virtually unique in Africa and adds an intriguing twist to the usual safari experience, pitting the plentiful wildlife against a backdrop of looming skyscrapers, speeding matatus and jets coming into land at Kenyatta airport. As the animals seem utterly unperturbed by all the activity around them, you stand a good chance of seeing gazelles, warthogs, zebras, giraffes, ostriches, buffaloes, lions, cheetahs and leopards. The landscape is mixture of savanna and swampland and is home to the highest concentration of black rhinos in the world (over 50). The wetland areas sustain over 550 recorded species of bird, more than in the whole of the UK!

Nairobi National Park is not fenced and wildlife is still able (for the time being) to migrate along a narrow wildlife corridor to the Rift Valley. The concentrations of wildlife are higher in the dry season as animals migrate into the park where water is almost always available. Keeping the migration pathway open is one of the principal aims of the **Friends of Nairobi National Park** (Fonnap; ☎ 500622; Kenya Wildlife Service Headquarters, Langata Rd, PO Box 42076) campaign.

By the main gate you will find the site where former President Moi famously burned 10 tons of ivory in 1989 in protest at the

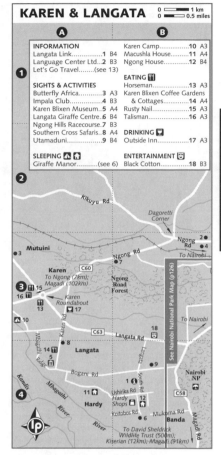

KAREN & LANGATA

0 —— 1 km
0 —— 0.5 miles

INFORMATION
Langata Link..............1 B4
Language Center Ltd..2 B3
Let's Go Travel........(see 13)

SIGHTS & ACTIVITIES
Butterfly Africa...........3 A3
Impala Club................4 B3
Karen Blixen Museum...5 A4
Langata Giraffe Centre.6 B4
Ngong Hills Racecourse.7 B3
Southern Cross Safaris..8 B4
Utamaduni................9 B4

SLEEPING
Giraffe Manor..........(see 6)

Karen Camp................10 A3
Macushla House.........11 A4
Ngong House.............12 B4

EATING
Horseman..................13 A3
Karen Blixen Coffee Gardens
    & Cottages.............14 A4
Rusty Nail..................15 A3
Talisman....................16 A3

DRINKING
Outside Inn................17 A3

ENTERTAINMENT
Black Cotton...............18 B3

international trade in ivory. Nearby is the **Nairobi Safari Walk** (nonresident adult/child US$8/5, resident KSh500/100; 8.30am-5.30pm), a sort of zoo-meets-nature boardwalk with lots of birds as well as other wildlife, including a pygmy hippo and a white rhino. The nearby **Animal Orphanage** charges the same rates, but it's basically a rather poor zoo and not a patch on the David Sheldrick Wildlife Trust (see p127).

The headquarters of the **Kenya Wildlife Service** (KWS; ☎ 600800; www.kws.org) are at the park entrance. There's an office right by the gate that sells and recharges smartcards, plus a small education centre.

Nairobi Park Services has a fine campsite (p129) on the edge of the park.

AROUND NAIROBI

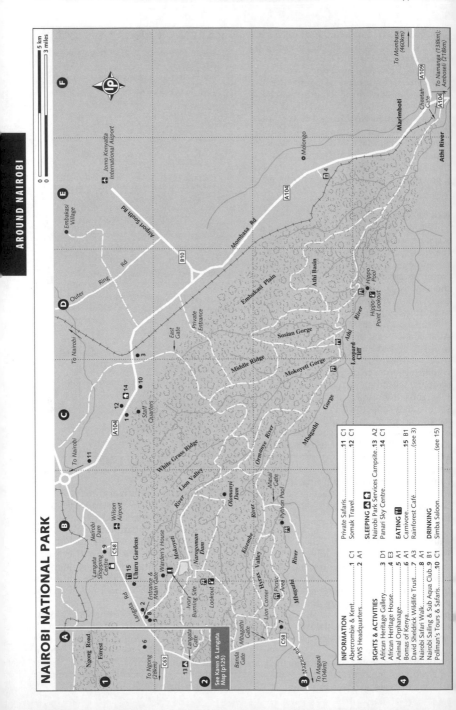

NAIROBI NATIONAL PARK

INFORMATION
Abercrombie & Kent..........................1 C1
KWS Headquarters...........................2 A1

SIGHTS & ACTIVITIES
African Heritage Gallery...................3 D1
African Heritage House....................4 E3
Animal Orphanage...........................5 A1
Bomas of Kenya..............................6 A1
David Sheldrick Wildlife Trust..........7 A3
Nairobi Safari Walk...........................8 A1
Nairobi Sailing & Sub Aqua Club....9 B1
Pollman's Tours & Safaris..............10 C1

Private Safaris................................11 C1
Somak Travel.................................12 C1

SLEEPING 🛏️
Nairobi Park Services Campsite...13 A2
Panani Sky Centre..........................14 C1

EATING 🍴
Carnivore......................................15 B1
Rainforest Café..........................(see 3)

DRINKING 🍷
Simba Saloon..............................(see 15)

GETTING THERE & AWAY

The cheapest way to see the park is with the 'Park Shuttle,' a big KWS bus that leaves the main gate at 3pm Sunday for a 2½-hour tour of the park. The cost is US$20/5 per adult/child and you'll need to book in person at the main gate by 2.30pm. Matatu Nos 125 and 126 pass the park entrance (KSh40, 45 minutes).

Alternatively, most safari companies (p59 and p107) offer various tours of the park. The half-day packages usually depart twice a day at 9.30am and 2pm and cost US$55 to US$75. Combined trips with the Bomas of Kenya and lunch at the Carnivore restaurant (p129) are also popular, costing US$75 to US$130.

The roads in the park are OK for 2WDs, but travelling in a 4WD is never a bad idea. The main entrance to the park is on Langata Rd, but there are also public gates on Magadi Rd. The Athi River Gate at the far end of the park is handy if you're planning to continue on to Mombasa, Amboseli or the Tanzanian border.

Butterfly Africa

This **butterfly sanctuary** (Map p125; ☎ 884972; www .african-butterfly.org; 256 Dagoretti Rd; adult/child nonresident KSh400/200, resident KSh200/100; ⏱ 9am-4.30pm) is housed in a large greenhouse of tropical plants. There are up to 1000 butterflies fluttering around at any one time, with some interesting display boards to help identify them, plus the usual information centre, shop and café. It's out past the Karen roundabout on Dagoretti Rd; you can get here from Moi Ave on the No 111 bus or matatu.

Karen Blixen Museum

This **museum** (Map p125; ☎ 882779; karenblixen@bidii .com; Karen Rd; adult/child nonresident KSh200/100, resident KSh50/20; ⏱ 9.30am-6pm) is the farmhouse where Karen Blixen, author of *Out of Africa*, lived between 1914 and 1931. She left after a series of personal tragedies, but the lovely colonial house has been preserved as a museum. It was presented to the Kenyan government at independence by the Danish government along with the adjacent agricultural college. It's set in lovely gardens and is an interesting place to wander around.

Just down the road you'll find the Karen Blixen Coffee Garden (p130) and also Karen Blixen Cottages (p129).

KAREN BLIXEN

The suburb of Karen takes its name from Karen Blixen, aka Isak Dinesen, a Danish coffee planter and lady aristocrat, who went on to become one of Europe's most famous writers on Africa. Although she lived a life of genteel luxury on the edge of the Ngong Hills, her personal life was full of heartbreak. After her first marriage broke down, she began a secret affair with the British playboy Denys Finch-Hatton, who was subsequently killed in a plane crash during one of his frequent flying visits to Tsavo National Park.

Blixen then returned to Denmark, where she began her famous memoir *Out of Africa*. The book is probably one of the definitive tales of European endeavour in Africa, but Blixen was passed over for the 1954 Nobel Prize for Literature in favour of Ernest Hemingway. She died from malnutrition at her family estate in Denmark in 1962.

Out of Africa was subsequently made into a movie starring Meryl Streep, Robert Redford and one of the retired trains from the Nairobi Railway museum!

AROUND NAIROBI

The museum is about 2km from Langata Rd. The easiest way to get here is via the Karen Metro Shuttle bus from City Hall Way (KSh20, 40 minutes). A taxi will cost about KSh900 one way. You can also come on an organised tour.

Utamaduni

A charitable organisation set in a large colonial house near the Langata Giraffe Sanctuary, **Utamaduni** (Map p125; ☎ 890464; Bogani East Rd; ⏱ 9.30am-6pm) is essentially a large crafts emporium, with 16 separate rooms selling all kinds of excellent artworks and souvenirs from around Africa. You can visit the workshops in the garden, and there's a playground and restaurant. It's a regular stop for the more upmarket tour companies, so prices start relatively high, but there's none of the hard sell you'd get in town. A portion of all proceeds goes to the Kenya Wildlife Foundation.

David Sheldrick Wildlife Trust

Occupying a plot within Nairobi National Park, this nonprofit conservation trust was established shortly after the death of David Sheldrick in 1977. David and his wife Daphne pioneered techniques of raising orphaned black rhinos and elephants and reintroducing them back into the wild, and the Trust has close links with Tsavo National Park for these and other projects. Rhinos and elephants are still reared on site and can be viewed between 11am and noon, at their daily mud bath. There's no charge for visiting, but a donation of around KSh300 per person would be appropriate. There's a gift shop and **information centre** (Map p126; ☎ 891996; www.sheldrickwildlifetrust.org) and usually someone around to answer questions.

From Moi Ave, take bus or matatu No 125 or 126 and ask to be dropped off at the KWS central workshop, on Magadi Rd (KSh40, 50 minutes). It's about 1km from the workshop gate to the Sheldrick centre; it's signposted and KWS staff can give you directions.

Langata Giraffe Centre

The **giraffe centre** (Map p125; ☎ 890952; www .giraffecentre.org; Koitobos Rd; nonresident adult/child KSh500/250, resident KSh100/20; ⊙ 9am-5.30pm), run by the African Fund for Endangered Wildlife (AFEW), is about 18km from central Nairobi, reached by Langata South Rd. Here you can observe, hand-feed or even kiss Rothschild's giraffes from a raised circular wooden structure, which is quite an experience, especially for children. There's a display of information about giraffes, and across the road is an interesting self-guided forest walk through the Gogo River bird sanctuary. Booklets are available from the ticket office.

To get here from central Nairobi, take matatu No 24 to the Hardy shops in Langata and walk from there, or take matatu No 126 to Magadi Rd and walk through from Mukoma Rd.

African Heritage House

Designed by Alan Donovan, an African heritage expert and gallery owner, this stunning **exhibition house** (Map p126; ☎ 0721-518389; www .africanheritagebook.com; off Mombasa Rd) overlooking Nairobi National Park can be visited by prior arrangement only. The mud architecture combines a range of traditional styles from across Africa, and the interior

is furnished exclusively with tribal artefacts and artworks. For those with the money, it's possible to negotiate overnight stays (single/double US$125/250), meals (US$25 to US$30) and steam train or even helicopter transfers.

For information, you can drop in at the **African Heritage Gallery** (Map p126; ☎ 890528; Libra House, Mombasa Rd), which sells the same kind of upmarket *objets d'art* you'll see in the house.

Sleeping

As you might expect, Karen and Langata have some rather exclusive accommodation options tucked away amid their leafy lanes, and if you want to splash out for something special you're certainly better off here than in Nairobi. Reservations are mandatory for most places here, as you're rarely permitted just to walk in off the street.

Giraffe Manor (Map p125; ☎ 891078; www.giraffe manor.com; Mukoma Rd; full board s/d US$385/595) Built in 1932 in the style of a typical English country manor, this elegant house is situated on 56 hectares, much of which is given over to the giraffe centre next door. The food is excellent (you dine as the personal guests of the owners) and you may have a Rothschild's giraffe peering through your bedroom window first thing in the morning. Literary buffs should ask for the Karen Blixen room, decked out with furniture the famous author gave the house's owners when she left Africa for the last time.

Ngong House (Map p125; ☎ 891856; ngonghouse@ form-net.com; Ndovo Rd; s/d US$450/600) Also a short walk from the giraffe centre, this is an altogether different sort of hotel. The four luxurious two-tier tree houses are set on 4m-high stilts, with fine views out across the Ngong Hills. Rates include transfers and all meals and drinks, and a number of free excursions are provided. It's a magical place, but you certainly pay for the experience.

Macushla House (Map p125; ☎ 891987; fax 891971; Nguruwe Rd; s/d US$95/170; ☒) A beautiful place, more like a private house, catering for just 10 guests. Located west of the Langata Giraffe Centre, it has beautiful gardens, an excellent restaurant and the rates, which include breakfast, are really very reasonable all things considered.

Karen Camp (Map p125; ☎ 883475; www.karencamp .com; Marula La; camping US$3, dm US$5, r US$20) Backpacker options are few and far between in affluent Karen, so it's good to see a new venture aiming to draw the budget crowd out into the suburbs. The quiet location and smart facilities are already attracting travellers; as well as the standard accommodation, there are also permanent safari-style tents (US$15) and a regular 'pig spit'. We hope they mean 'hog roast'…

Nairobi Park Services (Map p126; ☎ 890325; nps@swiftkenya.com; Magadi Rd; camping per person US$3, dm US$6, d/tr US$15/18) You'll find this place in a quiet residential area on the edge of Nairobi National Park. Established by two former overland drivers, it's set in a garden with a great wood-finished bar and restaurant with satellite TV, cold beers and cheap meals. The vehicle work bays make it a good pit stop for overland trucks and self-drivers. Security is tight and parking costs US$2 per vehicle per night. To get here from the centre, take a No 125 or 126 bus or matatu from near the train station; the entrance is opposite the Langata Gate.

Karen Blixen Cottages (Map p125; ☎ 882130; www.blixencoffeegarden.co.ke; 336 Karen Rd; per person US$170; 🏊) Near the Karen Blixen Museum, this is a lovely complex for up to 34 guests, set in a pretty formal garden with the coffee-garden restaurants conveniently to hand. Rates include breakfast.

Panari Sky Centre (Map p126; ☎ 553894; www.panarihotel.com; Mombasa Rd) Now that it's finally commencing operations, this extravagant modern glass'n'chrome building will be the nearest Nairobi has to an airport hotel, and a lot more besides – the complex includes space for a massive shopping centre, a casino, two cinemas and the first ever ice rink in East Africa!

Eating

Many of the expats and white Kenyans who live out in Karen and Langata never set foot in central Nairobi at all if they can help it, so there are a number of very good restaurants, cafés and bars catering for this exclusive but friendly resident community. Prices are high but so are standards, and high security means you're virtually guaranteed a break from prostitutes, hawkers and all the other day-to-day attentions of the city.

Carnivore (Map p126; ☎ 605933; www.carnivore.co.ke; off Langata Rd; set meals KSh1325) Owned by the Tamarind chain, this is hands-down

the most famous *nyama choma* restaurant in Kenya, beloved of tourists, expats and wealthier locals alike for the last 25 years. Just to reinforce the point, it has twice been voted among the 50 best restaurants in the world. At the entrance is a huge barbecue pit laden with real swords of beef, pork, lamb, chicken and farmed game meats; sadly new laws mean zebra, hartebeest, kudu and the like are now off the menu, which makes things distinctly less exotic, but you can still sample camel, ostrich and crocodile. As long as the paper flag on your table is flying, waiters will keep bringing the meat, which is carved right at the table. It's worth knowing that you can tip the flag over temporarily to give yourself a break to digest everything! If you do manage to save some space, dessert and coffee are included in the set price. Note that a hefty 26% tax and service charge is added to the bill.

At lunchtime, you can get here by matatu No 126 from the centre – the turn-off is signposted just past Wilson Airport, from where it's a 1km walk. At night, you're best off hiring a cab for the return trip. With waiting the fare should be about KSh1200, or KSh650 one way. The very popular Simba Saloon (p130) is next door.

Talisman (Map p125; ☎ 883213; talisman@swiftkenya.com; 320 Ngong Rd; mains KSh500-900; ⏰ from 9am Tue-Sun) This classy new café/bar/restaurant is incredibly fashionable with the Karen in-crowd right now, and rivals any of Kenya's top eateries for imaginative international food. The comfortable lounge-like rooms mix modern African and European styles, the courtyard provides some welcome air, and specials such as *tajine* (Moroccan stew) perk up the palate no end. The cakes and desserts also come highly recommended.

Rusty Nail (Map p125; ☎ 882461; rustynail@wananchi.com; Dagoretti Rd; mains KSh450-900) The combination Moroccan/Turkish styling of this pavilion restaurant belies the range of food on offer – lunch and dinner menus change every week, offering anything from falafel and steak to snapper and coronation chicken. Cream teas and traditional Sunday roasts cater for nostalgic English foodies.

Rainforest Café (Map p126; ☎ 555872; Libra House, Mombasa Rd; buffet KSh880) The fact that Rainforest is owned and operated by NAS Airport Services might ring alarm bells at first, but you won't find any pre-packed trays here.

In fact, locals reckon this is one of the few places in town you can get a decent sandwich, and the all-encompassing buffets are good value (there's no à la carte menu, though you can order individual dishes from the display).

Horseman (Map p125; ☎ 884560; Karen shopping centre, Langata Rd; mains KSh300-500, game meat KSh680-1000) Three restaurants in one, set in a leafy patio garden straight out of rural England, with a surprisingly authentic pub to match. One section specialises in game meat, one serves pizzas and the third offers Chinese, Indian and Kenyan food. It's currently fashionable for expats to sneer at the food, but this apparently has no effect on its popularity, and unlike its British counterparts the cosy bar is open till late. There's a takeaway section on the main road outside offering fast-food versions of various dishes (KSh150 to KSh300).

Karen Blixen Coffee Garden (Map p125; ☎ 882138; www.blixencoffeegarden.co.ke; Karen Rd; mains KSh300-900; ☼ 7am-10pm) Just down the road from the Karen Blixen Museum, this upmarket option offers diners and snackers five different areas to enjoy a varied menu, including the plush L'Amour dining room, the historic 1901 Swedo House and the main section, which is a smart, upmarket restaurant set in a veritable English country garden. The food is excellent, a stone pizza oven is under construction and there's a friendly and very popular pub.

Drinking & Entertainment

Simba Saloon (Map p126; ☎ 501706; off Langata Rd; admission KSh200-300; ☼ Wed-Sun) Next door to Carnivore, this huge, partly open-air bar and nightclub pulls in a huge crowd, particularly on Wednesday, Friday and Saturday. There are video screens, several bars, a bonfire and adventure playground in the garden and unashamedly Western music on the dance floor. It's usually rammed with wealthy Kenyans, expat teenagers, travellers and NGO workers, plus a fair sprinkling of prostitutes. You can also get a range of well-priced food at all hours, and there's a Dorman's coffee stall to keep those eyelids open til closing.

Black Cotton (Map p125; Langata Rd) A real insider tip; the sign opposite the junction with Langata South Rd is the only evidence this monthly club night even exists. If you're around on the first Friday of the month and feel like cutting loose, Black Cotton is without a doubt the biggest, messiest expat party in the whole Nairobi area.

Outside Inn (Map p125; ☎ 882110; Plains House, Karen Rd) Perfect for a bit of rowdy drinkage, this semi-open barn of a bar is a firm favourite with residents for its relaxed, boozy atmosphere, and stays friendly even when it's packed for televised football or rugby fixtures. Try the toffee vodka.

NGONG HILLS

The green and fertile Ngong Hills were where many white settlers set up farms in the early colonial days. It's still something of an expat enclave, and here and there in the hills are perfect reproductions of English farmhouses with country gardens full of flowering trees – only the acacias remind you that you aren't rambling around the Home Counties of England.

Close to Pt Lamwia, the summit of the range, is the grave of Denys George Finch-Hatton, the famous playboy and lover of Karen Blixen. A large obelisk east of the summit on the lower ridges marks his grave, inscribed with one of his favourite poems, *The Rime of the Ancient Mariner*. The hills still contain plenty of wildlife (antelopes and buffaloes are common) and there are legends about a lion and lioness standing guard at Finch-Hatton's graveside.

The hills provide some excellent walking, but robbery has been a risk in the past, so consult locals for the latest information. If you're worried take an organised tour or pick up an escort from the Ngong police station or KWS office.

Ngong Races

Several Sundays a month, hundreds of Nairobi residents flee the noise and bustle of the city for the much more genteel surroundings of the **Ngong Hills Racecourse** (Map p125; ☎ 573923; jck@karibunet.com; Ngong Rd), just east of Karen. In the past, races had to be cancelled because of rogue rhinos on the track, but the biggest danger these days is stray balls from the golf course in the middle! The public enclosure is free; entry to the grandstand is KSh100, or you can pay KSh250 for a platinum pass, which gives you access to the cushioned members' seating and the restaurant overlooking the course. A race card costs KSh30 and you can bet as little as KSh20 with some bookies (minimum KSh100 with the course Tote), so everyone should be able to afford a flutter. There are usually three races every month during the season, which runs from October to July. You can get here on the Metro Shuttle bus (KSh40, 30 minutes) and matatus No 24 or 111 (KSh20) from Haile Selassie Ave.

Sleeping

Whistling Thorns (☎ 072-721933; www.whistling thorns.com; Isinya/Kiserian Pipeline Rd, near Kiserian; camping KSh250, with tent KSh450, d cottage per person KSh2500-3500; ◙) An excellent place to stay in the Maasai foothills of the Ngong Hills. Horse riding is on offer at KSh1200 per hour, and there are numerous walking trails in the area. Cottage rates include breakfast. To get here, take bus or matatu No 111 or 126 from Moi Ave to Kiserian (KSh50, one hour) and change to a Isinya/Kajiado matatu. Ask to be dropped at Whistling Thorns, which is 200m from the roadside. Count on a two-hour trip door to door from central Nairobi.

SOUTH OF NAIROBI

OLORGASAILIE PREHISTORIC SITE

Several important archaeological finds were made at this site 40km north of Magadi by the Leakeys in the 1940s, including hand axes and stone tools thought to have been made by *Homo erectus* about half a million years ago. Fossils have also been discovered and some are still there, protected from the elements by shade roofs (sadly the 'elephant butchery' site, which contains the preserved remains of an elephant killed and eaten by primitive men, is not one of these). A guided tour (KSh200) is available and there are numerous notice boards and displays.

The **Olorgasailie campsite** (camping KSh200, bandas s/d KSh500/800) is not a bad place to stay for the night; you'll need to bring your own food, bedding and drinking water. It can get pretty windy out here, but you'll certainly feel like you're properly in the bush, and it's likely you'll have the place to yourself.

LAKE MAGADI

☎ 045

The most southerly of the Rift Valley lakes in Kenya, Lake Magadi is rarely visited by tourists because of its remoteness, although

it actually makes an easy day trip from Nairobi if you have your own vehicle. The most mineral-rich of the soda lakes, it is almost entirely covered by a thick encrustation of soda that supports many flamingos and other water birds and gives the landscape a weird lunar appearance, somewhere between Ice Station Zebra and Mission to Mars!

A causeway leads across the most visually dramatic part of this strange landscape to a viewpoint on the western shore. It's worth a drive if you have a 4WD, otherwise you can head to the hot springs further south. The springs aren't particularly dramatic, but you can take a dip in the deeper pools, and there are large numbers of fish that have adapted to the hot water. You may run into local tribespeople, particularly Maasai, who will offer to show you the way and 'demonstrate' everything for you for a fee.

The thick soda crust is formed when the mineral-rich water, pumped up from hot springs deep underground, evaporates rapidly in the 38°C temperature to leave a mineral layer. A soda-extraction factory 'harvests' this layer and extracts sodium chloride (common salt) and sodium carbonate (soda), which are then put straight onto trains to Mombasa.

The town of Magadi is purely a company town for factory staff and their families; it was originally built by the multinational ICI, and is now run by the unimaginatively named Magadi Soda Co. Facilities here are limited, but there are a couple of small bars, cafés, shops and a large swimming pool.

If you want to stay here, camping is your only option. There's no shortage of space – ask at the roadblock for the best spot. The best accommodation within a reasonable distance (around 60km to 70km) is Whistling Thorns (left), near Kiserian.

Getting There & Away

The C58 road from Nairobi is in good condition, although there is very little traffic on it after Kiserian. Akamba no longer runs bus services here and there seems to be only one matatu a day to Nairobi (KSh200), leaving in the morning and returning to Magadi in the evening.

ATHI RIVER

This industrial export zone has nothing of interest to visitors in itself, but does have one interesting accommodation option, convenient for breaking the journey down to Mombasa or Arusha.

Maasai Ostrich Resort (Map p124; ☎ 020-350014; www.mericagrouphotels.com; off Namanga Rd, near Kitengela; camping adult/child KSh400/250, s/d/ste US$35/40/55; ☒) Combining an ostrich farm and a hotel is a fairly unusual idea, but then again why not? Certainly the luxury farmhouse accommodation and gardens provide a nice setting, and there's a range of activities to keep you busy in an otherwise unpromising area, from tennis to ostrich rides (KSh100). The rates quoted on the website are double those given at reception, so make sure you check prices if you book in advance! To get here, take the road towards Namanga and turn left at the sign, about 10km past Kitengela town; southbound public transport can get you to the turn-off, but it's another 7km to the farm itself.

MACHAKOS
☎ 044

This small, busy town was the centre of the former Akamba territory (see p43 for more), and was chosen by the Imperial British East Africa Company as an upcountry trading post a decade or so before Nairobi was even established. The main motivation was the reputation of the Akamba people as mediators between the coastal Swahili and the inland Maasai and Kikuyu – the cooperation of the latter two tribes seemed essential for anyone wishing to reach the shores of Lake Victoria. When this attempt at diplomacy failed, the British simply built a railway right through the middle of the Maasai and Kikuyu territory. Topography meant that the railway had to bypass Machakos, so the provincial headquarters shifted to Nairobi in 1901.

The white settlers may have gone but Machakos is still bustling on a good day, its lively centre served by an active crew of *boda-bodas* and tuk-tuks. Being at a lower altitude than Nairobi, it avoids the cloud that hangs over the capital, providing a breath of country air. Once you've seen the decorative mosque and the large Catholic cathedral there are no attractions as such, but the unhurried pace and African atmosphere make it a good place to come and unwind.

As the town is hemmed in by attractive valleys, there are plenty of walking options, especially south of the centre, where numerous trails lead up to farms in the surrounding hills. Apparently there's a magnetic hill a few kilometres from town that has its own laws of gravity, but you'll need local help to find the spot and we can't vouch for what you'll find when you get there!

Information
There are branches of Barclays and Standard Chartered banks on the main street and a Kenya Commercial Bank on Syokimau Ave. The post office and Telkom centre are opposite each other off the main road, near the cathedral.

Cooperative Curio Shop (C97 Hwy) A handy place to buy crafts, employing local artisans.

eNet Cybercafé (Susu Centre; per min KSh1.50; ⏰ 24hr)

Telkom Centre (☎ 20161; Kinyali Hse, Mbolu Malu Rd) Opposite the post office.

Sleeping
Garden Hotel (☎ 20037; www.gardenhotelmachakos .com; Mwatu Wa Ngoma Rd; s/d KSh1940/3350, ste s/d KSh4340/5590) Past the council offices to the north of the centre, this is the best hotel in town. It is a huge and busy conference hotel with its own restaurant, bar and beer garden and a range of rooms including some big suites with garden-facing balconies. Rates include breakfast. If you ask nicely you may be allowed to camp in the quiet grounds.

Central Park Guest House (☎ 21866; Shanbad House, off Syokimau Ave; s/d KSh1400/1700) The name comes not from New York but from the tiny Mulu Mutisya Gardens opposite this decent central option. Rooms have TVs and prices include breakfast in the small terrace café.

Sunnyland Hotel (☎ 20402; s/d KSh500/700) One of the best places to stay, out along the road to Konza next to the Daima Bank. All rooms have mosquito nets and hot water, making them good value, and the modest hotel restaurant is popular with guests and locals alike.

Ikuuni Hotel (☎ 21166; r with shared/private bathroom KSh600/1000) The accommodation takes second place to the restaurant/bar/club trade here, but the small rooms circling the internal courtyard are tidy and serviceable enough, with some TVs for added entertainment. Breakfast costs an extra KSh260 per person.

KAFOCA Club (☎ 21933; d KSh800, s/d with shared bathroom KSh300/400) The Kenya Armed Forces

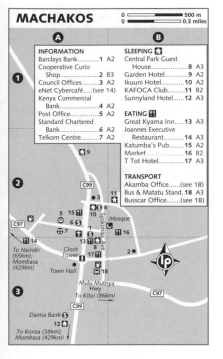

MACHAKOS

INFORMATION	**SLEEPING**
Barclays Bank...........**1** A2	Central Park Guest
Cooperative Curio	House..................**8** A3
Shop....................**2** B3	Garden Hotel............**9** A2
Council Offices.........**3** A2	Ikuuni Hotel...........**10** A2
eNet Cybercafé.....(see 14)	KAFOCA Club........**11** B2
Kenya Commercial	Sunnyland Hotel......**12** A3
Bank....................**4** A2	
Post Office...............**5** A2	**EATING**
Standard Chartered	Great Kyama Inn.....**13** A3
Bank....................**6** A2	Joannes Executive
Telkom Centre.........**7** A2	Restaurant............**14** A3
	Katumba's Pub........**15** A2
	Market................**16** B2
	T Tot Hotel............**17** A3
	TRANSPORT
	Akamba Office......(see 18)
	Bus & Matatu Stand.**18** A3
	Busscar Office.......(see 18)

0   500 m
0   0.3 miles

To Nairobi (65km); Mombasa (429km)

Clock Tower

Town Hall

Mosque

Syokimau Ave

Mulu Mutisya Hwy

To Kitui (86km)

Daima Bank

To Konza (38km); Mombasa (429km)

C97   C99

Old Comrades Association Club seems a bit short on military types these days, but it's a good secure compound with a bar, beer garden and cafeteria. Rooms are unfancy but reasonable, and could even be quite good if/when the ongoing renovations are complete.

Eating & Drinking

Apart from the various hotel restaurants, there are a handful of small canteens, cafés and pubs around town.

T Tot Hotel (Ngei Rd; snacks & meals KSh20-100) Right in the centre of town, this place is hard to beat. It's clean, well organised and seems to have an incredible number of waiters! The samosas, stews and side dishes are top class.

Joannes Executive Restaurant (Susu Centre, C97 Hwy; mains KSh165-200) 'Joanne' plies her trade from this little courtyard cafeteria in the Susu office complex, and may well count a number of budding executives among her regular clients, especially at lunchtime.

Great Kyama Inn (☎ 20086; C99 Hwy; mains KSh100-200) This popular pub-restaurant is

an institution in the Machakos scene, with regular DJs and live bands, including local stars and former Band of the Year the Everest Kings Band.

Katumba's Pub (C99 Hwy; nyama choma per kg KSh200-220) On the main road, features an upstairs bar and restaurant with a veranda overlooking the street. There's also a pool table.

For self-caterers, the town market is open from 6.30am to 6.30pm on Monday, Wednesday and Friday, and there are plenty of stores and supermarkets to fill the gaps.

Getting There & Away

The Machakos bus station is off Syokimau Ave, behind the Mobil petrol station. The best way to get here is to a take a matatu from the country bus station on Landhies Rd in Nairobi (KSh80, one hour). There are also very frequent buses from companies such as Busscar.

There's an Akamba office at the bus station where you can book transport to destinations throughout Kenya, mostly travelling via Nairobi. There's a direct service to Mombasa at 10am and 8.30pm (KSh500, six hours).

NORTH OF NAIROBI

KIAMBU
☎ 066

The main reason to come to Kiambu, 15km northeast of Nairobi, is to visit **Paradise Lost** (☎ 315273; paradiselostcaves@yahoo.com; Kiambu Rd; admission US$10, camping KSh400), an attractive picnic spot that's around 20km from Nairobi. Here are some 2.5-million-year-old caves set in 52 acres of forest and there's a waterfall and scenic dam where you can go fishing or swim (the owners insist there are no crocodiles!). Free boats are provided and horse and camel rides are also possible. If you want to camp, tents can be provided. You can get here by matatu No 100 from Racecourse Rd in Nairobi.

LIMURU
☎ 066

About 30km northwest of Nairobi, Limuru possibly has even more of a European feel than the Ngong Hills, except here there are vast coffee and tea plantations blanketing the rolling hills, cut by swathes of conifer and eucalypt forest. The village itself is un-remarkable, but there are some interesting detours in the surrounding hills.

The best places to see the **escarpments of the Rift Valley** are the roads that descend into the valley just past Limuru. The views are stunning; if you're on the new road, which runs direct to Naivasha, Mt Longonot is directly in front, while the plains of the Maasai sweep away to the south towards the Masai Mara National Reserve.

The old road, northwest of Limuru, was originally built by Italian POWs in WWII (there's a memorial chapel halfway down) and goes past the turn-offs for Mt Longonot, the Masai Mara and Hell's Gate. It's now been resurfaced and is in better condition than the 'new' road.

A number of **viewpoints** are signposted along these roads and are generally the safest places to stop. Predictably, there are souvenir stalls at all these places, selling Maasai blankets, sheepskin hats and other trinkets; there are few bargains to be found because of the number of tourists passing through.

Southern Kenya

At first glance the southern corner of Kenya may look like an expanse of blank space bisected by the Nairobi–Mombasa road, but really nothing could be further from the truth. This relatively small stretch between Kenya's two most important cities is largely taken up by the country's biggest national park and its most famous views, hugging the border with Tanzania where the slopes of Mt Kilimanjaro meet the Amboseli plains, and while it may not be as contoured as the highlands there's no shortage of remarkable things to see.

The parks are the best reason to visit southern Kenya, whether you opt for the classic but crowded vistas of Amboseli, explore the dark lava fields and caves of the Chyulu Hills, seek out leopards and rhinos in the diverse habitats of Tsavo West or skirt the green swathe of the Galana River in the vast emptiness of Tsavo East. With a range of tented camps, lodges, bandas and campsites awaiting the weary traveller, it's certainly no hardship finding somewhere to wake up in the wild, and off the main trails you'll rarely be bothered by others.

Outside the parks, community reserves and projects fight the good conservation fight at a grass-roots level, offering opportunities for visitors to give something back to the region. Walkers can also lose themselves in the surprising greenery of the hills around Voi.

However badly you want to get to Mombasa, stopping off to sample some of this area's attractions could transform your journey from a chore to a revelation. Bear it in mind as you negotiate yet another set of roadworks on the highway.

SOUTHERN KENYA

HIGHLIGHTS

- Shooting wildlife – with a camera of course – and Kilimanjaro in **Amboseli National Park** (p137)
- Doing your bit for local communities at the many private **wildlife sanctuaries** (p149)
- Exploring the varied delights of **Tsavo West National Park** (p143), including the epic Shetani Lava Flow and the hippo pools at Mzima Springs
- Braving the country's scariest lions and elephants in the wilds of **Tsavo East National Park** (p145)
- Getting away from the open plains in the moist greenery of the **Taita Hills** (p149)

★ Amboseli National Park

★ Tsavo East National Park

★ Tsavo West National Park
★ Taita Hills

★ Wildlife Sanctuaries

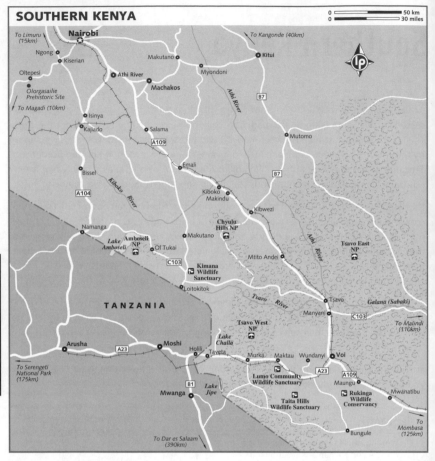

SOUTHERN KENYA

Climate

Falling between central Kenya and the coast, this area tends to be hot and dry, with average temperatures around 30ºC, but still experiences heavy rainfall from March to June and from October to November.

National Parks & Reserves

Between Nairobi and Voi you'll find Amboseli, Chyulu Hills, Tsavo West and Tsavo East National Parks and the Ngai-Ndethya National Reserve. There are also a number of private conservation areas around, including Kimana Wildlife Sanctuary, Lumo Community Wildlife Sanctuary, Taita Hills Wildlife Sanctuary and Rukinga Wildlife Conservancy.

Getting There & Around

The main towns here are easily accessible by public transport, especially those strung out along the Nairobi–Mombasa road. However, trying to visit the national parks independently can be a logistical nightmare without your own transport; most people take the easy option and visit on an organised safari from Nairobi or Mombasa.

BISSEL

☎ 045

On your way from Nairobi to Namanga, it's worth stopping in the little community of Bissel, a vibrant Maasai township with a busy market where you can buy all sorts of tribal objects and everyday goods. Facilities include a petrol station, a handful of *dukas* (shops), a freight container selling wholesale soft drinks and plenty of small bars and *hotelis* (eateries). You'll be a bit of a novelty, but people are very friendly, and if you feel like stretching your legs the hilly grasslands surrounding the town are good for a light walk.

There are matatus running from Bissel to Nairobi (KSh200, one hour) and Namanga (KSh100, one hour).

NAMANGA

☎ 045

A large township has grown up around the Tanzanian border at Namanga, and it's a good place to break the journey to Arusha or Amboseli, with some nice places to stay and a surprisingly relaxed atmosphere away from the frontier itself. The border crossing is open 24 hours and the two posts are almost next to each other, so you can walk across. Moneychangers do a brisk trade on the Kenyan side of the border if you need them, but don't believe anyone who says you can't take Kenyan shillings into Tanzania or vice versa!

Numerous Maasai women come here to sell bead jewellery and other Maasai crafts, and will materialise like magic around tourist vehicles, especially at the petrol stations. There's some great stuff on offer, but you'll have to haggle like a pro to get a bargain.

Namanga River Hotel (☎ 5132070; namangariver hotel@yahoo.com; camping KSh300, s/d KSh1550/2300) This is a poshish affair with nice cottages, a good restaurant and bar, and a shady camping area, often booked out by overland groups. Half and full board are available, and for an extra KSh500 per person you can live it up in the 'Exclusive' rooms, excellent stone-floored accommodation with individual boilers in the bathrooms. Animal lovers should ignore the rugs and concentrate on the happy resident dogs and rabbits.

Namanga Safari Lodge (☎ 0735-249527; camping KSh300, d/tw KSh600) Just next door. The grand name doesn't quite fit the cheap and cheerful accommodation here, though a garden full of stucco animals goes some way towards creating a safari atmosphere. Meals are available on request, and the staff are generally eager to please.

Aslam Hotel (meals KSh100-140) A loyal crowd swears by this very friendly little cafeteria

where you can get the works without worrying about the price – meat, rice, fried cabbage, beans, sauce and a drink should easily come in under KSh160. It's on the left just past the police barrier.

Getting There & Away

The large Kobil petrol station marks the turn-off to Amboseli and is a good place to ask around for transport – overland trucks and safari groups pass through quite regularly, so there's a vague chance of finding a lift into the park or across the border. Otherwise, locals may be willing to take you into Amboseli, though this won't be particularly cheap. Fill your tank here if you're driving into the park.

Buses between Nairobi and Arusha pass through daily (KSh250, two hours). Matatus also run here from the junction of River Rd and Ronald Ngala St in Nairobi (KSh250); Peugeots (shared taxis) on the same route charge KSh300.

Akamba has an office at the Kobil station, where you can book seats on the morning bus to Arusha. Several other companies also cover this route, as do matatus and Peugeots from the Tanzanian side of the border (KSh200 to KSh250, 1½ hours). For more details on getting to/from Tanzania see p373.

AMBOSELI NATIONAL PARK

Amboseli (☎ 045-622251; nonresident adult/child US$30/10, smartcard required) is the most popular park in Kenya after the Masai Mara, mainly because of the spectacular backdrop of Africa's highest peak, Mt Kilimanjaro, which broods over the southern boundary of the park. Cloud cover can render the mountain's massive bulk invisible for much of the day, but the two lodges in the centre of the park are perfectly placed for those classic early morning views.

As well as being a prominent part of the country's tourist portfolio, the park has been at the centre of some controversy since President Kibaki's 2005 decision to downgrade it from a national park to a national reserve, transferring its administration from the KWS to local authorities. Supporters claim that the move rightfully returns control of the land to the Maasai community, but many conservation bodies have argued that it's simply a political move aimed at securing the Maasai vote, and that degazetting parks

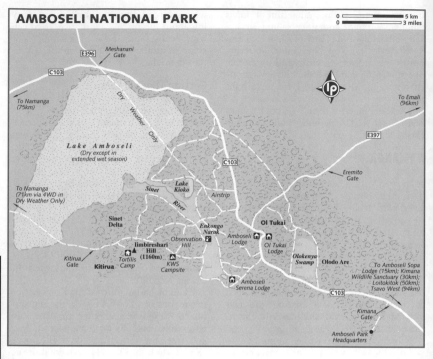

AMBOSELI NATIONAL PARK

is an illegal move that could undermine Kenya's whole wildlife preservation system. In the wake of his crushing defeat on the constitution referendum, Kibaki's next move on this issue will doubtless come under heavy scrutiny.

At 392 sq km, Amboseli is a small park and lacks the profusion of animal species found in the Masai Mara, but as the landscape provides limited cover for wildlife you have a good chance of seeing some of the larger predators. The vegetation here used to be much denser, but rising salinity, damage by elephants and irresponsible behaviour by safari vehicles has caused terrible erosion. Amboseli can turn into a real dustbowl in the dry season.

Buffaloes, lions, gazelles, cheetahs, wildebeests, hyenas, jackals, warthogs, zebras, Masai giraffes and baboons are all present, but the last few black rhinos were moved to Tsavo West in 1995 after a sustained period of poaching. In the permanent swamps of Enkongo Narok and Olokenya, large elephant herds can be seen grazing with Mt Kilimanjaro in the background, probably the

definitive Kenyan wildlife shot (and available on innumerable postcards if you can't snap it yourself!).

Erosion and grass die-off is having a dramatic effect at Amboseli; the rains seem to provide less relief every season, and it's only a matter of years before the lack of food makes the animals move on. It's important for vehicles to stick to the defined tracks to avoid making things any worse. Hopefully others will follow suit and the grasslands that drew all these animals here in the first place can be preserved.

Sleeping & Eating

All lodge prices given here are for full board. For nonguests, a buffet lunch at any of the big lodges will cost US$18 to US$25.

Tortilis Camp (Nairobi ☎ 020-604053; www.chelipea cock.com; s/d low season US$340/520, high season US$400/640) This wonderfully conceived site is one of the most exclusive ecolodges in Kenya, commanding a superb elevated spot with perfect Kilimanjaro vistas. The name comes from the *Acacia tortilis* trees surrounding the luxury permanent tents. Food is cooked without firewood, solar power heats the water and there's a huge organic vegetable garden. The rather daunting prices include transfers, wildlife drives, guided walks, cultural visits, laundry and most drinks, but not park fees or fancy wine. During the 'premium' season (Christmas/New Year and August to mid-September) rates rise by US$65 per person.

Ol Tukai Lodge (Nairobi ☎ 020-4445514; oltukai@ mitsuminet.com; s/d low season US$114/143, high season US$176/220; 🏊) This lodge belongs to the Block Hotels group. It's a splendid place, with soaring *makuti* (thatched palm-leaved) roofs and tranquil shaded gardens. The split-level bar has wonderful views and the overall atmosphere is of peace and luxury. Two of the attractive wooden cottages have wheelchair access.

Amboseli Serena Lodge (Nairobi ☎ 020-2710511; www.serenahotels.com; s/d low season US$80/160, high season US$210/260; 🏊) Posh Serena hotel in jungle-like gardens near the southern perimeter of the park. The low red adobe-style cottages make a change from the usual *makuti*, the very stylish lobby bar makes great use of hanging gourds and the nearby Enkongo Narok swamp ensures constant bird and animal activity.

Amboseli Lodge (☎ 045-622440; s/d/tr low season US$70/90/122, high season s/d US$117/180; 🏊) This lodge consists of a number of comfortable wooden cabins dotted around an expansive lawn and garden with sweeping Kili views. Quite a few tour groups drop in for lunch.

Amboseli Sopa Lodge (Nairobi ☎ 020-3750460; www .sopalodges.com; s/d low season US$78/120, high season US$162/260; 🏊) Just outside the park boundaries, the Sopa is a friendly chain lodge offering spacious thatched accommodation in round orange clay huts. If you're heading out of Amboseli the Tsavo convoy convenes nearby, and it's a good spot to refuel.

KWS campsite (camping per adult/child US$10/2) Just inside the southern boundary of the park, with toilets, an unreliable water supply (bring your own) and a bar selling warm beer and soft drinks. It's fenced off from the wildlife so you can walk around safely at night. *Don't* keep food in your tent, though, as baboons visit during the day looking for a feed.

Getting There & Away
AIR
Airkenya has daily flights between Wilson Airport in Nairobi and Amboseli (US$88,

one hour), departing from Nairobi at 7.30am. The return flight leaves Amboseli at 8.30am. Mombasa Air Safari flies here from Mombasa and Diani (US$220) on the coast.

You'll need to arrange with one of the lodges or a safari company for a vehicle to meet you at the airstrip.

CAR & 4WD
The usual approach to Amboseli is via Namanga. The road is sealed and in surprisingly good condition from Nairobi to Namanga; the 75km dirt road to the Meshanani Gate is pretty rough but passable (allow around four hours from Nairobi). In the dry season it's also possible to enter through Kitirua Gate, but this is a bumpy old road and it's hard to follow. The track branches right off the main Amboseli road after about 15km.

Some people also enter from the east via the Amboseli–Tsavo West road, although this track is in a bad way and shouldn't be considered in a conventional vehicle. During the 1990s there were bandit attacks in this area, so vehicles have to travel together, accompanied by armed guards. Convoys leave from the Tsavo turn-off, near the Sopa Lodge, at around 7am, 9am and 1pm. Allow 2½ hours to cover the 94km from Amboseli to the Chyulu Gate at Tsavo West.

Self-drivers will need a 4WD to make the most of the park. Petrol is available at the Serena and Sopa lodges.

KIMANA WILDLIFE SANCTUARY
About 30km east of Amboseli, near the road connecting Amboseli to Tsavo West, is this 40-hectare **wildlife sanctuary** (admission US$10, vehicle KSh100). It's owned and run by local Maasai, and wildlife is just as plentiful here as in Amboseli. It was set up with the help of Usaid and the KWS in 1996 and has been an encouraging template for similar initiatives, particularly now that the African Safari Club has set up several properties here.

The only access to this area is the poorly maintained dirt track leading west from Emali (on the Nairobi–Mombasa road) to Loitokitok on the Tanzanian border, or the even more diabolical road between Amboseli and Tsavo West.

There's officially no need to join the Tsavo convoy if you're coming here from Amboseli, but the area south of Kimana has a reputation for banditry.

Sleeping

There are three guarded **campsites** (KSh150) within the sanctuary itself, and numerous luxury camps are dotted around the bush just off the road towards Tsavo West.

Nyati Safari Camp (☎ 042-32506; www.nyaticamp .com; s/d low season US$85/150, high season US$100/180) This is a very stylish Italian-run operation with just 10 tents aligned to face Mt Kilimanjaro. It's 16km outside Tsavo West.

Campi ya Kanzi (Nairobi ☎ 020-605349; www.campi yakanzi.com; s/d from US$480/740) A luxury tented camp on a 400-sq-km Maasai-run conservation project. It's centred on a nostalgically decorated stone cottage and offers extremely comfortable tents with fine views. Rates include, well, almost everything except transfers, champagne, insurance and tips. A US$30 conservation fee applies.

Elsewhere in the sanctuary, Kimana Zebra Lodge, Leopard Lodge, Kilimanjaro Camp and Twiga Camp are all run by the private African Safari Club (p346).

LOITOKITOK
☎ 045

This rambling little border post, nestling in a permanent layer of powdery moon dust with Kilimanjaro peeking through the clouds above, is about halfway between Namanga and Tsavo East and has a certain offbeat charm, though it's not the most convenient base for the region's attractions.

Annoyingly, non-Kenyans aren't allowed to cross into Tanzania here, except as part of a tour with Kibo Slopes Safaris. This company operates out of **Kibo Slopes Cottages** (☎ 045-622091; kibocot@nbnet.co.ke; s/d/tr low season KSh1000/ 1800/2100, high season US$35/60/75, cottages low/high season KSh3300/US$60), a neat bungalow lodge on the main road into town. Rates here include breakfast and other meals are available.

It's possible to get here by matatu from Emali, just off the Nairobi–Mombasa road (KSh300), but it's a bumpy, dusty ride.

MAKINDU
☎ 045

This dusty junction town 45km northwest of Mtito Andei is worth a visit for the **Makindu Handicraft Cooperative Society**, a community project that employs 120 displaced Akamba people who produce excellent woodcarvings from renewable woods (see p57). The Sikh and Muslim faiths are vying for the attention of the townspeople here with two huge hospitals and religious centres. The ornate Sikh *gurdwara* (pilgrim's hostel) welcomes visitors and you can stay here overnight for a small fee; it's even recommended on www .sikhnet.com!

The best place to stay in this area is the **Hunter's Lodge** (☎ 622490; www.madahotels.com; camping KSh1000, s/d/tr KSh2500/3400/4200), situated 14km before Makindu (coming from Nairobi) on the Nairobi–Mombasa road. It's a relaxed hotel with comfortable rooms that overlook the river (fishing trips are available) and there are massive marabou storks in the acacia trees. The restaurant serves big buffet meals.

CHYULU HILLS NATIONAL PARK

Found northwest of Tsavo West National Park are the dramatic **Chyulu Hills** (adult/child US$15/5), a collection of ancient volcanic cinder cones. The hills were gazetted as a national park in 1983 and have splendid views of Mt Kilimanjaro and populations of elands, giraffes, zebras and wildebeests, plus a small number of elephants, lions and buffaloes.

Within the Chyulu Hills is Leviathan, the longest **lava tube** in the world, formed by hot lava flowing beneath a cooled crust. You'll need full caving equipment to explore it. Caving and trekking trips in the hills are possible with **Savage Wilderness Safaris Ltd** (Nairobi ☎ 020-2521590; www.whitewaterkenya.com; Sarit Centre, Westlands).

Although there's loads to see, the park lacks even basic infrastructure, though there has been a serious drive to open it up for tourism in the last few years. Forced evictions in 1997 have still not removed the problems of local communities damaging the ecosystem, and poaching is a big problem here, taking such a toll on the park's smaller animals that poachers have had to start targeting larger game. In May 2005 alone over 500 illegal snares were found.

The **park headquarters** (PO Box 458, Kibwezi) are 1.3km inside the northwest gate, not far from Kibwezi on the Nairobi–Mombasa road. For the time being, the best access is on the west side of the park, from the track between Amboseli and Tsavo West. The track into the hills from the headquarters is extremely tough going.

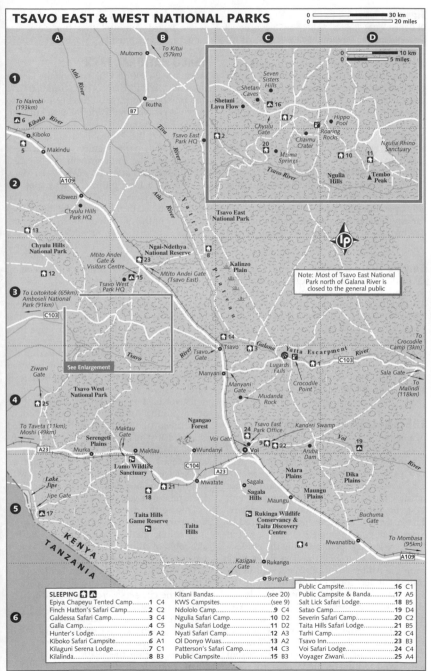

TSAVO EAST & WEST NATIONAL PARKS

0 _____ 30 km
0 _____ 20 miles

0 _____ 10 km
0 _____ 5 miles

SOUTHERN KENYA

Note: Most of Tsavo East National Park north of Galana River is closed to the general public

See Enlargement

KENYA

TANZANIA

SLEEPING
Epiya Chapeyu Tented Camp	1 C4
Finch Hatton's Safari Camp	2 C2
Galdessa Safari Camp	3 C4
Galla Camp	4 C5
Hunter's Lodge	5 A2
Kiboko Safari Campsite	6 A1
Kilaguni Serena Lodge	7 C1
Kilalinda	8 B3
Kitani Bandas	(see 20)
KWS Campsites	(see 9)
Ndololo Camp	9 C4
Ngulia Safari Camp	10 D2
Ngulia Safari Lodge	11 D2
Nyati Safari Camp	12 A3
Ol Donyo Wuas	13 A2
Patterson's Safari Camp	14 C3
Public Campsite	15 B3
Public Campsite	16 C1
Public Campsite & Banda	17 A5
Salt Lick Safari Lodge	18 B5
Satao Camp	19 D4
Severin Safari Camp	20 C2
Taita Hills Safari Lodge	21 B5
Tarhi Camp	22 C4
Tsavo Inn	23 B3
Voi Safari Lodge	24 C4
Voyager Ziwani	25 A4

Sleeping

Ol Donyo Wuas (Nairobi ☎ 020-600457; www.richard bonhamsafaris.com; s/d from US$400/640; 🐾) With no facilities inside the park, this is perhaps the most convenient option, an innovative ecolodge that recycles water and uses solar power. The cottages here are built from local materials and a US$20 conservation fee is charged to fund local community projects, including conservation, water projects and health services. Rates include wildlife drives and horse riding in the surrounding wildlife sanctuary.

Kiboko Safari Campsite (☎ 0721-312842; camping KSh500) A basic campsite outside the park at Kiboko, near Hunter's Lodge. It's supposedly open but staff seem utterly unprepared for anything as complicated as visitors.

Another nearby option is Nyati Safari Camp (p140).

Getting There & Away

Until the road from Kibwezi is brought up to standard, your best bet to get here is the 4WD track that branches off the Amboseli–Tsavo West road about 10km west of Chyulu Gate. Ol Donyo Wuas can be reached via this track, although most guests fly in on air charters from Nairobi.

The park headquarters is signposted just outside Kibwezi, about 41km northwest of Mtito Andei on the main Nairobi–Mombasa road.

SHETANI LAVA FLOW & CAVES

About 4km west of the Chyulu Gate of Tsavo West National Park on the road to Amboseli are the spectacular **Shetani lava flows**. This vast expanse of folded black lava spreads for 50 sq km across the savanna at the foot of the Chyulu Hills, looking strangely as if Vesuvius dropped its comfort blanket here. The last major eruption here is believed to have taken place around 200 years ago, but there are still few plants among the cinders. It's possible to follow the lava flows back from the Amboseli–Tsavo West road to the ruined cinder cone of Shetani (from the Swahili for 'devil'), at the foot of the Chyulu Hills. The views are spectacular, but you need to be wary of wildlife in this area.

Nearby are the **Shetani Caves**, which are also a result of volcanic activity. You'll need a torch (flashlight) if you want to explore, but watch your footing on the razor-sharp rocks and keep an eye out for the local fauna – we've heard rumours that the caves are sometimes inhabited by hyenas!

TSAVO NATIONAL PARK

At nearly 22,000 sq km, Tsavo is the largest national park in Kenya. For administrative and practical purposes, it has been split into Tsavo West National Park (9000 sq km) and Tsavo East National Park (11,747 sq km), divided by the Nairobi–Mombasa road (A109). Both parks feature some excellent scenery but the undergrowth is considerably higher than in Amboseli or Masai Mara, so it takes a little more effort to spot the wildlife, particularly the big predators. The compensation for this is that the landscapes are some of the most dramatic in Kenya, the animals are that little bit wilder (you really don't want to mess with a Tsavo elephant) and the parks receive comparatively few visitors compared to the hordes who descend on Amboseli and the Masai Mara.

The northern half of Tsavo West is the most developed, with a number of excellent lodges and several places you can get out of your vehicle and walk. The landscape here is made of volcanic hills and sweeping expanses of savanna. The southern part of the park, on the far side of the dirt road between Voi and Taveta on the Tanzanian border, is rarely visited.

Tsavo East is more remote, but there are a number of lodges, and, refreshingly, a number of independent budget tented camps. Most of the action here is concentrated along the Galana River; the north part of the park is bandit country and isn't really secure. The landscape here is drier, with rolling plains hugging the edge of the Yatta Escarpment, a vast prehistoric lava flow.

During the dry season, the landscape in both parks is dusty and parched, but it erupts into colour at the end of the wet season, although, of course, that means there's more greenery to hide the wildlife.

Both parks were once the lands of the Orma, Watta, Maasai and Kamba people, but all the villagers were displaced when the park was gazetted. Some of these communities have now established wildlife sanctuaries and group ranches on the outskirts of the park. Tsavo had terrible problems with poachers during the 1980s, when the elephant population dropped from 45,000 to just 5000 and rhinos were almost wiped out entirely.

Populations are slowly recovering and there are now about 9000 elephants in the two parks, but less than 100 rhinos, down from about 9000 in 1969. The last few years have once again seen a worrying upsurge in poaching.

Information

Entry is US$27/10 per adult/child per day, vehicles cost KSh200 and camping is US$10 per adult; as the two parks are administered separately you have to pay separate entrance fees for each. Both use the smartcard system – you'll need enough credit for your vehicle, entry fee and any camping charges for as long as you're staying. Smartcards can be bought and recharged at the Voi Gate to Tsavo East.

There's a small **visitor centre** (admission free; ✆ 8am-5pm) near the Mtito Andei Gate to Tsavo West, with interesting displays on conservation issues and some of the animals and birds in the park.

All the track junctions in Tsavo East and Tsavo West have numbered and signposted cairns, which in theory makes navigation fairly simple. In practice, some signposts are missing and the numbering system is often confusing, so a map is helpful. Survey of Kenya publishes a *Tsavo East National Park* map (KSh500) and a newer *Tsavo West National Park* map (KSh700). Both are available from the main entrance gates and the visitor centre at Tsavo West. Tourist Maps' *Tsavo National Parks* (KSh250) covers both parks.

Fuel is available at Kilaguni Serena and Ngulia Safari lodges in Tsavo West, and at Voi Safari Lodge in Tsavo East.

Tsavo West National Park

This fine national park covers a huge variety of landscapes, from swamps and natural springs to rocky peaks, extinct volcanic cones to rolling plains and sharp reddish outcrops dusted with greenery. It's easily the more attractive of the two parks, but wildlife can be hard to spot because of the dense scrub. Birds are very common and there are large populations of elephants, zebras, hippos and leopards. Lions are out there, but they tend to stay hidden.

The focus is **Mzima Springs**, which produces an incredible 93 million gallons of fresh water

a day. The springs are the source of the bulk of Mombasa's fresh water and you can walk down to a large pool that is a favourite haunt of hippos and crocodiles. There's an underwater viewing chamber, which unfortunately just gives a view of thousands of primeval-looking fish. Be a little careful here – both hippos and crocs are potentially dangerous.

Chaimu Crater, just southeast of Kilaguni Serena Lodge and the **Roaring Rocks** viewpoint, can be climbed in about 15 minutes. The views from either spot are stunning, with falcons, eagles and buzzards whirling over the plains. While there is little danger when walking these trails, be aware that the wildlife is still out there so keep your eyes open.

Another attraction is the **Ngulia Rhino Sanctuary**, at the base of Ngulia Hills, part of the Rhino Ark program. It's close to Ngulia Safari Lodge, but a long drive from anywhere else. The 70-sq-km area is surrounded by a 1m-high electric fence and provides a measure of security for the park's last 49 black rhinos. There are driving tracks and waterholes within the enclosed area and there's a good chance of seeing one of these elusive creatures. Large numbers of elephants, buffaloes and other species have also moved into the enclosure.

Some of the more unusual species to look out for in the park include the naked mole rat, which can sometimes be seen kicking sand from its burrows, and the enigmatically named white-bellied go-away bird, which is often seen perched in dead trees. Red-beaked hornbills and bateleur eagles are also common. Look out for dung beetles rolling huge balls of elephant dung along the tracks.

It's possible to go **rock-climbing** at Tembo Peak and the Ngulia Hills but you'll need to arrange this in advance with the **park warden** (✆ 043-622483). This area is also fantastic for birdlife and there's a very reliable hippo pool on the Mukui River, near the Ngulia Safari Lodge.

Lake Jipe *(ji-pay)*, at the southwest end of the park, is reached by a desperately dusty track from near Taveta. You can hire boats at the campsite to take you hippo and crocodile spotting on the lake (US$5). Huge herds of elephants come to the lake to drink and large flocks of migratory birds stop here from February to May.

SLEEPING
Budget & Midrange
Apart from camping in the park itself, the only vaguely budget options are the basic board and lodgings in the roadside town of Mtito Andei, near the Mtito Andei Gate, but most are pretty seedy and often serve as brothels for long-haul truck drivers.

Ngulia Safari Camp (Voi ☎ 043-30050; tsavoh@ africaonline.co.ke; r KSh3500-6000) Formerly Ngulia Bandas, new management and a complete renovation have turned this hillside camp into Tsavo's best luxury bargain. Unusually, it's the self-catering accommodation that really shines, offering thatched tent-fronted stone cottages on the edge of the escarpment overlooking a stream where leopards are known to hide out. There are rooms without kitchen and a bar-restaurant for the won't-cooks (dinner KSh750) and some more building is in progress. All in all, the setting and standards outdo plenty of the more ambitious lodges at a fraction of the price, with lots of wildlife (inside and out!).

Kitani Bandas (Mombasa ☎ 041-5485001; www .severin-kenya.com; bandas d/tr US$50/65) Run by the same people as the top-end luxury Severin Safari Camp. Accommodation here is obviously much simpler than the flash, tented kind but it's great value and there's a small shop providing supplies at not-too-inflated prices. Bandas No 2 and 3 hog the nicest spots, with possibly the cheapest Kili views in the park. It's about 2km past its sister site, near a waterhole.

Public campsites (per adult/child US$10/5) The public sites are at Komboyo, near the Mtito Andei Gate, and at Chyulu, just outside the Chyulu Gate.

Special campsites (per adult/child US$15/5) The locations of these bush sites change from time to time so check with the **warden** (☎ 045-622483). Write to: Assistant Director, Tsavo West National Park, PO Box 71, Mtito Andei.

Down on Lake Jipe are some simple **bandas** (KSh1000) and a **campsite** (KSh200).

Top End
All prices listed following are for full board accommodation.

Severin Safari Camp (Mombasa ☎ 041-5485001; www.severin-kenya.com; s/d low season US$80/160, high season US$156/240) At Kitani, this is a fantastic complex of thatched luxury tents with affable staff, Kilimanjaro views from the communal

lounge area and nightly hippo visitations. Room facilities are excellent (you even get a bidet), and the only reason it's not classed as a four or five-star establishment is the lack of a pool, which seems unduly harsh. The camp also has a self-catering annexe, Kitani Bandas (see left).

Kilaguni Serena Lodge (☎ 045-340000; www.serena hotels.com; s/d low season US$80/160, high season US$210/260, ste US$565; 🖳 🖳) Kilaguni has recently been renovated and is as attractive a place as ever, with a splendid bar and restaurant overlooking a busy illuminated waterhole – the vista stretches all the way from Mt Kilimanjaro to the Chyulu Hills, and guided walks in the nearby Seven Sisters Hills are possible. The extravagant suites are practically cottages in their own right, boasting chintzy living rooms, minibars, TVs and large balconies.

Finch Hatton's Safari Camp (Nairobi ☎ 020-553237; www.finchhattons.com; s/d/tr low season US$210/285/ 427, high season US$260/370/555; 🖳) An upmarket tented camp with bone china and gold shower taps, named after Denys Finch-Hatton, the playboy hunter and lover of Karen Blixen, who died at Tsavo. It's situated among springs and hippo pools in the west of the park, in grounds so sprawling you have to take an escort at night to keep you safe from the animals. In keeping with the colonial mood, guests are requested to dress for dinner. The camp has its own air-strip (flights from Nairobi cost US$300).

Voyager Ziwani (☎ 043-30506; www.heritage-east africa.com; s/d low season US$130/180, high season US$220/295; 🖳) By the Zimani Gate at the southwest end of the park is another luxury tented place, overlooking the Ziwa Dam. As well as wildlife walks, you can visit WWII battlefields and Grogan's Castle, a fortress-like hilltop residence built in the 19th century by swashbuckling British adventurer Ewart Grogan, who became famous for walking from Cape Town to Cairo to prove his love for a woman!

Ngulia Safari Lodge (☎ 043-30000; ngulialodge@ kenya-safari.co.ke; full board s/d low season US$80/160/228, s/d/tr high season US$150/200/280; 🖳) A curiously unattractive block in a spectacular location, constructed in the bad old days of emerging mass tourism when hotels made little effort to blend in. The surrounding Ngulia Hills attract loads of birds and the lodge puts out bait for leopards, which guarantees you a sighting, if not exactly a place in ecoawareness heaven. There's a waterhole right by the restaurant and sweeping views over the Ngulia Rhino Sanctuary on the other side.

GETTING THERE & AWAY

The main access to Tsavo West is through the Mtito Andei Gate on the Mombasa–Nairobi road in the north of the park, where you'll find the park headquarters and visitor centre. The main track cuts straight across to Kilaguni Serena Lodge and Chyulu Gate. Security is a problem here, so vehicles for Amboseli travel in armed convoys, leaving Kilaguni Serena Lodge at 8am and 10am.

Another 48km southeast along the main road is the Tsavo Gate. It is handy for the Ngulia Hills lodges and the rhino sanctuary. Few people use the Maktau Gate on the Voi–Taveta road in the south of the park.

The tracks here are only really suitable for 4WDs, and the roads in the south of the park are particularly challenging.

Tsavo East National Park

The landscape in Tsavo East is flatter and drier than in Tsavo West, despite the fact that one of Kenya's largest rivers flows through the middle of the park. The main track through the park follows the Galana River from the Tsavo Gate to the Sala Gate. The park headquarters, where you can charge and buy smartcards, is at Voi Gate.

Much of the wildlife spotting is concentrated on the Galana River, which cuts a green gash across the dusty orange plains of the park and supports plentiful crocs and hippos. There are several places along the flat-topped escarpments lining the river where you can get out of your vehicle, with due caution of course. Most scenic are **Lugards Falls**, a wonderful landscape of water-sculpted channels, and **Crocodile Point**, where you may see hippos and crocs. There are usually armed guards around, but you shouldn't get too close to the water. Kudus, waterbucks and dik-diks are common along the river banks. Also of interest is the **Mudanda Rock**, towering over a natural dam near the Manyani Gate, which attracts elephants in the dry season.

The bush is thinner than in Tsavo West, so wildlife is easier to spot, although it's not as plentiful. The rolling hills in the south of the park are home to large herds of elephants,

---

MAN-EATERS OF TSAVO

The lions of Tsavo National Park are unique in many ways. For a start, the males lack the typical mane that usually distinguishes this species, a fact often attributed to the dense thorn-filled vegetation of their habitat, which makes long hair a real hindrance to free movement. As an Earthwatch study recently revealed, they are also the only lions known to move in social groups with just one single male – most normal prides have one or two younger hangers-on as well as the alpha male.

Remarkably, scientists now believe there may be a single cause for all these idiosyncrasies: testosterone. When tested, Tsavo lions showed noticeably elevated levels of the male sex hormone, which could well be responsible for their hair loss and increased territorial behaviour.

This theory would also explain the famed aggression of the Tsavo lions, which has earned them a reputation as the fiercest predators in Africa. The best-known story concerns just two lions, who ate their way through 140 railway workers in a single year during the 19th century! The surviving workers soon decided that the lions had to be ghosts or devils. A series of ever more ingenious traps was devised by the chief engineer, Colonel JH Patterson, but each time the lions evaded them, striking unerringly at weak points in the camp defences.

Patterson was finally able to bag the first lion by hiding on a flimsy wooden scaffold baited with the corpse of a donkey. The second man-eater was dispatched a short time later, although it took six bullets to bring the massive beast down. Research has shown that the lions had badly damaged teeth, which may have driven them to abandon their normal prey and become man-eaters. Patterson wrote a best-selling book about the experience, *The Man-Eaters of Tsavo,* which was later rather freely filmed as *The Ghost and the Darkness.*

Although there's been nothing to compare to this since, quite a few local people have been attacked over the last decade, so be a little cautious when walking at Chaimu Crater, Mzima Springs or Lugards Falls. Hormonal or not, the Tsavo lions are not to be trifled with.

usually covered in red dust. The action is concentrated around the waterhole at Voi Safari Lodge, and the **Kanderi Swamp**, which is home to a profusion of wildlife and the public campsite. You can expect elephants to stroll through the campsite in the evenings. Further into the park, 30km east of Voi gate, is the **Aruba Dam** built across the Voi River, which also sees loads of wildlife. A lodge has been under construction here for some time.

The area north of the Galana River is dominated by the Yatta Escarpment, a vast prehistoric lava flow, but unfortunately much of this area is off limits because of the ongoing campaign against poachers. During the 1980s, the rhino population here was decimated and there are worrying signs that poaching is once again on the increase. Some observers suggest this resurgence is due to America's so-called 'war on terror', which has closed down other sources of funding for many warlord factions in Somalia.

Until their partial translocation to Tsavo East, the sole surviving population of hirola antelope was found near the Kenya–Somalia border in the south Tana River and Garissa districts. Intense poaching (for meat) and habitat destruction have reduced their numbers from an estimated 14,000 in 1976 to a pitiful 450 today, 100 of them being in Tsavo East. There are also around 48 black rhinos, moved here from Nairobi National Park, although how long they last in this hard-to-police sanctuary remains to be seen.

On the positive side, the recent translocation of 400 elephants from the Shimba Hills National Reserve (see p169) has replenished the populations depleted by poaching, and should herald the start of efforts to rehabilitate the wild northern sector of the park and open it up for tourist activity.

SLEEPING
Budget & Midrange
Camping is essentially your only option if you want to stay in the park but can't spring for a proper lodge. If you don't want to camp but are happy sleeping outside the park, head for Voi (opposite).

Ndololo Camp (☎ 043-30050; tsavoh@africaonline .co.ke; full board s/d/tr low season US$35/60/80, high season US$40/70/90) A great-value tented camp run by the owners of the Tsavo Park Hotel in Voi. The 22 comfortable tents have knot-

ted wooden furniture, mosquito nets and canvas toilet and shower cubicles. A buffet lunch here costs KSh850, and there's a good bar. The camp also offers nature walks with Maasai guides. Annoyingly, you have to pay the US$10 park camping fee on top of the room rates.

Tarhi Camp (Mombasa ☎ 041-5486378; kedev@afri caonline.co.ke; half board s/d US$60/100) Owned and run by a German company, this is another reasonably priced tented camp right on the edge of the Voi River, about 14km east of Voi Gate. It's a lovely peaceful spot. Rates include meals and wildlife walks with a Maasai guide. It's technically a special campsite, so an additional camping fee of US$15 is levied.

KWS campsites (☎ 043-30049; tenp@africaonline.co .ke; campsite per adult/child US$10/5) There's a single camping area with basic toilets near Kanderi Swamp. Elephants wander through here all the time. You can always pop in for a beer or a meal at Ndololo Camp if you book in advance. There are also a few special campsites (adult/child US$15/5), which move from year to year – inquire in advance.

Top End
Prices given here are all full board.

Voi Safari Lodge (Mombasa ☎ 041-471861; voilodge@ kenya-safari.co.ke; s/d low season US$80/110, high season US$105/150; 🏊) Just 4km from Voi Gate, this is a cracking lodge owned by Kenya Safari Lodges and Hotels. It's a long, low complex perched on the edge of an escarpment overlooking an incredible sweep of savanna, with a rock-cut swimming pool and a natural waterhole that attracts elephants, buffaloes and the occasional predator. Rather chubby rock hyraxes sun themselves on ledges. Facilities include several restaurants and bars.

Kilalinda (Nairobi ☎ 020-882598; www.private wilderness.com; s/d low season US$350/524, high season US$393/612; 🏊) Proof that even top-end resorts can take environmental issues seriously, this very fine ecolodge was built without felling a single tree. Accommodation is in luxury cottages; if you really want to splash out, opt for the Twiga Suite (single/double US$525/786), which has its own private Jacuzzi. All guests pay a US$20 conservation fee that goes into assisting local community projects and maintaining the surrounding wildlife conservancy.

Satao Camp (Mombasa ☎ 041-475074; www.satao camp.com; s/d low season US$80/120, high season US$160/200)

On the Voi River, this is a popular upmarket tented camp run by top-class operator Southern Cross Safaris. It's nicely laid out, with 20 canopied tents surrounding a waterhole, and you can take guided bush walks (US$30) and hire jeeps for wildlife drives (US$100 per day). A sister camp, Satao Rock Camp, in the Taita Hills reserve should now be open for business.

Galdessa Safari Camp (Nairobi ☎ 020-7123156; www.galdessa.com; s/d low season US$336/512, high season US$446/684; ☒ closed May) On the Galana River, 15km west of Lugards Falls, this place is close to the rhino sanctuary and is heavily involved in rhino conservation projects. It's very ecofriendly but frighteningly expensive, especially if you wish to book the eight tents for exclusive use. These rates include wildlife drives.

The following places are booked through **Let's Go Travel** (☎ 020-340331; www.lets-go-travel.net) in Nairobi.

Epiya Chapeyu Tented Camp (s/d US$72/144; ☒ closed Apr-Jul) A decent tented camp in a lovely glade by the Galana River, shaded by some vast palm trees. Wildlife walks and drives are available. The camp is run by an Italian company, and caters mainly for fellow Italians.

Patterson's Safari Camp (s/d low season US$65/90, high season US$85/120) Further west is another tented camp with the usual self-contained safari perma-tents. It's a relaxed place, only 9km from Tsavo Gate, and it sits on the spot where Patterson finally hunted down the man-eaters of Tsavo. So far no vengeful lion spirits (or relatives) have turned up to try and get their own back…

The African Safari Club (p346) owns the tented Crocodile Camp, close to the Sala Gate; there are several more private camps just outside the park here.

GETTING THERE & AWAY

Most tourist safaris enter Tsavo East via the Sala Gate, where a good dirt road runs east for 110km to Malindi (see p208 for details). If you're coming from Nairobi, the Voi Gate (near the town of same name) and the Manyani Gate (on the Nairobi–Mombasa road) are just as accessible.

Roads within the park are decidedly rough, and a 4WD with decent ground clearance is recommended. Expect longish journey times however you're travelling.

VOI
☎ 043

Small but always busy, Voi is a key service town at the intersection of the Nairobi–Mombasa road and the road to Moshi in Tanzania. The Voi Gate to Tsavo East National Park is just east of the town, and Voi has plenty of cheap places to stay, which is great for travellers who can't afford the safari lodges inside the park. There's a lively market area and a general air of activity, and there are some nice walks in the surrounding hills.

Information

Ashtec Computers (Fariji House) Email facilities.
Bafaigh supermarket Sells camera film.
Doctor (☎ 30139; Fariji House)
Kenya Commercial Bank (☎ 30138; Nairobi–Mombasa road)
Post office (☎ 30253)
Telkom office (Nairobi–Mombasa road)

Sleeping

Tsavo Park Hotel (☎ 30050; info@tsavoparkhotel.com; s/d/tr KSh1200/1800/2500) Don't worry about the missing top storey of this central hotel – it's on the way, and until it materialises it's business as usual on the existing floors. The large rooms aren't bad value, with some satellite TVs, but ongoing building means that the plumbing's a bit dodgy (no cold water!). Rates include breakfast, and there's a good-value restaurant. At busy times you may be charged official nonresident rates (single/double/triple US$40/70/90). The same people run the Ndololo Camp (opposite) in Tsavo East and Ngulia Safari Camp (p144) in Tsavo West, and transfers can be arranged.

Voi Town Lodge (☎ 30705; s/d KSh650/1000, s with shared bathroom KSh400) Resembling a converted meat warehouse, Voi Town Lodge is a friendly and economical alternative to the Tsavo Park Hotel with a handful of odd windowless rooms. Some of the walls don't reach the ceilings and it can get a bit echoey, but it's comfortable enough.

Vision Classic Hotel (☎ 30072; s/d KSh300/500) Upstairs next door to the Tsavo Park Hotel, this is an OK-value place offering clean, basic rooms. The customary dodgy shower-heater attachments provide hot water when the fancy takes them.

Johari's Guest House (☎ 30489; s/d with shared bathroom KSh250/350) A cheap courtyard place

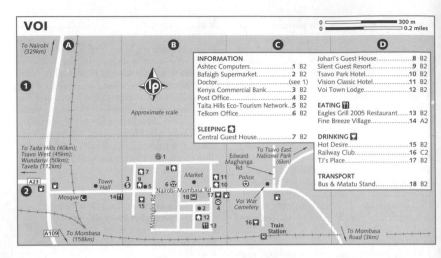

behind a drycleaners, one block north of the main road through Voi. Large signs remind guests that smoking inside a mosquito net may not be the best idea.

Silent Guest Resort (☎ 30112; silentresort@yahoo.com; s/d KSh2200/3200) Technically this has a good claim to be the best hotel in town in terms of facilities, with piped music as an unusual extra, but there's not much justification for the exorbitant price tag and rooms are smaller than at the Tsavo Park Hotel. Safari companies often put up their groups here, hence the inflated rates. Prices include breakfast at the agreeable terrace restaurant.

Central Guest House (s/d with shared bathroom KSh150/200) Ultrabudget, ultrabasic accommodation near the Kenya Commercial Bank.

Eating & Drinking
Most of the guesthouses have reasonable restaurants, particularly the Tsavo Park Hotel, and there are a number of small food *dukas* and cafés around the bus and matatu stand.

Eagles Grill 2005 Restaurant (Voi Town Lodge; mains under KSh100) Also known as Central Vision Café, Voi Town Lodge's house eatery does all the basics, but doesn't serve alcohol.

Fine Breeze Village (☎ 31041; Nairobi–Mombasa road; meals from KSh150) This big leafy beer garden is Voi's top spot for *nyama choma,* and it's not bad for a few Tuskers either.

As Voi is a transport hub, there's a low-key prostitution scene servicing the truck drivers, which can be a hassle in some bars.

For a lively night out, TJ's Place, near the market, is a popular 24-hour spit'n'sawdust bar with a pool table. Hot Desire, a massive *makuti*-thatched club with booming bass, is where the night-time action is, in every sense of the word. The Railway Club, by the station, also hosts occasional big events.

Getting There & Away
Frequent buses and matatus run to Mombasa (KSh250, three hours), and buses to Nairobi (KSh500 to KSh800, six hours) pass through town at around 10.30am and midnight. Busstar, Busscar, Mombasa Raha and Akamba all have offices around the bus stand. There are daily matatus to Wundanyi (KSh100, one hour) and Taveta (KSh250, two hours), on the Tanzanian border.

The **train station** (☎ 30098) is south of the town cemetery, at the eastern end of Voi. There are trains to Mombasa (1st/2nd class KSh1410/1130) at around 4am on Tuesday, Thursday and Saturday, and to Nairobi (1st/2nd class KSh2100/1475) at around 11pm on Tuesday, Thursday and Sunday.

At the time of writing, the twice-weekly train to Taveta had been suspended, with no indication when (or if) services will resume.

See p373 for information about travel to Tanzania.

AROUND VOI
☎ 043
In the bush on the edge of Tsavo West, there are a number of private and community-

owned nature reserves, all easily accessed from Voi if you have your own transport. The road between Voi and Taveta cuts through the lush hilly areas surrounding Voi and bisects the southern part of Tsavo West, providing some interesting detours for walkers and wildlife spotters.

Rukinga Wildlife Conservancy

This private reserve southeast of Voi covers 68,000 hectares of ranch land between Tsavo East and Tsavo West. **Savannah Camps & Lodges** (Nairobi ☎ 020-331191; www.savannahcamps .com) has an exclusive tourism concession in the area, which is rich in wildlife. The Taita Discovery Centre in the sanctuary offers volunteer workers environmental education and bush adventure courses (see p367), and can also take visitors by arrangement.

Accommodation is provided at **Galla Camp** (s/d US$132/190), a luxury tented camp within the sanctuary. It is very well run and you can get involved with loads of conservation activities. Rates include full board, transport within the ranch, conservancy fee and guide services. There are bandas for longer stays, though these are primarily for volunteers.

Sagala Hills

If you feel like getting away into rural Kenya but still want to be back in time for dinner, the long rounded ridges of the Sagala Hills provides a convenient but still untouristy diversion into real agricultural life, with all the unbeaten walking tracks your heart could desire. A daily matatu from Voi (KSh80, 45 minutes) struggles its way up the steep winding road to Sagala village, a tiny outpost with a handful of kiosks, where you'll doubtless be greeted with curiosity by the locals and should be able to persuade someone to guide you through the bush or around the *shambas* (farm plots) that cover the undulating hills.

Wundanyi

The provincial capital, Wundanyi, is an interesting place set high in the Taita Hills. It's a nice retreat if the heat of Tsavo gets too much and numerous trails criss-cross the cultivated terraced slopes around town leading to dramatic gorges, waterfalls, cliffs and jagged outcrops. It's easy to find someone to act as a guide, but stout walking boots and a head for heights are essential. Needless to say, the views are spectacular.

Other attractions in the hills include the butterflies of **Ngangao Forest**, a 6km matatu ride northwest to Werugha (KSh60); the huge granite **Wesu Rock** that overlooks Wundanyi; and the **Cave of Skulls** where the Taita people once put the skulls of their ancestors. The original African violets were discovered here, and the UNDP/GEP East Africa Cross Border Biodiversity Project office has more information about local fauna and flora.

The town market, hidden away behind the buildings on the hilltop, sells very cheap *loofas* (sponges made from a kind of squash).

SLEEPING & EATING

Taita Rocks (☎ 0735-651349; r KSh800-2000, per person with shared bathroom KSh400-500) Perched up a slope off the road on the way into town, with views towards Wesu Rock, Taita Rocks is the best of Wundanyi's limited accommodation offerings. The rooms are decent sizes, sleeping up to four people, the staff are frighteningly keen and there's a restaurant and bar, usually with constant TV and/or music.

Hotel Hills View (☎ 0735-273802; s/d with shared bathroom KSh300/450) Just next door, Hills View does indeed have hill views but the six horribly basic rooms are less easy on the eyes. Iffy power and dodgy plywood don't help, but it's cheap and has a terrace restaurant.

New Bistro 35 Cafeteria (mains from KSh80) This cheerfully painted eatery is on the left just past the post office as you head up the hill to the main market.

GETTING THERE & AWAY

Frequent matatu services run between Wundanyi and Voi (KSh120, one hour). Leave Wundanyi by around 8.30am if you want to connect with the morning buses to Nairobi from Voi. There are also direct matatus to Mombasa (KSh300, four to five hours) and an irregular morning service to Nairobi (KSh600, seven hours).

Taita Hills

South of the dirt road from Voi to Taveta, are the Taita Hills, a fertile area of verdant hills and scrub forest, a far cry from the semiarid landscape of Tsavo. Within the hills is the private **Taita Hills Game Reserve** (adult/child US$23/12), covering an area of 100 sq km. The landscape is dramatic and all the plains wildlife is here in abundance. If you stay at one of the lodges here, you can take a nocturnal wildlife drive, something that's not allowed in the national parks.

The two lodges at Taita Hills are owned by the Hilton Hotel chain; the **Salt Lick Safari Lodge** (☎ 30270; saltlick@africaonline.co.ke; s/d/tr high season US$185/226/286, low season US$132/161/195), further within the reserve itself, is the one normally used for visitors. It's a weird complex of mushroom-like houses on stilts surrounding a waterhole, but the facilities are luxurious.

The bougainvillea-covered Taita Hills Safari Lodge is a more conventional hotel building and is usually only used if the Salt Lick Safari Lodge is full. Children under five are not admitted to either property.

For information, excursions and homestays, contact the **Taita Hills Eco-Tourism Network** (☎ 043-30750; thenp@wananchi.com; Potter's House, Nairobi–Mombasa road, Voi).

Lumo Community Wildlife Sanctuary

This innovative new **reserve** (adult/child US$20/10) of 657 sq km was formed from three community-owned ranches in 1996, but only opened to the public in 2003. It's partly funded by the EU and involves local people at every stage of the project, from the park rangers to senior management. Birdlife is plentiful and all the 'Big Five' are here, as well as several war relics from WWI. For more information, call the **sanctuary offices** (☎ 30936) in the village of Maktau, near Maktau Gate. If you contact them in advance, the rangers may be able to arrange a wildlife drive or guide for around KSh500.

Accommodation within the sanctuary is provided by the private **Lion Rock Lodge** (☎ 0735-453089; full board d US$120), a *makuti* and canvas compound owned by the Tsavo Park Hotel in Voi.

The sanctuary lies on the Voi–Taveta road so you can get here by public bus or matatu.

TAVETA
☎ 043

This dusty little town sits on the Tanzanian border on the way to Moshi and Arusha. Unofficial car exporters drive the route constantly and there's a busy market here on Wednesday and Saturday, when people trek into town from remote villages on both sides of the border, but it's no more than a con-

venient stopping point for travellers. If you need money, the Kenya Commercial Bank has a bureau de change.

Tripple J Paradise (☎ 5352463; s KSh300-400, d KSh450-600) A pastel orange building conveniently situated on the main road. The Tripple J is hardly paradise (in fact half of it's still being built) but it's shiny-clean and better than you might expect, offering a range of rooms all with nets and fans. The bigger doubles have sofas and balconies overlooking the town.

There are also several basic board and lodgings around the main road and the market, charging around KSh100 to KSh200.

Getting There & Away

The Tanzania border is open 24 hours, but the border posts are 4km apart so you'll have to take a *boda-boda* (bicycle taxi; KSh40). On market days, trucks provide the same service for KSh20. From Holili on the Tanzanian side, there are matatus to Moshi (TSh1000), where you can change on to Arusha (TSh1500).

From Taveta, numerous matatus head to Voi (KSh300, 2½ hours) and Mombasa (KSh500, four hours) throughout the day. Six weekly buses also head on to Malindi.

There is currently no passenger train service to Voi, though it's possible the route may recommence in future.

LAKE CHALLA

This deep, spooky crater lake is about 10km north of Taveta, providing an atmospheric detour if you do decide to stop on the way in or out of Tanzania. There are grand views across the plains from the crater rim, near the defunct Lake Challa Safari Lodge, with the mysterious waters shimmering hundreds of metres below. The lake gained notoriety in early 2002 when a gap-year student was killed by crocodiles here. You can walk around the crater rim and down to the water but be very careful near the water's edge, and under no circumstances consider swimming – those crocs haven't gone anywhere, and they're unlikely to refuse another easy meal…

The road to Challa turns off the Voi–Taveta road on the outskirts of Taveta, by the second police post. On Taveta market days (Wednesday and Saturday) there are local buses to Challa village (KSh50), passing the turn-off to the crater rim.

The Coast

Be honest now, when you first thought of coming to Kenya, did you even remember it has a coast? Well if not, shame on you – it may seem at odds with the immediate mental image of safari Africa, but Kenya's Indian Ocean shoreline is one of its greatest assets, and the unique flavour of this steamy, sultry region never fails to weave a spell over its visitors. Even the most jaded beach bum can find something to delight in amid the palm-fringed white-sand stretches that run pretty much all the way from Tanzania to Somalia.

Don't be fooled into thinking it's all about the beaches, though. In fact, it's likely these will only play a minor part in your trip; for the adventurous independent traveller, the real draw of the coast is the Swahili culture that permeates every aspect of daily life here, from the bustling markets of Mombasa to the living history enshrined in Lamu's ever-captivating old town. Wandering narrow streets, exploring ancient ruins and setting sail in traditional dhows are the experiences that truly define a visit here, and you should take every opportunity to soak up the atmosphere that sets the region apart from the rest of Kenya.

For the active, the lure of coral reefs, remote islands and unlimited water sports is incentive to splash beneath the surface. Even away from the ocean, the region musters up enough surprises to enthral its fans and convert its critics, with something unexpected at every turn. Sunbathing be damned – with coastal rainforest, tribal shrines, coral mosques, thumbless monkeys, elephants and elephant shrews, Kenya's coast should barely leave you time to relax, and, if you don't make the most of all it has to offer, well, shame on you again.

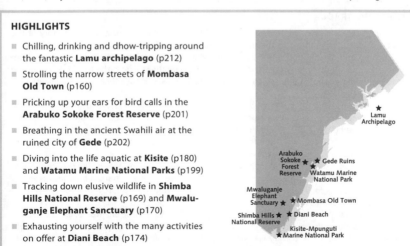

HIGHLIGHTS

- Chilling, drinking and dhow-tripping around the fantastic **Lamu archipelago** (p212)
- Strolling the narrow streets of **Mombasa Old Town** (p160)
- Pricking up your ears for bird calls in the **Arabuko Sokoke Forest Reserve** (p201)
- Breathing in the ancient Swahili air at the ruined city of **Gede** (p202)
- Diving into the life aquatic at **Kisite** (p180) and **Watamu Marine National Parks** (p199)
- Tracking down elusive wildlife in **Shimba Hills National Reserve** (p169) and **Mwalu-ganje Elephant Sanctuary** (p170)
- Exhausting yourself with the many activities on offer at **Diani Beach** (p174)

- POPULATION: 2.5 MILLION
- AREA: 83,600 SQ KM

THE COAST

History

The Swahili culture of the coast was a product of the trading routes initiated by Persian and Arab merchants. They used the monsoon winds to reach African shores and quickly established trading posts. By the 9th century, a series of fully fledged city-states had spread out along the coast from Somalia to Mozambique, and the first African slaves began to appear in Arabia (see below).

Intermarriage between Arabs and Africans gradually created the Swahili race, language and culture, and established some powerful dynasties. In the early 16th century the Portuguese swanned over the horizon, attracted by the wealth and determined to end the Arab trade monopoly. Unsurprisingly, the Swahilis did not take kindly to becoming slaves themselves and rebellions were very common throughout the 16th and 17th centuries.

It's fashionable to portray the Portuguese as the bad guys, but the sultans of Oman, who defeated them in 1698, were no more popular with the locals. Despite their shared faith, the Swahilis staged countless rebellions, even passing Mombasa into British hands from 1824 to 1826 to keep it from the sultans. Things only really quietened down after Sultan Seyyid Said moved his capital from Muscat to Zanzibar in 1832.

Said's huge coastal clove plantations created a massive need for labour, and the slave caravans of the 19th century marked the peak of the trade in human cargo. News of massacres and human rights abuses soon reached Europe, galvanising the British public to demand an end to slavery. Through a mixture of political savvy and implied force, the British government was eventually able to pressure Said's son Barghash to ban the slave trade, marking the beginning of the end for Arab rule on the coast.

Of course, this 'reform' didn't hurt British interests: as part of the treaty, the British East Africa Company took over administration of the Kenyan interior, taking the opportunity to start construction of the all-important East African Railway. A 16km-wide coastal strip was recognised as the territory of the sultan and was leased by the British from 1887. Upon independence in 1963, the last sultan of Zanzibar gifted the land to the new Kenyan government.

Today the coast province remains culturally and socially distinct from the rest of the country, still heavily influenced by its Swahili past. Indians are the largest minority, descendants of railway labourers and engineers brought here by the British, and the population as a whole is predominantly Muslim.

THE SLAVE TRADE

The Swahili coast may seem like the epitome of tropical paradise today, but the history of the region is inextricably linked to the Indian Ocean slave trade. Between the 7th and 19th centuries, Arab and Swahili traders removed somewhere in the region of four million slaves from East Africa, selling them for work in households and plantations across the Middle East and the Arab-controlled coastal states, which continued to use slave labour long after its abolition in Europe and the USA.

At first, slaves were often obtained through trade with the warlike inland tribes, but as the slave trade industry developed, vast slave caravans set off into the African interior, bringing back tons of plundered ivory and tens of thousands of captured men, women and children. Of these, fewer than one in five survived the forced march to the coast, most either dying of disease or being executed for showing weakness along the way.

Although some slaves married their owners and gained freedom, the experience for the majority was much harsher. Thousands of African boys were surgically transformed into eunuchs to provide servants for Arabic households, and an estimated 2.5 million young African women were sold as concubines for harems.

After the East African slave trade was finally brought to a close in the 1870s, the Swahili communities along the coast went into steady decline, although illicit trading continued right up until the 1960s, when slavery was finally outlawed in Oman. These days, this dark chapter of African history is seldom discussed by Kenyans except as a painful fragment of a past long left behind.

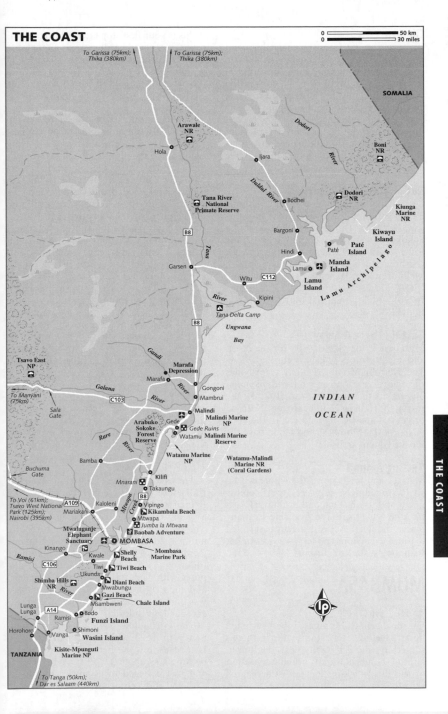

THE COAST

Climate

If you're coming from the cooler highland areas you'll notice the change in climate straight away – the coast maintains tropical temperatures of up to 32°C for most of the year, with humidity levels of around 75% and an average eight hours of sunshine per day between September and March. The coolest time of year is during the rainy season, from April to August. Conditions are also influenced by the monsoon winds, which reverse direction between March and April.

National Parks & Reserves

KWS parks in the region include Shimba Hills National Reserve (p169), Mwaluganje Elephant Sanctuary (p170), Arabuko Sokoke Forest Reserve (p201) and Tana River National Primate Reserve (p212). Offshore you'll find the Mombasa (p184), Malindi (p207), Watamu (p199) and Kisite (p180) Marine National Parks, and Kiunga (p228) and Mpunguti (p180) Marine National Reserves.

Getting There & Away

Mombasa is the gateway city for the coast, and most visitors will pass through here. The Nairobi–Mombasa highway provides the main access to the region, with plenty of bus services, though you can also take the overnight train to Mombasa from Nairobi, or get a domestic flight to one of the various airports (Mombasa and Lamu have the most frequent arrivals).

Getting Around

Matatus and buses cover the whole coastal strip, providing easy access to all points north and south. Boat and traditional Arabic dhow trips are also available in many places, though these are generally best suited to tours, excursions and ferry services rather than long-distance transport.

MOMBASA

☎ 041 / pop 653,000

For most people, Mombasa is best summed up as a feeling – love it or loathe it, there's something about the salty heat, the humid air, the sounds of the city and the sensation of the dust sticking to your suncreamed skin that evokes an instant sense of place.

If this is your first stop after visiting the interior, you could hardly ask for a more distinctive introduction to Kenya's coast, and it's the perfect place to help you fall into the naturally languid rhythm of Swahili life while still enjoying the modern comforts of home.

Mombasa is the largest city on the Kenyan coast and also the largest coastal port in East Africa. The city sprawls across a low-lying island at the mouth of a broad inlet, providing a natural anchorage for ships. Traders have been coming here since at least the 12th century and goods from Uganda, Rwanda, Burundi and eastern Congo (Zaïre) still pass through here on their way overseas.

The city's population is overwhelmingly African, many of whom are Swahilis, but there is a remarkable range of races and cultures here, from Africans to British expats, Omanis, Indians and Chinese.

Most package tourists stay in the beach resorts north or south of town, but leaving Mombasa out of your itinerary completely would be a shame. The most interesting part is the characterful Old Town, with its narrow, winding alleyways, historic Swahili houses and the remains of the mighty Fort Jesus.

History

Mombasa has always been at the centre of the coast's key events, a crucial stronghold for local and invading powers ever since the Arab-Swahili Mazrui clan emerged as one of the most powerful families in 9th-century East Africa.

The first Portuguese forays into Arab territory took place here in 1505, when Dom Francisco de Almeida arrived with a huge armada and levelled the city in just 1½ days. The plundered remains were soon rebuilt, but in 1528 Lisbon struck again as Nuña da Cunha captured the city, first by diplomacy (offering to act as an ally in Mombasa's disputes with Malindi, Pemba and Zanzibar) and then by force. Once again Mombasa was burned to the ground while the invaders sailed on to India.

The Portuguese made a bid for permanency in 1593 with the construction of Fort Jesus, but the hefty structure quickly became a symbolic target for rebel leaders and was besieged incessantly. During the 17th and 18th centuries, Mombasa changed

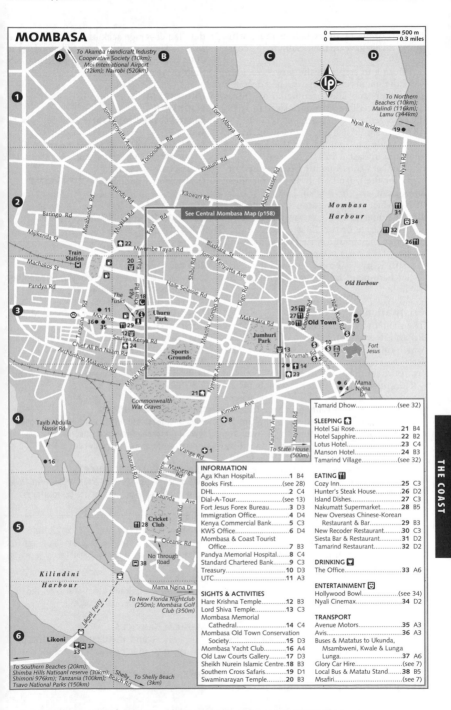

MOMBASA

0 — 500 m
0 — 0.3 miles

To Akamba Handicraft Industry
Cooperative Society (10km);
Moi International Airport
(12km); Nairobi (520km)

To Northern
Beaches (10km);
Malindi (116km);
Lamu (344km)

Mombasa
Harbour

See Central Mombasa Map (p158)

Old Harbour

Train
Station

The
Tusks

Uhuru
Park

Old Town

Fort
Jesus

Jumhuri
Park

Sports
Grounds

Commonwealth
War Graves

Mama
Ngina
Dr

Tayib Abdulla
Nassir Rd

To State House
(500m)

THE COAST

Cricket
Club

No Through
Road

Kilindini
Harbour

Mama Ngina Dr
To New Florida Nightclub
(250m); Mombasa Golf
Club (350m)

Likoni

To Southern Beaches (20km);
Shimba Hills Natioanl reserve (30km);
Shimoni 976km); Tanzania (100km);
Tsavo National Parks (150km)

Shelly   To Shelly Beach
Beach Rd (3km)

Tamarid Dhow.....................(see 32)

SLEEPING
Hotel Sai Rose......................**21** B4
Hotel Sapphire.....................**22** B2
Lotus Hotel..........................**23** C4
Manson Hotel.......................**24** B3
Tamarind Village................(see 32)

INFORMATION
Aga Khan Hospital................**1** B4
Books First..........................(see 28)
DHL....................................**2** C4
Dial-A-Tour.........................(see 13)
Fort Jesus Forex Bureau.........**3** D3
Immigration Office................**4** D4
Kenya Commercial Bank.........**5** C3
KWS Office..........................**6** D4
Mombasa & Coast Tourist
  Office................................**7** B3
Pandya Memorial Hospital......**8** C4
Standard Chartered Bank........**9** C3
Treasury.............................**10** D3
UTC...................................**11** A3

SIGHTS & ACTIVITIES
Hare Krishna Temple............**12** B3
Lord Shiva Temple................**13** C3
Mombasa Memorial
  Cathedral.........................**14** C4
Mombasa Old Town Conservation
  Society.............................**15** D3
Mombasa Yacht Club............**16** A4
Old Law Courts Gallery.........**17** D3
Sheikh Nurein Islamic Centre.**18** B3
Southern Cross Safaris..........**19** D1
Swaminarayan Temple..........**20** B3

EATING
Cozy Inn.............................**25** C3
Hunter's Steak House............**26** D2
Island Dishes.......................**27** C3
Nakumatt Supermarket..........**28** B5
New Overseas Chinese-Korean
  Restaurant & Bar.................**29** B3
New Recoder Restaurant........**30** C3
Siesta Bar & Restaurant.........**31** D2
Tamarind Restaurant.............**32** D2

DRINKING
The Office............................**33** A6

ENTERTAINMENT
Hollywood Bowl...................(see 34)
Nyali Cinemax.....................**34** D2

TRANSPORT
Avenue Motors.....................**35** A3
Avis...................................**36** A3
Buses & Matatus to Ukunda,
  Msambweni, Kwale & Lunga
  Lunga..............................**37** A6
Glory Car Hire......................(see 7)
Local Bus & Matatu Stand......**38** B5
Msafiri...............................(see 7)

hands dozens of times before the Portuguese finally gave up their claim to the coast in 1729.

Waiting to step into the power vacuum were the sultans of Oman, who had defeated the Europeans and occupied Fort Jesus after an incredible 33-month siege in 1698. The city remained in their control until the 1870s, when British intervention ended the slave trade and gained for the Empire a foothold in East Africa.

Mombasa subsequently became the railhead for the Uganda railway and the most important city in British East Africa. In 1920, when Kenya became a fully fledged British colony, Mombasa was made capital of the separate British Coast Protectorate.

Today the cut and thrust of politics and power play largely passes Mombasa by, but it's still Kenya's second city and a crucial social barometer for the coast province as a whole.

Orientation

The main thoroughfare in Mombasa is Digo Rd and its southern extension Nyerere Ave, which run north–south through the city. The ferry to Likoni and the south coast leaves from the southern end of Nyerere Ave.

Running west from the junction between Nyerere Ave and Digo Rd is Moi Ave, where you'll find the tourist office and the famous sculpted 'tusks', two huge pairs of aluminium elephant tusks forming an M over the road, which were erected to mark a visit by Britain's Princess Margaret in 1956. Heading east from the same junction, Nkrumah Rd provides the easiest access to the Old Town and Fort Jesus.

North of the centre, Digo Rd becomes Abdel Nasser Rd, where you'll find many of the bus stands for Nairobi and destinations north along the coast. There's another big group of bus offices west of here at the intersection of Jomo Kenyatta Ave and Mwembe Tayari Rd. The train station is at the intersection of Mwembe Tayari and Haile Selassie Rds.

MAPS

Choices are limited if you're looking for a decent map, but your best option is the 1:10,000 *Streets of Mombasa Island* map (KSh350), which was updated in 2004 and is available from the tourist office. For more

detailed coverage seek out the *Mombasa A to Z* (KSh300), which was fully revised in 2003 – it may be easier to find in Nairobi than in Mombasa itself.

Information

BOOKSHOPS

Bahati Book Centre (Map p158; ☎ 225010; Moi Ave)

Books First (Map p155; ☎ 313482; Nyerere Ave; 🖳) Well-stocked outlet with separate café, in the Nakumatt supermarket.

City Bookshop (Map p158; ☎ 313149; Nkrumah Rd)

EMERGENCY

AAR Health Services (☎ 312409; 🕙 24hr)

Police (☎ 222121, 999)

INTERNET ACCESS

Blue Room (Map p158; ☎ 224021; www.blueroom online.com; Haile Selassie Rd; per min KSh2; 🕙 9am-10pm)

Cyber Dome (Map p158; Moi Ave; per min KSh1; 🕙 8am-9pm Mon-Sat, 9am-6pm Sun)

FOTech (Map p158; ☎ 225123; Ambalal House, Nkrumah Rd; per min KSh1)

Info Café (Map p158; ☎ 227621; infomombasa@ yahoo .com; Ambalal House, Nkrumah Rd; per min KSh1)

Wavetek (Map p158; ☎ 0735-295007; TSS Towers, Nkrumah Rd; per min KSh1) Also offers international calls from KSh15 per minute.

INTERNET RESOURCES

www.mombasainfo.com Descriptive tourist information.

www.mombasaonline.com Includes some useful features, such as maps and weekly tide times.

KENYA WILDLIFE SERVICE

KWS office (Map p155; ☎ 312744/5; Nguua Court, Mama Ngina Dr; 🕙 6am-6pm) Sells and charges smartcards.

LIBRARIES

Mombasa Area Library (Map p158; ☎ 226380; Msanifu Kombo Rd; 🕙 8am-6.30pm Mon-Thu, to 4pm Fri, to 5pm Sat) Has a fairly extensive English-language section.

MEDIA

Coastweek (www.coastweek.com) Weekly news and features from the whole coast province.

MEDICAL SERVICES

All services and medication must be paid for upfront, so have travel insurance details handy.

Aga Khan Hospital (Map p155; ☎ 312953; akhm@mba .akhmkenya.org; Vanga Rd)

Pandya Memorial Hospital (Map p155; ☎ 229252; Kimathi Ave)

MONEY

Outside business hours you can change money at most major hotels, although rates in the hotels are usually poor. Exchange rates are generally slightly lower here than in Nairobi, especially if you're changing travellers cheques.

Barclays Bank Nkrumah Rd (Map p158; ☎ 311660); Digo Rd (Map p158; ☎ 224573)

Fort Jesus Forex Bureau (Map p155; ☎ 316717; Ndia Kuu Rd)

Kenya Commercial Bank Nkrumah Rd (Map p155; ☎ 312523); Moi Ave (Map p158; ☎ 220978)

Postbank (Map p158; ☎ 3434077; Moi Ave) Western Union money transfers.

Pwani Forex Bureau (Map p158; ☎ 221727; Digo Rd)

Standard Chartered Bank (Map p155; ☎ 224614; Treasury Square, Nkrumah Rd)

PHOTOGRAPHY EQUIPMENT

Despite Mombasa being a major tourist centre, slide film and fast-print film (above ASA 100) can be hard to find – bring supplies from Nairobi.

Photocine (Map p158; ☎ 315438; Moi Ave) Usually has slide film in stock.

POST

DHL (Map p155; ☎ 223933; Nkrumah Rd)

FedEx (Map p158; ☎ 228631; Moi Ave)

Post office (Map p158; ☎ 227705; Digo Rd)

TELEPHONE

Post Global Services (Map p158; ☎ 230581; inglobal@africaonline.co.ke; Maungano Rd; 7.30am-8pm;) International calls are around KSh85 per minute. Owner Rashmi is re-establishing his travel agency, and can act as a capable and friendly 'fixer' for travellers.

Telkom Kenya (Map p158; ☎ 312811) Locations on Nkrumah Rd and Moi Ave.

TOURIST INFORMATION

Mombasa & Coast Tourist Office (Map p155; ☎ 225428; mcta@ikenya.com; Moi Ave; 8am- 4.30pm) Provides information and can organise accommodation, tours, guides and transport.

TRAVEL AGENCIES

Dial-A-Tour (Map p155; ☎ 221411; dialatour@ikenya.com; Oriental Bldg, Nkrumah Rd)

Express Travel (Map p158; ☎ 315405; PO Box 90631,

Nkrumah Rd) Amex agent – mail can be held here for card-holders.

Fourways Travel (Map p158; ☎ 223344; Moi Ave)

VISA EXTENSIONS

Immigration office (Map p155; ☎ 311745; Uhuru ni Kari Bldg, Mama Ngina Dr)

Dangers & Annoyances

Mombasa is relatively safe compared to Nairobi, but the streets still clear pretty rapidly after dark so it's a good idea to take taxis rather than walking around alone at night. You need to be more careful on the beaches north (p181) and south (p169) of town. The Likoni ferry is a bag-snatching hotspot.

Visitors should also be aware of anti-Western sentiment among some Kenyan Muslims: hostile graffiti and Osama bin Laden T-shirts abound, and demonstrations against Israel and America are increasingly common. Keep a low profile during any escalation of violence in the Middle East or terrorist activity in the West.

Malaria is a big risk on the coast so remember to take your antimalarial drugs (see p389).

Sights & Activities

FORT JESUS

Mombasa's biggest tourist attraction dominates the harbour entrance at the end of Nkrumah Rd. The metre-thick coral walls make it an imposing edifice, despite being partially ruined. The fort was built by the Portuguese in 1593 to enforce their rule over the coastal Swahilis, but they rarely managed to hold onto it for long. It changed hands at least nine times in bloody sieges between 1631 and 1875, finally falling under British control.

The fort was the final project completed by Italian architect Joao Batista Cairato in his long career as Chief Architect for Portugal's eastern colonies. There are some ingenious elements in its design, especially the angular configuration of the west walls, which makes it impossible to attack one wall without being a sitting duck for soldiers on the opposite battlements.

These days the fort houses a **museum** (Map p155; ☎ 222425; nmkfortj@swiftmombasa.com; nonresident adult/child KSh200/100; 8am-6pm), built over the former barracks. The exhibits are mostly ceramics, reflecting the variety of cultures

THE COAST

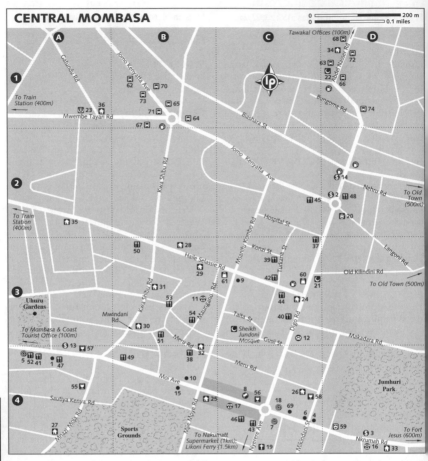

CENTRAL MOMBASA

that traded along the coast, but include other interesting odds and ends donated from private collections or dug up from sites along the coast. Also displayed are finds from the Portuguese frigate *Santo António de Tanná*, which sank near the fort during the siege in 1698, and the far end of the hall is devoted to the fascinating culture and traditions of the nine coastal Mijikenda tribes, including a map of sacred forests (see the boxed text on p160).

Exploring the battlements and ruined buildings within the compound is just as interesting, though the fort feels much smaller than it looks from the outside. The **Omani house** in the San Felipe bastion, in the northwestern corner of the fort, was built

in the late 18th century and houses a small exhibition of Omani jewellery and artefacts. Nearby is a ruined church, a huge well and cistern, and an excavated grave complete with skeleton. The **eastern wall** of the fort includes an Omani audience hall and the **Passage of the Arches**, a passage cut through the coral to give access to the sea.

Most coach tours arrive here late in the morning, so if you come early you may have the place to yourself. Many official and unofficial guides will offer their services, often for free, though a tip is always expected. Alternatively, you can buy the 1981 *Fort Jesus* guide booklet (KSh60) from the ticket desk and go it alone. At 7pm there's a daily 'sound and light show' illustrating the

INFORMATION
Ambalal House.................................(see 7)
Bahati Book Centre.............................**1** A4
Barclays Bank....................................**2** D2
Barclays Bank....................................**3** D4
Blue Room Cyber Café...................(see 42)
City Bookshop.....................................**4** C4
Cyber Dome..**5** A4
Express Travel (Amex)........................**6** C4
FedEx...(see 15)
FOTech...(see 7)
Fourways Travel................................(see 15)
Info Café..**7** C4
Italian Consulate.................................**8** C4
Kenya Commercial Bank...................(see 56)
Mombasa Area Library.........................**9** C3
Photocine..**10** B4
Post Global Services..........................**11** B3
Post Office..**12** C3
Postbank..**13** A3
Pwani Forex Bureau...........................**14** D2
Safari Seekers...................................**15** B4
Telkom Kenya...................................**16** D4
Telkom Kenya...................................**17** C4
Wavetek...**18** C4

SIGHTS & ACTIVITIES
Holy Ghost Cathedral.........................**19** C4
Jain Temple......................................**20** D2
Khonzi Mosque.................................**21** C3
Noor Mosque....................................**22** D1
Sikh Temple.....................................**23** A1

SLEEPING 🛏
Beracha Guest House.........................**24** C3
Castle Royal Hotel.............................**25** B4
Dancourt Hotel.................................**26** C4
Evening Guest House.........................**27** A4
Excellent Hotel.................................**28** B3
Glory Bed & Breakfast.......................**29** B3
Glory Guest House.............................**30** B3
Hotel Dorse......................................**31** B3
Hotel Splendid..................................**32** B4
New Palm Tree Hotel........................**33** D4
New People's Hotel...........................**34** D1
Royal Court Hotel.............................**35** A2
Tana Guest House.............................**36** A1

EATING 🍴
A-1 Supermarket...............................**37** C3
Anglo-Swiss Bakery...........................**38** B4
Aridi 4 Restaurant.............................**39** C3
Baron Restaurant & Pub....................**40** C3
Barrels Wines & Spirits......................**41** A4
Blue Room Restaurant.......................**42** C4
China Town Restaurant......................**43** C4
City Grocers.....................................**44** C3
Fayaz Baker & Confectioners.............**45** C2
Fontanella Steakhouse & Beer Garden.**46** C4
Little Chef Dinners Pub......................**47** A4
Main Market....................................**48** D2
Mombasa Coffee House......................**49** B4
New Chetna Restaurant......................**50** B3
Pistacchio Café.................................**51** B3
Rozina House Restaurant...................**52** A4
Shehnai Restaurant...........................**53** B3
Singh Restaurant.............................(see 23)

Splendid View Restaurant...................**54** B3

DRINKING 🍷
Casablanca Restaurant & Club............**55** A4
Salambo Club....................................**56** C4
Sky Bar & Restaurant.........................**57** A4
Toyz Disco..**58** C4

ENTERTAINMENT 🎭
Kenya Cinema...................................**59** D4

SHOPPING 🛍
Mombasa Tailoring Mart.....................**60** C3
Umed Mode......................................**61** C3

TRANSPORT
Akamba..**62** B1
Buses & Matatus to Malindi................**63** D1
Buses to Arusha & Moshi (Mwembe Tayari
  Health Centre)..............................**64** B1
Buses to Dar es Salaam & Tanga.........**65** B1
Busscar..(see 72)
Busstar..**66** D1
Coastline Safaris...............................**67** B1
Falcon...**68** D1
Kenatco Taxis..................................(see 7)
Kenya Airways..................................**69** C4
Kobil Petrol Station..........................(see 71)
Mash Express....................................**70** B1
Matatu to Voi & Wundanyi.................**71** B1
Mombasa Raha..................................**72** D1
Mombasa Raha..................................**73** B1
Oman Air...(see 8)
TSS Express......................................**74** D1

fort's history, organised by Jahazi Marine (see p161). Tickets cost US$15.

RELIGIOUS BUILDINGS

Mombasa has some interesting mosques; non-Muslims are usually not permitted to enter, although you can look from the outside. The dozen or so mosques in the Old Town are the most traditional, while more modern examples in town include the **Sheikh Nurein Islamic Centre** (Map p155) opposite Uhuru Gardens and the **Khonzi Mosque** (Map p158; Digo Rd) on Digo Rd.

You'll get a warm reception at the Hindu **Lord Shiva Temple** (Map p155; Mwinyi Ab Rd), which has an interesting sculpture garden, and **Swaminarayan Temple** (Map p155; Haile Selassie Rd), which has some wonderfully ornate painted doors and vivid paintings from Hindu mythology. For even more esoteric design, there's a **Sikh Temple** (Map p158; Mwembe Tayari Rd), a **Jain Temple** (Map p158; Langoni Rd) and a **Hare Krishna Temple** (Map p155; Sautiya Kenya Rd). Shoes should be removed before entering any of these buildings, and it's worth asking about any other appropriate signs of respect.

The two main Christian churches are also worth seeing, for rather different reasons. The **Holy Ghost Cathedral** (Map p158; Nyerere Ave) is a very European hunk of neo-Gothic buttressed architecture, with massive fans in the walls to cool its former colonial congregations. The **Mombasa Memorial Cathedral** (Map p155; Nkrumah Rd), on the other hand, tries almost too hard to fit in, resembling a mosque with its white walls, arches and cupola dome.

OLD LAW COURTS

The old law courts on Nkrumah Rd have been converted into an informal **gallery** (Map p155; Nkrumah Rd; admission free; 🕑 8am-6pm), with regularly changing displays of local art, Kenyan crafts, school competition pieces and votive objects from various tribal groups.

GOLF

Drive, chip and putt to your heart's content at **Mombasa Golf Club** (Map p155; ☎ 228531; Mama Ngina Dr), perched on the southeastern edge of the island. Day membership is KSh1500, clubs cost KSh800 per day and caddies cost KSh100 per nine-hole round.

SAILING

If you can sail, it may be worth joining **Mombasa Yacht Club** (Map p155; ☎ 223580; Tayib Abdulla Nassir Rd). Temporary membership cost KSh100/500 per day/week. Wednesday is club night, where qualified sailors may be able to talk themselves into some crewing, and there are usually races on Sunday. Those

THE COAST

COUNTING KAYAS

One belief that still persists among the Mijikenda (the nine coastal tribes) is the importance of sacred forests, known as *kayas*. There are strict rules about who can enter these mystical places, and sacrifices and ritual burials were regularly conducted in the forests in the past. Today few *kayas* remain, but you can still often see discarded bottles of rosewater used for offerings at particular spots. The incredible biodiversity of the coastal woodland outside Mombasa is partly a result of centuries of conservation by the Mijikenda, a welcome side-effect of their traditional respect for nature.

In 1992 the government designated all surviving *kayas* as National Monuments, and they have been listed by Conservation International as one of 25 conservation hotspots worldwide. However, with little protective infrastructure, deforestation continues to eat away at these sacred spaces. For a glimpse of the real thing, visit Kaya Kinondo, near Diani Beach (p173), or the Shimba Hills Triangular Forest Project (p169).

---

hoping to hitch a lift on a passing yacht will have a better (though remote) chance in Mtwapa (p195) or at Kilifi Boatyard (p198).

Walking Tour

While Mombasa's Old Town doesn't quite have the medieval charm of Lamu or Zanzibar, it's still an interesting area to wander around. The houses here are characteristic of coastal East African architecture, with ornately carved doors and window frames and fretwork balconies, designed to protect the modesty of the female inhabitants. Sadly, many of these have been destroyed; there is now a preservation order on the remaining doors and balconies, so further losses should hopefully be prevented. The **Mombasa Old Town Conservation Society** (Map p155; ☎ 312246; Sir Mbarak Hinawy Rd) is encouraging the renovation of many dilapidated buildings.

From the outside there's little evidence of what any of these buildings were once used for. To flesh out their history, it's worth picking up a copy of the booklet *The Old Town Mombasa: A Historical Guide* (KSh200) from the tourist office or the Fort Jesus ticket office. This excellent guide features old photos,

a good map and a building-by-building account of the various structures – as well as a description of the unusual trolley service that used to run through the city.

Early morning or late afternoon is the best time to walk around as there's more activity, although most houses are residential these days and the streets are rather quiet, except for the honking of horns as cars edge their way round blind corners. This tour can take anything from 30 minutes up to 1½ hours, depending how many stops you make along the way.

We start our walk at **Fort Jesus (1)**, the obvious gateway landmark for the Old Town area. When you've had your fill of the ramparts and relics, head past the colonial **Mombasa Club (2)** onto Sir Mbarak Hinawy Rd, once the main access road to the port and now a lively thoroughfare punctuated with shops and football graffiti.

On the left, **Anil's Arcade (3)** is a three-storey building that dates back to 1900, when it was occupied by a British shipping agency. Further along, **Dalal House (4)** was once the National Bank of South Africa; the pleasant orange facade was restored in 2000. Another former financial institution, the **Standard Bank (5)**, is just along from here, next to the Old Town conservation office. On the other side of the street you'll see the minaret of the 16th-century **Mandhry Mosque (6)**, one of the oldest still in use in Mombasa. The decorative freshwater **well (7)** for worshippers' ablutions is on the other side of the conservation office.

Turn the corner at the end of the street and you'll enter Government Square, the largest open space in the Old Town, facing towards the harbour. The buildings lining the square used to hold some of the city's key administrative offices, including the **Customs House (8)**, the **Dhow Registrar's Office (9)**, the **Treasury (10)** on Thika St and the **Italian Consulate (11)**. As you head northwest you'll also pass the **Scent Emporium (12)**, founded in 1850 and still trading today, and the rather less refined odours of the new **fish market (13)**, an annexe of the still-operational original market further north.

Uphill next to the market is the **Bohra Mosque (14)**, a prominent modern structure with a tall minaret, built on the site of a previous mosque. Turn left down the winding streets here to reach Ndia Kuu Rd, where

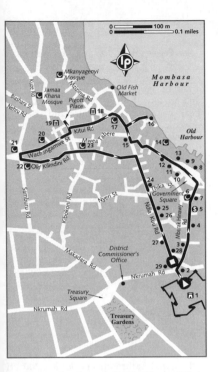

you'll see the former **Public Library (15)** in front of you, the first of its kind in Kenya. Heading north, a right turn takes you to the **Leven Steps (16)** by the waterfront, site of the former British colonial administration.

Returning to Ndia Kuu Rd, turn left past the **Ithna Asheri Mosque (17)** and head down Kitui Rd into the area known as Kitovuni. Just off this street is the **Pillar House (18)**, a three-storey building with unusual wooden pillars. At the end of the street you'll find Piggot Place, another colonial square. The building on the west side is **Glen's Building (19)**, which bears little resemblance to its original design and is chiefly noted for being named after a dog!

From here, mosque fans can detour down Wachangamwe St to catch the colourful, modern **Memon Mosque (20)** and the more traditional **Badala (21)** and **Badri (22)** mosques, before heading back down Old Kilindini Rd past the 16th-century **Basheikh Mosque (23)** to rejoin Ndia Kuu Rd.

Once you're on this straight home stretch, the final stages of your route can be as direct or as tangential as you wish – diverting into side streets to see the real life of the Old Town is highly recommended, and it's hard to get truly lost. The winding alleyways linking the Old Town to Digo Rd are wonderfully lively, with market traders selling everything from *kangas* (printed wraps worn by women) and mobile-phone accessories to baobab seeds and fried taro roots.

If you do stick to Ndia Kuu Rd, there are a lot of nicely restored traditional buildings, most now occupied by souvenir shops. Heading south, you'll pass **Hansing & Co (24)**, the former German import/export office; the **Criterion (25)**, once a well-known hotel; an Indian-style house known as the **Balcony House (26)**, for obvious reasons; **Edward St Rose (27)**, the former chemist, which retains its original engraved glass panel; and **Ali's Curio Market (28)**, one of the better preserved balcony houses and formerly Mombasa's police headquarters. Pass the Muslim **cemetery (29)** and you're back at Fort Jesus, hopefully refreshed and enlivened by a glance into Mombasa's recent past.

Tours

A number of tour companies have branches in Mombasa (see p59 for more details) and offer standard tours of the Old Town and Fort Jesus (from US$50 per person), plus safaris to Shimba Hills National Reserve and Tsavo East and Tsavo West National Parks. Most safaris are expensive lodge-based affairs, but there are a few camping safaris to Tsavo East and West.

Numerous activities are possible both north and south of Mombasa; most operators will pick you up from wherever you're staying for a small extra charge. See p181 and p169 for more details.

HARBOUR CRUISES

Luxury dhow cruises around the harbour are very popular in Mombasa and, notwithstanding the price, they are an excellent way to see the harbour, the Old Town and Fort Jesus and to get a slap-up meal at the end of it.

Topping the billing is the **Tamarind Dhow** (Map p155; ☎ 475074; www.tamarinddhow.com), run by the posh Tamarind restaurant chain of the same name. The cruise embarks from the jetty below the Tamarind restaurant in Nyali, and includes a harbour tour and a fantastic meal. The lunch cruises leave at 1pm and cost US$40/20 per adult/child, or

THE COAST

US$80/40 when combined with a city tour. Longer and more splendid evening cruises leave at 6.30pm and cost US$70/35. There is a choice of seafood, steak and vegetarian dishes. Prices include a complimentary cocktail and transport to and from your hotel.

The other big operator is **Jahazi Marine** (☎ 5485001; www.severin-kenya.com), which offers evening trips for US$75. The price includes transfers, a sunset cruise, a walk through the Old Town and entry to Fort Jesus for the light show and a five-course meal; for an extra US$10 you can sample a casino and head on to the Bora Bora International Nightclub in Bamburi, on the northern beaches.

Festivals & Events

The **Mombasa Carnival** (zainab@africaonline.co.ke) is the city's major annual event, held every November. The festival sees Moi Ave come alive for the day with street parades, floats and lots of music from the diverse cultural groups of the coastal region and the rest of Kenya.

For sporty types or keen spectators, the **Mombasa Triathlon** (☎ 230658) in August is an open competition with men's, women's and children's races.

Beauty pageants also seem to do a lively trade on the beach strips during summer, with prestigious titles such as Miss Coast and Miss Morality Mombasa up for grabs.

Sleeping

There are plenty of budget choices in Mombasa, as well as some excellent midrange hotels, but there are few top-end options. Many people choose to skip Mombasa and head straight for the beaches to the north (p181) and south (p169). All the places listed here have fans and mosquito nets as a minimum requirement, though their condition varies widely.

BUDGET

Most of the really cheap choices are in the busy, noisy area close to the bus stations on Abdel Nasser Rd and Jomo Kenyatta Ave. Lone female travellers might want to opt for something a little further up the price scale.

Tana Guest House (Map p158; ☎ 490550; cnr Mwembe Tayari & Gatundu Rds; s/d/tr KSh400/500/600) A simple but friendly place in the slightly seedy area close to the Jomo Kenyatta Ave bus stations. Rooms are clean, tidy and

pretty much what you'd expect for the price.

New People's Hotel (Map p158; Abdel Nasser Rd; s/d KSh350/500, with shared bathroom KSh200/350) This basic dosshouse gets loads of noise from traffic and the Noor Mosque next door, but you can't argue with the prices. There's a good, cheap restaurant downstairs and it's very convenient for buses to Lamu and Malindi.

Evening Guest House (Map p158; ☎ 221380; Mnazi Moja Rd; s KSh700-800, d KSh1000, with shared bathroom s/d KSh600/800) Set in a thatched courtyard behind its own large restaurant area, the Evening does have something of the night about it but is still mostly good value, despite a few cramped singles. All rooms have power points 'for mobile phones only'.

Beracha Guest House (Map p158; ☎ 0722-673798; Haile Selassie Rd; s/d KSh500/750) This popular central choice has variable but clean rooms in a range of unusual shapes. There's a cheap restaurant, and ongoing building work should add a few more strange angles to the geometry.

Glory Bed & Breakfast (Map p158; ☎ 228282; Haile Selassie Rd; s/d/tr KSh700/1000/1400) Adequate, if a little cramped: rooms have fans but no nets, and rates include breakfast. Taking a room with shared bathroom knocks KSh200 off the price. There have been no reports concerning security issues lately, but always be cautious when travelling.

MIDRANGE

At all the following places breakfast is included in the price.

Castle Royal Hotel (Map p158; ☎ 220373; info@680hotel.co.ke; Moi Ave; s/d/tr KSh2300/3000/4200; 🏊 🖵) Quite simply the best hotel in town, and at these prices one of the best deals in the whole of Kenya. The newly renovated Castle Royal is a joy to stay in, with TV, phone, fridge, safe, iron-framed bed and stylish decor in every room, plus an excellent breakfast in the cool terrace restaurant at the front. A shop, travel agent and Chinese restaurant round out the amenities, and when the second wing is completed you'll get a gym, lifts and possibly even a swimming pool. High-speed Internet lines are available (US$15 per day).

New Palm Tree Hotel (Map p158; ☎ 312623; Nkrumah Rd; s/d KSh1160/1740) The appealing New Palm Tree may be a step down from the competition in facilities, but it has character and charm in spades, with all the rooms set around a fantastic roof terrace. The nets are variable and hot water can be unreliable, but the rooms are big, the bar and restaurant are well priced and it has the most sociable atmosphere in town, ideal for travellers taking a break from budget slumming.

Lotus Hotel (Map p155; ☎ 313207; lotus_hotel@ hotmail.com; Cathedral Rd; s/d/tr KSh1800/2500/3000; ✿) A welcome change from dull everyday hotel design – if bright orange isn't your thing you might want to avert your eyes on entering. The rooms don't quite live up to the delightful inner courtyard with its Muslim-style fountain, but they're quiet and well sized, with two bars and a restaurant catering amply for other needs.

Manson Hotel (Map p155; ☎ 222356; vnmulji@ africa online.co.ke; Kisumu Rd; s KSh1050-1650, d KSh1650-2300; ✿) This balconied block is hidden away in a quiet residential neighbourhood. It's well looked after, with plain, spacious standard rooms. Security is tight, and amenities include a restaurant, TV and pool room.

Hotel Dorse (Map p158; ☎ 222252; hoteldorse@ africaonline.co.ke; Kwa Shibu Rd; s/d/tw KSk2500/3000/ 3500; ✿) Marketed at a conference clientele, this is a good low-lying building with balconies, big beds and showers designed for very tall people. As a minor downside, it's currently overlooked by shabby tenement blocks and a building site. Knock about KSh500 off the price in low season.

Hotel Sapphire (Map p155; ☎ 491657; hotelsapphire@ africaonline.co.ke; Mwembe Tayari Rd; s/d/tr KSh2200/ 3300/4200; ✿ ✉) The Sapphire offers passable rooms conveniently close to the train station, but the big multistorey building looks better from outside than inside, and could do with a bit of a touch-up in places. The swimming pool's often empty.

Dancourt Hotel (Map p158; ☎ 226278; swam boi2002@yahoo.com; Meru Rd; s/d KSh1500/2000) Only half built, the existing rooms show laudable ambition, with carved doors and huge TVs, but blocked views detract. When the upstairs balcony rooms are finished they'll be much nicer and the charming pastel-orange patio café should come into its own.

Hotel Splendid (Map p158; ☎ 221694; Msanifu Kombo St) This place was closed for renovation at the time of writing, but has always tried to live up to its name in the past. There's a range of rooms, and the rooftop restaurant catches a nice breeze.

Glory Guest House (Map p158; ☎ 228202; Kwa Shibu Rd; s KSh900-1500, d KSh1300-2000, tr KSh2100, s/d/tr with shared bathroom KSh600/1000/1400; ✿) This place shares a dodgy air with its fellow Glory properties, but most rooms are reasonable, especially the VIP rooms further up the scale. As the massive padlocks suggest, be conscious of the security of your belongings while travelling.

Excellent Hotel (Map p158; ☎ 227683; Haile Selassie Rd; s/d/tr KSh1000/1500/2100; ✿) Sadly standards here are not excellent – scummy bathtubs, dodgy locks and a fair bit of noise disappoint at this price, though the rooftop bar is a nice touch. For air-con add KSh300. Somewhat optimistically, reception sells 'I loved my stay at…' bumper stickers.

TOP END

Royal Court Hotel (Map p158; ☎ 223379; royal court@swiftmombasa; Haile Selassie Rd; s US$60-70, d US$75-95, ste US$130; ✿) The swish lobby is the highlight of this stylish business hotel – executive rooms are reasonably plush, but the standard rooms are beaten hands down by those at the Castle Royal, which cost half as much. Still, service and facilities are good, disabled access is a breeze and you get great views and excellent food at the Tawa Terrace restaurant on the roof.

Tamarind Village (Map p155; ☎ 473161; www.tama rind.co.ke; Silos Rd, Nyali; apt KSh8000-16,000; ✿ ✉) The highly superior Tamarind restaurant chain now has its own highly superior accommodation complex, with a range of luxury serviced apartments for anyone too full, rich or highly superior to stagger back to town. Full kitchenettes give you the option of cooking, but really, with Tamarind and the resort's private Harbour restaurant next door, why on earth would you want to?

Hotel Sai Rose (Map p155; ☎ 222897; hotelsairose@ iconnect.co.ke; Nyerere Ave; s US$30-40, d US$40-60, ste US$75; ✿) It has to be said that this is a bit of an oddity; a long narrow building with tight pastel corridors stuck between two patches of waste ground. For the price, though, rooms aren't bad at all, especially the Swahili-themed executive rooms and the blue honeymoon suite.

Eating

Eating on the coast can be a completely different experience from dining inland, with more variety, fresh seafood and a whole

THE COAST

new range of spices and flavours (see p89). There's a wide selection of restaurants in Mombasa, reflecting both Swahili tradition and the cosmopolitan ethnic make-up of the city itself.

RESTAURANTS
Kenyan & Swahili

Explore the Old Town for cheap, authentic Swahili cuisine; if in doubt, follow the locals to find the best deals. Most places are Muslim-run, so no alcoholic drinks are sold and they're closed until after sunset during Ramadan.

Island Dishes (Map p155; ☎ 0720-887311; Kibokoni Rd; mains KSh50-180) Once your eyes have adjusted to the dazzling strip lights, feast them on the tasty menu at this whiter-than-white Lamu-themed canteen. *Mishkaki* (kebabs), chicken tikka, fish, fresh juices and all the usual favourites are on offer to eat in or take away, though the biryani (curry and rice) is only available at lunchtime.

New Recoder Restaurant (Map p155; Kibokoni Rd; mains KSh50-180) A local favourite in a new location, slightly tattier than Island but with much the same coast cuisine.

Singh Restaurant (Map p158; ☎ 493283; Mwembe Tayari Rd; mains KSh50-150) The Sikh temple near the bus stands operates this small cafeteria restaurant, tipped by Mombasans in the know as one of the best places in town for vegetarians. KSh250 is more than enough to get you a massive feed.

Aridi 4 Restaurant (Map p158; Turkana St; mains KSh80-250) A friendly, popular and good-value local canteen, with superb juices and the standard Kenyan array of grills, burgers and fried chicken.

Indian

Shehnai Restaurant (Map p158; ☎ 224801; Fatemi House, Maungano Rd; mains from KSh290; ☽ noon-2pm & 7.30-10.30pm Tue-Sun) Mombasa's classiest curry house specialises in tandoori and *mughlai* (North Indian) cuisine and has a huge menu, complimented by a tasteful line in drapery. It's very popular with well-heeled Indian families and the food is authentic and very good.

Splendid View Restaurant (Map p158; ☎ 5487270; splendidrestaurants@yahoo.com; Maungano Rd; mains KSh100-300; ☽ 11.30am-2pm & 5.30-10.30pm) You'll be looking in vain if you expect magnificent vistas from the street seating here –

the name merely refers to the Splendid Hotel opposite. Luckily the food compensates for this sly misnomer, covering styles from tandoori to Chinese-influenced *pili pili*, a kind of curry.

New Chetna Restaurant (Map p158; ☎ 224477; Haile Selassie Rd; mains KSh200-300) This is a very popular South Indian canteen restaurant with a long list of vegetarian goodies, including *masala dosa* (curried vegetables inside a lentil-flour pancake) and *idli* (rice dumpling). The various *thali* (set meals) are great value.

Chinese

There are several good Chinese restaurants in Mombasa, although most also double as bars, so you may be the only person eating.

New Overseas Chinese-Korean Restaurant & Bar (Map p155; ☎ 230729; Moi Ave; mains KSh220-480) Despite the overblown name and the hilariously clichéd interior design, the New Overseas delivers on its Oriental promises and is particularly strong on seafood – a full Chinese or Korean feast will cost you up to KSh1000.

China Town Restaurant (Map p155; ☎ 315098; Nyerere Ave; mains KSh400-600) More incredibly chintzy decor, more great Korean and Chinese food. It's opposite the Holy Ghost Cathedral on Nyerere Ave.

International

Tamarind Restaurant (Map p155; ☎ 471747; Silos Rd, Nyali; mains KSh900-1800, lobster per 100g KSh330) Perhaps the finest of the various Tamarind ventures, eating on the terrace of this grand Moorish building overlooking the water is a romantic splurge you can't afford to miss. Seafood is the focus here, but meat eaters won't go hungry and vegetarians even get their own menu. The only bum note is the rather cheesy keyboard music, which takes a few *dawas* (vodka, lime and honey cocktails) to drown out. If you've got some spare cash there's a casino upstairs – just remember you'll need KSh350 for the taxi back to town.

Little Chef Dinners Pub (Map p158; ☎ 222740; Moi Ave; mains KSh100-210) Thankfully this funky green-hued pub-restaurant has nothing to do with the British motorway diners of the same name, dishing up big, tasty portions of Kenyan and international dishes from pilau to stroganoff. The 1st-floor bar has a pool table and a great breezy balcony, one of the

THE COAST

most relaxed places in town for a beer. The company has a couple more outlets in the area, but this is by far the nicest.

Baron Restaurant & Pub (Map p158; ☎ 314971; Digo Rd; mains KSh250-650) While it appears at first like a pretty average drinking hall, a glance at Baron's ambitious menu reveals a lot more than cold Tusker passing through the kitchen. Crocodile, ostrich, guinea fowl and lobster (KSh1750) all feature, and even the drinks list takes up a page or two.

Siesta Bar & Restaurant (Map p155; ☎ 474896; Nyali Rd, Nyali; mains KSh350-600; ☼ from 5pm Tue-Sun) You say *mzungu*, they say *gringo*…we just say *olé!* This is quite possibly the only Mexican restaurant in East Africa, set in a fine garden above the harbour by the Nyali Bridge. It's great for a sunset beer (or tequila if you've got the *cojones*) and the near-authentic food comes highly recommended.

Fontanella Steakhouse & Beer Garden (Map p158; ☎ 222740; City House, Moi Ave; mains KSh100-250) A popular open-air place in a courtyard off Moi Ave, with *nyama choma* (barbecued meat), steaks and Western offerings such as spag bol. There's a large bird cage for entertainment, though without many outside lights you can hardly see it (or the menus) at night.

Hunter's Steak House (Map p158; ☎ 474759; 'Königsallee', Mkomani Rd, Nyali; mains KSh450-1500; ☼ Wed-Mon) Hunter's is another high-class restaurant close to Tamarind, clearly displaying the influence of its German owners in the hefty parade of meat dishes. Aimed mainly at tourists, it's often closed for a month or so in June.

Rozina House Restaurant (Map p158; ☎ 311107; Moi Ave; mains KSh500-1200) Walk along Moi Ave in the evening and you're bound to be approached by touts for this would-be upmarket eatery. The food is reputedly very good, with plenty of seafood (KSh1000 to KSh2000, two-person platter KSh4000), but if you've just been dragged in off the street the prices are distinctly off-putting. Cheaper meals are available at the café next door.

CAFÉS
Cozy Inn (Map p155; ☎ 0733-925707; Kibokoni Rd; mains KSh80-195; ▣) A new addition to the Old Town, classical music soothes the senses in this friendly café. Lunch and dinner are planned weekly, with just four Italian-themed main dishes available each day.

Pistacchio Café (Map p158; ☎ 221989; cnr Meru Rd & Mwindani Rd; buffet lunch KSh450; ☼ Mon-Sat) A Swiss-run place with excellent ice cream and popular lunchtime buffets, usually consisting of a mixture of Indian and Western dishes. À-la-carte staples such as spaghetti are also served.

Mombasa Coffee House (Map p158; Moi Ave; meals from KSh100; ▣) Take the opportunity to escape above Moi Ave for fresh coffee and snacks, or local meals away from the daily grind.

QUICK EATS
There are dozens of inexpensive local cafés and restaurants serving quick meals and snacks. Street food is an even faster option: stalls around town sell snacks such as cassava, samosas, *bhajis* and kebabs, while a few set up trestle tables to dish out stew and *ugali* (maize meal). For dessert, vendors can ply you with *haluwa* (an Omani version of Turkish delight), fried taro roots, sweet baobab seeds and sugared donuts.

Blue Room Restaurant (Map p158; ☎ 224021; www .blueroomonline.com; Haile Selassie Rd; snacks KSh20-50, mains KSh110-325; ▣) The Blue Room is hugely popular for its fast food – anything from cakes and sandwiches to curries, steaks and pizzas. Drinks are made with filtered water and there are no fewer than two back-up generators in case of power cuts. There's also a highly recommended ice-cream parlour.

Fayaz Baker & Confectioners (Map p158; ☎ 220382; Jomo Kenyatta Ave) Mombasa's 'Master Baker' cooks up excellent cakes and muffins in several locations around town – great for breakfast on the run or a leisurely mid-morning snack.

Anglo-Swiss Bakery (Map p158; Meru Rd) Perhaps not the obvious entente cordiale, but another good place for cakes.

SELF-CATERING
Nakumatt supermarket (Map p155; ☎ 228945; Nyerere Ave) Close to the Likoni ferry, with an astounding selection of provisions, drinks, consumer goods and hardware items – just in case you need a TV, bicycle or lawnmower to go with your groceries.

Main market (Map p158; Digo Rd) Mombasa's dilapidated 'covered' market building, formerly the Mackinnon Market, is packed with stalls selling fresh fruit and vegetables. Roaming produce carts also congregate in

THE COAST

the streets around it, and dozens of *miraa* (leafy twigs and shoots chewed as a stimulant) sellers join the fray when the regular deliveries come in.

A-1 supermarket (Map p158; ☎ 313478; Digo Rd) Reasonable central supermarket.

City Grocers (Map p158; ☎ 223200; Haile Selassie Rd) A well-stocked shop.

Barrels Wines & Spirits (Map p158; ☎ 316187; Moi Ave) Convenient central off-licence.

Drinking

There are plenty of good drinking holes in Mombasa, and many restaurants cater primarily to drinkers in the evening. Keep an eye out for flyers advertising reggae concerts and other events.

New Florida Nightclub (☎ 313127; Mama Ngina Dr; admission men/women KSh150/70; ⏰ 24hr; 🅿) This vast seafront complex houses Mombasa's liveliest nightclub, which boasts its own casino, restaurants and even an open-air swimming pool. It's owned by the same people as the infamous Florida clubs in Nairobi and offers much the same atmosphere, clientele and Las Vegas–style floorshows, with the added bonus of outdoor bars, table football and real German *Currywurst* (curry sausage)! Friday, Saturday and Sunday are the big party nights. A taxi fare here is around KSh400.

The Office (Map p155; ☎ 451700; Shelly Beach Rd, Likoni) Perched above the Likoni ferry jetty and matatu stand, the entirely unaptly named Office is a real locals' hangout with regular massive reggae and dub nights shaking the thatched rafters. Any business that goes on here is definitely not the executive kind.

Casablanca Restaurant & Club (Map p158; Mnazi Moja Rd; admission KSh50-100) Amid the *makuti* and cartoon animals, this loud split-level bar-club pulls in plenty of Westerners, but also a *lot* of prostitutes – all-male groups will be mobbed mercilessly, especially on the dance floor. Still, the music is good, there's tables downstairs and the beers are wonderfully cold.

Toyz Disco (Map p158; ☎ 313931; Baluchi St; admission KSh100) A loud and lively Kenyan nightspot just off Nkrumah Rd. The 'Be Casual' sign outside announces in graphic form that drugs, nudity, fighting and weapons are banned, which seems to work as it's perfectly friendly inside. Entry is free for women. Expect plenty of gangsta rap and jangly Congolese music.

Salambo Club (Map p158; ☎ 220180; Moi Ave) Head down the steps to investigate this popular Kenyan basement bar, rinsing your eardrums with loud lingala music and your throat with cold beers.

Sky Bar & Restaurant (Map p158; ☎ 315165; Moi Ave) Not far from the tusks statue, this is a pretty seedy drinking hole with plastic chairs and lots of prostitutes. Most travellers only come here to play pool.

Entertainment

Nyali Cinemax (Map p155; ☎ 470000; info@nyalicinemax .com; Nyali Centre, Nyali Rd, Nyali; tickets KSh250-350) A plush, modern cinema complex close to Tamarind, also incorporating a casino, sports bar, cybercafé, Indian deli and restaurant, plus the Hollywood Bowl (see below).

Kenya Cinema (Map p158; ☎ 312355; Nkrumah Ave; tickets stalls/balcony KSh120/150) An appealing old movie house that screens Hindi movies regularly (usually with English subtitles) and Western blockbusters occasionally.

Hollywood Bowl (Map p155; ☎ 476056; Nyali Centre, Nyali Rd, Nyali; games KSh199-350) A typical American-style bowling alley with a range of special offers, including KSh999 family deals at weekends.

Shopping

Biashara St (see Map p158), a busy street west of the Digo Rd intersection, is Kenya's main centre for *kikoi*, brightly coloured woven sarongs for men, and *kangas*, printed wraps worn by women. *Kangas* come as a pair, one for the top half of the body and one for the bottom, and are marked with Swahili proverbs. You may need to bargain, but what you get is generally what you pay for; bank on about KSh350 for a pair of *kangas* or a *kikoi*.

Mombasa has an incredible number of skilled tailors and you can have a safari suit or shirt custom-made in a day or two for an incredible price. There are numerous choices on Nehru Rd, behind the market.

Moi Ave has loads of souvenir shops, but prices are high and every shop seems to stock exactly the same stuff. Almost every building on Ndia Kuu Rd in the Old Town is now a curio emporium! There are stalls selling sisal baskets and spices in and around the main market, but you'll rarely pay fair prices as touts loiter here and 'accompany' tourists for a commission.

Bombolulu Workshops & Cultural Centre (Map p183; ☎ 471704; www.apdkbombolulu.com; admission nonresident adult/child KSh360/180; ☻ 8am-6pm Mon-Sat, 10am-3pm Sun) This nonprofit organisation produces crafts of a very high standard and gives vocational training to of physically disabled people. Visit the workshops and showroom for free to buy jewellery, clothes, carvings and other crafts, or enter the cultural centre to tour mock-ups of traditional homesteads in the grounds, where various activities take place. The turn-off for the centre is on the left about 3km north of Nyali bridge. Bombolulu matatus run here from Msanifu Kombo St, and Bamburi services also pass the centre (KSh20).

Akamba Handicraft Industry Cooperative Society (☎ 432241; akamba@wananchi.com; Port Reitz Rd; ☻ 8am-5pm Mon-Fri, to noon Sun) This cooperative employs an incredible 10,000 people from the local area. It's also a nonprofit organisation and produces very fine animal woodcarving. Kwa Hola/Magongo matatus run right past the gates from the Kobil petrol station on Jomo Kenyatta Ave. Many coach tours from Mombasa also stop here.

Mombasa Tailoring Mart (Map p158; ☎ 226859; Digo Rd) This is recommended for tailored African-style shirts from around KSh1200 and full safari suits from KSh2800.

Umed Mode (Map p158; ☎ 228037; Haile Selassie Rd) Even cheaper but still reliable, if you catch the right special offer you can get a safari suit here for as little as KSh1000.

Getting There & Away
AIR
Kenya Airways (Map p158; ☎ 221251; www.kenya-airways.com; TSS Towers, Nkrumah Rd) flies between Nairobi and Mombasa at least six times daily (KSh6835, one hour). It's much cheaper if you book more than 14 days in advance. Remember to reconfirm your return seat 72 hours before travelling.

Mombasa Air Safari (☎ 433061; www.mombasaair safari.com; Moi International Airport) flies to Malindi (US$21, 25 minutes), Lamu (US$90, 1¼ hours) and Amboseli (US$220, one hour), Tsavo (US$220, on request) and the Masai Mara (US$229) national parks; they can also arrange complete safari packages.

BOAT
In theory it's possible to get a ride on a dhow to Pemba, Zanzibar or Dar es Salaam in Tanzania, but it's generally more trouble than it's worth. You might have a better chance down the coast at Shimoni. There were no ferry services at the time of writing.

BUS & MATATU
Most bus offices are either on Jomo Kenyatta Ave or Abdel Nasser Rd. Services to Malindi and Lamu leave from Abdel Nasser Rd, while buses to Tanzania leave from the junction of Jomo Kenyatta Ave and Mwembe Tayari Rd. With all Kenya Bus Service (KBS) buses suspended, Metro Mombasa has largely taken over the cheap multi-stop coastal routes.

For buses and matatus to the beaches south of Mombasa, you first need to get off the island via the Likoni ferry (p168). Frequent matatus run from Nyerere Ave to the transport stand by the ferry terminal.

Nairobi
There are dozens of daily departures in either direction (mostly in the early morning and late evening). Companies include the following:

Akamba (Map p158; ☎ 490269; Jomo Kenyatta Ave)
Busscar (Map p158; ☎ 222854; Abdel Nasser Rd)
Busstar (Map p158; Nairobi ☎ 02-219525; Abdel Nasser Rd)
Coastline Safaris (Map p158; ☎ 312083; Mwembe Tayari St)
Falcon (Map p158; Nairobi ☎ 02-229662; Abdel Nasser Rd)
Mash Express (Map p158; ☎ 491955; Jomo Kenyatta Ave)
Mombasa Raha (Map p158; ☎ 225716) Offices in Abdel Nasser Rd and Jomo Kenyatta Ave.
Msafiri (Map p155; ☎ 314691; Aga Khan Rd)

Daytime services take at least six hours, and overnight trips take eight to 10 hours and include a meal break about halfway. Fares vary from KSh500 to KSh1000; Coastline is the most expensive but its luxury buses are very comfortable. Mash and Mombasa Raha also offer different classes of bus, some with snacks and DVD movies. Most companies have at least four departures daily.

All buses travel via Voi (KSh300), which is also served by frequent matatus from the Kobil petrol station on Jomo Kenyatta Ave (KSh200). Several companies have buses across the country to Kisumu and towns near Lake Victoria, but all go via Nairobi.

Heading North

Red Metro Mombasa city buses run north from the Likoni ferry, which lands roughly every 45 minutes, passing through town on Digo Rd and heading to Mtwapa (KSh30, 40 minutes) or Malindi (KSh120, two hours).

There are numerous daily matatus and small lorry-buses up the coast to Malindi, leaving in front of the Noor Mosque on Abdel Nasser Rd. Buses take up to 2½ hours (KSh100), matatus about two hours (KSh120). You can also catch an 'express' matatu to Malindi (KSh150), which takes longer to fill up but is then supposedly non-stop all the way.

Tawakal, Falcon, Mombasa Raha and TSS Express have buses to Lamu, most leaving at around 7am (report 30 minutes early) from their offices on Abdel Nasser Rd. Buses take around seven hours to reach the Lamu ferry at Mokoke (KSh400 to KSh500), stopping in Malindi (KSh150).

Heading South

Regular buses and matatus leave from the Likoni ferry terminal and travel along the southern coast.

For Tanzania, Falcon and a handful of other companies have daily departures to Tanga (KSh500, two hours) and Dar es Salaam (KSh1000, eight hours) from their offices on Jomo Kenyatta Ave, near the junction with Mwembe Tayari Rd. Dubious-looking local buses to Moshi and Arusha leave from in front of the Mwembe Tayari Health Centre in the morning or evening.

TRAIN

The popular overnight train to/from Nairobi is a great place to meet other travellers and hook up for safaris or travel on the coast. Trains leave from Mombasa at 7pm on Tuesday, Thursday and Sunday, arriving the next day somewhere between 8.30am and 11am. The fares are KSh3160/2275 in 1st/2nd class including dinner, breakfast and bedding – reserve as far in advance as possible. The **booking office** (Map p155; ☎ 312220; ☒ 8am-5pm) is at the station in Mombasa.

Getting Around

TO/FROM THE AIRPORT

There is currently no public transport to or from the airport, so you're best taking a taxi – the fare to central Mombasa is around KSh650. Coming from town, the usual fare is KSh800, but you'll have to bargain down from KSh1000.

If you don't have much luggage, you can take a Kwa Hola/Magongo matatu from the Kobil petrol station on Jomo Kenyatta Ave to just beyond the Akamba Handicrafts Co-operative on Airport Rd for KSh20 and walk the last few kilometres.

BOAT

The two Likoni ferries connect Mombasa Island with the southern mainland, running at frequent intervals throughout the day and night. There's a crossing roughly every 20 minutes between 5am and 12.30am, less frequently outside these times. It's free for pedestrians and KSh35 per car. To get to the jetty from the centre of town, take a Likoni matatu from Digo Rd (KSh10).

CAR & MOTORCYCLE

There's not much to choose between the car-hire companies in town apart from the possible insurance excesses (see p379). Rates are the same as in Nairobi – about KSh7000 per day for a small jeep and KSh6000 per day for a saloon car. Companies with offices in central Mombasa include the following:

Avenue Motors (Map p155; ☎ 225126; Moi Ave)

Avis (Map p155; ☎ 314950; Southern House, Moi Ave)

Budget (☎ 221281; budgetmba@budget-kenya.com; Moi International Airport)

Glory Car Hire (Map p155; ☎ 313561; Moi Ave) Insurance excess KSh150,000.

Hertz (☎ 4332405; mombasa@hertz.co.ke; Moi International Airport)

MATATU

Matatus charge between KSh10 and KSh20 for short trips. For the Likoni ferry and Nakumatt supermarket, loads of matatus run south along Nyerere Ave (the main post office on Digo Rd is a good place to board them).

TAXI

Mombasa taxis are just as expensive as those in Nairobi, only harder to find. A good place to start looking is in front of Express Travel on Nkrumah Rd. Assume it'll cost KSh200 to KSh300 from the train station to the city centre. One reliable company with ranks all over town is **Kenatco** (Map p158; ☎ 227503; www .kenatco.co.ke; Ambalal House, Nkrumah Rd).

SOUTH OF MOMBASA

The main attraction south of Mombasa is the string of gorgeous beaches stretching most of the way to the Tanzanian border. However, the immaculate white sand can vanish under mounds of seaweed between March and December. Attempts at removing it have been met with mixed results as the weed beds play an important role in protecting the sand. Some resorts have been left sitting high and dry as the sand has been eroded from the beaches.

Offshore are the Kisite and Mpunguti marine parks, which protect some impressive coral reefs. Scuba diving, snorkelling and glass-bottomed boat trips are all popular activities. The reef protects the beaches from sharks, so there is no danger to swimmers at the beach resorts along the coast.

Diani Beach is where you'll find most of the big resorts and hotels, but the beach is better and more tranquil at low-key Tiwi Beach, just to the north, which has several budget places to stay. Dhow trips to the mangrove islands of Funzi and Wasini near the Tanzanian border offer a chance to experience what the coast was like before the big hotels arrived.

SHELLY BEACH

Right across the water from Mombasa island, Shelly Beach isn't a bad place to swim if you just want a day trip from Mombasa, though there's lots of seaweed and it's a poor substitute for the northern and southern beaches if you actually want to spend any time here. The Shelly Beach Hotel has the best reputation for accommodation and food, but at the time of writing it was closed. To get here take a matatu from the turn-off (KSh30), just south of the Likoni ferry jetty.

SHIMBA HILLS NATIONAL RESERVE

This 320-sq-km **reserve** (adult/child US$23/10; ☺ 6am-6pm) lies directly inland from Diani Beach. It covers a wonderful landscape of steep-sided valleys, rolling hills and lush pockets of tropical rainforest, and is rated one of the country's best surviving biodiversity zones. The hills are home to a healthy population of leopards and a vast abundance of birdlife, and you may also spot the reserve's most famous resident, the rare sable antelope. This tall, regal antelope has

a striking black-and-white coat and long, curved horns, and is now protected after the population plummeted to less than 120 animals in the 1970s.

The other main attraction here is the large community of elephants. In 2005 numbers reached an amazing 600, far too many for this tiny space. Instead of culling the herds, Kenya Wildlife Service (KWS) organised an unprecedented US$3.2 million translocation operation to reduce the pressure on the habitat, capturing no fewer than 400 elephants and moving them to Tsavo East National Park.

Most people enter the park through the main gate, about 5km beyond Kwale, but you can also enter via Shimba Gate, about 1km further on, or the Kidongo Gate at the southern end of the park (turn off the coast highway at Mwabungu, about 7km south of Ukunda). Numerous 4WD tracks connect the various observation points in the reserve; Marere Dam and the forest of Mwele Mdogo Hill are good spots for birdlife.

Highly recommended guided forest walks are run by the **Kenya Wildlife Service** (KWS; ☎ 040-4159; PO Box 30, Kwale) from the Sheldrick Falls ranger post at the southern end of the park down to scenic Sheldrick Falls on the Machenmwana River. Walks are free but a tip would be appropriate.

SAFETY ON THE COAST

Security along the coast has improved in recent years, but you still need to be careful around the popular resorts. Muggings are a risk on the minor roads that run between the main highway and the various beach hotels. Take a taxi or matatu, particularly at night.

All the resorts and cottages on the coast employ *askaris* (guards) to keep out undesirables, but once you're on the beach, it's easy to become a target for 'snatch and run' crimes. Leave watches, wallets, jewellery and other items of value in your room.

Beach boys – young Kenyan men who walk along the beaches selling everything from woodcarvings to marijuana as well as sexual favours – are a fact of life at the big resorts and their dogged persistence can be wearing. All you can do is refuse politely; they should move on quickly enough.

THE COAST

One more initiative that should be fully operational by the time you read this is the **Shimba Hills Triangular Forest** project, a community project run by the forest guides on the northeastern boundary of the reserve. This biologically rich area is being developed as an ecotourism attraction, with 90-minute tours taking in a replica *kaya* shrine, troupes of resident Sykes monkeys and over 40 species of butterfly.

Sleeping

Shimba Rainforest Lodge (☎ 040-4077; Kinango Rd; full board with shared bathroom per person US$120) A good Treetops-style affair built from indigenous woods, with a walkway through the rainforest, a viewing platform and a bar. Children under seven years are not permitted. The floodlit waterhole here attracts quite a lot of wildlife, including leopards.

Mukurumuji Tented Camp (☎ 040-2412; www.dianihouse.com; full board per person US$94) Set on a forested hill, this place is perched above the Mukurumuji River on the southern boundary of the park. Guests can take advantage of walking trips along the river and over to Sheldrick Falls. Transfers from Diani cost US$10 each way, or you can take an excursion package from Diani House (☎ 040-320 3487; info@dianihouse.com) at Diani Beach for around US$200 per person.

The **public campsite** (per person US$8) and excellent round **bandas** (per person US$20) are superbly located on the edge of an escarpment close to the main gate, with stunning views down to Diani Beach. Monkeys sit in the trees around the camp, and very tame zebras occasionally warm themselves by your fire. It's also possible to camp at Hunter's Camp, close to Sheldrick Falls.

Getting There & Away

You'll need a 4WD to enter the Shimba Hills National Reserve, but hitching may be possible at the main gate. From Likoni, small lorry-buses (No 34) to Kwale pass the main gate (KSh40). Most visitors come on overnight safari packages, but the Mukurumuji Tented Camp can organise transfers from Diani if you're staying there.

MWALUGANJE ELEPHANT SANCTUARY

This **sanctuary** (☎ 040-41121; nonresident adult/child US$15/2, vehicles KSh150-500; ☻ 6am-6pm) is a good example of community-based conservation

and most local people are stakeholders in the project. It was opened in October 1995 to create a corridor along an ancient elephant migration route between the Shimba Hills National Reserve and the Mwaluganje Forest Reserve, and comprises 2400 hectares of rugged, beautiful country along the valley of the Cha Shimba River.

More than 150 elephants live in the sanctuary and you're also likely to see a large variety of other fauna and flora, including rare cycad forest. (This primitive, palm-like plant species is over 300 million years old.) There's a good information centre close to the main gate and a second ticket office on the outskirts of Kwale. Don't miss the chance to buy the unique postcards and paper goods as souvenirs for the folks back home – they're all made from recycled elephant dung!

Mwaluganje Elephant Camp (Mombasa ☎ 041-5485121; www.travellersbeach.com; per person US$110) is a rather fine place to stay. There's a waterhole and accommodation is in permanent tents. Most travellers come here on day or overnight packages (US$115/213 per person), which include transfers from the south coast and wildlife drives.

There's a **campsite** (per person KSh300) near the main gate and another at the southern end of the park, surrounded by an electric fence to keep curious pachyderms out.

The main entrance to the sanctuary is about 13km northeast of Shimba Hills National Reserve, on the road to Kinango. A shorter route runs from Kwale to the Golini gate, passing the Mwaluganje ticket office. It's only 5km but the track is 4WD only.

TIWI BEACH
☎ 040

This wonderfully undeveloped beach is reached by two dirt roads that wind their way through the coastal scrub about 20km south of Likoni. It's a world away from the bustle of Diani Beach, and while the seclusion does mean you have to be a bit careful walking around, it's worth it for the real sense of peace and quiet on this beautiful stretch of white sand. With the Diani reef very close to shore at this point, Tiwi is also an excellent and very safe spot for swimming.

Tiwi is a tranquil haven but it's still very popular with those in the know, so you should book well ahead if you intend to visit during the high season (Easter, August to

TIWI & DIANI BEACHES

0 — 3 km
0 — 2 miles

INFORMATION
Barclays Bank..........................(see 45)
CMS Cybercafé...........................**1** A3
Diani Beach Hospital...................**2** B3
Diani Beach Post Office..............**3** A3
Diani Forex Bureau......................**4** B4
Hot Gossip...................................**5** B3
I-Point.......................................(see 45)
Kenya Commercial Bank.............**6** A3
Marine iCenter..........................(see 47)
Police..**7** A3
Postbank...................................(see 46)
TechnoScan...............................(see 45)
Ukunda Post Office....................**8** B3

SIGHTS & ACTIVITIES
Chale Paradise Island................(see 46)
Colobus Trust.............................**9** B4
Diani Falconry...........................(see 6)
Diani Marine..............................(see 18)
Diving The Crab.........................(see 32)
Dolphin Dhow............................(see 45)
Funzi Sea Adventures................(see 12)
Golf Course................................(see 27)
H2O Extreme.............................(see 32)
Intra Safaris..............................**10** B3
Ketty Tours................................(see 46)
Kisite Dhow Tours.....................(see 25)
Kongo Mosque...........................**11** B2
Paradise Divers..........................(see 45)
Pilli-Pipa...................................**12** B3
Seahorse Safaris........................(see 47)

SLEEPING
Africana Sea Lodge....................**13** B4
Capricho Beach Cottages...........**14** B2
Cliff Beach Villas.......................(see 35)
Coral Beach Cottages................(see 28)
Coral Cove Cottages..................(see 35)
Corner Guest House..................**15** A3
Diani Beach Campsite & Cottages..**16** B3
Diani Beachalets........................**17** B4
Diani Marine Village..................**18** B3
Diani Reef Beach Resort............**19** B3
Diani Sea Resort........................**20** B3
Eden Drops B&B........................**21** A3
Forest Dream Cottages..............**22** B4
Glory Palace Hotel.....................**23** A3
Indian Ocean Beach Club..........**24** B2
Jadini Beach Hotel.....................**25** B4

Kennaway....................................**26** B4
Kijiji Cottages............................(see 28)
Leisure Lodge Beach Resort.......**27** B3
Leopard Beach Resort................**28** B3
Maweni Beach Cottages.............**29** B2
Moonlight Bay Cottages............(see 31)
Safari Beach Hotel.....................**30** B4
Sand Island Beach Cottages.......**31** B2
Sands at Nomads.......................**32** B4
Shaanti Holistic Health Retreat...**33** B4
Tiwi Beach Resort......................**34** B2
Twiga Lodge...............................**35** B2
Vindigo Cottages.......................**36** B3
Warandale Cottages..................(see 28)
Wayside Apartments..................**37** B3

EATING
African Pot II..............................**38** A3
African Pot Restaurant...............(see 28)
Ali Barbour's Cave Restaurant....**39** B3
Forty Thieves Beach Bar............(see 39)
Galaxy Chinese Restaurant.........(see 48)
Globe International Restaurant...(see 47)
Nagina Supermarket..................**40** A2
Rongai Fast Food.......................**41** A3
Shan-e-Punjab Restaurant.........(see 48)

DRINKING
Germany Sports Pub..................**42** A3
New Dido Pub............................**43** A3
Shakatak.....................................**44** B4

ENTERTAINMENT
Kim4Love..................................(see 9)
Legend Casino Complex.............(see 47)

SHOPPING
Barclays Centre..........................**45** B3
Diani Bazaar..............................**46** B3
Diani Beach Shopping Centre....**47** B3
Diani Complex...........................**48** B3
Diani Shopping Centre..............(see 46)

TRANSPORT
Aeronav....................................(see 46)
Bus Stop....................................**49** A2
Fredlink Tours............................(see 20)
Fun Sports Centre......................**50** B3
Glory Car Hire...........................(see 5)
Leisure Car Hire.........................(see 20)

September and Christmas and New Year). Beach boys and souvenir sellers are fairly prevalent at the southern end of Tiwi, but are almost unheard of at the northern end of the strip.

Sleeping & Eating

Unlike the all-inclusive resorts down the road at Diani, self-catering is the name of the game here, and accommodation consists mainly of individual guest cottages, some with their own restaurants and bars in case you can't be bothered cooking. The options are divided into two groups, linked by a bumpy track just inland from the beach (walking is not recommended). The northern enclave has the nicest beach, a secluded sandy private stretch cut off from the south by the tide. It's reached by a dirt track off the main road, about 18km south of Mombasa.

Sand Island Beach Cottages (☎ 3300043; www .sandislandtiwi.com; cottages low season KSh2750-5500, high season KSh3000-6050) A lively posse of dogs enhances the warm welcome you'll get at these lovely colonial-style cottages, set in a tidy garden. Cottages sleep up to seven people; linen, mosquito nets and fans are all provided, there's an in-house cook who can prepare meals for you, and fresh fruit is available from the orchard. Nearby Sand Island is a lovely place to relax and catch some sun.

Maweni Beach Cottages (☎ 3300012; www.maweni beach.com; cottages low season KSh2000-4700, high season

THE COAST

KSh2500-5200) Owned by the Tiwi Beach Resort, this place consists of attractive *makuti*-roofed cottages overlooking a peaceful cove, with a choice of garden or sea views. There's no direct beach frontage but facilities are good and you definitely feel like you're getting your money's worth. High-flyers can opt for a posh 'executive' cottage (low/high season KSh12,000/10,000).

Moonlight Bay Cottages (☎ 3300040; cottages low season KSh3000-5400, high season KSh3400-6200) Just next door to Sand Island, this is a decent plot with well-equipped one- to three-bedroom cottages and a shady open-air bar-restaurant area. The larger houses have nice big dining rooms for more private socialising.

Capricho Beach Cottages (☎ 3300011; capricho .tiwibeach.com; cottages low season €22.50-39, high season €25.50-49; ☑) A peaceful and well-run operation that caters well for families, maintaining a very pleasant garden around the airy thatched cottages. Watch out for hidden costs, though – almost everything, from linen to use of the pool, is chargeable.

The other group of places is about 2km further south, near the village of Tiwi.

Coral Cove Cottages (☎ 3205195; coralcove.tiwi beach.com; cottages KSh3500-5200) A fantastically friendly place, with tame monkeys, cats, dogs, geese and ducks and a wide variety of comfy, nicely decorated cottages sleeping one to five people. The larger cottages have kitchens and cooks/cleaners can be hired for KSh500 per day. It's a fine place to stay and the owners go out of their way to help their guests.

Twiga Lodge (☎ 3205126; campsites KSh200, s/d KSh800/1500, cottages KSh1500) The only really backpacker-oriented place in Tiwi, Twiga is a good place to meet younger independent travellers. Almost everyone ends up in the bar-restaurant in the evenings, including guests from Coral Cove and Cliff Beach Villas. Accommodation runs the gamut from the beachfront campsite and basic four-bed cottages to the superior 'show rooms' (bed and breakfast KSh3000 to KSh4500). There's also a lot of building and renovation work going on. Local taxi drivers tout quite heavily for this place, and there always seems to be a crowd of hangers-on; you'd be sensible not to leave valuables lying around.

Tiwi Beach Resort (☎ 3202801; www.tiwibeach resort.com; s/d half board low season US$46/79, high season US$54/96; ☒ ☐ ☑) This package-holiday complex is the diametric opposite of the little family-run concerns here, with long whitewashed accommodation blocks, three restaurants, a nightclub, a branch of Somak Travel, palm trees galore and a rather snazzy pool design using linking canals and channels. Full-board and all-inclusive rates are also available.

Cliff Beach Villas (☎ 0721-409068; cottages per person KSh700; ☑) Good-value but unspectacular accommodation perched on a small coral cliff above the beach. The tiny pool's a plus, but there's no direct beach access and the cottages don't have cooking facilities.

Self-caterers can pick up supplies from the **Nagina supermarket** (A14 Hwy) and the *duka* (small shop) near the turn-off to the Tiwi Beach Hotel. Men on bicycles also tour the cottage complexes during the day selling fruit, vegetables and fresh fish.

Getting There & Away

Buses and matatus on the Likoni–Ukunda road can drop you at the start of either track down to Tiwi (KSh30) – keep an eye out for the signs to Capricho Beach Cottages or Tiwi Beach Resort. The southern turn-off by the supermarket, known locally as Tiwi 'spot', is much easier to find.

Although it's only 3.5km to the beach, both access roads are notorious for muggings so take a taxi (KSh300) or hang around for a lift. If you're heading back to the highway, any of the places listed can call ahead for a cab.

DIANI BEACH
☎ 040

As the principal package resort on the southern coast, Diani Beach tends to inspire mixed feelings among visitors. There's certainly not much that's Kenyan about the massive hotel complexes that line the long beach, but the setting as a whole is definitely more exotic than your average Mediterranean holiday strip, the inland national parks and southern islands are within easy reach and the number of activities on offer should be enough to keep even the most cynical tourist from grumbling. Besides, if you're just out for a drink, a laugh and a bit of time out between 'serious' travel, the atmosphere here is as good as you'll find anywhere on the coast, particularly if you get involved in socialising with the sizeable expat population as well as the transitory holiday crowds. One thing Diani won't apologise for is being good, straightforward fun, and you really can't knock it for that.

As at Tiwi Beach, make advance bookings for any of the cheaper places at Diani during the high season. If you intend to stay for some time and are part of a big group, scan the ads beside the road and in the shopping centres to secure a cheap private lease at one of the beach houses along the strip. Good package deals are often available at travel agencies.

Orientation

The town of Ukunda, which is on the main Mombasa–Tanzania road, is the turn-off point for Diani Beach. In the town you will find a post office, a bank and several shops, as well as a number of basic lodging houses and restaurants. From there, a tarmac road runs about 2.5km to a T-junction with the beach road, where you'll find everything Diani has to offer.

Information

EMERGENCY

Diani Beach Hospital (☎ 3202435; www.dianibeach hospital.com; ⏱ 24hr)
Police (☎ 3202121, 3202229; Ukunda)

INTERNET ACCESS

CMS Cybercafé (Palm Ave, Ukunda; per min KSh1.50; ⏱ 8am-8pm Mon-Sat, 10.30am-7pm Sun)
Hot Gossip (☎ 3203307; wellconnectednet@hotgossip .co.ke; Legend Casino Complex; per min KSh5; ⏱ 9am-6pm Mon-Fri, to 2pm Sat) Also offers international phone and fax services.
TechnoSoft (☎ 3203386; diani@technosoftkenya.com; Barclays Centre, Diani Beach Rd; per min KSh5)

INTERNET RESOURCES

www.dianibeach.com Includes information on Tiwi Beach and Funzi Island.

MONEY

Barclays Bank (☎ 3202448; Barclays Centre) ATM accepts Visa, MasterCard and Cirrus.
Diani Forex Bureau (☎ 3203595)
Kenya Commercial Bank (☎ 3202197; Ukunda) ATM accepts Visa.
Postbank (Diani shopping centre)

POST

Diani Beach post office (Diani Beach Rd)
Ukunda post office (Ukunda)

TOURIST INFORMATION

i-Point (☎ 3202234; Barclays Centre; ⏱ 8.30am-6pm Mon-Fri, 9am-4pm Sat) Private information office with plenty of brochures. Also sells the slightly dated *Diani Beach Tourist-Guide* (KSh50).
Marine iCenter (Diani Beach shopping centre; ⏱ 9am-1pm Mon-Sat, 2-5.30pm Mon-Fri) Information on diving and water sports in the area.

TRAVEL AGENCIES

Intra Safaris (☎ 3202630; Diani Beach Rd)

Dangers & Annoyances

Crime is an occasional problem at Diani; see p169 for more information. Souvenir sellers around the shopping centres are an everyday nuisance, engaging you in 'friendly' conversation to try and persuade you to visit their stalls; if that fails they may ask for money, food, a newspaper or even your socks!

Sights

As a beach resort Diani isn't exactly geared towards cultural tourism, but there are a few interesting spots worth seeking out.

The **Colobus Trust** (☎ 3203519; www.colobustrust .org; tours KSh500; ⏱ 8am-5pm Mon-Sat), a conservation project aimed at protecting Diani's population of endangered colobus monkeys (see boxed text on p174), offers informative guided walks from its research station off the southern part of Diani Beach Rd. They provide an excellent introduction to the coral rainforest habitat and a good chance of seeing other indigenous wildlife alongside the resident monkeys.

Inaugurated in 2001, **Kaya Kinondo** (☎ 0722-344426; kayakinondo@hotgossip.co.ke) is a superb grass-roots ecotourism project south of Diani. Guided walks take you through the *kaya* itself, sacred to the Digo people, and include visits to a traditional village, a tribal medicine man and the area's main primary school. The local community is involved at every level, managing the conservation process, training guides and producing crafts and other goods for sale to visitors. Projects like this are springing up all over Kenya, and should definitely be supported.

At the far northern end of the beach road strip, the 16th-century **Kongo Mosque** is the last surviving relic of the ancient Swahili civilisations that once controlled the coast here, and is one of a tiny handful of traditional coral mosques still in use in Kenya.

The land, which also encompasses its own *kaya*, was sold for development some years ago, but the resulting furore saw the sale overturned and the mosque is now a listed monument. It's an interesting squat building with a unique barrel-vaulted design.

If you're short of things to do in Ukunda, you could visit the **Diani Falconry** (☎ 0733-755791; Ukunda; adult/child KSh300/150; ☺ 8am-6pm), behind the Kenya Commercial Bank.

Activities

There's a championship-level **golf course** at the Leisure Lodge Beach Resort (see p176). It's open to nonguests for KSh3250 per day, and caddies and clubs can be hired for around KSh2000 for 18 holes. Minimum handicaps and dress code apply. The club also hosts the annual Diani Beach Masters tournament.

Camel rides are available along the beach for around KSh500 per hour (negotiable).

DIVING

All the big resorts either have their own dive schools or work with a local operator. Rates are fairly standard – Professional Association of Diving Instructors (PADI) open-water courses cost €490, and reef trips with two dives cost €90. Most dive sites here are under 29m and there's even a purposely sunk shipwreck, the 15m former fishing boat MFV *Alpha Funguo*, at 28m.

The following are the main operators:
Diani Marine (☎ 3203450; www.dianimarine.com; Diani Marine Village) Very professional German-run centre with its own accommodation (see opposite).
Diving The Crab (☎ 3202003; www.divingthecrab.com; Nomads Beach Hotel) The most commonly used outfit for the big hotels. Offers the cheapest open-water course (€350).
SX Scuba (☎ 3202719; www.southerncrossscuba.com; Aqualand) An offshoot of Southern Cross Safaris.

WATER SPORTS

With such a long stretch of beach, water sports are unsurprisingly popular, and everything from banana boats to jet skis are on offer. Kitesurfing seems to be the latest craze; full-day courses start around €180. As with diving, all the big hotels either have their own equipment (for common activities such as snorkelling and windsurfing) or arrange bookings with local firms.

Main operators:
H20 Extreme (☎ 0721-495876; www.h20-extreme.com; Nomads Beach Hotel)
Wet & Wild (☎ 0722-705350; www.wetandwilddiani .com; Aqualand)

Tours

Several companies offer dhow trips further down the coast to Funzi (p179) and Wasini Islands (p179). Day safaris to Shimba Hills National Reserve or Mwaluganje Elephant Sanctuary typically cost around US$100 including lunch and park entry fees; **Ketty Tours**

COLOBUS CLIMBING FRAMES

As your matatu barrels along Diani Beach Rd, you might be surprised to notice monkeys using rope ladders overhead, crossing the road with practised ease several feet above the traffic. This initiative was the founding project of the Colobus Trust, established in 1997 to try to combat the high monkey mortality rate.

The main victim of roadkill was the Angolan black-and-white colobus monkey *(Colobus angolensis palliatus)*, a once-common species now restricted to a few isolated pockets of forest south of Mombasa. As well as being quite clumsy beasts on the ground, colobus monkeys will only eat the leaves of certain coastal trees and so are particularly vulnerable to habitat destruction, another big problem in this area.

Staffed by international volunteers, the Colobus Trust has set up 23 'colobridges' between the trees lining Diani Beach Rd, allowing the monkeys to safely cross from one side to the other. With 150,000 recorded crossings per year, the scheme seems to be working, and there are now believed to be around 450 colobus here.

Of course, in such a developed area traffic is just one hazard, and the biggest threat now facing the local primates comes from uninsulated power lines, which kill or maim dozens of monkeys every year. The Trust is working with the power company to cut back vegetation around these lines, and also runs wildlife education and awareness programs for local people and resort staff. Progress is good, but the colobus are by no means out of the woods just yet.

(☎ 3203582; Diani shopping centre) is a reliable operator. Cheaper trips may be available with smaller safari companies at Diani.

Festivals & Events

Diani Rules (www.dianirules.com) is an entertaining charity sports tournament in aid of the Kwale District Eye Centre, held at the Pinewood Village resort on the first weekend of June. It's more of an expat event than a tourist attraction, but if you're staying locally there's every chance you'll be invited along or even asked to join a team. Games include football (played with a rugby ball), blindfold target throwing and 'tenfoot' plank walking; the real endurance event, though, is the three days of partying that accompanies proceedings…

Sleeping

BUDGET

Unless you're travelling in a group, Diani offers very few budget options. Beach access can be a problem as few of the big hotels will let nonguests walk through their compounds – your best bet is the path by Diani Beach Campsite.

Corner Guest House (☎ 3203355; Ukunda; s/d with shared bathroom KSh400/500) If you really need to sleep cheap, Ukunda's your only option, and this is the best of a number of basic lodgings near the Diani junction. Rooms are simple but clean, with fans and piped music until midnight. Add KSh50 from November to March. Breakfast is available for KSh200.

Diani Beach Campsite & Cottages (☎ 3203192; dianicampsite@yahoo.com; campsites low/high season KSh300/400, cottages low season KSh1500-2500, high season KSh3000-6000) The only budget choice anywhere near the beach, although unless you're camping, even the low-season prices are steep. The tent space is a small, simple lawn site with toilets and an eating area; tent hire costs an extra KSh200 (KSh100 in low season). The compact cottages sleep up to four people.

Glory Palace Hotel (☎ 3203392; Palm Ave; low season s KSh800, d KSh1200-2000, tr 2000, high season s KSh1000, d KSh2000-3000, tr KSh2500; 🐕 🏊) Not exactly a bargain but the cheapest hotel option for solo travellers, and at least you get breakfast, security and use of the swimming pool for your money. With constant matatus passing by, it's easy to get to the beach strip or the Ukunda transport stage.

Eden Drops B&B (☎ 0720-987174; edendrops@ yahoo.com; Palm Ave; s/d KSh1200/1500) Just opposite Glory Palace, this is another mid-quality place pushed into the budget category by a lack of alternatives. The atmosphere's nicer and the garden restaurant's lovely, but you don't get a pool.

MIDRANGE

All of Diani's other accommodation is spread out along the beach road. South of the T-junction from Ukunda most places front directly onto the beach; the further north you go, the steeper the slope down to the sand.

Unless otherwise indicated, all places in this category are self-catering.

North of Ukunda Junction

Kijiji Cottages (☎ 3300035; forbes@wananchi.com; cottages KSh5000-7000; 🏊) These characterful cottages, which sleep up to five people, are set along paths in their own garden complex, giving them an exclusive feel. The tiled floors, rock-effect showers and sea-facing balconies are nice touches; even better, the secluded beach is often cut off from the beach boys by the tide. Rates drop by KSh1000 in May and June but almost double over Christmas and New Year. Apparently the British owners may be selling up, so management could change in the future.

Warandale Cottages (☎ 3202187; cottages low season KSh2500-7000, high season KSh3500-10,000; 🏊) Just next door to Kijiji, this is a similarly nice selection of one- to three-bedroom bungalows.

Coral Beach Cottages (☎ 3202205; cottages low season KSh4000-5000, high season KSh7000-10,000) Just north of the junction, this has large, well-appointed cottages set in a garden. The atmosphere is pleasant and relaxed. The original branch of the African Pot restaurant (see p177) is at the entrance gate.

South of Ukunda Junction

Diani Marine Village (☎ 3202367; www.dianimarine .com; s/d low season €25/30, high season €30/35) Although it's primarily a dive resort, the huge guest rooms here are very appealing, with fans, stone floors and four-poster mosquito nets. Unlike most places in this class it's not self-catering – rates include breakfast, and other meals are also available.

Vindigo Cottages (☎ 3202192; vindigocottages@ kenyaweb.com; cottages low season KSh1500-3500, high season KSh2000-4000) A rather sweet collection of little orange cottages sloping down to the sea, each sleeping between two and eight people. There are no fans but the sea breeze keeps you cool, and all the cottages have nets. The quirky cottage names add to the charm, though we'd rather sleep in a Dhow than a Lobster Pot.

Sands at Nomads (☎ 3203312; www.thesandsat nomad.com; s/d from US$100/150, bandas/cottages per person from €24/35) This is a relaxed, informal place right on the beach, catering mainly for divers and water-sports fans and made up of comfortable concrete cottages (up to four people) and thatched twin-bed bandas on the edge of the beach. The attractive grounds are shaded by palms, and the beach bar-restaurant is a local favourite. There are no kitchen facilities for guests here; rates include breakfast.

Diani Beachalets (☎ 3202180; dianibeachalets@ wananchi.com; bandas per person KSh550, cottages low season KSh900-2500, high season KSh1300-3400) Towards the southern end of the strip, this place is a little old but there's plenty of space. The accommodation options vary hugely, from two-person bandas with shared facilities to four-bedroom seafront cottages with kitchen. As well as marauding monkeys, a resident army of lethargic cats occupies the front lawn for most of the day.

Kennaway (☎ 3202070; exclusive hire KSh15,000) One of a number of private houses in this area offering rental accommodation for visitors, with space for up to 10 people in attractive rooms. The owners are well clued-up about the local scene.

Wayside Apartments (☎ 3203119; www.kenya urlaub.de in German; apt per person per week €176; 🖳) A neat, well-run complex of smart modern apartments for longer stays, opposite the derelict Tradewinds Hotel. Prices include transfers from Mombasa; bed and breakfast, half-board and all-inclusive rates are also available.

TOP END

If you do have money to spend, Diani is amply stocked with fine properties: there are at least 13 flashy resort complexes spread out along the beach strip. The hotels here cater mostly to European package tourists, offering restaurants, bars, discos, pools, water sports and 'animations' – song-and-dance extravaganzas loosely based on African dances. Most hotels have desks for tours and activities in the area (see p174). Unless otherwise stated, prices listed are all-inclusive rates for standard rooms. Note that many of these places close for renovation between May and June.

North of Ukunda Junction

Diani Reef Beach Resort (☎ 3202723; www.dianireef .com; half board s/d low season from US$100/160, high season from US$190/250; 🔀 🖳 🖳 🕭) One of the sharpest resorts on the south coast, Diani Reef is well executed in every respect and boasts excellent facilities, including an Asian restaurant (complete with teppanyaki tables), health club, casino, water slide, six bars, three presidential suites, an open-air disco and even a 'wedding island' in the pool. The rooms themselves are nicely laid out, with spotless bathrooms and ethernet connections, and there's good disabled access. If you're in reception, look down to see possibly the coolest floor on the coast!

Indian Ocean Beach Club (☎ 3203730; www.jaca randahotels.com; full board s/d low season from US$96/150, high season from US$130/200; 🔀 🔀 🖳 🖳) A tasteful, low-key hotel in a Moorish style, near the mouth of the Mwachema River and the Kongo mosque. This is one of the more sensitively designed places, consisting of 100 well-spaced cottage-style rooms with some nice wicker features and other Swahili touches. Rooms have minibars and baths, and some are specially equipped for disabled guests.

Leopard Beach Resort (☎ 3202721; www.leopard beachhotel.com; half board s/d low season from US$60/110, high season from US$105/150; 🔀 🖳 🖳 🕭) Perched on some small cliffs above the ocean, Leopard Beach's compound of low *makuti*-thatched buildings, divided by ponds and pools, is tipped by locals as one of the area's top choices. 'We welcome you with both hands where lobsters meet leopards' must score points as one of the strangest slogans on the strip.

Leisure Lodge Beach Resort (☎ 3203624; www .leisurelodgeresort.com; s/d low season from €64/100, high season from €110/144; 🔀 🖳 🖳 🕭) Bring your sense of direction if you want to stay here: the complex is so vast it's practically a small town in its own right, and even the staff sometimes have to consult the handy pathside maps to check where they're going! The sports facilities are particularly good and include an 18-hole golf course across the road (see p174). There is some disabled access.

South of Ukunda Junction

Shaanti Holistic Health Retreat (☎ 3202064; shaanti hhr@yahoo.co.uk; low season s KSh7000-7900, d KSh12,200-13,700, high season s KSh11,500-13,300, d KSh19,400-22,300; ☒ ☲) If you don't have any hippy in you, get some fast – this brand-new Ayurvedic sanctuary is the antithesis of the usual resort blocks, appealing to New Agers and pleasure seekers alike. There are just eight rooms, designed and decorated in an Indian-influenced sandstone style, plus a tower restaurant offering excellent vegetarian food, a relaxation room with enticing divans, a yoga platform, a Jacuzzi with sea view and several massage bandas right on the beach. Rates include the full day's yoga spa program; other packages are available, and nonguests can also visit for the various classes and treatments. It's enough to make even the most hardened sceptic melt in the hand.

Forest Dream Cottages (☎ 3203224; www.forest dreamcottages.com; cottages €124-290; ☒ ☲) If you're not bothered about the beach, Forest Dream is a fantastic luxury choice, set in an actual forest reserve. The six thatched houses are set up to an excellent standard, sleeping between four and 12 people, and there's even an amazing Sultan's Palace building for a taste of the regal life. Koi ponds, Jacuzzis and fully fitted kitchens are just some of the other treats on offer.

Pinewood Village Resort (☎ 3203720; www .pinewood-village.com; half board s/d US$79/112, ste US$164; ☒ ☐ ☲ ☷) On Galu Beach, down past the far end of the Diani strip, this tasteful, comprehensively equipped villa resort is run by Southern Cross Safaris. The fancy suites come with personal chefs, so you can dictate your own meal times! The Aqualand watersports centre (☎ 3202719) is one of the best in the area.

Neptune Paradise Village (☎ 3203061; www .neptunehotels.com; s/d low season KSh5000/7600, high season KSh6000/9000; ☒ ☲ ☷) At the Galu Beach end of Diani Beach Rd, Neptune has rooms in two-storey *makuti*-thatched huts spread over two adjoining sites. There are several large pools, restaurants and bars down by the beach. Superior rooms are more spacious and generally nicer.

Africana Sea Lodge (☎ 3202021; ahl@africaonline .co.ke; s/d low season €100/174, high season €120/210; ☒ ☐ ☲ ☷) Arguably the best of the three hotels owned by the Alliance group here, though none of them are exactly sloppy.

Diani Sea Resort (☎ 3203081; dianisea@africaonline .co.ke; s/d low season €54/84, high season €75/114; ☒ ☐ ☲ ☷) This is an attractive red-tiled place tucked away behind a shopping arcade. There are nice stepped gardens and the atmosphere is peaceful and unhurried, although the rooms don't quite live up to the layout.

The other two Alliance properties, operating on a half-board basis, are **Jadini Beach Hotel** (☎ 3203081; s/d low season €77/134, high season €92/162) and **Safari Beach Hotel** (☎ 3202726; s/d low season €83/144, high season €99/174).

Eating

African Pot Restaurant (☎ 3203890; Coral Beach Cottages; mains KSh200-220) Meals here work to a simple formula: you order your meat (chicken, beef or goat), then choose from one of five or six ways to have it prepared and add any accompaniments you like. The house speciality, *karanga*, a tomato-based sauce with garlic, coriander and onions cooked in a real earthenware pot, is highly recommended.

African Pot II (☎ 3202882; Palm Ave; ☲) African Pot's open-air sister restaurant, halfway down the Ukunda road, has an identical menu but also offers a pool hall (the kind with balls) and an actual pool (the kind with water).

Ali Barbour's Cave Restaurant (☎ 3202033; www .georgebarbour.com; mains KSh550-900; ☾ from 7pm) This is a very sophisticated semi-open restaurant, built into a cave near the Diani Sea Resort. Seafood is the main attraction, with lobster available for KSh1800. Dining under the stars amid the jagged coral and fairy lights is quite an experience, but you should use the courtesy bus or take a taxi to/from the door as people have been mugged walking down the track.

Forty Thieves Beach Bar (☎ 3203419; mains KSh280-500) Part of the Ali Barbour empire, this has a good standard menu of grills and international dishes, plus regular specials like pub grub on Friday and a curry buffet on Sunday (KSh350). You can hire plastic 'topper' boats here, and the bar is a local institution (see p178).

Galaxy Chinese Restaurant (☎ 3202529; Diani Complex; mains KSh305-615; ☾ noon-6.30pm) A smart Chinese restaurant with an outdoor 'island' pavilion bar and seating area. Duck will set you back KSh1350, while lobster costs KSh200 per 100g; at the other end of the scale there's a good-value buffet (adult/child KSh500/200). A courtesy bus is available.

Shan-e-Punjab Restaurant (☎ 3202116; Diani Complex; mains KSh300-600) A very popular Indian restaurant opposite the Diani Reef Beach Resort. A wide range of curries are on offer, including some vegetarian options. The owners also run the supermarket of the same name in the Diani Complex.

Globe International Restaurant (☎ 0733-740938; Diani Beach shopping centre; mains KSh380-850) As the name suggests, the Globe spans quite a number of far-flung cuisines, though much of the emphasis is on good old British cooking. Try the lamb with mint sauce (KSh480).

Rongai Fast Food (Palm Ave, Ukunda) Head for the painted flames to sample this local butchery restaurant, highly recommended for *nyama choma*. You can also buy fresh meat for beach barbecues here.

Self-caterers can stock up at the supermarkets in Diani's shopping centres, or at any of the shops, *dukas* and market stalls in Ukunda.

Drinking & Entertainment

Forty Thieves Beach Bar (☎ 3203419) Of all the phrases you might hear in Diani, 'Meet you at Forty's?' is probably the most common, and the most welcome – this is easily the best bar on the strip, frequented on a daily basis by a crowd of expats and regulars known affectionately as the Reprobates. Wednesday, Friday and Saturday are disco nights, Tuesday and Thursday are movie nights, there are live bands on Sunday afternoons and pub quizzes are held once a month. It's open until the last guest leaves, ie pretty damn late.

Shakatak (☎ 3203124) Essentially the only full-on nightclub in Diani not attached to a hotel, Shakatak is quite hilariously seedy, but can be fun once you know what to expect. Like most big Kenyan clubs, food is served at all hours.

Kim4Love (www.kim4love.com) Not a venue but a person, this local DJ and musician puts on regular summer concerts and events to promote tourism. They're usually held at Kim's own beach bar, by the former Two Fishes hotel – look out for the sign along Diani Beach Rd.

Ukunda has a handful of real locals' bars on the main road where you can find African music and (unfortunately) lots of prostitutes. Options include the **New Dido Pub** (A14 Hwy) and **Germany Sports Pub** (A14 Hwy).

Getting There & Around

AIR

Mombasa Air Safari's routes to Lamu and the southern national parks originate in Diani, passing through Mombasa (see p167). **Aeronav** (☎ 3202655; Diani shopping centre) offers scheduled flights to Lamu and the Masai Mara, also via Mombasa.

BUS & MATATU

Numerous matatus run south from the Likoni ferry directly to Ukunda (KSh50, 30 minutes) and onwards to Msambweni and Lunga Lunga. From the Diani junction in Ukunda, matatus run down to the beach all day for KSh20; check before boarding to see if it's a Reef service (heading north along the strip, then south) or a Neptune one (south beach only).

CAR & MOTORCYCLE

Fun Sports Centre (☎ 0734-769457) rents out motorbikes for KSh2500 per day, and quad bikes for KSh1000 per hour or KSh6000 per day. A valid passport, drivers licence and a KSh2000 deposit are required to be able to rent a vehicle; note that you can't take them onto the beach.

Motorcycles can be hired from **Fredlink Tours** (☎ 3202647; www.motorbike-safari.com; Diani Plaza). With the first 100km included, 350cc trail bikes cost KSh2700 per day and Yamaha scooters cost KSh1500. You can have unlimited mileage for an extra KSh1200. A full motorcycle licence, passport and credit card or cash deposit are required for rental. The company also arranges motorcycle safaris (see p70).

Car rental firms:

Glory Car Hire (☎ 3203076; Diani Beach shopping centre)

Leisure Car Hire (☎ 3203225; Diani Sea Resort)

TAXI

Taxis hang around Ukunda junction and all the main shopping centres; most hotels and restaurants will also have a couple waiting at night. Fares should be between KSh150 and 650, depending on distance. You can also take a smiley yellow tuk-tuk from **Mobby Safaris** (☎ 0734-700700).

BETWEEN DIANI BEACH & FUNZI ISLAND

About 20km south of Ukunda, at the tip of a mangrove peninsula, is gorgeous **Chale Island**, a tropical getaway with a fine beach, sulphur springs and supposedly therapeutic mud. Most visitors come here on health retreats at the upmarket resort of **Chale Paradise Island** (☎ 040-3203235; www.chaleislandparadise.com; office Diani Bazaar, Diani Beach; per person low/high season US$70/100). A full course of beauty treatments using the famous 'Fangomud' is available for US$60 per day, including massage and a vitamin cocktail. Transfers from Diani cost KSh720.

A few kilometres further south, down another dirt track branching off the main road, is Gazi Beach, where you'll find **Seahorse Safaris** (☎ 0733-319116; seahorse@swiftkenya.com; office Diani Beach shopping centre, Diani Beach). This company offers dhow trips to nearby Bird Island, including a seafood lunch, snorkelling and a guided walk (US$65 from Gazi, US$70 with transfers from south-coast hotels). There are also powerboat trips to Kisite Marine National Park (p180) with lunch and snorkelling for US$70 (US$80 from south-coast hotels).

FUNZI ISLAND

Funzi is a small mangrove island about 35km south of Diani, and has only really appeared on the tourist map over the last few years. Like Wasini to the south, it's mainly popular with groups and day-trippers, so if you arrive under your own steam you'll find a tranquil idyll far removed from the usual resort atmosphere.

Boat tours here are becoming increasingly popular, and crocodiles and dolphins can be spotted in the inlets. Arranging your own boat trip is a breeze if you're in a group: boatmen in the mainland village of **Bodo**, west of Funzi, ask around KSh5000 per day per boat (up to eight people), or you can negotiate individual dolphin-spotting trips and crocodile-spotting expeditions up the Ramisi River. The tidal sandbar in the main bay is a common stopping point, especially around sunset, and you may even be able to have dinner on it!

Funzi Sea Adventures (☎ 0722-762656; funzicamp@ africaonline.co.ke; office Diani Villas, Diani Beach) runs more luxurious dhow trips to Funzi Island and up the Ramisi River. Trips cost US$70 including food, drink and transfers, or US$80

if you're staying north of Mombasa. Children are half-price. Staying overnight at their island camp with full board costs US$140 per person.

If you arrive independently, you can generally count on the permanent presence of an accompanying guide from the moment you land, which is actually no bad thing, as they'll show you round the island and can arrange accommodation in the village for around KSh500 to KSh700, with meals available for a further KSh500 (all negotiable).

To get here, take a matatu from Ukunda towards Lunga Lunga and ask for the Bodo turn-off (KSh100). The village is another 2.5km along a sandy track – you can take a *boda-boda* (bicycle taxi), though they'll try and charge you KSh100, or get someone to show you the way. Try to arrive before 9am if you're planning a boat trip. On the way out, northbound matatus are often full when they pass the turn, but there are plenty of them so you shouldn't be stuck for long.

SHIMONI & WASINI ISLAND
☎ 040

The village of Shimoni sits at the tip of a peninsula about 76km south of Likoni. Dhow trips to Wasini Island and Kisite Marine National Park have become a big industry here, and every morning in high season a convoy of coaches arrives carrying tourists from the resorts at Diani Beach. The trips are well run, but you can easily organise your own trip directly with the boatmen.

It's worth waiting until the day-trippers have gone home to explore Shimoni, as the dusty streets have their own unique atmosphere outside tourist times. Villagers have opened up the old **slave caves** (adult/child KSh100/25; ⏰ 8.30-10.30am & 1.30-6pm) as a tourist attraction, with a custodian who'll take you around the dank caverns to illustrate this little-discussed part of East African history. Actual evidence that slaves were kept here is a little thin, but as the pile of empty votive rosewater bottles indicates, even today the site definitely has significance for more superstitious locals.

Wasini Island, too, becomes even more appealing in the peace of the evening. There are no roads or running water and the only electricity comes from generators. There are several worthwhile things to see, including some ancient **Swahili ruins** and the **coral gardens** (adult/child KSh100/20), a bizarre landscape

THE COAST

of exposed coral reefs with a boardwalk for viewing. Most people come here on organised dhow trips from Diani.

Kisite Marine National Park

Just off the south coast of Wasini Island, this **marine park** (adult/child US$5/2) is one of the best in Kenya, also incorporating the **Mpunguti Marine National Reserve**. The park covers 28 sq km of pristine coral reefs and offers excellent diving and snorkelling. You have a reasonable chance of seeing dolphins in the Shimoni Channel, and humpback whales are sometimes spotted between August and October.

There are various organised trips to the marine park (see p174) but these tend to be outside ventures and don't always contribute a great deal to the local community. It's easy to organise your own boat trip with a local captain – the going rate is KSh1500 per person or KSh6000 per boat, including lunch and a walk in the coral gardens on Wasini Island. Masks and snorkels can be hired for KSh200 (fins are discouraged as they may damage the reef).

A good place to start looking for a boatman is at the office of **KWS** (☎ 52027; ⊙ 6am-6pm), which is about 200m south of the main pier, where you'll also have to come to pay the entry fee.

The best time to dive and snorkel is between October and March. Avoid diving in June, July and August because of rough seas, silt and poor visibility.

Activities

SNORKELLING & DIVING

Masks and snorkels are available for rent on the beach for KSh100. You'll need a boat to get out to the reef. Most trips to the park provide their own snorkelling gear. Certified divers can take dives with local tour companies (see right), or more expensively at Coral Reef Lodge or Pemba Channel Fishing Club (opposite). Dive courses and longer scuba safaris are also possible in the Pemba Channel.

DEEP-SEA FISHING

The Pemba Channel is famous for deep-sea fishing, and Pemba Channel Fishing Club (opposite) holds over 50% of Kenya's marlin-fishing records. Boats cost from US$500 for nine hours (valid for up to four fishers).

This company promotes tag and release, which we strongly encourage (see p200).

Tours

Various companies offer organised dhow tours for snorkelling, all leaving Shimoni by 9am. Transfers from north- and south-coast hotels are available (US$10 to US$20), and longer trips with overnight stays can also be arranged. Children pay half the adult price. Certified divers can take one/two scuba dives for an extra US$30/50 with any of these companies.

The Friends of Kenyan Dolphins have set up the **Dolphin Dhow** (☎ 52255, office 3202144; www.dolphindhow.com; office Barclays Centre, Diani Beach), a dolphin-spotting and snorkelling trip around Wasini Island. The dhow leaves from Shimoni jetty at 8.45am daily and costs US$75. The price includes snorkelling equipment, drinks, a Swahili seafood lunch and the marine park fees.

Kisite Dhow Tours (☎ 3202331; www.wasini-island.com; office Jadini Beach Hotel, Diani Beach) runs popular ecotourist snorkelling trips to the marine park, including a nature walk on Wasini and a very good seafood lunch at Charlie Claw's Original Wasini Island Restaurant. Trips cost US$55 from Shimoni jetty, or US$75 with breakfast, drinks and visits to the coral gardens and slave caves.

Pilli-Pipa (☎ 3202401; www.pillipipa.com; office Colliers Centre, Diani Beach) is another expat-owned company offering full-day trips. The price is US$80 from Shimoni, including lunch, park fees, snorkelling and drinks. Diving trips are available at US$130/145 for one/two dives.

Paradise Divers (☎ 3202740; www.paradisedivers.net; office Barclays Centre, Diani Beach), also based in Diani, offers similar trips for US$80.

Sleeping & Eating

Mpunguti Lodge (☎ 52288; Wasini Island; campsites KSh300, half board r with shared bathroom per person KSh1200) This is the only accommodation in Wasini village, run by local character Masood Abdullah and his many nephews. The rooms are uncomplicated, with mosquito nets and small verandas; there is running water but it's collected in rain barrels and doesn't always look too pleasant! The food here is excellent, and it's a common lunch stop for boat trips. You'll need to bring your own towel, soap and any alcoholic drinks from the mainland.

Camp Eden (KWS ☎ 52027; Shimoni; campsites adult/child US$8/5, bandas per person US$10) Behind KWS headquarters, this camping ground offers accommodation with 'birdsong and insect noise' in the tropical forest south of the main jetty. The airy bandas are well maintained and have mosquito nets. There's a campsite, a covered cooking area, pit toilets and showers. It's easiest to bring supplies from Mombasa or Ukunda.

Pemba Channel Fishing Club (☎ 0722-205020; www.pembachannel.com; Shimoni; full board per person low season US$85, high season US$150; 🏊) A proper slice of elegant colonial style, with a handful of airy cottages set around a swimming pool and three big daft dogs to make you feel welcome. Deep-sea fishing is almost mandatory (see opposite) and the trophy-studded restaurant and bar is excellent. Nonguests are welcome but the cooks need prior warning.

Coral Reef Lodge (☎ 52015; www.oneearthsafaris.com; Shimoni; per person low season US$52-64, high season US$80-104; 🏊) A pleasant resort-type place on a bluff overlooking the Shimoni Channel. Facilities include a pool table, a small TV room and a roof terrace with great bay views. The Arabic-style cottages are open-plan and surround a pool, and there's a restaurant overlooking the ocean, but it can seem a little lonely out of season.

Betty's Camp (☎ 0720-900771; www.bettys-camp.com; Shimoni; bungalows US$75, r/ste US$95/120; 🏊) Not really what you'd call a campsite, this Swiss-owned luxury complex right on the waterfront offers a choice of tented bungalows and fancier hotel rooms. Rates include breakfast.

Smugglers Bar & Restaurant, close to the KWS compound in Shimoni, is a big *makuti* bar serving beers, *nyama choma* and snack food.

Getting There & Around

There are matatus every hour or so between Likoni and Shimoni (KSh100, one hour) until about 6pm. It's best to be at Likoni by 6.30am if you want to get to Shimoni in time to catch one of the dhow sailings.

The price of getting across the channel to Wasini Island depends to a degree on who you meet on arrival, how many are in your group and how affluent you look. Crossings should cost between KSh300 and KSh500 each way, less if you negotiate return journeys.

There are occasional dhows between Shimoni and Pemba in Tanzania (KSh2500, three hours), but finding a boat, organising passage and haggling over the price generally makes the process one huge, long hassle unless you can find someone trustworthy to do it for you. Ask at the customs office in Shimoni to see if there are any sailings. There is a small immigration office at Shimoni, but you may have to get your exit stamp back in Mombasa if it's closed.

LUNGA LUNGA

There isn't much at Lunga Lunga apart from the Tanzanian border crossing, which is open 24 hours. It's 6.5km from the Kenyan border post to the Tanzanian border post at Horohoro – matatus run between the two border posts throughout the day (KSh20). From Horohoro, there are numerous matatus to Tanga (TSh200). Frequent matatus run to Lunga Lunga from Likoni, but most people take through buses from Mombasa to Tanga or Dar es Salaam.

NORTH OF MOMBASA

Like the south coast, the coastline north of Mombasa has been extensively developed, although this trails off once you get north of Shanzu Beach. It's mostly set up for European package tourists on all-inclusive holidays, but there are some decent choices for independent travellers.

The northern beaches are also dogged by seaweed at certain times of the year. They are usually clear between December and April, but at other times the sand can vanish under piles of black seaweed. The expensive resort hotels employ people to burn or bury the troublesome weed on the beach.

If you're on a budget chances are you'll be staying away from the beach, as the big hotels have grabbed most of the sand. The resorts are luxurious by Kenyan standards but not always in European terms, and most of them are so self-contained that guests don't see anything of the real Africa except the airport, the taxi driver and a few Kenyan waiters.

Going north from Mombasa, the beaches are Nyali, Bamburi, Shanzu, Kikambala and Vipingo.

NYALI BEACH

☎ 041

Out past the suburb of Nyali, this is the first beach encountered as you head north from Mombasa. Like all the northern beaches, it's a long, straight stretch mainly taken up by hotels, with an extensive and expensive residential area to the south.

The **Nova shopping centre** (Malindi Rd; ☼ 8.30am-10pm Sun-Thu, to midnight Fri & Sat), which also caters for nearby Bamburi Beach, has a big Nakumatt supermarket and the excellent Books First bookshop, with an upstairs **Internet café** (per minute KSh2).

Also in Nyali is the very posh **Nyali Golf Club** (☎ 471589; green fees US$33; ☼ 8am-6pm), set in ornamental gardens on Links Rd. Club hire is KSh1200.

The various hotels are clearly signposted from the relevant roundabouts on Links Rd.

Mamba Village Crocodile Farm

A bizarre combination of commercial crocodile farm, animal park, sports bar and nightclub (see p184). **Mamba Village** (☎ 475184; mambavillage2001@hotmail.com; Links Rd; nonresident adult/child KSh450/250; ☼ 8am-6pm), is located opposite Nyali Golf Club. Around 10,000 scaly inmates bare their teeth for the public at the complex. There's a feeding show at 5pm, which rouses the lethargic beasts quite dramatically. While it's interesting to see the crocodiles in various stages of their development, the knowledge of their impending reincarnation as belts and handbags is a little off-putting, and the fact that you can eat the exhibits in the house restaurant is downright creepy.

You can also visit the small botanical garden, aquarium and snake park (adult/child KSh200/100) or pop next door for some horse and camel riding (KSh50 per round or KSh950 for an hour-long beach tour).

Sleeping

Unless otherwise stated, all rates here are for half board.

Voyager Beach Resort (☎ 475114; www.heritage -eastafrica.com; Barracks Rd; s/d low season US$185/260, high season US$230/310; ✂ ▣ ⍟ ♿) The nautical theme is possibly stretched a bit far, but Voyager can happily cruise through life on its deserved reputation as Nyali's best luxury resort. Facilities are comprehensive, prices are all-inclusive, staff are well drilled,

the grounds are huge and the beach is right there – if you actually have any time for it in between everything else.

Nyali Beach Hotel (☎ 471541; www.blockhotelske .com; Beach Rd; s/tw low season US$118/147, high season US$184/234; ✂ ▣ ⍟ ♿) At the southern end of the beach, this is Voyager's main competition, managing to take up even more space and offer even more facilities – you'd practically have to stay for a week just to try all the different restaurants and bars. The Sunday poolside barbecues are surprisingly good value at KSh650.

Nyali Beach Holiday Resorts (☎ 472325; nbhr@ wananchi.com; Beach Rd; s/d low season KSh3500/5800 high season KSh4500/6800, cottages from KSh5500 ✂ ▣ ⍟ ♿) A good option if you want the Kenyan beach experience without the European price tag. It's less luxurious than the other resorts around here, but you still get a restaurant, bar and games room, and the self-catering cottages (one to three bedrooms) work well for groups. Reception helpfully shows the time in Helsinki for any disoriented Finns who happen by.

Bahari Beach Hotel (☎ 472822; baharihol@africa online.co.ke; Barracks Rd; s/d low season KSh4700/7100 high season KSh5500/8100; ✂ ▣ ⍟ ♿) Germans on all-inclusive packages form the core clientele at this low-slung *makuti* complex which makes good design use of the coral rocks that separate it from the beach. The cave-like Italian restaurant is a particularly nice feature.

Fisherman's Leisure Inn (☎ 220721; lexuscarhire@ hotmail.com; Mwamba Dr; B&B s/d low season KSh2000, 2800, high season KSh3500/4200; ⍟) Reached via a turn-off just before the Nova shopping centre, this is a quiet, friendly Indian-run guesthouse with an attractive Moorish foyer and well-appointed tiled rooms. The Lobster Pot restaurant provides meals on site. Walk through the Reef Hotel to get to the beach.

Reef Hotel (☎ 471771; www.oneearthsafaris.com Barracks Rd; s/d low season US$59/88, high season US$68/115 ▣ ⍟ ♿) This rather faded hotel seems to be going for a Club Med vibe, though some of the facilities look a little aged. Luckily the interior is much better kept, and the relatively down-to-earth rates make it popular with Kenyans as well as foreign tourists.

Glory Villas (☎ 474758; s KSh800, d KSh1200-2000, cottages KSh3000; ✂ ⍟) The only vaguely budget option for miles, this entry in the Glory empire is a complex of odd conical towers

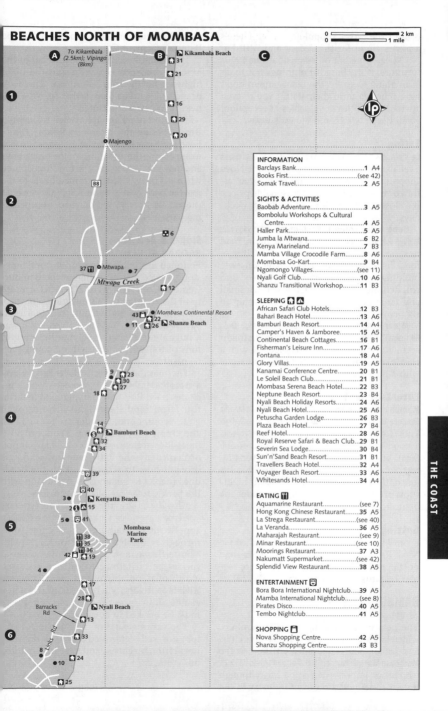

BEACHES NORTH OF MOMBASA

0 — 2 km
0 — 1 mile

To Kikambala
(2.5km); Vipingo
(8km)

Kikambala Beach

Majengo

B8

Mtwapa

Mtwapa Creek

Mombasa Continental Resort

Shanzu Beach

Bamburi Beach

Kenyatta Beach

Mombasa
Marine
Park

Nyali Beach

Barracks
Rd

INFORMATION
Barclays Bank..................................**1** A4
Books First...............................(see 42)
Somak Travel..................................**2** A5

SIGHTS & ACTIVITIES
Baobab Adventure...........................**3** A5
Bombolulu Workshops & Cultural
  Centre......................................**4** A5
Haller Park.....................................**5** A5
Jumba la Mtwana...........................**6** B2
Kenya Marineland...........................**7** B3
Mamba Village Crocodile Farm........**8** A6
Mombasa Go-Kart...........................**9** B4
Ngomongo Villages....................(see 11)
Nyali Golf Club.............................**10** A6
Shanzu Transitional Workshop.......**11** B3

SLEEPING
African Safari Club Hotels.............**12** B3
Bahari Beach Hotel.......................**13** A6
Bamburi Beach Resort..................**14** A4
Camper's Haven & Jamboree........**15** A5
Continental Beach Cottages..........**16** B1
Fisherman's Leisure Inn.................**17** A6
Fontana......................................**18** A4
Glory Villas.................................**19** A5
Kanamai Conference Centre..........**20** B1
Le Soleil Beach Club.....................**21** B1
Mombasa Serena Beach Hotel.......**22** B3
Neptune Beach Resort..................**23** B4
Nyali Beach Holiday Resorts..........**24** A6
Nyali Beach Hotel........................**25** A6
Petuscha Garden Lodge.................**26** B3
Plaza Beach Hotel.........................**27** B4
Reef Hotel..................................**28** A6
Royal Reserve Safari & Beach Club..**29** B1
Severin Sea Lodge........................**30** B4
Sun'n'Sand Beach Resort...............**31** B1
Travellers Beach Hotel..................**32** A4
Voyager Beach Resort...................**33** A6
Whitesands Hotel.........................**34** A4

EATING
Aquamarine Restaurant................(see 7)
Hong Kong Chinese Restaurant.......**35** A5
La Strega Restaurant...................(see 40)
La Veranda..................................**36** A5
Maharajah Restaurant..................(see 9)
Minar Restaurant........................(see 10)
Moorings Restaurant.....................**37** A3
Nakumatt Supermarket................(see 42)
Splendid View Restaurant.............**38** A5

ENTERTAINMENT
Bora Bora International Nightclub.....**39** A5
Mamba International Nightclub........(see 8)
Pirates Disco................................**40** A5
Tembo Nightclub..........................**41** A5

SHOPPING
Nova Shopping Centre...................**42** A5
Shanzu Shopping Centre................**43** B3

THE COAST

behind the Nova shopping centre. There's a prayer room for the devout and 'VIPs' in No 34 can dine out on some hilarious 1970s furniture. If the long list of things not to do is anything to go by, the management don't have much faith in their staff – you're even advised not to leave valuables at reception! Nyali Beach is a 15-minute walk away.

Eating

La Veranda (☎ 5485482; mains KSh350-650) This is a reliable Italian restaurant behind the Nova shopping centre, with a big pizza oven, alfresco veranda dining and reasonable prices. It's closed between 3pm and 6pm on weekdays.

Hong Kong Chinese Restaurant (☎ 5485422; Malindi Rd; mains KSh280-595) On the main road next to the shopping centre, the Chinese food dished up in this round pavilion-style building is a good example of its breed and will definitely fill a hole. Choose from small and large portions or set menus for up to six people (KSh1900 to KSh6850).

Minar Restaurant (☎ 471220; Nyali Golf Club, Links Rd; mains KSh280-800) An Indian restaurant might seem an unusually ethnic choice for such a classic colonial golf club, but you can't argue with a good curry after 18 holes.

Entertainment

Mamba International Nightclub (☎ 475180; Mamba Crocodile Village, Links Rd; admission KSh100-200) Who knows what twisted genius thought it was a good idea to have a disco in a crocodile farm, but the result is this totally over-the-top place, now Nyali's main dance floor. It's one of the most popular independent nightspots around Mombasa – it's a wonder the poor crocs get any sleep!

Getting There & Away

From Mombasa, Nyali Beach is reached via Nyali Rd, which branches off the main road north just after Nyali Bridge. There are regular matatus to/from Mombasa (KSh30).

BAMBURI BEACH

☎ 041

The next beach heading north is Bamburi, which has huge hotels, boisterous nightclubs and some good restaurants. Offshore is the **Mombasa Marine Park** (☎ 312744; adult/child US$5/2), which has impressive marine life, although it cops some pollution from industry in the

area. On land, Bamburi is dominated by the Bamburi Cement Company.

The beach hotels begin just north of the junction between Links Rd and the main highway north from Mombasa. There's a branch of **Barclays Bank** (Malindi Rd; ☎ 485434) next to Whitesands Hotel.

The most popular public beach is Kenyatta Beach, beside the infamous Pirates Disco. Loads of Kenyans come here, and while you won't escape the attentions of the beach boys and hawkers it's usually a fun atmosphere when it's busy. Glass-bottomed boats to the marine park cost around KSh3000 per boat (negotiable) for a 2½-hour trip, not including park fees.

Sights & Activities
BAOBAB ADVENTURE

Founded in the 1950s to process coral limestone, the cement workings at the Bamburi Cement Company were a derelict eyesore until the creation of this ingenious complex of nature trails and wildlife sanctuaries at **Baobab Adventure** (☎ 5485901; Malindi Rd). It was a huge undertaking, involving bringing in tons of topsoil before anything could even be planted.

The main attraction is **Haller Park** (nonresident adult/child KSh450/225; ☉ 8am-5pm), which includes a wildlife sanctuary, crocodile farm, fish farm, reptile park and drive-through giraffe compound. Giraffes are fed at 11am and 3pm; hippos at 4pm. You can also meet local celebrity, Owen, a baby hippo orphaned by the 2004 tsunami who was brought here to recover and hit the headlines thanks to his unusual friendship with the park's 100-year-old giant tortoise.

Also here are the **Bamburi Forest Trails** (nonresident adult/child KSh200/100; ☉ 6am-5.30pm) a network of walking and cycling trails through reforested cement workings, with a butterfly pavilion displaying many coastal species and a terrace to catch the sunset. North of the main cement plant is **Nguun Wildlife Sanctuary**, where herds of ostriches, elands and oryxes are farmed. Tours here must be booked in advance.

The various parts of the Baobab Adventure are well signposted from the highway north from Mombasa and have well-marked bus stops.

(Continued on page 193)

Maasai woman dancing and singing, Masai Mara National Reserve (p285)

MITCH REARDON

Witch doctor, Kikuyu tribe, Central Highlands (p251)

DAVID WALL

ERIC L WHEATER

Pokot girls looking in rear-view mirror north of Kitale (p310), western Kenya

Traditional dress with beaded necklace, Rift Valley (p229)

CHRISTER FREDRIKSSON

Soda crust of Lake Magadi (p131)

Chyulu Hills National Park (p140)

Lewis Glacier and the jagged ridges of Nyahururu, Aberdare National Park (p256)

Snorkelling, Malindi Marine National Park (p207)

Herd of wildebeest fleeing an approaching storm, Masai Mara National Reserve (p286)

Hot water erupts into the air along the western shore of Lake Baringo, Lake Bogoria National Reserve (p246)

The sign says it all on Koinange Street, Nairobi (p95)

ELLIOT DANIEL

Posters and corrugation, Nairobi (p95)

ELLIOT DANIEL

Blue and red phone booths, Watamu (p198)

ANDERS BLOMQVIST

Three-wheeler transport not unlike a tuk-tuk, Nairobi (p95)

ELLIOT DANIEL

WAYNE WALTON
Mother carrying baby and basket, Mombasa (p154)

Local man, Lamu (p213)

ARIADNE VAN ZANDBERGEN

Group of schoolchildren, Mombasa (p154)

ERIC L WHEATER

Young girl in front of adobe wall and door near Kisii (p299)

ERIC L WHEATER

RAY TIPPER

African fish eagle making a meal of a juvenile lesser flamingo, Lake Nakuru National Park (p243)

Nests of spectacled weaver hanging from acacia trees, Buffalo Springs National Reserve (p324)

MITCH REARDON

Flamingo, Lake Nakuru National Park (p243)

MARK NEWMAN

African jacana, or lilytrotter, Amboseli National Park (p137)

GRAHAM BELL

Long-tailed fiscal, Amboseli National Park (p137)

DAVID TIPLING

Grass woven weaver's nest, Samburu National
Reserve (p324)

TOM COCKREM

MITCH REARDON

Buff-bellied kingfisher, Samburu National
Reserve (p324)

Black-headed weaver, Masai Mara National Reserve (p286)

ANDERS BLOMQVIST

192

Olive baboons grooming each other, Masai Mara
National Reserve (p286)

Elephant wallowing in mud to cool down,
Nairobi National Park (p125)

A yawning lioness, Buffalo Springs National
Reserve (p324)

Reticulated giraffe peering over a bush, Samburu National Reserve (p324)

(Continued from page 184)

MOMBASA GO-KART
If you haven't had your fill of excitement on the Kenyan roads, this 1500ft **go-kart track** (☎ 0721-485247; www.mombasa-gokart.com; adult/child KSh1000/500; ☺ 4-10pm Tue-Sun) should satisfy any need for speed.

Sleeping
BUDGET & MIDRANGE
There are no budget choices here at all, but groups in particular can find some reasonable accommodation for a moderate price.

Bamburi Beach Resort (☎ 0733-474482; www.bamburiresort.com; r US$20-90; ❄ ⬟) This tidy little complex has direct access to the beach, and a choice of appealing bamboo-finished hotel rooms and self-catering rooms (with outdoor kitchens). There's a nice beachfront bar with a big shaggy *makuti* thatch.

Fontana (☎ 5487554; Malindi Rd; d low/high season KSh2500/3000; ❄ ⬟) While the rooms are thoroughly liveable, the highlight of this small German-owned establishment is the big thatched lobby restaurant (mains KSh420-700), which resembles a musty safari lodge stuffed with a huge job lot of Africana. The beach is 100m beyond the compound.

Camper's Haven & Jamboree (☎ 5486954; campers_haven@yahoo.com; campsites per tent KSh500, r low/high season KSh2500/5500) A large, slightly bumpy camping ground on the beach. The four-person tents are KSh1500; room prices include breakfast in low season and half board in high season. If you're wondering where 'jamboree' comes into it, wait until the evening – with disco nights Wednesday to Sunday and local stars the Utamaduni Band playing every Sunday afternoon, peace and quiet isn't high on the agenda!

TOP END
Unless otherwise stated, all prices here are for half board.

Whitesands Hotel (☎ 485926; www.sarovahotels.com; s/d low season from US$90/140, high season from US$140/180; ❄ ⬜ ⬟ ♿) It's multi-award-winning and invariably busy, and could be justified in dubbing itself the best resort hotel on the coast, offering consistently good service, thoughtful design, full luxury facilities and high standards throughout. Fancy wood reliefs, hand-painted panels and marble add to the airy sophistication.

There are an amazing five pools and the grounds front directly onto the sand.

Severin Sea Lodge (☎ 5485001; www.severin-kenya.com; s/d low season US$54/108, high season US$165/206; ❄ ⬟ ♿) This place is so classy it has a Swiss consulate in it – surely high praise. Appealing round cottages running down to the beach and there are some nice bars and restaurants, including a funky restaurant in a converted dhow. The comfort-class doubles are the nicest rooms, with more elaborate decor and more expensive rates.

Travellers Beach Hotel (☎ 5485121; www.travellersbeach.com; s/d low season KSh5500/7300, high-season KSh7300/9700; ❄ ⬜ ⬟ ♿) A modern, quite stylish place fronted by a huge triangular *makuti* building. Attractive channels link the pools. Not all rooms have sea views.

Plaza Beach Hotel (☎ 5485321; www.plazabeach.co.ke; s/d low season US$60/110, high season US$85/140; ❄ ⬜ ⬟ ♿) Looking a little cramped on the plot next to Severin and Neptune, the Plaza's grounds are a little dry but the Moorish design and decent rooms work just fine. With ships' wheels as headboards, it's certainly not a problem drifting off.

Neptune Beach Resort (☎ 5485701; www.neptunehotels.com; s/d/tr low season KSh2700/4400/6600, high season KSh4300/7000/10,500; ❄ ⬟ ♿) An endearing eyesore, the haphazard colour scheme and panda-shaped pool do at least help Neptune stand out from the competition. High-season rates are all-inclusive.

Eating
Splendid View Restaurant (☎ 5487270; Malindi Rd; mains KSh100-500; ☺ noon-2pm & 7-10pm Tue-Sun) Sister to the original branch in Mombasa, this is the more attractive sibling and has a wider menu, serving the customary Indian cuisine and a handful of Western dishes. It's right at the start of the strip, next to the Nova complex; ironically, the views here aren't that much better than in town.

La Strega (☎ 5487431; stephanie@africaonline.co.ke; Pirates complex; mains KSh350-1000) You wouldn't think so to look at it, but the thatched restaurant next to the Pirates nightclub is a great Italian eatery, with a small but well-tempura'd Japanese menu to boot.

Maharajah Restaurant (☎ 5485895; mains from KSh350; ☺ dinner Wed-Mon, lunch Sat & Sun) A stylish Indian restaurant at the entrance to the Indiana Beach Hotel with good veggie and nonveggie food.

THE COAST

Entertainment

Bamburi is a town that's known for its infamous nightclubs, which pull in a slightly wild crowd of locals, tourists, prostitutes and hustlers.

Pirates (☎ 5486020; Kenyatta Beach; admission Fri & Sat KSh200) A huge complex of water slides and bars that transforms into the strip's rowdiest nightclub from Wednesday to Saturday in high season, blazing into the small hours. During the day it's surprisingly wholesome, with family 'fun shows' every Saturday.

Bora Bora International Nightclub (☎ 5486421; admission men/women KSh180/100; ♥ from 9pm, closed Tue) This is another big late-night party place, and it's known for its over-the-top cabaret shows.

Tembo Nightclub (☎ 5485078; men/women KSh150/100; ♥ to 5am Sun-Thu, to 6am Fri & Sat) This open *makuti* complex is not just a club, it's an 'entertainment plaza', with pool tables, a playground, barbecue area, beauty salon and 24-hour bar.

Getting There & Around

Buses and matatus to Malindi or Mtwapa stop at Bamburi (KSh30). For the Baobab Adventure, there are bus stops in front of both the Haller Park and the main Bamburi Cement Company gate.

SHANZU BEACH

☎ 041

This busy beach resort is dominated by the private African Safari Club, which operates no less than six luxury hotels in the area. The beach itself is lovely, but away from the all-inclusive places Shanzu is actually depressingly seedy, with a thriving trade catering for European sex tourists and con-

---

> ### COAST PHONE NUMBERS
>
> There have been huge problems with the fixed telephone lines on the coast in recent years, and while Telkom Kenya has now upgraded its equipment there's still a chance that phone numbers between Nyali and Malindi may be out of order. We've given mobile numbers wherever they're still used as a primary contact, though, as these are often just the staff's personal numbers, the ensuing conversations may be a little confusing!

---

stant hassle from souvenir sellers, touts and *boda-boda* boys.

If you're just down at Shanzu Beach for the day you can get to the beach through the grounds of the defunct Mombasa Continental Resort. Looking around the abandoned grounds of the hotel itself is actually quite fascinating (though watch out for the 'massage' girls who set up shop there), and the security guards are only too happy to have a chat.

Ngomongo Villages (☎ 5486480; www.ngomongo .com; adult/child KSh500/250; ♥ 9am-5pm) is a curious enterprise that attempts to give visitors a glimpse of nine of Kenya's different tribal groups in one place. Although it's touristy stuff, the tours are good fun and you can try your hand at various tribal activities such as Maasai dancing, archery and pounding maize.

Nearby, the **Shanzu Transitional Workshop** (♥ 8am-12.30pm & 2-4.30pm), run by the Girl Guides Association, provides training for handicapped women and sells their crafts for them. Among the items on offer are attractive clothes made using traditional Swahili fabrics.

Sleeping & Eating

Mombasa Serena Beach Hotel (☎ 485721; www.se renahotels.com; half board s/d low season US$95/190, high season US$200/260; ♥ ♨ ♀ ♣) Serena's only Kenyan beach resort is so extensive that it's styled on a traditional Swahili village – the pathways around the tree-filled complex even have street names. The split-level rooms are equally impressive, and the design lends an incongruous intimacy.

Petuscha Garden Lodge (☎ 0722-734755; petuscha hotel@yahoo.com; s/d KSh2000/3000, apts €40; ♀) A small private complex marketed mainly at Germans. There's a range of different rooms, and rates are pretty negotiable out of season.

The upmarket Coral Beach, Shanzu Beach, Palm Beach, Paradise Beach, Dolphin and Flamingo Beach hotels are all owned by the African Safari Club (p346).

Most visitors eat at the hotel where they are staying, but there are several restaurants in the Shanzu shopping centre offering almost identical menus of pizzas and other European favourites for between KSh350 and KSh500.

THE COAST

Getting There & Away

Public transport plying the route between Mombasa and Malindi or Mtwapa pass the turn-off to Shanzu (KSh30), where a crowd of *boda-bodas* tout for rides to the hotels (KSh10). Hourly matatus from Mtwapa stop at the resort stage before heading to Mombasa (KSh30). The No 31 Metro Mombasa bus to Mtwapa also comes through here – look out for the yellow 'Via Serena' sign in the windscreen.

MTWAPA

☎ 041

At first glance Mtwapa just looks like a busy roadside service town, but the small fishing village at its heart has a lovely setting with fine views of **Mtwapa Creek**, and makes a great stop for a scenic supper.

Most travellers come for the gourmet meals and dhow tours offered by **Kenya Marineland** (☎ 5485248; www.kenyamarineland.com), tucked away on a private estate towards the mouth of Mtwapa Creek. These trips include a visit to the Marineland **aquarium** (admission KSh300), morning and afternoon cruises along the coast with various entertainment and lunch at the waterside Aquamarine restaurant. It's not a bad trip and the food at the restaurant is excellent – the price is US$85/42.50 per adult/child, including transfers.

Moorings Restaurant (☎ 5485260; mains KSh380-720) is a popular expat hang-out on a floating pontoon on the north shore of Mtwapa Creek, offering prime views of the lofty road bridge. It's a fine place for a beer and serves great seafood. It's a base for various water sports and fishing trips, and sailors have a small chance of finding crewing work or a lift along the coast here. The turn-off is just after the Mtwapa bridge – follow the signs down to the water's edge.

Several companies based in Mtwapa offer deep-sea fishing for marlin and other large billfish. Try **Hallmark Charters** (☎ 5485680), **James Adcock** (☎ 5485527) or **Howard Lawrence-Brown** (☎ 5486394). As always, we recommend that fish are tagged and released (see p200).

Jumba la Mtwana

This **national monument** (nonresident adult/child KSh200/100; 🕑 8am-6pm) is just north of Mtwapa Creek. The ruins are from a 15th-century Swahili settlement, and some interesting structures remain, of which the **Mosque by the Sea** stands out. There are three other mosques on the site, and evidence of extensive sanitation facilities in all the main buildings. A handy guidebook may be available from the ticket office for KSh20, or the custodian will happily give you the tour for a small gratuity. A cafeteria is being built and should be completed by the time you read this – construction was delayed by the discovery of an ancient mass grave under the site!

The nearby beach is delightful. The site is a 3km walk down a dirt track, signposted from the highway about 1km north of Mtwapa bridge; a taxi there and back should cost around KSh200.

Getting There & Away

Very regular matatus and buses run from Mtwapa to Mombasa (KSh30) and Malindi (KSh70).

KIKAMBALA & VIPINGO

☎ 041

These two remote beaches are reached by long, winding dirt roads and both have a peaceful, unspoilt atmosphere. The coast at Vipingo is particularly beautiful and the reef comes right up to the beach. The tranquillity was disrupted when the Paradise Hotel in Kikambala was the target of a car bomb attack in 2002 (see p31), but life seems to have returned to normal remarkably rapidly.

Sleeping & Eating

All these hotels are at Kikambala, on a long track off the main highway.

Royal Reserve Safari & Beach Club (☎ 32022; www.royalreserve.com; apts US$66-100; ❄ 🏊 👶) Possibly the best-value self-catering on the coast – the smart modern apartments here have all-new fittings, including microwave and utensils, complemented by a full range of facilities and activities. If you need provisions, there's a small shop on site and a weekly shuttle bus to the supermarket. It's heavily marketed for timeshares, so book early in high season.

Sun'n'Sand Beach Resort (☎ 32621; www.sunnsand.co.ke; half board s/d low season US$45/90, high season US$70/100; ❄ 💻 🏊 👶) Despite its 900-head capacity there's a really nice feel to the pastel-orange Sun'n'Sand, and it's known as one of the best hotels on the north coast for kids. The mock-mud Moorish buildings are intelligently laid out so it doesn't feel crowded. Children are charged 50% of the adult rate.

The company also contributes a lot to the local community, providing drinking water, a health centre and a school.

Kanamai Conference Centre (☎ 32046; kanamai@ iconnect.co.ke; dm KSh700, s/d KSh1800/3000, cottages KSh1800-2700) This is a quiet Christian conference centre with a tranquil, laid-back atmosphere. Alcohol is prohibited, but there's a cafeteria serving breakfast meals, or you can join in with prayer and fasting (KSh200!). All the rooms are simple but comfortable, and the self-catering cottages are particularly immaculate. It's at the southern end of the track, signposted just before Majengo township.

Continental Beach Cottages (☎ 32190; manasseh@ wananchi.com; B&B/full board per person KSh950/1450, cottages KSh1700-3850; ⚡ ⚡) Next door to the very faded Whispering Palms Hotel, Continental is a quiet little place with a beach bar. The cottages are neat and well looked after, with kitchens and palm gardens facing onto the beach.

Le Soleil Beach Club (☎ 32604; www.lesoleilkenya .com; s/d/tr low season US$72/120/168, high season US$84/140/196; ⚡ ⚡ ⚡) A big beach resort with modernist white blocks and the usual array of facilities. Sadly these prices make it the most expensive hotel on the strip, which is hardly justified.

Getting There and Away

It is possible to come here by public transport (Mombasa–Malindi matatus and buses pass along the highway) but all of the places to stay are a long way from the highway and walking isn't recommended on the smaller tracks. Probably the best option is to get off at the clearly marked turn-off to Sun'n'Sand and pick up a taxi in front of the resort.

If you have your own transport, Kanamai is reached by a signposted track near Majengo. Continental Beach Cottages and Royal Reserve are reached via another turn-off 3km further north. Sun'n'Sand and Le Soleil are down a third road, signposted about 1km further along the highway. Smaller tracks link all these places directly.

KILIFI
☎ 041

Like Mtwapa to its south, Kilifi is a gorgeous river estuary with effortlessly picture-perfect views from its massive road bridge. Many white Kenyans have yachts moored in the creek and there are numerous beach houses belonging to artists, writers and adventurers from around the globe.

The main reasons that most travellers come here are to stay at one of the pleasant beach resorts at the mouth of the creek or to visit the ruins of Mnarani, high on a bluff on the south bank of the creek.

Information

Kilifi consists of the small village of Mnarani (or Manarani) on the southern bank of the creek, and Kilifi village on the northern bank, where you'll find the post office, bus station, markets and the budget hotels.

Kilifi Creek is a popular anchorage spot for yachties sailing along the coast, and if you're looking for a ride you *may* find one at the **Kilifi Boatyard** (☎ 522552), southwest of Kilifi town.

Barclays Bank (Ronald Ngala St) ATM only; accepts Visa, MasterCard and Cirrus.
Kenya Commercial Bank (☎ 522034; Ronald Ngala St) ATM accepts Visa cards.
Kilifi Books & Stationery Store (☎ 525408; kilifibks@ africaonline.co.ke; Biashara St; Internet access per min KSh5) Internet café.
Tourist police (Kilifi Shopping Arcade)

Sights
MNARANI

The **ruins** (nonresident adult/child KSh100/50; ⏲ 7am-6pm) are high on a bluff just west of the old ferry landing stage on the southern bank of Kilifi Creek. Only partly excavated, the site was occupied from the end of the 14th century to around the first half of the 17th century, when it was abandoned following sieges by Galla tribespeople from Somalia and the failure of the water supply.

The best preserved ruin is the **Great Mosque** with its finely carved inscription around the *mihrab* (the niche showing the direction of Mecca). Also here are a group of **carved tombs** (including a restored pillar tomb), a small mosque dating back to the 16th century and parts of the town wall.

Tucked away in the woods are all manner of other ruins and unexcavated structures, including a small mosque, plus a huge baobab tree, one of several rumoured to be the oldest or largest on the coast. There's a human-made hole in the side of the tree where local people leave offerings to the local spirits. The path up to the ruins (about

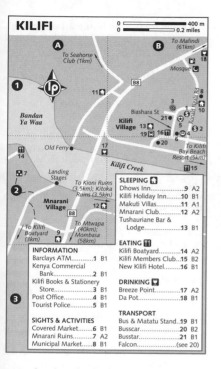

KILIFI

0 _____ 400 m
0 _____ 0.2 miles

INFORMATION
Barclays ATM............1 B1
Kenya Commercial
Bank.....................2 B1
Kilifi Books & Stationery
Store....................3 B1
Post Office................4 B1
Tourist Police............5 B1

SIGHTS & ACTIVITIES
Covered Market...........6 B1
Mnarani Ruins...........7 A2
Municipal Market.....8 B1

SLEEPING
Dhows Inn..................9 A2
Kilifi Holiday Inn........10 B1
Makuti Villas............11 A1
Mnarani Club...........12 A2
Tushauriane Bar &
Lodge...................13 B1

EATING
Kilifi Boatyard...........14 A2
New Kilifi Hotel........16 B1

DRINKING
Breeze Point.............17 A2
Da Pot..................18 B1

TRANSPORT
Bus & Matatu Stand..19 B1
Busscar..................20 B2
Busstar..................21 B1
Falcon...................(see 20)

300m long) is clearly signposted off the tarmac road behind Mnarani village.

Mnarani was associated with the smaller settlements of **Kioni**, past Mnarani Club, and **Kitoka**, about 3km southeast of Mnarani Club on the northern bank of Takaungu Creek. All these settlements were ruled over by Mombasa and are now ruined. If you want to visit, it's best to find a guide to show you the way.

KILIFI CREEK
The **beach** on either side of the creek is very pleasant and doesn't suffer the same seaweed problems as the beaches further south, but most of the frontage is private property. Hotels and local boatmen can arrange **sailing trips** around the creek for about KSh500 per person.

MARKETS
Kilifi has two main markets: the **covered market** on Biashara St, a bustling hall crammed with produce stalls, and the **municipal market** on Ronald Ngala St, an open compound of shops, stalls and kiosks selling everything

from meat and clothes to mobile phone cards. They're both atmospheric and unaffectedly African places to peruse.

Sleeping
BUDGET & MIDRANGE
Dhows Inn (☎ 522028; dhowsinn_kilifi@yahoo.com; Malindi Rd; s/d KSh650/900) This place is on the main road south of Kilifi Creek. It's a small, well-maintained hostelry with simple but decent thatched blocks set around a garden. The Mnarani ruins are within easy walking distance, and there's a popular bar and restaurant on site.

Makuti Villas (☎ 522415; s/d KSh800/1000; ☐) Also known as Mkwajuni Motel or Dhows Inn Annex, this bungalow complex isn't nearly as grand as it sounds, but you're certainly not short on space in the big thatched buildings. Prices include breakfast at the complex's bar-restaurant.

Kilifi Holiday Inn (☎ 525490; s KSh400) According to the signs this is 'the celebrated' Holiday Inn, although it's quite patently nothing to do with the US chain. Rooms have fans, nets and squat toilets, and rates include breakfast; other meals must be ordered in advance.

Tushauriane Bar & Lodge (☎ 522521; s/d with shared bathroom KSh150/300) This is a bright yellow building behind the bus station. Unsurprisingly at this price, rooms are basic as you like, with just beds, nets and plenty of market noise.

TOP END
Mnarani Club (☎ 522318; mnarani@africaonline.com; s/d low season US$62/99, high season US$79/115; ☒ ☐) Atop the cliff on the southern side of Kilifi Creek, this very stylish resort complex has a choice of garden and creek views and an amazing *trompe l'oeil* pool which seems to blend into the ocean. There's a beach below and loads of water sports are possible. The hotel has an adults-only policy.

Kilifi Bay Beach Resort (☎ 522264; www.mada hotels.com; full board s/d low season US$82.50/110, high season US$120/160; ☒ ☐ ☒) About 5km north of Kilifi on the coast road, this is a pleasant, small resort with a nice beach and plenty of facilities. Prices are a bit high for what you get.

Seahorse Club, on the northern side of the creek, is a particularly good hotel in the African Safari Club group (p346).

Eating & Drinking

Kilifi Members Club (☎ 525258; mains KSh100-260)
A fantastic spot for sunset, perched on the
northern cliff edge with a clear sightline to
the creek bridge. There's a good menu with
lots of *nyama choma* (up to KSh460 per kg)
and the Tusker's very reasonable for these
parts (KSh70). Despite the name you don't
have to be a member.

Kilifi Boatyard (☎ 522552; mains KSh350) A very
nice sand-floored café serving excellent seafood and cold beers to expat boating types.
It's a long walk from town down a dirt road
off the highway just south of Kilifi. A taxi
will cost around KSh600 return.

New Kilifi Hotel (☎ 0733-793700; Biashara St; mains
KSh80-140) Just past the bus station is this very
popular local canteen with good pilau and
biryanis (rice and curried meat), plus the
usual stew and *ugali* options.

For a beer and bop, Kilifi's main nightspots are **Breeze Point** (Malindi Rd), a *makuti* bar
overlooking the creek with regular Giriama
dancing, and **Da Pot** (Malindi Rd), a louder, row-
dier club in the usual hip-hop vein.

Getting There & Away

All buses and matatus travelling between
Mombasa (up to 1½ hours) and Malindi
(1¼ hours) stop here at Kilifi; the fare to
either destination is KSh70. Falcon, Busstar
and Busscar all have offices here for their
Nairobi–Malindi route; buses to Mombasa
and on to Nairobi leave at around 7.45am
and 7.45pm (KSh600).

WATAMU

☎ 042

About 24km south of Malindi, Watamu is
another popular beach village with sandy
beaches and plenty of hotels, though the
atmosphere is a lot more resort-like than
in Kilifi. Offshore is the southern part of
Malindi Marine Reserve, and the unspoilt
forests of Arabuko Sokoke Forest Reserve
and the Swahili ruins of Gede are both a
short distance away.

The coast here is broken up into three
separate coves divided by eroded rocky
headlands. Each bay becomes a broad
white strand at low tide, and many people walk across to the offshore islands. Like
the southern resorts, Watamu is inundated
with seaweed at certain times, but the sand
is usually clear from December to April.

Although Watamu is primarily a package
resort, Swahili fishers still moor their dhows
just metres from the sunbathing tourists and
a village of mud-walled houses sits immediately behind the resorts. You're equally likely
to see a herd of goats or an expat sports car
on the main road.

Orientation

Most resorts are south of Watamu, on the
road that runs down to KWS headquarters,
but the Watamu Beach Hotel and the cheap
guesthouses are reached by Beach Way Rd,
which leads down to the old village and is
lined with souvenir stalls. The old village
itself is something of a maze, with unofficial street names in graffiti (look out for
Cash Money Rd and New Bla Bla Bla Rd
2000), but the main track is easy enough
to follow.

Information

There are now no banks in Watamu, so
your only options are the forex bureaus at
the big hotels and Tunda Tours. If you need
to use an ATM, your nearest choices are
in Kilifi or Malindi. The post office is on
the Gede road. Online information can be
found at www.watamu.net.

Corner Connections (Map p199; Watamu Supermarket;
Internet access per min KSh5) Access the Internet here.

Telkom Kenya office (Map p199; Beach Way Rd)

Tunda Tours (Map p199; ☎ 32079; Beach Way Rd;
Internet access per min KSh5)

Sights

BIO KEN SNAKE FARM & LABORATORY

This excellent **snake farm** (Map p202; ☎ 32303;
snakes@africaonline.co.ke; adult/child KSh500/free; ☉ 10am-
noon & 2-5pm) is by far the best of all the snake
parks situated along the coast. The farm
was established by the late James Ashe,
who was a reptile expert and former cura-
tor from the National Museums of Kenya.
Ashe achieved such level of recognition
in his field that he even has a bush viper
named after him.

The farm is a nonprofit organisation,
providing free antivenin wherever it is
needed in Kenya. As well as touring the
facilities, staff can take you on a day safari
to look for snakes in their natural habitat
(KSh4500).

The centre is just north of Watamu village on the main beach road.

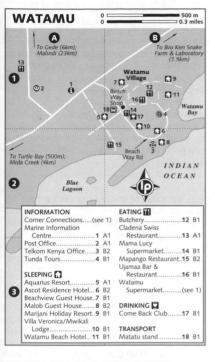

WATAMU

INFORMATION
Corner Connections.....(see 1)
Marine Information
  Centre........................1 A1
Post Office....................2 A1
Telkom Kenya Office.....3 B2
Tunda Tours.................4 B1

SLEEPING
Aquarius Resort.............5 A1
Ascot Residence Hotel... 6 B2
Beachview Guest House.7 B1
Malob Guest House.......8 B2
Marijani Holiday Resort..9 B1
Villa Veronica/Mwikali
  Lodge....................10 B1
Watamu Beach Hotel...11 B1

EATING
Butchery...................12 B1
Cladena Swiss
  Restaurant..............13 A1
Mama Lucy
  Supermarket...........14 B1
Mapango Restaurant.15 B2
Ujamaa Bar &
  Restaurant..............16 B1
Watamu
  Supermarket..........(see 1)

DRINKING
Come Back Club.......17 B1

TRANSPORT
Matatu stand............18 B1

WATAMU MARINE NATIONAL PARK

The southern part of Malindi Marine Reserve, this **marine park** (Map p202; adult/child US$5/2) includes some magnificent coral reefs and abundant fish-life. It lies around 2km offshore from Watamu. To get to the park you'll need to hire a glass-bottomed boat, which is easy enough at the **KWS office** (Map p202; 32393), at the end of the coast road, where you pay the park fees. For marine park trips, boat operators ask anything from KSh1800 to KSh3500 per person, excluding park fees; it's all negotiable.

All the big hotels offer 'goggling' (snorkelling) trips to nonguests for around KSh1500. The best are the snorkel safaris run by zoologist Richard Bennett from the **Turtle Bay Discovery Centre** (Map p202; 32003; adult/child KSh1700/850; 8am-noon & 4-8pm) at Turtle Bay Beach Club.

MIDA CREEK

The extensive mangrove forests around Mida Creek, just south of Watamu, support a huge number of bird species, including the spectacular malachite kingfisher, yellow-billed

stork and African fish eagle. It's paradise for bird-watchers and there is also some good snorkelling and scuba diving at the mouth of the creek.

The head of the creek, the best area for viewing waterbirds, is reached by a dirt road opposite the Mida entrance to the Arabuko Sokoke Forest Reserve. The guides who work out of the reserve can organise guided walks in the mangroves (see p201).

Many people also come here on boat tours (arranged through Watamu hotels), which visit a boardwalk and picnic ground on Sudi Island. Turtle Bay Beach Club's Discovery Centre runs tours for KSh2750 per person.

TURTLES

Several species of marine turtle lay their eggs on the beaches around Watamu and **Watamu Turtle Watch** (Map p202; www.watamuturtles .com), part of the Local Ocean Trust, has set up initiatives with local people to protect these threatened animals. Female turtles lay thousands of eggs here between January and April. Contact the trust's **Marine Information Centre** (Map p199; 32118; paradise@swiftmalindi .com; 9.30am-12.30pm & 2-5pm Mon-Sat) if you're interested in seeing this incredible spectacle or volunteering with local projects.

Activities

DIVING

With the marine park just offshore, diving is popular. **Aqua Ventures** (Map p202; 32420; www .diveinkenya.com), at Ocean Sports Hotel, offers guided dives in the marine park for UK£18 and an open-water PADI dive course for UK£275. The best time to dive and snorkel is between October and March. Avoid diving from June to August because of rough seas and poor visibility. Dive trips to the **Tewa Caves** (Map p202) at the mouth of Mida Creek are popular, where a group of giant rock cod loiter menacingly at the bottom.

DEEP-SEA FISHING

If you want to ape the fish-wrestling antics of Ernest Hemingway, deep-sea fishing is possible at Ocean Sports Hotel and Hemingway's for around UK£540 per boat (high season, up to four anglers). People are a little more environmentally sensitive now than in old Ernie's day – tag and release is standard procedure (see p200).

THE COAST

TAG & BRAG

While the idea of wrestling a huge marlin on the open sea has a powerful macho allure, catches of billfish in the Indian Ocean are getting smaller all the time. The biggest threat to game fish is relentless overfishing by commercial tuna companies, who routinely hook other pelagic fish as so-called 'bycatch'. Pollution and falling stocks of prey species are also having a serious knock-on effect. Some large species are believed to have declined by as much as 80% since the 1970s; sharks are particularly vulnerable.

Instead of bashing some unfortunate fish over the head with a boathook, you can do your bit to help sustain shark and billfish populations by tagging your catch and releasing it back into the ocean. Most deep-sea fishing companies provide anglers with a souvenir photo and official recognition of their catch, then release the fish to fight another day, carrying tags that will allow scientists to discover more about these magnificent predators.

Sleeping

BUDGET & MIDRANGE

Marijani Holiday Resort (Map p199; ☎ 32448; marijani@swiftmalindi.com; s/d €18.50/20.50, cottages €38.50-52) The best place to stay in the village, distinctive coral facing, traditional furnishings, balcony sofas and local art set this very personal guesthouse above any competition. If you read German, you can buy the book describing the owners' adventures setting up home in Kenya. To get here, take the path beside the Mama Lucy supermarket and turn left at the Beach Way Shop.

Ascot Residence Hotel (Map p199; ☎ 32326; info@ ascotresidence.com; Beach Way Rd; s/d KSh1600/2800, apt KSh3500-7000; ⊠) A very comfortable complex of tidy rooms and apartments set in a garden with a dolphin-shaped pool. Security is good and there's a fine pizza restaurant.

Malob Guest House (Map p199; ☎ 32260; Beach Way Rd; s KSh600) Opposite Ascot, Malob is a good small budget choice. Rooms are clean and well looked after, and are set around a peaceful courtyard.

Villa Veronika/Mwikali Lodge (Map p199; ☎ 0735-499836; Beach Way Rd; d KSh600) A friendly and secure family-run lodging. Rooms come with fans, nets and fridges; they're a bit scrappy and don't always have power, but you could do worse. In high season breakfast is available for KSh100. Some rooms get noise from the nearby Come Back Club.

Scuba Diving Watamu (Map p202; ☎ 32099; www .scuba-diving-kenya.com; cottages €29-52; ⊠) No prizes for figuring out what the main line of business is here – luckily for keen self-caterers the German owners also offer accommodation in five charming one- and two-bedroom cottages. Prices include daily cleaning, and cooks are available. There's

also a good café and a separate villa for up to 22 people (€150).

Beachview Guest House (Map p199; ☎ 32383; watamubeachview@yahoo.com; d KSh1500; ⊠) This big block off Beach Way Rd offers spacious stone-floored rooms at pretty reasonable prices.

TOP END

Top-end hotels take up much of the beach frontage along the three coves. Watamu is very seasonal and many of these places are closed from at least May to mid-July.

Turtle Bay Beach Club (Map p202; ☎ 32003; www .turtlebay.co.ke; r per person low season €58-85, high season €93-122; ⊠ ⊠ ⊠ ⊠) At the far end of the cove, Turtle Bay is one of the best resorts of its kind in the area, with palm-planted gardens to disguise the size of the site. There are various classes of rooms here, facilities are excellent and it's particularly strong on kids' entertainment. Loads of excursions are on offer at the community-oriented Discovery Centre, most of which are open to non-guests. Prices quoted are all-inclusive.

Ocean Sports Hotel (Map p202; ☎ 32008; oceansps@ africaonline.co.ke; half board s/d low season US$82/111, high season US$100/160; ⊠ ⊠) A small, informal family-run resort with a deep-sea fishing slant. It's very modest considering the prices, but the atmosphere's very relaxed and the clientele consists mainly of British expats, including local residents who often drop in for a drink. Good cheap snorkelling trips are available here (KSh800).

Hemingways Resort (Map p202; ☎ 32624; www .hemingways.co.ke; half board s/d low season UK£57/82, high season UK£143/203; ⊠ ⊠) Next door to Ocean Sports, this very stately luxury lodge has a strong deep-sea fishing theme (well, duh), snappy service and an exclusive ambi-ence. Loads of activities are possible – prices include free transfers from Malindi airport, snorkelling in the marine park and trips to Malindi and Gede.

Aquarius Resort (Map p199; ☎ 32069; www.aquarius watamu.com; full board s/d low season €64.50/86, high season €78/104; ✇ ✇ ✇) A brand-new place set back from the water. The *makuti*-roofed buildings are set in a lovely garden and there are peaceful communal balconies overlooking the pool. The Mapango Restaurant (Map p199), in a separate compound nearer the beach, is highly recommended.

Watamu Beach Hotel (Map p199) is a posh African Safari Club hotel that takes up most of the northeast peninsula (p346). Watamu's small but persistent posses of touts and taxi drivers hang around opposite the complex entrance.

Eating

As the better hotels cater more than amply for their clients, there's not much of an independent restaurant scene in Watamu, and most places close relatively early.

For local cuisine, several tiny stalls along Beach Way Rd sell ultra-cheap meals of kebabs, chicken, chips, samosas, chapati and the like. KSh150 to KSh200 should be more than enough to fill you up, possibly with a drink thrown in.

Ujamaa Bar & Restaurant (Map p199; mains KSh150-600; ✇ noon-2pm & 5-9pm) A central village eatery with some tourist standards such as steak and spaghetti thrown in to complement the local favourites (and up the prices).

Cladena Swiss Restaurant (Map p199; ☎ 32500; cladena@africaonline.co.ke; mains KSh200-600) It's not often you get a taste of the Alps in coastal Kenya, so if you have a hankering for fondue and sausage this is the place to come. It's also the site restaurant for the self-catering cottages run by the same owners.

For a splurge, try the Sunday lunch buffets at the Ocean Sports Hotel or Hemingway's – the going rate is around KSh1000.

Mama Lucy (Map p199; ☎ 32584; Beach Way Rd) and Watamu (Map p199) supermarkets are handy for self-caterers. There's a good *halal* butchery (Map p199) near the village mosque.

Getting There & Around

There are matatus between Malindi and Watamu throughout the day (KSh50, one hour). All matatus pass the turn-off to the Gede ruins (KSh10).

For Mombasa, the easiest option is to take a matatu to the highway (KSh10) and flag down a bus or matatu from there.

Taxis charge KSh800 to the Gede ruins and KSh1800 to Malindi. There are also a handful of motorised rickshaws, which are cheaper and can be handy for the long beach road; a ride to the KWS office should cost around KSh250.

Bicycles can be hired at various hotels and shops for around KSh60 per hour.

ARABUKO SOKOKE FOREST RESERVE

Close to the marine park at Watamu, **Arabuko Sokoke Forest Reserve** (Map p202; adult/child US$10/5) is the largest tract of indigenous coastal forest remaining in East Africa, with four distinct vegetation zones. Gazetted in 2002 as an International Heritage Site, it's administered jointly by the Forestry Department and KWS, and contains an unusually high concentration of rare species, especially birds (240 species) and butterflies (260 species). A good deal of work has gone into involving the local community in the protection of the forest.

The most high-profile birds here are Clarke's weaver (found nowhere else in the world), the beautiful miniature Sokoke scops owl (only 15cm tall), the east coast akalat, the Sokoke pipit, the Amani sunbird and the spotted ground thrush. The reserve's signature animal is the charming golden-rumped elephant-shrew – amazingly, it's related to the full-sized elephant. You may see its much larger cousin trundling around the forest, as there's a herd of 80 here.

The **Arabuko Sokoke Visitor Centre** (Map p202; Malindi Rd; ☎ 042-32462; ✇ 8am-4pm) is very helpful; it's at Gede Forest Station, with displays on the various species found here. The shop sells the excellent KWS/Forestry Department guide *Arabuko Sokoke Forest & Mida Creek* (KSh300) and Tansy Bliss' *Arabuko-Sokoke Forest – A Visitor's Guide* (KSh120). The noticeboard in the centre shows the sites of recent wildlife sightings.

From the visitor centre, a series of nature trails, running tracks and 4WD paths cut through the forest. There are more bird trails at **Whistling Duck Pools**, reached via the Mida Creek entrance to the reserve, and at **Kararacha Pools** and **Spinetail Way**, located

THE COAST

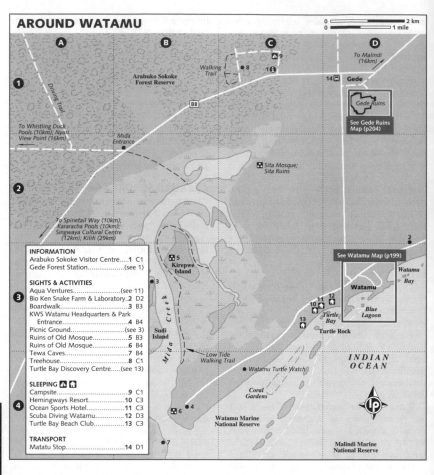

AROUND WATAMU

INFORMATION
Arabuko Sokoke Visitor Centre.....**1** C1
Gede Forest Station..................(see 1)

SIGHTS & ACTIVITIES
Aqua Ventures........................(see 11)
Bio Ken Snake Farm & Laboratory.**2** D2
Boardwalk.............................**3** B3
KWS Watamu Headquarters & Park
    Entrance..........................**4** B4
Picnic Ground.........................(see 3)
Ruins of Old Mosque..................**5** B3
Ruins of Old Mosque..................**6** B4
Tewa Caves...........................**7** B4
Treehouse.............................**8** C1
Turtle Bay Discovery Centre.....(see 13)

SLEEPING
Campsite..............................**9** C1
Hemingways Resort...................**10** C3
Ocean Sports Hotel..................**11** C3
Scuba Diving Watamu..............**12** D3
Turtle Bay Beach Club..............**13** C3

TRANSPORT
Matatu Stop..........................**14** D1

16km further south. Near Kararacha is the **Singwaya Cultural Centre**, where traditional dances can be arranged.

Trained bird and wildlife **guides** (☎ 0734-994931) can be hired at KSh600 for up to three hours, KSh1200 for a full day and KSh800 for a half day or a highly recommended night walk (leaving the visitor centre at 6pm). They're very knowledgeable about the forest, and also offer walks in Mida Creek on the opposite side of the highway.

There are basic **campsites** (per person US$8) close to the visitor centre and further south near Spinetail Way. With permission, camping is also allowed deeper within the forest or at the **treehouse** by Sand Quarry. (Acro-

batic nymphomaniacs take note: a painted warning prohibits sex here!)

The forest is just off the main Malindi–Mombasa road. The main gate to the forest and visitor centre is about 1.5km west of the turn-off to Gede and Watamu, while the Mida entrance is about 3km further south. All buses and matatus between Mombasa and Malindi can drop you at either entrance. From Watamu, matatus to Malindi can drop you at the main junction.

GEDE RUINS

Some 4km from Watamu, just off the main Malindi–Mombasa road, are the famous **Gede ruins** (adult/child KSh200/100; ☼ 7am-6pm), one of the principal historical monuments on the coast. Hidden away in the forest is a vast complex of derelict houses, palaces and mosques, made all the more mysterious by the fact that there seem to be no records of Gede's existence in any historical texts.

Gede (or Gedi) was established and actively trading by at least the 13th century. Excavations have uncovered Ming Chinese porcelain and glass and glazed earthenware from Persia, indicating not only trade links, but a taste for luxury among Gede's Swahili elite. Within the compound are ruins of ornate tombs and mosques and the regal ruins of a Swahili palace, further evidence of Gede's prosperity.

The city was inexplicably abandoned in the 17th or 18th century. The current wisdom is that a series of events weakened the city-state, including disease, guerrilla attacks by the Galla tribe from Somalia and the cannibalistic Zimba people from near Malawi, punitive expeditions from rival city Mombasa and the removal of the sheikh of Malindi by the Portuguese in 1593. Then again, the reason could simply be that Gede ran out of water – at some stage the water table here dropped rapidly and none of the wells at Gede today contain water.

Whatever the reason for Gede's abandonment, the forest took over and the site was lost to the world until the 1920s. Since then, there have been extensive excavations, revealing the remains of substantial Swahili houses and complex sanitation facilities, including toilets and cisterns for ritual washing. The toilets are particularly impressive, consisting of paired cubicles containing a squat toilet and a stand for a washbasin. All the buildings here were constructed of coral rag, coral lime and earth, and some have pictures incised into the plaster finish of their walls.

Two walls surround the site, the inner one of which may have divided the wealthier, ruling-class section of town from the rest of the populace. Another theory is that it was built to enclose a smaller area after the city was temporarily abandoned in the 15th or 16th century. Most of the excavated buildings are concentrated in a dense cluster near the entrance gate, but there are dozens of other ruins scattered through the forest.

Walking Tour

The tree-shrouded ruins are very atmospheric and you will often have the site to yourself if you visit early in the morning. Guides are available at the gate for KSh300; they definitely help bring the site to life, pointing out the various trees and plants as well as interesting features of the buildings, but will generally stick to a standard circuit of the most important ruins. If you want to see the whole 45-acre site you'll either have to be insistent or go round by yourself. Be a little careful if you choose the latter, as there are dozens of deep wells here.

Gedi – Historical Monument (KSh50), a guidebook to the ruins with a map and descriptions of many of the buildings, should be available at the ticket office or the museum shop.

On your right as you enter the compound is the **Dated Tomb (1)**, so called because of the inscription on the wall, featuring the Muslim date corresponding to 1399. This tomb has provided a reference point for dating other buildings within the complex. Near it, inside the wall, is the **Tomb of the Fluted Pillar (2)**, which is characteristic of such pillar designs found along the East African coast. The tomb is largely intact and was once decorated with ceramic dishes and coral bosses.

Past the tomb, next to the **House of the Long Court (3)**, the **Great Mosque (4)** is one of Gede's most significant buildings. It originally dates from the mid-15th century but was rebuilt a century later, possibly after damage sustained at the time of Gede's first abandonment. The mosque is of typical East African design with a *mihrab* or echo-chamber facing Mecca. You can see where porcelain bowls were once mounted in the walls flanking the *mihrab*. On the edge of

---

TOILET DIPLOMACY?

One intriguing feature of the palace at Gede is the antechamber where distinguished guests are believed to have waited for a personal audience with the town's ruler. Not only is it small and narrow, but the vent in the inside wall leads directly to the ruler's personal toilet, which has no other ventilation! You can just visualise the poor visiting dignitaries shifting uncomfortably on the stone benches as the noises and smells of a higher power wafted over them – surely a political master stroke…

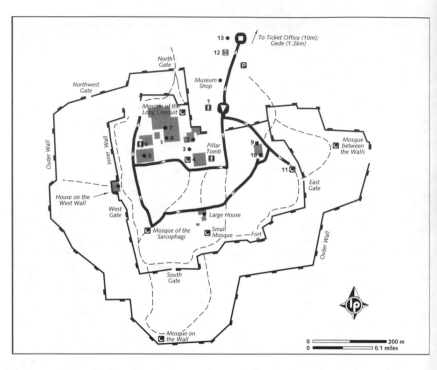

the mosque is a ritual washing area, served by a conduit from a nearby well.

Behind the mosque are the ruins of an extensive **palace (5)** spread out over a quarter of an acre and thought to have been owned by the former ruler of Gede. This regal structure is entered through a complete arched doorway and many of its interesting features have been preserved, including the great audience hall and a strongroom with no doors or windows, used to store valuables (the only entry would have been a small hatch high up in the wall). Beside the palace is an annexe believed to be the Women's Quarters, consisting of four apartments with private courtyards built later than the main structure.

Some of the walls contain square niches used for oil lamps, and there's also a well-preserved Swahili toilet. One of the most interesting things found within the ruins was an earthenware jar containing a *fingo* or charm, thought to attract *djinns* (guardian spirits) who would drive trespassers insane. The palace also has a particularly fine **pillar tomb (6)**; its hexagonal shape is unique in East Africa.

Following the path past the tomb, around 11 old **Swahili houses (7)** have been excavated here, in a compact group beside the Great Mosque and the palace. They're each named after particular features of their design, or after objects found in them by archaeologists. The **House of the Cistern (8)** is particularly interesting, with ancient illustrations incised into the plaster walls. Like most houses at Gede, these dwellings follow a traditional Swahili pattern, with a reception court at the front and separate living quarters for the master of the house and his wives.

The other excavations on the site are more spread out, with numerous paths running through the woods from the main complex. Some of he most interesting structures are east of the Great Mosque, including the **House of the Dhow (9)**, the **House of the Double Court (10)** and the nearby **Mosque of the Three Aisles (11)**, which has the largest well at Gede. There are a handful of other structures in the forest if you wish to explore further.

As you head back out past the car park, there's a small **museum (12)** and 'interpretation centre' with displays of artefacts found on the site, although the best stuff was taken to the Fort Jesus museum in Mombasa.

Other Attractions
Right by the entrance to the Gede complex is the **Kipepeo butterfly farm** (**13**; ☎ 32380; nonresident adult/child KSh100/50; ☻ 8am-5pm), named for the Swahili word for butterfly. It was set up by a zoologist from the University of Nairobi. Locals are paid to collect live pupae from the Arabuko Sokoke Forest Reserve, which are hatched into butterflies and sold to foreign collectors and live exhibits in the UK and USA. The money is then ploughed back into conservation of the forests.

Getting There & Away
The ruins lie just off the main highway near the village of Gede, on the access road to Watamu. The easiest way to get here is to take a Watamu-bound matatu to Gede Village and follow the well-signposted dirt road from there – it's a 10-minute walk.

It's also possible to get a taxi to take you on a round trip from Malindi for about KSh1000, with an hour or more to look around the site. This could be worthwhile if your time is limited.

MALINDI & AROUND
☎ 042
Malindi is one of those holiday towns that inspire wildly opposite reactions in people. For many, especially Italians, this is their Kenyan beach paradise and even their adopted home, defended with the unswerving loyalty of a shrine; for others it's a cynical tourist trap with few redeeming features, at best a transport hub for Lamu. If you're new to Africa the high-season hassle may well incline you towards the latter angle, but it would be a shame to dismiss Malindi out of hand, and once you get under its skin you may well find there's more to the town than pizzas and sunloungers.

The Swahili city-state of Malindi had its heyday in the 14th century, when it often rivalled Mombasa and Paté for control of this part of the East African coast. An important trading post, it attracted shipping from as far afield as China, and was one of the few places on the coast to offer a friendly welcome to the early Portuguese mariners.

From a tourist perspective, modern Malindi is all about the beaches, with little in the way of cultural attractions. Offshore are the coral reefs of the Malindi Marine National Park, one of Kenya's best marine parks, with plenty of opportunities for snorkelling and diving.

The town is best visited during the high season, from August to January, and it can often seem pretty dead if you visit outside these times.

Orientation
The actual centre of Malindi is the area around the old market on Uhuru Rd; the tourist accommodation, restaurants and malls are spread out north and south along the coast. Mama Ngina Rd (which is also known as Government Rd, Vasco da Gama Rd, Sea Front Rd or Ocean View Rd on certain sections) provides access to the resorts south of the town, while the KWS headquarters is at the south end of parallel Casuarina Rd. The big shopping arcades and restaurant complexes are north of the centre on Lamu Rd.

Information
EMERGENCY
Ambulance (☎ 30575)
Fire (☎ 31001, 0733-550990)
Police (☎ 31555; Kenyatta Rd)

INTERNET ACCESS
Bling Net (☎ 30041; Lamu Rd; per min KSh2) Also does food.
Dragonbyte (☎ 30778; dragonbyte@swiftmalindi.com; Malindi Complex, Lamu Rd; per min KSh2)
Inter-Communications (☎ 31310; Lamu Rd; per min KSh1; ☻ 8am-11pm)
Telephone Solutions (☎ 30782; Sabaki Centre, Lamu Rd; per min KSh2)
Y-Net (☎ 30171; y-netinternational@yahoo.com; Stanchart Arcade, Lamu Rd; per min KSh2)

MONEY
Barclays Bank (☎ 20656; Lamu Rd)
Dollar Forex Bureau (☎ 30602; Lamu Rd) Rates may be slightly better here than at the banks.
Kenya Commercial Bank (☎ 20148; Lamu Rd) With ATM (accepts Visa cards).
Postbank (Malindi Complex, Lamu Rd)
Standard Chartered Bank (Stanchart Arcade, Lamu Rd) With ATM (accepts Visa cards).

POST
Post office (Kenyatta Rd)

MALINDI

0 _____ 500 m
0 _____ 0.3 miles

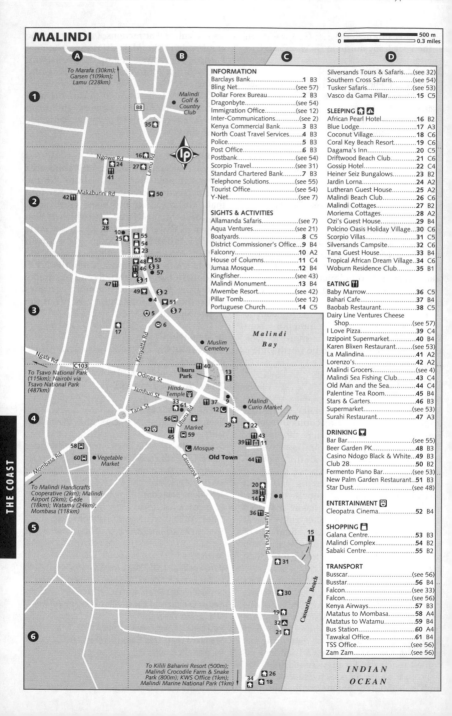

INFORMATION
Barclays Bank	**1** B3
Bling Net	(see 57)
Dollar Forex Bureau	**2** B3
Dragonbyte	(see 54)
Immigration Office	(see 12)
Inter-Communications	(see 2)
Kenya Commercial Bank	**3** B3
North Coast Travel Services	**4** B3
Police	**5** B3
Post Office	**6** B3
Postbank	(see 54)
Scorpio Travel	(see 31)
Standard Chartered Bank	**7** B3
Telephone Solutions	(see 55)
Tourist Office	(see 54)
Y-Net	(see 7)

SIGHTS & ACTIVITIES
Allamanda Safaris	(see 7)
Aqua Ventures	(see 21)
Boatyards	**8** C5
District Commissioner's Office	**9** B4
Falconry	**10** A2
House of Columns	**11** C4
Jumaa Mosque	**12** B4
Kingfisher	(see 43)
Malindi Monument	**13** B4
Mwembe Resort	(see 42)
Pillar Tomb	(see 12)
Portuguese Church	**14** C5

SLEEPING
Silversands Tours & Safaris	(see 32)
Southern Cross Safaris	(see 54)
Tusker Safaris	(see 53)
Vasco da Gama Pillar	**15** C5

African Pearl Hotel	**16** B2
Blue Lodge	**17** A3
Coconut Village	**18** C6
Coral Key Beach Resort	**19** C6
Dagama's Inn	**20** C5
Driftwood Beach Club	**21** C6
Gossip Hotel	**22** C4
Heiner Seiz Bungalows	**23** B2
Jardin Lorna	**24** A2
Lutheran Guest House	**25** A2
Malindi Beach Club	**26** C6
Malindi Cottages	**27** B2
Moriema Cottages	**28** A2
Ozi's Guest House	**29** B4
Polcino Oasis Holiday Village	**30** C6
Scorpio Villas	**31** C5
Silversands Campsite	**32** C6
Tana Guest House	**33** B4
Tropical African Dream Village	**34** C6
Woburn Residence Club	**35** B1

EATING
Baby Marrow	**36** C5
Bahari Cafe	**37** B4
Baobab Restaurant	**38** C5
Dairy Line Ventures Cheese Shop	(see 57)
I Love Pizza	**39** C4
Izzipoint Supermarket	**40** B4
Karen Blixen Restaurant	(see 53)
La Malindina	**41** A2
Lorenzo's	**42** A2
Malindi Grocers	(see 4)
Malindi Sea Fishing Club	**43** B4
Old Man and the Sea	**44** C4
Palentine Tea Room	**45** B4
Stars & Garters	**46** B3
Supermarket	(see 53)
Surahi Restaurant	**47** A3

DRINKING
Bar Bar	(see 55)
Beer Garden PK	**48** B3
Casino Ndogo Black & White	**49** B3
Club 28	**50** B2
Fermento Piano Bar	(see 53)
New Palm Garden Restaurant	**51** B3
Star Dust	(see 48)

ENTERTAINMENT
Cleopatra Cinema	**52** B4

SHOPPING
Galana Centre	**53** B3
Malindi Complex	**54** B2
Sabaki Centre	**55** B2

TRANSPORT
Busscar	(see 56)
Busstar	**56** B4
Falcon	(see 33)
Falcon	(see 56)
Kenya Airways	**57** B3
Matatus to Mombasa	**58** A4
Matatus to Watamu	**59** B4
Bus Station	**60** A4
Tawakal Office	**61** B4
TSS Office	(see 56)
Zam Zam	(see 56)

To Marafa (30km);
Garsen (109km);
Lamu (228km)

Malindi Golf & Country Club

B8

Ngowe Rd

Makaburini Rd

Lamu Rd

Ngala Rd

C103

To Tsavo National Park (115km); Nairobi via Tsavo National Park (487km)

Kenyatta Rd

Odinga St

Jamhun St

Tana St

Mombasa Rd

To Malindi Handicrafts Cooperative (2km); Malindi Airport (2km); Gede (18km); Watamu (24km); Mombasa (118km)

Muslim Cemetery

Malindi Bay

Uhuru Park

Hindu Temple

Uhuru Rd

Market

Mosque

Vegetable Market

Malindi Curio Market

Jetty

Old Town

Casuarina Rd

Mama Ngina Rd

Casuarina Beach

INDIAN OCEAN

To Kilili Bahari Resort (500m); Malindi Crocodile Farm & Snake Park (800m); KWS Office (1km); Malindi Marine National Park (1km)

THE COAST

TOURIST INFORMATION
Tourist office (☎ 20689; Malindi Complex, Lamu Rd; ☺ 8am-12.30pm & 2-4.30pm Mon-Fri) Staff here are friendly but really don't have much information to dispense.

TRAVEL AGENCIES
North Coast Travel Services (☎ 30312; ncts@ swiftmalindi.com; Lamu Rd)

Scorpio Travel (☎ 21250; scorpio@swiftmalindi.com; Scorpio Villas, Mama Ngina Rd)

VISA EXTENSIONS
Immigration office (☎ 30876; Mama Ngina Rd) Note that travellers seeking visa extensions are often referred to Mombasa.

Dangers & Annoyances
Don't walk back to your hotel along the beach at night. In the past many people have been mugged, although there haven't been any incidents lately. The long, dark walk from the north end of town to the resorts south of the centre should also be avoided at night.

Beach boys are a fact of life and, as well as sex and souvenirs, drugs are widely offered. This is often part of a sting in which phoney policemen appear, confiscate the drugs and extract a large 'fine'. Drugs *are* illegal here, and being ripped off is nothing compared to what will happen if you are arrested by a bona fide cop – either way, it isn't worth the risk.

Sights & Activities
HOUSE OF COLUMNS
One of a handful of traditional Swahili houses left in Malindi, the recently restored **House of Columns** (Mama Ngina Rd) contains the new **Malindi museum** (adult/child KSh200/100; ☺ 8am-6pm), a fairly haphazard collection of pictures, objects and exhibits covering the region's past and present. So far it hasn't made the most of the space, but the poster displays on Vasco da Gama and Islam are interesting, there's a multilingual reference library and the curators will doubtless grow into their role.

PORTUGUESE CHURCH
The tiny thatched **Portuguese church** (Mama Ngina Rd; admission KSh200) is so called because Vasco da Gama is reputed to have erected it, and two of his crew are supposedly buried here. This may or may not be the case, but it's certainly true that St Francis Xavier

visited on his way to India. The rest of the compound is taken up by the graves of Catholic missionaries.

JUMAA MOSQUE
Opposite the boat jetty on the seafront is the town's principal mosque, and the remains of the ancient **Jumaa Mosque and Palace** (Mama Ngina Rd). Within the compound is a large pillar tomb; non-Muslims are not allowed to enter, but you may be able to catch a glimpse when approaching from the north.

MONUMENTS
Malindi's most famous monument, although it isn't particularly impressive, is the bell-shaped **Vasco da Gama Pillar**, erected by the Portuguese explorer as a navigational aid in 1498. The coral pillar is topped by a cross made of Lisbon stone, which almost certainly dates from da Gama's time, and stands on the rocks at the northern end of Casuarina Beach. From the rocks there are good views along the coast. To get here, follow the signs from the alley beside Scorpio Villas (p210).

Even less spectacular is the **Malindi Monument**, a white concrete sail erected in 1960 to commemorate Henry the Navigator and Vasco da Gama's Swahili guide Ahmed Ibn Majid. It was originally visible from the sea, which is hard to imagine now. The **District Commissioner's Office**, one of the oldest buildings in town, is nearby.

MALINDI MARINE NATIONAL PARK
Immediately offshore from Malindi and extending south as far as Watamu, this important **marine park** (adult/child US$5/2; ☺ 7am-7pm) covers 213 sq km and protects some impressive coral reefs, although the piles of seashells on sale in Malindi may make you wonder just how much that protection is worth.

Despite the extensive damage there is still some amazing marine life here, and there's always a chance you may see megafauna such as whale sharks and mako sharks. Note that underwater visibility is severely reduced by silt from the Galana River between March and June.

Most people visit on a snorkelling or glass-bottomed boat trip, which can be arranged at the **KWS office** (☎ 31554; malindimnp@kws.org) on the coast road south of town. Boats only

THE COAST

go out at low tide, so it's a good idea to call in advance to check times. The going rate is around KSh3500 per boat (five to ten people) for a two-hour trip, and masks and snorkels are provided. Alternatively, you can take a tour with any of the agencies in town.

The use of fins (flippers) is discouraged as there has been lots of damage caused by inexperienced snorkellers. Walking atop the reef at low tide also does irreparable damage and should be avoided.

The KWS compound sits on a lovely stretch of beach and there's a KWS campsite and bandas (opposite). You can also charge national park smartcards here for trips to Tsavo East and West.

MALINDI CROCODILE FARM & SNAKE PARK

This commercial **crocodile farm** (☎ 20121; non-resident adult/child US$5/2; ☼ 9am-5.30pm) is just off the main road leading to the marine park, and the crocs obligingly engage in a feeding frenzy at 4pm every Wednesday and Friday. Kids are more likely than adults to enjoy the spectacle without making the link between the smiling reptiles in the pens and the belts and wallets on sale in the foyer…

FALCONRY

Malindi's **falconry** (☎ 0722-346491; adult/child KSh300/150; ☼ 9am-5.30pm), near the town centre, has a number of caged birds of prey and a late-opening bar-restaurant. The displays can be dramatic, but the drab atmosphere's a bit depressing.

DIVING

With the marine park just offshore, scuba diving is a popular activity, although, as mentioned, the visibility is greatly reduced by silt between March and June. All the big hotels have dive centres, usually run in conjunction with local companies. Single dives cost €40 plus the park entry fee, while a PADI open-water diver course will cost around €330.

Main operators:

Aqua Ventures (☎ 32420; www.diveinkenya.com; Driftwood Beach Club)

Blue Fin (☎ 0722-261242; www.bluefindiving.com) Operates out of several resorts in Malindi.

DEEP-SEA FISHING

As you might expect with all the Hemingway allusions, deep-sea fishing is popular.

Kingfisher (☎ 31275; Mama Ngina Rd), below the Malindi Sea Fishing Club, is one of the best places on the coast to find a cheap, private deep-sea fishing charter. It has a large fleet of boats and charges US$350 for a 'short day' of around six hours (up to four anglers). You can also ask around the boatyard for cheaper local crews. Tag and release is recommended in all cases (see p200).

Tours

Numerous safari companies operate from Malindi to Tsavo East National Park, entering the park via the Sala Gate. The going rate for a day trip is US$120 per person. Trips to the Malindi Marine National Park are also a standard option (US$20).

Reliable companies include the following:

Allamanda Safaris (☎ 31272; allamanda@swiftmalindi .com; Stanchart Arcade, Lamu Rd)

Silversands Tours & Safaris (☎ 30014; Mama Ngina Rd)

Southern Cross Safaris (☎ 30547; sxsmld@swiftmalindi .com; Malindi Complex, Lamu Rd)

Tusker Safaris (☎ 30525; tuskersaf@swiftmalindi.com; AG Complex, Lamu Rd) Can organise transport to the Marafa Depression (US$25 per vehicle).

Sleeping

BUDGET

Tana Guest House (☎ 30940; Jamhuri St; s/d/tr KSh550/ 550/650, s/d with shared bathroom KSh350/450) Just round the corner from the market area, this is a severely convenient location for buses and cheap food. Rooms are decent for the price, with fans, nets, squat toilets and what appear to be changing rooms. You can buy day-old chicks at reception, if you so wish.

Lutheran Guest House (☎ 30098; tw KSh1000, tw/ tr/q with shared bathroom KSh800/1200/1500, bungalows KSh1500) The Lutheran religious centre, set in a quiet garden near the falconry, provides accommodation to travellers of all persuasions. The simple rooms have fans, nets and little else; the bungalows have living rooms and kitchens. Alcohol is prohibited here.

Dagama's Inn (☎ 31942; Mama Ngina Rd; s/d KSh600/800) Big, bare doubles and smaller singles in a modern block, now under new management, with a decent Indian restaurant downstairs (mains KSh190 to KSh495). Only one room has a fan, but there's plenty of breeze through the slatted walls.

Blue Lodge (☎ 30246; s/d KSh350/400, s with shared bathroom KSh300) On the dirt streets behind

Lamu Rd, this is a basic but acceptable budget option away from the bustle of the town centre.

KWS compound (☎ 31554; Casuarina Beach; campsites adult/child US$8/5, bandas per person KSh600) KWS provides a shady campsite, with lights and a cooking area, and eight popular bandas. Water and bedding are provided and there's a kitchen and mess hall you can use for KSh300. Mountain bikes can be hired for KSh200 per day.

Silversands Campsite (☎ 20412; campsites adult/child KSh200/100, bandas KSh500-600) On the southern beach strip, this is a much-loved site for travellers. There are good facilities but limited shade. The simple tented bandas have recently been fully refurbished. Bicycles can be rented for KSh200 per day.

MIDRANGE

There are relatively few places in this price range. All rates are for high season and include breakfast.

African Pearl Hotel (☎ 0733-966167; www.african pearl.com; Lamu Rd; s/d from KSh1800/2200, cottages KSh2000-4500; 🐾 🛒) Blessed with a personal touch, this is the kind of pearl that's worth shuckin' a few shellfish for. Rooms are spacious, all with their own balconies, and foregoing air-con to get an atmospheric wood-panelled fan room is no hardship. Self-catering facilities are available for longer stays.

Ozi's Guest House (☎ 20218; ozi@swiftmalindi.com; Mama Ngina Rd; s/d/tr with shared bathroom KSh600/1200/1800) Barely out of the budget category, this friendly hostelry is a travellers' favourite, though with the mosque right next door light sleepers may want to start praying.

Jardin Lorna (☎ 30658; harry@swiftmalindi.com; Mtangani Rd; r KSh2500-3500; 🐾 🛒) Don't be fooled by the French *nom de plume* – Lorna is very unpretentious, providing accommodation mainly for students of the Hospitality Training and Management Institute. Rooms are endearingly quirky, zebra rugs and local art punctuate the interior, and the large family room even has a panic button! The restaurant (p210) is also very good.

Heiner Seiz Bungalows (☎ 20978; Lamu Rd; s/d KSh1400/1600; 🐾 🛒) These quiet German-run cottages are subdivided into unfancy but well-kept rooms with fridges. Some kitchens are also available to guests.

Moriema Cottages (☎ 31326; s/d KSh1400/2500) These large cottage-style rooms are a pretty good deal, but whoever thought of putting in carpets and dull green furnishings was way off the mark aesthetically. They're tucked away in a quaint garden behind the Sabaki shopping centre.

Polcino Oasis Holiday Village (☎ 31995; oasis@ africaonline.co.ke; Mama Ngina Rd; apts €28-39; 🐾 🛒) A vast but crumbling four-storey *makuti*-roofed apartment block on the southern beach strip, surrounding a truly enormous pool. The shopping arcade has a pizzeria and a good ice-cream parlour.

Gossip Hotel (☎ 0723-516602; Mama Ngina Rd; s/d KSh700/1200) Just down from Ozi's, the Gossip aims for much the same backpacker clientele. Rooms have four-poster nets, dark wood and plastic chairs, and the downstairs restaurant boasts an intriguing TV lounge/junk corner. A couple of rooms share bathrooms, but prices are the same.

Malindi Cottages (☎ 21071; malindicottages@yahoo .com; Lamu Rd; r KSh1500, cottages KSh3000; 🛒) Looking at the terrible 1970s curtains, the seatless toilets, the dodgy kitchenettes and the dank (or empty) pool, you'd have to say this place was a touch overpriced. Still, the rooms themselves are liveable, and at least there's a couple of swings for the kiddies.

TOP END

Malindi experienced a phenomenal tourist boom in the 1980s and has received regular cash injections from Italian tour operators. As a result, there are fancy resorts all along the beachfront both north and south of the town centre, stretching all the way to the marine park. The hotels south of town open right onto a wonderful stretch of beach, but those north of the centre are separated from the ocean by a wide swathe of dunes.

Unless otherwise stated, the following rates include breakfast. Note that most of these places close or scale down operations between April and June or July.

Tropical African Dream Village (☎ 31673; www .planhotel.ch; Casuarina Rd; s/d/tr low season from €94/130/175, high season from €116/160/216; 🐾 🖳 🛒 🐾) This place consists of three resorts around the intersection of Mama Ngina and Casuarina Rds. The Tropical African Dream Village section is a rather grand complex of *makuti*-roofed plantation-style houses, with a soaring multi-level bar and restaurant. Around the corner, the fancy Malindi Beach Club section has a glorious Swahili doorway and accommodation in stylish Moorish cottages, while the cheaper Coconut Village is a more predictable collection of *makuti*-roofed villas.

Kilili Baharini Resort (☎ 20169; www.kililibaharini .com; Casuarina Rd; half board s/d from US$153/182; 🞐 🞐) This is a splendid Italian resort, with flamboyant decor and Swahili beds set all over the complex so you can read and catch the sea breeze. It fronts directly onto the sand, and the light, spacious rooms are clustered in small groups around attractive pools.

Coral Key Beach Resort (☎ 30717; www.coralkey malindi.com; Mama Ngina Rd; s/d low season from €23/31, high season from €44/58; 🞐 🞐 🞐 🞐) A huge mass-tourism resort catering particularly for young Italians. It's very lively, with activities such as water-volleyball and a climbing wall. Rooms are divided into groups within five themed areas, each block with its own separate pool, which adds up to a *lot* of water. The Sporting Club has the best design.

Driftwood Beach Club (☎ 20155; www.driftwood club.com; Mama Ngina Rd; s/d/tr KSh5300/7600/9120, cottages KSh16,500; 🞐 🞐 🞐) One of the best-known resorts in Malindi, Driftwood prides itself on an informal atmosphere and attracts a more independent clientele than many of its peers. The restaurant, bar and other facilities are all open to nonguests for a temporary membership fee of KSh200 per day.

Woburn Residence Club (☎ 31085; www.woburn residencemalindi.com; s/d from €79.20/104, apt low season €152-232, high season €190-290; 🞐 🞐) If you're not bothered about direct beach access, this swish complex offers pristine modern rooms and apartments with giant marble bathrooms and the smart Two Dolphins restaurant (mains KSh450 to KSh850).

Scorpio Villas (☎ 20194; s/d low season €26.40/48, high season €41.80/76; 🞐 🞐) Villa-type accommodation set in dense, well-tended tropical gardens with three pools, a restaurant and a travel agent. The beds are huge and lovely Silversands Beach is just 50m from the gate. Staff aren't always as service-oriented as they could be, though.

Eating
KENYAN & SWAHILI
For those on a budget (or just bored of pasta), there are some good Swahili places in the old part of town. Many of these places close during the month of Ramadan.

Palentine Tea Room (☎ 31412; Uhuru Rd; mains KSh60-140; 🖳) A recommended all-hours Muslim canteen opposite the old market, serving stews, curries, pilau and soups in tiled surroundings. It's friendly and almost always busy.

Baobab Restaurant (☎ 31699; Mama Ngina Rd; KSh250-600) On the seafront near the boatyards, Baobab is reasonably popular and offers decent Western and African food and beers.

Bahari Cafe (Mama Ngina Rd; meals KSh70-220) Close to the souvenir shops at Uhuru Park, Bahari is a bright little fast-food café serving biryanis.

Stars & Garters (☎ 31336; Lamu Rd; mains KSh190-300; 🕑 24hr) A large *makuti*-roofed bar with pool tables, cable TV, beers and a quite reasonable menu offering all the usual grills and spills.

WESTERN/ITALIAN
Old Man and the Sea (☎ 31106; Mama Ngina Rd; mains KSh300-590, seafood KSh550-1100) Definitely the daddy of Malindi's restaurants, this old Moorish house on the seafront has no competition in its class. The food's superb, service is attentive, you can get decent wine by the glass (KSh110) and the guestbook is entertaining reading – apparently Tupac Shakur returned from the grave to eat here. A 16% VAT charge is added to the bill.

Jardin Lorna Restaurant (☎ 30658; Mtangani Rd; mains KSh150-550) Amid the trees and obsolete beer pumps, this peaceful garden restaurant serves up a limited but unusual selection of French, Italian and African dishes, from standard grills to 'Chinese fondue' (beef with a range of sauces). Lobster starts at KSh600, which is pretty good value.

Malindi Sea Fishing Club (☎ 30550; Mama Ngina Rd; mains KSh240-400; 🕑 noon-8pm) A popular hang-out for the deep-sea fishing crowd. The walls feature some huge stuffed sharks and billfish in dramatic poses. The seafood is excellent. It's a great place for a sundown beer, but it closes early and you have to pay a KSh100 temporary membership fee.

I Love Pizza (☎ 20672; Mama Ngina Rd; nwright@ africaonline.co.ke; pizzas KSh300-550, mains from KSh600) A very popular Italian restaurant on the seafront, full of diners pointedly ignoring the cringeworthy name. Luckily the pizzas are excellent.

Baby Marrow (☎ 0733-542584; Mama Ngina Rd; mains KSh350-800) Everything about this place is quirkily stylish, from the thatched veranda and the plant-horse to the Italian-based menu and the tasty seafood (KSh1400 to KSh1800). We're hoping the 'titramisu' is a misprint though.

Karen Blixen Restaurant (☎ 0733-974756; celty3@ yahoo.it; Galana Centre, Lamu Rd; mains KSh600-950) A fine (wait for it…) Italian terrace restaurant hinting at Art Deco style. The menu has all the usual and an added dose of Chinese, seafood and grill dishes, plus crocodile and warthog (!) for KSh1000. It's also good for a morning cappuccino.

Surahi Restaurant (☎ 30452; mains KSh270-370) What, no spaghetti? Break the habit with an Indian meal at this big restaurant, which has a variable menu and a particularly good range of naan and *paratha* (Indian flatbread). It's down a long, bumpy dirt track off Lamu Rd, and sadly seems to go to pieces slightly outside high season.

In the network of streets behind Lamu Rd are two very upmarket Italian restaurants, **La Malindina** (☎ 20045; www.malindina.com in Italian) and **Lorenzo's** (☎ 31758; Mwembe Resort, Makaburini Rd). Both are open from 9pm in high season only, and serve set meals for around KSh2000. Lorenzo's is part of the private Mwembe Resort, off Lamu Rd, while La Malindina is just around the corner from Jardin Lorna.

SELF-CATERING
The following are useful outlets:
Dairy Line Ventures Cheese Shop (☎ 31264; Lamu Rd)
Izzipoint supermarket (☎ 30652; Uhuru Rd)
Malindi Grocers (☎ 20886; Lamu Rd)
Supermarket (Galana Centre, Lamu Rd)

Drinking & Entertainment
BARS & CLUBS
Bar Bar (Sabaki Centre, Lamu Rd) A perennially popular high-season courtyard bar, restaurant and ice-cream parlour with nonstop Italian cable TV in the background. For a snack lunch, the panini and foccacia are recommended.

Fermento Piano Bar (☎ 31780; Galana Centre, Lamu Rd; admission KSh200; ⌚ from 10pm Wed, Fri & Sat; ⚼) 'For those of the night' – Fermento has the town's hippest dance floor, apparently once frequented by Naomi Campbell. It's young, trendy and Italian, so wear your showiest outfit. Morgan's Bar, part of Fermento, is a ritzy cocktail joint with

a very well-tended bar (cocktails KSh300 to KSh800).

Casino Ndogo Black & White (☎ 0724-236476; Lamu Rd; admission KSh100; ⌚ 24hr) A typical semi-open *makuti* bar-club with regular live Congolese lingala bands.

Many tourist bars on Lamu Rd can seem like they're just glorified pick-up joints for prostitutes; **Beer Garden PK** (Lamu Rd) and **New Palm Garden Restaurant** (Lamu Rd) could be put in this category, though things may lighten up a little out of season.

The main nightclubs outside the resorts are **Star Dust** (Lamu Rd) and **Club 28** (Lamu Rd), which open erratically out of season but are generally rammed when they do. As with the bars above, you can expect plenty of unwanted attention.

CINEMAS
Cleopatra Cinema (Casuarina Rd; admission KSh20) This small cinema screens Indian blockbusters and English, Italian and Spanish premier-league football (soccer).

Shopping
There are numerous posh souvenir shops and a curio market along Uhuru Rd and Mama Ngina Rd near the old town. Avoid the shell vendors around Uhuru Park – the shells on sale here are mostly plundered from the national park.

Malindi Handicrafts Cooperative (☎ 30248) Another good place to buy handicrafts is this community project found on the outskirts of Malindi. The cooperative employs numerous local artisans, and the woodcarvings are of a high quality. To get there, turn off the main road to Mombasa near the BP petrol station; you'll find the centre 2km along a dirt road, just opposite the community clinic.

Getting There & Away
AIR
Airkenya (☎ 30646; Malindi Airport) has daily afternoon/evening flights to Nairobi (US$85, 1¼ hours). **Kenya Airways** (☎ 20237; Lamu Rd) flies the same route at least once a day (from KSh4010).

Mombasa Air Safari (☎ 041-433061) has daily flights to Mombasa (US$21, 25 minutes) and Lamu (US$62, 30 minutes) in high season; booking in Malindi is through **Southern Cross Safaris** (☎ 30547; Malindi Complex, Lamu Rd).

THE COAST

BUS & MATATU

The new bus station on Mombasa Rd is currently only used by Mombasa Raha (Mombasa Liners), which has numerous daily buses to Mombasa (KSh150, two hours). Metro Mombasa buses and Mombasa matatus (KSh100 to KSh150) stop at the road stage near here.

Companies such as Busstar, Busscar, TSS and Falcon have offices opposite the old market in the centre of Malindi. All have daily departures to Nairobi at around 7am and/or 7pm (KSh800, 10 to 12 hours), going via Mombasa.

Matatus to Watamu (KSh50, one hour) leave from the old market in town and also stop at the Mombasa stage.

Thanks to improvements on the Malindi–Garissa road, taking a bus to Lamu is an easier and safer proposition than a few years ago, though buses are still accompanied by armed guards for some of the way. Among the various companies offering services, Tawakal buses leave at 8.30am, Falcon at 8.45am and Zam Zam at 10.30am; the fare is KSh300 to KSh400. The journey takes at least four hours between Malindi and the jetty at Mokowe. The ferry to Lamu from the mainland costs KSh50 and takes about 20 minutes.

Getting Around

You can rent bicycles from the Silversands Campsite, the KWS and most of the bigger hotels for KSh200 to KSh500 per day. This is probably the best way to get around town unless you prefer to walk. Cycling at night is not permitted.

Taxis are mainly concentrated along Lamu Rd and in front of any of the big hotels south of town (the best place to start is Coral Key Beach Resort). From the southern resorts, it costs KSh200 to Malindi town, KSh300 to Lamu Rd and KSh500 to the airport.

Malindi also has Kenya's biggest fleet of Indonesian-style tuk-tuks, which are cheaper than taxis – a trip from town to the KWS office should cost around KSh100.

MARAFA DEPRESSION

This beautiful geological anomaly, also called Hell's Kitchen, Devil's Kitchen or Nyari (the Place Broken by Itself), lies about 30km directly northeast of Malindi near Marafa. Over the millennia wind and rain have eroded a ridge of sandstone into an amazing set of gorges. Most people visit on organised tours, with a self-drive car or by taxi (KSh6000).

Alternatively, there are one or two morning matatus from Mombasa Rd in Malindi to Marafa village (KSh100, three hours), and from there it's a 30-minute walk to Hell's Kitchen. Guides are available in the village, but you may have to spend the night in one of the basic lodges, as all matatus travel in the morning.

TANA RIVER

From Garsen, a nondescript town (with very basic hotels) on the road to Lamu, a rough road leads inland to hot and humid Garissa and on to Thika. About 40km north of Garsen on this road is the **Tana River National Primate Reserve** (☎ 046-2035), established in 1976 to protect the remaining populations of the endangered crested mangabey and Tana River red colobus. Funded by the World Bank, the **Muchelelo Research Camp** was set up here in 1992 to study these rare primates, but plans to create a full-blown national park have faced considerable opposition from locals (see opposite).

While the reserve itself is not yet a viable option for tourists, Bush Homes of East Africa has taken advantage of the area's isolation to create the **Tana Delta Camp** (Nairobi ☎ 020-600457; www.bush-homes.co.ke; s/d low season US$285/480, high season US$380/640), a remote and exclusive lodge right at the scenic mouth of the Tana River. Prices include all meals and activities; it's at least three hours from Malindi by road, or air transfers are available for US$40.

All roads into the area are prone to attacks by bandits and cannot currently be considered safe for independent travel; however, the security situation has improved up as far as Lamu, so things may be looking up. Contact the **KWS** (☎ 020-600800) in Nairobi to find out the latest situation.

LAMU ARCHIPELAGO

There's something magical in the air on Lamu, and it's not just the seductive sea breeze. Consisting of six main islands and countless smaller ones, the archipelago is the unrivalled jewel of the Kenyan coast, offering both tourist facilities and unspoiled tropical havens for those who know where

---

TANA RIVER PROTESTS

The Tana River National Primate Reserve has been earmarked for development into a national park, backed by the World Bank and International Monetary Fund (IMF), but the plans would require thousands of local tribespeople to be relocated from their ancestral lands. There have been extensive protests against the plan by local people, who are already suffering from a vicious ongoing tribal war between the Orma and Pokomo people over land rights.

Things came to a head in February 2001, when 300 naked women from surrounding villages stormed the research centre and attacked the scientists, a traditional gesture designed to shame enemies. Faced by such protests, the World Bank has suspended its funding and the KWS has put its plans on indefinite hold.

---

to find them. For many people a stay here is the highlight not just of the coast, but of their entire time in Kenya, and a large proportion of visitors are regulars entranced by the whole feel of the place.

Among the archipelago's many charms are Lamu's Swahili old town, Shela's exclusive beach community and the remote shores of Kiwayu Island. All are supported and enlivened by a cast of bizarre characters including a man called Satan, a cat called Smacker and a blind man who can 'see' women. At its best, Lamu has the ability to make you feel like you've always belonged here, and it's small wonder so many people keep coming back.

LAMU
☎ 042

Lamu town is the core of everything the archipelago stands for in the hearts and minds of inhabitants and visitors alike, a living throwback to the Swahili culture that once dominated the entire Indian Ocean coast. The winding streets, carved woods and traditional houses are simply captivating. Few experiences can compare with wandering the narrow lanes immersed in the sights and sounds of everyday life, from the mysterious rustle of *bui-bui*-clad women to the echoing of some unseen donkey's hooves, all set against the crackle of wind-blown palm trees, the slow bobbing of dhows at sunset, the smell of seafood and the changing textures of a hundred coral and plaster walls. It's simply a different world, and one you'll be in no hurry to leave.

Traditionally, Lamu houses had flat roofs that created a private space where women were free to talk and socialise; many have been replaced by shady *makuti*-covered terraces, which serve the same purpose for the many travellers who cross paths here. Although there have been concerns about the increasing use of imported materials in building and maintenance work, conservation efforts have largely paid off and surviving examples of the town's famous carved doors and painted wooden beams are probably safe from plunder.

History

Lamu itself was a bit of a late starter; originally, the major power-centres in the archipelago were the Swahili settlements of Takwa, Paté, Faza and Siyu (on Paté Island), which date back to the 7th and 8th centuries. In pre-Arab times, the islands were home to Bajun tribespeople, but that culture vanished almost entirely with the ascendancy of Arabic ideas.

Arab settlers established a busy trading post on Lamu island at the start of the 16th century, exporting ivory, mangrove poles, tortoiseshell and thousands of African slaves, who were whisked away by dhow to Iraq, Oman and the burgeoning Arabic colonies elsewhere on the East African coast.

Initially, Lamu was a minor player in the East African power game, dominated by the nearby sultanate of Paté, but it rose to prominence in the 19th century after defeating the forces of Paté in a battle at Shela beach. At this time the twin cash-cows of ivory and slavery made Lamu a splendidly wealthy place, and most of the fine Swahili houses that survive today were built during this period.

It all came to an end in 1873, when the British forced Sultan Barghash of Zanzibar to close down the slave markets. With the abolition of slavery, the economy of the island went into rapid decline. The city-state was incorporated into the British Protectorate

THE COAST

LAMU

0 ——————— 200 m
0 ——————— 0.1 miles

INDIAN OCEAN

To Mokowe (mainland) (5km)

Main Jetty

To Manda Island (Airport)(1km)

To Matondoni (6km)

Bohora Mosque

Jamaa Mosque

Catholic Church

Shiaithna-Asheri Mosque

District Commissioner's Office

Main Square

Dhow Moorings

To Kipungani Village (10km)

To Manda Beach (4km)

To Lamu Dhow (200m); Civil Servants' Club (800m); Dodo Villas/ Talking Trees Campsite (1km); King Fadh Lamu District Hospital (1.5km); Shela (3km)

To Muslim Cemetery (150m); Police Administration Club (500m); Shela (Inland Road) (3.5km)

INFORMATION

Immigration Office	1 D4
Kenya Commercial Bank	2 D3
Lamu Medical Clinic	3 C2
Langoni Nursing Home	4 D5
Lynx Infosystems	5 C4
Mani Books & Stationers	6 D4
Post Office	7 D4
Tourist Information Office	8 D5

SIGHTS & ACTIVITIES

Donkey Sanctuary	9 C2
German Post Office Museum	10 D4
Lamu Fort	11 C4
Lamu Museum	12 C3
Lamu Museum Information Centre	13 C2
Riyadha Mosque	14 B5
Swahili House Museum	15 B2

SLEEPING

Amu House	16 C3
Casuarina Rest House	17 C2
Jannat House	18 B1
Kitendetini Bahari Hotel	19 C1
Lamu Archipelago Villa	20 D6
Lamu Castle Hotel	21 C4
Lamu Guest House	22 C3
Lamu World	23 C1
New Lamu Palace Hotel	24 D5
Petley's Inn	25 C3
Pole Pole Guest House	26 B1
Stone House Hotel	27 C2
SunSail Hotel	28 D4
Sunshine Guesthouse	29 C2
Yumbe House	30 B2

EATING

Bosnian Café	31 D6
Bush Gardens Restaurant	32 D3
Hapa Hapa Restaurant	33 D3
Mangrove Centre	34 D3
Market	35 C4
New Minaa Café	36 C6
Olympic Restaurant	37 D6
Whispers Coffeeshop	38 D5

ENTERTAINMENT

Zinj Cinema	39 D6

SHOPPING

Baraka Gallery	(see 38)

TRANSPORT

Airkenya	(see 38)
Falcon	40 D5
Kenya Airways	41 D4
Khadi Star	42 D4
Tawakal	43 D4
TSS	44 D5
Zam Zam	(see 40)

from 1890, and became part of Kenya with independence in 1963.

Until it was 'rediscovered' by travellers in the 1970s, Lamu existed in a state of humble obscurity, escaping the runaway development that happened elsewhere on the coast. Today, only Zanzibar can offer such a feast of Swahili culture and uncorrupted traditional architecture. In 2001 Lamu town was added to Unesco's list of World Heritage Sites.

Orientation

Although there are several restaurants and places to stay along the waterfront (Harambee Ave), most of the guesthouses are tucked away in the confusing maze of alleys behind. Lamu's main thoroughfare is Kenyatta Rd, a long winding alley known popularly as 'Main St', which runs from the northern end of town, past the fort, and then south to the Muslim cemetery and the inland track to Shela.

MAPS

The leaflet-map *Lamu: Map & Guide to the Archipelago, the Island & the Town* (KSh500), available from the tourist office, is worth buying if you want to explore properly.

Information
BOOKSHOPS

Lamu Museum shop (Harambee Ave) Specialises in Lamu and Swahili culture.
Mani Books & Stationers (☎ 632238; Kenyatta Rd) Good for newspapers.

INTERNET ACCESS

Lynx Infosystems (☎ 833134; per min KSh2; ☼ 8am-10pm) Temperamental connections over a Safaricom line – worth a look when the post office is closed. To find it, head west down the street next to the Khadi Star office and turn left at the end.

MEDICAL SERVICES

King Fadh Lamu District Hospital (☎ 633012) One of the most modern and well-equipped hospitals on the coast.
Lamu Medical Clinic (☎ 633438; Kenyatta Rd; ☼ 8am-9pm)
Langoni Nursing Home (☎ 633349; Kenyatta Rd; ☼ 24hr) Offers clinic services.

MONEY

If you're stuck outside bank times, ask around; local shopkeepers may be able to help you out with changing money, sometimes at surprisingly reasonable rates.
Kenya Commercial Bank (☎ 633327; Harambee Ave) The only bank on Lamu. No ATM, Visa advances only. Beware of large commissions on cards and travellers cheques.

POST

Post office (Harambee Ave) Postal services, cardphones and the best Internet connections in town.

TOURIST INFORMATION

Tourist information office (☎ 633449; ☼ 9am-1pm & 2-4pm) A commercial tour and accommodation agency that also provides tourist information.

VISA EXTENSIONS

Immigration office (☎ 633032; off Kenyatta Rd) There's an office near the fort where you should be able to get visa extensions, although travellers are sometimes referred to Mombasa.

Dangers & Annoyances

Beach boys are the primary nuisance in Lamu. Most loiter around the waterfront offering dhow trips, marijuana and other 'services'. Men can generally get away with a bit of friendly chat, but single women and even groups of female travellers are likely to have constant company, which can get *very* wearing. Unfortunately there's not a lot you can do except be firm, stay polite and always keep on walking.

Lamu has long been popular for its relaxed and tolerant atmosphere, but it's still a Muslim island, with all the associated views of acceptable behaviour. In an extreme case in 1999, a gay couple who planned a public wedding here had to be evacuated under police custody. Whatever your sexuality, it's best to keep public displays of affection to a minimum and respect local attitudes to modesty – ignoring local sensibilities makes you just as much of an annoyance as those pesky beach boys.

Sights

All of Lamu's museums are open from 8am to 6pm daily. Admission to each is KSh200/100 for a nonresident adult/child.

LAMU MUSEUM

Housed in a very grand Swahili warehouse on the waterfront, the Lamu Museum is an excellent introduction to the culture and history of Lamu Island. It's one of the most interesting small museums in Kenya, with displays on Swahili culture, the famous coastal carved doors, the Maulid Festival, Lamu's nautical history and the tribes who used to occupy this part of the coast in pre-Muslim days, including the Boni, who were legendary elephant-hunters.

The pride of the collection are the remarkable and ornate *siwa* (ceremonial horns) of Lamu and Paté, dating back to the 17th century. Lamu's *siwa* is made of engraved brass, but it pales beside the glorious ivory *siwa* of Paté, carved from a single massive elephant tusk. Swahili relics from Takwa and other sites in the archipelago are displayed the gallery downstairs.

The upstairs rooms, recreating the wedding quarters of a traditional Swahili house, are particularly worthwhile – not least for factoids like the custom of showing the nuptial sheet to the women of the bride's family to prove consummation had occurred.

The museum also has its own library and **Information Centre** (Harambee Ave; ⊗ 8.30am-12.30pm & 2.30-4.30pm Mon-Fri, 8.30am-12.30pm Sat; ▣) just down the waterfront, supported by the American Embassy.

SWAHILI HOUSE MUSEUM
If the Lamu Museum stokes your interest in Swahili culture, this beautifully restored traditional house tucked away off to the side of Yumbe House hotel will put you firmly back in the past. Inside you'll find a recreation of a working Swahili home, with cookware, beds and other furniture. The attendant will give you a whistle-stop but informative tour in between small talk, including some fascinating descriptions of the regimented lives of Swahilis in the 18th and 19th centuries.

Traditional Swahili homes were built along rigid social lines, with separate quarters for men and women and audience halls allowing men to receive guests without infringing on their womenfolk's privacy. Other unusual details are the ceremonial death bed, where the deceased lay in state before burial, and the echo chamber, used by women to receive visitors without being seen when their menfolk were away. The museum is signposted from Kenyatta Rd.

LAMU FORT
The bulky, atmospheric Lamu Fort squats on Lamu's main square like a weary intruder among the airy Swahili roofs. The building of this massive structure was begun by the Sultan of Paté in 1810 and completed in 1823. From 1910 right up to 1984 it was used as a prison, and it now houses the island's library and some lacklustre displays on natural history and the environment, which a guide will show you around. The highlight is scaling the ramparts for some sweeping town views.

GERMAN POST OFFICE MUSEUM
In the late 1800s, before the British decided to nip German expansion into Tanganyika in the bud, the Germans regarded Lamu as an ideal base from where they could successfully and safely exploit the interior. As part of their efforts the German East Africa Company set up a post office on Kenyatta Rd, and the old building is now a museum exhibiting photographs and memorabilia from that fleeting period of colonial history.

DONKEY SANCTUARY
A man without a donkey, *is* a donkey.
Swahili proverb

With around 3000 donkeys active on Lamu, *Equus asinus* is still the main form of transport here, and this **sanctuary** (☎ 633303; Harambee Ave; admission free; ⊗ 9am-1pm Mon-Fri) was established by the International Donkey Protection Trust of Sidmouth, UK, to improve the lot of the island's hard-working beasts of burden. The project provides free veterinary services to donkey owners and tends to injured, sick or worn-out animals; there's even a small ambulance for donkey-mergencies.

Activities
DHOW TRIPS
Taking a dhow trip is almost obligatory and drifting through the mangroves is a wonderful way to experience the islands. You'll be approached by touts and would-be captains almost as soon as you arrive, but it's worth shopping around to find a captain you like and a price you're happy with. Prices vary depending on where you want to go and how long you go for; with a bit of bargaining you should pay around KSh500 per person in a group of four or five people. Groups of more than five aren't recommended as the boats aren't very big.

Solo travellers joining an existing group to make up numbers will often be offered a great price, on the condition that they don't tell their fellow passengers how much they paid. As this generally means the others paid the extortionate asking price of KSh1000 each, it probably shouldn't be encouraged!

Whatever you arrange, make sure you know exactly how much you'll be paying and what that will include, to avoid misunderstandings and overcharging. Don't hand over any money until the day of departure, except perhaps a small advance for food. On long trips, it's best to organise your own drinks. Make sure you take a hat and some sunscreen, as there is rarely any shade on the dhows.

Most day trips meander around the channel between Lamu and Manda Islands, and the price includes fishing and snorkelling, although both can be disappointing as the fish tend to hide amongst the coral during the day. Lunch is usually served up on a beach on Manda Island. Longer trips head for Manda Toto Island, which has better snorkelling.

For something a bit more flashy, Peponi Hotel, at Shela, offers full-moon dhow cruises for KSh4500 (minimum eight people) including drinks, wine and a lobster dinner.

Multi-day trips head out to Paté or the still more remote island of Kiwayu (see p228). When it is properly up and running, **Lamu Dhow** (☎ 0734-583780; rocksure@hotmail.com; Harambee Ave) will offer luxury trips with accommodation actually on board a massive vessel.

Dhows without an outboard motor are entirely dependent on wind to get them anywhere, although poling the boat is fairly common along narrow creeks and channels. It's common to get becalmed or stuck on sand banks, so you'll just have to patient and wait until the wind picks up or the tide rises to move on. With this in mind, it's probably unwise to go on a long trip if you have a flight or other appointment to meet.

Likewise, dhows are dependent on the tides. You can't sail up creeks if the tide is out and there's not enough water to float the boat. This will be the main factor determining departure and return times (see right for more information about these crafts).

PLAIN SAILING

Arabic dhows have been negotiating the coast of East Africa for centuries, and numerous dhow ferries still operate between the mangrove islands that line the Kenyan coast. These ancient vessels are distinguished by their triangular sails (lateens), although today many rely on a mixture of wind and motor power to get around. Dhows range considerably in size, from huge ocean-going *jahazi*, with broad hulls designed to withstand constant bumping along rocky shores and coral reefs, to small *kijahazi*, used as ferries and fishing boats up and down the coast. Kenyan *jahazi* can be recognised by their perpendicular bows, distinct from the sloping bows of their Zanzibari counterparts, but you're only likely to see these larger boats on dhow tours around Mombasa. *Kijahazi* are much more common and are widely used around the Lamu archipelago. There are excellent models of the various types of the dhow in the Lamu Museum (p215).

Walking Tour

The best, indeed only, way to see Lamu town is on foot. Few experiences compare with exploring the far back streets, where you can wander unnoticed amid wafts of cardamom and carbolic and watch the town's agile cats scaling the vertical coral walls. This tour will take you past some of the more noteworthy buildings in under an hour, but don't feel bound to follow it too rigidly. In fact, getting slightly lost is a vital part of the process, and we downright insist that you take as many detours and digressions as possible!

Most of Lamu's buildings date back to the 18th century and are constructed out of local materials, with cut coral-rag blocks for the walls, wooden floors supported by mangrove poles and intricately carved shutters for windows. Lavish decorations were created using carved plaster, and carpenters were employed to produce ornately carved window and door frames as a sign of the financial status of the owners. There are so many wonderful Swahili houses that it's pointless for us to recommend specific examples – keep your eyes open wherever you go, and don't forget to look up.

THE COAST

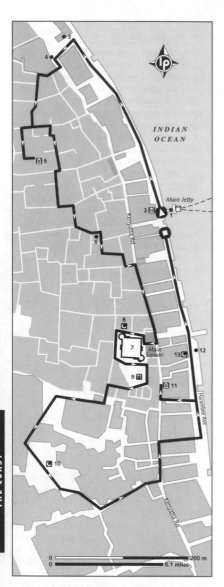

From here head onto Kenyatta Rd, passing an original Swahili **well (4)**, and into the alleys towards the **Swahili House Museum (5)**. Once you've had your fill of domestic insights, take any route back towards the main street – if you can hit the road leading towards Matondoni you'll pass a particularly elaborate original carved **door (6)** in the Arabic style.

Once you've hit the main square and the **fort (7)**, take a right to see the crumbled remains of the 14th-century **Pwani Mosque (8)**, one of Lamu's oldest buildings; an Arabic inscription is still visible on the wall. From here you can head round and browse the covered **market (9)**, then negotiate your way towards the bright Saudi-funded **Riyadha Mosque (10)**, the centre of Lamu's religious scene, founded by the great scholar Habib Swaleh in 1891.

From here you can take as long or as short a route as you like back to the waterfront; this end of town is a little shabbier, but it has just as much life as the northern part. Then stroll back up along the promenade, diverting for the **German Post Office Museum (11)** if you haven't already seen it – the door is another amazing example of Swahili carving. If you're feeling the pace, take a rest and shoot the breeze on the **baraza ya wazee (12**; 'Old Men's Bench') outside the appealing stucco minarets of the **Shiaithna-Asheri Mosque (13)**. Benches of this kind were a crucial feature of any Swahili home, providing an informal social setting for men to discuss the issues of the day, and this newly inaugurated seat is already well used by Lamu's loquacious elders.

Carrying on up Harambee Ave will bring you back to the main jetty and the end of our tour. We suggest you celebrate a hard day's walk with a large juice at one of the seafront restaurants!

Festivals & Events

The Maulid Festival celebrates the birth of the Prophet Mohammed. Its date shifts according to the Muslim calendar and it will fall on 12 April 2006, and 20 March in 2007 and 2008. The festival has been celebrated on the island for over 100 years and much singing, dancing and general jollity takes place around this time. Among the interesting traditional dances are the *goma* or cane-fighting dance and the quivering-sword

Starting at the **main jetty (1)**, head north past the **Lamu Museum (2)** and along the waterfront until you reach the **door carving workshops (3)**. In recent years, there has been a real revival in woodcarving and you can once again see traditional carved lintels and doors being made in workshops like these all over Lamu.

dance, where sword-wielding dancers set up a chorus of vibrating steel.

Organised events include swimming galas, poetry reading, calligraphy competitions, donkey races for young boys and dhow races for all the dhow captains. Most of the celebrations are centred around the Riyadha Mosque, although there is much loud rejoicing at all of Lamu's mosques. On the final day a procession heads down to the tomb of the man who started it all, Habib Swaleh.

The Lamu Cultural Festival is another colourful cultural event, held in the last week of August. It's actually a recent initiative, established in 2000 and aimed more at tourists than local people. Attractions include traditional dancing, displays of crafts such as *kofia* embroidery (a *kofia* is a cap worn by Muslim men) and dhow races.

The Donkey Awards in March/April are an unusual spectacle, organised by the Lamu Donkey Sanctuary (p216) in conjunction with the KSPCA to promote animal welfare. Prizes are given for the best-cared-for donkey, and a surprising number of locals turn out to parade their well-tended beasts.

Sleeping
BUDGET

Lamu has been catering for budget travellers for several decades and still has loads of inexpensive guesthouses. Prices are remarkably consistent because of the competition for clientele, although you obviously get what you pay for. All the places have fans (where necessary) and mosquito nets, though remarkably few have the towels and soap you'd usually expect as standard.

Rates rise by up to 50% from August to September and around Christmas and New Year. At other times, there's plenty of scope for negotiation, especially if you plan to stay for more than a day or two. Touts will invariably try and accompany you from the jetty to get commission; the best way to avoid this is to book at least one night in advance, so you know ahead of time what you'll be paying.

If you plan on staying in Lamu for a while it's worth making inquiries about renting a house, so long as there's a group of you to share the cost. The price per person will usually be similar to staying at a lodge, but you'll have the advantage of a place to yourself and the luxury of a kitchen. Houses

are available in both Lamu and Shela – ask around and see what's available.

Casuarina Rest House (☎ 633123; s/d KSh400/800, s/d/tr with shared bathroom KSh300/500/700) What can we say – we just love this place, less for the accommodation than for the atmosphere, which is exactly the kind of friendly personal vibe that gets people backpacking in the first place. The roof terrace acts as a social lounge, the staff are great fun and the breezy top-floor balcony double is romantic as all hell, even if the shower is virtually outdoors. Unfortunately (and unsurprisingly), it's often full, both in and out of season; ongoing expansion should create a few more berths.

Pole Pole Guest House (☎ 0722-652477; s/d KSh500/1000) Pole Pole is north of the centre of town and back from the waterfront. One of the tallest buildings in Lamu, it has bright doubles with fans and nets. There's a spacious *makuti*-roofed terrace area with great views and its own mini 'tower'. It's a good place to stay, but relies heavily on touts.

Lamu Guest House (☎ 633338; Kenyatta Rd; s/d KSh500/1000, s/d/tr with shared bathroom KSh400/800/900) Behind Petley's Inn, the basic rooms here are very plain, but the upper-floor ones are better and catch the sea breeze. The 'official' rates posted in reception are a good KSh500 more than quoted here and definitely not worth paying.

Lamu Castle Hotel (☎ 0722-355240; s/d with shared bathroom KSh300/400) A lick of fresh pink paint has left the Castle looking rather spruce, but inside it's just the basics, and even some of the walls seem to be left a little short. You'll find it off the main square, behind the market.

Sunshine Guesthouse (d/tr KSh500/700) Around the corner from Stone House Hotel, Sunshine is a bit old-looking, but it is cheap and there's a kitchen with a fridge for guests. Entry is via the steps up over the alleyway, which doubles as a neat vantage point to peer at the street below.

MIDRANGE

Yumbe House (☎ 633101; lamuoldtown@africaonline.co .ke; s/d/tr low season KSh1100/2100/2900, high season KSh1290/2700/3860) Close to the Swahili House Museum, Yumbe is a tall, traditional house set around a leafy courtyard. The pleasant rooms have fridges and are spotlessly clean, decked out with kangas, woven rugs and

Lamu furniture. If you can, go for the big, chic 'tower' room right under the thatch. If the house is full, staff can refer you to its sister hotel a few blocks away.

Jannat House (☎ 633414; www.jannathouse.com; s/d KSh2625/4500, with shared bathroom KSh2175/3675; 🔊) The architects clearly had a field day designing the Jannat House; it's essentially two houses spliced together around a courtyard, with several levels and multiple terraces. The lower rooms are disappointing, but the upper levels are as nice as you'd hope for. Follow the signs from Kenyatta Rd – you'll need to keep looking up.

Stone House Hotel (☎ 633544; half board s/d US$45/66) Another wonderful old Swahili place, with Escher-like stairways and a fine leafy courtyard. The hotel has its own superb rooftop restaurant (no alcohol) with excellent views over the town and waterfront. Rooms can be booked with Kisiwani Ltd (☎ 020-4446384) in Nairobi.

Amu House (☎ 633420; amuhouse@aol.com; s/d/tr KSh1700/2300/2700) Of all the refurbished Swahili hotels, this beautifully restored 16th-century house has had perhaps the greatest attention to detail paid to it. The original woodwork and plaster have been lovingly brought out, with local antiques completing the look. Rates include breakfast, transfers from Manda airstrip and a free water-skiing lesson at Shela Beach. Knock KSh500 or so off in low season.

Kitendetini Bahari Hotel (☎ 633172; s/d KSh700/ 1200) A borderline budget option set around a neat rectangular courtyard. All rooms have fans, nets and fridges, though the toilets lack seats. Prices include breakfast and are usually negotiable.

SunSail Hotel (☎ 632065; sunsailhotel2004@hotmail .com; Harambee Ave; s/d downstairs KSh1800/2500, upstairs KSh2000/3000) The effort put into the SunSail sadly doesn't do justice to the waterfront location – there are some great views from upstairs rooms, but the downstairs rooms are pretty cramped. Still, the rooftop terrace is huge (if a little bare) and it's generally quiet.

Lamu Archipelago Villa (☎ 633247; Harambee Ave; s/d KSh900/1500) Just along the waterfront, this friendly hotel has trouble entirely justifying even this modest price tag, and there's certainly nothing villa-like about it. Useful as a fall-back or cheaper alternative to the popular Swahili places.

TOP END

Lamu World (☎ 633491; www.lamuworld.com; Harambee Ave; s/d low season US$90/100, high season US$150/200, ste low/high season US$150/250; 🖳 🔊) Oh my gosh. It almost rankles to recommend something so new in such a traditional town, but the pale stone design of this luxury establishment is such a perfect modern interpretation of Swahili style that it frankly outshines even some of the authentic places. There are just 10 rooms shared between two houses, all with immaculate fittings, super-thick mattresses and huge shower heads; exclusive hire of each house costs US$1000, or US$1200 with a dhow thrown in.

Petley's Inn (☎ 633107; www.chaleislandparadise .com; Harambee Ave; s/d US$70/90; 🔊) Originally set up in the late 19th century by Percy Petley, a somewhat eccentric English colonist, Petley's has plenty of traditional touches but is looking a bit worn these days, despite extensive renovation after a fire in 2003. It's a fine place though, especially the 'penthouse' room and rooftop bar. Rates include transfers to and from Manda Island airstrip. Petley's is also a drinking venue.

New Lamu Palace Hotel (☎ 633164; Harambee Ave; s/d US$70/90) Owned by the same people as Petley's Inn. This modern hotel is not as sensitively designed as its peers, but rooms are smart and comfortable and there's a good restaurant (mains KSh650 to KSh1200) and a bar serving alcohol. The problem, as with all the top-end options here, is that you could rent a whole Swahili house for these prices.

Eating

It's important to know that *all* the cheap places to eat, and many of the more expensive restaurants, are closed all day until after sunset during the month of Ramadan. If your hotel doesn't provide breakfast and lunch, you'll have to head to Whispers Coffeeshop, Petley's Inn or New Lamu Palace Hotel, or Peponi Hotel in Shela.

Bush Gardens Restaurant (☎ 633285; Harambee Ave; mains KSh180-800) The Bush Gardens is the template for a whole set of restaurants along the waterfront, offering breakfasts, seafood – excellent fish, top-value 'monster crab' (KSh400) and the inevitable lobster in Swahili sauce (KSh750) – and superb juices and shakes mixed up in panelled British pint mugs. Somehow just about every traveller on Lamu ends up here at some point, and it remains a great meeting point and a firm favourite with repeat visitors. We hear the samosas are quite good, with a squeeze of lime of course.

Hapa Hapa Restaurant (Harambee Ave; mains KSh150-750) Very much in the same vein as Bush Gardens, and advocated just as vehemently by its regulars, this waterfront eatery is a bit more informal and African under its low thatch.

New Minaa Café (meals under KSh120; ⏰ 6.30am-midnight) On the road towards the Riyadha Mosque, this busy, clean rooftop café serves Swahili favourites such as beef kebabs, *maharagwe* (beans in coconut milk), chicken tikka and *samaki* (fried fish). It's cheap and popular with both locals and travellers.

Mangrove Centre (Harambee Ave; mains KSh250-380) Facing the main jetty, you'll find a video store and an informal cinema behind the eating area here, though sadly you can't watch the films as you eat. The restaurant does a lively trade at lunchtime, and it's handy for a juice while you wait for a boat, or while you find your feet on arrival.

Olympic Restaurant (Harambee Ave; mains KSh250-700) Further south near the waterfront woodyards, the Olympic serves the usual favourites. It's less popular than its more central rivals, but no worse off for that. The owners are very friendly and it's a favourite with a slightly older crowd.

Whispers Coffeeshop (Kenyatta Rd; mains KSh240-550; ⏰ 9am-9pm) In the same building as the posh Baraka Gallery, this is a great place for an upmarket meal, a freshly baked cake or a real cappuccino. There's a lovely palm-shaded courtyard and simple meals such as pasta, fish and chips and pizza are available even during Ramadan, though it closes in low season.

Stone House Hotel (☎ 633544; mains KSh250-750; ⏰ noon-2pm & 7-9pm) A fine rooftop restaurant that really catches the breeze. The wonderful panorama of the town and seafront is matched by the quality of the food. There are usually several choices for lunch or dinner, and menus often feature crab and grilled barracuda. Only soft drinks are available.

Bosnian Café (Kenyatta Rd) One of several dirt-cheap local canteens at the far end of the main street that set up takeaway stalls in the evening, selling samosas, chapatis,

mishkaki (kebabs), chips and the like from 10 bob apiece.

At some point most travellers will come across Ali Hippy, who offers meals at his house for around KSh500 and will almost certainly point out his presence in this book. The whole family entertains you while you eat and some people come away quite satisfied, but plenty are put off instantly by the sales pitch!

Self-caterers should head to the main market next to the fort. The fruit and vegetables are cheap and fresh, and there's a slightly gory section where you can get meat and fish.

Drinking & Entertainment
As a Muslim town, Lamu caters very poorly for drinkers.

Petley's Inn (☎ 633107; Harambee Ave) and **New Lamu Palace Hotel** (☎ 633164; Harambee Ave) both have nice bars where you can sink a cold beer. Petley's has the edge as its terrace catches the breeze and the pool table is well used. Beers cost a steep KSh120.

Even bureaucrats need to let their hair down – the **Civil Servants' Club** (admission KSh100), along the waterfront towards Shela village, is virtually the only reliable spot for a drink and a dance at weekends, and occasionally plays host to big names like the Ogopa DJs. It's small, loud, rowdy and great fun, though lone women should run for cover and the harbour wall outside is a potential death trap after a few Tuskers.

The informal disco at the **Police Administration Club** (admission KSh50; ⏰ Fri & Sat) is the only other option, though for some reason it's only open during school terms.

Lamu has several small cinemas, all screening Bollywood blockbusters and big football matches for KSh20 a seat. The **Zinj Cinema** (Kenyatta Rd), at the southern end of town, is easy to find.

Shopping
Along the seafront and in the suburbs surrounding Lamu town, you can see craftsmen carving traditional Lamu doors, furniture and window frames. Many now do a healthy sideline in picture frames, *bao* board games, Quran stands, and traditional *ito* – round painted 'eyes' from Swahili dhows, originally used as talismans to avoid underwater obstacles and protect against the evil eye.

For upmarket souvenirs from all over Africa, **Baraka Gallery** (☎ 633264; Kenyatta Rd) has a fine selection, but stratospheric prices.

Lamu is also a good place to buy *kikois*, the patterned wraps traditionally worn by Swahili men. The standard price is around KSh350, more for the heavier Somali style.

Getting There & Away
AIR
Airkenya (☎ 633445; Baraka House, Kenyatta Rd) offers daily afternoon flights between Lamu and Wilson Airport in Nairobi (US$143, 1¾ hours). The inbound flights also continue on to Kiwayu Island (US$65, 15 minutes). **Safarilink** (Nairobi ☎ 020-600777) runs virtually identical services (US$140).

Kenya Airways (☎ 633155; Casuarina House, Harambee Ave) has daily afternoon flights between Lamu and the domestic terminal at Nairobi's Kenyatta International Airport (KSh10,860, 2¼ hours). Fares come down dramatically if you can book in advance. Remember to reconfirm your flights at least 72 hours before flying.

Mombasa Air Safari (Mombasa ☎ 041-433061) flies to Mombasa (US$90, 1¼ hours) via Malindi (US$21, 30 minutes). Book through **Ndau Safaris** (☎ 633576).

The airport at Lamu is on Manda Island and the ferry across the channel to Lamu costs KSh100. You will be met by 'guides' at the airport who will offer to carry your bags to the hotel of your choice for a small consideration (about KSh200). Many double as accommodation touts, so be cautious about accepting the first price you are quoted when you get to your hotel.

BUS
The main bus companies operating between Mombasa, Malindi and Lamu are TSS, Falcon, Zam Zam, Khadi Star and Tawakal.

There are booking offices for all these bus companies on Kenyatta Rd, apart from Khadi Star, which has its office on the waterfront. The going rate for a bus trip to Mombasa is KSh400 to KSh500; most buses leave between 7am and 8am, so you'll need to be at the jetty at 6.30am to catch the boat to the mainland. Tawakal also has 10am and 1pm bus services. It takes at least four hours to get from Lamu to Malindi, plus another two hours to Mombasa. Book early as demand is heavy.

Getting Around
There are ferries (KSh40) between Lamu and the bus station on the mainland (near Mokowe). Boats leave when the buses arrive at Mokowe; in the reverse direction, they leave at around 6.30am to meet the departing buses. Ferries between the airstrip on Manda Island and Lamu cost KSh100 and leave about half an hour before the flights leave. Expect to pay KSh200 for a custom trip if you miss either of these boats.

Between Lamu village and Shela there are plenty of motorised dhows in either direction throughout the day until around sunset; these cost about KSh100 per person and leave when full. Alternatively, you can hire a whole boat for KSh250 to KSh300, or KSh400 after dark.

There are also regular ferries between Lamu and Paté Island (see p226).

AROUND LAMU
Shela
This ancient Swahili village, often spelled Shella, sits at the start of glorious Shela Beach. In some places it seems even more medieval than Lamu, with few signs of modernity along its maze-like alleyways. Ironically, the pleasing authenticity is mostly due to the large and affluent expat population, who have restored many of the old houses – left to its own devices Shela would probably be far more dilapidated.

Shela's first residents were migrants from the abandoned settlement of Takwa on Manda Island. The local people speak a distinct dialect of Swahili and you can see strong evidence of Omani ancestry in many people's faces. Although it's something of a European enclave, with almost unseemly amounts of building going on to cater for foreign demand, it's still an atmospheric place to visit and wander around, and the mood is just as languorous and laid-back as it's always been.

SIGHTS & ACTIVITIES
There are no cultural attractions in Shela, but wandering around the village is a very amenable way to pass the time. Look out for the pillar-style **Mnarani Mosque** behind Peponi Hotel.

Most people are here for the **beach** – this spectacular dune-backed strip runs for 12km around the headland, so you're guar-

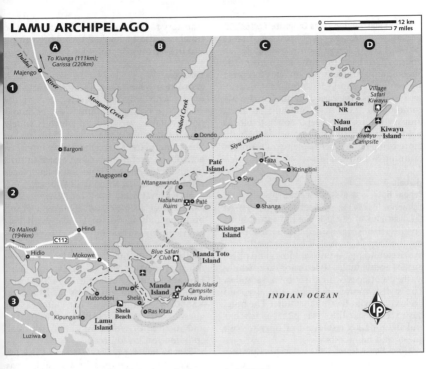

LAMU ARCHIPELAGO

| 0 | 12 km |
| 0 | 7 miles |

A · B · C · D

To Kiunga (111km);
Garissa (220km)
Majengo

Daudai River

Mongani Creek

Dodori Creek

Bargoni

Dondo

Siyu Channel

Paté Island

Faza

Kizingitini

Magogoni

Mtangawanda

Siyu

Nabahani Ruins

Paté

Shanga

Kisingati Island

Kiunga Marine NR

Village Safari Kiwayu

Ndau Island

Kiwayu Island

Kiwayu Campsite

To Malindi (194km)
C112
Hindi

Hidio

Mokowe

Blue Safari Club

Manda Toto Island

Matondoni

Shela

Manda Island

Manda Island Campsite
Takwa Ruins

INDIAN OCEAN

Kipungani

Shela Beach

Ras Kitau

Luziwa

Lamu Island

anteed a private stretch of sand, and it's a good place to comb the beach for shells. The Indian Ocean tsunami washed away a lot of sand here, revealing some sharp rocks, but it's expected to return to normal within a few seasons.

At the start of the beach is a ridiculous mock **fort**, which was built by an Italian entrepreneur who had lots of money but dubious taste.

There's no surf at Shela village because it lies in the channel between Lamu and Manda Islands, which makes it a prime spot for **windsurfing**. For traditional surfing, there are real breakers at the mouth of the channel, although this is also the realm of some substantial sharks.

Peponi Hotel's **water-sports centre** runs water-skiing (KSh8000 per hour), windsurfing (KSh650 to KSh800 per hour), snorkelling (equipment KSh200 per day), deep-sea fishing (from US$200 per boat) and scuba diving for certified divers between December and March (US$50/90 for one/two dives, including lunch). Cheaper windsurfing gear is available at Talking Trees Village.

SLEEPING
Guesthouses

Stopover Guest House (☎ 633459; mtendeni@ikenya .com; d KSh3000) This is the first place you come to on the waterfront, above the popular restaurant of the same name. The rooms are nice and light with big beds; like all the places in this category, prices include breakfast and should be thoroughly negotiable when it's not busy.

Shella Bahari Guest House (☎ 632046; bahari guest@swiftlamu.com; d low season KSh2000-3000, high season KSh2500-4000) Another waterfront place with a very similar setup to the Stopover. Rooms open onto a wide balcony above the bay and have sea views, nets, fans and Swahili furniture. Again, you can often bargain down – aim for around KSh500 per person.

Shella Pwani Guest House (☎ 633540; d low/high season KSh2000/2500) Behind the shop selling *kikois*, immediately behind Peponi Hotel, is this lovely Swahili house with carved plasterwork. Some rooms have fine sea views, as does the airy roof terrace, and all have fans and nets.

THE COAST

Dodo Villas/Talking Trees Campsite (☎ 633500; campsites per tent KSh400, r KSh600-1200, apt per person KSh200) This is Lamu's only budget beach option, 50m back from the seafront on the Shela–Lamu track, with an extra lounge area on the sand. Its nominal identity crisis reflects the varied nature of the accommodation: the main building has large, unfussy rooms and several concrete blocks hold apartments for up to ten people, with more being built. There's plenty of room for camping but no shade.

Hotels

Peponi Hotel (☎ 633421; www.peponi-lamu.com; s/d high season US$220/300; ☒ closed May & Jun; ☒) At the east end of Shela is *the* top resort hotel on the island, right on the waterfront facing the Lamu Channel. It blends neatly into the surrounding Swahili buildings and offers just 24 individually styled rooms, in whitewashed cottages with their own verandas. The stylish rooms are bright and airy, and decked out with Swahili furniture. The hotel has excellent facilities (see p223) plus a bar and an upmarket restaurant, all open to both guests and nonguests.

Kijani House Hotel (☎ 633235; www.kijani-lamu .com; d US$160-180; ☒ closed May & Jun; ☒) Set in splendid gardens, Kijani was painstakingly rebuilt over 10 years from the remains of three separate Swahili houses, and it looks a treat. Rooms are beautifully appointed, with fine traditional furniture. Like Peponi, all manner of activities and trips can be arranged, and rates include boat transfers to and from Manda Island airstrip.

Fatuma's Tower Yoga & Retreat House (☎ 632044; r per person from US$50) Seekers of the esoteric or just something that little bit different should bend and stretch their way to this unique complex, a collection of coral cottages seemingly cobbled together as a single fortress-like entity. Rooms are very variable, but the ones on upper floors are well worth a sprain or two. Yoga classes cost KSh500 per person. The retreat is towards the back of the village; ask for directions.

Island Hotel (☎ 633290; half board s/d US$37/52) In the centre of Shela is a superb Lamu-style house with a romantic rooftop restaurant (opposite). It's only five minutes' walk from the waterfront, along the alley beside Kijani House, but you'll probably have to ask for directions. The room rates include boat

transfers to and from Manda airstrip. The hotel can also be booked through Kisiwani Ltd in Nairobi (☎ 020-4446384).

Houses

As so many houses in Shela are owned by expats who only live here for part of the year, there's a huge amount of accommodation available, very little of which is widely advertised outside the island. This makes Shela one place where the beach boys can actually be useful – it's often easier to turn up and let someone show you a few places rather than trying to do it all yourself.

Shella Royal House (☎ 0722-698059; www.shella royalhouse.com; d KSh1000-5000) This is a grand building behind Kijani House, with balcony dining areas on every floor. The owners, Shella Guest Houses (☎ 633091; shella@africaonline.co.ke), also run two other properties, the White House Guest House (rooms KSh1000 to KSh4000) and Shella Rest House (rooms KSh1500 to KSh5000). All the houses have kitchens for guests. Rates vary according to the season and include breakfast and staff, who can cook for you if required.

Banana House (☎ 0723-471814; s/d US$70/100) Seven stunning rooms in a Swahili-style coral house in the so-called New Town area. The garden's particularly lovely, and, as with most private houses, exclusive hire is available. Rates include breakfast.

Kisiwani Ltd (Nairobi ☎ 020-4446384; www.lamu homes.com) Rents out whole houses in Shela from US$180 to US$280 per day. Cooks and cleaners are provided and the houses sleep six to 10 people. Properties include Mnarani House, behind the Mnarani Mosque, and Mtakuja House and Jasmine House, behind the Kijani House Hotel. You should book all these houses well in advance.

EATING & DRINKING

Stopover Restaurant (☎ 633459; mains KSh250-800) This is where Shela's extended posse of beach boys meet for afternoon *chai* (tea), which can actually be quite fun if you're on sociable rather than business terms. Even if you're ignoring them completely it's a good place to eat, with the usual complement of seafood and plenty of curries.

Bahari Guest House & Restaurant (☎ 632046; mains KSh250-600) Again, Bahari's house restaurant is pretty much identical to Stopover, and sadly has adjusted its prices upwards to match. Still, you can't sniff at lobster for KSh700.

Barracuda Restaurant (☎ 633290; mains KSh350-850) Just in case Lamu itself isn't romantic enough for you, this rooftop restaurant at the Island Hotel provides the perfect setting for an intimate night out. The terrace looks out over the old village, and the seafood is excellent. Nonguests are welcome and prices are reasonable.

Rangaleni Café (meals KSh60) Hidden away in the alleys behind the shorefront mosque is this tiny blue café, which does the usual stews and *ugali*.

Ali Samosa (☎ 632236; set dinners KSh1000) Shela's answer to Ali Hippy is Ali Samosa, a former samosa-seller whose whole family has done rather well out of the tourist boom. Shela's Ali is a lot smoother than his Lamu counterpart, and the extremely good Swahili meals are served in a rooftop dining room in a house near the Shela Primary School. He can often be found at Peponi Hotel, or you can ask at any of the Shella Guest Houses properties.

Peponi's Bar (☎ 633421) Naturally the bar at a Swiss-owned Kenyan hotel with an Italian name has to resemble an English pub. The terrace overlooking the water is a splendid place to watch the sunset, but at KSh140 for a Tusker it's not solar glare that'll bring tears to the eyes.

GETTING THERE & AWAY
To get to Shela, you can take a motorised dhow from the moorings in Lamu for KSh100 per person (or KSh250 to KSh300 for a solo ride). Alternatively, you can walk it in about 40 minutes. The easiest way is to take Harambee Ave and then follow the shoreline, though this may be partly flooded at high tide. When the tide is in, you can either wade through the sunken bits or cut across to the inland path. If you want to follow the inland path all the way, it starts near the Muslim cemetery in Lamu.

Matondoni
You'll see many dhows anchored along the waterfront at Lamu and at Shela, in the harbour at the southern end of town, but if you want to see them being built or repaired the best place is at the village of Matondoni, in the northwest of the island.

To get there from Lamu town you have a choice of walking (about two hours), hiring a donkey (KSh400) or hiring a dhow (KSh2000 per boat, up to five people). Dhow captains often provide lunch.

Walking there is a little more problematic, as there are lots of confusing trails in the sandy terrain behind town. First you have to find the track at the back of town, then head for the football pitch and follow the telephone wires that go to Matondoni. Ask directions from locals until you're sure you're on the right track.

Set off early if you are walking. There's a small café in Matondoni village, but no guesthouses. An impromptu group of travellers generally collects later in the afternoon, so you can usually share a dhow ride back to Lamu.

Kipungani
At the southwest tip of Lamu Island is this small village where local people make straw mats, baskets, hats and *kifumbu*, used to squeeze milk from mashed coconut. It's a friendly place, and tea and snacks can be arranged, plus there's a beautiful empty beach nearby. It's a long, hot walk and the path is very hard to find. A better option is to visit on a dhow tour for about KSh5000 per boat (good for around five people). Prices include lunch.

The only accommodation here is at the very exclusive **Kipungani Explorer** (Nairobi ☎ 020-4446651; www.heritage-eastafrica.com; full board s/d US$335/470; ☺ closed Apr-Jun). It's predictably luxurious, and rates include transfers and 'non-motorised marine activities'. There's a booking office next to Lamu Archipelago Villa in Lamu town.

MANDA ISLAND
This is the easiest island to get to, since it's just across the channel from Lamu. Almost everyone takes a half-day trip to the Takwa ruins at the head of Manda Creek. A dhow trip to Manda Island costs an average of around KSh1500, shared by however many people you can gather. Sometimes (but not always) this includes a barbecued lunch, so settle this issue before you leave. You can also get there by motor launch, which isn't as romantic but will give you a little more time at the site before the tide gets too low for boats to negotiate the creek.

Sights & Activities

The extensive **Takwa ruins** (adult/child KSh200/100) are the remains of an old Swahili city that flourished between the 15th and 17th centuries. At its peak, there were at least 2500 people here, but the town was inexplicably abandoned in the 17th century and the people moved to Shela. The site is maintained by the National Museums of Kenya and the ruins include the remains of about 100 limestone and coral houses, all aligned towards Mecca.

The largest structure is the **Jamaa mosque** (*Jamaa* means 'Friday'), which is well preserved and includes a pillar tomb unusually situated atop the *mihrab*. Also here is a tomb dating back to 1683 (1094 by the Islamic calendar). The settlement is surrounded by the remains of a wall and huge baobab trees dot the site.

Just off the northeast coast of Manda is **Manda Toto Island**, which offers some of the best snorkelling possibilities in the archipelago. The only way to get here is by dhow, and you need a full day to get there and back from Lamu. Boat owners typically charge around KSh700 per person if there's a group of four or more, and masks and snorkels are provided.

Across the channel from Shela is **Manda Beach**, which has fine sand and is home to the Manda Beach Club, where you can get a chilly Tusker or something fancy with a little umbrella in it. Shuttle boats leave from New Lamu Palace Hotel at 10am (KSh600 one way), returning at 6pm. You can also hire a boat in front of Peponi Hotel.

Sleeping

The only standard place to stay is the campsite adjacent to Takwa, but few people stay here because facilities are minimal. Contact the Lamu Museum for bookings, information and transport.

Blue Safari Club (Nairobi ☎ 020-890184; www.blue safariclub.com; r per person US$300-400) On the northern end of the island is this intimidatingly exclusive resort, only accessible by boat. Rates include activities and transfers, and you can also arrange luxury sailing cruises from US$325 per person.

Getting There & Away

The trip across to Manda from Lamu takes about 1½ hours by boat and can only be

done at high tide because the inlet is too shallow at low tide. You may well have to wade up the final stretch, so wear shorts. Since you have to catch the outgoing tide, your time at Takwa will probably not be more than an hour.

It's possible to walk to the Takwa ruins from the airstrip, but it's around 5km and the path isn't properly cleared. A boat transfer to the airport jetty costs KSh100.

Peponi Hotel and Kijani House in Shela offer tours to Takwa for around KSh1200 per person.

PATÉ ISLAND

Paté, an engaging mangrove island northeast of Lamu and Manda, is one of those rare places where the cultural isolation equals the geographical seclusion, preserving an uncomplicated traditional lifestyle as much by necessity as by choice. The only foreigners who come to this island are dhow-trippers and the occasional archaeologist, so you can expect to be a novelty and to be treated with friendly curiosity, especially by the local children. The local mosquitoes also appreciate the fresh meat, so bring insect repellent.

There is a number of historical sites on Paté Island, including Paté town, Siyu, Mtangawanda and Faza. All are still inhabited, mainly by fishers and mangrove-pole cutters, but very little effort has been put into preserving or clearing the remains of these once-powerful Swahili city-states.

Accommodation and food on the island are easy to arrange with local families, and there are one or two simple restaurants offering basic meals and tea. Paté town is little more than a crumbling old settlement, but the **Nabahani ruins**, just outside town, are interesting, although they've never been seriously excavated or cleared.

Getting There & Away

A motor launch leaves Lamu more or less daily for Mtangawanda (KSh50, about two hours), from which it's about an hour's walk to Paté town along a narrow footpath through thick bush and across tidal flats.

Boats continue to Faza (about another two hours) and Kizingitini (KSh150, another one hour), also stopping at the mouth of the channel to Siyu, where small boats transfer passengers to shore. Boats leave from the main jetty in Lamu town; times depend on the tides, but it can be quite tricky finding out when they go, as Swahili time is commonly used and everyone you ask will tell you something different!

Coming back from Paté, ask locally to make sure the boat will be calling at Mtangawanda on the return trip. If not, you may have to wait an extra day.

Siyu

Founded in the 15th century, Siyu was once famous as a centre of Islamic scholarship and crafts. In its heyday (between the 17th and 19th centuries) it boasted some 30,000 inhabitants and was the largest settlement on the island. Today, however, less than 4000 people live here and there are few signs of its previous cultural and religious influence.

The modern village displays little of Siyu's former glory, consisting of simple mud-walled and *makuti*-roofed houses. What does remain is the ruin of a huge crenellated **fort**, which sits dramatically on the waterfront. Even this grand structure couldn't halt Siyu's demise in 1847, when it was occupied by the sultan of Zanzibar's troops. The fort has been well restored and there are some Swahili relics inside.

South of Siyu is the intriguing village of **Shanga**, apparently originally settled by stranded Chinese traders (the name itself is a corruption of China). You'll need local help to find it.

GETTING THERE & AWAY

The boat from Mtangawanda to Faza stops at the mouth of the mangrove-lined channel leading up to Siyu, where small canoes transfer passengers to the village. From Lamu the fare is KSh100. This service isn't always available, so you may have to walk from Paté or Faza.

From Paté it's about 8km to Siyu along a dirt track through the bush. The first part is tricky since certain turn-offs are easy to miss, so it's a good idea to take a guide with you as far as the tidal inlet (the boat captain can help to arrange this). From there on it's easy, as the path bears left and then continues straight through to Siyu.

Faza

The biggest settlement on Paté Island, Faza has a chequered history, being almost totally destroyed by Paté in the 13th century and then again by the Portuguese in 1586. It was subsequently re-established and switched its allegiances to the Portuguese during their attempts to subdue Paté in the 17th century. With the demise of slavery, Faza faded away, but its new status as an administrative centre is breathing some life back into the place.

The modern town is quite extensive and includes a post office, telephone exchange, a simple restaurant, several general stores and two guesthouses. The only historical relic is the ruined **Kunjanja Mosque** on the creek next to the district headquarters. Among the rubble is a beautifully carved *mihrab* and some fine Arabic inscriptions. Outside town is the **tomb of Amir Hamad**, commander of the sultan of Zanzibar's forces, who was killed here in 1844 while campaigning against Siyu and Paté.

SLEEPING & EATING

The two guesthouses, Lamu House and Shela House, are essentially family residences, but they can provide meals and a bedroom if you need somewhere to stay. The price is negotiable (expect to pay around KSh200 per person) and the families are very friendly.

A simple restaurant in the centre of town offers bean stews, tea and *mandazi* (a semi-sweet flat donut) for just a fistful of shillings, and is a popular meeting place for the local menfolk.

GETTING THERE & AWAY

The inlet leading up to Faza from the main channel is deep enough to allow the passage of dhows and motor launches at high tide, but at low tide it is impassable, so you'll have to walk in to Faza over the mud and sandbanks.

The Paté motor launch continues to Faza after Mtangawanda and Siyu, charging KSh150 from Lamu (four hours). Boats usually leave mid-morning from Lamu and from Faza in either direction, but the exact ferry times depend on the tides, so you should ask around the day before you leave.

Getting to Siyu from Faza involves a two-hour walk through *shambas* (small farms) and thick bush along a dirt track. The path is confusing so it may be best to come with a guide from Faza – volunteers are sure to approach you.

KIWAYU ISLAND

At the far northeast of the Lamu archipelago, Kiwayu Island has a population of just a few hundred people and is part of the Kiunga Marine National Reserve. Gloriously remote, it's a long, narrow ridge of sand and trees surrounded by reefs, with a long beach stretching all down the eastern side of the island. Standing at the tallest point and surveying your surroundings at sunset will probably be one of the defining experiences of your time on the coast.

The main reason to come here is for the three-day dhow trip itself, and to explore the coral reefs off the eastern side of the island, rated as some of the best along the Kenyan coast. For our money, the reefs at Manda Toto Island and further south at Watamu are better, but a visit here is still highly recommended.

The village on the western side of the island where the dhows drop anchor is very small, but it does have a general store with a few basics.

Sleeping & Eating

Kiwayu Campsite (campsites KSh150, bandas from KSh500) Unless you can stretch to US$600 per night, the only place to stay is this rudimentary tourist site on the bay where the dhows land. The thatched bandas are a bit run down, but clean sheets are provided as well as kerosene lanterns, and the treehouse is fabulous. There are basic toilet and bucket-shower facilities, and a covered dining area where you or your dhow crew can cook up the catch of the day. The same owner also operates a second set of more solid bandas (high season only) by the long beach on the other side of the island, a 10-minute walk away.

Kiwayu Safari Village (Nairobi ☎ 020-600107; www .kiwayu.com; s/d US$408/632) If money is no object, you could do worse than stay at this exclusive collection of open luxury bandas, known as a hideaway for rock stars and other glitterati. It's a splendid getaway, although you pay a premium for the privacy and isolation.

Getting There & Away

The most interesting way to get to Kiwayu is by dhow. The island forms part of a three- or five-day dhow trip from Lamu, usually with stops along the way. If there's sufficient wind, the return trip to Kiwayu from Lamu takes three days and two nights; it's a lot quicker on the way there, as the return journey is against the wind and involves a lot of tacking down the Manda Channel, which can take up to 14 hours to navigate. Bank on around KSh1000 per person per day, based on a group of five or more.

If you'd rather spend more time on the island and less on the boat, you can take the motor ferry to Kizingitini on Paté (p226) and catch a dhow from there (KSh500 to KSh600, one hour).

High fliers tend to arrive by air. Airkenya flies from Manda airstrip to Kiwayu (US$65, 15 minutes), usually as an add-on to flights originating from Nairobi. Safarilink also offers flights here from Nairobi (US$170, 4¼ hours).

Rift Valley

Raise a glass to toast Earth's failure. About eight million years ago, by repeating the process it had successfully used to tear the ancient continent of Pangaea into seven shards, Mother Earth tried to rip Africa in two. Africa bent, Africa buckled, but Africa never gave in.

Africa's battle scar, stretching thousands of kilometres from Ethiopia to Mozambique, forms a stunning landscape. Some of the most attractive wounds are in Kenya's Rift Valley, where serrated escarpments and volcanoes tower over ochre soils, grassy plains and soda lakes. Steam and fluids spurt from its surface at Lake Bogoria and Hell's Gate National Park.

The valley's fertile floor, dotted with large freshwater and soda lakes, is alive with some of Kenya's most spectacular wildlife. Lake Nakuru's shores are often dyed pink with hundreds of thousands of fluorescent flamingos wading in the shallows, while its forested slopes host bigger treats such as rhinos, giraffes, buffaloes, antelopes and leopards. And if you walk or cycle unguided through the gorges of Hell's Gate National Park, you'll never see a zebra or giraffe in the same way again – being on foot is the ultimate amplifier of observation.

Hikes up the valley's dormant volcanoes are rewarding and offer tremendous views over the rift. Similar views without the peaceful solitude are also available from the viewpoints signposted on the Old Naivasha Rd as it drops into the valley from the town of Limuru.

After visiting, we're sure you'll thank Mother Earth for her royal botch-up!

HIGHLIGHTS

- Realising that you're not wearing rose-coloured spectacles and that wildlife at **Lake Nakuru National Park** (p243) is truly that brilliant
- Attempting to squeeze crocodiles, hippos, a hunting fish eagle and an amazing sunrise into one photograph at **Lake Baringo** (p247)
- Dancing along the crater rim of **Mt Longonot** (p231) to a glorious Rift Valley audience 1000m below
- Staring slack-jawed atop a precipice overlooking **Menengai Crater** (p242), a place of past volcanic and tribal hostility
- Gaining an entirely new respect for nature while walking through the wildlife and striking gorges of **Hell's Gate National Park** (p237)

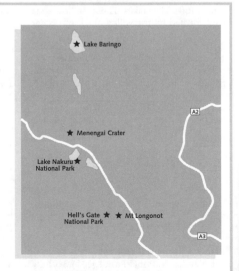

RIFT VALLEY

Geography

Kenya's Rift Valley is actually part of the Afro-Arabian rift system that stretches 6000km from the Dead Sea in the Middle East to Mozambique in southern Africa, passing through the Red Sea, then Ethiopia, Kenya, Tanzania and Malawi. A western branch forms a string of lakes in the centre of the continent, including Albert and Edward on the Uganda–Congo (Zaïre) border, Kivu on the Congo (Zaïre)–Rwanda border, and Tanganyika on the Tanzania–Congo (Zaïre) border, which joins the main system at the northern tip of Lake Malawi. The East African section of the rift failed and now only the Red Sea rift continues, slowly separating Africa from the Middle East.

In Kenya, the Rift Valley can be traced through Lake Turkana, the Cherangani Hills and lakes Baringo, Bogoria, Nakuru, Elmenteita, Naivasha and Magadi. A string of volcanic peaks and craters also line the valley. While most are now extinct, no fewer than thirty remain active, and according to local legend, Mt Longonot erupted as recently as 1860. This continuing activity supports a considerable number of hot springs and provides ideal conditions for geothermal power plants, which are increasingly important in Kenya's energy supply.

Besides providing fertile soil, the volcanic deposits have created alkaline waters in most Rift Valley lakes. These shallow soda lakes, formed by the valley's lack of decent drainage, experience high evaporation rates, which further concentrates the alkalinity. The strangely soapy and smelly waters are, however, the perfect environment for the growth of microscopic blue-green algae, which in turn feed lesser flamingos, tiny crustaceans (food for greater flamingos) and insect larvae (food for soda-resistant fish).

Climate

Although slightly hotter than the Central Highlands, the Rift Valley enjoys a pleasant climate and temperatures typically don't surpass 28°C. Like the highlands, rain usually falls in two seasons: March to the beginning of June (the 'long rains') and October to the end of November (the 'short rains').

National Parks & Reserves

Lake Nakuru National Park (p243), with its sweeping pink shores of pecking flamingos,

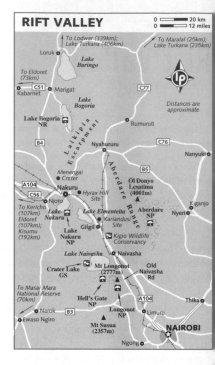

regular rhino sightings and abundance of other wildlife, is the region's biggest hitter. While Hell's Gate National Park (p237) sees much fewer visitors, it does offer the unique opportunity to walk unguided through striking landscapes and among African plains wildlife in all their natural glory. Standing in stunning contrast to these two national parks is the harsh and desolate beauty of Lake Bogoria National Reserve (p246). Steam plumes rise from its hydrothermal shores, which play second home to Lake Nakuru's massive flamingo population.

Getting There & Away

While you can charter planes into Lake Nakuru National Park, the valley's close proximity to Nairobi means virtually everybody enters the region using the extensive road network. Regular buses and matatus (minibuses) link the towns to Nairobi, western Kenya and the Central Highlands.

Getting Around

You'll have no trouble getting around this region. Convenient matatus and buses ply all major (and most minor) routes. Most roads are in great shape, except the potholed A104 Nakuru–Naivasha section, though it's scheduled for resurfacing.

LONGONOT NATIONAL PARK

Few places offer better Rift Valley views than the serrated crater rim of Mt Longonot, rising 1000m above the baking valley floor. In dog years this dormant volcano is ancient, while in geological terms it's just a wee pup at 400,000 years of age.

Since the best vistas in the **park** (adult/child US$15/5) are only reached with some effort on foot, peace and quiet accompany the panoramas. The steep climb to the rim takes just under an hour, while the rewarding jaunt to the summit (2776m) and around the crater takes another three hours. Despite the bounty of Rift Valley views, your eyes may just be drawn inward to the 2km-wide **crater**, a little lost world hosting an entirely different ecosystem. Including time for gawking, this 11km trek should take about six hours.

Although security has improved and KWS (Kenya Wildlife Service) no longer require rangers to escort you, double-check the situation at the gate.

The basic **Oloongonot Campsite** (adult/child US$8/5) sits just beyond the gate and has basic facilities (no water or firewood). The nearest roofed accommodation to the park is **Longonot Ranch** (☎ 050-50077; longonot@samawati.co.ke; full board s/d US$250/370), which is a lovely old-style farmhouse and cottage built by one of Hemingway's wives. It's sublime, and even has a floodlit waterhole regularly patronised by giraffes, zebras and other plains animals.

The cheapest hotels are found in nearby Naivasha.

Getting There & Away

Driving, it's 75km northwest of Nairobi on the Old Naivasha Rd. If you're without a vehicle, take a matatu from Naivasha to Longonot village, from where there's a path (ask locals) to the park's access road. Continue south past Longonot village to the actual access road for a longer but more straightforward route. From there it's a 7km walk to the gate.

MT SUSUA

Less frequented than Longonot but more interesting, this unique volcano is well worth the effort of getting there. The steep outer crater protects a second inner crater, whose rim peaks at 2357m and begs to be trekked. There's also a network of unexplored caves on the east side of the mountain.

There's no designated route and all land is owned by local Maasai, so you'll have to find someone to guide you in the nearby villages that dot the B3 Nairobi–Narok road. You'll need a 4WD to tackle the outer crater, although it's easy afterwards.

NAIVASHA

☎ 050

Bypassed by the new A104 Hwy to Nairobi, Naivasha has become an agricultural backwater. The streets have descended into cratered madness and services primarily focus on the area's blossoming flower industry. Although a convenient base for visits to Longonot National Park, staying around nearby Lake Naivasha (p233) is more enjoyable.

The only conceivable reason to stop is for supplies en route to Lake Naivasha, as there are very limited stocks in the lakeshore road *dukas* (shops).

Information

Barclays Bank (Moi Ave) Exchange cash and travellers cheques (KSh50 per leaf commission). With ATM.
Cyber Cafe (Kenyatta Ave; per hr KSh120) Slow connections, but open Sundays.
Kenya Commercial Bank (Moi Ave) Exchange cash and travellers cheques (1% commission, minimum charge KSh250). With ATM (Visa only).
Medical Clinic (Biashara Rd; ☿ 9am-7pm Mon-Sat, 11am-4pm Sun) Crude clinic and lab services.
Post office (Moi Ave) With card phones and Internet.

Sleeping

BUDGET

We've punted the real dives (there were many) and chosen these.

Kafico Lodge (☎ 2021344; Biashara Rd; s/tw KSh350/600) One of the odd places that 'seal' the rooms after 'cleaning', meaning you can only see the room after paying. The rooms are tattered and the toilets lack seats, but they're comfy enough. Security is good and if you use secure parking, you'll wake to a clean car (a KSh50 tip is appropriate).

Sam's Holiday Inn (☎ 0721-474556; Mbaria Kaniu Rd; s/tw KSh250/400) It's a bit gloomy, but should do the trick. Rooms have mosquito nets.

Othaya Annexe Hotel (☎ 0721-979916; Kariuki Chotara Rd; s KSh300) A bit brighter than Sam's,

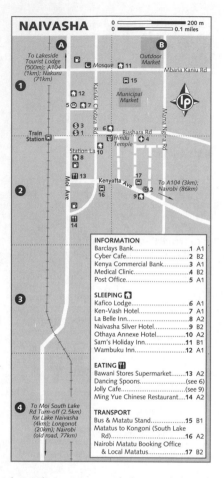

INFORMATION
Barclays Bank..............................1 A1
Cyber Cafe..................................2 B2
Kenya Commercial Bank...........3 A1
Medical Clinic.............................4 B2
Post Office..................................5 A1

SLEEPING
Kafico Lodge..............................6 A1
Ken-Vash Hotel..........................7 A1
La Belle Inn................................8 A2
Naivasha Silver Hotel.................9 B2
Othaya Annexe Hotel...............10 A2
Sam's Holiday Inn.....................11 B1
Wambuku Inn...........................12 A1

EATING
Bawani Stores Supermarket......13 A2
Dancing Spoons...................(see 6)
Jolly Cafe.............................(see 9)
Ming Yue Chinese Restaurant...14 A2

TRANSPORT
Bus & Matatu Stand.................15 B1
Matatus to Kongoni (South Lake
Rd)..16 A2
Nairobi Matatu Booking Office
& Local Matatus.....................17 B2

but Othaya Annexe only has single rooms and lacks mozzie nets.

Naivasha Silver Hotel (☎ 2020580; Kenyatta Ave; s/tw KSh600/1000) A slightly more pleasant option than other budget lodgings. Rooms and beds vary in size, so scope out a few. It has a decent restaurant and secure parking.

Wambuku Inn (☎ 2030287; Moi Ave; s/d/tw KSh800/1200/1400) Although this place is better maintained than the Naivasha Silver Hotel, the rooms at the Wambuku are quite dark and overpriced.

MIDRANGE
Naivasha's midrange accommodation is pricier than average, but includes breakfast and secure parking.

La Belle Inn (☎ 2021007; Moi Ave; s/d KSh2500/2900) A classic colonial-style option, with rooms of various sizes sporting plank floors, local artwork and a level of cleanliness unseen anywhere else in town. Prices quoted include breakfast.

Ken-Vash Hotel (☎ 2030049; off Moi Ave; s/d/tw KSh1400/2000/2200) A large tourist-class place with slightly better-equipped rooms (with TVs) and thick shag carpets, but lacking La Belle's character.

Lakeside Tourist Lodge (☎ 2020856; Moi Ave; s/d/tw KSh1600/2500/3400) This newish lodge is so smart and clean that it ends up being entirely characterless – some balconies even boast truck park views – enjoy!

Eating & Drinking
Although most people seem to eat and drink at their hotels, some good options lurk outside.

La Belle Inn (Moi Ave; meals KSh180-400) Whether your stomach is rumbling for an Indian curry (veggie or non-veggie), steak, pork spare ribs, beef kebab, fresh tilapia from the lake or even apple pie, this great colonial veranda is for you. It's also a top place for drinks, despite occasional dust clouds from the road. The Happy Valley Bar inside is also worth a Tusker or two in the evenings.

Ming Yue Chinese Restaurant (Moi Ave; meals KSh300-700; ☺ Mon-Sat) With a menu boasting the likes of bean curd satay, fried *bok choi* and scrumptious spring rolls, it's safe to say that there's nothing like it for miles. We dare you to order 'whole fish looks like squirrel'.

Dancing Spoons (Biashara Rd; meals KSh60-130) Located below the Kafico Lodge, this is the restaurant of choice for simple Kenyan fare.

Jolly Cafe (Kenyatta Ave; meals KSh80-220) While Martha Stewart would gasp at the overdone window treatments and fluorescent chairs, she wouldn't choke on their food. The menu is a good mix of Kenyan and Western dishes.

Bawani Stores Supermarket (Moi Ave) This is the perfect place for self-caterers to stock up.

There's a cluster of cheap bars and butcheries on Kariuki Chotara Rd, although you'd have to be pretty brave to venture into most of them.

Getting There & Away
The main bus and matatu station is off Mbaria Kaniu Rd, close to the municipal

market. Frequent buses and matatus leave for Nakuru (KSh120, 1¼ hours), Nairobi (KSh150, 1½ hours), Nyahururu (KSh200, 1¾ hours) and places west. Advance tickets can be bought for Nairobi matatus at the matatu booking office on Kenyatta Ave. Some Nairobi matatus, and all those for Kongoni via Fisherman's Camp (KSh70, 45 minutes), leave from Kenyatta Ave.

LAKE NAIVASHA
☎ 050

With shores fringed with papyrus and yellow-barked acacias, and freshwater that supports protected hippo populations, fish eagles and a blossoming horticultural industry, Lake Naivasha's beauty is as undeniable as its importance to the region.

A vast range of plains animals and a plethora of birdlife have long called the verdant shoreline home, as have the Maasai, who considered it prime grazing land. Unfortunately for the Maasai, the splendour of the surroundings wasn't lost on early settlers either and it was one of the first areas they settled, eventually becoming the favourite haunt of Lord Delamere and the decadent Happy Valley set in the 1930s. Amazingly between 1937 and 1950 the lake was Kenya's main airport, with BOAC's Empire and Solent flying-boats landing here after their four-day journey from Southampton. Lake Naivasha is still one of the largest settler and expat communities in Kenya, and can have a

resort-like feel to it in high season, when it essentially becomes Kenya's St Tropez.

Not only does Lake Naivasha's fresh water bestow it with a unique ecosystem in comparison with the vast majority of Rift Valley lakes, which are highly alkaline, but it also means the lake can be used for irrigation purposes. While the surrounding countryside has historically been a major production area for beef cattle and fresh fruit and vegetables, today the flower industry rules the roost. Shade houses have proliferated in the hills recently, and Lake Naivasha is now the centre of Kenya's US$360-million flower industry. Astoundingly, flowers that are picked here in the early morning can be at Europe's flower auctions the same day. One flower grower alone produced a million rose stems for Valentine's Day in 2005!

However, the success of the agricultural and horticultural industry is threatening the very survival of the source of their creation, as pesticides and fertilizers are seeping into the lake and reeking havoc with the ecosystem. Irrigation has further destabilised erratic water levels, which had seen the lake almost dry up in the 1890s before rebounding to cover almost 1000 sq km in the early 20th century. The lake is currently receding again, and now only spreads over 170 sq km.

The lake's ecology has been interfered with on a number of other occasions, notably with the introduction of foreign fish (for sports and commercial fisheries), crayfish, the South American coypu (an aquatic rodent that initially escaped from a fur farm) and various aquatic plants, including the dreaded water hyacinth.

For these reasons Naivasha has been the focus of conservation efforts and in 1995, after years of lobbying from the Lake Naivasha Riparian Association (LNRA), the lake was designated a Ramsar site, officially recognising it as a wetland of international importance. Besides educating the locals dependent on the lake about the environmental issues involved, the LNRA, Elsamere Conservation Centre and other organisations work to establish a code of conduct among the local growers that will maintain the lake's biodiversity. The results are promising, but much work remains to be done.

ME, A DELAMERE?

You'd think being repeatedly mistaken for Lord Delamere's great-grandson would have some fringe benefits…sadly not. Especially when the great-grandson in question has just had murder charges controversially dropped after shooting a Maasai KWS agent on his ranch.

People stared. People chased. People yelled. For the first time in my Lonely Planet career I was hoping to be recognised as an author! While I could only muster, 'I am Canadian!', my driver, who I'd hired to visit the parks and the remote north, had it down to a tee: 'Not Tom! Not Tom! He's not the killer!'

Fringe benefits my arse!

Matt Phillips

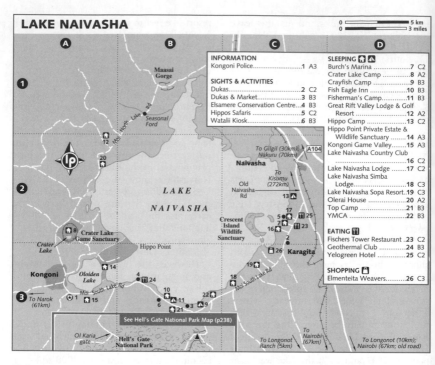

LAKE NAIVASHA

0 — 5 km
0 — 3 miles

INFORMATION
Kongoni Police...........................1 A3

SIGHTS & ACTIVITIES
Dukas..2 C2
Dukas & Market..........................3 B3
Elsamere Conservation Centre....4 B3
Hippos Safaris............................5 C2
Watalii Kiosk..............................6 B3

SLEEPING
Burch's Marina...........................7 C2
Crater Lake Camp.......................8 A2
Crayfish Camp............................9 B3
Fish Eagle Inn...........................10 B3
Fisherman's Camp.....................11 B3
Great Rift Valley Lodge & Golf
  Resort...................................12 A2
Hippo Camp...............................13 C2
Hippo Point Private Estate &
  Wildlife Sanctuary 14 A3
Kongoni Game Valley...............15 A3
Lake Naivasha Country Club
  ....16 C2
Lake Naivasha Lodge...............17 C2
Lake Naivasha Simba
  Lodge....................................18 C3
Lake Naivasha Sopa Resort......19 C3
Olerai House.............................20 A2
Top Camp.................................21 B3
YMCA.......................................22 B3

EATING
Fischers Tower Restaurant .23 C2
Geothermal Club 24 B3
Yelogreen Hotel 25 C2

SHOPPING
Elmenteita Weavers..........26 C3

Sights

CRATER LAKE GAME SANCTUARY

Surrounding a beautiful volcanic crater lake, on the western side of Lake Naivasha and north of the village of Kongoni, is this small **sanctuary** (admission KSh100), with many trails including one for hikers along the steep but diminutive crater rim. Besides the impressive 150 bird species recorded here, giraffes, zebras and other plains wildlife are also regular residents. While walking, remember that buffaloes lurk in the woods. The tiny jade-green crater lake is held in high regard by the local Maasai, who even believe its water helps soothe ailing cattle.

CRESCENT ISLAND WILDLIFE SANCTUARY

The protruding rim of a collapsed volcanic crater forms this island on the eastern side of Lake Naivasha. It's a private **sanctuary** (adult/child US$14/7), where you can walk beneath yellow-barked acacias (yellow fever trees) in search of giraffes, Thomson's and Grant's gazelles, elands, waterbucks and countless bird species. Oh, and there are some rather gigantic pythons too!

Almost all accommodation options rent boats for island trips (around KSh2500 per hour). The best is **Hippos Safaris** (☎ 0733-813100; off Moi South Lake Rd) as they charge a flat rate of KSh2000 per boat, which includes waiting time. It's technically possible to drive here along a small causeway, but the land owner is now charging extortionate fees for crossing his property.

ELSAMERE CONSERVATION CENTRE

A couple of kilometres past Fisherman's Camp on Moi South Lake Rd you'll find **Elsamere Conservation Centre** (☎ 2021055; elsa@ africaonline.co.ke; admission KSh500; ☼ 8am-6.30pm), the former home of the late Joy Adamson of *Born Free* fame. She bought the house in 1967 with a view to retiring here with her husband, George. Adamson did much of her writing from Elsamere right up until her murder in 1980.

Now a conservation centre focused on lake ecology and environmental awareness programs, the site is open to the public and entry includes afternoon tea on the lawn (with a chance to see eastern black-and-white colobus monkeys), a visit to the memorial room and a showing of the weathered 40-minute *Joy Adamson Story*.

Book ahead for a meal – lunch costs KSh650/800 on weekdays/weekends, and dinner is KSh1000 – and you can visit the centre for free.

Sleeping

BUDGET & MIDRANGE

Due to its popularity, Lake Naivasha has the Rift Valley's best range of budget accommodation. All sites are located on or near Moi South Lake Rd unless otherwise specified.

Fisherman's Camp (☎ 2030088; camping KSh200, dm KSh500, s/tw with shared bathrooms from KSh800/1600) Spread along the grassy tree-laden southern shore, this is a perennial favourite of campers, overland companies and hungry hippos. While hippo movements have been restricted by electric fences for safety reasons, you still stand a real chance of seeing one of these great beasts grazing at night. The site is huge, thus enabling you to get away from the overlander crowds and the noise from the popular bar and restaurant. With overpriced simple rooms and basic bandas, camping is clearly the best option. The tin-shack toilets and showers are pass-

able, but are the site's weakest point. You can also rent tents (KSh200 per person) and bikes (KSh500 per day). Nonguests are charged KSh100 admission.

Top Camp (☎ 2030276; camping KSh200, s/tw bandas from KSh500/1000, 5-person cottages KSh5000) It lacks Fisherman's lakeside location, but Top Camp boasts crazy lake views from its hilltop perch. It's a quiet place with various tin-roofed, bamboo-walled bandas (almost all have bathrooms). There are also cooking utensils, plates and a charcoal burner available for self-caterers. The large cosy cottage has a full kitchen and books a-plenty.

Crayfish Camp (☎ 2020239; craycamp@africaonline.co.ke; camping KSh250, s with shared bathroom KSh750, s/d KSh2500/3000; 💻) Following Fisherman's lead, the Crayfish Camp can seem more like a beer garden than a campsite, but it's not a bad option. The pricey new rooms are a bit minimalist, but have some charm, while the petite rooms with shared facilities are very plain Jane. While the communal bathrooms would make Fred Flintstone smile, you may not be so happy – very cavemanish. It has a restaurant and two bars, kitchen facilities, pool tables and tent, bedding, bicycle and boat hire (same rates as Fisherman's). Horseback riding is also offered (KSh500 per hour).

YMCA (camping KSh250, dm KSh250, bandas per person KSh300-450) For basic roofed accommodation, you'll do no better than the Y. It's also convenient for walks into Hell's Gate. There are two dorms and a number of Spartan bandas; firewood and bedding can be provided for a small charge. Meals are also available (lunch KSh150, dinner KSh200). It's popular with Kenyans and gets busy with school groups during holidays.

Burch's Marina (☎ 0733-660372; camping KSh200, 2-person rondavels KSh600, cottages d/tr/q KSh2200/2600/3000) About 1km past Hotel Yelogreen is this idiosyncratic place, ideal for those fleeing the noise of Fisherman's Camp and its ilk. There's a store with basic provisions and a range of accommodation. The campsite is pleasant and well-shaded, with hot showers, a communal cooking area and well. It has basic twin-bed rondavels or thatched four-bed family cottages (bedding isn't normally supplied, but can be requested). It's pretty busy here, especially on Tuesdays and weekends, so advance booking is mandatory.

Hippo Camp (off Old Naivasha Rd; camping KSh200) Run by KWS, this is a reasonable site with some slightly shabby permanent tents for rent (five-person tent KSh500, plus camping fees). There's a path down to the lake for some free wildlife viewing.

Fish Eagle Inn (☎ 2030306; fish@africaonline.co.ke; camping KSh220, dm KSh450, s KSh2110-2660, d KSh3550-4100; 🏊) If you have money to burn and find plywood charming, you'll love the overpriced DIY standard rooms. The 'Jumbo House' rooms are even more pricey, but have creature comforts like satellite TV and canopy beds. Even numbered rooms 302 to 312 also have pleasant balconies. Swimming for those camping or in dorms is KSh100.

TOP END

Kongoni Game Valley (☎ 2021070; www.kgvalley.com; full board per person US$150; 🏊) Nothing around the lake can compare with this grand colonial farm house for utter African safari charm. Wander the house and soak up the atmosphere before sinking into some wicker with a cup of tea on the sweeping veranda – the views will leave you spellbound. Most rooms surround the house's lovely courtyard and boast hardwood floors, rich rugs, comfortable beds and bear-claw bathtubs. The Pili Pili stone cottage, with its three bedrooms, lovely sitting room and fireplace is also fabulous. The farmhouse sits within a private wildlife reserve, so sightings are plentiful and everything from horseback riding to safari walks and drives can be arranged. Package rates, including all activities and trips to Hell's Gate National park, are US$300 per person.

Olerai House (☎ 020-891112; www.olerai.com; Moi North Lake Rd; full board s/d US$240/320) Rose petals dust the beds and floors of these five sublime suites, each unique and a mix of Kenyan and Mediterranean influences. Despite being rather luxurious, the old wood timbers, grass mats and warm personal atmosphere make it feel more homelike than other luxury lodges. Spend evenings outside with your back to a cushion and your face to the campfire. Prices are slightly negotiable.

Elsamere Conservation Centre (☎ 2021055; elsa@africaonline.co.ke; full board s/d US$85/140) Small bungalows, each with its own diminutive veranda, dot the lovely lawn and offer great lake views. Although lacking the 'wow' factor of others, it's comfortable, extremely friendly and a relative bargain. Trips to Hell's Gate National Park and Mt Longonot are available upon request.

Hippo Point Private Estate & Wildlife Sanctuary (☎ 2021295; www.hippo-pointkenya.com; per person US$500; 🖳 🏊) We could try and tell you about the absolute lavishness of the main house and the tower, but you'd never believe us – we still can't believe it, and we saw it! Perhaps the most luxurious accommodation in Kenya, the entire estate is rented out exclusively to one group at a time (minimum four people). Rates include food, drinks, wildlife drives, water skiing…you name it.

Lake Naivasha Sopa Resort (☎ 2050358, Nairobi 020-3750235; full board s/d US$188/250; 🏊) Towering cacti and manicured gardens front the massive luxury cottages at this new resort that opened in 2004. Upstairs suites boast balconies, king-sized beds, modern bathrooms, TVs and pure comfort, while downstairs options only differ in that they have twin queen-sized beds and spill right into the gardens. Besides the pool, there's also a gym, sauna and lakeside path. The arc-shaped bar and restaurant, with massive vaulted ceilings, is gorgeous.

Crater Lake Camp (☎ 2020613; crater@africaonline .co.ke; full board low season s/d KSh4930/8925, high season KSh5880/10500) A luxury tented camp nestled among trees and overlooking the tiny jade-green crater lake. The food is good and the service excellent, and you can explore the whole of the sanctuary on foot. This place *is* a gem, but we're not sure how the owner's recent tragic death will affect the sanctuary and camp.

Lake Naivasha Lodge (☎ 2030298; fax 2020611; camping KSh200, full board low season s/d US$55/80, high season US$85/120) It's pleasant, but the cottage-style rooms and bathrooms are much more dated than other lodges. Another drawback is its lack of lake frontage.

Other luxurious recommendations:

Great Rift Valley Lodge & Golf Resort (☎ 2050048; rvgolf@heritagehotels.co.ke; high season s/d US$133/180, low season US$222/300; 🏊)

Lake Naivasha Country Club (☎ 020-650500; blocknaivasha@africaonline.co.ke; half board high season s/d US$131/162, low season US$161/212; 🏊)

Lake Naivasha Simba Lodge (☎ 020-4343960; enquiries@marasimba.com; full board s/d US$180/250; 🏊)

Eating & Drinking

Since food and drinks can be had at most of the accommodation options mentioned above, there's little in the way of independent wining and dining.

Fisherman's Camp (meals KSh250-425) Everything from fruit smoothies and chicken tikka to burgers and chilli con carne make their way onto plates at this atmospheric restaurant and bar.

Geothermal Club (meals KSh140-270) Set in a beautiful spot looking down over the lake about 45 minutes' walk from Fisherman's Camp, this relaxed restaurant caters for KenGen thermal power plant's employees but will happily serve visitors. Cold beer (KSh65) is always available.

A small market and some *dukas* (shops) are found near Fisherman's Camp for basic supplies.

The following local restaurants serve cheapish meals:

Fischers Tower Restaurant (meals KSh150-200)

Yelogreen Hotel (meals KSh150-400)

Shopping

Visit **Elmenteita Weavers** (off Moi South Lake Rd; ☯ 8am-5pm) and you'll see weavers producing hand-woven rugs, carpets, *kangas* (printed cotton wraparounds), baskets and the like. Prices reflect the high quality.

Getting There & Away

Frequent matatus (KSh80, one hour) run along Moi South Lake Rd between Naivasha town and Kongoni on the lake's western side, passing the turn-offs to Hell's Gate National Park and Fisherman's Camp.

It's a 5km walk from Kongoni to Crater Lake, but don't do this alone as there have been recent muggings.

There's one daily matatu along Moi North Lake Rd, leaving from the Total petrol station in Naivasha around 3pm. Returning to town, you'll need to be on the road by about 7am, otherwise it's a long dusty walk.

Getting Around

Most budget and midrange accommodation options rent reasonable boats for lake trips (KSh2500 per hour). Top-end lodges charge between KSh3000 and KSh4000 per hour for similar rides.

If you'd like to row row row your boat, Fisherman's Lodge can help you out (KSh300 per hour).

Most sites also hire mountain bikes; Fisherman's Camp and Fish Eagle Inn both charge KSh500 per day. You'll find cheaper rides at various places signposted off Moi South Lake Rd, but check the contraptions carefully before paying.

HELL'S GATE NATIONAL PARK

There's visiting national parks, and then there's experiencing national parks – Hell's Gate is an experience indeed. The park is truly unique, as it allows you to walk or cycle unguided across its breadth. Sure you can still drive, but why would you? Senses are heightened tenfold when you're face to face with grazing zebras, towering giraffes, galloping gazelles and massive eland antelopes. The knowledge that cheetahs, lions and leopards aren't unheard of here only adds to the excitement of it all! And be sure to give buffaloes plenty of room.

Keep an eye out for the massive lammergeyers (bearded vultures), which are slowly being reintroduced. Their wingspans can reach almost 3m.

The scenery here is dramatic, with rich ochre soils and savannah grasses squeezed between looming cliffs of rusty columnar basalt – it's all aglow in the early morning.

Marking the eastern entrance to **Hell's Gate Gorge** is **Fischer's Tower**, a 25m-high volcanic column named after Gustav Fischer, a German explorer who reached here in 1882. Commissioned by the Hamburg Geographical Society to find a route from Mombasa to Lake Victoria, Fischer was stopped by territorial Maasai, who comprehensively and most efficiently kyboshed his campaign by slaughtering almost his entire party. Fischer's tower is one of the park's many popular rock-climbing sites.

Rising from the gorge's southern end is the large **Central Tower** (rock-climbing prohibited). A picnic site and ranger's post are close by, from where an excellent walk descends into the **Lower Gorge** (Ol Njorowa). This narrow sandstone ravine has been stunningly sculpted by water, and the incoming light casts marvellous shadows. You'd do well to spend a couple of hours exploring here. It's a steep and very slippery descent, but some steps have been cut into the rock and whole school parties manage it on a regular basis. Flash floods are common, so check with rangers before proceeding.

If you want to explore further, the **Buffalo Circuit** offers fine views over Hell's Gate Gorge, the surrounding countryside and the serrated profile of a distant Mt Longonot.

RIFT VALLEY

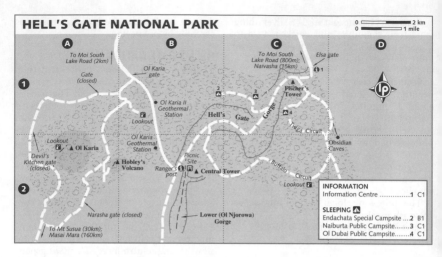

HELL'S GATE NATIONAL PARK

INFORMATION
Information Centre 1 C1

SLEEPING
Endachata Special Campsite 2 B1
Naiburta Public Campsite........3 C1
Ol Dubai Public Campsite........4 C1

This circuit has more soft sections of sand, which isn't conducive to cycling.

The park's western half is much less scenic and hosts the **Ol Karia Geothermal Station**, a power project utilising one of the world's hottest sources of natural steam. The plumes of rising steam can be seen from many of the park's viewpoints. It's usually possible to have a look around the site – ask the guards at Ol Karia II.

The park's striking scenery has played a role in several movies, the most recent being *Lara Croft Tomb Raider: The Cradle of Life*.

Information

The usual access point to the **park** (adult/child US$15/5) is through the main Elsa gate, 2km from Moi South Lake Rd, where there's an **information centre** (☎ 050-2020284). With the two gates on the northwest corner of the park closed, the only other gate is Ol Karia. It's always wise to have exact change.

Sleeping

Although it's convenient to sleep at Lake Naivasha's many lodges and camps (p235), the park's two gorgeous **public campsites** (adult/child US$8/5) can't be recommended enough.

Naiburta, sitting halfway up the Hell's Gate Gorge and looking west past Fischer's Tower, is the most scenic site, with basic toilets, an open banda for cooking and fresh-water taps.

Ol Dubai, resting on the gorge's opposite side, offers identical facilities and views east

to the orange bluffs and the puffs of steam from the power station.

The **Endachata Special Campsite** (adult/child US$10/5, plus set-up fee KSh5000) has no services, and besides absolute solitude, offers no more ambience than the cheaper public sites.

Getting There & Around

The round trip from the park's turn-off on Moi South Lake Rd to the shore of Lake Naivasha via Elsa gate and Ol Karia gate is 22km; the distance between the two gates via Moi South Lake Rd is 9km. If you intend to walk through the park, allow a full day, and take plenty of supplies. Drinking water is available at the park's two public campsites. A good alternative is to hire a mountain bike from one of Lake Naivasha's camps, or ask around at Fisherman's Camp for a lift.

NAIVASHA TO NAKURU

Besides the odd zebra and gangs of hardened road warriors (baboons) dotting the road-side between Naivasha and Nakuru, there are some obvious and not so obvious sights. The frequent matatus plying this route will happily drop you anywhere you like.

Kigio Wildlife Conservancy

Hiding off the A104, just south of the toll booth, is this up-and-coming 3500-acre **wild-life conservancy** (☎ 050-2030312; www.malewariver lodge.com). Started on a struggling dairy and beef ranch in 1997, the conservancy has set out to protect local wildlife and ecosystems, educate local communities about wildlife as a resource, and prove that humans, domestic stock and wildlife can thrive in the same environment.

Things have been successful and zebras, hippos, impalas, Thomson's gazelles, elands and buffaloes are now regularly sighted. In August 2002, with KWS' help, eight endangered Rothschild giraffes were relocated here from Lake Nakuru National Park as part of Kigio's goal to re-introduce endemic species to the area. Now that the Rothschilds are breeding, plans have shifted to the re-introduction of white rhinos.

Denuded areas, especially along the Malewa River's edge, are being replanted with pencil cedar and wild olive trees that once stood here centuries ago.

The conservancy supports three local primary schools and hopes environmental education will pave the way to a greener Kenya.

To visit the conservancy you must be staying at its ecolodge or campsites. Besides wildlife walks and drives, other possible activities here include horseback riding, fishing, rock-climbing, abseiling and mountain biking. You can even try your hand at cattle herding.

SLEEPING

There are four great **campsites** (camping incl conservancy fee KSh400) spread along the river's banks, each shaded by leafy trees. There's free firewood, long-drop toilets, hot showers and water at each.

The **Malewa River Lodge** (☎ 050-2030312; www .malewariverlodge.com; full board s/d US$160/210) consists of six rustic thatched cottages, each privately spaced among the riverside trees. Everything is made from local materials – the beautiful beds are actually made from refurbished fence posts. Water is supplied by a water-driven turbine in the river and only kerosene lamps are used – no noisy or polluting generator. Just to add to the safari experience, the cottages are partially open-fronted, with only bamboo blinds separating you from the night's wilds – listen and enjoy.

Kariandusi Prehistoric Site

The **Kariandusi site** (adult/child KSh200/100; ⏲ 8am-6pm) is signposted off the A104 Hwy near Lake Elmenteita. It was here in the 1920s that the Leakeys (a family of renowned archaeologists) discovered numerous obsidian and lava tools made by early humans between 1.4 million and 200,000 years ago. Two excavations sites are preserved and there's a new gallery displaying a brief history of early human life.

From the lower excavation you'll glimpse the sci-fi-looking excavations of **African Diatomite Industries** (☎ 050-4015290). If you ask at its gate, they'll usually be happy to give you a tour. Diatomite has many plaster-like properties and is formed from deposits of aquatic diatoms – yes, this region all used to be underwater. Most tunnels were dug by hand and are now home to thousands of bats.

Lake Elmenteita

It's bleached shoreline often fringed in pink, thanks to thousands of brilliant flamingos, Elmenteita is another of the major Rift Valley soda lakes. It's not a national park, so there are no entry fees, and you can walk around parts of the shoreline that aren't privately owned. For some water action, Flamingo Camp rents canoes for a paltry KSh100.

SLEEPING

Flamingo Camp (☎ 0722-832001; camping KSh200, s/d KSh2000/4000) Set right on the shore of Lake Elmenteita, small rooms are spread between three stone rondavels. Although it's comfortable and the tiny terraces offer good views, it's overpriced. The campsite isn't bad but would be a more attractive option with some shade. A restaurant and bar are on site.

Lake Elmenteita Lodge (☎ 051-8508630; full board high season s/d US70/100, low season US$120/155; ⚟) Surrounded by lovely gardens and overlooking Lake Elmenteita, these bungalows have dated but well-maintained rooms. Horseback riding (KSh1500 per hour) and walks to the lake are offered.

NAKURU

☎ 051

Although Nakuru is Kenya's fourth-largest town (population 163,000 at the last census), it still has a relaxed atmosphere and makes a pleasant base for a few days. It's on the doorstep of the delightful Lake Nakuru National Park and is only a few kilometres from the deep, dramatic Menengai Crater.

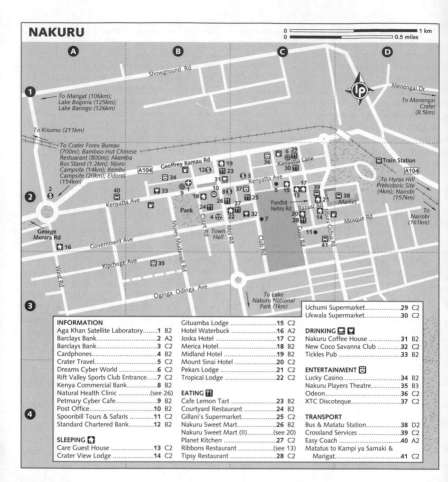

NAKURU

INFORMATION	
Aga Khan Satellite Laboratory.....1	B2
Barclays Bank.....2	A2
Barclays Bank.....3	C2
Cardphones.....4	B2
Crater Travel.....5	C2
Dreams Cyber World.....6	C2
Rift Valley Sports Club Entrance.....7	C2
Kenya Commercial Bank.....8	B2
Natural Health Clinic.....(see 26)	
Petmary Cyber Cafe.....9	B2
Post Office.....10	B2
Spoonbill Tours & Safaris.....11	C2
Standard Chartered Bank.....12	B2

SLEEPING ⌂	
Care Guest House.....13	C2
Crater View Lodge.....14	C2
Gituamba Lodge.....15	C2
Hotel Waterbuck.....16	A2
Joska Hotel.....17	C2
Merica Hotel.....18	B2
Midland Hotel.....19	B2
Mount Sinai Hotel.....20	C2
Pekars Lodge.....21	C2
Tropical Lodge.....22	C2

EATING ⊞	
Cafe Lemon Tart.....23	B2
Courtyard Restaurant.....24	B2
Gillani's Supermarket.....25	B2
Nakuru Sweet Mart.....26	B2
Nakuru Sweet Mart (II).....(see 20)	
Planet Kitchen.....27	C2
Ribbons Restaurant.....(see 13)	
Tipsy Restaurant.....28	C2

Uchumi Supermarket.....29	C2
Ukwala Supermarket.....30	C2

DRINKING ⊟ ⊟	
Nakuru Coffee House.....31	B2
New Coco Savanna Club.....32	C2
Tickles Pub.....33	B2

ENTERTAINMENT ⊡	
Lucky Casino.....34	B2
Nakuru Players Theatre.....35	B3
Odeon.....36	C2
XTC Discoteque.....37	C2

TRANSPORT	
Bus & Matatu Station.....38	D2
Crossland Services.....39	C2
Easy Coach.....40	A2
Matatus to Kampi ya Samaki & Marigat.....41	C2

Information

Changing cash and travellers cheques in Nakuru is easy, with numerous banks and forex bureaus. Barclays Bank's ATMs are the most reliable. Plenty of card phones are scattered around town.

Aga Khan Satellite Laboratory (off Court Rd) Various lab services. Malaria tests cost KSh160.

Crater Travel (☎ 2215019; off Kenyatta Ave) One of the few reputable travel agencies in town.

Dreams Cyber World (Kenyatta Lane; per hr KSh120; ☽ 8am-8pm, closed 1-2pm Fri) Fast connections and open Sunday.

Natural Health Clinic (Moi Rd; ☽ 9am-6pm Mon-Thu, 9am-4pm Fri) Natural remedies.

One World Tours & Safaris (☎ 0733-621598; PO Box 13047, Nakuru) Cheapest vehicle hire for Lake Nakuru trips.

There's no office, so you'll have to call. Usually rendezvous at Rift Valley Sports Club.

Petmary Cyber Cafe (Kenyatta Ave; per hr KSh120; ☽ 7.45am-5.30pm Mon-Sat) Nakuru's fastest Internet connections.

Post office (Kenyatta Ave) Town's cheapest Internet.

Spoonbill Tours & Safaris (☎ 0733-502768; Carnation Hotel, Mosque Rd) They seem to have a monopoly on activities around Nakuru. Most travel agents, including Crater Travel, use their services.

Sleeping
BUDGET

Lurking within the maze of noisy and dirty budget options were these standouts.

Mount Sinai Hotel (☎ 2211779; Bazaar Rd; s/tw/tr KSh350/500/650) A big, clean place with sound security (iron bars all over!). The rooms on the scenic roof terrace are the brightest of the bunch.

Joska Hotel (☎ 2212546; Pandhit Nehru Rd; s KSh400) Foam mattresses have shag-carpet covers in these basic rooms. Everything is rather clean, but you'll have to be a porcelain jockey – the toilets lack seats. Ask for an upstairs or in-ward-facing room, as they're more quiet.

Tropical Lodge (☎ 2216847; Moi Rd; s/tw with shared bathroom KSh250/350) While the bathrooms are shared, they do have toilet seats (a rarity in these parts). Rooms are simple, quiet and baby blue. It's run by a cheerful woman, which makes up for the odd cockroach.

Crater View Lodge (☎ 2216352; Mburu Gichua Rd; s/tw KSh300/350) All rooms face a bright inner courtyard, and noise here is less than you'd suspect. The twin rooms are a bargain, even if the bathrooms are a bit rough. Secure parking is available.

Gituamba Lodge (Gusii Rd; s/tw with shared bathroom KSh260/345, s/tw KSh310/400) The rooms here are all bare-bones basics, but they're rather large and some have big bright windows. It can be noisy, so take a top floor room.

Other budget hotels that won't curl your toes include the following.

Care Guest House (☎ 0721-636447; Pandit Nehru Rd; s/tw KSh300/400) Ask for room 66.

Pekars Lodge (☎ 2215455; Mburu Gichua Rd; s/tw incl breakfast KSh360/720) A good deal for single rooms.

Campers can drop tent in nearby Lake Nakuru National Park (p245), at Hyrax Hill Prehistoric Site (p243), or 20km west of town at **Kembu Campsite** (☎ 0722-361102; kembu@africaonline.co.ke; camping US$4, 1-/2-bedroom cottages KSh3000/6000). Kembu has a great atmosphere and it's particularly popular with overlanders due to its truck workshop and airy bamboo-clad bar/restaurant (order your food in advance). The semi-secluded one-bedroom acacia cottage, with French doors, polished-wood floors, a gorgeous bed and a lovely bathroom, is easily the Nakuru region's most charming room. The larger cottages have kitchens and are great for families. Mountain-bike hire and various treks into the surrounding area can be arranged. To get here, take a matatu heading to Molo (via Njoro; KSh80) and ask to be dropped at the metal gecko sign, about 6km northwest of Njoro on the C56. It's also signposted from the A104.

MIDRANGE & TOP END

There's a limited amount of midrange and top-end accommodation within Nakuru, but great options at Lake Nakuru National Park (p245) and Kembu Campsite add to the selection.

Hotel Waterbuck (☎ 2215672; West Rd; s/d/tw incl breakfast KSh2000/2500/2500; 🏊) Beneath the boring exterior lurk large kitschy African-themed doubles. Although a bit brash, they are, in fact, comfortable and more memorable than any other room in town. The singles and twins are small, boring and lack balconies. Kindergarten colours surround the courtyard and swimming pool. Non-guests can take a dip for KSh100.

Midland Hotel (☎ 2212125; Geoffrey Kamau Rd; s/d incl breakfast from KSh2300/3700) This popular place has a range of rooms (most with carpet) with varying levels of comfort. A third wing has recently been added; the names 'old wing' and 'new wing' are already taken, so we're wondering what they'll call it.

Merica Hotel (☎ 2216013; merica@kenyaweb.com; Kenyatta Ave; half board s/d US$65/110; 🍴 🏊) Opened in 2003 this contemporary tower hosts Nakuru's only top-end rooms. Ride the glass elevators up the sunlit atrium to your large, well-appointed room. Besides modern comfort, there's classic fun in Nakuru's best swimming pool (nonguests KSh200).

Eating

We could state the obvious and tell you that you'll have no trouble getting pleasantly stuffed in Nakuru, but we won't.

Merica Hotel (Kenyatta Ave; meals KSh185-500) Take pizza, pasta, a tender steak or a fine Indian curry at a poolside table in Nakuru's highest-rated restaurant.

Bamboo Hut Chinese Restaurant (Map p244; Giddo Plaza, George Morara Rd; meals KSh300-700) Highly recommended by Nakuru's expat community, this place serves great Chinese fare.

Courtyard Restaurant (off Court Rd; meals KSh250-500) This place scratches a variety of itches, from Indian to Italian and from beef stew to seafood. The chicken *pili pili* (pan-fried chicken flavoured with coconut cream, green chillies and turmeric) is rather enjoyable. As the name suggests, it's got a nice courtyard.

Ribbons Restaurant (Gusii Rd; meals KSh50-200) One of the best restaurants for cheap Kenyan dishes. There's a balcony overlooking the street and the servers are pretty in pink.

Cafe Lemon Tart (Moi Rd; meals KSh100-200) A bright and popular cafe serving Kenyan fare. No alcohol is served, which guarantees a peaceful ambience.

Tipsy Restaurant (Gusii Rd; mains KSh100-250) A fast-food feel, complete with 1970s swivelling chairs. It's well liked by locals, and offers reasonable value for Indian and Western food, although dishes can be greasy.

Nakuru Sweet Mart (Gusii Rd) A perennial favourite, this bakery dishes out Indian sweets, puff pastries and tasty gingerbread men.

Nakuru Sweet Mart (II) (Moi Rd; meals KSh120-220) This second outlet is more of a sit-down option and serves sandwiches, burgers, greasy fried chicken and chips.

Planet Kitchen (off Moi Rd; meals KSh75-200) Serving simple local dishes, Planet Kitchen is usually busy with the after-work business crowd.

There are several well-stocked supermarkets for self-caterers.

Drinking

There are plenty of places pouring wobbly pops (beers), including the top-end hotels, and even one wee shop which brews great coffee.

Tickles Pub (Kenyatta Ave) This mellow pub is the friendliest choice and has several TVs keeping local footy fans happy. Things pick up on weekends when they host local DJs.

New Coco Savanna Club (Government Ave) A cavernous place with pounding music, the odd pool shark and prostitutes.

Nakuru Coffee House (Kenyatta Ave) For a straightforward caffeine fix, this café sells excellent freshly roasted coffee.

Entertainment

For a rural town there's actually a choice of evening options.

Nakuru Players Theatre (Kipchoge Ave) Four evenings a month this theatre stages entertaining Kenyan plays.

Odeon (Geoffrey Kamau Rd; ☻ 6pm Tue-Sun) It's a bit of a dump, but it usually screens Western movies.

Lucky Casino (off Kenyatta Ave) For those who like to be more pro-active with their cash.

XTC Discoteque (Kenyatta Ave) With strobe lights and a dark dance floor, this is the nearest you'll get to a proper nightclub in Nakuru. They were playing JLo when we visited – we'll try not to hold it against them. Will you?

Getting There & Away

Regular buses, matatus and the odd Peugeot (shared taxi) leave the chaotic stands off Mburu Gichua Rd for Naivasha (KSh120, 1¼ hours), Nyahururu (KSh100, 1¼ hours), Kericho (KSh200, two hours), Nyeri (KSh250, 2½ hours), Eldoret (KSh200, 2¾ hours), Nairobi (KSh200, three hours), Kitale (KSh350, 3½ hours), Kisumu (KSh350, 3½ hours) and Kisii (KSh375, 4½ hours).

Matatus for Molo (KSh100, one hour) leave from **Crossland Services** (Mburu Gichua Rd), while services to Kampi ya Samaki (for Lake Baringo) via Marigat (for Lake Bogoria) leave further south on Mburu Gichua Rd. Kampi ya Samaki (KSh200, 2½ hours) costs slightly more and takes 30 minutes longer to reach than Marigat.

Akamba (Map p244; George Morara Rd) buses leave from their depot behind the Kenol petrol station west of town. Destinations include Nairobi (KSh200, thee hours), Eldoret (KSh200, 2¾ hours) and Kisumu (KSh300, 3½ hours). **Easy Coach** (Kenyatta Ave) offers the same destinations and a little extra comfort for almost double the cost.

Parking is tricky, with yellow-jacketed wardens charging KSh50 on most streets.

AROUND NAKURU
Menengai Crater

You'd be forgiven for yawning when looking at the gentle forested slopes of this dormant volcano from Nakuru (yes, it's that boring). However, when standing high atop a promontory on the edge of its hidden crater some 8km away, your mouth will open for completely different reasons (yes, it's that jaw-droppingly gorgeous). Striking red cliffs radiate outward and encircle a 90-sq-km cauldron of convoluted black lava flows. While lush vegetation is now proliferating on the harsh crater floor, some 480m below, the violent and dramatic volcanic history is easily seen.

A grim local legend states that the plumes of steam rising from the bottom are the souls of defeated Maasai warriors, thrown into the crater after a territorial battle, trying to make their way to heaven.

While hiking to the viewpoint from town offers great views back over Lake Nakuru, it's rather isolated and tourists have been mugged. To be safe, the 9km walk from town should only be done in groups of at least four or five. Alternatively, you can take a taxi up and back for KSh1000. There's a small group of *dukas* (shops) at the main viewpoint selling drinks and trinkets.

Hyrax Hill Prehistoric Site

This **archaeological site** (Map p244; adult/child KSh100/ 50; ☽ 8.30am-6pm) is 4km outside Nakuru and contains a museum and the remains of three settlements excavated between 1937 and the late 1980s, the oldest being possibly 3000 years old, the most recent only 200 to 300 years old.

The tiny museum discusses the distribution and cultures of Rift Valley peoples over the centuries. Try not to laugh at the plastic spitting cobra.

You're free to wander the site, but it's rather cryptic and a guide is useful – a tip of KSh100 is plenty. The North-East Village, which is believed to be about 400 years old, sits closest to the museum and once housed 13 enclosures. Only the 1965 excavation of Pit D remains open. It was here where great number of pottery fragments were found, some of which have been pieced together into complete jars and are displayed in the museum.

From Pit D the trail climbs to the scant remains of the stone-walled hill fort near the top of Hyrax Hill itself. You can continue to the peak, from where there's a fine view of flamingo-lined Lake Nakuru in the distance.

Looking down the other side of the hill, you'll see two 'C' shaped Iron Age stone hut foundations at the base. Just north of the foundations, a series of Iron Aged burial pits containing 19 skeletons was found. The majority were male and lots of them had been decapitated, so a number of colourful explanations have been offered.

Nearby, two Neolithic burial mounds and several other Iron Age burial pits were also discovered. The large collection of items found in these pits included a real puzzle – six Indian coins, one of them 500 years old, and two others dating from 1918 and 1919.

On a more lively note, there's a *bao* (a traditional African game that's played throughout East Africa) board carved into a rock outcrop between the Iron Age settlements and the museum.

It's now possible to **camp** (per tent KSh500) here, though facilities are limited.

Local matatus to Naivasha or Nairobi will take you past the turn-off (about 1km from the site), just south of Nakuru.

LAKE NAKURU NATIONAL PARK

With a pink sea of flamingos lapping at its shores, rich areas of grassland, euphorbia and acacia forests, and rocky cliffs supporting a myriad of animal and bird species, there's little doubt why Lake Nakuru National Park is rivalling Amboseli as Kenya's second most visited park after the Masai Mara.

Sightings of grazing or lazing white rhinos at the lake's southern end now seem to be commonplace since the species was reintroduced several years ago. The shy black rhinos, browsers by nature, are more difficult to spot. If you're very, very lucky, you'll catch a glimpse of a rare tree-climbing lion. Warthogs are common all over the park, providing light relief from the 'serious' animals with their amusing gait and upright tails (known to locals as Kenyan antennas). Along shore you'll come across waterbucks and buffaloes, while Thomson's gazelles and reedbucks can be seen further into the bush, where there's also a good chance of seeing leopards. Around the cliffs you may catch sight of hyraxes and birds of prey amid the countless baboons. A small herd of hippos generally frequents the lake's northern shore.

There's no better view of the park than that seen from atop **Baboon Cliff** as the afternoon sun casts a warm glow over the lake.

Since the 180-sq-km park's creation in 1961, the population of lesser and greater flamingos has risen and fallen with the soda lake's erratic water levels. When the lake dried up in 1962 (happy first birthday!), the population plummeted, as it later did in the 1970s when heavy rainfall diluted the lake's salinity and affected the lesser flamingos' food source (blue-green algae). Over much of the last decade healthy water levels have seen flamingo numbers blossom again. If future droughts or flooding make them fly the coop again, you'll probably find them at Lake Bogoria.

Sadly, not all is picture perfect, as in recent years pressures on the lake have increased. Pollution from Nakuru town, pesticide run-off from surrounding farms, and massive deforestation within the water catchment area have all caused concern. A World Wildlife Fund (WWF) project is

LAKE NAKURU NATIONAL PARK

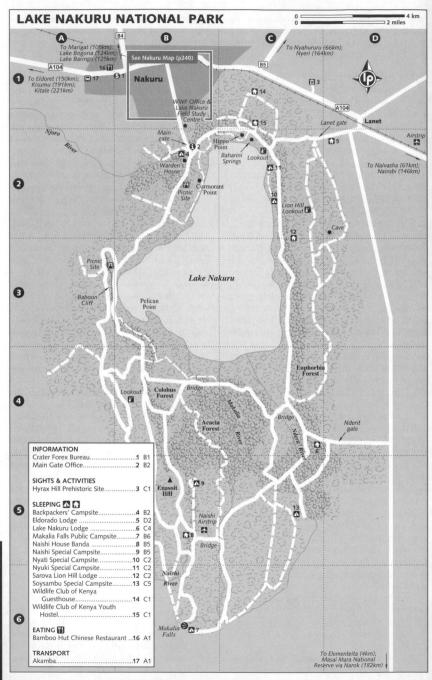

INFORMATION
Crater Forex Bureau.........................**1** B1
Main Gate Office..............................**2** B2

SIGHTS & ACTIVITIES
Hyrax Hill Prehistoric Site.................**3** C1

SLEEPING
Backpackers' Campsite......................**4** B2
Eldorado Lodge................................**5** D2
Lake Nakuru Lodge...........................**6** C4
Makalia Falls Public Campsite............**7** B6
Naishi House Banda..........................**8** B5
Naishi Special Campsite.....................**9** B5
Nyati Special Campsite.....................**10** C2
Nyuki Special Campsite.....................**11** C2
Sarova Lion Hill Lodge......................**12** C2
Soysambu Special Campsite...............**13** C5
Wildlife Club of Kenya
 Guesthouse..................................**14** C1
Wildlife Club of Kenya Youth
 Hostel...**15** C1

EATING
Bamboo Hut Chinese Restaurant....**16** A1

TRANSPORT
Akamba...**17** A1

making considerable progress in countering these problems, and the local afforestation program continues to plant thousands of indigenous tree seedlings.

Information

The main **park** (adult/child US$30/10, smartcard required) gate is about 2km south of the centre of Nakuru. KWS smartcards and official guidebooks (KSh750) are available at the main gate's **office** (☎ 051-2217151), but not at the Lanet or Nderit gates.

Sleeping

BUDGET & MIDRANGE

None of the following options provide any meals, so you'll have to bring your own food. If camping, always make sure your tents are securely zipped or the vervet monkeys and baboons will make a right mess while cleaning you right out. And remember to carry out all your garbage.

Makalia Falls Public Campsite (adult/child US$10/5) While it may be hard to get to and have cruder facilities than Backpackers', this is the best place to camp in the park. It's picturesque and sits next to the seasonal Makalia Falls.

Backpackers' Campsite (adult/child US$10/5) This large public campsite sits inside the main gate and also has the park's best camping facilities.

Special campsites (adult/child US$15/5, plus set-up fee KSh5000) These are dotted all over the park and have no facilities, but offer a true bush experience – just you and the animals.

Wildlife Club of Kenya Guesthouse (☎ 051-851559; PO Box 33, Nakuru; s/tw with shared bathroom KSh800/1600) This place is great – facilities include hot showers, TV lounge and use of the kitchen's fridge, gas cooker and microwave. The rooms are clean and comfortable.

Wildlife Club of Kenya Youth Hostel (☎ 051-850929; dm KSh150, s with shared bathroom KSh300, s/tw KSh500/1000) This hostel is a nice, very friendly site with clean dorms, simple single rooms and two-bedded bandas, complete with cooking areas.

Eldorado Lodge (☎ 051-851263; camping KSh300, s/d KSh1000/1500; ⊠) Just outside the park's Lanet gate, this place is a viable option for camping if you roll up to closed park gates in the evening. The rooms are overpriced and the pool is a little too green for our liking.

TOP END

Naishi House Banda (bookings ☎ 051-2217151; 6-person cottage plus 2-person annex Jan-Jun US$200, Jul-Dec US$250) Sit on the shady terrace and watch zebras and rhinos grazing on your very doorstep – there are no fences here. This charming self-catering cottage is very comfortable, complete with a lovely fireplace, sitting room and full kitchen. The annex was designed for safari drivers and is pretty basic. The park's main gate handles bookings and payments.

Sarova Lion Hill Lodge (☎ 020-2713333; www .sarovahotels.com; high season full board s/d from US$80/140, low season US$160/220; ⊠) Sitting high up the lake's eastern slopes, this lodge offers first-class service and comfort. The views from the open-air restaurant/bar and from most rooms are great. Rooms are understated but pretty, while the flashy suites are large and absolutely stunning.

Lake Nakuru Lodge (☎ 051-850228, Nairobi 020-2733695; www.lakenakurulodge.com; full board high season s/d from US$80/120; low season US$160/190; ⊠) South of the lake, this lodge's standard rooms, housed in cute shingle-roofed octagonal cottages, are a big step down in quality from those at Lion Hill. The only options worth the asking price are the new 'deluxe' rooms (make sure you ask for the ones that aren't in the farmhouse). The usual facilities are available, along with activities such as horse riding (KSh1550 per hour) and nature walks (KSh800).

Getting There & Away

Walking in the park isn't permitted, so you'll have to rent a taxi, go on a tour or be lucky enough to hitch a ride. A taxi for a few hours will likely cost KSh2000, though you'll have to bargain hard for it. More enjoyable options are **One World Tours & Safaris** (☎ 0733-621598; PO Box 13047, Nakuru), who charge KSh6000 for an open-topped eight-seat 4WD (about six hours), and **Crater Travel** (☎ 051-2215019; off Kenyatta Ave, Nakuru), who organise three-seater jeeps for KSh4500 (also for six hours).

If you're driving, there's access from the main gate, just outside Nakuru, the Lanet gate, a few kilometres south on the Nairobi road, and the Nderit gate, near the southern end of the lake.

NORTH TO MARIGAT

The journey north from Nakuru along the excellent B4 Hwy takes you through some dramatic changes of scenery, particularly around the equator, where the landscape turns dry and dusty, getting more forbidding the further north you go. Suddenly, out of the sea of reds, browns and meek greens, the blues of Lake Baringo appear in the distance. Soon you'll start to descend and, as the roadside to the east drops away, you'll see brief glimpses of the red plains and distant hills. At the bottom sits **Radat**, a tiny village known to produce some of Kenya's best *asali* (honey). They sell it from roadside kiosks by the vodka-bottle full (KSh100). If you blink and miss Radat, don't worry as you'll find sweet *asali* for sale throughout the region.

As you approach Marigat the spectacular ridges and escarpments of the Tugen Hills come into view, and you'll see an extraordinary number of huge termites' nests towering up from the reddish plains.

LAKE BOGORIA NATIONAL RESERVE

In the late 1990s this reserve's shallow soda lake achieved fame as 'the new home of the flamingo', with a migrant population of up to two million birds. In 2000 it was designated a Ramsar site, establishing it as a wetland of international importance. While lesser flamingo numbers have since dropped significantly, now that Lake Nakuru has recovered from earlier droughts, this **reserve** (☎ 0722-377252; PO Box 64, Marigat; adult/child KSh1500/200) is still a fascinating place to visit and a world away from any other Rift Valley lake.

Backed by the bleak Siracho Escarpment, moss-green waves roll down Lake Bogoria's rocky, barren shores, while nearby **hot springs** and **geysers** spew boiling fluids from the earth's insides – keep your distance! Amazingly, this inhospitable alien environment is a haven for birdlife and at **Kesubo Swamp**, just north of the park, more than 200 species have been recorded. One lucky soul spotted 96 species in one hour – a Kenyan record.

The lack of dense brush around Lake Bogoria also makes this one of the best places in Kenya to see the greater kudu. The isolated wooded area at the lake's southern end is also home to leopards, klipspringers, gazelles, caracals and buffaloes. Oh, and you'll see your fair share of donkeys and cattle too.

While the odd Kenyan tourist visits the springs, few people venture further south, meaning you may well have the place to yourself. You now have the bonus of being able to explore on foot or bicycle, though stay clear of the small buffalo population. If you'd like a guide (half-/full-day KSh500/1000), enquire at Loboi gate.

Sleeping & Eating

Camping is the only sleeping option within the reserve. If you'd prefer a roof, there's a top-end hotel nearby and various dives near the Loboi gate.

Fig Tree Camp (camping KSh500) Nestled beneath a stand of massive fig trees is this fantastic site. Sure the loos lack doors and baboons can be a nuisance, but there are brilliant views down the lake and a permanent freshwater stream. The 2km drive (4WD only) or hike from the main park road is worth the trip alone.

Acacia Camp (camping KSh500) A pretty lakeside site shaded by acacias, with some soft grass on which your tent can rest. You'll have to bring your own water. Acacia and Fig Tree blow the socks off the dismal Hot Springs and VIPS campsites.

Papyrus Inn (☎ 051-2216980; s/tw with shared toilets KSh500/800) This overpriced place is in a bit

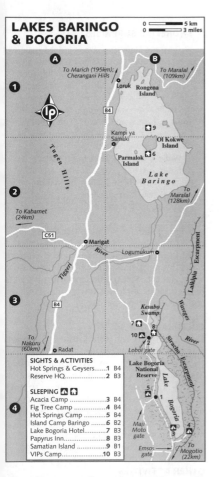

LAKES BARINGO & BOGORIA

0 —— 5 km
0 —— 3 miles

To Marich (195km);
Cherangani Hills

To Maralal
(109km)

Loruk
Rongena
Island

B4

Kampi ya
Sámaki

Ol Kokwe
Island

Parmalok
Island

*Lake
Baringo*

To
Maralal
(128km)

Tugen Hills

To Kabarnet
(24km)

C51

Marigat

Logumukum

Tigeri River

Loboro Escarpment

B4

Kesubo
Swamp

To
Nakuru
(60km)

Radat

Waseges River

Loboi gate

Siracho Escarpment

SIGHTS & ACTIVITIES

Hot Springs & Geysers......1	B4
Reserve HQ.....................2	B3

SLEEPING

Acacia Camp 3	B4
Fig Tree Camp 4	B4
Hot Springs Camp 5	B4
Island Camp Baringo 6	B2
Lake Bogoria Hotel.........7	B3
Papyrus Inn...................8	B3
Samatian Island 9	B1
VIPs Camp....................10	B3

Lake Bogoria
National
Reserve

*Lake
Bogoria*

Maji
Moto
gate

Emsos
gate

To
Mogotio
(22km)

of a sad state, really, with crumbling walls and filth pervading the rooms. Its proximity to the Loboi gate is probably its only redeeming feature.

Lake Bogoria Hotel (☎ 051-2216441; lakebogoria@ wanachi.com; s/d incl breakfast US$70/90; ☒) Set in lovely grounds around 2km before the Loboi gate, this hotel is a quality option with two swimming pools, one of them spring-fed. The rooms in the hotel are large and bright, while those in the new cottages (which are the same price) are more modern and much more comfortable. The on-site restaurant (lunch/dinner buffets KSh600/700, mains KSh100 to KSh350) serves a variety of dishes, including several vegetarian options.

The town of Marigat, located nearby, is a good place to buy local produce or to have a local meal:

Kamco Hotel (off B4 Hwy; meals KSh40-150)
Union Hotel (off B4 Hwy; meals KSh40-150)

Getting There & Away

There are three entrance gates to Lake Bogoria – Emsos in the south, Maji Moto in the west and Loboi in the north. The turn-off for Emsos and Maji Moto gates is at Mogotio, which is about 38km past Nakuru on the B4 highway, but both of these routes are poorly signposted and inaccessible without a serious 4WD.

Loboi gate is a far more straightforward point of entry, reached by taking a turnoff shortly before Marigat. It's 20km from here to the actual gate along a good sealed road. The sealed road continues to the hot springs, but is horrendous shape in this section.

The nearest petrol is found in Marigat.

Without your own vehicle, Loboi gate can be accessed by matatu from Marigat (KSh50, 30 minutes). Regular matatus serve Marigat from Nakuru (KSh180, two hours) and Kabarnet (KSh140, 1¼ hours).

LAKE BARINGO

☎ 051

This rare freshwater Rift Valley lake, encircled by mountains and its surface dotted with picturesque islands and hippos batting their eyelids, is a spectacular sight indeed. Topping the scenic surrounds is an amazing abundance of birdlife, with over 450 of the 1200 bird species native to Kenya present. For years bird-watchers have come here from all over the world to glimpse the rare and beautiful feathered flyers.

Despite being listed as Kenya's fourth Ramsar site in January 2002, Lake Baringo has been plagued with various problems over the past few years. Irrigation dams and droughts caused the water level to drop alarmingly, pulling the shoreline back several hundred metres; severe siltation due to soil erosion around the seasonal *luggas* (creeks) has meant that the water is almost always muddy; and the lake has been overfished so badly that any tilapia caught these days is rarely more than 15cm long. The water level has risen again recently, but the situation is still very delicate, and with

RIFT VALLEY

further droughts expected the ecosystem remains at risk.

Lake access is easiest from **Kampi ya Samaki** on the lake's western shore, some 15km north of Marigat. This small, quiet town used to be a fishing village, but now it depends almost entirely on tourism. Sadly the recent problems have caused visitor numbers to drop, resulting in even tougher times for the community.

It's still a lovely place to visit and locals would greatly appreciate the business.

Information

Kampi ya Samaki has traditionally charged a toll (KSh200) to enter the town, but this no longer seems to be the case. The nearest banking facilities are in Kabarnet about 40km west, while Internet access is found in Marigat's post office.

Sights & Activities

BOAT RIDES

The most popular activities around Lake Baringo are **boat rides**, which are touted as competitively as the Masai Mara is in Nairobi – there are boat offices all over town, and literally everyone you talk to will claim to have access to a boat and be able to undercut anyone else's price. A speciality is a trip to see fish eagles feeding; the birds dive for fish at a whistle, making for great (if slightly contrived) photo opportunities.

The most reliable trips are organised by the following:

Community Boats & Excursions (☎ 0720-523874; Kampi ya Samaki; per boat per hr KSh2200)

Lake Baringo Club (☎ 850880; Kampi ya Samaki; per boat per hr KSh7000)

Roberts' Camp (☎ 851879; Kampi ya Samaki; per boat per hr KSh2400)

Most boats accommodate up to seven passengers. A one-hour trip allows you to cruise the shoreline, while two hours allows you to check out Parmalok Island. With three hours you can visit Ol Kokwe Island.

BIRD WALKS

There's a constant twittering from birds in the trees around the lake, in the rushes and on the face of the escarpment near Kampi ya Samaki. Even if you're not an avid twitcher, it's hard to resist setting off on a dawn **bird walk**, when you will have a good chance of

---

SHORELINE SURPRISES

While some life in the lake is indeed struggling, crocodile populations are healthier than ever – so you'd best be careful when standing close to the shore. We got lost in the beauty of an early-morning sunrise one day while at the water's edge, and before we knew it there were 12 to 15 snouts poking from the glassy surface directly in front of us – cue speedy retreat!

While crocodiles (and hippos) do pose a threat, malarial mosquitos actually pose more of a risk here – whatever you do, remember your bug repellent.

---

seeing hornbills or a magnificent fish eagle in action. Lake Baringo Club offers the most knowledgeable guides, and it charges KSh1100 per person for a 60- to 90-minute walk. Roberts' Camp and Community Boats & Excursions leads less rewarding walks for about KSh300 per person.

CULTURAL TOURS

Lake Baringo Club offers tours to Pokot, Tugen and Njemps villages close to the lake (KSh 600); the Njemps are cousins of the Maasai and live on Ol Kokwe and Parmalok Islands and around the lakeshore, mainly practising pastoralism and fishing. You'll usually be able to walk around freely and take photos, but you'll probably be hassled to buy handicrafts. There's an additional KSh500 charge for entering each village.

OTHER ACTIVITIES

If nothing mentioned so far has floated your boat, there's even an uninhabited and uncharted **'Devil's Island'** with a fearsome reputation among the normally prosaic locals, who won't go near the place at night, claiming you can see flames and hear screaming. So far no visitors have confirmed these sightings, but it sounds a bit more exciting than bird-watching!

The rock forming the cliffs outside of the town is also apparently suitable for **technical rock-climbing**.

Sleeping

BUDGET & MIDRANGE

Roberts' Camp (☎ 851879; camping KSh350, bandas s/tw with shared bathroom KSh1000/2000, 4-person cottages KSh5000) Easily spotted off Kampi ya Samaki's main drag, next to Lake Baringo Club, is this fantastic site. It's right on the lake and offers great camping facilities, comfortable cottages as well as an open-air restaurant/bar. They also rent four-person tents, with bedding, for KSh850 per person (including camping fees) and there are even shared cooking facilities for self-caterers. If the odd bat doesn't bother you, the wooden Hammerkop cottage, with its massive deck, large loft and airy ambience, is the most atmospheric place for a snooze. Campers need to exercise some common sense regarding the hippos, which may graze within just a metre of your tent at night. Ideally you should stay at least 20m away from them when you can, especially if they have young, and don't frighten them with headlights, torches (flashlights), loud noises or flash photography. No one's been seriously hurt by a hippo in almost 15 years here, but some readers have had decidedly close calls! Remember that they are wild animals and should be treated with respect.

Bahari Lodge & Hotel (☎ 851425; Kampi ya Samaki; s/tw with shared bathroom KSh200/400) Bahari is popular with the drivers of safari vehicles, which is generally a good sign! The rooms are a little shabby but OK. The toilets are rather odoriferous.

Weavers Lodge (☎ 0721-556153; Kampi ya Samaki; s/tw KSh350/700) Down a rocky alley off the town's main drag, Weavers has good-sized rooms that come with fans, mosquito nets and comfortable beds; sadly toilet paper, soap and hot water are often lacking and the constant loud music from the bar can be a pain.

Lake View Lodge (☎ 851413; s with shared bathroom KSh100) Think prison cell block with distorted lake views. Although crude, the rooms are quite clean. The loos are outside and a little rough.

TOP END

Lake Baringo Club (☎ 850880, Nairobi 020-650500; block baringo@africaonline.co.ke; Kampi ya Samaki; high season & Nov–mid-Dec full board s/d US$120/150, mid-Dec–Mar & Jul-Oct US$150/180; ⊠) Set in sprawling lakeside gardens, this is a grand old place. The rooms are pleasant, if uninspired, with angled wooden ceilings, comfortable beds, wee terraces and linoleum floors. Facilities include a swimming pool, games room, badminton

court and library, and are open to nonguests for KSh200. There's a nightly slide show featuring beautiful birds sighted around Lake Baringo.

Island Camp Baringo (bookings ☎ 020-4447151; full board s/d US$220/295; ⊠) This luxury tented lodge sits on Ol Kokwe Island's southern tip, and it makes a perfect hideaway. It's beautifully conceived with 23 double tents set among flowering trees, all overlooking the lake. Facilities include two bars and watersports equipment. The price includes transfers from town.

Samatian Island (bookings ☎ 020-4447151; Kampi ya Samaki; full board s/d US$255/510) For a truly exclusive experience, this is the place to be. The three chalets on this tiny island are rented as a unit, and the hefty price tag is worth it for the glorious isolation. Transfers from Kampi ya Samaki are included.

Soi Safari Lodge (☎ 020-318774; www.soisafarilodge.com; Kampi ya Samaki; half board s/tw US$60/80; ⊠ ⊠) Strangely this new lodge, owned by ex-president Moi's son, thought the parking lot should have the lake views instead of the rooms – so sad but so true. Rooms are bland and the place has zero ambience. Air-con is its only redeeming feature.

Eating & Drinking

Thirsty Goat (Roberts' Camp, Kampi ya Samaki; meals KSh300-450) This lovely open-air restaurant and bar serves a welcome variety of foreign fare. It's a bit pricey, but when your nose gets a whiff of the Moroccan meatballs, your taste buds will step on your whingeing wallet's tongue.

Lake Baringo Club (Kampi ya Samaki; lunch/dinner buffets KSh1300/1460, mains KSh300-700) As you'd hope for this price, the food is mostly excellent. While you may shed a tear paying KSh120 for a large Tusker, one sip of it on the shady terrace or lakeside lawn and you'll soon be laughing again.

Bahari Lodge & Hotel (meals KSh150-200) Of Kampi ya Samaki's few remaining local restaurants, this is the best place for cheap stodge.

Self-caterers should keep in mind that while some foodstuffs may be available at Roberts' Camp, fresh vegetables and fruit are generally in short supply, and there's only a very limited stock available in Kampi ya Samaki. Bring much of what you need – Marigat usually has a good selection.

Getting There & Away

A 25-seater bus leaves for Nakuru each morning between 6.30am and 9.30am (it departs when it's full). Bar that, hop onto one of the regular pick-up trucks heading to Marigat (KSh50, 30 minutes) and catch more frequent matatus from there on to Nakuru (KSh160, two hours) or Kabarnet (KSh140, 1¼ hours).

A gravel track connects Loruk at the top end of the lake with the Nyahururu to Maralal road. If you have your own transport, it's a rough but bearable road; there's no public transport along it and hitching is extremely difficult. You can usually buy petrol at Lake Baringo Club; if you're heading northeast, it's worth noting that after Marigat, there's no reliable supply until Maralal.

Central Highlands

Forming the eastern wall of the Rift Valley and climbing from the heat of the northern plains are the Central Highlands, Kenya's heartland. What better monument to the region's importance than Mt Kenya, the country's highest mountain and Africa's second-highest peak.

Densely populated and intensively cultivated, the Central Highlands are home to the Kikuyu people, Kenya's largest and most politically favoured group (see p43). Squeezed into the mix are the Mt Kenya, Aberdare and Meru National Parks, which hold landscapes, wildlife, flora and fauna unseen elsewhere, as well as some amazing trekking possibilities.

The Laikipia Plateau, stretching into northern Kenya from Nanyuki, is also home to a conservation project that has communities and ranches working together to protect and foster wildlife outside national parks. This effort can only bode well for the region's future.

That said, the Central Highlands does have its problems, mostly tied to the purchase, division and distribution of many white farmers' lands to the Kikuyu after independence. This subdivision and its encroachment on one of Kenya's few remaining large forested areas has led to water crises and soil erosion. Many plots are also too small to support a family. Although a lot of forest still remains, demand for timber to be used as construction material and firewood (the most common form of fuel for cooking and heating) puts it at risk.

For ease of reference, the areas of the highlands that lie north of Nyahururu, Nanyuki and Meru are discussed in the Northern Kenya chapter.

HIGHLIGHTS

- Holding a frozen Kenyan flag in your frozen hands atop the frozen summit of Point Lenana on **Mt Kenya** (p261), just 16km from the Equator

- Disappearing into the depths of the riverside jungle in search of leopards at **Meru National Park** (p277)

- Testing your fear of heights while watching water fall into oblivion at Karura Falls in **Aberdare National Park** (p256)

- Meeting one of your closest relatives in the chimpanzee sanctuary at **Ol Pejata Conservancy** (p274)

- Soaring in silence over the Aberdares with the **Gliding Club of Kenya** (p254)

- Living like a Somali nomad at **Nanyuki River Camel Camp** (p272)

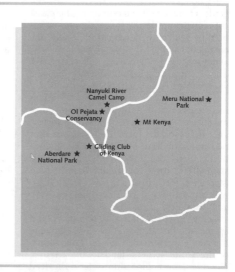

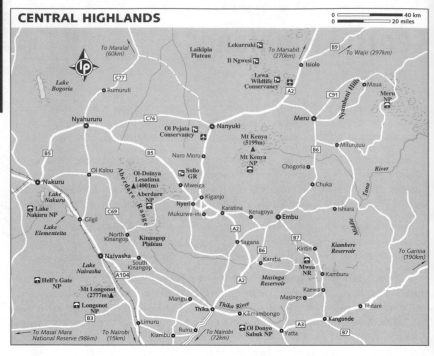

CENTRAL HIGHLANDS

History
Before Europeans arrived much of the Central Highlands was occupied by Kikuyu people, who had been accomplished farmers and herders here for several centuries. The pleasant climate and fertile soils didn't go unnoticed by settlers, who were arriving after the completion of the Mombasa–Uganda railway, and soon the Kikuyu were sadly displaced. The Central Highlands quickly became known to some as the 'White Highlands'.

The Kikuyu resented the lack of land on their reserves and many formed a resistance movement known as the Mau Mau. Resistance first took the form of strikes, but after no results the Mau Mau turned to violence in the 1950s (see p29). While not even the staunchest patriot could claim that the Mau Mau won, the uprising forced British colonial authorities to reassess their position and ultimately grant Kenya independence.

After independence this region's stand against the British wasn't overlooked by the Kenyan government, who returned much of the white settlers' land to the Kikuyu. However, the reallocation of land did lead to problems and agricultural production has yet to totally recover.

Climate
The Central Highlands enjoys perhaps the most agreeable climate in the country. Average temperatures rarely exceed 23°C and nights are pleasantly cool. Rain essentially falls in two seasons: March to the beginning of June (the 'long rains') and October to the end of November (the 'short rains').

National Parks
Mt Kenya National Park (p261) is more than just the home of Kenya's highest mountain and unique flora and fauna: it is the region's biggest attraction and treks to the summit of Pt Lenana (4985m) are the highlight of many people's trips to Africa.

While Aberdare National Park (p256) is best known to the outside world as the place Princess Elizabeth became queen, those who've been lucky enough to visit will recall it far more for its lush Salient rainforest, Kinangop Plateau and abundant wildlife.

Lesser-known Meru National Park (p277), with diverse landscapes and wildlife, is one of Kenya's best kept secrets.

The tiny national park of Ol Donyo Sabuk (p281) straddles its namesake hill and plays home to a lush forest, buffaloes, birds and primates.

Getting There & Away
AIR
Daily **Airkenya** (☎ 020-605745; www.airkenya.com) and **Safarilink** (☎ 020-600777; www.safarilink.co.ke) services link Nanyuki with Nairobi (Wilson Airport), Lewa Wildlife Conservancy and Samburu National Park. Airkenya also has three flights a week connecting the Meru National Park with Samburu and Nairobi. See Getting There & Away under the relevant sections for more details.

BUS & MATATU
The Central Highlands are linked to Nairobi, western Kenya and the southern reaches of northern Kenya by countless matatus (minibuses) and regular bus services. Limited bus services also connect the region to Mombasa and the coast.

Getting Around
This region's roads are in particularly good shape and, thanks to the new matatu safety regulations, it is safer than ever to get around. Countless buses and matatus ply the routes between all major towns.

ABERDARES

The Aberdares stretch from South Kinangop, east of Naivasha, up to the Laikipia Escarpment northwest of Nyahururu. Known to the Kikuyu as Nyandarua (meaning Drying Hide), the Aberdares were named by explorer Joseph Thomson in 1884. The lower eastern slopes of the Aberdares were long cultivated by the Kikuyu, while the higher regions (now part of Aberdare National Park), boasting 4000m peaks, 300m waterfalls, dense forests, bamboo thickets, mist-covered moors and serious trekking potential, were left to leopards, buffaloes, lions, rhinos and elephants. The Aberdares remain one of Kenya's best places to spot black rhinos.

European settlers established coffee and tea plantations on the eastern side of the Aberdares and the wheat and pyrethrum (chrysanthemum) farms on the western slopes.

NYERI & AROUND
☎ 061
A well-provisioned, lively place and one of the Central Highlands' largest towns, Nyeri is the administrative headquarters of Central Province and gateway to Aberdare National Park. In colonialism's early days Nyeri was a garrison town, but it quickly became a trading and social centre for white cattle ranchers, coffee growers and wheat farmers. The verdant surrounds are intensively cultivated for vegetables, sugar cane, citrus fruits, bananas, tea, coffee and macadamia nuts.

On a clear morning, you can see distant Mt Kenya in all its snow-capped glory. However, few travellers linger more than two nights.

Information
Internet access is available for KSh1 per minute at numerous cafés and at the three post offices, which also host card phones.
Barclays Bank (cnr Sulukia & Sharpe Rds) Exchange cash and travellers cheques (KSh34 per leaf commission). With ATM.
Kenya Commercial Bank (Kenyatta Rd) With ATM (Visa only).
Standard Chartered Bank (Kenyatta Rd) With ATM (Visa only).
Wanga Cyber Hut (Batian Exhibition Centre, Gakere Rd; per CD burned KSh50) Burn images to CD using USB connections.

Sights & Activities
SOLIO GAME RESERVE
This private 17,500-acre **reserve** (☎ 55271; B5 Hwy; adult/child/vehicle KSh1600/free/500), 22km north of Nyeri, plays a major part in preserving and breeding black rhinos in Kenya. Most of the hook-lipped horned beasts wandering national parks were actually born here. Its current population of rhinos would make some sub-Saharan countries blush!

The reserve also hosts animals like oryxes, gazelles, hartebeests, giraffes and buffaloes. While visiting you'll probably see the beautiful crowned crane and several varieties of paradise birds.

Self-drive safaris are permitted, with free maps available at the front gate. Allmendinger's guesthouse (p255) offers half-day

BEHIND THE BEANS

Kenya is a great place to buy coffee, and it is one thing you'll have no problem taking out of the country. However, next time you're sipping a frappuccino or demanding extra froth on your US$4 skinny latte, spare a thought for Kenyan coffee farmers, who number among the planet's worst-exploited commodity producers.

Coffee became something of a *cause célèbre* in 2002 when Oxfam International launched its Make Trade Fair campaign, highlighting the huge gulf between farmers' earnings and the massive profits enjoyed by multinational 'roasters'. According to Oxfam, coffee prices had slumped to a 30-year low, with farmers worldwide receiving around US$1 per kilogram, while the international industry, worth over US$2 billion annually, charged consumers almost US$15 per kilo.

The global market remains hugely oversupplied and buyers effectively force farmers to accept whatever price they offer. With most exporters buying through local cooperative societies, Kenyan growers receive as little as 4% of auction prices – a serious crisis for a country exporting up to 32,000 tons of coffee annually.

Thankfully the Make Trade Fair campaign has made gains and some major roasters now deal partially in Fair Trade Coffee, albeit as an infinitesimal fraction of their business. The sooner you demand Fair Trade Coffee for your skinny latte (don't forget that extra froth), the sooner the unjust imbalance facing Kenyan farmers will be rectified. So get ordering – you can sleep later!

---

trips for US$60 per person (minimum two people, plus admission).

BADEN-POWELL MUSEUM

Sitting within the Outspan Hotel's beautiful grounds, this **museum** (admission KSh100; ☉ 8am-6pm) was the former cottage of Lord Baden-Powell, founder of the international Scout Association. You'll find oodles of scouting paraphernalia and great mid-20th-century photos. The man himself is buried behind **St Peter's Church** (B5 Hwy).

OTHER ACTIVITIES

Nyeri's three top-end hotels offer **Wildlife drives** into Aberdare National Park (p256). Outspan Hotel is the most reasonable at KSh2500 per person (minimum two passengers) for two hours, plus park fees.

If you fancy getting your head in the clouds, the **Gliding Club of Kenya** (Map p257; ☎ 0733-760331; gliding@africaonline.co.ke; PO Box 926, Nyeri), based 2km south of Mweiga, fits the bill. A 10-minute flight costs US$50.

Every Sunday and public holiday the **Green Hills Hotel** (Bishop Gatimu Rd) hosts a day-long mini-festival of traditional dance, music and puppetry. It's free and great for kids. A dip in the swimming pool is KSh200.

Sleeping

BUDGET & MIDRANGE

Most of the cheap options will curl your toes, so here are some of the better picks.

Central Hotel (☎ 2030296; Kanisa Rd; s/tw incl breakfast KSh600/850) Central hosts bright, clean, yet slightly cramped twins, and more roomy singles, with many boasting balconies. Service here is a step up from most.

Ibis Hotel (☎ 2034858; s/tw KSh500/800) Representing good value, Ibis has comfortable and clean rooms with brilliant power-showers.

Paresia Hotel (☎ 2032765; off Gakere Rd; s/tw KSh300/500) With red cement floors and blue linoleum showers, Paresia is as colourful as it is cheap. Some rooms smell a bit musty, so sniff a few. Room 212 is the brightest of the bunch.

Nyeri Star Restaurant & Board & Lodging (☎ 2031083; Gakere Rd; s/tw KSh300/500) Slightly rougher round the edges than nearby Paresia, it still has hot showers and some sizeable rooms. The upstairs outward-facing rooms are brightest and most quiet. It is conveniently close to the bus station and parking is available.

Green Oaks (☎ 2030093; off Kimathi Way; s/tw KSh300/450) The rooms are bare-bones basic, but they're close to the upper bus stand. Its lively restaurant can get a little loud.

Batian Grand Hotel (☎ 2030743; batianhotel@ wanachi.com; Gakere Rd; s/tw KSh700/1000) Front rooms face Mt Kenya at this well-appointed place with good facilities (when the boilers aren't leaking). The small inward-facing singles are darker than the larger carpeted twins and doubles. A coffee shop, restaurant and pub are downstairs.

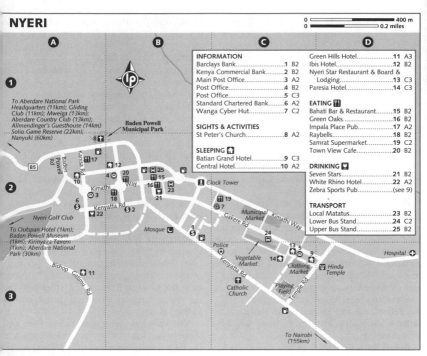

NYERI

INFORMATION
Barclays Bank...........................1 B2
Kenya Commercial Bank..........2 B2
Main Post Office......................3 A2
Post Office...............................4 B2
Post Office...............................5 C3
Standard Chartered Bank........6 A2
Wanga Cyber Hut....................7 C2

SIGHTS & ACTIVITIES
St Peter's Church......................8 A2

SLEEPING
Batian Grand Hotel..................9 B2
Central Hotel..........................10 A2

Green Hills Hotel.....................11 A3
Ibis Hotel................................12 B2
Nyeri Star Restaurant & Board &
   Lodging..............................13 C3
Paresia Hotel...........................14 C3

EATING
Bahati Bar & Restaurant.........15 B2
Green Oaks.............................16 B2
Impala Place Pub....................17 A2
Raybells..................................18 B2
Samrat Supermarket...............19 C2
Town View Cafe.....................20 B2

DRINKING
Seven Stars.............................21 B2
White Rhino Hotel...................22 A2
Zebra Sports Pub..............(see 9)

TRANSPORT
Local Matatus.........................23 B2
Lower Bus Stand.....................24 C2
Upper Bus Stand.....................25 B2

Green Hills Hotel (☎ 2030604; Bishop Gatimu Rd; s/tw from KSh1350/2300; ☒) Some distance from the town centre lies the only true midrange option. The palm-lined 'standard' rooms are comfortable and sport shady balconies with garden views. The larger 'executive' options have lounge chairs and TVs.

TOP END
These options are located within the Aberdare National Park (Map p257).

Outspan Hotel (Map p257; ☎ 2032424, Nairobi 020-4452103; www.aberdaresafarihotels.com; Apr–mid-Jul full board s/tw from US$98/130, mid-Jul–Mar US$130/160) Formerly part of Block Hotels, this lovely property has new owners, who are keen to up the standard while maintaining the historic character. The 'standard' rooms (15 to 21), with stone fireplaces and doors opening onto beautiful gardens, have the most character. While modern 'deluxe' rooms have cable TV, time is better spent on the gorgeous balconies. Outspan is found on the road to Aberdare's Kiandongoro gate.

Aberdare Country Club (Map p257; ☎ 2055620; Nairobi 020-216940; www.fairmont.com; low season full

board s/tw US$87/172, high season US$162/230; ☒) Surrounded by its own 500-hectare sanctuary east of Mweiga, this club sits atop a hill and proffers glorious views. Its new owners, Fairmont, plan on pumping millions into the place. The view and character should remain, but the rooms and service will be truly first class. Plenty of wildlife and leisurely activities (golf, tennis, horse riding etc) are in order here. Temporary membership is KSh500 per day.

Allmendinger's Guesthouse (Map p257; ☎ 0733-760331; gliding@africaonline.co.ke; PO Box 926, Nyeri; full board s/tw US$98/148) Just west of the Aberdare Country Club, this comes highly recommended, although the road here can be difficult during the rains. Prices include walking, hiking and bird-watching. Horse riding, gliding safaris and wildlife drives to surrounding parks and reserves can be arranged.

Eating
Although Nyeri is basically a chicken and chips den, there's still a good mix of cheap local eateries.

Green Oaks (Gakere Rd; meals KSh80-220) A local favourite, with tasty curries and stews, a lively bar and a great vantage point from the balcony.

Raybells (Kimathi Way; meals KSh90-220) An excellent Western-style 'family' restaurant and takeaway, serving everything from samosas to pizza.

Town View Cafe (Kimathi Way; meals KSh60-180) A small but welcoming option for traditional Kenyan fare.

Impala Place Pub (Kanisa Rd; lunch buffets KSh200; 12.30-4pm Mon-Fri) While aiming to please the business lunch crowd, it should put a smile on your face too.

Ibis Hotel (meals KSh145-245) Within the hotel's covered courtyard, a restaurant pumps out quality Kenyan dishes. It is not a bad option for breakfast.

Central Hotel (Kanisa Rd; meals KSh90-200) There's a pleasant outdoor option fronting this popular hotel. Simple sandwiches, grilled meat and savoury stews are on the menu.

Green Hills Hotel (Bishop Gatimu Rd; buffets KSh550) Touted as the top restaurant in town, the bottomless buffets are sure to leave you as full as an egg.

Bahati Bar & Restaurant (Kimathi Way; chicken & chips from KSh150) When we asked to see the menu, staff stated, 'We do chicken and chips.' Need we say more?

Samrat Supermarket (off Kimathi Way) The best stocked supermarket in town.

Drinking & Entertainment

Slide into a posh hotel for a cold beverage and a slice of the high life, or wade into a rough-and-ready dive to shoot some stick – you pick. Local hotels provide the happy middle ground.

Green Oaks (off Kimathi Way) The most friendly local bar in town, usually with European football on the box.

Kirinyaga Tavern (Outspan Hotel) While located behind the posh hotel's gates, this is actually reasonable and is separate from the hotel's bar. It has a bonfire and traditional dancing on Saturday nights.

Zebra Sports Pub (Batian Grand Hotel, Gakere Rd) An upmarket self-proclaimed sports bar.

Seven Stars (off Kimathi Way) Next to Green Oaks, this place is of the rowdy variety and is suitably messy.

White Rhino Hotel (Kenyatta Rd) The bar is the only reasonable remnant of this old hotel.

Look out for their ever-popular reggae nights.

Getting There & Away

The upper bus stand deals with big buses and sporadic matatus to most places, while the lower stand houses local buses and a multitude of matatus heading in all directions. Some local matatus are also found on Kimathi Way.

Matatus run to Nanyuki (KSh100, one hour), Nyahururu (KSh130, 1¼ hours), Thika (KSh200, two hours), Nakuru (KSh250, 2½ hours), Nairobi (KSh250, 2½ hours) and Eldoret (KSh400, five hours). Buses duplicate most of these lines; you may occasionally have to change at Karatina for Nairobi.

ABERDARE NATIONAL PARK

Created in 1950, this park essentially encloses two different environments: the striking 60km stretch of moorland, peaks and forest atop the western Kinangop Plateau and the eastern outcrop of dense rainforest known as the Salient.

The park has varieties of fauna, flora and scenery not found elsewhere. Elephants and buffaloes dominate, but other species, including black rhinos, spotted hyenas, bongo antelopes, bush pigs, giant forest hogs, black servals and rare black leopards, can also be seen. Look out for the few remaining lions (most were removed from the park to protect endangered bongo antelopes) from the viewing platforms next to the dramatic **Chania Falls** and **Karura Falls**. **Gura Falls**, which drops a full 300m down into thick forest, is less accessible.

Hundreds of bird species thrive, including giant kingfishers and regal crowned cranes.

Viewing wildlife here isn't like you'll find it on the open savannah of Amboseli and Masai Mara. The dense rainforest of the Salient provides excellent cover for the animals, so it's best to take your time and stay a few nights.

Thanks to rough terrain and minor roads turning into mud traps during the rains, KWS (Kenya Wildlife Service) restricts entry to all but 4WD vehicles. The park thus rarely features in safari itineraries and is even less visited by independent travellers. However, if you're prepared to hire a vehicle, join the lodges' tours, or hoof it on foot, your efforts will be rewarded.

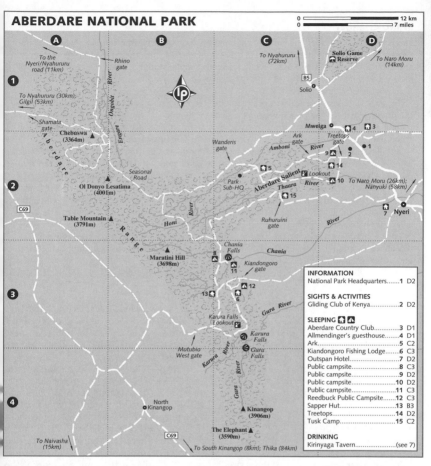

ABERDARE NATIONAL PARK

INFORMATION	
National Park Headquarters.......**1** D2	

SIGHTS & ACTIVITIES	
Gliding Club of Kenya..............**2** D2	

SLEEPING	
Aberdare Country Club.............**3** D1	
Allmendinger's guesthouse.......**4** D1	
Ark.................................**5** C2	
Kiandongoro Fishing Lodge.......**6** C3	
Outspan Hotel.....................**7** D2	
Public campsite...................**8** C3	
Public campsite...................**9** D2	
Public campsite...................**10** D2	
Public campsite...................**11** C3	
Reedbuck Public Campsite......**12** C3	
Sapper Hut.........................**13** B3	
Treetops............................**14** D2	
Tusk Camp...........................**15** C2	

DRINKING	
Kirinyaga Tavern....................(see **7**)	

Information

To enter the **park** (adult/child US$30/10, smartcard required) through the Treetops or Ark gates, ask permission at **national park headquarters** (☎ 061-2055024; Mweiga, PO Box 22, Nyeri). The headquarters, between Mweiga and Nyeri on the B5, sells the KWS Smartcard and excellent 1:25,000 maps (KSh450). Map proceeds go to the Rhino Ark Charitable Trust.

Africans are thankfully now allowed to visit the entire park and the road barrier below Tusk Camp has been removed.

Activities

TREKKING

KWS currently advises against trekking in the Salient, as the dense cover does make walking dangerous for visitors, but the high moorland and four main peaks (all 3500m to 4000m) are excellent trekking spots. As is the case on Mt Kenya, heavy rain can arrive at any time, so you must be prepared. Mud and reduced visibility are two good reasons not to trek during the heavy rains (from March to May). You'll need advance permission from the warden at park headquarters, who'll provide an armed ranger (KSh1000 per day) to guide you and protect you against inquisitive wildlife. Lonely Planet's *Trekking in East Africa* has full details of the walks. See p261 for general details on trekking or contact the Mountain Club of Kenya (p97), which is a good source of information.

RHINO CHARGE!

Locals scratch their heads, the earth screams in vain and rhinos blush with envy – yes, the Rhino Charge is no ordinary race. First run in 1989, this entertaining annual event pitches human and vehicle versus mud and bush. While it sounds simple enough – using the least amount of distance to drive your 4WD to 13 strategically-placed posts within a 100-sq-km area – doing it is another matter entirely.

To win you must theoretically steer straight between each post, just like rhinos charge through the jungle. However, the organisers have a sense of humour, so the course takes advantage of natural obstacles too insane for most to tackle straight on. The fact that some try is where the entertainment value arises! If you're in Kenya when it takes place, don't miss it.

It's all in the name of charity and funds go to **Rhino Ark Charitable Trust** (www.rhinoark.org), who are constructing an electric fence around the perimeter of the Aberdare National Park and greater Aberdare Conservation Area. Once finished, the 340km fence will keep animals safely within the park (and out of fragile local farms) and stop local villagers encroaching on the forest. Over 230km of fence has been completed and Rhino Ark hope to finish in 2007. Don't worry, the charge will continue after the fence is done – large funds are required for the fence's maintenance and other Rhino Ark projects.

For environmental reasons the charge is held at a different venue each year and only the top 60 fund-raising vehicles can participate. Check out Rhino Ark's website for information and entry details – charge!

FISHING

Trout fishing is very popular, especially high up on the moors, but requires a permit from park headquarters (KSh100). Kiandongoro Fishing Lodge makes a good base and the Chania River is great for brown trout, but watch your back – there are tales of fishers being stalked by lions! Lions or not, best get an armed ranger to escort you.

Sleeping

BUDGET & MIDRANGE

The following accommodation must be booked through park headquarters.

Public campsites (adult/child US$10/5) Basic sites with minimal facilities – some have water.

Tusk Camp (exclusive use per night KSh6000) Near Ruhuruini gate, these four cottages provide beds for eight to 10 people, a kitchen area (no pots, utensils etc), toilets, hot water, a dining/lounge area and great views.

Sapper Hut (exclusive use per night KSh2000) A simple banda, with an open fire, two beds and a hot-water boiler, overlooking a waterfall on the Upper Magura River. You'll need to bring everything from drinking water to bedding.

Kiandongoro Fishing Lodge (7-person cottages Jan-Jun US$200, Jul-Dec US$250) Sitting in an excellent spot on the high moor by the Gura River, these two large stone cottages offer bathrooms, gas-powered kitchens, dining rooms and fireplaces.

TOP END

Prices below include transfers (self-drive isn't permitted) from Outspan Hotel in Nyeri (for Treetops) and Aberdare Country Club near Mweiga (for Ark). Children under seven are prohibited at both lodges.

Treetops (☎ 020-4452095; www.aberdaresafarihotels .com; mid-Jul–mid-Dec full board s/tw with shared bathroom US$135/180, mid-Dec–mid-Jul US$198/250) It was at this very floodlit waterhole in 1952 that a sleeping princess became Queen Elizabeth II, upon the death of George VI. In 1957, three years after Mau Mau guerrillas turned the original into ashes, a much larger rendition was built on the opposite side of the waterhole.

Today, with faded, peeling bark siding and cast-iron spiral staircases, Treetops' exterior resembles a weathered shipwreck. The narrow wood-lined hallways, miniature rooms, bench-seated dining hall and shared bathrooms are just as shiplike, but thankfully they don't scream nautical disaster. Despite its quirks, Treetops reeks of charm and there's still one lone tree meandering its way through the floors, ceilings and walls near reception. Besides a great rooftop wildlife viewing area and photographic hides, there's an onsite naturalist who gives talks and happily answers questions.

Ark (☎ 020-216940; www.fairmont.com; low season full board s/tw US$75/150, high season US$185/250) What this modern upscale version of Treetops lacks in history and charm, it makes up for in comfort and wildlife viewing. Sitting higher in the Aberdares, Ark's floodlit waterhole is surrounded by grasses and mountain forest, which attracts a wider array of animals than Treetops. Nightly visitors typically include elephants, rhinos, buffaloes and spotted hyenas. Spotting a leopard is less likely, but still a real possibility. Like Treetops, they dubiously spread salt to attract wildlife, but here it's confined to a smaller area, meaning there's less trampling of vegetation along the waterline (crucial for timid species to approach).

Getting There & Away

Access roads from the B5 Hwy to the Wanderis, Ark, Treetops and Ruhuruini gates are in decent shape, while the road from Nyeri to Kiandongora gate is horrendous.

Regular Nyeri–Mweiga matatus (KSh50, 35 minutes) pass KWS headquarters and the main park gates. Since trekking the Salient is inadvisable, most trekkers use the Wanderis gate.

Nyeri's Outspan Hotel charges KSh2500 per person (minimum two people) for wildlife drives into the lower Salient, while the Aberdare Country Club charges US$160 per vehicle; both rates exclude park entry fees.

NYAHURURU (THOMSON'S FALLS)

☎ 065

Set next to Thomson's Falls, one of Kenya's most impressive waterfalls and the town's former namesake, is Nyahururu. At 2360m, this is Kenya's highest major town, and it has a cool and invigorating climate. Besides the falls and some nice forested walks, most travellers find little reason to linger more than a day or two.

One of the last white settlements to be established in the colonial era, Nyahururu didn't take off until the arrival of the Gilgil railway spur in 1929; now the trains carry only freight, and the town is once again becoming an agricultural backwater. The surrounding plateau is highly cultivated with maize, beans and sweet potatoes – they are all well represented in Nyahururu's lively markets.

The best approach to town is along the amazingly scenic road from Nakuru, which snakes up and down through the Sukukia

Valley's undulating farmlands and dense forests.

Information

Barclays Bank (cnr Sulukia & Sharpe Rds) Exchange cash and travellers cheques (KSh34 per leaf commission). With ATM.

Clicks Cyber Cafe (Mimi Centre, Kenyatta Rd; per hr KSh180) Best Internet other than post office.

Kenya Commercial Bank (Sulukia Rd) With ATM (Visa only).

Post office (Sulukia Rd) With Internet and card phones.

Sights & Activities

THE FALLS

Located on the town's outskirts and formed by the waters of the Ewaso Narok River, **Thomson's Falls** plummets over 72m into a ravine and the resulting spray bathes the dense forest below in a perpetual mist. Get down, get close and get wet, we say! A series of stone steps leads to the bottom of the ravine – don't attempt to go down any other way as the rocks on the side of the ravine are often very loose.

There are some fantastic **walks** downstream through the forested valley of the Ewaso Narok River and upstream a couple of kilometres to one of the highest hippo pools in Kenya. Take time to explore a little. Guides are fairly easy to find, especially around the souvenir shacks overlooking the falls, but you'll have to bargain hard.

The falls were named by Joseph Thomson, the first European to walk from Mombasa to Lake Victoria in the early 1880s.

Sleeping

Nyahururu has a couple of places with single rooms for KSh150, but that's really scraping the bottom of the barrel.

Safari Lodge (Go Down Rd; s/tw KSh300/500) This massive new place is very clean, very bright and very affordable. Hot water is on demand and there are even sockets to charge your mobile.

County Hostel (off Sulukia Rd; s KSh200) Behind the Nyandarua County Council headquarters, this place has quiet rooms with bathrooms and even toilet seats. At this price that's saying something! Couples can squeeze into the beds.

Nyaki Hotel (☎ 22313; off Kenyatta Rd; s/tw KSh350/800) This relatively modern five-storey building hosts small but comfy singles and large

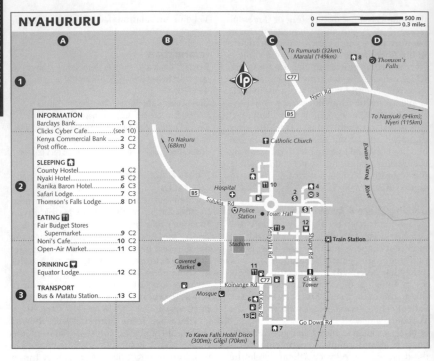

NYAHURURU

0 _____ 500 m
0 _____ 0.3 miles

INFORMATION
Barclays Bank.........................1 C2
Clicks Cyber Cafe.............(see 10)
Kenya Commercial Bank 2 C2
Post office............................3 C2

SLEEPING
County Hostel.......................4 C2
Nyaki Hotel..........................5 C2
Ranika Baron Hotel...............6 C3
Safari Lodge.........................7 C3
Thomson's Falls Lodge..........8 D1

EATING
Fair Budget Stores
    Supermarket....................9 C2
Noni's Cafe.........................10 C2
Open-Air Market..................11 C3

DRINKING
Equator Lodge.....................12 C2

TRANSPORT
Bus & Matatu Station...........13 C3

To Rumuruti (32km);
Maralal (149km)

Thomson's
Falls

To Nanyuki (94km);
Nyeri (115km)

Nyeri Rd

C77

B5

To Nakuru
(68km)

Catholic Church

Hospital

Sulukia Rd

Police
Station

Town Hall

Train Station

Stadium

Kenyatta Rd

Sharpe Rd

Covered
Market

Koinange Rd

C77

Clock
Tower

Mosque

Go Down Rd

To Kawa Falls Hotel Disco
(300m); Gilgil (70km)

Ewaso Narok River

---

clean twins that are essentially poor-man's suites. Rooms 131, 128, 119 and 116 are the brightest singles. It also features hot-water showers and secure parking.

Ranika Baron Hotel (☎ 32883; Ol Kalou Rd; s/tw/ste KSh350/500/850) This place is a little tattered, but the beds in the singles are large and married couples can share for no extra cost.

Thomson's Falls Lodge (☎ 22006; tfalls@africaonline .co.ke; off B5 Hwy; camping KSh300, s/tw incl breakfast KSh2200/2800) While the white planters are long gone, this nostalgic and cosy lodge that overlooks the falls still has character to spare. The main building and several cottages scattered around the manicured grounds have rooms with log fireplaces and decent facilities. The grassy campground is a right bargain, with free firewood and hot showers. As you'd expect, the lodge also has a charming bar, lounge and restaurant.

Eating
Noni's Cafe (Mimi Centre, Kenyatta Rd; meals KSh60-150) Easily the cleanest and most welcoming of Nyahururu's local eateries. It's a great spot for breakfast.

Thomson's Falls Lodge (off B5 Hwy; mains KSh150-500, buffets KSh800) This is the best (and only) place to go for a minor splurge. Stuff yourself at a buffet or delve into Irish stew, mutton specialties or beef burgers. Packed lunches (KSh350) are available for guests. The grounds are a great place for a picnic, though it will cost KSh50 per group.

Nyaki Hotel (off Kenyatta Rd; meals KSh80-200) Probably the best of the many hotels serving standard Kenyan fare.

Ranika Baron Hotel (☎ 32883; Ol Kalou Rd; meals KSh75-200) Like Nyaki, it serves quality Kenyan eats.

For those who want to prepare their own meals, there are fruit and vegetables at the **open-air market** (off Koinange Rd). The brave can also find meat at the **covered market** (off Koinange Rd). The **Fair Budget Stores supermarket** (Kenyatta Rd) is fairly well-stocked.

Drinking & Entertainment
Thomson's Falls Lodge (off B5 Hwy) With plank floors, comfortable armchairs and blazing log fires, this is *the* place to enjoy a cold Tusker.

Equator Lodge (Sharpe Rd) We'll give this local bar an 'A' for effort regarding their kitschy forested facade. Inside they get a 'C' for late night carnage.

Kawa Falls Hotel disco (Ol Kalou Rd; admission KSh100; ☺ weekends) This popular disco occasionally hosts well known Kenyan DJs.

Getting There & Away

Numerous matatus run to Nakuru (KSh100, 1¼ hours) and Nyeri (KSh150, 2 hours) until late afternoon. Less plentiful are services to Naivasha (KSh200, 1½ hours), Nanyuki (KSh250, three hours) and Nairobi (KSh250, three hours). The odd morning matatu reaches Maralal (KSh300, three hours).

Several early morning buses also serve Nairobi (KSh230-250, three hours).

If you're driving north, fill up on petrol here, as it is much pricier in Maralal.

MT KENYA NATIONAL PARK

Astoundingly, just 16km from the equator, 12 glaciers continue to shape the jagged roots of what was once Africa's tallest mountain. After seeing the 5199m worth of dramatic remnants that today comprise Mt Kenya (now Africa's second-highest mountain), it's easy to understand why the Kikuyu people deified it and still believe it's the seat of their supreme god Ngai.

Fortunately for the many travellers who try the ascent every year, Ngai doesn't seem to be concerned by trekkers. However, you'd be wise not to temp fate, so treat Mt Kenya with the utmost respect (see Responsible Trekking p265). Besides being venerated by the Kikuyu, Mt Kenya has the rare honour of being both a Unesco World Heritage Site and a Unesco Biosphere Reserve.

Mt Kenya's highest peaks, Batian (5199m) and Nelion (5188m), can only be reached by mountaineers with technical skills. However, Point Lenana (4985m), the third-highest peak, can be reached by trekkers and is the usual goal for most mortals, offering a fantastic experience without the risks of technical climbing. As you might imagine, there are superb views over the surrounding country from Point Lenana, although the summit is often cloaked in mist from late

morning until late afternoon. Above 3000m is mountain moorland, characterised by remarkable flora (see p262).

As marvellous as the summit is, a common complaint from trekkers is that they didn't allow enough time to enjoy the entire mountain. Walks through the foothills, particularly those to the east and northeast of the main peaks, and the Summit Circuit around Batian and Nelion, are dramatic and tremendously rewarding. You won't regret setting aside a week or 10 days rather than just four days for a summit rush.

If time is short or you don't want to do all the planning yourself, see p264.

INFORMATION

The daily fees for the **national park** (☎ 061-55645; PO Box 253, Nyeri; adult/child US$15/8) are charged upon entry, so you must estimate the length of your stay. If you overstay, you must pay the difference when leaving. You'll have to pay an additional KSh50 per day for each guide and porter you take with you. Always ask for a receipt.

Before you leave Nairobi buy a copy of *Mt Kenya 1:50,000 Map & Guide* (1993) by Mark Savage & Andrew Wielochowski. It has a detailed topographical map and full descriptions of the routes, mountain medicine, flora and fauna, and accommodation. It is stocked by the main bookshops in Nairobi and by some shops abroad, like Stanford's in London.

Lonely Planet's *Trekking in East Africa* has more information, details on wilder routes and some of the more esoteric variations that are possible on Mt Kenya.

Technical climbers and mountaineers should get a copy of **Mountain Club of Kenya's** (MCK; Nairobi ☎ 020-602330; www.mck.or.ke) *Guide to Mt Kenya & Kilimanjaro*, edited by Iain Allan. This substantial and comprehensive guide is available in bookshops or from the MCK offices (p97). MCK also has reasonably up-to-date mountain information posted on its website.

SAFETY

Mt Kenya's accessibility and the technical ease with which Point Lenana can be reached create their own problems for enthusiastic trekkers. Many people ascend much too quickly and end up suffering from headaches, nausea as well as other (sometimes

CENTRAL HIGHLANDS

MT KENYA'S FLORA

The volcanic soil and rivers that radiate from the central cone of Mt Kenya have created a fertile environment, especially on the rainy southern and eastern slopes. Despite farms encroaching on the mountain up to an altitude of 1900m, the lower slopes are well wooded. Above this zone, apart from the odd spot where logging occurs, is untouched rainforest. Among the abundant species of plants here are giant camphors, along with vines, ferns, orchids and other epiphytes. On the drier northern and western slopes, conifers are the predominant trees.

On the southern and western slopes, as altitude increases, the forest gradually merges into a belt of dense bamboo. This eventually gives way to more open woodland consisting of hagena and hypericum trees, along with an undergrowth of flowering shrubs and herbs. Further up still is a belt of giant heather that forms dense clumps up to 4m high, interspersed with tall grasses.

Open moorland forms the next zone and this is often very colourful, with a profusion of small flowering plants. Here you'll find the amazing groundsel tree with enormous cabbagelike flowers and the bizarre giant lobelias and senecios. This moorland zone extends up to the snow line at around 4600m. Beyond the snow line, the only plants you'll find are mosses and lichens.

---

more serious) effects of altitude sickness. By spending at least three nights on the ascent, you'll enjoy yourself much more.

Another problem can be unpredictable, harsh, cold, wet and windy weather. The trek to Point Lenana isn't an easy hike and people die on the mountain every year. With proper clothes and equipment, you stand a much better chance of making it back down. The best time to go is from mid-January to late February or from late August to September.

Unless you're a seasoned trekker with high altitude experience and a good knowledge of reading maps and using a compass, you'd be flirting with death by not taking a guide or by hiking with someone who isn't qualified. Even those with ample experience should take a guide if attempting the Summit Circuit.

CLOTHING & EQUIPMENT

Seeing that Mt Kenya's summits are surrounded by glaciers and often covered by snow, you shouldn't be surprised to hear that nightly temperatures often drop to below -10°C (it certainly feels like it in Mackinder's hut), so bring a good sleeping bag. A closed-cell foam mat or thermarest is also vital for insulation if you're camping. A good set of warm clothes (wool or synthetics – never cotton, as it traps moisture), including quality headgear and gloves, is equally important. As it can rain heavily at any time of year, you'll also need waterproof clothing (breathable fabric like Gore-Tex is best). While a decent pair of boots isn't strictly necessary, hiking in sodden joggers isn't fun

and neither is losing your grip on wet or icy rocks near the summit. Bringing a pair of sandals or light shoes to wear in the evening when your boots get wet is a great idea. At this altitude the sun can do some serious damage to your skin and eyes, so sun block and sunglasses are also crucial items.

If a porter is carrying your backpack, always keep essential clothing (warm and wet weather gear) in your day-pack because you may become separated for hours at a time.

It's not a good idea to sleep in clothes you've worn during the day because the sweat your clothes absorbed keeps them moist at night, reducing their heat-retention capabilities.

If you don't intend to stay in the huts along the way, you'll need a tent and associated equipment.

You'll also need a stove, basic cooking equipment, utensils, a 3L water container (per person) and water-purifying tablets. Stove fuel in the form of petrol and kerosene (paraffin) is fairly easily found in towns, and methylated spirits is available in Nairobi, as are gas cartridges, although the supply of these isn't guaranteed. Fires are prohibited in the open except in an emergency; in any case, there's no wood once you get beyond 3300m. If you engage porters, you'll have to supply each of them with a backpack to carry your gear and theirs.

If you have a mobile phone, take it along, suitably protected of course; reception on the mountain's higher reaches is actually very good, and a link to the outside world is invaluable during emergencies.

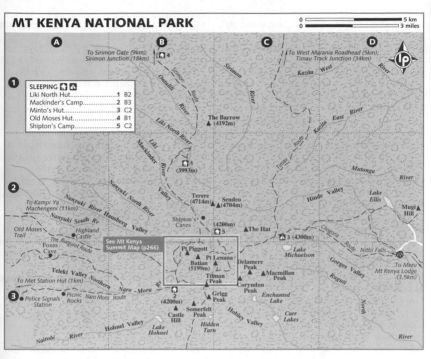

MT KENYA NATIONAL PARK

SLEEPING
Liki North Hut.........................1 B2
Mackinder's Camp..................2 B3
Minto's Hut............................3 C2
Old Moses Hut.......................4 B1
Shipton's Camp......................5 C2

Equipment Hire

Well-maintained rental gear is available at
the **Naro Moru River Lodge** (Map p271; ☎ 062-62212;
mt.kenya@africaonline.co.ke; PO Box 18, Naro Moru), although it can't be reserved and is relatively
expensive (US$4 per day for a sleeping bag).
Most guiding companies will have cheaper
equipment for hire, although you'll have less
choice and lower standards.

GUIDES, COOKS & PORTERS

Taking on a guide and a porter will improve
your chances of getting to the top and avoiding altitude sickness. For starters, having a
porter carrying your heavy gear is like travelling in a chauffeured Mercedes instead of a
matatu. A good guide will help set a sustainable pace and hopefully dispense interesting
information about Mt Kenya and its flora,
fauna and wildlife. With both on your team,
your appreciation of this mountain will be
enhanced a hundredfold and, for the price,
it is a bargain.

If you hire a guide or porter who can also
cook, you'll won't regret it. It's one thing to
arrive at camp safe, sound and enlightened,

but arriving to steaming coffee and a hot
meal is beyond nice – it's heaven.

Considerable effort has been made in recent years to regulate guides and porters
operating on the mountain. The KWS now
issues vouchers to all registered guides and
porters, who should also hold identity cards;
they won't be allowed into the park without
them.

Female guides are becoming more common, and technical guides for climbing Batian and Nelion are widely available.

Costs

Basic qualified guides, like those from **Mt
Kenya Guides & Porters Safari Club** (Map p271;
☎ 062-62015; PO Box 128, Naro Moru), will cost you
KSh750 per day. Cooks cost about the same,
while porters charge KSh650. Guides with a
little more knowledge, such as those from
Mountain Rock Lodge (Map p271; ☎ 062-62625; info@
mountainrockkenya.com), will set you back US$15
per day, while cooks and porters cost US$12
per day.

These fees don't include park entry fees
and tips (budget around a day's wages per

person as a tip, but make it clear it is only for good service).

If you ascend the mountain along one route and descend along a different one, you'll be responsible for arranging and paying the transport costs for your porter and guide back to where they started from. It is wise to sort this out before you start, and agree on a price for return transport plus any additional wages (a day spent travelling home counts as a working day), food and hotel costs along the way.

Porters will carry up to 18kg for three-day trips or 16kg for longer trips, excluding the weight of their own food and equipment. If you want them to carry more, you'll have to negotiate an added cost. A normal day's work is regarded as one stage of the journey; if you want to go further you'll have to pay two days' wages, even if porters don't do anything the following day.

SLEEPING

You can **camp** (adult/child US$10/5) anywhere on the mountain – the nightly fee is payable to KWS at any gate. Most people camp near the huts or bunkhouses, as there are often toilets and water nearby. If setting up remote camps, see opposite for tips on waste disposal and camp location.

There are several huts on the mountain owned by MCK, but the only one that's in reasonable shape nowadays sits 5188m up on Nelion's summit – not for the typical punter!

Accommodation along the major trekking routes, whether in huts or larger bunkhouses, is described in detail in each route's accommodation section.

For information about pre- and post-trekking accommodation, see p269.

EATING

In an attempt to reduce luggage, many trekkers forgo taking stoves and cooking equipment and exist entirely on canned and dried foods. You can certainly do this by keeping up your fluid intake, but it's not a good idea. That cup of hot soup in the evening and pot of coffee in the morning can make all the difference between enjoying the trek and hating it, or at least feeling irritable.

There are, however, a few things to bear in mind about cooking at high altitudes. The

major consideration is that the boiling point of water is considerably reduced. At 4500m, for example, water boils at 85°C; this is too low to sufficiently cook rice or lentils (pasta is better) and you won't be able to brew a good cup of tea either (instant coffee is the answer). Cooking times and fuel usage are considerably increased as a result, so plan accordingly.

The best range of suitable mountain foods is to be found in Nairobi's supermarkets, especially Nakumatt and Uchumi (p115). Elsewhere, there's a good range in the towns around the mountain (Nyeri, Nanyuki, Embu and Meru), but precious little at Naro Moru or Chogoria.

When you're buying dehydrated foods, get the pre-cooked variety to cut down on cooking time – two-minute noodles are a solution. It's a good idea to bring these from home.

Take plenty of citrus fruits and/or citrus drinks as well as chocolate, sweets or dried fruit to keep your blood-sugar level high. Fresh fruit and vegetables are available in all reasonably sized towns and villages.

To avoid severe headaches caused by dehydration or altitude sickness, drink at least 3L of fluid per day and bring rehydration sachets.

ORGANISED TREKS

If time is limited or you'd prefer someone else to make all the trekking arrangements, there are plenty of possibilities. It is hard to go anywhere in this region without being approached by several prospective guides. All-inclusive packages – which include park entry and camping fees, food, huts, a guide, cook and porters, and transfers to and from the mountain – can be a good deal, particularly if you don't have any equipment.

As always, you need to watch out for sharks; picking the right company is even more important here than on a normal wildlife safari, as an unqualified or inexperienced guide could put you in real danger as well as spoil your trip.

Mountain Rock Safaris Resorts & Trekking Services (☎ 020-242133; www.mountainrockkenya.com; PO Box 15796-00100, Nairobi), in Jubilee Insurance House in Nairobi, is a real specialist at Mt Kenya climbs and runs the Mountain Rock Lodge (p271) near Naro Moru. Its day rates for all-inclusive trips start at US$135 per person per day, but drop to as low as US$80 if five or more people are in your group. These prices are a good benchmark for quality service.

Naro Moru River Lodge (Map p271; ☎ 062-62212; mt.kenya@africaonline.co.ke; PO Box 18, Naro Moru) also runs a range of all-inclusive trips. Its prices are more expensive than most (US$135 to US$220 per person per day depending on group size), but it's the only company that can guarantee you beds in the Met Station Hut and Mackinder's Camp on the Naro Moru route.

There are several safari companies in Nairobi that offer Mt Kenya treks, but many just sell the treks operated by Naro Moru and Mountain Rock Lodges, charging you an extra commission on top. Companies that do run their own treks include the following.

IntoAfrica (☎ 0114-255 5610; www.intoafrica.co.uk; 40 Huntingdon Crescent, Sheffield, UK, S11 8AX) This environmentally and culturally sensitive company places an emphasis on fair trade and offers both scheduled and exclusive seven-day trips (six days of trekking) ascending Sirimon route and descending Chogoria. Joining scheduled trips costs US$139 per day (minimum two people), while private treks

range from US$128 to US$256 per person per day, depending on group size.

KG Mountain Expeditions (☎ 062-62403; www.kenyaexpeditions.com; PO Box 199, Naro Moru) This company, run by a highly experienced mountaineer, offers all-inclusive packages from US$265 per day (depending on group size), as well as no-frills budget options for around US$80.

Mountain View Tours & Trekking Safaris (☎ 062-62088; PO Box 48, Naro Moru) Recommended by readers as being cheap and reliable. Prices are negotiable, but expect to pay around US$60 to US$70 per day.

Sana Highlands Trekking Expeditions (☎ 020-227820; www.sanatrekkingkenya.com; Contrust House, Moi Ave, PO Box 5400-00100, Nairobi) Sana operate five-day all-inclusive treks on the Sirimon and Chogoria routes that start at US$325 per person (based on a group of five).

THE ROUTES

There are at least seven different routes up Mt Kenya. Of those, we cover Naro Moru, the easiest and most popular, as well as Sirimon and Chogoria, which are excellent alternatives. The Burguret and Timau routes

---

RESPONSIBLE TREKKING

Mt Kenya's trekking popularity is placing great pressure on the environment. You can help preserve the ecology and beauty of the area by taking note of the following information.

- Carry out all your rubbish. Never ever bury it.

- Minimise the waste you must carry out by taking minimal packaging and no more food than you'll need.

- Where there's no toilet, at lower elevations bury your faeces in a 15cm deep hole (consider carrying a lightweight trowel for this purpose). At higher altitudes soil lacks the organisms needed to digest your faeces, so leave your waste in the open where UV rays will break it down – spreading it facilitates the process. Always carry out your toilet paper (Ziplock bags are best). With either option make sure your faeces is at least 50m from any path, 100m from any watercourse and 200m from any building.

- Don't use detergents or toothpaste within 50m of watercourses, even if they're biodegradable.

- Stick to existing tracks and avoid short cuts that bypass a switchback. If you blaze a new trail straight down a slope, it will erode the hillside with the next heavy rainfall.

- Avoid removing plant life, as it keeps topsoil in place.

- Open fires aren't permitted. Cook on lightweight kerosene, alcohol or Shellite (white gas) stoves.

- Never feed wildlife, as it messes with their digestive system and leads them to become dependent on hand-outs.

- If camping, try to camp on existing sites. Where none exist, set up away from streams on rock or bare ground, never over vegetation.

CENTRAL HIGHLANDS

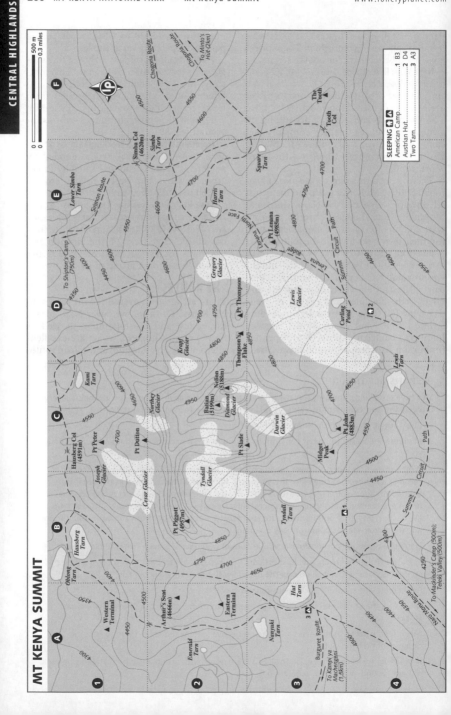

MT KENYA SUMMIT

0   500 m
0   0.3 miles

SLEEPING
American Camp..........1 B3
Austrian Hut............2 D4
Two Tarn................3 A3

are less well known and are described in Lonely Planet's *Trekking in East Africa*.

We also delve into the exciting but demanding Summit Circuit, which circles Batian and Nelion, thus enabling you to mix and match ascending and descending routes.

With the mountain usually shrouded in mist after 10am, you should set off early each morning to make the most of the trek. For the final Point Lenana assault, make a very early start to see the sunrise and the views from the top, which (if you're lucky) can include Mt Kilimanjaro.

Naro Moru Route

Although the least scenic, this is the most straightforward and popular route and is still a spectacular and very enjoyable trail. Begin in the town of Naro Moru (p270) and allow a minimum of four days for the trek. While possible in three, if you arrange transport between Naro Moru and the Met Station, doing it this quickly risks serious altitude sickness.

SLEEPING

There are three good bunk houses along this route: **Met Station Hut** (Map p271; dm US$12) is at 3000m, **Mackinder's Camp** (Map p263; dm US$12) is at 4160m and **Austrian Hut** (Map p266; dm KSh1000) is at 4790m. Austrian Hut (booked and paid for at any gate) has just been overhauled and is finally in good shape. Beds in Met Station and Mackinder's are harder to find, as they're booked through **Naro Moru River Lodge** (Map p271; ☎ 062-62212; mt.kenya@africaonline.co.ke; PO Box 18, Naro Moru). If you're denied beds, you can still climb this route if you're willing to camp and carry all the appropriate equipment.

GUIDES & PORTERS

Apart from the Naro Moru River Lodge in Naro Moru itself, guides, porters and cooks can be booked through **Mt Kenya Guides & Porters Safari Club** (Map p271; ☎ 062-62015; PO Box 128, Naro Moru). Its office is 5km along the road towards the Naro Moru gate, but its staff also scout for business at hotels in town.

Mountain Rock Lodge (Map p271; ☎ 062-62625; info@mountainrockkenya.com) also provides guides/porters for this route at a cost of US$15/12 per day. However, like most places, the lodge 'encourages' you to take an expensive all-inclusive package.

THE TREK

Starting in Naro Moru town, the first part of the route takes you along a relatively good gravel road through farmlands for some 13km (all the junctions are signposted) to the start of the forest. Another 5km brings you to the park entry gate (2400m), from where it's 8km to the road head and the Met Station Hut (3000m), where you stay for the night.

You can also get up to the park gate (18km from Naro Moru) in 2WD in dry weather, although you won't make it to the Met Station in anything other than a 4WD. Both roads are deteriorating and often become impassable in wet weather. You can get a matatu from the post office in Naro Moru to Kiambuthi (KSh50), 3km short of the park gate. This takes you past Blue Line Hotel (p270), Mt Kenya Guides & Porters Safari Club and Mt Kenya Hostel & Campsite (p270).

On the second day, set off up the Teleki Valley to the edge of the forest (at about 3200m). From here you scale the so-called **Vertical Bog** onto a ridge, where the route divides into two. You can either take the higher path, which gives better views but is often wet, or the lower, which crosses the Naro Moru River and continues gently up to Mackinder's Camp (4160m). This part of the trek should take about 4½ hours. Here you can stay in the dormitories or camp. There are toilets, and drinking water is available. The caretaker checks your bunkhouse booking receipts.

On the third day you can either rest at Mackinder's Camp to acclimatise or aim for **Point Lenana** (4895m). This stretch takes four to five hours, so it is common to leave around 2am (you'll need a torch or flashlight) to reach the summit in time for sunrise. From the bunkhouse, continue up past the ranger station to a fork in the path. Keep right, and go across a swampy area, followed by a moraine, and then up a very long scree slope – this is a long, hard slog. KWS' Austrian Hut (4790m) is three to four hours from Mackinder's and about one hour below the summit of Lenana, so it's a good place to rest before the final push. Alternatively, you could arrive here on the third day, then go for the summit on the morning of the fourth. Facilities are basic, although the hut has been recently refurbished.

The section of the trek from Austrian Hut up to Point Lenana takes you up a narrow rocky path that traverses the southwest ridge parallel to the Lewis Glacier, which has shrunk more than 100m since the 1960s. A final climb or scramble brings you up onto the peak. In good weather it's fairly straightforward, but in bad weather you shouldn't attempt to reach the summit unless you're experienced in mountain conditions or have a guide. Plenty of inexperienced trekkers have come to grief on this section, falling off icy cliffs or even disappearing into crevasses.

From Point Lenana most people return along the same route – assuming you summit early, you can reach the Met Station on the same day. Alternatively, you can return to Austrian Hut, then take the Summit Circuit around the base of the main peaks to reach the top of one of the other routes before you descend.

Sirimon Route

A popular alternative to Naro Moru, this route has more spectacular scenery, greater flexibility and a gentler rate of ascent, although it is still easy to climb too fast, so allow at least five days for the trek. It's well worth considering combining it with the Chogoria route for a six- to seven-day traverse that will really bring out the best of Mt Kenya.

Nanyuki (p272) is the best launching point for this route.

SLEEPING

Old Moses Hut (Map p263; dm US$10) at 3300m and **Shipton's Camp** (Map p266; dm US$12) at 4200m serve trekkers on this route. They're both booked through the **Mountain Rock Lodge** (Map p271; ☎ 062-62625; info@mountainrockkenya.com), near Naro Moru.

Depending on how you ascend or descend, you may also sleep at **Austrian Hut** (Map p266; dm KSh1000), which is almost an hour below the summit. It's booked and paid for at any park gate.

GUIDES & PORTERS

In Nanyuki, guides operating out of **Mt Kenya Mountaineering Information Office** (Map p273; ☎ 0733-340849; Mt Kenya Paradise Hotel) are generally quite reliable, but ask to see their KWS registration and go over your planned route in detail. The people at **Montana Trek &**

Information Centre (Map p273; ☎ 062-32731; Jambo House Hotel, Lumumba Rd, Nanyuki) seem to know their stuff but are a bit more pushy.

Guides/porters are also available from Mountain Rock Lodge for US$15/12 per day. As with the Naro Moru route, they prefer it if you take all-inclusive packages.

THE TREK

It is 15km from Nanyuki to the Sirimon Gate, and transport is included with pre-booked packages. Otherwise take a matatu towards Timau or Meru, or arrange a lift from town. From the gate it's about 9km through the forest to Old Moses Hut (3300m), where you can spend the first night.

On the second day you could head straight through the moorland for Shipton's Camp, but it is worth taking an extra day to go via **Liki North Hut** (Map p263; 3993m) a tiny place on the floor of a classic glacial valley. The actual hut is a complete wreck and is only meant for porters, but it's a good campsite with a toilet and stream nearby. You can also walk further up the valley to help acclimatise.

On the third day, head straight up the western side of the Liki North Valley and over the ridge into Mackinder's Valley, joining the direct route about 1½ hours in. After crossing the Liki River, follow the path for another 30 minutes until you reach the bunkhouse at Shipton's Camp (4200m), which is set in a fantastic location right below Batian and Nelion. The camp is also within sight of two glaciers, which can often be heard cracking.

From Shipton's you can push straight for **Point Lenana** (4895m), a tough three- to four-hour slog via Harris Tarn and the tricky north face approach, or take the Summit Circuit in either direction around the peaks to reach Austrian Hut (4790m), about one hour below the summit. The left-hand (east) route past Simba Col is shorter but steeper, while the right-hand (west) option takes you on the Harris Tarn trail nearer the main peaks.

From Austrian Hut take the standard southwest traverse up to Point Lenana – see p267. If you're spending the night here, it's worth having a wander around to catch the views up to Batian and down the Lewis Glacier into Teleki Valley, as well as the spectacular **ice cave** by the Curling Pond.

Chogoria Route

This route is justly famous for crossing some of the most spectacular and varied scenery on Mt Kenya, and is often combined with the Sirimon route (usually as the descent). The only disadvantage is the long distance between Chogoria village (p279) and the park gate. Allow at least five days for a trek here. Side trips to Lake Michaelson and Lake Ellis would take up a couple of extra days.

SLEEPING

The only option besides camping on this route is **Meru Mt Kenya Lodge** (Map p271; s/tw US$22/44), a group of comfortable cabins administered by **Meru County Council** (Map p276; Kenyatta Hwy, Meru).

GUIDES & PORTERS

The best place to organise guides and porters is the **Mt Kenya Chogoria Guides & Porters Association** (Map p271; ☎ 064-22096) at the Transit Motel (p280) near Chogoria village. Guides and porters aren't available beyond Chogoria Forest Station.

If you want porters to walk the whole stretch between Chogoria and the park gate, you may be charged two extra days' wages – make sure you negotiate everything before you leave.

THE TREK

The main reason this route is more popular as a descent is the 29km bottom stage. While it is not overly steep, climbing upwards for that distance is much harder than descending it. Either way, it's a beautiful walk through farmland, rainforest and bamboo zones. You can camp near the Forest Station 6km out of town, but you'll still have 23km to walk the next day. Transport is available from the village, but it'll cost you, and even a Land Rover may struggle in the wet.

Camping is possible at the gate, or you can stay nearby in Meru Mt Kenya Lodge (3000m) – with transport to town available and a small shop selling beer, which is also popular with people coming down.

On the second day, head up through the forest to the trailhead (camping is possible here). From here it's another 7km over rolling foothills to the Hall Tarns area and **Minto's Hut** (Map p263; 4300m). Like Liki North, this nasty hut is only intended for porters, but the area makes a decent campsite. It has a stream for water and a long-drop loo – which, incidentally, finally has a door (though it won't close!). Don't use the tarns here to wash anything, as they have already been polluted by careless trekkers.

From here you follow the trail up alongside the stunning **Gorges Valley** (another possible descent route for the adventurous) and scramble up some steep ridges to meet the Summit Circuit, which can take you in either direction. It is possible to go straight for the north face or southwest ridge of Point Lenana, but stopping at Austrian Hut or detouring to Shipton's Camp is probably a better idea and gives you more time to enjoy the scenery – see Sirimon (opposite) and Naro Moru routes (p267) for details.

Summit Circuit

While everyone who summits Pt Lenana gets a small taste of the spectacular Summit Circuit, few trekkers ever grab the beautiful beast by the horns and hike its entire length. The trail encircles the main peaks of Mt Kenya between the 4300m and 4800m contour lines and offers challenging terrain, fabulous views and a splendid opportunity to familiarise yourself with this complex mountain. It is also a fantastic way to further acclimatise before bagging Pt Lenana.

One of the many highlights along the route is a peek at Mt Kenya's southwest face, with the long, thin Diamond Couloir leading up the Gates of the Mists between the summits of Batian and Nelion.

Depending on your level of fitness, this route can take between four and nine hours. Some fit souls have bagged Point Lenana (from Austrian Hut or Shipton's Camp) and then completed the Summit Circuit in the same day.

The trail can be deceptive at times, especially when fog rolls in, and some trekkers have become seriously lost between Tooth Col and Austrian Hut. It is imperative to take a guide if attempting this route.

AROUND MT KENYA

Mt Kenya's vast bulk looms over the entire region, and the snow-covered peaks can be seen for miles until late-morning clouds obscure the view. The sheer distance involved, and the variety of landscapes covered while circumnavigating the mountain, says something of its majesty.

To the west sit the undulating grassy plains of the Laikipia Plateau, home to the friendly town of Nanyuki, oodles of agriculture and one of sub-Saharan Africa's most important wildlife conservation sites. Skirting north of the mountain are the vast northern plains, dotted with volcanic cones and the Matthews Range in the distance. To the east and south, the landscape is more steep and home to thick forests, although logging (both legal and illegal) is paving the way for more crops of coffee and *miraa* (a leafy shoot with amphetamine-like effects), and threatening what is one of the country's most important water catchment areas. Further east is one of Kenya's most diverse and underrated national parks, Meru.

If we haven't made it clear already, there's much to see around Mt Kenya besides Mt Kenya. Break the mould and delve a little deeper into this unique region.

NARO MORU
☎ 062

The village of Naro Moru, on the western side of the mountain, is little more than a dusty string of shops and houses, with a couple of very basic hotels and a market, but it's the most popular starting point for treks up Mt Kenya. There's a post office with Internet, but no banks (the nearest are at Nanyuki and Nyeri).

Sights & Activities

Apart from gawking at Mt Kenya and starting the Naro Moru route up to its summit (p267), there are some fine things to do here. Mt Kenya Hostel & Campsite organises a number of excursions, including **nature walks** and hikes to the **Mau Mau caves**. Mountain Rock Lodge and Naro Moru River Lodge also run similar trips, as well as offering **horse riding** and **fishing**.

Sleeping & Eating

Although there are a number of basic hotels in Naro Moru town, the best options are in the surrounding few kilometres. Eating options are incredibly slim, with only some hotels offering meals. There's a tiny store selling foodstuffs next to the post office, but you're better off shopping in Nanyuki or Nyeri.

BUDGET

Note that both of the midrange and top-end options have great campsites.

Mt Kenya Hostel & Campsite (Map p271; ☎ 62412; mtkenyahostel@wananchi.com; camping KSh250, dm KSh400) About 8.5km from town and 7.5km from the park gate, this place offers simple accommodation, a large campsite, kitchen facilities and a bar. The restaurant (lunch/dinner KSh200/KSh300) provides much needed calories, but don't expect your tastebuds to sing. They rent limited mountain gear as well as a 4WD vehicle. Mt Kenya treks can be arranged here too.

Mountain View Hotel (☎ 62088; A2 Hwy; s KSh520) This is the best option in town and is very basic. Patent red cement floors host large single beds (couples can squeeze in for no extra dough) and the bathrooms have hot showers. Treks and equipment can be arranged here.

Blue Line Hotel (Map p271; ☎ 62420; camping KSh150, s/d KSh400/800) Similar in scope to its sister hotel the Mountain View, but hot showers are only available in the morning here. Blue Line is 3km from town and 1.5km from the Mt Kenya Guides & Porters office (convenient for organising guides the day before), but lies 13km short of the park gate. The hotel is generally pleasant and quiet, and has a bar and restaurant (meals KSh180 to KSh280). Rooms are clean.

Mt Kenya Guides & Porters Safari Club (Map p271; ☎ 62015; camping KSh150) You may also camp here. The club can provide tents (two-person tent KSh600). The site is rather primitive and the loos are rather grim – showers come in buckets.

Joruna Lodge (s/tw with shared bathroom KSh200/300, s KSh250) Just east of Mountain View, the singles with bathrooms and twin rooms pass the cringe test, but the rest don't. You get what you pay for and that's not much.

MIDRANGE & TOP END

Naro Moru River Lodge (Map p271; ☎ 62212, Nairobi 020-4443357; mt.kenya@africaonline.co.ke; camping US$10, dm US$8, May-Jun & mid-Sep–mid-Dec half board from s/tw US$55/82, Mar-Apr US$66/96, rest of year US$90/120; 🏊) This relaxing lodge is about 1.5km north of town and is set on the sloping bank of the Naro Moru River in beautifully landscaped gardens. The Standard rooms are well-equipped, while the pricier 'superior' rooms also have shady balconies. The 'deluxe' rooms are larger and also boast

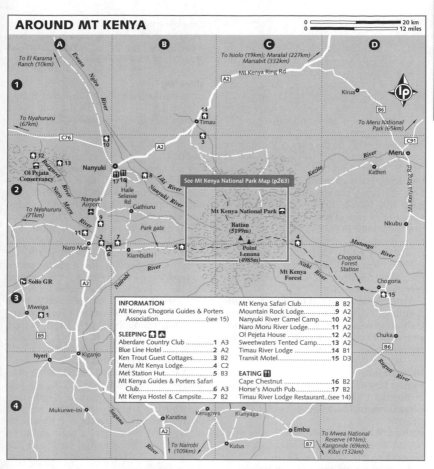

AROUND MT KENYA

0 _____ 20 km
0 _____ 12 miles

INFORMATION
Mt Kenya Chogoria Guides & Porters
Association.........................(see 15)

SLEEPING 🛏️ ⛺
Aberdare Country Club 1 A3
Blue Line Hotel 2 A2
Ken Trout Guest Cottages..........3 B2
Meru Mt Kenya Lodge................4 C2
Met Station Hut.........................5 B3
Mt Kenya Guides & Porters Safari
Club.......................................6 A3
Mt Kenya Hostel & Campsite......7 B2

Mt Kenya Safari Club.................8 B2
Mountain Rock Lodge................9 A2
Nanyuki River Camel Camp......10 A2
Naro Moru River Lodge............11 A2
Ol Pejeta House 12 A2
Sweetwaters Tented Camp........13 A2
Timau River Lodge 14 B1
Transit Motel...........................15 D3

EATING 🍴
Cape Chestnut 16 B2
Horse's Mouth Pub..................17 B2
Timau River Lodge Restaurant..(see 14)

vaulted ceilings and fireplaces. In addition, there's a well-equipped campsite as well as a dormitory block offering hot showers, toilets and firewood. Campers are able to use all the hotel facilities, which include two bars and a restaurant (breakfast/dinner KSh500/KSh1000).

Mountain Rock Lodge (Map p271; ☎ 62625; info@ mountainrockkenya.com; camping US$5; standard s/tw US$24/32, superior s/tw or tr US$32/48) This place is located 6km north of Naro Moru, tucked away in the woods less than 1km from the Nanyuki road. The standard rooms at the lodge are decent value, while the 'superior' rooms have a bit of character to go with their fireplaces. You could also save a few dollars if you rent a fixed-tent (s/tw/tr

US$15/20/24) or setting up your own in the campsite. Camping facilities include hot water, toilets, cooking facilities, electricity and ample firewood. It is a friendly and reliable place with a spacious dining room, two bars and a lounge. See p264 for information about the lodge's guided treks.

Getting There & Away
There are plenty of buses and matatus heading to Nanyuki (KSh60, 30 minutes), Nyeri (KSh80, 45 minutes) and Nairobi (KSh300, three hours).

Naro Moru River Lodge operates transfers between the lodge and Nairobi (US$80) or Nanyuki airstrip (US$25), but you must book 24 hours in advance.

CENTRAL HIGHLANDS

NANYUKI

☎ 062

Founded by white settlers in 1907, Nanyuki is a small but very energetic country town. It is a popular and friendly place to base Mt Kenya treks, especially if taking on the Sirimon and Burguret routes, though you'll probably experience some initial hassle from the slew of guides, touts and hawkers.

Besides lapping against Mt Kenya's slopes, Nanyuki also sits on the edge of the massive Laikipia Plateau, which is currently one of Africa's most important wildlife conservation sites. Local communities and ranches here are being encouraged to share their space with wildlife, like lions, elephants and Grevy's zebras, and to adjust their activities to allow wildlife to flourish while at the same time decreasing potential human-animal conflict (see p323). Ol Pejata Conservancy (p274), 17km south of Nanyuki, is a prime example of this sweeping and successful conservation movement.

You may be surprised to hear local kids spouting Cockney rhyming slang. They owe their linguistic prowess to the annual invasion of British army units who visit the region on joint manoeuvres.

Information

Barclays Bank (Kenyatta Ave) Exchange cash and travellers cheques (KSh34 per leaf commission). With ATM.

Kenya Commercial Bank (Kenyatta Ave) With ATM (Visa only).

Marina Grill & Restaurant (Kenyatta Ave; Internet per hr KSh60) Internet access, cheap international calls and burning images to CD (KSh80) using USB port.

Mt Kenya Cyberworld (Kenyatta Ave; per hr KSh60) Internet and cheap international calls.

Post office (Kenyatta Ave) With Internet and card phones.

Standard Chartered Bank (Kenyatta Ave) With ATM (Visa only).

Sights & Activities

Besides tackling Mt Kenya's Sirimon (p268) or Burguret routes, you could stroll 3km south to the **Equator** and check the antics of draining water. (If a flushing toilet's water moves clockwise in the northern hemisphere and anti-clockwise in the south, what will it do here?)

If you'd rather punish your backside instead of your feet, the **Nanyuki River Camel Camp** (Map p271; ☎ 0722-361642; camellot@wananchi .com; off C76 Hwy) offers great half-/full-day camel journeys for US$16/20. And if punishment isn't in your dictionary, how about a day of the high life at **Mt Kenya Safari Club** (Map p271; ☎ 30000; temporary membership KSH495).

Sleeping

In town there are no shortage of budget or midrange options, while the only swank option, Mount Kenya Safari Club, is 11km away.

BUDGET

Nanyuki River Camel Camp (Map p271; ☎ 0722-361642; camellot@wananchi.com; off C76 Hwy; camping US$6, half board huts with shared bathroom US$22) The only camping near Nanyuki is at this fabulous place 4km out of town. The firewood is free and there are decent facilities. The woven huts are modelled on a traditional Somali nomadic village and they're highly authentic – spending the night in one is an experience indeed. The food is excellent and the 200 camels are available for hire.

Ibis Hotel (☎ 31536; Lumumba Rd; s/tw KSh500/900) Bright rooms and a brighter covered courtyard lurk behind Ibis Hotel's facade of fresh tiles and woodwork. It is a comfortable, clean place and all rooms have mozzie nets. Angle for a room with a Mt Kenya view.

Mt Kenya Paradise Hotel (☎ 0722-899950; off Kenyatta Ave; s/tw KSh400/600) Formerly the Nanyuki Riverside Hotel, this place is a little dog-eared but has large clean rooms and is a good place to meet other travellers. It backs onto the Nanyuki River – grab a chair and sit on the terrace to the sound of birds and gurgling water. It's best avoided on weekends due to the disco.

Joskaki Hotel (☎ 31473; Lumumba Rd; s/tw/d KSh300/400/450) This is the best of the budget establishments. If you wander, you may hit the Joskaki jackpot: a room with some sun and a toilet seat! There's secure parking as well as a lively bar and restaurant.

Nyahururu Horizon Hostel (☎ 0723-741542; Lumumba Rd; s/tw KSh250/400) A step down from Joskaki but a decent place for a night's snooze. Expect the odd roach perusing the pavement floors.

MIDRANGE & TOP END

Equator Chalet (☎ 31480; Kenyatta Ave; s/tw/d incl breakfast KSh800/1200/1450) This newish place in the centre of town gives substantial comfort bang for minimal buck. Rooms surround a

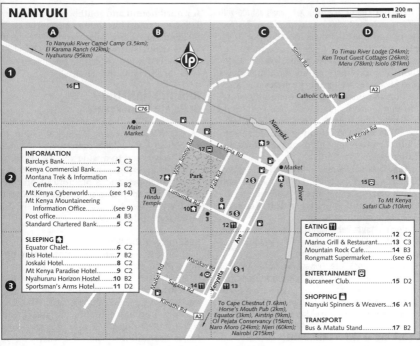

NANYUKI

INFORMATION
Barclays Bank...........................1 C3
Kenya Commercial Bank..........2 C2
Montana Trek & Information
Centre..................................3 B2
Mt Kenya Cyberworld...........(see 14)
Mt Kenya Mountaineering
Information Office...............(see 9)
Post office...............................4 B3
Standard Chartered Bank.........5 C2

SLEEPING
Equator Chalet.........................6 C2
Ibis Hotel.................................7 B2
Joskaki Hotel............................8 C2
Mt Kenya Paradise Hotel...........9 C2
Nyahururu Horizon Hostel.......10 B2
Sportsman's Arms Hotel..........11 D2

EATING
Camcorner..............................12 C2
Marina Grill & Restaurant........13 C3
Mountain Rock Cafe................14 B3
Rongmatt Supermarket...........(see 6)

ENTERTAINMENT
Buccaneer Club.......................15 D2

SHOPPING
Nanyuki Spinners & Weavers....16 A1

TRANSPORT
Bus & Matatu Stand................17 B2

breezy internal courtyard that opens onto two balcony areas and a roof terrace. The doubles have four-poster canopy beds and more modern bathrooms.

Sportsman's Arms Hotel (☎ 32348; www.sportsmansarms.com; off Laikipia Rd; s/d/tw incl breakfast KSh3000/4000/4600, 4-person cottages KSh7000; ⊠) Set in landscaped gardens along the road east of town, this was once the white settlers' main rendezvous, and is still popular with tourists and soldiers. The modern single and double rooms outclass the older twin rooms, but the cottages are best: there's a choice of older thatched cottages and stunning modern ones dripping with facilities. The complex boasts a sauna, a gym, a Jacuzzi, tennis, squash, a restaurant and three bars (with table football).

Mt Kenya Safari Club (Map p271; ☎ 30000, Nairobi 020-216940; www.fairmont.com; full board s/d US$270/390, 4-person cottages US$995; ⊠ ⊠) Originally the homestead of a white settler family, this club was founded in the 1950s by a group including the late actor William Holden. Already one of the flashiest top-class resorts in Kenya, it's recently been bought by Fairmont

and they have big posh plans. If golf, tennis, croquet, snooker, swimming, fishing, bowls, an art gallery and a private wildlife sanctuary with a herd of rare bongo antelopes tickle your fancy, sign right up (though most cost extra). The views up Mt Kenya are excellent and there's a hedge maze that kids will love. Couples should ask for the riverside cottages (no more pricey than standard rooms), while families will love the charming family cottages. Access is from a well-signposted turn-off about 2km south of Nanyuki, from which it's 9km along a paved road.

Eating

You'll find that most of Nanyuki's best restaurants are attached to hotels.

Sportsman's Arms Hotel (off Laikipia Rd; meals KSh150-450) Having Nanyuki's widest ranging menu, the Sportsman's Arms has long been heralded as the town's top restaurant. After having one of their curries, we won't argue.

Ibis Hotel (Lumumba Rd; meals KSh70-240) Steaks are the Ibis' claim to fame, though most meals are equally pleasing.

Equator Chalet (Kenyatta Ave; meals KSh100-200) The marinated chicken with garlic butter, herbs and roast potatoes hits the spot. It's a pleasant place for a meal.

Camcorner (Kenyatta Ave; meals KSh60-260) A delightful oddity serving up the usual stews and steaks, as well as fiery curries and a selection of camel products (including camel *biltong* – jerky).

Marina Grill & Restaurant (Kenyatta Ave; meals KSh90-350) Sit on the rooftop and delve into a burger or steak. The pizzas are tasty but embarrassingly small.

Cape Chestnut (Map p271; off Kenyatta Ave; ☺ Mon-Sat) This is an excellent coffee garden and snack place catering mostly for white farmers, expats and tourists. It's off Kenyatta Ave, 1km south of town.

Horse's Mouth Pub (Map p271; Haile Selassie Rd; meals KSh150-400) This place near Cape Chestnut caters for a similar clientele.

Mountain Rock Cafe (Kenyatta Ave; meals KSh60-200) Popular with locals, this is a good spot for cheap Kenyan fare.

Rongmatt Supermarket (Kenyatta Ave) A decent supermarket where trekkers can stock up.

Drinking & Entertainment

The eateries Cape Chestnut and Horse's Mouth Pub are pleasant places to enjoy a daylight beer, while in the evening the rooftop of Marina Grill & Restaurant is a good choice.

The **Buccaneer Club** (Laikipia Rd; ☺ Wed & Sat evenings) may look like a UFO, but its disco is nothing out of this world.

Shopping

There are a number of souvenir stalls and shops around town, catering mostly to the British army – if you have gear to swap, this is the place to do it.

Nanyuki Spinners & Weavers (Laikipia Rd) For something less tacky, try this women's craft cooperative that specialises in woven woollen goods. The product and pattern design is high quality and is cheaper than the same work in Nairobi.

Getting There & Away

Airkenya (☎ 020-605745; www.airkenya.com) and **Safarilink** (☎ 020-600777; www.safarilink.co.ke) fly daily from Wilson Airport in Nairobi to Nanyuki. A return trip on Airkenya/Safarilink costs US$130/149, while one way fares

for northbound and southbound flights are US$60/70 and US$80/90 respectively.

There are daily buses and matatus to Nyeri (KSh100, one hour), Isiolo (KSh150, 1½ hours), Meru (KSh120, 1½ hours) and Nairobi (KSh350, three hours).

AROUND NANYUKI
Ol Pejata Conservancy

Formerly called the Sweetwaters Game Reserve, this impressive 97-sq-km (soon to be 300-sq-km) **wildlife conservancy** (adult/child US$25/13) is home to a wide variety of plains wildlife, including the Big Five, massive eland antelopes and a plethora of birdlife. There's also an important **chimpanzee sanctuary** (☺ 9-10.30am & 3-4.30pm), operated by the Jane Goodall Institute.

SLEEPING & EATING

There are two top-end accommodation options in the reserve.

Sweetwaters Tented Camp (Map p271; ☎ 062-32409, Nairobi 020-2710511; sweetwaters@serena.co.ke; low season full board s/d US$90/180, high season US$235/310) Recently purchased by Serena Hotels, this equator-straddling place is up for some major renovations. There are currently 30 permanent tents beneath thatched roofs that sit beside a floodlit waterhole (tent numbers one and two have the best view). It has a lovely small bar and a lounge where wicker abounds. Activities available include wildlife drives (US$45), walking safaris (US$21) and camel rides (US$11 per hour).

Ol Pejeta House (Map p271; ☎ 062-32400, Nairobi 020-2710511; swtc@kenyaweb.com; low season full board s/d US$210/270, high season US$270/390) Once home to Lord Delamere and subsequently the holiday getaway of the now bankrupt international arms dealer Adnan Kashoggi, this house has also just been bought by Serena Hotels. Whether they'll keep Adnan's lavish decorations and his massive 4m x 4m bed is anyone's guess. Rates include wildlife drives.

GETTING THERE & AWAY

You can visit the reserve independently if you have your own vehicle. Access is off the A2 Hwy south out of Nanyuki. Mt Kenya Safari Club (p273) runs half-day wildlife drives for US$55 per person (minimum two passengers); guests staying two or more nights get free entry to the conservancy and lunch at Sweetwaters Tented Camp.

Timau

This tiny town is a convenient stop between Isiolo and Nanyuki and has a couple of interesting accommodation options, offering a range of activities.

SLEEPING & EATING

Timau River Lodge (Map p271; ☎ 062-41230; timau riverlodge@hotmail.com; off A2 Hwy; camping KSh300, cottages incl breakfast per person KSh1400) A wonderfully offbeat place, consisting of several lovely thatched cottages of varying sizes and a well-equipped campsite with a large covered cooking area. The restaurant (meals KSh150 to KSh450) is good and it happily caters to vegetarians. Besides offering all-inclusive treks (US$70 per day) up Mt Kenya on the rarely used Timau route, the lodge also offers camel treks (KSh850 per day), cultural visits (KSh600 per day) and safaris to Ol Pejeta Conservancy (US$68, minimum two people). There's a good chance of seeing elephants and other wildlife nearby.

Ken Trout Guest Cottages (Map p271; ☎ 0720-804751; off A2 Hwy; camping KSh300, half board cottages per person KSh2500) This place, 3km south of Timau, is a more mainstream establishment with an excellent restaurant (meals KSh450; 11am to 5pm). There is some very good fishing here, although you pay for everything you catch. The main house (which sleeps up to eight) is rented exclusively and has old plank floors and brick fireplaces in most rooms. The cottages are much smaller but more cosy.

GETTING THERE & AWAY

Any matatu running between Nanyuki and Isiolo, or Nanyuki and Meru, will happily drop you in Timau or at the turn-off to either sleeping option.

El Karama Ranch

About 42km to the northwest of Nanyuki, **El Karama Ranch** (☎ 062-32526, Nairobi 020-340331; info@ letsgosafari.com; bandas per person KSh2500) is on the Ewaso Ngiro River. Although still a working ranch, wildlife conservation is paramount and the 5668-hectares play home to lions, leopards, elephants, hippos, buffaloes and rare northern species like Grevy's zebras and reticulated giraffes. Billed as a 'self-service camp', it's an old family-run settlers' ranch with a number of basic but comfortable riverside bandas. Seated long-drop toilets and showers are close by. Bring everything you need, including food. Activities here include wildlife walks, horse riding and camel safaris (see www.horsebackinkenya.com). Let's Go Travel (p101)in Nairobi provides a map with directions. During the rainy seasons you'll need a 4WD to get here; however, as driving around the ranch is discouraged and there's little public transport, it's usually better to phone and arrange to be picked up, generally from Nanyuki.

MERU

☎ 064

Stretched out along the eastern side of the Mt Kenya ring road, Meru isn't so much a base of operations for Mt Kenya or Meru National Park, but rather a travel hub. Whether you end up having to spend the night here, or just stop to stock up on various commodities, it's worth a look around.

Because it's a regional service centre and not a tourist destination you'll rarely be hassled on the streets, despite them being alive with activity. The colourful main market is worth a stroll and if you ever thought of chewing *miraa* (see p277), Meru is the epicentre of Kenyan production.

It's quite a climb up to Meru from either Isiolo or Embu, and in the rainy season you'll find yourself lost in the clouds. However, when the weather is clear there are superb views for miles over the surrounding lowlands, and you may catch glimpses of Mt Kenya.

The town is a focal point for the Meru people (see p43).

Information

Barclays Bank (Tom Mboya St) Exchange cash and charge 1% commission on travellers cheques. With ATM.
Cafe Candy (Tom Mboya St; Internet per hr KSh180) Decent Internet connections.
Kenya Commercial Bank (KCB; Njiru Ncheke St) Exchange cash and travellers cheques (KSh50 per leaf commission).
Meru County Council (Kenyatta Hwy) Bookings for Meru Mt Kenya Lodge on the Chogoria route.
Post office (Kenyatta Hwy) With Internet and card phones.
Standard Chartered Bank (Moi Ave) Exchange cash and travellers cheques (KSh50 per leaf commission).

Sights

The small **Meru National Museum** (☎ 20482; off Kenyatta Hwy; adult/child KSh200/100; ☺ 9.30am-6pm,

CENTRAL HIGHLANDS

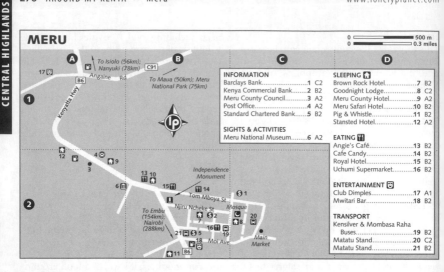

MERU

0 ————— 500 m
0 ————— 0.3 miles

To Isiolo (56km);
Nanyuki (78km)

Angaine Rd

C91

To Maua (50km); Meru
National Park (75km)

Kenyatta Hwy

To Embu
(154km);
Nairobi
(288km)

Independence
Monument

Tom Mboya St

Njiru Ncheke St

Mosque

Moi Ave

Main
Market

INFORMATION
Barclays Bank.....................1 C2
Kenya Commercial Bank.......2 B2
Meru County Council...........3 A2
Post Office.........................4 A2
Standard Chartered Bank.....5 B2

SIGHTS & ACTIVITIES
Meru National Museum........6 A2

SLEEPING
Brown Rock Hotel...............7 B2
Goodnight Lodge................8 C2
Meru County Hotel..............9 A2
Meru Safari Hotel..............10 B2
Pig & Whistle...................11 B2
Stansted Hotel.................12 A2

EATING
Angie's Café....................13 B2
Cafe Candy.....................14 B2
Royal Hotel.....................15 B2
Uchumi Supermarket.........16 B2

ENTERTAINMENT
Club Dimples...................17 A1
Mwitari Bar.....................18 B2

TRANSPORT
Kensilver & Mombasa Raha
Buses...........................19 B2
Matatu Stand...................20 C2
Matatu Stand...................21 B2

1-6pm public holidays) is worth visiting. The usual displays are present, with an explanation of evolution and copious stuffed and mounted wildlife, but there's also a small and informative section concerning the clothing, weapons, and agricultural and initiation practices (including clitoridectomies) of the Meru people.

Sleeping

Nothing here will truly float your boat, but hopefully those listed below won't sink it either.

Goodnight Lodge (☎ 30057; Mosque Hill Rd; s incl breakfast KSh350) Probably the best budget option. Rooms and bathrooms (hot water showers but no toilet seats) are clean and the upstairs options take in some sun. Breakfast is a bit of a joke (two boiled eggs and buttered bread).

Brown Rock Hotel (☎ 20247; Njiru Ncheke St; s/tw KSh350/450) Although the brown-and-white floor tiles are failing, this is still your best bet for cheap twin-bedded rooms. Some are brighter and have balconies, so check out a few. Hot water is sketchy at times.

Meru Safari Hotel (☎ 31500; Kenyatta Hwy; s/tw KSh600/800) Considering your hot water showers come from the kitchen in buckets, this place is overpriced. Rooms are slightly more comfortable than those seen at Goodnight and Brown Rock. The terrace bar is its greatest asset.

Stansted Hotel (☎ 31119; Kenyatta Hwy; s KSh200) Any cleanish rooms at this price with

bathrooms (and toilet seats) are a blessing indeed. It's quiet too, but the beds aren't comfortable.

Pig & Whistle (☎ 31411; off Kenyatta Hwy; s/tw incl breakfast KSh1000/1200) This place has a distinctly ramshackle charm to it, with nice quiet grounds and a colonial-style bar/restaurant and lounge. Most of the cottages are uninspiring concrete blocks, but TV, phone and a dining area go some way towards compensating. More memorable stays are to be had in the old (1934) wooden cabins.

Meru County Hotel (☎ 20432; Kenyatta Hwy; s/tw incl breakfast from KSh1000/1500) This is the other midrange contender in town, with a bit less style but a few more creature comforts. The 'studio' suites, with balconies and TVs, are well worth the extra KSh100.

Eating & Drinking

With French, Thai, Chinese, Indian and Kenyan fare gracing menus, you won't go hungry here. OK, we're joking about the Thai, Chinese and French bits (how cruel of us!) but that still leaves you with Indian and Kenyan.

Pig & Whistle (off Kenyatta Hwy; meals KSh60-250) Flowering hedges separate tables in this scenic garden eatery that serves up tasty Kenyan fare. It's also a great place for an afternoon beer.

Meru County Hotel (Kenyatta Hwy; meals KSh60-280) Thatched umbrellas hover over each table on this pretty *nyama choma* (barbecued meat) terrace. If you want to give the flaming flesh a rest, Western, Kenyan and Indian meals are also on offer.

Royal Hotel (Tom Mboya St; meals KSh80-150) Deep pots ensure they still have food late in the evenings when most places are coming up empty. The bar is very popular at weekends.

Cafe Candy (Tom Mboya St; meals around KSh50-180) A very popular place with locals, this is a good place for cheap vegetarian curries, stews and fish during the day.

Angie's Café (Kenyatta Hwy; meals KSh50-150) Sedated goldfish patrol the aquarium and watch over some simple menus. Locals recommend the biryani.

Uchumi supermarket (off Mosque Hill Rd) A very well-stocked option for self-caterers.

Entertainment

The **Mwitari Bar** (off Moi Ave), behind the Shell petrol station, is an odd, weirdly Swiss Family Robinson–style structure, which sometimes hosts live bands. The only other evening action is at **Club Dimples** (Angaine Rd; cover KSh50; ✪ Wed, Fri & Sat evenings), which is an energetic disco joint up the hill.

Getting There & Away

Kensilver (Mosque Hill Rd) has 13 daily departures from 6.45am onwards, covering Embu (KSh250, two hours), Thika (KSh280, 3½ hours) and Nairobi (KSh300, 4½ hours). **Mombasa Raha** (Mosque Hill Rd) has daily 5pm services to Mombasa (KSh900, 10 hours).

Regular matatus serve the same destinations for similar costs and leave from the main stand, near the main market, and from opposite the Shell petrol station. Matatus also serve Nanyuki (KSh120, 1½ hours) and Isiolo (KSh120, 1½ hours).

MERU NATIONAL PARK

This national park is the cornerstone of the Meru Conservation Area, a 4000-sq-km expanse that also includes the adjacent Kora National Park, and Bisanadi, Mwingi and North Kitui National Reserves (which are

---

MIRAA – MAKING MANY PLANS

The small twigs and leaves you'll see people chewing around Mt Kenya are *miraa*, the product of an evergreen tree native to East and Southern Africa, Afghanistan and Yemen. It's also known as *coas* and *khat*, and over 40 other names around the world. Chewing *miraa* is an increasingly popular pastime in Kenya, but it's not nearly as important as in Somalia, where the drug is ingrained in the culture: in 1983 consumption reached such epidemic proportions that the government tried to ban it.

Some of the best *miraa* in the world is grown around Meru and it's a whopping US$250-million export industry. Of course much of the demand is from Somalia and, since *miraa*'s potency is diminished 48 hours after picking, massively overladen pick-up trucks race nightly to Wilson Airport in Nairobi for the morning flight to Mogadishu.

Miraa is a mild stimulant. Chewing it predates coffee drinking and is deeply rooted in the cultural traditions of some societies, especially in Muslim countries. It's usually chewed in company to encourage confidence, contentment and a flow of ideas. Locals selling the stuff are often heard saying, 'when you chew miraa you'll make many plans…' Make plans is right, though getting around to doing anything about your much-vaunted plans is another thing entirely! The active ingredient, *cathinone,* is closely related to amphetamine, and the euphoric effects can last for up to 24 hours, depending on how much is chewed.

Chewing too much can be habit-forming and has serious consequences, known medically as '*khat* syndrome'. Aggressive behaviour, nightmares and hallucinations are common mental side-effects, while reduced appetite, malnourishment, constipation and brown teeth are common physical consequences. Even less pleasant are claims that *miraa* can cause spermatorrhoea (abnormal leakage of sperm – just delightful), leading to infertility.

Miraa is illegal in the USA, but is legally imported into several European countries, including the UK – though they are thinking of banning it. In Kenya it's sold in handfuls known as *kilos* or *gizas* for between KSh100 and KSh300, depending on size. Meru is a good place for curious travellers to give it a go, but those who don't gag at their first taste (there aren't many) usually only notice that it keeps them awake for prolonged periods. The texture is rather unpleasant too – funnily enough, it's just like chewing twigs.

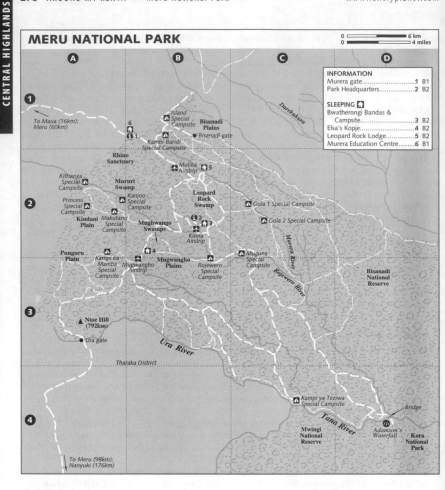

MERU NATIONAL PARK

INFORMATION
Murera gate..........................**1** B1
Park Headquarters................**2** B2

SLEEPING 🏠
Bwatherongi Bandas &
    Campsite...........................**3** B2
Elsa's Kopje..........................**4** B2
Leopard Rock Lodge.............**5** B2
Murera Education Centre........**6** B1

closed), covering the lowland plains east of Meru town.

KWS has big plans for this park. In the 1970s the populations of rhinos and elephants could pull in up to 40,000 visitors a year, but banditry and poaching during the 1980s effectively put paid to tourism here, wiping out the white rhinos and leaving the area almost abandoned until the late 1990s. Today, substantial foreign investment, notably from French development agencies and the International Fund for Animal Welfare (IFAW), has enabled a flurry of rehabilitation projects: a new rhino sanctuary opened in 2001 and now houses 25 rhinos (24 of them white), a new sealed access road is half completed, all the main park roads have been

upgraded, and there's now a bridge across the Tana River at **Adamson's Falls** (worth a visit) accessing Kora National Park.

With security long since settled, these improvements are starting to pay off and visitor numbers are steadily climbing, from a meagre 1000 in 1997 to well over 10,000 in 2004. With two luxury lodges and some of the best budget options in any of Kenya's national parks, Meru's fortunes should soon be on the up again. Visit soon and you'll still feel like you have this blissful place to yourself.

This resurgence is definitely a good thing, as the park is a complete contrast to the nearby savannah reserves of Samburu, Buffalo Springs and Shaba. Abundant rainfall and numerous permanent watercourses flowing down from the Mt Kenya massif support a luxuriant jungle of forest, bush, swamp and tall grasses, which, in turn, provide fodder to a wide variety of herbivores and shelter to them and their predators. This is one of the most geographically diverse parks in Kenya and a favourite with the safari cognoscenti; you need to spend a few days here to fully appreciate what the park has to offer.

While on the rise, wildlife is still not as abundant here as in other parks. To make things more challenging, the limited elephant numbers have led to an increase in vegetation cover, making it difficult to spot those species that do exist. However, with a little patience you can see elephants (often found in the marshy Bisanadi Plains at the north of the park), leopards, lions and cheetahs, along with lesser kudus, elands, waterbucks, gazelles and oryxes. Buffaloes, reticulated giraffes, and Grevy's zebras are common, while monkeys, crocodiles and a plethora of bird species, including the palm nut vulture and Marshal eagle, can be found in the dense vegetation along the watercourses. A drive through the overgrown jungle that shadows the Tana River is well worth the trip to Meru alone.

Information

Entrance to **Meru National Park** (☎ 062-21320; adult/child US$27/10) doesn't entitle you to enter the adjacent **Kora National Park** (☎ 062-21320; adult/child US$27/10). Visits into Kora must be prearranged with Meru's warden.

At present you need to have a 4WD or be on a tour to visit. Most road junctions are numbered, so KWS' *Meru National Park* map (KSh450), sold at the gate, is essential if you want to find your way around.

Sleeping

Bwatherongi Bandas & Campsite (adult/child US$10/5, bandas per person US$15; 🏊) Perhaps the best KWS camp in all of Kenya, this site has great showers, toilets, barbecue pits, a swimming pool and an *askari* (security guard) in attendance. There are also four excellent thatched bandas with shady verandas, twin beds, kerosene lamps, mosquito nets, decent bathrooms and small sofas.

Special campsites (adult/child US$15/5, plus set-up fee KSh5000) There are about a dozen of these bush campsites (no facilities) located throughout

the park. The gate will let you know which are currently open.

Murera Education Centre (bandas per person US$15) This centre's bandas by the main gate should only be considered if Bwatherongi's bandas are full. Ask at the gate for details.

Elsa's Kopje (☎ 020-604053; safaris@chelipeacock .co.ke; mid-Mar–mid-Jun & Nov–mid-Dec full board s/d US$320/600, Jan–mid-Mar, mid-Jun–Jul & mid-Sep–Oct US$450/760, rest of year US$520/920; 🏊) Wake to glorious panoramic views and sweet breezes in these gorgeous open-fronted thatched cottages that blend seamlessly into the upper reaches of Mughwango Hill. This place is the definition of sensitively designed luxury. A rock outcrop seemingly bursts through the floor of cottage number one, where steps lead down to a stunning outdoor bathtub hewn into the cliff itself. The pool and surrounds are equally sublime. The hefty prices include three wildlife drives (one at night), walking safaris, fishing and transfers.

Leopard Rock Lodge (☎ 020-600031; leopardmico@ wananchi.com; Apr–Jun full board s/d from US$285/440, Jul–Mar US$340/515; 🏊) With landscaped gardens, a stilted restaurant on the Murera River and comfortable cottages, this lodge would shine anywhere else in Kenya, but here it's entirely outmatched by the stunning beauty of Elsa's Kopje. The lodge arranges similar activities to Elsa's, but charges extra.

Getting There & Away

Simply put, there's no point reaching the park without a vehicle. If you don't want to join a tour, your cheapest option is to acquire a 4WD (and driver) from a local in the village of Maua, which is 31km from the gate. Regular matatus service Maua from Meru town (KSh100, one hour).

Every Wednesday, Friday and Sunday **Airkenya** (☎ 020-605745; www.airkenya.com) connects Meru to Nairobi (one way/return US$150/300) and Samburu (one way/return US$60/120). From Nairobi to Samburu with a stopover in Meru is US$190 one way. Give your lodge your flight details for pick-up.

CHOGORIA
☎ 064
The only reason to come to this small town on the lower eastern slopes of Mt Kenya is to access one of the mountain's most scenic climbs – the Chogoria route (p269).

CENTRAL HIGHLANDS

It has a lively Sunday **market** and a couple of half-decent cafés in the village, but Chogoria has quite a reputation for hassle, with every man and his dog offering to take you up the mountain. On arrival, it's much better to bypass the village altogether, get yourself sorted at the Transit Motel, then head back if you need basic supplies.

The well-signposted **Transit Motel** (Map p271; ☎ 22096; PO Box 190, Chogoria; camping per tent KSh500, s/tw incl breakfast KSh1000/1600) is as great for arranging Mt Kenya treks as it is for flaking out when the long, enjoyable slog is over. The large rooms are clean with hot showers, mozzie nets and balconies. The TV lounge is comfy and the bar serves cold beers, but watch out for 'skunked' (stale) bottles. There's also a decent restaurant (meals range from KSh100 to KSh300). It's a 1.5km walk from the signposted turn-off just south of Chogoria or a 2km walk from the town's centre. Don't believe rival mountain touts claiming the motel has burnt down – it's a cement structure!

Regular buses and matatus ply the road heading north to Meru (KSh60, 30 minutes) and south to Embu (KSh150, 1½ hours) and Nairobi (KSh280, four hours).

EMBU
☎ 068

Surrounded by highly cultivated hills on the fringes of Mt Kenya's southeastern slopes is Embu, the unlikely capital of the Eastern Province. Given that this agricultural backwater town barely sits in the province, our only guess is that it was chosen as capital because of its agreeable climate.

Despite its local significance, there's not a lot for travellers here, and it's a long way from the mountain. However, it can make a good stopover on the way to Thika or Nairobi, and if you have your own transport, use it as a base for exploring Mwea National Reserve (opposite) or for visiting the coffee nurseries off the B6 and A2 highways.

Information

Barclays Bank (B6 Hwy) Exchange cash and travellers cheques (KSh34 per leaf commission). With ATM.
Cyberlink (off Kenyatta Hwy; per hr KSh120) Embu's fastest Internet connections.
Embu Provincial Hospital (Kenyatta Hwy)
Post office (Kenyatta Hwy) With Internet and card phones.

EMBU

INFORMATION		
Barclays Bank	1	B3
Cyberlink	2	B2
Post Office	3	B1
SLEEPING		
Embu Motel	4	A3
Highway Court Hotel	5	B3
Prime Lodge	6	A3
EATING		
Classic Cafe	7	A3
Eastern Inn	8	B2
Kamuketha Hotel	9	A3
Maguna-Andu Supermarket	10	B3
Mario's Cafe	11	B3
Morning Glory Hotel	12	B2
DRINKING		
Eagles Nest	13	B1
TRANSPORT		
BP Petrol Station	(see 15)	
Bus & Matatu Stand	14	B3
Buses	15	B3

To Kenya Scouts Training Centre (300m); Embu Provincial Hospital (1km); Izaak Walton Inn (1.5km); Meru (154km)

Town Hall
Library
Kenyatta Hwy
Mama Ngina St
Morning Glory Plaza

To Mwea National Reserve (51km); Kitui (142km)
To Thika (94km); Nairobi (134km)
To Embu Motel (150m)

Sleeping

There are quite a few cheap hotels spread out along Kenyatta Hwy in town but most of them are very basic and cannot be recommended.

Kenya Scouts Training Centre (☎ 30459; Kenyatta Hwy; camping KSh100, dm KSh250) This spotless place has great facilities and is a bargain. Four- or five-bed dorms are only rented to one group at a time, so if you're alone you'll get the room to yourself for only KSh250. Judging from all the anti-drug posters, it's not a good idea to saunter in here with your mouth full of *miraa*!

Embu Motel (☎ 0722-462277; off B6 Hwy; s/d incl breakfast from KSh700/900) Quietly set back off the main road, this is another great option. Cleanliness pervades throughout and the toilets even have seats. The motel has a comfy TV room, a spartan dining area and a safe spot to park your metal steed.

Highway Court Hotel (☎ 20046; Kenyatta Hwy; s/tw from KSh400/800) The rooms are clean but they don't really gleam like those at Embu. It's a comfortable place, with hot-water showers, mozzie nets and TVs (only in large twins, KSh1200). Some are brighter than others, so peruse a little. Security is excellent, but the lively bar and restaurant are noisy.

Prime Lodge (☎ 30692; off B6 Hwy; s/tw KSh650/1050) Prices have jumped here, but quality clearly hasn't. The same linoleum lines the cement floors, and most toilets still lack seats. On the upside, it's clean and most rooms catch some sun. Some rooms have baths instead of showers.

Izaak Walton Inn (☎ 20128; izaakwalton@winnet.co.ke; Kenyatta Hwy; s/d incl breakfast from US$32/50) About 1.5km north of town is this well-known place set in fantastic old colonial grounds. Some standard rooms have a cabin feel, with wood-lined walls, while others are more contemporary and have glass walls leading onto small terraces. All of the rooms here have TVs and there's a great cosy bar where wood and wicker pervade.

Eating & Drinking

Izaak Walton Inn (Kenyatta Hwy; mains KSh100-400, set-meal US$7) A great place for a great meal. The French onion soup and Mt Kenya stew are recommended by well-to-do locals. The bar is a great place to introduce a cold beverage to your insides.

Eastern Inn (Mama Ngina St; meals KSh40-150) Fronted by a shady awning, this Christian restaurant serves up sandwiches, samosas, fried chicken and fish.

Morning Glory Hotel (Kenyatta Hwy; meals KSh80-200; ☯ 24hr) This is the spot for fried chicken and chips in Embu. The hotel also does decent breakfasts, but, after seeing their green goldfish tank, you might not want to order the fish.

Kamuketha Hotel (B6 Hwy; meals KSh80-200) They say they fry up the best tilapia in town – many locals would agree.

Classic Cafe (off B6 Hwy; meals KSh20-80) A dark and tiny hole in the wall serves up popular Kenyan dishes like *madado* (beans) and *ndengu* (lentils) with chapattis, rice or *ugali*.

Mario's Cafe (off Mam Ngina St; meals KSh35-130) Basic Kenyan eats served in the shadows of a fading TV.

Maguna-Andu Supermarket (B7 Hwy) A well-stocked supermarket.

Eagles Nest (off Kenyatta Hwy) The local favourite for a cold Tusker and *nyama choma*.

Getting There & Away

Regular Kensilver buses heading to Meru (KSh250, two hours) and Nairobi (KSh250, three hours) pick up passengers at the BP petrol station in the centre of town.

Mombasa Liners leave the BP station for Mombasa (KSh700, 10 hours) each morning at 7.30am.

There are numerous matatus serving Chogoria (KSh150, 1½ hours), Meru (KSh250, two hours), Thika (KSh200, two hours), Nyeri (KSh150, two hours), Nanyuki (KSh220, 2½ hours), Nyahururu (KSh300, three hours), Nairobi (KSh250, three hours) and Nakuru (KSh400, 4½ hours).

MWEA NATIONAL RESERVE

The Kamburu Dam, at the meeting point of the Tana and Thiba Rivers, forms the focus for this 48-sq-km **reserve** (adult/child US$15/5). Enclosed by an electric fence, elephants, hippos, buffaloes, lesser kudus and a myriad of birdlife are present here. Evenings at Hippo Point, when the animals amble down to the water's edge, are a particular highlight.

There's a **campsite** (adult/child US$10/5) with basic facilities (no water) close to the reserve headquarters and another site with similar facilities, close to Hippo Point.

In wet season the nearest formal accommodation is in Embu (opposite), while in dry season there's a 14km shortcut from the gate southwest to the **Masinga Dam Lodge** (Nairobi ☎ 020-341781; camping KSh500, s/d KSh650/800; ☲). It's a simple place that looks over the dam and plains.

Getting There & Away

Mwea is best accessed from the 11km dirt road that's signposted off the B7 Hwy some 40km south of Embu. Ignore the signposted 27km dirt track to the park that's 14km south of Embu – trust us! A 4WD is just about essential to get to Mwea and around the park.

OL DONYO SABUK NATIONAL PARK

This tiny **park** (adult/child US$15/5) was gazetted in 1967 and covers an area of just 20.7 sq km. The focus of the park is the summit of **Ol Donyo Sabuk** (2146m), surrounded by an oasis of dense primeval forest that supports a huge variety of birds and numerous primates, including black and white colobus and blue monkeys. The Kikuyu call the mountain

Kilimambongo (buffalo mountain) and buffaloes are indisputably the dominant animals here. Below the picnic site and communications tower on the summit is a salt lick that attracts regular herds.

It's possible to explore on foot if accompanied by a ranger (per half-/full-day KSh500/KSh1000). It's a 9km hike (three or four hours) to an amazing 360-degree view at the summit.

There's a pretty **campsite** (adult/child US$10/5) just before the main gate, with soft grass, and shady trees. Facilities include one long-drop toilet, a rusty tap and free firewood.

Getting There & Away

From Thika, take a matatu to the village of Ol Donyo Sabuk (KSh70, 50 minutes), from where it's a 2km walk along a straight dirt road to the gate. You could also take a matatu heading to Kitui and hop off at Kilimambongo (KSh50, 45 minutes), which is 6km from Ol Donyo Sabuk village.

THIKA

☎ 067

Thika isn't much more than a busy little agricultural service town, and there aren't many of those famous flame trees to be seen. That said, it's a leafy place and quite pleasant for a stroll. The only true 'attractions' are **Chania Falls** and **Thika Falls**, about 1km north of town on the busy Nairobi–Nyeri road. It's also a good place to base a visit to Ol Donyo Sabuk National Park (p281).

Information

Barclays Bank (Kenyatta Hwy) Changes cash and travellers cheques (KSh30 per leaf commission). With ATM.

Cyber Cafe (Uhuru St; per hr KSh60) Thika's best Internet connections.

Post office (Commercial St) With Internet and card phones.

Sleeping & Eating

December Hotel (☎ 22140; Commercial St; s/d KSh600/800) This is the best and brightest of the budget bunch. The large rooms and bathrooms are well kept. Some rooms see more sun than others, so check a few (number seven is best).

Thika Inn (☎ 31590; Kenyatta Hwy; s/tw incl breakfast KSh650/1200) Just south of town, behind the Caltex petrol station, Thika Inn has reasonable rooms. While the bedding is fresh and clean, the bathrooms are slightly grungy. Thankfully the rooms are sheltered from their lively restaurant (meals KSh150 to KSh350) and disco known as the Vybestar Club.

New Fulia Hotel (☎ 31286; Uhuru St; s KSh300) Simple singles with bathrooms (no toilet seats). It's clean enough, but most are rather dark and lack mosquito nets.

Blue Post Hotel (☎ 22241; blueposthotel@africa online.co.ke; s/d KSh1600/1900; 💻) Set in lovely gardens next to the Chania River, 2km north of town, this place has comfortable rooms with four-poster canopy beds, polished-wood floors and TVs. Rooms 101 to 106 cost no more, yet offer shady balconies and glimpses of Chania Falls. It has a great bar and a decent restaurant (meals KSh120 to KSh240) serving Western selections.

Primos Hotel (Kame Nkrumah; meals KSh50-220) With comfy seats and views over the street, Primos prepares Kenyan dishes, burgers and basic sandwiches. They also take a stab at beef stroganoff.

Quality Cafe (Mama Ngina Rd; meals KSh40-150) A popular place serving simple Kenyan fare.

Getting There & Away

There are plenty of matatus heading to Nairobi (KSh70, 45 minutes), Embu (KSh200, two hours) and Nyeri (KSh200, 1¾ hours). The odd service reaches Naivasha (KSh200, 1½ hours).

Western Kenya

Imagine western Kenya and you'll probably only think of Masai Mara's savanna and wildlife. After all, the Mara is astounding and the only part of this region most travellers ever see.

Those few of you who imagine 4000m peaks, rainforests crawling with birdlife and rare primates, rolling hills draped in tea plantations, and fishing boats dotting Lake Victoria's horizon – you're the lucky ones. You've probably already experienced this amazing region.

Western Kenya's highlands sit atop the Elgeyo and Mau Escarpments. The verdant north is a cultivated patchwork of farms and the south an abode to countless tea plantations. Kakamega Forest Reserve and Saiwa Swamp National Park are two bastions of pristine wilderness and wildlife amidst this agricultural heartland. With Mt Elgon and the Cherangani Hills rising skyward from its northern reaches, unique trekking possibilities also abound.

Sitting in the shadows of the highlands are Lake Victoria's captivating lowlands, home to the city of Kisumu, Ruma National Park, Mfangano Island and numerous fishing villages.

The Luo, the third-largest tribe in Kenya, live around Lake Victoria, while the Luyha, Gusii and Kalenjin live in the highlands (see p43). With the exception of the Maasai, who've been inundated with tourists, western Kenya is your best chance to get to know the locals.

Go on. Be one of the lucky ones. Delve a little deeper into western Kenya.

HIGHLIGHTS

- Witnessing the glorious spectacle of rush-hour, wildebeest style, during their annual migration at **Masai Mara National Reserve** (p286)
- Watching trees battle to the death while wandering the depths of **Kakamega Forest Reserve** (p304)
- Waking to clear skies and astounding views on the crater rim at **Mt Elgon National Park** (p312)
- Wasting an hour indulging in divine freshly made cheese at **Eldoret** (p306)
- Wading into the crowds and smoky surrounds on the shore of Lake Victoria for some fried tilapia in **Kisumu** (p290)
- Walking through the manicured tea fields that carpet the rolling hills of **Kericho** (p300)

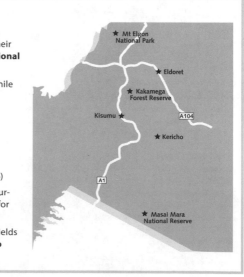

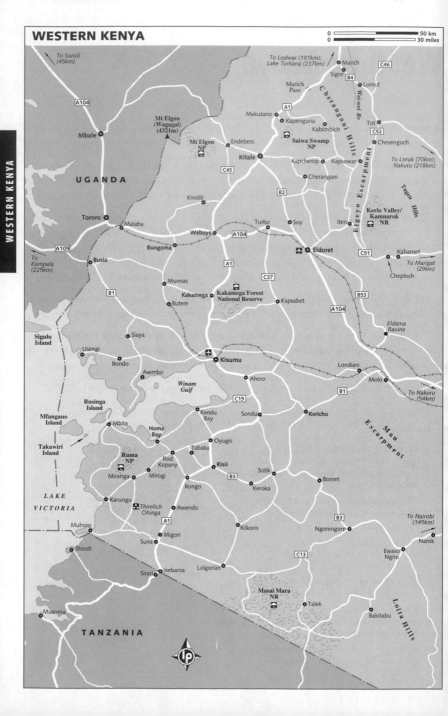

WESTERN KENYA

WESTERN KENYA

To Soroti (45km)

A104

Mbale

Mt Elgon (Wagagai) (4321m)

Mt Elgon NP

UGANDA

Tororo

Malaba

A109

To Kampala (225km)

Busia

B1

Sigulu Island

Usengi

Bondo

Mfangano Island

Rusinga Island

Mbita

Homa Bay

Takawiri Island

Ruma NP

Miranga

Mirogi

LAKE VICTORIA

Karungu

Thimlich Ohinga

Muhoro

Shirati

Sirari

Musoma

TANZANIA

To Lodwar (181km); Lake Turkana (237km)

Marich

Sigor

B4

Lomut

C46

Marich Pass

Cherangani Hills

Wei-wei Rv

Tot

C52

Chesengoch

Makutano

A1

Kapenguria

Kabichbich

Endebess

Saiwa Swamp NP

Kitale

Kapcherop

Kapsowar

Eldama Escarpment

To Loruk (70km); Nakuru (218km)

Tugen Hills

Kapchorwa

Cherangani

B2

Kerio Valley/ Kamnarok NR

Iten

C45

Kimilili

Turbo

Soy

Webuye

A104

Eldoret

C51

Kabarnet

Bungoma

A1

To Marigat (29km)

Cheploch

Mumias

C37

Kakamega

Kakamega Forest National Reserve

Kapsabet

B53

A104

Butere

Siaya

Eldama Ravine

KISUMU

Ahero

Londiani

Winam Gulf

Asembo

C19

Sondu

Molo

To Nakuru (54km)

Kendu Bay

Kericho

Mau Escarpment

Tabaka

Oyugis

Rod Kopany

Kisii

Sotik

Rongo

B3

Keroka

Bomet

Awendo

Kilkoris

Ngorengore

B3

To Nairobi (145km)

A1

Migori

Suna

C13

Ewaso Ngiro

Narok

Isebania

Lolgorian

Masai Mara NR

Talek

Bakitabu

Loita Hills

0 ──── 50 km

0 ──── 30 miles

Climate

Throughout the year the lowlands around Lake Victoria are fairly hot and humid, while the area around the Western Highlands are decidedly cooler. The heaviest rains fall between March and May, with almost 200mm falling in April. The lesser rains fall in November and December before things really dry out in January.

National Parks & Reserves

With the Big Five roaming the stunning savanna of Masai Mara National Reserve (right), prolific birdlife, primates and flying squirrels soaring through the dense rainforests of Kakamega Forest Reserve (p304) and 4000m peaks beckoning trekkers at Mt Elgon National Park (p312), it is clear western Kenya's parks have it all.

More wildlife and unique surrounds can be found at Ruma National Park (p297), home to Kenya's only roan antelope population, and at Saiwa Swamp National Park (p315), which hosts rare sitatunga antelopes and De Brazza's monkeys.

If you want to truly disown the beaten track, hit Lake Kamnarok and Kerio Valley National Reserves (p309).

Getting There & Away

AIR

Kenya Airways (☎ 020-3274747; www.kenya-airways.com) connects Nairobi (Wilson Airport) with Kisumu and Eldoret, while both **Airkenya** (☎ 020-605745; www.airkenya.com) and **Safarilink** (☎ 020-600777; www.safarilink.co.ke) link Wilson Airport with Masai Mara National Reserve. See Getting There & Away under the relevant sections for more details.

BUS & MATATU

The road to western Kenya inevitably leads through Nakuru. From there countless buses and matatus (minibuses) run north to Kitale, via Eldoret or Marigat, west to Kisumu and south to Kericho and Kisii.

Masai Mara is the one exception, with most transportation coming via Narok.

Getting Around

Being the most densely populated part of the country, the road system is good and there is a multitude of matatus, buses and occasional Peugeots (shared taxis) plying the routes. Since the new government's crackdown on speeding and overcrowding in matatus, accident rates have thankfully dropped dramatically.

MASAI MARA

Masai Mara is more than just the most popular wildlife park in Kenya; in many cases it's the reason people come to Kenya. Mara is the classic savanna you see in almost every African film and nature program that's ever been made, and its sheer density of wildlife is amazing. It is also the homeland of the Maasai, Kenya's most celebrated tribe. Their cattle herds largely displaced in favour of more profitable animals, many Maasai now rely on tourism (see p286).

NAROK
☎ 050

Two hours west of Nairobi, this ramshackle provincial town is the Masai Mara's main access point. It is not that great for independent travellers, as prices reflect the heavy tourist traffic the region sees and Narok is rife with souvenir sellers, transport touts and rip-off merchants – enjoy!

Information

Kenya Commercial Bank is the town's only bank and it has an unreliable ATM (Visa only). Card phones are found in front of the Spear Hotel and at the post office (which has Internet access).

Sleeping & Eating

Kim's Dishes Hotel (☎ 22001; s/d/tw KSh500/800/1000) With secure parking and recent renovations bestowing the comfy rooms with great bathrooms, 24-hour hot water and new mozzie nets, Kim's is Narok's best-value joint. But value doesn't equate to good taste – the frilly bedspreads will make grown men's toes curl. The restaurant (meals KSh80 to KSh200) downstairs serves tasty Kenyan dishes.

Spear Hotel (☎ 22035; s/tw with shared bathroom KSh250/500, s/tw KSh400/750) The rooms are spacious and have mosquito nets, but some mattresses are better than others – poke a few before deciding. Hot water only flows in the morning. Locals love the restaurant (meals KSh100–200) and you may see traditionally dressed Maasai gathered to watch Oprah! The food's almost as entertaining.

THE HARD SELL

A common complaint among travellers, particularly in the Mara, is that the Maasai can be incredibly hard-nosed in business, and 'cultural' visits to villages often become high-pressure sales ventures the moment you arrive.

While it would be unfair to generalise, it's certainly true that some Maasai, especially in high-density tourist areas, will treat you purely as a cash cow. Favourite techniques include dropping wares in your lap and refusing to take them back; coming into campsites to offer dances at non-negotiable rates; and charging for absolutely everything, from camping to crossing their land. While this behaviour isn't limited to Maasai, their aggressive and utterly unapologetic attitude upsets more travellers than day-to-day hassle elsewhere.

If you feel you're being taken for a ride, Maasai or otherwise, stand up for yourself. Or, ask yourself this: if your people had been consistently dispossessed for over a century and were now subjected to constant streams of gawping foreigners with seemingly bottomless pockets, wouldn't you do the same?

Chambai Hotel (☎ 22591; s KSh650, super s/tw KSh1000/1400) The standard rooms out the back are simple, spotless and sport mosquito nets. The new, sizeable super rooms in the main building have inviting beds, balconies, large TVs and huge bathrooms – sit on your throne and rule your porcelain kingdom. The bar and restaurant (meals KSh250, buffets KSh350) are civilised and worth trying.

Getting There & Away

Frequent matatus run between Narok and Nairobi (KSh250, 2½ hours) and less-frequent departures serve Naivasha (KSh200, three hours) and Kisii (KSh300, three hours). There is also usually daily transport to Sekenani and Talek gates for around KSh350.

Several petrol stations pump the elixir of vehicular life – fill up, it's much cheaper than in the reserve.

MASAI MARA NATIONAL RESERVE

Backed by the spectacular Esoit Oloololo (Siria) Escarpment, watered by the Mara River and littered with an astonishing amount of wildlife is this world-renowned national reserve. Its 1510 sq km of open rolling grasslands, the northern extension of the equally famous Serengeti Plains, are actually the agglomeration of the Narok (managed by Narok County Council) and Transmara National Reserves (managed by Mara Conservancy).

Although concentrations of wildlife are typically highest in the swampy area around the escarpment on the reserve's western edge, superior roads draw most visitors to the eastern side. Of the big cats, lions are

found in large prides everywhere, and it is not uncommon to see them hunting. Cheetahs and leopards are less visible, but still fairly common. Elephants, buffaloes, zebras and hippos also exist in large numbers.

Of the antelopes, the black-striped Thomson's gazelle and larger Grant's gazelle are most prevalent, although the numbers of impalas, topis, Coke's hartebeests and wildebeests aren't too far behind. Other common animals include Masai giraffes, baboons, warthogs, jackals, bat-eared foxes and matriarchal clans of spotted hyenas. The few dozen black rhinos are rarely seen.

The ultimate attraction is undoubtedly the annual wildebeest migration in July and August, when millions of the ungainly beasts move north from the Serengeti seeking lusher grass before turning south again around October. While you're more likely to see endless columns grazing or trudging along rather than dramatic TV-style river fordings, it is nonetheless a staggering experience.

During the migration there seem to be as many minibuses as animals, and many tend to take off, making new tracks wherever they feel fit. This shouldn't be encouraged.

Information

Because most of the gates are located inside the **reserve** (adult/child US$30/10) boundary it is easy to enter the Masai Mara unknowingly. Most confusion arises when people camping outside the gates are requested to pay park fees – cue confrontation. For the record, campsites outside Oloolaimutiek gate are inside the reserve, while Talek gate's sites north of the Talek River are outside it.

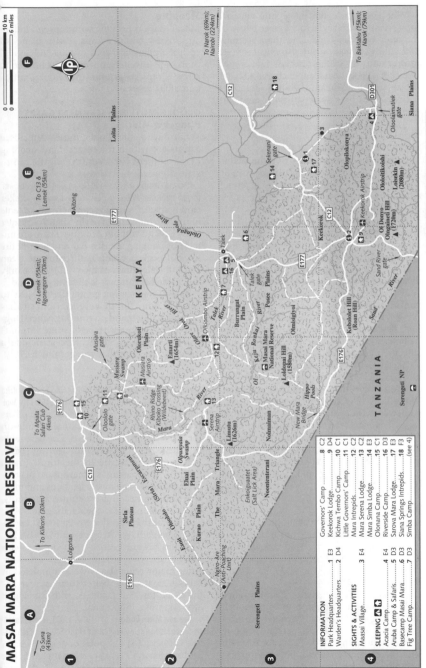

MASAI MARA NATIONAL RESERVE

WESTERN KENYA

INFORMATION	
Park Headquarters	1 E3
Warden's Headquarters	2 D4

SIGHTS & ACTIVITIES	
Maasai Village	3 E4

SLEEPING	
Acacia Camp	4 E4
Aruba Camp & Safaris	5 D3
Basecamp Masai Mara	6 D3
Fig Tree Camp	7 D3
Governors' Camp	8 C2
Keekorok Lodge	9 D4
Kichwa Tembo Camp	10 C1
Little Governors' Camp	11 C2
Mara Intrepids	12 C2
Mara Serena Lodge	13 C2
Mara Simba Lodge	14 E3
Olonana Camp	15 C1
Riverside Camp	16 D3
Sarova Mara Lodge	17 E3
Siana Springs Intrepids	18 F3
Simba Camp	(see 4)

Wherever you enter, make sure you ask for a receipt: it is crucial for passage between the reserve's Narok and Transmara sections and your eventual exit. It also ensures your money ends up in the reserve's hands, not elsewhere. Gates also seem to charge KSh500 for all vehicles instead of KSh250 for ones with less than six seats – be insistent but polite and all will be well.

Sights & Activities
WILDLIFE DRIVES & WALKS
Whether you're bouncing over the plains in pursuit of elusive elephant silhouettes or parked next to a pride of lions and listening to their bellowed breaths, wildlife drives are *the* highlight of a trip to the Mara.

All top-end places offer wildlife drives, which can be negotiated into the rate while booking – it's usually cheaper than arranging them on arrival. However, guided walks and activities such as **horse riding** and **bush dinners** are booked during your stay.

If you've arrived by matatu, you can organise drives with most lodges, as they're fairly friendly towards independent travellers. **Basecamp Masai Mara** (☎ 020-577490; www .basecampexplorer.com) is easiest because it is outside the park and only a 1.5km walk from Talek. Two-hour drives (day or night) typically cost US$35 per person, plus park fees. Doing a safari this way isn't recommended, though, as it is seldom cheaper than organised safaris. Alternatively, walk with a Maasai *moran* (warrior) outside the park, where there is still a large amount of wildlife. This can be a wonderful experience, but be aware that local Maasai groups may charge you for crossing their land. Talek is a good base for walking.

BALLOONING
If you can afford US$390, balloon safaris are superb and worlds away from the minibus circuit. Trips can be arranged through top-end lodges. See p348 for more details.

MAASAI VILLAGE
The Maasai village between Oloolaimutiek and Sekenani gates welcomes tourists, though negotiating admission can be fraught – prices start as high as US$20 per person. If you're willing to drop this kind of cash for free rein with the camera, go ahead, but don't expect a genuine cultural experience.

Sleeping
Masai Mara is heaving with top-end lodges and luxury tented camps – with plenty of cash the plains are your oyster. Budget and midrange travellers, however, are limited to a few campsites around the Oloolaimutiek and Talek gates.

OLOOLAIMUTIEK & SEKANANI GATES
Budget & Midrange
While outside the Oloolaimutiek gate, these camps are within the reserve and sleeping here will incur park fees (even if the camps state otherwise).

Acacia Camp (☎ 020-210024; camping US$5, s/tw with shared bathroom US$35/40) Thatched roofs shelter closely spaced, spartan semi-permanent tents in this quaint camp. They're slightly cheaper (s/tw US$30) without bedding. There are numerous cooking areas, a bar and a campfire pit, but no restaurant. Bathrooms are clean and hot water flows in the evening. The only downside for campers is the lack of shade.

Simba Camp (camping per tent KSh800) Next to Acacia Camp, this dishevelled campsite has tin-shack toilets and no running water. Dog-eared tents (some with beds, some without) are for rent at KSh900. Prices include a 'security' fee (not that you get much).

Top End
Siana Springs Intrepids (☎ 020-4446651; siana@africa online.co.ke; low season full board s/d US$150/210, high season US$260/350; 🏊) This tented camp offers comfort without letting luxury intrude on the African bush experience. The best tents dot the edge of a beautiful clearing (bamboo group) or nestle in the forest (palm group) – the spacing is generous, so privacy is guaranteed. The lovely log beds and massive shower heads are definite standouts. Siana is 16km outside Sekenani gate.

Keekorok Lodge (bookings ☎ 020-4447151; low season full board s/d US$140/180, high season US$200/250; 🏊) This has always been a great option, with bungalows, cabins and cottages on offer. After major renovations were completed in mid-2005, it's now better than ever. It has the usual top-end facilities, with the added attraction of a hippo pool.

Sarova Mara Lodge (☎ 020-2713333; reservations@ sarova.co.ke; low season full board s/d US$80/140, high season US$160/210; 🏊) The polar opposite of Siana Springs, Sarova's semi-permanent tents reek of luxury and lack bush charm.

Mara Simba Lodge (☎ 020-4343961; enquiries@ marasimba.com; low season full board s/d US$100/150, high season US$180/250; ☒) Large log-sided cabins house comfortable rooms with plank floors, balconies and fans – ask for upstairs rooms as they boast better views.

TALEK GATE
Budget & Midrange
Aruba Camp & Safaris (☎ 0723-997524; gerdi.simon@ web.de; camping KSh300) Just outside the reserve, on the Talek River's scenic north bank, is this up-and-coming option. Joining the bare-bones campsite will soon be Masai Mara's first midrange tented safari camp. For less than US$100 per person, you will get full board accommodation and wildlife drives. Currently campers must also pay KSh300 per group for security.

Riverside Camp (☎ 0720-218319; camping KSh350, bandas per person KSh2000) Run by Maasai, this campsite has good facilities, like running water, hot showers and a kitchen area, complete with utensils. Trees provide shade for campers, while simple bandas provide shelter for the tentless. There is a bar, and if you call ahead, meals are available. Groups must pay KSh300 for security.

Top End
Basecamp Masai Mara (☎ 020-577490; www.basecamp explorer.com; low season full board s/d US$90/140, Nov-Mar US$120/190, Jul-Oct US$140/200) Masai Mara's only ecolodge is an incredibly friendly place. Solar panels provide power, organic waste is composted and dirty water is reused to water the grounds. One of the superb observation towers has a small exhibition space where local conservationists give informal lectures. The 16 individually designed permanent tents have thatched roofs, beautiful outdoor showers and large verandas with day-beds. Although equally gorgeous, tents seven to 11 lack the lovely riverside locations and views afforded to others. Basecamp run the Bush Buck Forestation program and have already planted 15,000 trees in the hope of regenerating native woodland – a US$20 donation enables you to plant five trees.

Fig Tree Camp (☎ 020-605328; sales@madahotels .com; Jan-Jun full board s/d US$80/120, Jul-Dec US$165/220; ☒) Vegetate on your tent's veranda, watching the Talek's waters gently flow by. Cabins with equally basic interiors cost the same but lack the river views. To round things off,

there is a small but scenic pool and a trendy treetop bar.

Mara Intrepids (☎ 020-4446651; maraintrepids@ heritagehotels.co.ke; low season full board incl wildlife drives s/d US$245/370, high season US$450/615; ☒) The 30 permanent tents offer comfort, four-poster canopy beds and stone bathrooms. A lovely pool, complete with diving board, sits riverside. Recent renovations make tents 12, 26, 27 and 30 the brightest of the bunch. If you want wonderful river views, avoid 24 and 25. A heap of activities are available, including flying day-safaris to Rusinga Island (p297) on Lake Victoria (per person US$425).

MUSIARA & OLOOLOLO GATES
Sadly, there are no secure budget or midrange options here.

Mara Serena Lodge (☎ 020-22059; mara@serena .co.ke; low season full board s/d US$80/160, high season US$210/260; ☒) Built to resemble a futuristic Maasai village, Serena is the most colourful lodge in the reserve. Hip rooms, with vibrant curved walls and Juliet balconies, line a ridge and overlook the grassy plains below. Blending beautifully with its surroundings and offering 1st-class service, it's justifiably popular.

Kichwa Tembo Camp (☎ 020-3740920; alice@cons corp.co.ke; low season full board s/d US$120/240, Mar & Nov–mid-Dec US$155/310, rest of year US$185/370; ☒) Just outside the northern boundary, Kichwa has permanent tents with grass-mat floors, stone bathrooms and tasteful furnishings. Hop in a hammock and take in spectacular savanna views. The food has an excellent reputation.

Olonana Camp (☎ 020-6950244; kenya@sanctuary lodges.com; low season full board per person US$225, Oct–mid-Dec US$340, rest of year US$450; ☒) Twelve tents, with thatched shelters, large decks, wooden floors and beautiful stone bathrooms, call this camp home. Watch hippos swim in the Mara River from your grand bed or the bar's deck.

Governors' Camp (☎ 020-2734000; www.governors camp.com; low season full board s/d US$165/330, high season US$370/550; ☒) This camp, and Little Governors' Camp (low season full board s/d US$180/360, high season US$405/600, with a swimming pool) both have tents similar to those at Kichwa and offer great service, pleasing riverside locations and activities a-plenty. The hefty rates include three wildlife drives. Feel like some humidity? Take a flying day-safari (per person US$425) to Mfangano Island (p298) on Lake Victoria.

Mpata Safari Club (☎ 020-310867; mpata4@africa online.co.ke; Mar-May s/d US$240/380, Jun-Feb US$340/480; 🏊) Almost 10km north of Oloololo gate and sitting up the Esoit Oloololo Escarpment, Mpata offers the Mara's grandest views and most luxurious accommodation. With brave contemporary styling, spiralling roofs, circular skylights, glass walls and quirky furniture, you will be talking about more than just animals.

Eating & Drinking

If you can't afford the lodges' accommodation, drop in for drinks or a meal. Lovely lunches/dinners will set you back US$15/25, but the views and ambience are free.

There's a tiny shop, eatery and lively Maasai market in Talek village.

Getting There & Away

AIR

Airkenya (☎ 020-605745; www.airkenya.com) and **Safarilink** (☎ 020-600777; www.safarilink.co.ke) each have daily flights to Masai Mara. Return flights on Airkenya are US$191, while Safarilink will get you there and back for US$201.

You must state which Mara airstrip you require, and make sure you get to the airport early, because the aeroplane doesn't wait for late comers.

MATATU, CAR & 4WD

Although it's possible to arrange wildlife drives independently, keep in mind that there are few savings in coming here without transport. That said, it is possible to access Talek and Sekenani gates from Narok by matatu. From Kisii a matatu will get you as far as Kilkoris or Suna on the main A1 Hwy, but you will have problems after this.

For those who drive, the first 52km west of Narok on the B3 and C12 are smooth enough, but after the bitumen runs out you'll find that it gets pretty bumpy. The C13, which connects Oloololo gate with Lolgorian in the west, is very rough and rocky, and it's poorly signposted – a highway it's not.

Petrol is available (although expensive) at Mara Sarova, Mara Serena and Keekorok Lodges.

LAKE VICTORIA

Spread across 70,000 sq km and gracing the shores of Kenya, Tanzania and Uganda, Lake Victoria is East Africa's most important geographical feature. Despite its massive girth, the lake is never more than 80m deep. This stands in amazing contrast to the smaller Rift Valley lakes such as Lake Tanganyika, whose depths can reach 1500m.

The lake's 'evolving' ecosystem has proved to be both a boon and a bane for those living along its shores. For starters, its waters are a haven for mosquitos and snails, making malaria and bilharzia too common here. Then there are Nile perch (introduced 50 years ago to combat mosquitos), which eventually thrived, growing to over 200kg in size and becoming every small fishing boat's dream. Sadly, now it's only large commercial fishing vessels thriving. Horrifyingly, the ravenous perch have wiped out over 300 species of smaller tropical fish unique to the lake.

Last but not least is the ornamental water hyacinth. First reported in 1986, this 'exotic' pond plant had no natural predators here and quickly reached plague proportions; the Winam Gulf area by Kisumu was worst affected and the fishing industry 'suffocated', confining many large ships to port. Millions of dollars (much from the World Bank) have been ploughed into solving the problem, with controversial programs including mechanical removal and the introduction of weed-eating weevils. The investment seems to be paying off, with the most recent satellite photos showing hyacinth covering 384 hectares, compared with the 17,230 hectares it covered at its zenith.

Despite the ecological and economic turmoil, the lives of Kenyans living along the shore go on, whether in tiny fishing villages or in Kisumu, and a peek into their world is as fascinating as ever.

KISUMU

☎ 057

Set on the sloping shore of Lake Victoria's Winam Gulf, the town of Kisumu is the third-largest in Kenya. Declared a city during its centenary celebrations in 2001, it still doesn't feel like one; its relaxed atmosphere is a world away from that of places like Nairobi and Mombasa. Amazingly, like much of western Kenya, Kisumu receives relatively few travellers.

Despite the lake being its lifeblood from inception, geographically Kisumu has always had its back to the water, something that now echoes the sentiment and economy of the city today. Until 1977 the port was one of the busiest in Kenya, but decline set in with the demise of the East African Community (Kenya, Tanzania and Uganda), and it sat virtually idle for two decades. Although increasing cooperation between these countries (now known collectively as Comesa) has established Kisumu as an international shipment point for petroleum products, surprisingly the lake plays no part – raw fuel for processing is piped in from Mombasa and the end products are shipped out by truck. With Kisumu's fortunes again rising, and the water hyacinth's impact reduced, it is hoped Lake Victoria will once more start contributing to the local economy.

If you've arrived from the higher country east, you will immediately notice the humidity. Kisumu is a few degrees hotter than the highland cities, and the steamy conditions add to the generally languid air.

Despite its relative isolation, Kisumu has excellent travel connections to the east of Kenya, and there are enough attractions to make it an interesting place to stop for a few days.

Orientation

Kisumu is a fairly sprawling town, but everything you will need is within walking distance. Most shops, banks, cheap hotels and other facilities can be found around Oginga Odinga Rd, while the train station and ferry jetty are short walks from the end of New Station Rd.

Jomo Kenyatta Hwy is the major thoroughfare, connecting the town with the main market and the noisy bus and matatu station, both a 10-minute walk northwest from Oginga Odinga Rd.

The most pleasant access to the lake itself is at Dunga, a small village about 3km south of town along Nzola Rd.

Information
EMERGENCY
Police station (Uhuru Rd) The police force wasn't happy giving out its phone number – hopefully it'll be happier to help those in need.

WARNING

Although you're at far greater risk of contracting malaria here than bilharzia, it is still not wise to swim in the water or walk in the grass along its shores – this is the hide-out of the snails that host the damaging parasites that invade your body (see p385).

INTERNET ACCESS
Abacus Cyber Cafe (Al-Imran Plaza, Oginga Odinga Rd; per hr KSh60; ⏰ 8am-8pm) Speedy surfing.
Crystal Communications (Mega Plaza, Oginga Odinga Rd; per hr KSh60; ⏰ 8am-6pm) Fast Internet connections and soon to be able to burn CDs from cameras using USB connections.
Sanhedrin Cyber Joint (Swan Centre, Accra St; per hr KSh60; ⏰ 8am-10pm) Super friendly and offering cheap international Internet calls.

MEDICAL SERVICES
Aga Khan Hospital (☎ 2020005; Otiena Oyoo St) A large hospital with modern facilities and 24hr emergency room.
Clinipath Laboratory (☎ 2022363; Mega Plaza, Oginga Odinga Rd; ⏰ 8am-5pm Mon-Fri, 8am-1pm Sat, 10am-noon Sun) A satellite laboratory of the Aga Khan Hospital that does blood work. Malaria tests cost KSh160.

MONEY
Barclays Bank (Kampala St) Exchanges cash and travellers cheques (KSh30 per leaf commission). With ATM.
Kenya Commercial Bank (Jomo Kenyatta Hwy) Exchanges cash and travellers cheques (KSh50 per leaf commission). With ATM (Visa only).
Standard Chartered Bank (Oginga Odinga Rd) Offers the best exchange rate for travellers cheques, but only accepts Amex (KSh50 per leaf commission). With ATM (Visa only).

PHOTOGRAPHY
Ken's Photo Imaging (Al-Imran Plaza, Oginga Odinga Rd; ⏰ closed Sun) Decent development and currently the only place that burns digital images to CD.

POST
Post office (Oginga Odinga Rd) With Internet.

TELEPHONE
There are card phones on Oginga Odinga Rd across from the post office. Others are scattered around town.
Sanhedrin Cyber Joint (Swan Centre, Accra St; ⏰ 8am-10pm) Cheap long distance calls over the Internet – quality can vary from good to bad.

WESTERN KENYA

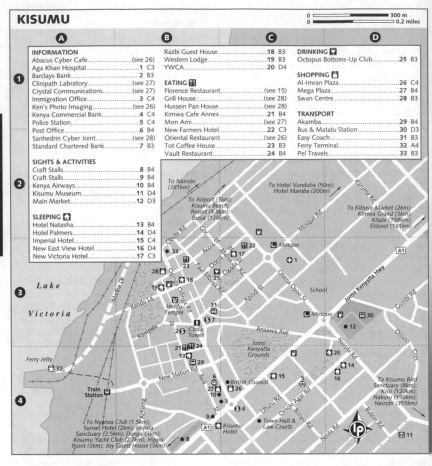

KISUMU

INFORMATION
Abacus Cyber Cafe..................(see 26)
Aga Khan Hospital...........................1 C3
Barclays Bank..................................2 B3
Clinipath Labratory.................(see 27)
Crystal Communications..........(see 27)
Immigration Office...........................3 C4
Ken's Photo Imaging................(see 26)
Kenya Commercial Bank..................4 C4
Police Station...................................5 C4
Post Office.......................................6 B4
Sanhedrin Cyber Joint..............(see 28)
Standard Chartered Bank.................7 B3

SIGHTS & ACTIVITIES
Craft Stalls......................................8 B4
Craft Stalls......................................9 B4
Kenya Airways...............................10 B4
Kisumu Museum.............................11 D4
Main Market...................................12 D3

SLEEPING
Hotel Natasha................................13 B4
Hotel Palmers.................................14 D4
Imperial Hotel................................15 C4
New East View Hotel......................16 D4
New Victoria Hotel.........................17 C3

Razbi Guest House..........................18 B3
Western Lodge...............................19 B3
YWCA..20 D4

EATING
Florence Restaurant.................(see 15)
Grill House................................(see 28)
Hussein Pan House....................(see 28)
Kimwa Cafe Annex........................21 B4
Mon Ami..................................(see 27)
New Farmers Hotel.........................22 C3
Oriental Restaurant..................(see 26)
Tot Coffee House...........................23 B3
Vault Restaurant............................24 B4

DRINKING
Octopus Bottoms-Up Club.............25 B3

SHOPPING
Al-Imran Plaza................................26 C4
Mega Plaza....................................27 B4
Swan Centre...................................28 B4

TRANSPORT
Akamba...29 B4
Bus & Matatu Station.....................30 D3
Easy Coach....................................31 B3
Ferry Terminal...............................32 A4
Pel Travels.....................................33 B3

TRAVEL AGENCIES

Pel Travels (☎ 2022780; travels@pel.co.ke; Oginga Odinga Rd) The most helpful and skilled travel agent in town. Vehicle hire is also available.

VISA EXTENSIONS

Immigration office (1st fl Reinsurance Plaza, cnr Oginga Odinga Rd & Jomo Kenyatta Hwy) Visa extensions are available at this office, behind the Format Supermarket.

Dangers & Annoyances

While open storm drains and steep curbs are probably your biggest worry when walking around at night, it's still best not to do it too often (robberies do occur). Kisumu, like most large Kenyan towns, has its share of glue-sniffing children and some travellers

find their persistence here troubling – if you want to help, donate some time or a kind word, but never give money.

Sights & Activities

KISUMU MUSEUM

Unlike many local museums, **Kisumu Museum** (Nairobi Rd; admission KSh200; 8am-6pm) is an interesting and often informative place.

The displays are wide ranging and most are well presented, though some could use some light. There is a very good collection of traditional everyday items that are used by the region's various peoples, including agricultural implements, bird and insect traps, food utensils, clothing, furniture, weapons and musical instruments. There is also a fairly motley collection of stuffed birds and animals, including an amazing airborne lion mauling a wildebeest.

Outside, a traditional Luo homestead has been constructed, consisting of the husband's thatched mud-house and separate houses for wife one, two and three!

There are also the usual crocodile and tortoise enclosures, which are small and a tad depressing.

HIPPO POINT & BOAT TRIPS

Grassy and palm-laden Hippo Point sticks into Lake Victoria at Dunga, about 3km south of town, and is a pleasant spot to head for, though you're not guaranteed to see any hippos. There also used to be a cool restaurant here, but it burnt down years ago. If reconstruction maintains its current pace, it will reopen March 18, 2073.

If you want virtually guaranteed hippo sightings, you will have to venture onto the lake. As you might imagine, plenty of people offer just such a boat trip. Since locals pay KSh150 per hour for a paddle boat, you'd be insane to pay their KSh1000 asking price – serious negotiations are in serious order! Power boats that can take you further afield can be found at nearby **Dunga fish market** (usual asking price KSh2500 – cue negotiations).

MARKETS

Kisumu's **main market** (off Jomo Kenyatta Hwy) is one of Kenya's most animated, and certainly one of its largest, now spilling out onto the surrounding roads. If you're curious or just looking for essentials like suits or wigs, it's worth a stroll around.

The **Kibuye Market** (Jomo Kenyatta Hwy) is a huge outdoor affair that draws people from all around the district each Sunday. Everything from second-hand clothes to furniture and food can be found spread out along the road, a couple of kilometres north of the main market.

The various **craft stalls** near Kisumu Hotel are some of the best places in Kenya for soapstone carvings. Quality varies but there are some gems to be found.

IMPALA SANCTUARY

On the road to Dunga is Kenya Wildlife Service's 1-sq-km **Impala Sanctuary** (adult/child US$5/2; ☽ 6am-6pm). Besides being home to a small

impala herd, it also provides important grazing grounds for local hippos. You will find a pleasant nature trail and a not so pleasant animal orphanage.

KISUMU BIRD SANCTUARY

This **sanctuary** (off A1 Hwy; ☽ 6am-6pm), 8km southeast of town, covers a large area of swampland and is an important breeding ground for herons, storks, cormorants and egrets. The best time to visit is April or May. Transport is easy along the A1, but it's then a 3km walk from the turn-off. Visitor fees may be implemented soon.

NDERE ISLAND NATIONAL PARK

Gazetted as a **national park** (adult/child US$15/5) back in 1986, tourism to this small 4.2-sq-km island has never taken off. It is forested and very beautiful, housing a variety of bird species, plus hippos, impalas (introduced) and spotted crocodiles, a lesser-known cousin of the larger Nile crocodile. Tsetse flies can be problematic after the rains.

Unfortunately there is nowhere to stay and chartered boats are your only option to get there. Kisumu Beach Resort (p294) charters 20 passenger boats for KSh3000 per hour, with typical return trips taking five hours (including three hours on shore) – keep an eye out for hippos en route.

OTHER ACTIVITIES

Join the **Nyanza Club** (☎ 2022433; off Jomo Kenyatta Hwy; temporary membership KSh100) for the day, which entitles you to belly flop in their huge **swimming pool**, vegetate on the lounge chairs and play pool and billiards to your heart's content. Tennis and Squash are also options, but you will need your own racquets.

Sleeping
BUDGET

After weeding out Kisumu's plethora of dives, we were left with the following options.

Western Lodge (☎ 2023707; Kendu Lane; s or d KSh500) This lodge has a number of smallish singles (or cosy doubles) with mozzie nets and bathrooms. There is a nice common balcony with plants, tables and a slice of lake view.

Razbi Guest House (☎ 2025488; Kendu Lane; s/tw with shared bathroom KSh400/500, s KSh600) A secure place with small, mosquito net–clad rooms, some decidedly brighter than others. The shared toilets pass the nostril test and there is a private TV lounge/restaurant upstairs.

YWCA (☎ 0733-992982; Anaawa Ave; dm KSh300, full board KSh500) Bare-bones bunks in airy rooms for bottom dollar. The shared bathrooms look clean, but are rather pungent.

Hotel Natasha (☎ 2020189; off Oginga Odinga Rd; s/tw KSh600/800) A simple place with bright rooms featuring fans (but no mozzie nets), hot water and old but clean bathrooms.

Kisumu Beach Resort (☎ 0733-749327; camping KSh300, s/tw KSh1250/1500) This scruffy lakeside 'resort' is set across the bay from town. With loads of space, wicker lounges, a pool table, volley ball net, decent restaurant (meals KSh160 to KSh500) and a well-stocked bar (large Tusker KSh80), it's easy to see why it's popular with overlanders and campers. The cottages are a bit grotty and aren't worth the price. To get here, take a Pipeline matatu (KSh20) from the main station to the airport, from where you can hire a *boda-boda* (KSh10), or walk the remaining 1.8km.

MIDRANGE

All prices below include breakfast unless stated otherwise.

Hotel Palmers (☎ 2024867; Omolo Agar Rd; s/tw KSh1000/1400) An understated place with a perceptible warmth to its atmosphere. The rooms are on the small side, but they see some sun, have decent bathrooms and are home to breezy fans. The hotel also has a comfortable lounge, an outdoor restaurant and secure parking.

New Victoria Hotel (☎ 2021067; Gor Mahia Rd; s with shared bathroom KSh600, s/tw/tr KSh850/1050/1550) Bright on the outside and gleaming green on the inside, this hotel has some good options. Rooms have fans, mozzie nets and comfy foam mattresses, and a few boast balconies with lake views. The hotel also has a good café and TV lounge.

Hotel Vunduba (☎ 2020043; Mosque Rd; s/tw/ste KSh800/1300/2500) Rooms here surround a sunny courtyard and offer good value. The singles are small but squeaky clean, while the twins are more sizeable and comfy. The suites are perfect for families and the courtyard is an ideal spot for weary vehicles to snooze.

New East View Hotel (☎ 0722-556721; Omolo Agar Rd; s/tw KSh1200/1600) Although it's less atmospheric than its neighbour, Hotel Palmers, this hotel's rooms offer more character. The bathrooms are rather aged.

Hotel Mamba (☎ 2020043; Off Mosque Rd; s/tw KSh800/1300) While rundown, this is a very friendly place to stay. The rooms are small and have TVs (only a bonus if you speak Swahili).

Joy Guest House (☎ 0720-272037; Dunga; tw KSh1000, with shared bathroom KSh800) Located 3km south of town near Hippo Point's turn-off, this welcoming place has a homey feel. Cooking facilities, solid-rock sofas (sit slowly or risk a broken arse) and cramped rug-clad rooms, with fans and the odd balcony, call Joy's home. Sadly, prices don't include breakfast.

TOP END

Imperial Hotel (☎ 2022211; www.imperialkisumu.com; Jomo Kenyatta Hwy; s/d incl breakfast from US$75/85; ste US$175; 🗙 🖳 🖭) Offering friendly 1st-class service, this old dame is Kisumu's most luxurious hotel. The full-length windows afford grand views and, if opened, heavenly breezes – turn off that air-conditioning! All rooms are well appointed, with 'deluxe' options offering better views and a fridge. The top-floor suites are simply swank. Weekend rates are a bargain.

Nyanza Club (☎ 2022433; off Jomo Kenyatta Hwy; s/tw incl breakfast KSh2500/3000; 🖭) While this blindingly white option is slightly past its prime, its leafy and sporty surrounds make for an entertaining stay. The rooms are huge and those upstairs have lovely shaded balconies with lake views. There is a plethora of activities available (see p293), but since they're strictly for members, you will have to become a temporary member (per day KSh100).

Sunset Hotel (☎ 2022174; Jomo Kenyatta Hwy; s/tw KSh3600/4000; 🗙 🖭) This modern hotel, 2.5km south of town, climbs numerous storeys above the trees to offer unmatched vistas over Lake Victoria. Although simple, all rooms are very comfortable and boast breezy balconies with astounding views.

Eating

The fact that Kisumu sits on Lake Victoria isn't lost on restaurants here and seafood is abundant.

If you want an authentic local fish fry, there is no better place than the dozen tin-shack restaurants siting on the lake's shore at the end of Oginga Odinga Rd. Open flames, a whole lot of smoke and boisterous locals all add to the experience. Dive in between 11am and 6pm; a 1½kg fish should set you back Ksh150.

Florence Restaurant (☎ 2022211; Jomo Kenyatta Hwy; mains KSh200-450) Housed within the glam Imperial Hotel, Florence is renowned as Kisumu's best restaurant. Their poached Nile perch is lovely, as are the chicken Kiev and mutton masala.

Kisumu Yacht Club (☎ 2022050; Dunga; meals KSh200-300) On the lake's edge, just past the Impala Sanctuary on the Dunga road, with a lovely patio and teak furnishings. The menu ranges from delicately stuffed fish to Indian selections such as chicken biryani and *palak paneer*. A temporary membership (KSh200) is necessary to indulge.

Grill House (Swan Centre, Accra St; meals KSh100-450; ⊙ Tue-Sun) Wicker furniture and shady umbrellas sit street-side at this German-owned eatery. The menu is a bit of a cultural hotchpotch – the spring rolls are quite nice.

Hussein Pan House (Swan Centre, Accra St; meals KSh150-300; ⊙ 6-11pm) Smoky stoves grace the sidewalk here each evening and pump out amazing Asian selections like chicken tikka and mutton pilau. The boneless chicken *mushkati* is divine.

Mon Ami (Mega Plaza, Oginga Odinga Rd; meals KSh150-350) A favourite expat pit-stop, with Western standards such as hamburgers, pastas and pizza.

Vault Restaurant (off Oginga Odinga Rd; meals KSh300-600) Pizza (with real cheese), pasta and even veal grace this Italian restaurant's menu. Housed in a former bank, the massive vault still lurks in the shadows.

New Victoria Hotel (Gor Mahia Rd; meals KSh150-300) Follow the local crowds and descend into the subdued interior of this brightly coloured hotel for a filling feed in the morning.

Oriental Restaurant (Al-Imran Plaza, Oginga Odinga Rd; meals KSh260-400) The dishes read like your Chinese favourites, and they almost look like your Thai favourites, but sadly none of them taste like your tongue's favourites. On the bright side, it still gives your palate some needed diversity.

Some of the better Kenyan restaurants serving cheap local dishes such as *matoke* (mashed plantains) and stew:

Kimwa Cafe Annex (off Oginga Odinga Rd; meals KSh60-250)

New Farmers Hotel (Odera St; meals KSh60-160)

Tot Coffee House (Accra St; meals KSh65-180)

Drinking & Entertainment

Kisumu's nightlife has a reputation for being even livelier than Nairobi's, but thanks to many of the best parties and live Congolese bands cropping up at various venues such as the **Kimwa Grand** (Jomo Kenyatta Hwy) along the roads out of town, it's harder to find. Check flyers and ask locals who are plugged into the scene.

Mon Ami (Mega Plaza, Oginga Odinga Rd) Easy to find and always good for having a drink, this is a lively bar with a pool table, welcoming expat crowd and satellite TV, which blasts European footy in the evenings.

Octopus Bottoms-Up Club (Ogada St) A short stroll from Oginga Odinga Rd, this popular bar has two pool tables, a foosball table, its own disco (admission KSh100) and more Michael Jackson posters than we're comfortable with. With a largely male crowd and lots of beer flowing, single females may not find it the most appealing of places.

The Imperial Hotel and Kisumu Yacht Club are good spots for a cold beverage and a taste of the high life, while the Kisumu Beach Resort can either be a great place to chill quietly with other backpackers or to rip it up, depending whether an overland truck and its boisterous crowd are on site. The only problem with the yacht club and beach resort is getting home!

Getting There & Away

AIR

Kenya Airways (☎ 2020081; Alpha House, Oginga Odinga Rd) has daily morning flights to Nairobi (KSh7500, one hour) and an evening flight on Friday and Sunday. Hopefully the fact that their model Kenya Airways plane has lost its starboard engine won't put you off!

BOAT

Despite the reduced hyacinth in the Winam Gulf, ferry services to Tanzania and Uganda haven't restarted. The only route active during research was a 9am sailing to Homa Bay (KSh250, four hours) each Monday. Check the port's booking office for the latest information.

BUS & MATATU

Most buses, matatus and Peugeots to destinations within Kenya leave from the large bus and matatu station just north of the main market.

Matatus offer the only direct services to Kakamega (KSh120, one hour) and Eldoret (KSh250, 2½ hours). Plenty of other matatus serve Busia (KSh250, two hours), Kericho (KSh200, two hours), Kisii (KSh200, two hours), Homa Bay (KSh250, three hours), Nakuru (KSh300, 3½ hours), Nairobi (KSh550, 5½ hours) and Isebania (KSh350, four hours), on the Tanzanian border. Peugeots do still serve some destinations, but they cost about 25% more than matatus.

There are very few direct services to Kitale (KSh300, four hours); it is best to take a vehicle to Kakamega or Eldoret and change there.

Akamba (off New Station Rd) has its own depot in the town's centre. Besides four daily buses to Nairobi (KSh500, seven hours) via Nakuru (KSh300, 4½ hours), Akamba also has daily services to Busia (KSh200, three hours) and Kampala (KSh750, seven hours). **Easy Coach** (off Mosque Rd) serves similar destinations, as well as Kakamega (KSh150, one hour), with some added comfort and cost.

TRAIN
After being shut down for years, the train service to Nairobi (1st-/2nd-class KSh1415/720, 13 hours) is once again on the roll. Trains are scheduled to depart on Sunday, Tuesday and Thursday at 6.30pm, though they usually leave late.

Getting Around
TO/FROM THE AIRPORT
A taxi is probably the easiest way to get to town from the airport (around KSh500). Pipeline matatus (KSh20) pick up and drop off passengers outside the airport gate.

BODA-BODA
Bicycle-taxis have proliferated and they are a great way to get around Kisumu. No journey in town should be more than 20 bob.

CAR
Pel Travels (☎ 2022780; travels@pel.co.ke; Oginga Odinga Rd) is your only option for a rental car here. It charges KSh4000 per day including insurance. Excess is set at KSh35,000.

There are no rental 4WDs in Kisumu.

MATATU
The No 7 and No 9 matatus (KSh20), which run north along Oginga Odinga Rd before turning up Anaawa Ave and continuing east down Jomo Kenyatta Hwy, are handy to reach the main matatu station, main market and Kibuye Market – just wave an arm and hop on anywhere you see one.

TAXI
A taxi around town costs between KSh100 and KSh200, while trips to Dunga or Kisumu Beach Resort range from KSh200 to KSh300.

LAKE VICTORIA'S SOUTH SHORE
Kendu Bay
This small lakeside village, two hours from Kisumu on the potholed road to Homa Bay, has little to offer apart from the strange volcanic **Simbi Lake** a couple of kilometres from town. The circular lake, sunk into the earth like a bomb crater, has a footpath around it and is quite popular with bird-watchers.

There is no real reason to stay, but if the need arises **Big Five Hotel & Bar** (☎ 059-22416; route C19; s/tw with shared bathroom KSh300/400) is your best option.

Homa Bay
☎ 059
This area, blanketed with green and dotted with conical volcanic plugs (the plumbing of ancient volcanos exposed through erosion) makes for an interesting visit and a great base to visit Ruma National Park (opposite) and Thimlich Ohinga (opposite).

Climb nearby Mt Homa (one hour) for a panoramic vista, take in the bustling harbour or just wander the dusty streets to the Caribbean beats radiating from various *dukas*. It is also a great place to find tapes of traditional Luo music.

INFORMATION
The Co-operative Bank of Kenya exchanges US dollars, while Postbank offers Western Union. The new Kenya Commercial Bank, with an ATM (Visa only), should be open by the time you read this. The post office has Internet and telephone services. The **warden's office** (☎ 22544) for Ruma National Park is found up the hill in the District Commissioner's compound.

SLEEPING & EATING
Bay Lodge (☎ 22568; s with shared bathroom KSh250, s/tw KSh300/450) An aquamarine sanctuary of

simplicity nestled between the bus station and the post office. It is tidy, quiet, has secure parking and the staff are lovely and helpful.

Little Nile Guest House (☎ 0720-997718; s/tw incl breakfast KSh800/1200) On the hill leading into town, this shiny new option is bright, comfortable and houses colourful murals.

Ruma Tourist Lodge (☎ 0734-590868; s/d KSh600/900) Lurking behind a messy entrance, Ruma's bungalows offer comfy rooms and great bathrooms. Unfortunately the town's best bar – which has cold beers, decent tunes, a pool table and a restaurant (meals KSh150 to KSh230) – also lives here, so noise can be problematic. It is signposted behind the Total station.

Hippo Buck Hotel (☎ 22032; s/d/tr KSh1000/1400/2000) About 1.5km out of town towards Mbita, Hippo Buck's spotless, simple rooms are surrounded by colourful flowering gardens. The restaurant (meals KSh150 to KSh230) is highly recommended.

Self-caterers can visit the well-stocked Shiviling Supermarket near the post office.

GETTING THERE & AWAY
Akamba's office is just down the hill from the bus station and its buses serve Nairobi (KSh550, 8½ hours, 7am and 7.30pm) via Kericho (KSh300, four hours) and Nakuru (KSh450, six hours). Several other companies and matatus (operating from the bus station) also ply these routes, as well as Mbita (KSh150, 1½ hours) and Kisumu (KSh250, three hours).

RUMA NATIONAL PARK
Bordered by the dramatic **Kanyamaa Escarpment**, and home to Kenya's only population of roans (one of Africa's rarest and largest antelopes), is the surprisingly seldom-visited **Ruma National Park** (adult/child US$15/5). While hot and often wet, it is beautiful and comprises 120 sq km of verdant riverine woodland and savanna grassland within the Lambwe Valley.

Besides roan, other rarities like Bohor's reedbuck, Rothschild's giraffe, Jackson's hartebeest and the tiny oribi antelope can be seen. Birdlife is prolific, with 145 different bird species present, including the mighty fish eagle and white egret.

The park is set up for those with vehicles, but contact the **warden** (☎ 059-22544; PO Box 420,

Homa Bay) in Homa Bay and you may be able to organise a hike, though you will have to pay a ranger to accompany you (KSh500/1000 per half-/full-day).

There are two simple **campsites** (adult/child US$8/5) near the main gate and the guesthouse will soon be rebuilt.

Tsetse flies can be a problem after the rains.

Getting There & Away
Head a couple of kilometres south from Homa Bay and turn right onto the Mbita road. About 12km west is the main access road, and from there it's another 11km. The park's roads are in decent shape, but require a 4WD in the rainy season.

If you don't have transport but have contacted the warden, hop on a Homa Bay–Mbita matatu and jump off at the access road.

THIMLICH OHINGA
East of Ruma National Park, this **archaeological site** (KSh250) is one of East Africa's most important sites. The remains of a dry-stone enclosure, 150m in diameter and containing another five smaller enclosures, was discovered here. Stylistically, the structure resembles traditional Luo buildings, but may date back as far as the 15th century. Those who have stood within the walls of Zimbabwe's ancient stone fortress, Great Zimbabwe, will note the similarities. The name is essentially a description of the site, which means 'stone enclosure in frightening dense forest'.

Getting to Thimlich is a problem without your own transport, although not completely impossible with patience. Head down the Homa Bay–Rongo road for 12km, then turn right at Rod Kopany village, heading southwest through Mirogi to the village of Miranga. The site is signposted from there.

MBITA & RUSINGA ISLAND
Set on the shoreline of Lake Victoria and marking Winam Gulf's entrance is Mbita is this lonely village with a warm frontier feel. While often treated as an access point for Rusinga and Mfangano Islands, Mbita is a great place to experience a traditional fishing village. The fact that there are some beaches in the area only adds to its appeal.

A short causeway connects Mbita to Rusinga Island, which is a great place for a day's wander – the craggy hill makes an attractive viewpoint. On the island's north side is **Tom Mboya's mausoleum**. A child of Rusinga and former sanitary inspector in Nairobi, Mboya was one of the few Luos ever to achieve any kind of political success in the government of Kenya. He held a huge amount of influence as Jomo Kenyatta's right-hand man and was widely tipped to become Kenya's second president before he was assassinated in 1969. He's still well remembered today.

Sleeping & Eating

Mbuta Campsite (☎ 0722-617953; camping per tent KSh100) This grassy camp 2.5km south of Mbita is set on a small section of beach and is a perfect place to laze away a day or two. Nice two-/four-person (KSh200/400) tents with beds are available for rent, and meals can be prepared if you call ahead. Look for the small camping sign en route to Lake Victoria's Safari Village.

Elk Guest House (tw KSh600, s/tw with shared toilet KSh300/400) Backing the bus stand in Mbita, this place will do perfectly for a night's kip. Besides being clean, it has mosquito nets and private showers.

Lake Victoria's Safari Village (☎ 0721-912120; www.safarikenya.net; s/d incl breakfast US$35/55) A Lake Victoria beachfront haven if there ever was one. Lovely traditionally thatched roofs tower over comfy beds and impressive bathrooms in each of the pretty cottages. The grassy garden is grand and the food looks good too. It is well signposted from town.

Rusinga Island Club (bookings ☎ 020-340331; info@letsgosafari.com; full board incl all activities s/d US$410/700) This is an exclusive place on the northern side of Rusinga Island. Fishing is the dominant activity, but if you're not a keen worm-dangler there are various water sports available and the birdlife is prolific. The flash rooms are in individual thatched huts, each with fine lake views.

Viking Hotel (meals KSh70-100) Popular with locals, this wee restaurant is next to the Elk Guest House.

Getting There & Away

There are four buses to Kisumu (KSh200, five hours) each morning between 6am and 11am. Matatus to Homa Bay are far more frequent (KSh100, 1½ hours). The odd matatu heads to Rusinga Island and past the mausoleum (KSh50).

MFANGANO ISLAND

Home to many a monitor lizard, curious locals, intriguing **rock paintings** and the imposing but assailable **Mt Kwitutu** (1694m), Mfangano Island is well worth a day or two. Thanks to the refreshing absence of vehicles, only footpaths crisscross the island. A guide is invaluable (KSh500 per day is fair).

It is about a 1½- to two-hour climb from the Sena village jetty to the sublime vista atop Kwitutu, on the southeastern side of the island. The rock paintings, both revered and feared by locals (which has hindered vandalism), are found northwest of Kwitutu towards the village of Ukula.

Sena village has little more than the post office and the chief's camp (housing the administrator of the island).

Sleeping & Eating

There are no guesthouses, but it may be possible to arrange home stays with the local residents. Campers might also stay on the grounds of St Linus' Church (check out the mural inside).

If you have a bunch of Benjamin Franklins burning a hole in your pocket, there is the **Mfangano Island Camp** (bookings ☎ 020-2734000; governors@reservation.com; full board s/d US$370/550; ☯ Jun-Mar) on the north side of the island. Built in traditional Luo style (albeit with a few modern amenities), this is primarily a fishing resort.

Getting There & Away

Until the ferries get their act together, sporadic 10m canoes are the only transport to Mfangano Island from Mbita (per person KSh150). If you don't want to wait for passengers, you will have to fork out KSh4000 for the entire boat. Market day in Mbita (Thursday) is a good day to travel because there are plenty of boats coming and going from its causeway.

WESTERN HIGHLANDS

Benefiting from reliable rainfall and fertile soil, the Western Highlands make up the agricultural heartland of Kenya, separating Kisumu and Lake Victoria from the rest of the country. The south is cash-crop country, with vast patchworks of tea plantations covering the region around Kisii and Kericho, while further north, near Kitale and Eldoret, insanely dense cultivation takes over.

The settlements here are predominantly agricultural service towns, with little of interest unless you need a chainsaw or water barrel. For visitors, the real attractions lie outside these places – the rolling tea fields around Kericho, the tropical beauty of Kakamega Forest, trekking on Mt Elgon, the prolific birdlife in Saiwa Swamp National Park and exploring the dramatic Cherangani Hills.

KISII
☎ 058
Whether inspired by nearby soils (some of the most fertile in Kenya) or by the growing non-Bantu-speaking tribes surrounding them (Maasai to the south, Luo to the west and north and Kipsigis to the east), the Bantu-speaking Gusii people of this region (see p43) are producing offspring at one of the world's fastest rates. An amazing 50% of the 1.5 million Gusii are below the age of 15. With all those new mouths to feed and house, the rapidly expanding town of Kisii is bursting with activity.

Besides being the region's transportation hub and hosting a variety of facilities, this hilly city (resembling a miniature Kigali in Rwanda) has little to offer travellers besides muddy, trash-laden streets, a lot of noise and an entertaining nightlife (its saving grace).

While the fêted Kisii soapstone obviously comes from this area, it's not on sale here. Quarrying and carving go on in the village of **Tabaka**, 23km northwest of Kisii, where you can usually visit the workshops. Since most carvings are sold to dealers and shops in Nairobi at rock-bottom prices, they'll happily accept a fair price from you.

Information
Barclays Bank (Moi Hwy) Exchange cash and travellers cheques (KSh34 per leaf commission). With ATM.
Cyber Cafe (Hospital Rd; per hr KSh90) Reasonable Internet connections.
National Bank of Kenya (cnr Hospital Rd & Sansora Rd) With ATM (Cirrus and Plus cards only).
Postbank (Hospital Rd) Western Union services.
Post office (Moi Hwy) With card phones and Internet.

Sleeping & Eating
There are few decent accommodation options, and the budget places are particularly poor. There is a lot of noise at night wherever you stay, not of the baby-making variety! Eating options are also slim.

Sabrina Lodge (s/tw with shared bathroom KSh300/ 500) Just up from Postbank, Sabrina has clean, concrete Santa specials, with rooms boasting red floors and bright green walls. The toilets (missing seats) are clean enough, but there is no running water. Hot bucket showers are available in the morning. The beds aren't great, but they do have mozzie nets.

Kisii Hotel (☎ 30254; off Moi Hwy; s/tw incl breakfast KSh750/950) Double the price, but triple the pleasure. This is a relaxed place boasting large gardens and sizeable rooms, each with

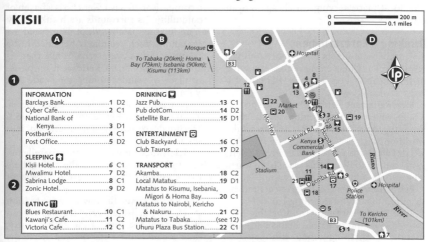

KISII

0 — 200 m
0 — 0.1 miles

INFORMATION	
Barclays Bank	1 D2
Cyber Cafe	2 C1
National Bank of Kenya	3 D1
Postbank	4 C1
Post Office	5 D2

SLEEPING 🏠	
Kisii Hotel	6 C1
Mwalimu Hotel	7 D2
Sabrina Lodge	8 C1
Zonic Hotel	9 D2

EATING 🍴	
Blues Restaurant	10 C1
Kawanji's Cafe	11 C2
Victoria Cafe	12 C1

DRINKING 🍷	
Jazz Pub	13 C1
Pub dotCom	14 D2
Satellite Bar	15 D1

ENTERTAINMENT 🎭	
Club Backyard	16 C1
Club Taurus	17 D2

TRANSPORT	
Akamba	18 C2
Local Matatus	19 D1
Matatus to Kisumu, Isebania, Migori & Homa Bay	20 C1
Matatus to Nairobi, Kericho & Nakuru	21 C2
Matatus to Tabaka	(see 12)
Uhuru Plaza Bus Station	22 C1

To Tabaka (20km); Homa Bay (75km); Isebania (90km); Kisumu (113km)

To Kericho (101km)

decent bathrooms. The restaurant (meals KSh150 to KSh300) is deservedly popular, but the performing turkey and ducks are still missing in action.

Mwalimu Hotel (Moi Hwy; d/ste KSh800/1500) Set in its own compound opposite the Mobile station at the southeastern end of town, this hotel isn't atmospheric but provides good value and secure parking. The rooms are bright and average-sized, and they also have mosquito nets. The hotel has a popular bar and terrace as well as a restaurant (meals KSh80 to KSh230) that serves a mix of Kenyan, Western and Indian dishes.

Zonic Hotel (☎ 30298; Hospital Rd; s/d US$25/40, ste from US$65; ⊠) The 'Cement, Lacquer & Plywood 101' architecture professor would be beaming with pride. Although bizarre, Zonic is home to town's most comfortable rooms, each large, clean and sporting a balcony. There is a rooftop swimming pool and a cavernous restaurant (meals KSh250 to KSh350), which produces some tasty Asian curries and a good beef tenderloin in pepper sauce.

Blues Restaurant (Hospital Rd; meals KSh150-250) With a feel more like a modern pub, this friendly restaurant cooks up some great Chinese stir-fries, complete with fresh ginger. The chicken stew isn't bad either.

Kawanji's Cafe (Ogemba Rd; meals KSh120-180) Lurking behind a wall of foliage, this pleasant restaurant serves the best Kenyan dishes in Kisii.

Victoria Cafe (Moi Hwy; meals Ksh60-160) A popular local place serving up cheap Kenyan meals.

Drinking & Entertainment

To compensate for its other shortcomings, Kisii has plenty of evening venues and some of the cheapest beer around (KSh60 for a large Tusker).

Blues Restaurant (Hospital Rd) A good spot for a beer, with a balcony overlooking the market and proper cable TV to catch up on the world outside.

Jazz Pub (Hospital Rd) A similar crowd (Kenyan yuppies) to Blues, this place has a warm vibe and an odd absence of jazz music.

Pub dotCom (Ogemba Rd) Reggae cuts radiate through this tiny, welcoming bar.

Zonic Hotel (Hospital Rd) Comfortable surrounds, but a bit of an old man's bar – not that there's anything wrong with that!

Satellite Bar (Sansora Rd) Even rain doesn't seem to dampen the late night spirits at this rooftop bar. Thankfully there is a shelter over the pool table.

Club Backyard (Hospital Rd; ⊠ weekends) The best nightclub in town, this place gets packed on Friday and Saturday nights. They usually host well-known DJs – look for posters throughout town.

Club Taurus (Ogemba Rd; ⊠ weekends) A decent second-place finisher in the nightclub department.

Getting There & Away

Matatus line the length of Moi Hwy – look for the destination placards on their roofs. Regular departures serve Homa Bay (KSh100, one hour), Kisumu (KSh200, two hours), Kericho (KSh180, two hours) and Isebania (KSh150, 1¾ hours) on the Tanzanian border.

Tabaka matatus leave from the Victoria Cafe, while local matatus (and additional Kericho services) leave from the stand at the end of Sansora Rd.

Akamba (Moi Hwy) has a daily bus to Nairobi (KSh550, eight hours) via Nakuru (KSh290, 5½ hours) departing at 7.30am – it's wise to book a day in advance. International bus departures for Mwanza in Tanzania also leave from here (see p375).

Various other bus companies have offices along Moi Hwy.

KERICHO

☎ 052

In comparison to Kisii, Kericho is a haven of tranquillity. Its surrounds are blanketed by an undulating patchwork of manicured tea plantations, each seemingly hemmed in by distant stands of evergreens. While there is little to actually do in Kericho, it's a pleasant place to wander among the shade cast by leafy trees.

There is little doubt why Kericho is the tea capital of western Kenya: the soil is perfect, the climate consistent and afternoon rain falls almost every day.

Luckily these downpours are generally too brief to be a nuisance, and the atmosphere is cool enough to keep it fresh instead of humid.

Settlers attribute the town's name to John Kerich, a herbalist and early tea planter who lived here at the turn of the 20th century, while locals believe it's derived from the

---

ANYONE FOR TEA?

Kenya is the world's third-largest tea exporter after India and Sri Lanka, with tea accounting for between 20% and 30% of the country's export income. Tea picking is a great source of employment around Kericho, with mature bushes picked every 17 days and the same worker continually picking the same patch. Good pickers collect almost double their own body weight in tea each day!

The Kenyan tea industry is unique in that its small landholders produce the bulk (60%) of the country's tea. All the leaves used to be sold to the Kenya Tea Development Authority (KTDA), which did the processing and supposedly guaranteed farmers 70% of the sale price.

Corrupt and inefficient, the KTDA was replaced in 2000 by the Kenya Tea Development Agency (spot the difference!), which is run as a private company. However, smallholders continue to take a bigger role in the management of Kenya's most important cash crop, and the problems which have beset the coffee industry aren't quite so prevalent here.

Despite Kericho producing some of the planet's best black tea, you will have trouble finding a cup of the finest blends here – most of it's exported.

Maasai chief Ole Kericho, killed here by the Gusii during an 18th-century territorial battle. Who's right is anyone's guess.

Eventually the Maasai and Gusii settled elsewhere and the Kipsigis people, part of the greater Kalenjin group of Nandi-speaking tribes that also includes the Pokot, the Nandi and the Marakwet (see p43), now call this rich region home.

Information

Aga Khan Satellite Laboratory (Moi Hwy) Malaria and other blood tests.
Barclays Bank (Moi Hwy) Exchange cash and travellers cheques (KSh34 per leaf commission). With ATM.
Kenya Commercial Bank (Moi Hwy) With ATM (Visa only).
Medicare Centre (☎ 21733; Moi Rd) Clinic, pharmacy and X-ray.
Post office (Moi Hwy) With card phones, Internet and Western Union.
Standard Chartered Bank (Moi Hwy) Exchange cash and Amex travellers cheques (KSh50 per leaf). With ATM (Visa only).
Tea Hotel (Moi Hwy; per hr KSh1200) The only other Internet option besides the post office.
Telecare Centre (Temple Rd) Calling cards and card phones.

Sights & Activities

Organised **tea plantation tours** are surprisingly uncommon in Kericho, but Kimugu River Lodge they can usually set something up for you. The Tea Hotel can do the same, although you will pay through the nose.

If you're only interested in seeing the fields up close, it's an easy walk to the nearest

plantation, which sits behind the Tea Hotel. Head through the hotel grounds and follow the path out the back gate through the tea bushes to the hotel workers' huts. If you're lucky, picking may be in progress.

You can also arrange **hikes** through tea estates and **guided river walks** at Kimugu River Lodge.

Africa's largest **Gurudwara** (Sikh place of worship) is found on Hospital Rd.

Sleeping & Eating

It is easier filling your grumbling tummy than finding a satisfactory room in this tea garden town.

Kericho Garden Lodge (☎ 32021; Moi Hwy; camping KSh275, s/tw KSh660/990) There is plenty of room for tents on this lodge's pleasant grounds. The simple rooms, with lumpy mattresses and sporadic hot water, are less of a bargain. It also houses a homey bar and lounge.

Mwalimu (☎ 30656; Moi Rd; s/tw KSh400/550) A secure place for a night's kip. The rooms are much brighter than the gloomy corridors and host soft foam mattresses. The bathrooms are dark and dreary, but hot water flows in the morning and evening.

New Sunshine Hotel (☎ 30037; Tengecha Rd; s/tw/d KSh600/900/1000) Boasting faux-wood paintwork that's almost funny enough to be charming, this place is worth a look. The rooms are clean, though they're a little dark. Hot water is available around the clock and there is secure parking. A bamboo roof and cheesy artificial waterfall grace the restaurant (meals KSh80 to KSh190), which serves Western snacks, sandwiches and burgers.

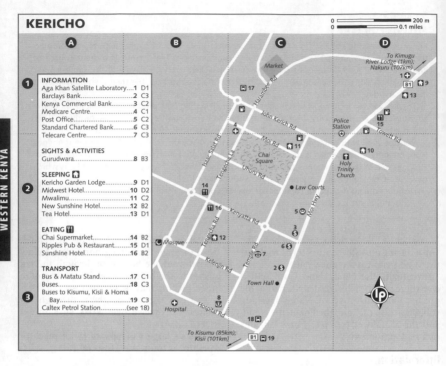

KERICHO

INFORMATION
Aga Khan Satellite Laboratory....**1** D1
Barclays Bank.............................**2** C3
Kenya Commercial Bank...........**3** C2
Medicare Centre.......................**4** C1
Post Office................................**5** C2
Standard Chartered Bank..........**6** C3
Telecare Centre........................**7** C3

SIGHTS & ACTIVITIES
Gurudwara................................**8** B3

SLEEPING
Kericho Garden Lodge...............**9** D1
Midwest Hotel..........................**10** D2
Mwalimu..................................**11** C2
New Sunshine Hotel..................**12** B2
Tea Hotel.................................**13** D1

EATING
Chai Supermarket.....................**14** B2
Ripples Pub & Restaurant.........**15** D1
Sunshine Hotel.........................**16** B2

TRANSPORT
Bus & Matatu Stand..................**17** C1
Buses......................................**18** C3
Buses to Kisumu, Kisii & Homa
Bay..**19** C3
Caltex Petrol Station.............(see 18)

Kimugu River Lodge (☎ 0733-504942; off Moi Hwy; camping KSh150; s/d/tr from KSh1000/1500/2000) Set on the scenic bank of the Kimugi River, which runs behind the Tea Hotel, this lodge is a good option for campers (if you can handle cold showers). Unfortunately, the bandas are unreasonably expensive. Enjoy the bar and devour a spicy south Asian meal at the **restaurant** (meals KSh160-300). Its access road is signposted opposite the BP station.

Midwest Hotel (☎ 30196; Off Moi Hwy; s/d KSh1500/ 2000, ste KSh2950-3550) Garden views and sunshine save these rather basic rooms from being laughably overpriced. The buffet dinners at the popular restaurant (meals KSh200 to KSh450) are another redeeming quality.

Tea Hotel (☎ 30004; teahotel@africaonline.co.ke; Moi Hwy; camping KSh300; s/d US$60/84; ste US$102-108; ⓦ) Glorious gardens envelop this grand property, built in the 1950s by the Brooke Bond company. The rooms in the stone cottages have aged more gracefully than the hotel rooms and cost the same. All rooms have TVs, fireplaces and dated bathrooms.

Ripples Pub & Restaurant (Moi Hwy; meals KSh130-350; ☺ Tue-Sun) Despite being part of

the Kobil petrol station, this is definitely Kericho's most colourful restaurant. There is a good range of pizzas and sandwiches, as well as tasty Indian dishes such as spicy chicken tikka.

Sunshine Hotel (Kenyatta Rd; meals KSh60-160) Locals pile in to devour fried tilapia (their speciality) and other Kenyan selections.

Chai Supermarket (Kenyatta Rd) Perfect for self-caterers to stock up.

Getting There & Away
While most buses and matatus stop at the main stand in the town's northwest corner, many also pick up passengers on the Moi Hwy near the Caltex petrol station. If you simply state your destination to anyone in town, they'll be happy to point you in the right direction.

Buses to Nairobi (KSh450, 4½ hours) are quite frequent, as are matatus to Kisumu (KSh150, two hours), Kisii (KSh180, two hours), Eldoret (KSh250, 3½ hours) and Nakuru (KSh200, two hours). The odd Peugeot also serves these destinations, but costs about 25% more.

KAKAMEGA

☎ 056

This small but busy town is spread out along the A1 Hwy north of Kisumu. There is no real reason to stay here, but if you arrive late in the day it can be convenient to sleep over and stock up with supplies before heading to nearby Kakamega Forest Reserve, one of western Kenya's star attractions.

The Kakamega region is part of the traditional Bungoma district (see below) and home to the Luyha people (see p43), who are quite Westernised and unobtrusive as a community.

Information

Barclays Bank (A1 Hwy) Exchange cash and travellers cheques (KSh34 per leaf commission). With ATM.

Kenya Commercial Bank (Kenyatta Ave) With ATM (Visa only).

KWS Area Headquarters (☎ 30603; PO Box 88, Kakamega) Kakamega Forest information.

Post office (A1 Hwy) With Internet.

Telkom Kenya (A1 Hwy) Calling cards and card phones.

Sights & Activities

Perched on a ridge south of town is the **Crying Stone of Ilesi**, a local curiosity that has become a regional emblem. The formation, looking like a solemn head resting on weary shoulders, consists of a large boulder balanced atop an 8m column of rock. While legend has it that tears never stop flowing down its length, it was dry during our visit – perhaps it was just happy to see us! Still, stains from years of eerie weeping are evident and it's

worth a look. Maybe it won't be so happy to see you…

Those wishing to beat the heat can take a dip in the Golf Hotel's **swimming pool** (KSh150).

Sleeping & Eating

There are slim pickings in the sleeping and eating departments, though try to taste *ugali wimbi* (made from sorghum) while here. Word on the street is that eating this reddish local specialty will slow the aging process.

Bendera Hotel (Sudi Rd; d KSh350) Consistently the best budget hotel in town. It was closed for renovations during our visit, so it should be better than ever when you arrive.

Salama Hotel (Cannon Awori Rd; s/tw with shared bathroom KSh200/300) Can you spell evid backwards? Rooms are very dark and the stinky squat toilets will inspire your bladder to new feats of endurance.

Golf Hotel (☎ 30150; Khasakhala Rd; s/d incl breakfast US$60/75; ▨) While the large rooms, each with a balcony and garden view (some even glimpse Mt Elgon), are bright and pleasant, this hotel is seriously overpriced. On a positive note, readers rave about the swimming pool and fish dishes in the restaurant (meals KSh180 to KSh350).

Snack Stop Cafe (Cannon Awori Rd; meals KSh65-130) The restaurant of choice for locals. Simple Kenyan standards, including *ugali wimbi*.

Pizza Hut Cafe (Cannon Awori Rd; meals KSh60-180) Don't count on pizza! Basic local dishes and slow service are the name of the game.

There are several supermarkets for self-caterers.

WESTERN KENYA

THE KINDEST CUT

The Bungoma/Trans-Nzoia district goes wild in August with the sights and sounds of the Bukusu Circumcision Festival, an annual jamboree dedicated to the initiation of young boys into manhood.

The tradition was apparently passed to the Bukusu by the Sabaot tribe in the 1800s, when a young hunter cut the head off a troublesome serpent to earn the coveted operation (too symbolic to be true?).

The evening before the ceremony is devoted to substance abuse and sex; in the morning the fortunate youngsters are trimmed with a traditional knife in front of their entire village.

Unsurprisingly, this practice has attracted a certain amount of controversy in recent years. Health concerns are prevalent, as the same knife can be used for up to 10 boys, posing a risk of AIDS and other infections. The associated debauchery also brings a seasonal rush of underage pregnancies and family rifts that seriously affect local communities.

Education and experience now mean that fewer boys undergo the old method, preferring to take the safe option at local hospitals. However, those wielding the knife are less likely to let go of their heritage. To quote one prominent circumciser: 'Every year at this time it's like a fever grips me, and I can't rest until I've cut a boy'. It seems that in Bukusuland some traditions die hard.

Getting There & Around

Easy Coach (off Kenyatta Ave) serves Kisumu (KSh150, one hour) and has early morning and evening buses to Nairobi (KSh650, 7½ hours) via Nakuru (KSh450, five hours). Nearby, **Akamba** (off Kenyatta Ave) has an 8pm bus to Nairobi (KSh600).

Behind the Total station on the northern edge of the town, matatus leave for Kisumu (KSh120, one hour), Kitale (KSh190, 2½ hours) and Eldoret (KSh180, 2½ hours).

Boda-bodas (bicycle taxis) are everywhere and crossing town costs about KSh15.

KAKAMEGA FOREST RESERVE

☎ 056

This superb small slab of virgin tropical rainforest is the only Kenyan vestige of the unique and once mighty Guineo-Congolian forest ecosystem. It is so wild here trees actually kill each other – really! Parasitic fig trees grow on top of unsuspecting trees and strangle their hosts to death. Potential victims include the lovely Elgon teak.

Less murderous and more exciting is the forest's array of wildlife. An astounding 330 species of birds, including casqued hornbill, Ross's turaco and great blue turaco, have been spotted here. During darkness, hammer-headed fruit bats and flying squirrels take to the air. The best viewing months are June, August and October, when many migrant species arrive. The wildflowers are also wonderful in October, supporting around 400 species of butterfly.

Dancing in the canopy are no less than seven different primate species, one being the exceedingly rare De Brazza's monkey. Others here include the red-tailed monkey, blue monkey and the thumbless black and white colobus.

The northern section of the forest around Buyangu is more accessible and comprises the **Kakamega Forest National Reserve**. Maintained by the KWS, this area has a variety of habitats but is generally very dense, with considerable areas of primary forest and regenerating secondary forest; there is a total ban on grazing, wood collection and cultivation in this zone. Isolated a few kilometres north, but still part of this reserve, is the small **Kisere Forest Reserve**.

The southern section, centred around Isecheno, forms the **Kakamega Forest Reserve** and is looked after by the Forest Depart-ment. Predominantly forested, this region supports several communities and is under considerable pressure from both farming and illegal logging.

Tribal practices in the forest persist: *mugumu* trees are considered sacred, circumcisions are sometimes performed in the forest and bullfights are still held on Sunday in Khayega and Shinyalu. Intervillage wrestling also used to be common, but was eventually banned, as the prize (the victor's pick of the young women present) tended to provoke more fights than the match itself.

Information

KWS currently only charges admission to the **Kakamega Forest National Reserve** (adult/child US$10/5, vehicle KSh300). An excellent guide to the forest, published by Kenya Indigenous Forest Conservation Programme, is available at the KWS office (KSh300) and Rondo Retreat (KSh500).

Sights & Activities

WALKING TRAILS

The best way to appreciate the forest is to walk, and trails radiate from Buyangu and Isecheno areas. It is possible to drive, but the roads are pretty tough going, and the engine noise will scare off any wildlife nearby as well as annoying everyone else present.

Official **guides** (per person for short/long walk KSh200/600), trained by the Kakamega Biodiversity Conservation and Tour Operators Association, are well worth the money. Not only do they prevent you from getting lost (many of the trail signs are missing), but most are excellent naturalists who can recognise birds by call alone and provide information about numerous animals.

Rangers state that trails vary in length from 1km to 7km, but the enjoyable **Isiukhu Trail**, which connects Isecheno to **Isiukhu Falls**, seems much longer. Short walks to **Buyangu Hill** in the north or **Lirhanda Hill** in the south for sunrise or sunset are highly recommended. River walks are also rewarding. As ever, the early morning and late afternoon are the best times to view birds, but night walks can also be a fantastic experience.

KAKAMEGA ENVIRONMENTAL EDUCATION PROGRAMME

A visit to the diminutive resource centre and library of the **Kakamega Environmental**

Education Programme (KEEP; keeporg@yahoo.com) is quite rewarding. Its mission is to educate the local communities on the importance of maintaining the fragile environment, and to create sustainable income for locals through ecotourism, honey production and butterfly farming.

Sleeping & Eating

BUYANGU AREA

Udo's Bandas & Campsite (☎ 30603; PO Box 879, Kakamega; camping adult/child US$8/5, bandas per person US$10) Named after Udo Savalli, a well-known ornithologist, this place is run by KWS. It is a tidy, well-maintained campsite with seven simple thatched bandas; nets are provided, but you will need your own sleeping bag and other supplies. There are long-drop toilets, bucket showers and a communal cooking and dining shelter.

ISECHENO AREA

Forest Rest House (☎ 30603; PO Box 88, Kakamega; camping KSh150, s/tw KSh350/700) Beds are housed in four rudimentary twin rooms, while bare-bones bathrooms (no hot water) are in a rickety stilted wooden building that looks directly out over the forest. You will need your own sleeping bag, food and preferably something to cook on, although fires are allowed and the small canteen here can cook for you. You can get basic supplies from the *dukas* (shops) about 2km back towards Shinyalu.

KEEP Bandas (keeporg@yahoo.com; s/tw KSh500/1000) Opened in May 2005, these bandas are a more comfortable option than the rest house and have more facilities, including a nice dining area.

Savona Isle Resort (☎ 31095; d/tw/tr KSh1500/1500/5000; ▣) This resort is too far from the forest to make it a walking base, but it is a fine option if you have a car. Rooms are in slightly aged thatched bandas, each with a balcony backing onto the bamboo-lined river. Extortionate 'family' triple rooms are merely created by opening the door between a regular single and double room – keep the door closed and save KSh2000! Meals are available in the atmospheric restaurant (meals KSh200 to KSh400).

Rondo Retreat (☎ 30268; tfrondo@multitechweb .com; full board s/tw KSh9000/11,600) Originally built as a sawmiller's residence in the 1920s, this charming choice is about 3km east of Isecheno. Seven cottages, each with striking

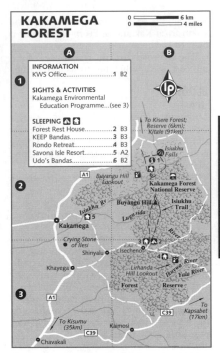

traditional fittings and large verandas, sit in gorgeous gardens through which plenty of wildlife passes. The main house oozes atmosphere (ask for Bob & Betty's room), though some of its rooms share a bathroom. The meals are excellent, although they prefer advance warning. Transfers from Kakamega, guides and forest tours can be arranged.

Getting There & Away

BUYANGU AREA

Matatus heading north towards Kitale can drop you at the access road about 18km north of Kakamega town (KSh50). It is a well signposted 2km walk from there to the park office and Udo's.

ISECHENO AREA

Regular matatus link Kakamega with Shinyalu (KSh60), but few go on to Isecheno. Shinyalu is accessed by a rare matatu service from Khayega. Odd vehicles run between Shinyalu and Isecheno (KSh30 to KSh60).

The improved roads are still treacherous after rain and you may prefer to walk once you've seen the trouble vehicles have. To

Shinyalu it's about 7km from Khayega and 10km from Kakamega. From Shinyalu it is 5km to Isecheno.

The dirt road from the rest house continues east to Kapsabet, but transport is rare.

ELDORET
☎ 053

Mmmmm…cheese! While the pull of a fine Gouda, Gruyere, Stilton, Brie or Cheddar can vary depending on how long you've been on your African safari, a stop in Eldoret is a must for all cheese lovers.

For you cheese haters, there is little else to draw you to this large service town besides the need of a bank or a good night's sleep before venturing into the nearby Kerio Valley and Kamnarok National Reserves.

Former president Moi hails from around this area, and during his presidency the city controversially received many beneficial developments such as Moi University and the international airport. Simultaneous construction of a munitions factory next to the airport also raised many eyebrows at the time – critics wondered just what sort of exports were intended.

Information

Barclays Bank (Uganda Rd) Exchange cash and travellers cheques (per leaf commission KSh34). With ATM.

Cyber Hawk Internet Café (Nandi Arcade, Nandi Rd; per hr KSh60) Fast connections and friendly service.

Eldoret Hospital (off Uganda Rd) One of Kenya's best hospitals. With 24hr Emergency.

Kenya Commercial Bank (Kenyatta St) With ATM (Visa only).

Nameme Cyber Café (Nandi Arcade, Nandia Rd; per hr KSh60) Burn images to CD using USB connection (KSh200).

Post office (Uganda Rd) With Internet.

Safari Forex Bureau (KVDA Plaza, Oloo Rd) Exchange cash and travellers cheques (no commission). Western Union services.

Standard Chartered Bank (Uganda Rd) With ATM (Visa only).

Telkom Kenya (cnr Kenyatta St & Elijaa Cheruhota St) Calling cards and card phones.

Sights & Activities

Cheese cheese cheese, get me some cheese – please! An odd but tasty attraction, the **Dorinyo Lessos Creameries Cheese Factory** (Kenyatta St; ☼ 8am-6pm) produces over 30 different types of cheese. You can taste most for free and the average price is KSh500 per kg, with a minimum purchase of 250g. The company also makes yummy ice cream (KSh23 for 100ml).

An afternoon of lounging and underwater activities can be had at Sirikwa Hotel's **swimming pool** (Elgeyo Rd; adult/child KSh150/200).

Sleeping
BUDGET

Mountain View Hotel (☎ 0720-486613; Uganda Rd; s/tw KSh450/550) While a little noisy and small, these bright clean rooms have mozzie nets, reasonable bathrooms and balconies complete with potted plants. Taking a cell-like inside-facing single without a balcony only saves 50 bob. Security is distinctly prison-like (you have to be let out as well as in). It also has a respectable terrace bar and restaurant.

EDUCATION FOR ALL!

After the 2002 elections the new government created a long-awaited provision guaranteeing free primary education for all Kenyans, a move applauded by parents across the nation. One great-grandfather by the name of Kimani Nganga Maruge clapped a little louder than most.

What the teacher thought on the first day of class when she saw this cane-wielding knobbly-kneed 84-year-old, dressed in school uniform – shorts and all, with striped knee-socks pulled high – sitting in the front row (he was hard of hearing, after all) is anyone's guess!

Mr Maruge was there to start collecting his long-overdue education and wouldn't let anyone say otherwise. Besides basic maths, he was keen on learning how to read. This would allow him to study the bible and see if his suspicions that his local preacher wasn't actually following it were true!

Not only does he continue to attend classes in the Eldoret area, but he's also been made prefect and his teacher is said to rave about his influence over the students. Mr Maruge is also a quick pupil and has scored some of the top marks in his class. Perhaps he's being tutored by his two grandchildren, who attend the same school.

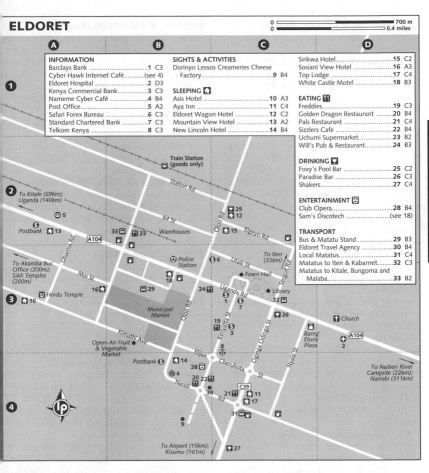

ELDORET

0 — 700 m
0 — 0.4 miles

INFORMATION
Barclays Bank 1 C3
Cyber Hawk Internet Café..........(see 4)
Eldoret Hospital 2 D3
Kenya Commercial Bank................3 C3
Nameme Cyber Café 4 B4
Post Office....................................5 A2
Safari Forex Bureau 6 C3
Standard Chartered Bank 7 C3
Telkom Kenya 8 C3

SIGHTS & ACTIVITIES
Dorinyo Lessos Creameries Cheese
Factory......................................9 B4

SLEEPING
Asis Hotel 10 A3
Aya Inn 11 C4
Eldoret Wagon Hotel 12 C2
Mountain View Hotel 13 A2
New Lincoln Hotel 14 B4

Sirikwa Hotel..............................15 C2
Sosiani View Hotel 16 A3
Top Lodge 17 C4
White Castle Motel 18 B3

EATING
Freddies.....................................19 C3
Golden Dragon Restaurant 20 B4
Pals Restaurant 21 C4
Sizzlers Cafe 22 B4
Uchumi Supermarket..................23 B2
Will's Pub & Restaurant..............24 B3

DRINKING
Foxy's Pool Bar 25 C2
Paradise Bar 26 C3
Shakers......................................27 C4

ENTERTAINMENT
Club Opera.................................28 B4
Sam's Discotech ....(see 18)

TRANSPORT
Bus & Matatu Stand....................29 B3
Eldoret Travel Agency 30 B4
Local Matatus.............................31 C4
Matatus to Iten & Kabarnet........32 C3
Matatus to Kitale, Bungoma and
Malaba....................................33 B2

WESTERN KENYA

New Lincoln Hotel (☎ 0723-676699; Oloo Rd; s/d KSh600/800) The most comfortable of the budget options, this pleasant place has decent rooms spread around its courtyard. The bathrooms and hot water plumbing are slightly disfigured but seem to do the job.

Aya Inn (Oginga Odinga St; s/tw incl breakfast KSh500/1000) With clean rooms, large (somewhat saggy) beds, hot water showers and a courtyard for vehicles, this place is a reasonable option. There are some cheaper singles (KSh400) with shared bathrooms.

Sosiani View Hotel (☎ 0723-112157; off Moi St; s/tw with shared bathroom KSh360/500) At the western end of the main matatu stand, this slightly grotty hotel has bare-bones rooms with some very firm mattresses.

Top Lodge (Oginga Odinga St; s/tw with shared bathroom KSh200/300) If money is tight, some of the rooms facing the street are bright and tolerable. The shared bathrooms are grim.

Naiberi River Campsite (☎ 2063047; campsite@africaonline.co.ke; camping KSh250, dm KSh500, cabins KSh1200;) This place, 22km southeast of town on the C54 to Kaptagat, is your best option for camping, as it has tonnes of facilities. It is, however, very popular with overland companies. Contact the campsite for directions.

MIDRANGE & TOP END

Eldoret Wagon Hotel (☎ 2062270; Oloo Rd; s/d incl breakfast KSh1550/2250) This option has a certain amount of colonial charm. It is overpriced, but retains some suitably eccentric memorabilia, and there is a casino to make you feel like a high roller.

White Castle Motel (☎ 2033095; Uganda Rd; s/d KSh850/1550) Lonely beds sit strangely away from all the walls in these sizeable austere rooms. Some rooms have decent views and all have aged but clean bathrooms. The expensive special singles are not worth the money.

Asis Hotel (☎ 2061807; Kimathi Ave; s/tw incl breakfast KSh750/1250) Alone on the west side of town, this conference-class place is very clean and comfortable. From some rooms farsighted guests will enjoy countryside views, while nearsighted guests will glare at the litter outside.

Sirikwa Hotel (☎ 2063614; hotelsirikwa@multitech web.com; Elgeyo Rd; s/tw incl breakfast KSh4000/5000, ste from KSh8500; ☒) This is Eldoret's only top-end hotel and it boasts a long list of facilities, including a lovely swimming pool and beautiful terrace. The rooms are comfortable but a bit dated, though renovations are planned for 2006. Hopefully they won't touch the suites, which feature velvet and scream 70s chic.

Eating

Sirikwa Hotel (Elgeyo Rd; meals KSh250-400) Slide onto their grand terrace and sink your teeth into some sumptuous selections. Local well-to-do's rave about the marinated lamb and chicken curry.

Will's Pub & Restaurant (Uganda Rd; meals KSh200-450) The burgers and shoestring fries here will leave you smiling. Thanks to the fried fish and lamb stew also being justifiably popular, tables come at a premium.

Golden Dragon Restaurant (Kenyatta St; meals KSh300-400; ☑ Wed-Mon) A tad pricey, but Chinese food will give your taste buds something new to sing about.

Freddies (Kenyatta St; meals KSh60-270) A fast food feel with Western snacks. Not a bad spot for breakfast.

Sizzlers Cafe (Kenyatta St; meals KSh100-235) Grab a curry and get stuffed for minimal coinage at this undeniable favourite.

Pals Restaurant (Oginga Odinga St; meals KSh50-100) Serving up stews and other Kenyan fare. It is oddly popular with Eldoret's elderly – perhaps the food is the secret of longevity?

Uchumi supermarket (off Uganda Rd) Well stocked and perfect for self-caterers.

Drinking & Entertainment

Shakers (Oginga Odinga Rd) An atmospheric, albeit isolated (take a taxi) place just waiting for introductions: arse meet wicker. Eyes meet European footy. Beer meet lips.

Will's Pub (Uganda St) A tame but lively place for a cold drink or three. It is a friendly spot for female travellers.

Foxy's Pool Bar (Oloo Rd) A quiet place to shoot some stick and savour a beer.

Paradise Bar (Oginga Odinga Rd) A rough and tumble place. Is it a good or bad sign that the bar is behind bars?

Sam's Discotech (Uganda Rd; ☑ weekends) Eldoret's energetic dance club.

Club Opera (Kenyatta St) Day-Glo paint, black lights and occasional live bands grace this raucous nightclub.

Getting There & Away

AIR

There are daily flights between Eldoret and Nairobi (KSh5700, one hour) with the little-known Aero Kenya. Bookings are handled by **Eldoret Travel Agency** (☎ 2062707; Kenyatta St).

BUS & MATATU

The main bus and matatu stand is in the centre of town, by the market.

Regular matatus/Peugeots serve Kitale (KSh150/200, 1¼ hours), Kisumu (KSh250/300, 2½ hours), Kericho (KSh250/300, 3½ hours), Nakuru (KSh200/400, 2¾ hours) and Nairobi (KSh400/700, six hours). Buses duplicate these routes.

Local matatus and more Kericho services leave from Nandi Rd. Irregular matatus to Iten and Kabarnet leave opposite Paradise Bar on Uganda Rd. Further west on Uganda Rd, matatus leave for Malaba (KSh300, 2½ hours) on the Ugandan border.

Akamba (Moi St) buses to Nairobi (KSh500, 10.30am and 9pm) via Nakuru (KSh250) leave from their depot. There is also a noon (KSh1000) and midnight (KSh1150) service to Kampala (six hours).

Getting Around

A matatu to or from the airport costs KSh50, and a taxi will cost around KSh1000. *Boda-bodas* (bicycle taxis) are rare here, though some linger near the bus stand.

Parking is tricky in town, and most streets have a KSh30 charge, collected by yellow-jacketed wardens.

WEST TO UGANDA
Malaba
☎ 055

This dusty town sits on the main border crossing to Uganda and you may get stuck here for one reason or another. The **Kenya Commercial Bank** (☎ 54204; A104 Hwy) can exchange small amounts of currency – you'll have to call ahead for larger sums. The **post office** (A104 Hwy) has the only Internet access.

Emael Tourist Hotel (☎ 54022; off A104 Hwy; s/d ncl breakfast KSh750/950) has the town's nicest rooms – the toilets even have seats. It is just north, off the A104 past Jaki Guest House. The restaurant (meals KSh150 to KSh300) is an equally good option.

A cheaper option is **Jaki Guest House** (☎ 54484; A104 Hwy; s KSh300-500, tw KSh500-1000), which has basic rooms with mozzie nets in their old wing and more comfortable, though tacky (a Martha Stewart paint 'effect' gone horribly wrong), options in the new wing. The restaurant (meals KSh150 to KSh300) out the back is suitably simple.

GETTING THERE & AWAY
Akamba (A104 Hwy) has daily buses to Nairobi (KSh550, eight hours, 11am and 8pm) and Kampala (KSh450, 4½ hours, 2.30pm). Sporadic matatus serve Eldoret (KSh300, 2½ hours) and Kitale (KSh300, 2½ hours).

Busia
☎ 055

This tiny town links Kisumu with Uganda and was primarily used by transport trucks, though matatus and Nairobi–Kampala buses now use this route too. There is a Kenya Commercial Bank, but they seem rather unhelpful – you will usually find locals on the buses offering decent rates to exchange Kenyan and Ugandan currency.

The **Lian Guest House** (off Moi Ave; s KSh250) is a basic but clean place to sleep. To get here, follow the signs for the Blue York Hotel.

Further up the road is the **Blue York Hotel** (☎ 22081; off Moi Ave; s/tw incl breakfast KSh700/1100), which boasts comfortable, spotless rooms.

The best place to eat is **Royal Cafe** (B1 Hwy; meals KSh80-150), which is just northeast of the bus stand.

GETTING THERE & AWAY
Akamba (B1 Hwy) has daily bus services to Nairobi (KSh600, eight hours, 8am and 10pm),

Kisumu (KSh200, three hours, noon) and Kampala (KSh500, four hours, 5am, 7am and 3pm).

KABARNET
☎ 053

With a spectacular location on the eastern edge of the Kerio Valley, Kabarnet is one of many little towns nestled in the Tugen Hills. The road here is excellent, and the journey from Marigat is absolutely stunning, with views right across the arid but tree-covered ridges and the region's valleys. Kabarnet is also the best launching point for treks into the Kerio Valley.

Information
Kenya Commercial Bank (town centre) Exchange cash and travellers cheques (KSh50 per leaf). With ATM (Visa only).
Post office (town centre) With Internet and card phones.
Standard Chartered Bank (town centre) With ATM (Visa only).

Sleeping & Eating
Sinkoro Hotel (☎ 22245; town centre; s/tw KSh400/612) The spacious rooms are airy, and the even-numbered rooms upstairs have views. It also has a nice restaurant (meals KSh90 to KSh160) and bar.

Sportsline Hotel (☎ 21430; town centre; s KSh300) This is a bargain for basic and bright singles. The restaurant (meals KSh50 to KSh185), which serves the usual Kenyan suspects, and its terrace are local favourites.

Kabarnet Hotel (☎ 22094; town centre; s/d incl breakfast KSh1500/2000; 🏊) Just outside town, this is a solid midrange option. Comfortable rooms, with sloped wooden ceilings and slightly dog-eared bathrooms, look onto gorgeous gardens.

The supermarket behind Postbank is well-stocked.

Getting There & Away
Matatus/Peugeots serve Eldoret (KSh200/250, two hours), Nakuru (KSh200/250, 2½ hours) and Marigat (KSh140, 1¼ hours).

LAKE KAMNAROK & KERIO VALLEY NATIONAL RESERVES
These two little-visited national reserves lie in the heart of the beautiful Kerio Valley, sandwiched between the **Cherangani Hills** and the **Tugen Hills**, and are divided by the Kerio

River. Prolific birdlife, crocodiles, wonderful landscapes and the chance to get totally off the beaten track are the main attractions.

Lake Kamnarok, on the river's eastern side, is the most accessible of the two reserves, although there are absolutely no facilities. Bush camping is possible by the lake and no park fees are currently charged by the KWS. At present you can walk anywhere on foot, but it is best to ask rangers and locals if there have been any recent wild dog attacks in the area.

It is possible to cross into Kerio Valley National Reserve from Kamnarok during dry season, but you will have to wade across the river north of the lake. To the south of the reserve is the beautiful **Cheploch Gorge**.

The rest of the Kerio Valley begs to be explored and there is still talk of two other national reserves being created: one around Kapkut (2799m), a beautiful mountain close to Eldama Ravine, and another in the Tugen Hills.

To reach Lake Kamnarok, go 25km north up the rough dirt track from the village of Cheploch, which sits just east of the Kerio River on the Kabarnet–Iten road. A 4WD is required in dry season – don't even think about it during the rains.

KITALE

☎ 054

Kitale is considerably smaller than its nearest neighbour Eldoret and has more of an agricultural feel, although there are more street kids than in most normal service towns. Although it has an interesting museum, Kitale's main function for travellers is as a base for explorations further afield – Mt Elgon and Saiwa Swamp National Parks – and as a take-off point for a trip up to the western side of Lake Turkana. As such, Kitale is a pleasant enough town and can be an enjoyable place to pass through.

Information

Barclays Bank (Bank St) Exchange cash and travellers cheques (KSh34 per leaf commission). With ATM.
Mt Elgon Northwest Ecotourism (Menowecto; ☎ 30996; Kitale Museum, A1 Hwy) Nonprofit organisation providing tourist information. Paying the museum fee isn't necessary to reach the office.
MultiTech (Askari Rd; per hr KSh60) The town's most reliable Internet connections.
Post office (Post Office Rd) With Internet.

Standard Chartered Bank (Bank St) With ATM (Visa only).
Telkom Kenya (Post Office Rd) Calling cards and card phones.
Western Union (Askari Rd) Money transfer services.

Sights & Activities
KITALE MUSEUM
The **museum** (☎ 30996; A1 Hwy; adult/child KSh200/20; ☽ 8am-6pm) was founded on the collection of butterflies, birds and ethnographic memorabilia left to the nation in 1967 by the late Lieutenant Colonel Stoneham. The more recent ethnographic displays of the Pokot, Akamba, Marakwet and Turkana peoples are a bit more interesting than the rows of dead things (although the stuffed cheetah is comical). The outdoor exhibits include some traditional tribal homesteads as well as the inevitable snakes, crocodiles and tortoises, plus an interesting 'Hutchinson Biogas Unit'.

The best thing here is the small **nature trail** that leads through some virgin rainforest at the back of the museum and links with the arboretum of the Olaf Palme Agroforestry Centre. The forest is teeming with birdlife, insects and the odd colobus monkey.

The craft shop here is worth a look, stocking some nice stuff at good, nominally fixed prices.

OLAF PALME AGROFORESTRY CENTRE
Next to the museum along the highway is the **Olaf Palme Agroforestry Centre** (A1 Hwy; admission free; ☽ 8am-5pm). This is a Swedish-funded program aimed at educating local people about protection and rehabilitation of the environment by integrating trees into farming systems. The project includes a small demonstration farm and agroforestry plot, an information centre and an arboretum containing 46 rare species of indigenous trees; it's well worth a visit.

Sleeping
Kitale lacks any top-end options and decent budget options are few and far between.

BUDGET
Bongo Lodge (☎ 30972; Moi Ave; s/tw KSh500/600) Good-value rooms offering hot showers surround a bright courtyard. Similar to the pricier Alakara, but a little more aged.

Executive Lodge (☎ 0720-536359; Kenyatta St; s/tw with shared bathroom KSh300/700, tw KSh800) The cheap small singles are a slight step up from those at Mamboleo, but a distant drop from all others we've mentioned. The twins aren't worth the money.

Hotel Mamboleo (☎ 30850; Moi Ave; s/tw with shared bathroom KSh200/300) This is the least revolting of Kitale's true cheapies. The rooms upstairs are a little brighter than the cell-like options below.

MIDRANGE
Alakara Hotel (☎ 31554; Kenyatta St; s with shared bathroom KSh500, s/tw/d KSh700/1000/1500) This is the best value in town. The comfortable rooms have phones, the staff are friendly and prices include breakfast. It has a good bar, restaurant, TV room and parking facilities.

Sunrise Motel (☎ 31841; Kenyatta St; s KSh700-850, tw KSh900-1000) Rooms have a little more flair than Alakara's, with hardwood floors, rugs and splashes of colour. The slightly more expensive options are size large and include bright balconies.

Vision Gate Hotel (☎ 0734-894177; Askari Rd; s/d incl breakfast from KSh1000/1250) While these spotless rooms are smaller and less decorated than those at Sunrise, they have slightly more comfortable beds. They also offer discounted rates for children.

Kitale Club (☎ 31330; A1 Hwy; s KSh1200-2700, tw KSh2000-3700; 🏊) The 'standard' rooms are rather bland and overpriced, while the 'executive' options are brighter and more comfortable. The large cottages are perfect for families and offer a TV lounge, fireplace and baby cot. You will need to pay (KSh500 per person) for temporary membership, which also gives you access to the pool, sauna, tennis and squash courts, and darts and snooker rooms.

Pinewood (☎ 30011; A1 Hwy; r KSh800-1500) At the time of research this place, between town and the Kitale Club, had started building accommodation out the back. If it's half as nice as the restaurant, it'll be a great option.

Eating & Drinking
Despite its few options Kitale packs a tasty culinary punch – whammo!

Lantern Restaurant (Kenyatta St; meals KSh190-300; ⏱ 6pm-midnight) With starters like tasty French onion soup and meals ranging from English fish and chips to Indian specialties, this is *the* place to eat. Aubergine masala is one of several delicious vegetarian selections. The

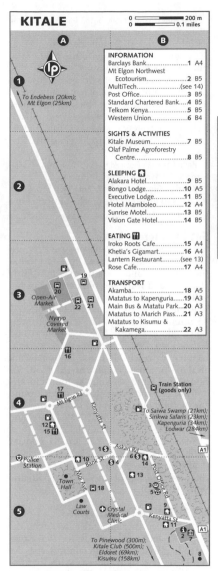

INFORMATION
Barclays Bank...................1 A4
Mt Elgon Northwest
   Ecotourism...................2 B5
MultiTech......................(see 14)
Post Office........................3 B5
Standard Chartered Bank....4 B5
Telkom Kenya...................5 B5
Western Union.................6 B4

SIGHTS & ACTIVITIES
Kitale Museum..................7 B5
Olaf Palme Agroforestry
   Centre..........................8 B5

SLEEPING
Alakara Hotel....................9 B5
Bongo Lodge...................10 A5
Executive Lodge...............11 B5
Hotel Mamboleo................12 A4
Sunrise Motel..................13 B5
Vision Gate Hotel..............14 B5

EATING
Iroko Roots Cafe...............15 A4
Khetia's Gigamart..............16 A4
Lantern Restaurant.........(see 13)
Rose Cafe.......................17 A4

TRANSPORT
Akamba..........................18 A5
Matatus to Kapenguria......19 A3
Main Bus & Matatu Park....20 A3
Matatus to Marich Pass......21 A3
Matatus to Kisumu &
   Kakamega...................22 A3

cocktail bar only adds to the fantastic atmosphere. It's found upstairs in the Sunrise Motel.

Iroko Roots Cafe (Moi Ave; meals KSh50-110) Feeling more like a coffee shop in the Rocky Mountains, this spotless, unique place serves up the best Kenyan dishes in town and is perfect for breakfast.

Pinewood (A1 Hwy; meals KSh180-480) A great new place for Indian or Chinese fare (complete with fresh ginger). Sit outside with views of Mt Elgon or head inside to the plethora of pine. The pub here is also great.

Alakara Hotel (Kenyatta St; meals KSh140-200) Lacks Lantern's vibe, but it has quality meals and is the best place for chicken and chips.

Kitale Club (A1 Hwy; set meals KSh390-600) What it lacks in cheapness it makes up for in taste. It is also a lovely place to have a drink (the Sports Bar is excellent).

Rose Cafe (Mt Elgon Rd; meals KSh50-130; ☽ 24hr) Simple Kenyan eats at all hours.

Khetia's Gigamart (☽ 7.30am-7pm) Stock up for trips to Elgon or the north at this massive supermarket.

Getting There & Away

Matatus, buses and Peugeots are grouped by destination, and spread in and around the main bus and matatu park. It is fairly chaotic, but if you state your destination you will be pointed in the right direction.

Regular matatus run to Endebess (KSh70, 45 minutes), Kapenguria (KSh80, 45 minutes), Eldoret (KSh 150, 1¼ hours) and Kakamega (KSh180, two hours). Less regular services reach Mt Elgon National Park (KSh80, one hour), Nakuru (KSh350, 3½ hours) and Kisumu (KSh300, four hours).

Most bus companies have offices around the bus station and serve Eldoret (KSh150, one hour), Nakuru (KSh350, 3½ hours) and Nairobi (KSh500, six hours).

Several buses now run up to Lodwar (KSh700, 8½ hours) each day.

Akamba (Moi Ave) run buses from outside their office to Nairobi at 9am (KSh550) and 9pm (KSh600).

MT ELGON NATIONAL PARK

With its deep volcanic crater straddling the Kenya/Uganda border and its forested flanks extending well into both countries, massive Mt Elgon is a sight indeed. With the dramatic 7km-wide caldera dotted with several peaks – including the basalt column of Koitoboss (4187m), Kenya's second highest, and Wagagai (4321m) in Uganda – this extinct volcano offers some of the best treks in Kenya. The national park boundaries extend from the lower slopes right up to the border.

Despite its lower altitude making conditions less extreme than Mt Kenya, Elgon sees a fraction of its bigger cousin's visitors, partly due to its greater distance from Nairobi, its wetter weather and the fact that most visitors are more interested in claiming they've climbed Kenya's tallest mountain. While this is sad, it means those unconcerned about bragging will have far fewer people to share the mountain with.

The extinct shield volcano's distinct shape landed it a Maasai name literally meaning 'mountain shaped like human breast'! Thankfully for your lungs and legs, Mt Elgon is more of a pre- than post-silicone Pam Anderson shape.

While rarely seen, the mountain's most famous attractions are the elephants known for their predilection for digging salt out of the lower eastern slopes' caves. The elephants are such keen excavators that some people have been fooled into believing they are totally responsible for the caves. Sadly, the number of these saline-loving creatures has declined over the years, mainly due to incursions by Ugandan poachers.

Four main lava tubes (caves) are open to visitors: **Kitum**, **Chepnyalil**, **Mackingeny** and **Rongai**. Kitum holds your best hope for glimpsing elephants (especially before dawn), while Mackingeny, with a waterfall cascading across the entrance, is the most spectacular. A good flashlight is essential and you should be wary of rock falls – the bones of a crushed elephant stand as evidence of this.

The mountain's fauna and flora are also great attractions. With rainforest at the base, the vegetation changes as you ascend, to bamboo jungle and finally alpine moorland featuring the giant groundsel and giant lobelia plants. Common animals include buffaloes, bushbucks, olive baboons, giant forest hogs and duikers, while Defassa waterbucks are also present. The lower forests are the habitat of the black and white colobus, and the blue and De Brazza's monkeys (most likely seen near waterways).

There are more than 240 species of birds here, including red-fronted parrots, Ross's turacos and casqued hornbills. On the peaks you may even see a lammergeyer raptor gliding through the thin air. The Elephant Platform and Endebess Bluff viewpoints are good places to survey the scene on the way up.

The streams that run off the mountain are filled with trout; fishing permits are available from the park headquarters for KSh100.

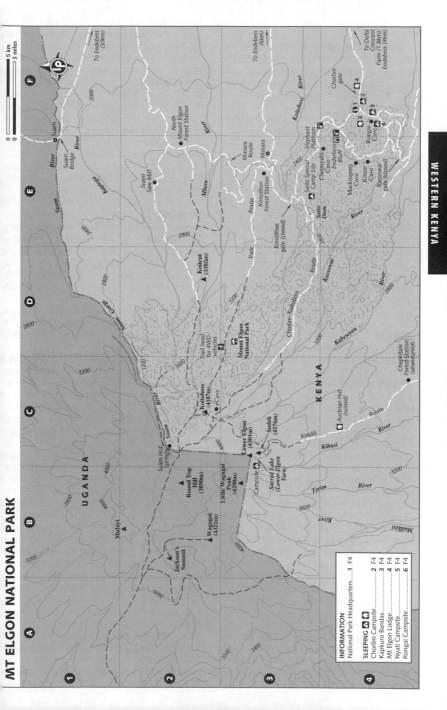

MT ELGON NATIONAL PARK

WESTERN KENYA

INFORMATION
National Park Headquarters....**1** F4

SLEEPING
Chorlim Campsite..................**2** F4
Kapkuro Bandas.....................**3** F4
Mt Elgon Lodge.....................**4** F4
Nyati Campsite.......................**5** F4
Rongai Campsite....................**6** F4

Information

The **park** (adult/child US$15/5) is wet much of the year, but driest between December and February. As well as bringing waterproof gear, you will need warm clothes, as it gets cold up here at night. Altitude may also be a problem for some people.

Access to the 169-sq-km national park is now permitted without a vehicle. Even if you have a 4WD, walking is the best way to get around as the roads are treacherous.

Due to the odd elephant, a **ranger** (per half/full day KSh500/1000) must escort you on walks on the lower slopes, such as to the caves.

For trekking the higher slopes you will need a tent and all your own camping gear. A **guide** (per day KSh1000) is also essential (see p265 for general advice).

Lonely Planet's *Trekking in East Africa* has more juicy details on the various trekking and walking routes, and Andy Wielochowski's *Mt Elgon Map & Guide* is an essential purchase, available in Nairobi for around US$5. *Kitum Cave Guide Book* is also a good buy.

Trekking

Trekkers are encouraged to stay within the park boundaries, as security has previously been a problem. Check out the situation with **KWS headquarters** (☎ 020-600800; kws@kws .org; PO Box 40241, Nairobi) in Nairobi or **Mt Elgon National Park** (☎ 054-31456; PO Box 753, Kitale) before you plan anything. Crossing into Uganda isn't currently permitted, but ask for the latest at the gate.

Allow at least four days for any round trip and two or three days for any direct ascent of **Koitoboss** if you're walking from the Chorlim gate. Arrange guide requirements at the park headquarters in advance.

The **Park Route** offers some interesting possibilities and there is a well-worn route from Chorlim gate up to Koitoboss Peak that requires one or two overnight camps. If you have a vehicle, you can drive up to 3500m, but the current state of the road means the 32km drive can take half a day, and then it's a two- to three-hour walk up to the peak.

Descending, you have a number of options. You can descend northwest into the crater to **Suam Hot Springs**. Alternatively, if the security situation improves, you could go east around the crater rim and descend the **Masara Route**, which leads to the small village of Masara on the eastern slopes of the mountain (about 25km) and then returns to Endebess. Or you can head southwest around the rim of the crater (some very hard walking) to **Lower Elgon Tarn**, where you can camp before ascending **Lower Elgon Peak** (4301m).

To return, head back the way you came. The alternative is the **Kimilili Route**, via the ruined Austrian Hut and the abandoned Chepkitale Forest Station, down to the KWS post at Kaberua Forest Station. Then it's a 5km walk down to **Kapsakwany**, with matatus to Kimilili and basic accommodation. You must check the safety of the Kimilili Route with KWS before attempting it.

Sleeping

If you're trekking your only option is to **camp** (adult/child US$8/5). This fee is the same whether you drop your tent in the official campsites or on any old flat spot during your trek. For non-campers sticking to the lower slopes, there is one roofed option inside the park and two outside.

Chorlim Campsite (next to Chorlim gate) This new campsite has the park's best facilities but is less scenic than the other two public sites, Nyati and Rongai.

Kapkuro Bandas (US$30) These excellent stone bandas can sleep three people in two beds and have simple bathrooms and small kitchen areas. Hot water is provided by a wood stove, while solar panels provide electricity. Bring food, as there is only one small shop that sells beer and a few basics for the park staff and their families.

Delta Crescent Farm (☎ 0722-2489317; camping KSh200, tw with shared bathroom incl breakfast KSh2000) Conveniently located between Endebess and Chorlim gate, this farm has three huge areas for campers and three basic, clean thatched bandas. Four-person and 12-person rental tents are also available for KSh800 and KSh2000 respectively (plus camping fees). The communal bathrooms have gargantuan shower heads and decent toilets. The owners keep horses (riding per hour KSh600) and there is even a small 'wildlife sanctuary' (admission KSh100) with imported giraffes and zebras. Transfers to Chorlim gate and Kitale are available (KSh1500 per vehicle) as are 4WD tours of the park.

Mt Elgon Lodge (☎ 0722-866480, PO Box 7, Endebess s/tw incl breakfast KSh3500/5000) Despite being perched next to Chorlim gate and offering mountain views, huge fire places and some colonial charm, this tattered lodge is severely overpriced, although after a few days of trekking, a meal in their restaurant (meals KSh350 to KSh450) is a godsend.

Getting There & Away

Sporadic matatus and Peugeots now reach the Chorlim gate from Kitale (KSh80, one hour). More regular services reach Endebess (KSh70, 45 minutes), a 9km walk from the gate. If you want to break up the walk, make for Delta Crescent Farm, spend the night there, and then walk the remaining 5.5km to the gate the next morning (you'll need time to organise guides in any case). Locals will happily point you in the right direction.

If you're driving, the road up to the park is OK, but once inside a 4WD is essential; the dirt roads haven't been graded in years, so it's slow going even in good weather.

SAIWA SWAMP NATIONAL PARK

This small **park** (adult/child US$15/5) north of Kitale is a real delight. Originally set up to preserve the habitat of the *nzohe* or sitatunga antelope, the 3-sq-km reserve is also home to blue, vervet and De Brazza's monkeys and some 370 species of birds. The fluffy black and white colobus and the impressive crowned crane are both present, and you may see the Cape clawless and spot-throated otters.

The best part is that this tiny park is only accessible on foot. Walking trails skirt the swamp, duckboards go right across it, and there are some extremely rickety observation towers (number four is the best). For an eyeful, come first thing in the morning.

Thanks to a new and energetic warden Saiwa Swamp is seeing better days. A new perimeter fence is protecting the sought after trees, and rangers are working to protect wild sage (sitatunga's typical food) from the suffocating growth of tall grasses that have blossomed thanks to fertilizers from nearby fields. Education programs are also having success in encouraging local people to get involved in the protection of the park.

Sleeping

Public Campsite (adult/child US$8/5) There is a beautiful site by the river here. Facilities include flush toilets, showers and two covered cooking bandas with barbecues and picnic tables.

Sirikwa Safaris (☎ 0733-793524; camping KSh415, tents s/d KSh1240/1650, farmhouse with shared bathroom s/d KSh2750/3850) Owned and run by the family that started Saiwa, this is a treasure trove of information and activities, but an expensive place to stay. Camping costs are typical, but basic furnished tents and two cosy farmhouse rooms are pretty steep for what you get. You may also have to pay a 10% service charge. Sirikwa whip up tasty meals, but at a cost – a dinner main is KSh550! Excursions can be arranged from here, including ornithological tours of the Cherangani Hills and Saiwa Swamp (bird guides KSh825 per half day). See p71 for more details.

Getting There & Away

The park is 18km northeast of Kitale; take a matatu towards Kapenguria (KSh60, 30 minutes) and get out at the signposted turn-off, from which it is a 5km walk.

CHERANGANI HILLS

Northeast of Kitale and forming the western wall of the spectacular **Elgeyo Escarpment** are the Cherangani Hills. This high plateau has a distinctly pastoral feel, with thatched huts, patchwork *shambas* (plots of land) and wide rolling meadows cut by babbling brooks. You could easily spend weeks exploring here and never come across a single tourist.

You won't be alone though, as the plateau is home to the interesting Marakwet or Markweta people (part of the greater Kalenjin grouping), who migrated here from the north. They settled here because the area was secure and the consistent rainfall and streams were ideal for agriculture.

There are a couple of great five-day **treks**, namely from Kabichbich to Chesengoch and Kapcherop to Sigor. These two treks are detailed in Lonely Planet's *Trekking in East Africa*; information on some of the shorter hikes in the northern reaches of the Cherangani Hills is found on p339.

Sirikwa Safaris (left) and Marich Pass Field Studies Centre (p339) can both arrange rewarding day and multi-day treks in the region.

Getting There & Away

Kabichbich is best reached from Kapenguria by matatu (KSh100, 1¼ hours), and Kapcherop is accessible from Kitale with patience and a matatu change in Cherangani. You can walk to the northern part of the hills from Marich Pass Field Studies Centre (p339).

Northern Kenya

Northern Kenya is more an experience than a series of destinations. There's constantly something catching your eye, whether it's Gabbra tribespeople walking the shattered lava fields, extinct volcanos rising from desert seas, or the road tracking across the plains. All who visit this wild, diverse region leave cherishing something different, that they'll never forget.

That said, some things will be ingrained in every visitor's psyche. The complete and utter beauty of the 'Jade Sea' (Lake Turkana), whose baking, barren shores stretch over the horizon to a distant Ethiopia some 250km away, can't be overstated.

The many tribes of northern Kenya are some of the most fascinating people on earth – a glimpse into their world is priceless. Unique wildlife, like the reticulated giraffe and endangered Grevy's zebra, also call northern Kenya home, mixing with lions, elephants and oryxes in the varied landscapes of Samburu, Buffalo Springs and Shaba National Reserves.

For those with energy to burn, there's great hiking around Marich, Maralal, Marsabit and the Ndoto Mountains. If walking isn't your thing, it's also perfect for a camel safari.

Where there's reward, there's usually risk and northern Kenya is no exception (see opposite). Don't expect it to be easy – the roads will batter your arse and your 4WD. But you'll love every minute of it!

NORTHERN KENYA

HIGHLIGHTS

- Thanking the heavens for the sight of **Lake Turkana** (p336) and thanking your lucky stars your tyres survived to get you there
- Witnessing the temperature dropping and volcanic cinder cones climbing on **Mt Marsabit** (p327), a forested island in a desert sea
- Sharing a smile and some shade with Kenya's most captivating tribes in **South Horr** (p335), **Loyangalani** (p336) or **Lodwar** (p340)
- Experiencing the spectacular scenery and wildlife while staying at the **Lewa Wildlife Conservancy** (p321), and learning about their community and conservation programs
- Realising zebras do change their stripes in **Samburu National Reserve** (p324), home to the rare Grevy's species
- Searching for words atop Mt Poi in the remote **Ndoto Mountains** (p327)
- Drooling uncontrollably at **Lesiolo** (p335)

Geography

Northern Kenya's diverse landscapes are truly amazing. Deserts range from large tracts of scrub, dissected by *luggas* (dry river beds that burst into violent life after heavy rains) and peppered with acacia trees, to Chalbi's inhospitable black stones and Karoli's soft sands.

Massive yet gently sloping, the dormant shield volcanos of Mt Kulal and Mt Marsabit climb from barren plains to provide forested havens for humans and animals, while countless steep, Martian-like stratovolcanos burst from lava fields and Lake Turkana's waters. In other areas, such as South Horr, craggy peaks shelter clear streams that flow through valley oases of lush vegetation.

Lake Turkana is the north's most renowned geographic feature and covers an amazing 6405 sq km, making it earth's largest permanent desert lake.

Climate

The climate here reflects the landscape's incredible contrasts. Temperatures on the plains can reach 50°C, without a breath of wind, only for the desert's dead calm to be shattered by sudden violent thunderstorms that drench everything and disappear as quickly as they came. It's not uncommon to experience several weather systems during the day and still sleep under clear, star-studded skies.

The lone constant is the stifling heat and strong winds around Lake Turkana.

National Parks & Reserves

From the celebrated African animals of today, thriving along the Ewaso Ngiro River's lush banks in the Samburu, Shaba and Buffalo Springs National Reserves (p324), to the fossilised evidence of early humans and prehistoric animals sitting beneath the scorching soils of Sibiloi National Park (p338) on Lake Turkana's northern shore, northern Kenya's national parks and reserves cover a breadth of landscapes, wilderness and history unimaginable elsewhere.

Also intriguing is Marsabit National Park (p329), whose rich forest and shy Big

---

WARNING

Unfortunately, the strong warrior traditions of northern Kenya's nomadic peoples have led to security problems plaguing the region for years. Things were only exacerbated in the 1990s by a massive influx of cheap guns from many conflict zones just outside Kenya, which dramatically altered traditional balances of power. Minor conflicts stemming from grazing rights and cattle rustling, formerly settled by compensation rather than violence, quickly escalated into ongoing gun battles and authorities had trouble restoring order.

While travellers rarely witnessed intertribal conflict, the abundance of guns led to increases in banditry that posed a significant risk to anyone moving through the region. This led to convoys or armed escorts being required on most major roads. However, the recent government has clamped down on lawlessness, and security in the north has turned for the better. Convoys and armed guards are no longer used between Marich and Lodwar and between Isiolo and Moyale on the Ethiopian border. Although the notoriously dangerous conditions on the road between Lodwar and Lokichoggio, near the Sudanese border, have improved enough for local trucks and matatus to travel unguarded, the UN and non-governmental organisations (NGOs) still travel in large convoys.

Sadly, all isn't on the mend and sporadic bloody tribal conflicts still arise, like in July 2005 when 44 people (including 27 children) were killed in Marsabit district's remote Turbi region. The whole northeastern region around Garsen, Garissa, Wajir and Mandera is still *shifta* (bandit) country and you should avoid travelling here. Buses heading to Lamu and between Garissa and Thika have also been attacked. Intrepid travellers heading up the Suguta Valley should be aware that armed gangs roam these lands and have assaulted foreigners. Thanks to a 1999 conflict between the Ethiopian government and Oromo Liberation Front (fighting for independence in southern Ethiopia) spilling over into Kenya around Moyale, landmines have been reported – stick to well-marked paths outside of town.

Improvements or not, security in northern Kenya is a dynamic entity and travellers should seek local advice about the latest developments before travelling and never take unnecessary risks.

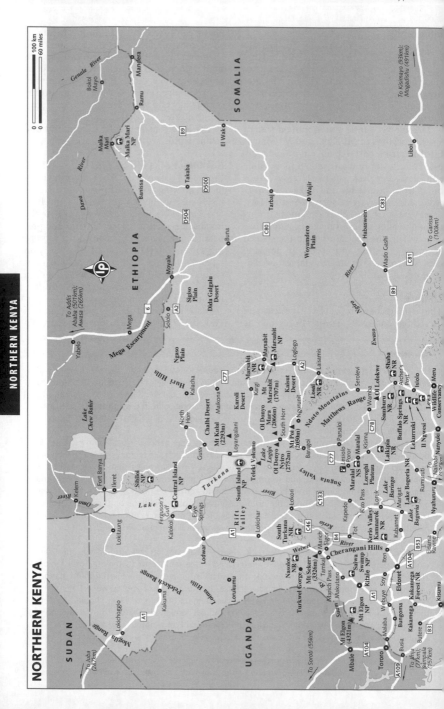

'ive population rest on the cool slopes of massive volcano rising gently out of the aking northern plains. Dramatic volcanic andscapes of an entirely different manifes-ation burst bleakly from Lake Turkana's vaters and form South Island (p336) and Central Island (p343) National Parks, which, ogether with Sibiloi, comprise a Unesco World Heritage Site.

Getting There & Away

AIR

Daily **Airkenya** (☎ 020-605745; www.airkenya.com) nd **Safarilink** (☎ 020-600777; www.safarilink.co.ke) ervices link Samburu National Reserve and Lewa Wildlife Conservancy with Nanyuki, Meru and Nairobi (Wilson Airport). See p326 and p322 for details.

BUS & MATATU

Countless bus and matatu services enter northern Kenya from the Central and West-rn Highlands. They are detailed on p261, p274, p277 and p312.

Getting Around

4WD

Having your own 4WD gives you flexibility, but comes with its own challenges thanks to wide-ranging road conditions. For starters you'll need a large 4WD (a Toyota RAV4 or Suzuki won't do) with high ground clear-nce and a skid plate to protect the under-arriage. You should have a high-rise jack, and ladders, a shovel, a long, strong rope or chain (to hitch up to camels or other vehicles) plus enough fuel, water and spare ires (one is rarely enough). A compass and ;ood map are also invaluable.

Road conditions between destinations are discussed in each town's Getting There & Away sections.

BUS & MATATU

There's now regular public transport as far north as Kalokol and Lokichoggio on Tur-kana's west side, but it's more limited up the lake's east side, only reaching Maralal via Nyahururu or Isiolo. With improved se-urity, buses now run from Isiolo to Moyale on the Ethiopian border via Marsabit.

HITCHING

Hopping onto the top of a dusty transport ruck with the locals has long been an un-comfortable, dirty and somehow mildly enchanting way to travel around northern Kenya. However, improved bus services mean that Loyangalani is the only major destination that still requires hitching.

To enjoy the experience you must throw out your schedule and accept that you'll spend days waiting for rides. It's no free ride either, with most drivers charging between KSh2 and KSh5 per kilometre. Security is another issue, as bandits are more inter-ested in cattle trucks than buses, and for this reason hitching can't be recommended unreservedly.

SAFARIS

A few organised safaris and overland trucks now go to Lake Turkana's west, but most still stick to the lake's east side. Average trips are seven- to 10-days long and they typically follow the same route. See p69 for a full rundown.

Other options include camel safaris, al-though treks down into the Suguta Valley should be approached with caution for se-curity reasons. See p67 for more camel safari information.

ISIOLO TO ETHIOPIA

Besides being a gateway to Ethiopia's riches, this route offers northern Kenya's best wild-life viewing, along with some incredible culture and landscapes. New hiking possibil-ities in the Ndoto Mountains and several pi-oneering community wildlife-conservation projects only add to the region's appeal.

ISIOLO

☎ 064

Isiolo is a vital pit stop on the long road north, as it's the last place with decent facili-ties until Maralal or Marsabit.

How you interpret this frontier town de-pends on which direction you arrive from. Arrive from the south and you'll get your first taste of the remote northeast of the country– and hopefully not a mouthful of dirt blown up by late-afternoon squalls. Be-sides the arid conditions, you'll undoubt-edly notice the large Somali population (descendants of WWI veterans who set-tled here) and the striking faces of Boran, Samburu and Turkana people walking the

NORTHERN KENYA

streets. Pull in from the north and you'll notice little other than the verdant Central Highlands and omnipresent Mt Kenya towering in the distance. Your mind will wander to thoughts of crisp air and cool nights – heaven ahead indeed!

Besides buying some supplies for the trip north, you should also have a quick gander at the fine, and surprisingly cheap (post-haggling), brass, copper and aluminium bracelets that Isiolo's ubiquitous street sellers hawk. KSh100 will land you three simple bracelets, while KSh200 will score a more elaborate example.

In respect of Isiolo's strong Muslim community, women should avoid wearing shorts or short skirts.

Information

Consolidated Bank of Kenya (A2 Hwy) No ATM. Changes cash and Amex travellers cheques (200KSh per leaf, plus 0.25% commission). Banks are scarce in the north, so plan ahead.

District Hospital (Hospital Rd; ⊗ 24hr) Isiolo's best medical facility.

Isiolo Telephone Exchange (Hospital Rd) Calling cards and card phones.

Post office (Hospital Rd) With Internet.

Sleeping

Isiolo has happy homes for budget and midrange travellers (and their vehicles), but desperately lacks top-end options.

Mocharo Lodge (☎ 52385; s/tw KSh350/450; P) Sizeable clean rooms proffer mosquito nets, comfortable beds and hot water (in the mornings only). Some toilets are seatless, so if you don't want to be a porcelain jockey check out a few rooms. There's also secure parking, a decent restaurant and a TV room.

Range Land Hotel (☎ 0721-434353; A2 Hwy; camping KSh200, tw cottage per person KSh1000) About 6km south of town, this is a nice option for campers and families. Shade is rare, but there's now grass to plant your tent on and one of the stone cottages, with a nice bathroom, chairs and TV, is set aside for your use. Meals can be prepared with advance notice and there's a wee kids' playground – note: use is 'at owner's risk'!

Jamhuri Guest House (s KSh250; s/tw with shared bathroom KSh120/200; P) Popular with budget travellers in the past, it's simple, clean enough and has secure parking.

Jabal-Nur Plaza Lodge (☎ 0724-916670; s KSh300 with shared bathroom KSh200) Their rooms are pleasant, but their bathrooms are weak – you'll either be straddling the toilet to shower in your room or plugging your nose in the shared toilets.

Transit Hotel (☎ 52083; s/tw KSh500/900) They've dropped their rates substantially, but their rooms are still just more expensive versions of Mocharo Lodge's. The exception is room 208 (single), which is blessed with a big bright window.

Bomen Hotel (☎ 52389; s/tw/ste KSh900/1500/2500; P) NGO's favourite home, the Bomen Hotel has the town's brightest (ask for one facing outward) and most comfortable rooms. Room prices are steep, especially since some toilets are seatless, but bonus options include TVs and shared terraces with views (single rooms 304–07). You'll be happy to know that your truck will sleep safely here too.

Eating & Drinking

You won't go hungry or have to walk far to fill your belly in Isiolo – most sleeping options serve up tasty, albeit uncreative eats.

Transit Hotel (☎ 52083; meals KSh120-250) A rare place serving more than the local usuals, with fried tilapia, pepper steak, vegetable cutlets and curries up for grabs.

Bomen Hotel (☎ 52389; meals KSh130-380) Think Transit Hotel with nicer seats and elevated prices.

Fremia Hotel (meals KSh50-100) Like most places, they'll have little left on the menu after 8pm. However, they'll actually run out and buy supplies to prepare your meal of choice – smile and be patient!

Silver Bells Hotel (meals KSh60-150) A good spot for grabbing yourself a cheap and greasy pre-departure breakfast.

Other popular local eating establishments include the following:

Roots Restaurant (meals KSh50-120)

Corner Restaurant (meals KSh50-120)

Northbound self-caterers should head to 101 Supermarket and the market near the mosque to purchase food and drink as there's very little available beyond here.

Thanks to a strong Muslim influence, drinking venues are rare – check out **Frontier Club** (A2 Hwy), which occasionally has live bands.

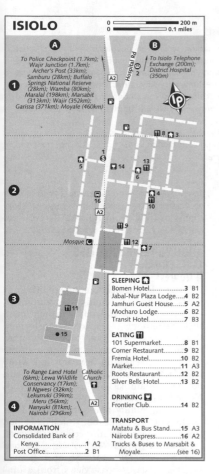

ISIOLO

0   200 m
0   0.1 miles

To Police Checkpoint (1.7km);
Wajir Junction (1.7km);
Archer's Post (33km);
Samburu (28km); Buffalo
Springs National Reserve
(28km); Wamba (80km);
Maralal (198km); Marsabit
(313km); Wajir (352km);
Garissa (371km); Moyale (460km);

To Isiolo Telephone
Exchange (200m);
District Hospital
(350m)

Hospital Rd

Mosque

To Range Land Hotel
(6km); Lewa Wildlife
Conservancy (17km);
Il Ngwesi (32km);
Lekurruki (39km);
Meru (56km);
Nanyuki (81km);
Nairobi (296km)

Catholic
Church

SLEEPING 🛏
Bomen Hotel..................3 B1
Jabal-Nur Plaza Lodge....4 B2
Jamhuri Guest House......5 A2
Mocharo Lodge.............6 B2
Transit Hotel..................7 B3

EATING 🍴
101 Supermarket.............8 B1
Corner Restaurant..........9 B2
Fremia Hotel..................10 B2
Market...........................11 A3
Roots Restaurant..........12 B2
Silver Bells Hotel...........13 B2

DRINKING 🍸
Frontier Club..................14 B2

TRANSPORT
Matatu & Bus Stand......15 A3
Nairobi Express.............16 A2
Trucks & Buses to Marsabit &
Moyale..................(see 16)

INFORMATION
Consolidated Bank of
Kenya...........................1 A2
Post Office....................2 B1

Getting There & Away
Although convoys are no longer being used north to Marsabit, check the security situation thoroughly with locals and the police checkpoint north of town before leaving. This is especially critical if heading towards Garissa, Wajir or Mandera, which are currently considered unsafe for travellers.

4WD
Isiolo marks the tarmac's northern terminus and the start of the corrugated dirt and gravel, which will shake the guts out of you and your vehicle. There are several petrol stations, so top up as prices climb and supplies diminish northward. If you're heading south, Central Highlands petrol is cheaper.

BUS & MATATU
The best option to Nairobi is **Nairobi Express** (A2 Hwy), operating daily buses (KSh500, 4½ hours) at 6.45am. The bus north to Marsabit (KSh600, 8½ hours) and Moyale (KSh1200, 17 hours) picks up passengers at Nairobi Express between 11pm and midnight.

For Maralal take an early-morning matatu to Wamba (KSh300, 2½ hours), and then the midday Maralal matatu (KSh300, 2½ hours). Regular matatus leave from a chaotic stand around the market and also serve Archer's Post (KSh80, 45 minutes), Meru (KSh120, 1½ hours), Nanyuki (KSh150, two hours) and Nairobi (KSh450, five hours). Peugeots (shared taxis) also service Meru (KSh150, 1¼ hours).

HITCHING
Trucks are filthy and uncomfortable but a viable option for the northbound adventurous. Although they pick up passengers at the police checkpoint north of town, better seats are available if you board when they stop near Nairobi Express. Drain your bladder, purchase enough food, water and sunscreen, and hop aboard.

LEWA WILDLIFE CONSERVANCY
While the massive 263-sq-km **Lewa Wildlife Conservancy** (LWC; ☎ 064-31405; www.lewa.org; admission incl in accommodation rates), just south of Isiolo, could boast about their luxury lodges, stunning scenery, astounding wildlife activities and having often hosted Prince William, they'd rather talk about their community and conservation projects. Founded in 1995, LWC now spends an amazing 30% of its budget on healthcare and education for surrounding villages, 40% towards community projects, with the remainder funding conservation and security. To help raise awareness and funds they host one of the world's most rewarding and exhausting marathons (see boxed text on p322).

The conservancy effort has been astounding and 20% of the world's Grevy's zebras, 8% of Kenya's black rhinos, a rare population of aquatic sitatunga antelopes and sizeable populations of white rhinos, elephants, buffaloes, leopards, lions and cheetahs now call this magical place home.

Wildlife drives in private vehicles aren't permitted and only guests of the LWC's lodges are allowed into the conservancy. A

NORTHERN KENYA

RUNNING FOR YOUR LIFE AND THEN SOME

It's one thing to run a marathon to the encouraging screams of people, it's entirely another to run it sharing the course with elephants, rhinos and the odd antelope! Established in 2000 to raise funds for wildlife conservation and community development, the Safaricom Marathon, run within the Lewa Wildlife Conservancy in late June/early July, attracts world-record holders and is renowned worldwide as one of the planet's toughest marathons. Thanks to experienced rangers, helicopters and spotter planes, your only worry should be the heat and the 1700m average elevation.

Will you be slowed by repeatedly gazing into the bewildered eyes of nearby giraffes or will your legs speed on at the thought of cheetahs and lions lurking in the grass? Why not try it and find out? Visit www.tusk.org for registration details.

plethora of activities, ranging from drives (day and night) and walks to horse riding and camel rides, are available at most lodges. Guests are encouraged to take part in conservation activities, like tracking and tagging animals.

Sleeping & Eating

Lewa House (☎ 064-31405; c.moller@lewa.org; exclusive use per night incl wildlife drives US$840;) Six sublime thatched-roof African chalets, comfortably sleeping 12 people, form Lewa House. Privacy is guaranteed since it's rented only to one group at a time. For full board, add US$120 per person per night.

Lewa Safari Camp (☎ 064-31405; www.lewasafaricamp.com; full board s/d incl wildlife drives US$285/570; closed Nov) Twelve luxurious octagonal tents hang beneath charming thatched roofs and offer up privacy and a slice of the African safari dream. The lounge, dining room, food and service are all top-notch.

Wilderness Trails (☎ 020-600457; www.bush-and-beyond.com; full board s/d incl activities US$430/860; closed Apr, May & Nov;) Although the thatched cottages and pool are as breathtaking as the views over the plains, none of Wilderness Trails' proceeds go towards LWC (unlike Lewa Safari Camp and Lewa House, which are non-profit and donate 100% of their proceeds), making it the least attractive accommodation option here.

There are some designated bush sites (no facilities) for **camping** (☎ 064-31405; info@lewa.org; US$90), but after compiling the costs of camping, food, a guide and wildlife drives, you're better off staying at Lewa Safari Camp.

Getting There & Away

LWC is only 12km south of Isiolo and is well signposted on A2 Hwy. **Airkenya** (☎ 020-605745; www.airkenya.com) and **Safarilink** (☎ 020-600777; www.safarilink.co.ke) have daily 'request stop' flights to LWC from Nairobi. Return fares on Airkenya/Safarilink are US$199/222.

AROUND LEWA WILDLIFE CONSERVANCY

Il Ngwesi

Il Ngwesi is a project linking wildlife conservation and community development. The Maasai of Il Ngwesi, with help from their neighbour LWC, have transformed this undeveloped land, previously used for subsidence pastoralism, into a prime wildlife conservation area hosting white and black rhinos, water bucks, giraffes and other plains animals. It's truly fitting that Il Ngwesi translates to 'people of wildlife'.

The community now supplements their herding income with tourist dollars gained from their award-winning ecolodge, **Il Ngwesi Group Ranch** (☎ 020-340331; info@letsgosafari.com; s/d incl all meals US$209/418;). Six open-fronted thatched cottages boast views from a dramatic escarpment that will have you smiling yourself to sleep and shaking your head when the sun rises (especially in cottages one and five, where the beds roll out beneath the stars). Natural materials are used throughout and you'll never be so in love with twisted, crooked wood – who likes straight lines anyway? The best part is that profits go straight to the Maasai community. Advance reservations are essential and getting here requires a serious 4WD.

Lekurruki

Home to descendants of the tiny Yaaku tribe, Lekurruki sits immediately north of Il Ngwesi. Although descendants of various Ethiopian, Somali and Rendille tribes, they've been swallowed by surrounding Maasai communities and have now named themselves Laikipiak Maasai. With most now speaking Maa (a Maasai dialect), funds are being sought to study the remaining 10 traditional Seiku speakers so that the endangered language might live to speak another day.

This community has followed in the footsteps of Il Ngwesi by embracing wildlife conservation and ecotourism. In 2002 they opened **Tassia Lodge** (☎ 020-340331; www.tassia kenya.com; exclusive use per night US$400; ⬤), which is perched on the Mukogodo escarpment, overlooking the plains to the sacred mountain Ol Lolokwe and Samburu National Reserve. The six open-fronted cottages are virtually identical to those at Il Ngwesi Group Ranch and the view from each bed, lounge and loo is equally mind-blowing. There's an amazing six-bed children's bunk-house that's part Antoni Gaudí and part childhood dream. The entire lodge is rented exclusively – not a bad deal for six couples and six kids. Wildlife drives and meals are not included, but they can be arranged. All funds benefit the Laikipiak Maasai community.

Although close to Isiolo, getting here is a difficult and requires a sturdy 4WD – get directions and a map when booking.

ARCHER'S POST

This dusty, ramshackle town sits 33km north of Isiolo and is perfect for budget travellers visiting Samburu, Buffalo Springs and Shaba National Reserves. At night there's definitely a Wild West feel about the place, with most vendors plying their goods by candlelight.

There's a small **market** (Map p325; off A2) but little else in the way of services.

Eight kilometres north of Archer's Post is the immense 384-sq-km **Kalama Community Wildlife Conservancy** (admission incl camping KSh1500), which opened in 2004 and hosts wildlife including Grevy's zebras, elephants and reticulated giraffes. The road network is still undeveloped, but guides (per day KSh500) lead walks and hikes up **Kalama Hill**. Camping in their three shady sites is free with admission. This community-run project supports hundreds of local families.

About 30km north of town and shrouded in Samburu folklore is the massive mesa of **Ol Lolokwe**. It's a great day hike and, at sunset, light radiating off its rusty bluffs is seen for miles around.

Don't want to camp with the lions and leopards in the national reserves? Want to save some moolah? Head to **Umoja Campsite** (Map p325; camping KSh200), which sits on the Ewaso Ngiro's banks between town and Archer's Post gate. It's run by women who've fled abusive husbands (see p324).

Those wanting a roof can crash at **Accacia Inns Lkimairr Lodge** (Map p325; ☎ 0721-659717; off A2 Hwy; s with shared bathroom KSh200). The mozzie net–clad rooms are simple and clean. Showers come in buckets and the toilets are

---

THE START OF A BEAUTIFUL FRIENDSHIP?

While other countries have been fighting a losing battle to preserve wildlife by separating animals and humans, local communities in parts of northern Kenya, like the Maasai of Il Ngwesi, Laikipiak Maasai of Lekurruki and the Samburu within the Matthews Range, are actually increasing animal populations (and their own standard of living) by embracing peaceful cohabitation.

These communities treat wildlife as a natural resource and take serious action to protect its wellbeing, whether by combating poaching with increased security or by modifying their herding activities to minimise human–animal conflict and environmental damage. With financial and logistical support from many sources, including LWC, **Laikipia Wildlife Forum** (LWF; www .laikipia.org) and the Northern Ranchlands Trust (NRT), these communities have built the magical ecolodges whose income now provides much-needed funds for their education, health and humanitarian projects.

The pioneering doesn't stop there. The LWF and NRT also coordinate wildlife conservancy on large private ranches and small farms (in northern Kenya and on the Laikipia Plateau), hoping to spark more sustainable development projects and further improve local standards of living. If these brave projects continue to prove that humans and wildlife can not only live in the same environment, but actually thrive from the mutual relationship, an amazing precedent will be set for the rest of sub-Saharan Africa.

GOODBYE MEN – HELLO HAPPINESS?

In 1990, 15 women who'd suffered too long from violent husbands abandoned their homes and started the village of Umoja (meaning 'unity' in Swahili), just outside Archer's Post. They hoped to survive together by producing and selling traditional Samburu jewellery to tourists. It all proved rather successful and Umoja thrived, even opening a campsite a few years later. Boosted by its success, 33 more women left unhappy situations and now call the women-only village home.

Local men were fairly tolerant initially, but apathy became jealousy and they even set up rival trinket stalls nearby. After their stalls' utter failure and the women's continued success, there have been reports of angry men warning tourist vehicles not to visit Umoja. Worse still are the recent raids of Umoja by men threatening these peaceful women with violence, something they had hoped to have left behind for good.

While these women still need your support, it would be wise to ask them about the security situation before dropping your tent.

crude, but they're clean enough. There's also a small thatched-roof cooking shelter for self-caterers. It's en route to Archer's Post gate and Umoja Campsite.

While **Uaso Cafe** (Map p325; A2 Hwy; meals KSh60-150) isn't the only restaurant in town, it's the only place to eat – enough said.

Getting There & Away

Matatus from Isiolo stop here en route to Wamba (KSh250, 1¾ hours) and those coming from Wamba also pick up for Isiolo (KSh80, 45 minutes).

SAMBURU, BUFFALO SPRINGS & SHABA NATIONAL RESERVES

These national reserves, comprising some 300 sq km, straddle the **Ewaso Ngiro River** and boast a breadth of wildlife, vegetation and landscapes. Shaba, with its great rocky *kopjes* (isolated hills), natural springs and doum palms, is the most physically beautiful, while open savannahs, scrub desert and verdant river foliage in Samburu and Buffalo Springs virtually guarantee close encounters with elephants, reticulated giraffes, Grevy's zebras, Somali ostriches, Beisa oryxes and the elegant giraffe-necked gerenuks. Chances of spotting a massive crocodile or leopard are substantially increased (albeit artificially) if you're staying at the posh lodges, as most unscrupulously leave bait out each evening.

After lodge hold-ups in Samburu several years ago, security has considerably improved. Ranger and Kenya Wildlife Service (KWS) lookouts are placed throughout the reserve. Poachers killed 25 elephants in early 2002, but things have been quiet since, and visitors are steadily returning.

Information

Conveniently, admission for Buffalo Springs, Shaba and Samburu (adult/child US$30/10) are interchangeable, so you only pay once, even if you're visiting all three in one day.

If you're driving, Survey of Kenya's map *Samburu & Buffalo Springs Game Reserves* (KSh85) is helpful, but hard to find. Getting around isn't difficult, but some minor roads are for 4WDs only. Signage has improved in Samburu but the maze of wayward minibus tracks can be confusing.

Petrol is available at Sarova Shaba Lodge and Samburu Game Lodge.

Sleeping & Eating

Each reserve is blessed with at least one luxury lodge and several campsites. For campers and day visitors, all the luxury lodges have buffet meals (around KSh1825).

BUFFALO SPRINGS NATIONAL RESERVE

Samburu Serena Lodge (☎ 064-30800, Nairobi 020-2710511; cro@serena.co.ke; full board low season s/d US$80/160, high season US$200/260; ☒) Though not as extravagant as Shaba Sarova Lodge, it's still lovely and offers plenty of activities, like slide shows, bird walks, hikes up L'Olgotoi Hill and camel rides. Comfy cottages, with breezy verandas, reed-lined ceilings and canopy beds, line the riverbank.

Buffalo Springs Lodge (Box 71, Isiolo; s/tw KSh1000/2000) The state of the pool speaks volumes – it's half-empty. On the positive side, the wood, reed-lined cottages are rather charming and the best value around. On the negative side, there's no food, the thatched cement cottages are dreary and have lumpy beds, and…let's not forget the pool!

SAMBURU & BUFFALO SPRINGS NATIONAL RESERVES

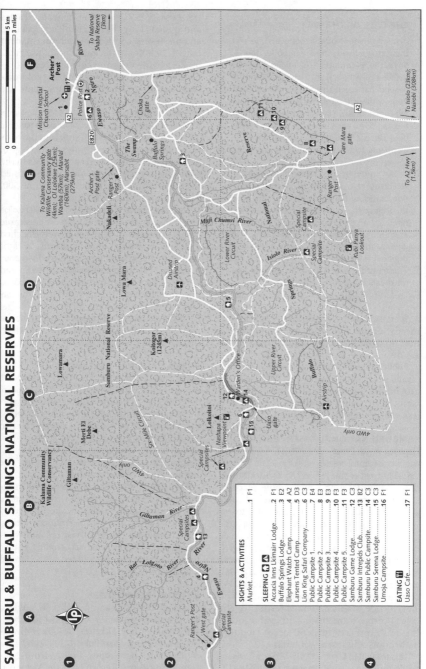

SIGHTS & ACTIVITIES
Market......................................1	F1

SLEEPING
Accacia Inns Lkimairr Lodge......2	F1
Buffalo Springs Lodge...............3	E2
Elephant Watch Camp...............4	A2
Larsens Tented Camp................5	D3
Lion King Safari Company..........6	C3
Public Campsite 1.....................7	E4
Public Campsite 2.....................8	E3
Public Campsite 3.....................9	E3
Public Campsite 4.....................10	F3
Public Campsite 5.....................11	F3
Samburu Game Lodge...............12	C3
Samburu Intrepids Club.............13	B2
Samburu Public Campsite...........14	C3
Samburu Serena Lodge..............15	C3
Umoja Campsite.......................16	F1

EATING
Uaso Cafe................................17	F1

NORTHERN KENYA

THE CALL OF THE WILD

Just when you thought that everyone and their dog already had a mobile phone, **Save the Elephants** (☎ 020-891673; www .savetheelephants.com) in Samburu National Reserve has given them to elephants! Each hour, without the mighty pachyderms having to bat an ear, SIM-card collars send text messages to each scientist's phone with their current location. This allows Save the Elephants to track elephants in real time, something never possible before.

By studying elephants' movements, scientists can discover important migration corridors between reserves and work to protect them. If these routes became denuded and migration ceased, the sheer magnitude of elephants' appetites would destroy their immediate environment and threaten their survival.

Interested visitors are welcome, but you must call in advance.

Special campsites (camping KSh825) While scenically located by freshwater springs along the Isiolo and Maji ya Chumvi Rivers, there are no facilities.

Public campsites (camping KSh440) The five public sites close to Gare Mara gate are overgrown, hard to find and have absolutely no facilities or water. For toilets, showers and less solitude, camp in Samburu.

SAMBURU NATIONAL RESERVE

Elephant Watch Camp (☎ 020-891112; www.elephant watchsafaris.com; full board incl guided walks s/d Apr & Nov US$320/640, rest of year US$360/720) Undoubtedly the most unique and memorable place to stay in the reserves. Massive thatched roofs cling to crooked acacia branches and tower over cosy, palatial, eight-sided tents and large grass mat–clad terraces. Natural materials pervade and the bathrooms are stunning.

Samburu Game Lodge (☎ 020-559529; wilderness@ mitsuminet.com; full board s/tw low season US$130/165, high season US$200/250; ☒) Several thatched log cottages and one large apartment-like block sit riverside in this perennial favourite. The bright cottages are much better value, offering more privacy, tasteful decor, modern bathrooms and larger verandas.

Larsens Tented Camp (☎ 020-559529; wilderness@ mitsuminet.com; full board low season s/tw US$169/226,

high season US$251/320) Sitting beneath acacias and spread along the riverbank are spacious and oh so very comfortable semipermanent tents. Each boasts scenic verandas, rugs, modern bathrooms and king-size beds, complete with headboards resembling colonial-style leather chests. Two of the tents are wheelchair accessible.

Samburu Intrepids Club (☎ 064-30453, Nairobi 020-446651; www.heritage-eastafricas.com; full board s/d US$300/450; ☒) Grab a G&T, sink into the bar's teak lounges and gaze over the Ewaso Ngiro. While thatched roofs and canopy beds in the luxurious tents scream Africa, the refined furniture unfortunately shrieks Fortune 500. Their friendly service is unmatched.

Lion King Safari Company (lionking@africaonline .co.ke; exclusive use per night US$300) This simple tented camp sleeps eight, has a lovely thatched chill area boasting comfy cushions, is right on the river and can be rented exclusively.

Samburu Public Campsite (camping KSh440) Spread along the Ewaso Ngiro River's northern bank, this site is blessed with new bathroom blocks and some secluded spots for tents.

Special campsites (camping KSh825) Special they're not – bush sites with no facilities or water, they're further west and tricky to find.

SHABA NATIONAL RESERVE

Shaba Sarova Lodge (☎ 020-713333; reservations@ sarova.co.ke; full board s/d Mar-Jun US$87/135, Jul-Feb US$130/185; ☒) This spectacular, almost-over-the-top (yet strangely underpriced) place nestles on the Ewaso Ngiro River. Next to the magnificent pool, natural springs flow through the gorgeous open-air bar and beneath the lofty 200-seat restaurant. The rooms? They're pretty lavish too!

Special campsites (camping KSh825) Of the several special sites (no facilities) here, Funan, set in Shaba's core, takes the cake. Shaded by acacias, it's next to a semipermanent spring, which provides water for visitors and wildlife alike. A ranger must accompany you to these sites; the cost is included in the fee but a tip is appropriate.

Getting There & Away

The vehicle-less can probably wrangle a 4WD and driver in Archer's Post for about KSh6000 per day. **Airkenya** (☎ 020-605745; www .airkenya.com) and **Safarilink** (☎ 020-600777; www .safarilink.co.ke) have daily flights from Nairobi to Samburu. Return fares on Airkenya/

Safarilink are US$199/222. Early-morning Safarilink flights are about US$15 less.

MATTHEWS RANGE

West of the remarkable flat-topped mountain Ol Lolokwe and north of Wamba is the Matthews Range. Its thick evergreen forests support elephants, lions, buffaloes and Kenya's most important wild dog population. These dramatic mountains (highest peak 2285m) offer great opportunities to explore the depths of Kenya's wilds. With few roads, only those willing to go the extra mile on foot will be rewarded with the spoils.

In 1995 the local Samburu communities collectively formed the **Namunyak Wildlife Conservation Trust**, now one of Kenya's most successful community conservation programs. The trust is unique because it's run by a democratically elected board, each community having one trustee. Now endorsed by KWS, it oversees 750 sq km and has substantially increased animal populations by successfully combating poaching.

To capitalise on their wildlife resources and fund community projects, the trust built **Sarara Tented Camp** (☎ 020-600457; info@bush-and -beyond.com; full board s/d incl conservancy fee US$490/780; ☺ closed May & Nov; ☒). With its grand open-fronted thatched lounge, enveloping comfort, private verandas, sublime surrounds and natural rock pool, guests benefit as much as the cause.

For budgeteers, the basic **El-Moran** (s KSh250, with shared bathroom KSh150) in Wamba is the only option besides bush camping. If it's full you could try the local mission (which incidentally has northern Kenya's best hospital, a fact worth remembering while in the bush).

Getting There & Away

While matatus from Isiolo (p321) and Maralal (p334) do reach Wamba, there's no point in coming without a vehicle. Getting to Sarara Camp isn't easy, even with a 4WD – it's probably best to arrange a transfer or get detailed directions when booking.

NDOTO MOUNTAINS

Climbing from the Korante Plain's sands are the magnificent rusty bluffs and ridges of the Ndoto Mountains. Kept a virtual secret from the travelling world by their remote location, the Ndotos abound with hiking, climbing and bouldering potential. **Mt Poi**

(2050m), which resembles the world's largest bread loaf from some angles, is a technical climber's dream, its sheer 800m north face begging to be bagged. If you're fit and have a whole day to spare, it's a great hike to the summit and the views are extraordinary.

The tiny village of **Ngurunit** is the best base for your adventures and is interesting in its own right, with captivating, traditionally dressed Samburu people living in simple, yet elegantly woven grass huts.

Salato Women's Group Campsite (☎ 0721-565383; lemunyete@wananchi.com; PO Box 352, Maralal; camping KSh100, s/tw KSh150/300) is about 3km west of Ngurunit and has decent facilities, fresh water and a small cooking area. There are also six cement Samburu-style bandas, complete with kerosene lamps and mosquito nets. Local guides (per day KSh500) can be arranged for hiking and camel treks (per 3km KSh200) are also on offer.

Getting There & Away

Ngurunit is best accessed from Loglogo, 47km south of Marsabit and 233km north of Archer's Post. From Loglogo it's a tricky 79km (1¾-hour) drive, with many forks, through the Kaisut Desert. Contact Salato for directions or offer a lift to someone in Loglogo looking for a ride to Ngurunit – they are cheap (free!) and helpful guides.

To access Ngurunit from Baragoi, head about 40km north towards South Horr and, after descending the first steep paved section and crossing the following *lugga* (dry river bed), look out for Lmerim Nursery School. Found it? The Ngurunit turn-off is 200m behind you!

MARSABIT

☎ 069

Approach Marsabit in fading light and you'll undoubtedly rub your weary eyes in disbelief. Scattered across the plains, surrounded by desert and strangely reminiscent of Egyptian pyramids (we did say weary eyes!), are fields of dramatic cinder cones (volcanic vents). Climbing towards town, the bleached yellows and browns turn to rich shades of green and the mercury takes a heavenly dip downward, adding pleasure to your continued feeling of astonishment.

The entire area surrounding Marsabit is actually a behemoth 6300-sq-km shield volcano, whose surface is peppered with no less

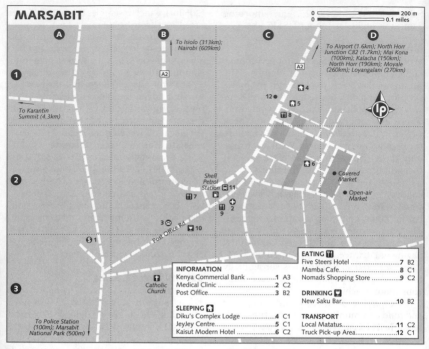

MARSABIT

INFORMATION
Kenya Commercial Bank 1 A3
Medical Clinic 2 C2
Post Office 3 B2

SLEEPING
Diku's Complex Lodge 4 C1
JeyJey Centre 5 C1
Kaisut Modern Hotel 6 C2

EATING
Five Steers Hotel 7 B2
Mamba Cafe 8 C1
Nomads Shopping Store 9 C2

DRINKING
New Saku Bar 10 B2

TRANSPORT
Local Matatus 11 C1
Truck Pick-up Area 12 C1

than 180 amazing cinder cones and 22 volcanic craters (*gofs* or *maars*), many housing lakes. Mt Marsabit's highest peak, **Karantin** (1707m), is a rewarding 5km hike from town through lush vegetation and moss-covered trees. The view from Karantin is astounding and if you play your cards right (and aren't scared of heights), 50 bob may have you wavering in the wind atop the communications tower.

While the town is less attractive than its lush surrounds, which comprise the enormous 1500-sq-km **Marsabit National Reserve**, it's fairly interesting due to an intriguing migrant population. The best place to take in the cornucopia of culture is the lively **market**. Unfortunately, the cultural mix has been volatile at times (see opposite).

Information

Kenya Commercial Bank (off Post Office Rd) No ATM. Changes cash and travellers cheques (KSh50 per leaf commission).

Medical clinic (Post Office Rd; 8am-7pm Mon-Sat, noon-7pm Sun) Clinic with laboratory services.

Post office (Post Office Rd) With Internet and card phones.

Sleeping

Since we were here last, several accommodation options have taken a turn for the worse – don't frown, this only makes your decision easier!

JeyJey Centre (2296; A2 Hwy; s KSh400, s/tw/tr with shared bathroom KSh250/400/600) Owned by government MP JJ Falana, this is the best lodge in town. Clean rooms with mozzie nets surround a colourful courtyard and bathrooms (even shared ones) sport on-demand hot water. There's also a TV room, a decent restaurant and an unattractive campsite (per person KSh150). Spot the guard 50 bob and your vehicle will sleep safely.

Diku's Complex Lodge (2465; A2 Hwy; s/tw with shared bathroom KSh300/600) North of JeyJey and tucked behind a wholesale store is this simple and slightly overpriced place. The spartan rooms (four walls and a bed) are spacious, but lack mosquito nets. The shared showers are clean, while the cement-block squat toilets could use a wee wash.

Kaisut Modern Hotel (s/tw with shared bathroom KSh150/200) Like the odd Smartie, this place is pretty purple on the outside and chocolate brown on the inside. However, that's where the Smartie similarity ends – once you've had your first taste of this place you won't be coming back for more. The rooms are passable, some being decidedly less dark than others, but the toilets are truly grim.

Eating & Drinking

While not offering much culinary diversity, Marsabit has a few places that should leave you full as an egg.

Five Steers Hotel (A2 Hwy; meals KSh70-130) Easily the best local eatery. The ½ Federation meal (a bulging pile of rice, spaghetti, beef, vegetables and chapati) is filling and surprisingly tasty.

JeyJey Centre (☎ 2296; A2 Hwy; meals KSh120-200) Inside the popular lodge, JeyJey serves local favourites as well as the odd curry. Elevated prices don't necessarily reflect a higher standard of food.

Mamba Cafe (A2 Hwy; meals KSh50-100) This small shack next to JeyJey Centre is perfect for breakfast and their chai is spot on.

If you're short of food or supplies check out the market and **Nomads Shopping Store** (Post Office Rd; ☺ Mon-Sat).

Thanks to a strong Muslim influence, beer can be hard to find. The best spot for a cold one is **New Saku Bar** (Post Office Rd), which has a lively interior and a relaxed outdoor section.

Getting There & Away

Although improved security meant convoys and armed guards weren't being used to Moyale or Isiolo during our research, it's still wise to get the latest security and Ethiopian border information from locals and the police station before leaving town.

4WD

The Moyale road is less corrugated than the one to Isiolo, but its sharp stones will devour your tyres and the deep ruts will scrub your undercarriage. The only fuel north is in Moyale, so stock up here. As a rule, if buses and trucks travel in a convoy or take armed soldiers on board, you should too! For advice on travel to Loyangalani, see p337.

BUS

With security on the mend, a bus now connects Marsabit to Moyale (KSh600, 8½ hours). There's no designated stop – simply

---

---

flag it down on the A2 Hwy as it comes through town around 5pm each day (en route from Nairobi!). The same service heads south to Isiolo (KSh600, 8½ hours) at 9am.

HITCHING

Trucks regularly ply the bus routes for about KSh100 less, but balancing your malnourished and bony arse on a metal bar above discontented cows for eight hours, while simultaneously battling the sun, wind and dust, is one tricky, tiring act. On the flip side, you'll have a lifetime of memories. There are also one or two trucks a week that leave Marsabit for Loyangalani (KSh700, seven hours) via Kargi. Most trucks pick up opposite JeyJey Centre.

MARSABIT NATIONAL PARK

This small **park** (adult/child US$15/5), nestled on Mt Marsabit's upper slopes, hosts thick forests and a variety of wildlife, including lions, leopards, elephants and rhinos. During our visit we were lucky enough to see a large cobra at close range, with its neck spread into the infamous 'hood'. We say lucky because we were in our truck at the time!

You won't see much big wildlife on a quick drive-through of the park, so stick around and camp at **Lake Paradise**. This small

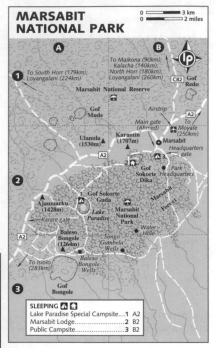

MARSABIT NATIONAL PARK

0 — 3 km
0 — 2 miles

To South Horr (179km);
Loyangalani (224km)

To Maikona (90km);
Kalacha (140km);
North Horr (180km);
Loyangalani (260km)

Marsabit National Reserve

Gof Redo

Gof Mude

Airstrip

Main gate (Ahmed)

Moyale (250km)

Ulanula (1530m)

Karantin (1707m)

Marsabit Headquarters gate

Gof Sokorte Dika

Park Headquarters

Ajaumarku (1428m)

Gof Sokorte Guda

Lake Paradise

Marsabit National Park

Karare gate

Marsabit Forest

Water Hole

Baleso Bongole (1264m)

Songa Gambela Wells

To Isiolo (283km)

Baleso Bongole Wells

Gof Bongole

SLEEPING
Lake Paradise Special Campsite....1 A2
Marsabit Lodge..........................2 B2
Public Campsite.........................3 B2

lake, which occupies the Gof Sokorte Guda's crater floor, is lovely, and the views from the escarpment above are stunning.

Sleeping & Eating

Marsabit Lodge (☎ 0735-555747; s/tw/tr incl breakfast KSh5500/5900/6950) The long shingle-roofed bungalows of the lodge arc around the lake occupying Gof Sokorte Dika, and offer up fine views. Even with the location, the simple and spartan rooms are overpriced. With its gargantuan fireplace and comfy chairs, the lounge is the lodge's most redeeming feature.

Lake Paradise Special Campsite (adult/child US$10/5, plus set-up fee KSh5000) Although there's nothing except lake water and firewood, this picturesque site is easily the best place to stay in the park. Thanks to roaming buffaloes and elephants, a ranger must be present when you camp here.

Public Campsite (adult/child US$8/5) This site, which is next to the main gate, has water and firewood, but the facilities, especially the showers, really are in severe need of an overhaul.

Getting There & Away

Despite it being a short walk to the park gate from town, you need your own 4WD to explore. In the wet season, you may find some park roads closed.

MOYALE

Let's be honest, nobody comes to Moyale to see Moyale; people come because it's the gateway to one of the world's most fascinating countries, Ethiopia. The drive from Marsabit is long and hard (on you and your 4WD), but it can be rewarding, with nomadic stone graves eerily rising out of the grassy plains, Dida Galgalu Desert's almost endless black shattered lava fields stretching out before you and the imposing Mega Escarpment seemingly climbing ever higher as you approach near Sololo. At times, as the journey rises in elevation, you'd be forgiven for thinking that an ocean, not a desert, sits in your path – it's simply that flat.

In stark contrast to the solitary journey here, Moyale's small, sandy streets burst with activity. The town's Ethiopian half is more developed, complete with sealed roads, and there's a palpable difference in its atmosphere.

Information

It's possible to enter Ethiopia for the day without a visa, but Ethiopian officials will hold your passport until you return. The border closes at 6pm – don't be late! For more information on crossing this border see p373. The Commercial Bank of Ethiopia, 2km from the border, changes travellers cheques (0.5% commission) as well as US dollars and euros. While it doesn't exchange Kenyan shillings, the Tourist Hotel will swap them for Ethiopian Birr (KSh8.4 to Birr1).

Holale Medical Clinic (A2 Hwy) Clinic with laboratory services.

Kenya Commercial Bank (A2 Hwy) No ATM. Changes cash and travellers cheques (KSh50 charge per leaf, plus KSh300 commission).

Post office (A2 Hwy) With Internet and card phones.

Sleeping & Eating

There are a few simple places to stay and eat on both sides of the border.

KENYA

Tawakal Hotel & Lodging (s/tw with shared bathroom KSh150/200) This place, with a lovely, relaxing

TV lounge, has comfortable beds in large, although slightly dark, rooms. Unfortunately the toilets are a cockroach committee room during the evenings, so go during daylight hours if you can! If that last bit didn't turn you off, the restaurant (meals KSh80 to KSh150) serves decent local meals.

Sherif Guest House (s/tw with shared bathroom KSh150/ 200) Sitting above the bank, this guest house has reasonably bright, clean rooms. Some rooms have mozzie nets, while others have mattresses too soft for their slat bases, so check out a few before choosing one. The communal toilet isn't pretty, but it's the best you'll find.

Medina Hotel (s/tw with shared bathroom KSh100/ 200) The cheapest rooms going, but they're dark and dirty.

Baghdad Hotel II (meals KSh80-150) This is the most popular local restaurant – sit down, swipe some flies and get stuffed.

Prison Canteen (meals KSh70-150) This kitsch place, complete with zebra motifs and thatched pavilions, is the canteen used by prison workers and it makes an atmospheric place for a meal (particularly *nyama choma* – barbecued meat, often goat) and a cold beer. You must be over 18 to enter the canteen.

ETHIOPIA

Since prices in the area are quoted in Ethiopian Birr, we've done the same here. For convenience the exchange rate is about KSh8.4 to Birr1.

Gihon Hotel (☎ 046-444 0065; d Birr20, with shared bathroom Birr15) This place is cheap, clean and has one of Moyale's best restaurants. The bathrooms (shared and private) or on the weak side but are passable.

Bekele Molla Hotel (☎ 046-4440030; camping Birr20, d Birr40) Located 2.3km from the border, this dog-eared hotel has large rooms with private bathrooms and mosquito nets. Sadly, there's no running water, so showers come in buckets.

Tourist Hotel (s with shared toilet Birr15) Sheltered behind its cool Rasta-inspired bar, this sleeping option has decent rooms that include private showers. The shared toilets are nothing to sing about, but thankfully they're nothing to scream about either.

Hagos Hotel (meals Birr8-12) Dig into some *injera* (Ethiopian bread-like staple) or some spice-laden roasted meat. There's a terrace

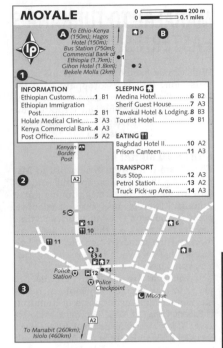

out back and some shady seating below a flowering tree. It's just up from the border and the Tourist Hotel.

Ethio-Kenya (breakfast Birr3-6) Across from the Hagos Hotel, Ethio-Kenya's leaf-laden terrace is a great place to eat breakfast and an animated location for having a few drinks later in the day.

Getting There & Away

A bus leaves town daily for Marsabit (KSh600, 8½ hours) and Isiolo (KSh1200, 17 hours) at 9.30am. Trucks servicing the same destinations pick up passengers near the main intersection in town. More details about hitching and driving between Moyale and Marsabit are found on p329. Drivers should note that petrol on the Ethiopian side of Moyale is half the cost of that in Kenya, handy to know if your budget is tight.

On the Ethiopian side, a bus leaves for Addis Ababa (Birr78.6) each morning at around 5.30am. The two-day journey is broken with a night's sleep at either Awasa or Shashemene.

NORTHERN KENYA

MARALAL TO TURKANA'S EASTERN SHORE

With vibrant Samburu and Turkana tribes, treks along lush cliffs dropping from the Loroghi Plateau, desert camel safaris, mesmerising barren volcanic landscapes and the north's jade jewel, Lake Turkana, this region of northern Kenya has it all.

NORTH TO MARALAL

The 130km drive from Nyahururu to Maralal along the C77 is bumpy but straightforward, despite the tarmac running out at Rumuruti (we do hope you said goodbye, because you won't see it again any time soon!). Punctures on this route are common and the scenery is ummm…well let's just say that once you've set eyes on the Jade Sea, you'll have forgotten all about it.

If you're not in a hurry, there are two places to make the journey more memorable. Eighteen kilometres north of Rumuruti is **Bobong Camp** (☎ 062-32718; olmaisor@africaonline .co.ke; PO Box 5, Rumuruti; camping KSh250, 4-person bandas KSh3000), which offers some of Kenya's cheapest self-catered **camel safaris** (per camel per day KSh1000) and **cultural visits** (per group KSh5000) to Turkana and Samburu communities. They have plans to open a **Cheetah Education Centre**, and if you're lucky you may spot Claudia, a cheetah that roams nearby. Thanks to its hilltop location, the camp offers grand views over the Laikipia plains to a distant Mt Kenya. Nyahururu–Maralal matatus (KSh60, 45 minutes) can drop you here, but may charge full fare (KSh300).

Forty-five kilometres further north is **Mugie Ranch** (☎ 062-31045; www.mugieranch.com; half-day adult/child US$15/7.50), a 200-sq-km working ranch that plays home to the Big Five, Grevy's zebras, endangered Jackson's hartebeest and Kenya's newest rhino sanctuary (21 black rhinos and two white). Part of the Laikipia Predator Project, they study the relationships between humans, livestock and predators to identify techniques for coexistence. Besides self-drive wildlife safaris, they offer exclusive top-end accommodation in the magnificent **Mutamaiyu House** (full board per person US$306; 🖳). Comfort is guaranteed and full board includes almost everything except champagne and clay-pigeon shooting!

MARALAL
☎ 065

Tin roofs poke from the forested Loroghi Hills overlooking Maralal's wide tree-lined boulevards below. Sounds pretty, but it's not. Where Maralal's charm lies is in its frontier rough 'n' ready atmosphere, with colourful Samburu people wandering the dusty streets and weathered characters sitting beneath shabby street-side verandas. It seems eerily reminiscent of the classic Wild West.

Maralal has gained an international reputation for its fantastically frenetic **International Camel Derby** (see boxed text p334) and a visit over its duration is truly unforgettable. Less crazy but almost as memorable are the year-round camel safaris and treks that are offered here.

Sadly, most visitors don't delve into Maralal, stopping only for a night en route to Lake Turkana. The opposite is true for independent travellers, who often end up spending more time here than planned, simply because transportation north is erratic at best. Let's face it though, there are worse places to get stuck.

People here are generally friendly, but you'll quickly encounter Maralal's professional tout posse. You'll be offered everything from bangles to guiding services, friendly 'advice' and Samburu weddings, and their persistence can be truly astounding – use your best judgment and keep your wits about you.

In the colonial era, white settlers coveted Maralal and the surrounding undulating grasslands and coniferous forests, but colonial authorities quashed their ambitions due to anticipated violent opposition from the Samburu, for whom the area holds special significance.

Information

Kenya Commercial Bank (behind market) No ATM. Changes cash and travellers cheques (KSh50 commission per leaf).

Maralal Medical Clinic (🕑 Mon-Sat) With laboratory services. If your truck is feeling better than you are, stop here.

Maralal Safari Lodge (☎ 62220) Change travellers cheques outside banking hours. Poor rates.

Post office (next to market) With Internet and card phones.

Yare Camel Club & Camp (☎ 62295) Can exchange travellers cheques, but has low rates.

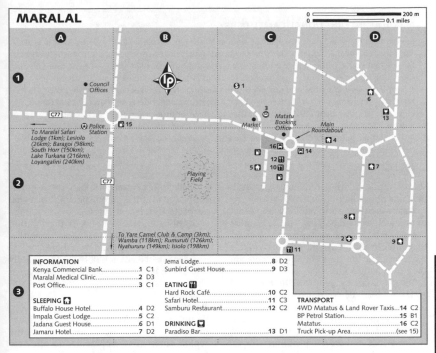

MARALAL

INFORMATION	
Kenya Commercial Bank	1 C1
Maralal Medical Clinic	2 D3
Post Office	3 C1

SLEEPING 🏠	
Buffalo House Hotel	4 D2
Impala Guest Lodge	5 C2
Jadana Guest House	6 D1
Jamaru Hotel	7 D2
Jema Lodge	8 D2
Sunbird Guest House	9 D3

EATING 🍴	
Hard Rock Café	10 C2
Safari Hotel	11 C3
Samburu Restaurant	12 C2

DRINKING 🍷	
Paradiso Bar	13 D1

TRANSPORT	
4WD Matatus & Land Rover Taxis	14 C2
BP Petrol Station	15 B1
Matatus	16 C2
Truck Pick-up Area	(see 15)

Sights & Activities

Trekking the Loroghi Hills Circuit, which takes in one of Kenya's most astounding vistas, Lesiolo (p335), is a rewarding five days and 78km. This trek is detailed in Lonely Planet's *Trekking in East Africa*.

Yare Camel Club & Camp (☎ 62295) organises guides and camels for independent camel safaris in the region. Self-catered day/overnight trips cost US$20/35 per person. Fully catered overnight trips are US$95.

Surrounding the town is the **Maralal National Sanctuary**, home to zebras, impalas, hyenas, elephants, elands, buffaloes and other varieties of plains wildlife, which you can see for free from the road leading into Maralal from the south. One of the best ways to take in the animals is with a cold beverage in hand at Maralal Safari Lodge's bar.

Sleeping

Advance booking is absolutely essential in Maralal during the derby.

Sunbird Guest House (☎ 62015; PO Box 74, Maralal; s/tw/d KSh350/450/600; 🅿) Easily the best budget option in town, this shiny and friendly new

place has quiet, clean and comfortable rooms with nice linen, mosquito nets, sparkling bathrooms, 24-hour hot water and sockets to charge your mobile phone. You won't even have to search your pack for toilet paper – it hangs on a dispenser in the loo – go figure! Oh, add secure parking to its lengthy list of attributes.

Yare Camel Club & Camp (☎ 62295; yare@africaonline.co.ke; camping KSh200, s/tw/tr US$20/28/35) This place is justifiably popular with campers and sits 3km south of town on the Isiolo–Nyahururu road. You can camp here or stay in cosy, expensive wooden bandas, which boast bathrooms, towels and free hot-water buckets for bathing. The campsite has its own cold showers and toilets. Thoughtfully constructed, Yare's facilities include a well-stocked bar and lounge, a restaurant, *nyama choma* on Wednesdays and Saturdays and a games room.

Jamaru Hotel (☎ 62093; s/tw/tr KSh300/600/1000, s/tw with shared bathroom KSh200/350) Behind its fancy façade lurk simple rooms with interesting but functional plumbing, as well as some cheaper options with less-pleasant

NORTHERN KENYA

MARALAL INTERNATIONAL CAMEL DERBY

Inaugurated by Yare Safaris in 1990, the annual Maralal International Camel Derby held in early August is one of the biggest events in Kenya, attracting riders and spectators from the world's four distant corners. The races are open to anyone and the extended after-parties at Yare Camel Club & Camp are notorious – you're likely to bump into some genuine characters here.

Not interested in parties and just want some fast-moving camel action? Then the derby's first race has your name written all over it – it's for amateur camel riders. Ante up KSh1500 for your entry and another KSh2500 for your slobbering steed and get racing! It's a butt-jarring 11km journey. Don't even start feeling sorry for your arse – the professional riders cover 42km.

For further information contact **Yare Safaris** (☎ 065-62295; yare@africaonline.co.ke; PO Box 63006, Nairobi) or Yare Camel Club & Camp in Maralal.

---

shared facilities. All rooms have mosquito nets and sporadic hot water.

Jadana Guest House (s/tw KSh250/400; P) A rare option with secured parking, Jadana is unfortunately a bit run-down, with shabby sheets that you can almost see through. The rooms are a bit dark but do have mozzie nets and their own bathrooms.

Maralal Safari Lodge (☎ 62220, Nairobi 020-211124; full board s/d Oct-Jun US$120/185, Jul-Sep & Christmas US$150/225; 🏊) This has large wooden chalets with vaulted ceilings, private balconies and a loft for children to snooze. It's very cosy, but we'd expect more for the price. The best feature of the lodge is the wildlife water hole at the bar, which nearly justifies paying KSh125 for a beer. The gate is 1km west of the BP station along the road to Baragoi.

Other sleeping options:

Jema Lodge (☎ 0723-868721; s KSh300)

Buffalo House Hotel (s/tw with shared bathroom KSh150/300)

Impala Guest Lodge (☎ 62292; s/tw with shared bathroom KSh150/300)

Eating

Unless you've got the *ugali* (maize meal set hard and served in brick-shaped pieces) or *nyama choma* itch, few of your tastebuds will be scratched here. That said, a few places hammer out quality local eats.

Hard Rock Café (meals KSh60-170) While the Hard Rock Café chain would cringe at their name's use, this Somali-run restaurant is the town's best restaurant. Enjoy their chapo-fry (spiced beef with chapati and side plate of diced tomatoes, onions and beans) while listening to Rick Astley and being peered over by mugs of Michael Jackson, the Spice Girls and 2Pac.

Samburu Restaurant (meals KSh80-200) A popular place, with the menu sporting the usual suspects and decent curries.

Safari Hotel (meals Ksh80-150) If the lighting and wallpaper don't ruin your appetite, you'll get a good Kenyan meal here.

Jadana Guest House (meals KSh80-170) Reputedly one of the best places in Maralal for *nyama choma*.

Drinking

Some years ago, the District Commissioner ordered Maralal's discos closed due to the region's insecurity. Apparently no-one here has thought to fight for their right to party, as this order is still in place.

Buffalo House Hotel, with a pool table, is probably the most popular boozer in town. Another place to shoot some stick and down a Tusker is Paradiso Bar. The bars at Yare Camel Club & Camp and Maralal Safari Lodge are nicer, but if you're staying in town transport back may pose a problem.

Getting There & Away

Matatus serve Nyahururu (KSh300, three hours), Rumuruti (KSh250, 2½ hours) and Wamba (KSh350, 3½ hours) on a daily basis, usually in the mornings and early afternoons. Reaching Isiolo involves overnighting in Wamba to catch the early-morning southbound matatu. There are no direct services to Nairobi – take a matatu or bus (KSh300, three hours) to Nyahururu and transfer there.

During the dry season a few 4WD matatus and Land Rover taxis head north each week to Baragoi (KSh300, three hours). If you're intending to head to Lake Turkana, you'll have to wait a few days to a week for a truck (KSh800 to KSh1000, nine to 12 hours). To shorten your wait, inquire around the town's petrol stations and its transportation hub (the main roundabout) when you arrive instead of waiting until you want to leave. While breaking the truck journey in Baragoi or South Horr may seem like a good idea, remember that you may have to wait there for week before another truck trundles through.

Most transport leaves from the main roundabout, while trucks usually pick up passengers at the BP station.

The **BP petrol station** (C77 Hwy) is the town's most reliable. Petrol is KSh10 more per litre here than in Nyahururu, but cheaper than you'll find it north.

AROUND MARALAL

There are views and then there are views. **Lesiolo** (or 'World's View'), which perches atop an escarpment marking the Loroghi Plateau's dramatic end, offers an outrageous 120km panoramic view over the Rift Valley and serrated Tiati Hills. Lesiolo is part of the Malasso Eco-tourism Project and a viewing fee (adult/child US$5/3) is now charged – pricey, but worth every penny.

The **Lesiolo Loop** (detailed in Lonely Planet's *Trekking in East Africa*) is a spectacular and gruelling 12km trek (eight to 10 hours) that takes you down the escarpment to the Rift Valley floor and then slowly brings you back up again. A local guide (Malasso Eco-tourism Project guides cost KSh1000 per day) is essential for this trek.

It's possible to **camp** (adult/child US$10/5) at Lesiolo and the viewing fee is waived if you do so. There's water (collected rain), crude toilets and a whole lot of cow patties to go with the astounding view.

Getting There & Away

To get here, head north from the town, towards Baragoi; the Malasso Eco-tourism Project sign marks the turn-off about 17km from Maralal. Several more signs and helpful locals will point you the rest of the way. Patience and erratic transport can get you to the village of Poror, an easy 9km (two to three hour) walk from Lesiolo. You'll need a 4WD if driving in the wet season.

BARAGOI

The long descent off the Loroghi Plateau towards Baragoi serves up some sweet vistas, but none can compare with the sheer magnitude of Lesiolo (left) – make sure you stop there en route. When you reach the bottom, the road ahead is laid out before you; it meanders across the acacia-dotted plains before disappearing into jagged hills that seemingly erupt from the horizon. Reaching Baragoi is a bit of an anticlimax as the dusty, diminutive town is clearly outdone by its surroundings.

Treks through the Suguta Valley to Lake Turkana are possible from Baragoi, and there are several English-speaking guides here to remind you! Make sure you get a good appraisal of the security situation before attempting this trek.

Be careful not to take photos in town as it's supposedly forbidden and police are keen to enforce the rule.

The **Mt Ngiro General Shop** (C77 Hwy) sells pricey petrol from the barrel and the **Morning Star Guest House** (C77 Hwy; s/tw with shared bathroom KSh200/400) provides a decent place for a night's kip. It's just south of the post office (no Internet) and offers secure parking, decent rooms and mozzie nets. Fine dining (spot blatant overstatement) is found at **Al-Mukaram Hotel** (C77 Hwy; meals KSh60).

Those with bulging pockets of Benjamin Franklins can stay at **Desert Rose** (☎ 0722-638774; www.desertrosekenya.com; full board incl activities low season US$400/600, high season US$450/700; ☀), a stunning ecolodge nestled on the southern slopes of Ol Donyo Nyiro. Each cottage is truly unique and blends into the natural surrounds. Whether sitting on the deck, bobbing in the pool or vegetating in your outdoor bathtub, the scenery will leave you gobsmacked. The Desert Rose turn-off is 18km north of Baragoi and is marked by a gas canister.

Getting There & Away

The dirt track from Maralal to Baragoi is much improved but still very rocky in places. The drive takes between 2½ and four hours. See opposite for details about riding trucks between Maralal, Baragoi and Loyangalani.

SOUTH HORR

South Horr is the next village north of Baragoi and sits in an acacia-paved valley beneath the towering peaks of **Ol Donyo Nyiro** (2752m) and **Ol Donyo Mara** (2066m). Despite the delightful craggy scenery high above, your eyes will rarely look up from the colourful and enchanting Samburu herders who gather in the wavering trees' shadows.

Easy hikes are possible on the valley's forested lower slopes, while more motivated souls can try to bag Ol Donyo Nyiro's peak.

Your only accommodation option here (besides staying with locals) is the **Forest Camping Site** (camping KSh150), signposted on the left just south of town. Eucalyptus and acacias provide the shade, a local stream provides the water and a tin shack provides the long-drop loo at this simple site. **Winana House** (meals KSh40-80) and **Green Olive Hotel** (meals KSh40-80) offer limited local meals.

The road between Baragoi and South Horr is in reasonable shape and consists of compacted sand and bumpy rocky sections (glistening metamorphic gneisses for you rock hounds).

NORTH TO LAKE TURKANA

Almost 23km north of South Horr, when the valley opens to the northern plains, you'll see massive Mt Kulal in the distance and Devil's Hand, a large rock outcrop resembling a fist attempting to punch its way out of the earth's surface, to your immediate right. Just north is the eastern turn-off to Marsabit via Kargi, so if you're heading for Turkana keep left. If you get mixed up, just remember that Mt Kulal on your right is good and that Mt Kulal on your left is very, very bad (unless of course you're heading to Marsabit).

Further north, the scrub desert suddenly scatters and you'll be greeted by vast volcanic armies of shimmering bowling ball–sized boulders, cinder cones and reddish-purple

---

DID YOU KNOW?

- Lake Turkana's shoreline is longer than Kenya's entire Indian Ocean coast.

- The lake's water level was over 100m higher some 10,000 years ago and used to feed the mighty Nile.

- The first Europeans to reach the lake were Austrian explorers Teleki and von Höhnel in 1888. They proudly named it Lake Rudolf, after the Austrian Crown Prince at the time. It wasn't until the 1970s that the Swahili name Turkana was adopted.

---

hues – if they could talk they'd welcome you to Mt Kulal's shattered lava fields. If this arresting and barren Martian landscape doesn't take your breath away, the first sight of the sparkling Jade Sea a few kilometres north certainly will.

As you descend to the lake, South Island stands proudly before you, while Teleki Volcano's geometrically perfect cone lurks on Turkana's southern shore. Since most of you are probably pulled over at the moment, looking for your swimming kit, we thought we'd warn you about Turkana's escalating crocodile population.

LOYANGALANI

An oasis of doum palms, natural springs and vivid Turkana tribespeople, Loyangalani is one of northern Kenya's most fascinating places. It overlooks Lake Turkana and is surrounded by small ridges of pillow lava (evidence that this area used to be underwater) peppered with Turkana families' traditional stick and palm dwellings.

The El-Molo tribe (see p44), which is one of Africa's smallest, lives on the lakeshore just north of here in the villages of **Layeni** and **Komote**. Although outwardly similar to the Turkana, the El-Molo are linguistically linked to the Somali and Rendille people. Unfortunately the last speaker of their traditional language died before the turn of the millennium.

As with the Maasai, tourism has wrought inevitable changes in the El-Molo and Turkana peoples' lifestyles, and many travellers feel that the tribal issue has been overly commercialised. You'll certainly pay handsomely for taking any photographs.

Information

Other than the post office (no Internet) and the Catholic mission occasionally selling petrol out of the barrel at exorbitant prices, there's little in the way of services.

Sights & Activities
SOUTH ISLAND NATIONAL PARK

Opened as a public reserve in 1983 and made a World Heritage Site by Unesco in 1997, this tiny 39-sq-km purplish volcanic island and **park** (adult/child US$15/5) is completely barren and uninhabited apart from large populations of crocodiles, poisonous snakes and feral goats. Spending the night at a **special**

campsite (adult/child US$8/5) makes for an even more eerie trip. All the sites lack water, firewood (there are no trees on the island) and toilets. The southern site is the most sheltered from the wind, so your tent is less likely to take flight here.

In calm weather a speedboat can reach the island in 30 minutes and circumnavigate it in another hour. If winds crop up, trip times can easily double. You can hire a boat from Oasis Lodge (per hour KSh2500) or from a local, but always check the vessel's seaworthiness and the impending weather.

MT KULAL

Mt Kulal dominates Lake Turkana's eastern horizon, and its forested volcanic flanks offer up some serious hiking possibilities. No matter what the local guides tell you, trekking up to the summit (2293m) from Loyangalani in a day isn't feasible. Plan on several days for a return trip, or part with substantial sums of cash (KSh8000 to KSh12,000) for a lift up Mt Kulal to the villages of Arapal or Gatab. From there you can head for the summit and spend a long day (eight to 10 hours) hiking back down to Loyangalani. The volcano's view over Lake Turkana and Chalbi Desert are sublime.

OTHER ACTIVITIES

Swimming is a perfect way to battle the heat and a dip in Oasis Lodge's two peaceful spring-fed pools will set you back KSh300. Swimming in the saline lake is free but you'll have to deal with crocodiles in the depths and with scorpions and vipers on shore – good luck! If you'd rather battle a large Nile perch, Oasis Lodge sells **fishing** licences for KSh400 and rents fishing boats for KSh2500 per hour.

Sleeping & Eating

Let's face it, you came north for adventure, not comfort. If you're camping remember to tie down your tent as early evening winds pick up tremendously and can be blowing at 60km/h by 8pm.

Palm Shade Camp (camping KSh350, s/tw rondavel with shared bathroom KSh500/1000) Drop your tent on some grass beneath acacias and doum palms or crash in their simple domed rondavels (round huts). The huts have simple wood beds with foam mattresses and unique walls with meshed cut-outs that let light and heavenly evening breezes in. Throw in the town's best toilets and showers, a cooking shelter and electricity until 10pm, and your decision is an easy one.

Oasis Lodge (☎ 020-503267; willtravel@swiftkenya .com; full board s/tw US$150/200; ⊠) This over-priced lodge offers simple cement-floor bungalows with dated bathrooms. The food, spring-fed swimming pools (KSh300 for nonguests) and view from the open air bar are its best assets.

Mosaretu Women's Group Campsite (camping KSh350, grass huts with shared bathroom s/tw KSh350/700) Next to Palm Shade and outside the gates of the Oasis Lodge, this place offers camping and crude beds in traditional Turkana grass huts. The toilets are a bit dire and even though there's no electricity, you still have to listen to Oasis Lodge's noisy generator.

New Saalama Hotel (meals KSh50-110) Although it lacks any signage (ask a local to point it out), this little shack with wood benches, crooked tables and candlelight is the best place for a local meal. They're usually out of food soon after sunset.

Cold Drink Hotel (meals KSh50-110) Run by a local Somali family, they serve up Kenyan dishes and a version of Ethiopian *injera* (a thin, cold, rubbery pancake). Their smoky chai is worth skipping.

If you ask around, you may find a villager who'll cook up a meal of Nile perch for you in their home.

Getting There & Away

There are one or two trucks a week that stop in Loyangalani en route to Maralal (KSh1000, 10 to 12 hours) from Marsabit. Trucks heading in any other direction are even more rare.

If you're travelling in your own vehicle, you have two options to reach Marsabit: continue northeast from Loyangalani across the dark stones of the Chalbi Desert towards North Horr, or head 67km south towards South Horr and take the eastern turn-off near Devil's Hand (see opposite). The 270km Chalbi route (seven to eight hours) is OK in the dry season but can be treacherous after rain. We met a UN convoy that spent three days stuck in mud out here, so make sure you're carrying adequate food and water with your spare tyres, compass and fuel when you set out. It's also wise to ask for directions every chance you get, otherwise it's possible to take the wrong track and not realise until hours later. The 241km southern route (six to seven hours) via Devil's Hand, the Karoli Desert and Kargi is composed of compacted sands and is less difficult in the rainy season.

For those with money to burn, Oasis Lodge arranges light-plane transport to the local airstrip and rents vehicles for KSh5000 per day plus KSh100 per km.

SIBILOI NATIONAL PARK

A Unesco World Heritage Site and probably Kenya's most remote **national park** (www.sibiloi .com; adult/child US$15/5), Sibiloi is located up the eastern shore of Lake Turkana and covers 1570 sq km. It was here that Dr Richard Leakey discovered the skull of a *Homo habilis* believed to be 2½ million years old, and where others have unearthed evidence of *Homo erectus*. Despite the area's fascinating prehistory, fossil sites and wonderful arid ecosystem, the difficulties involved in getting this far north tend to discourage visitors, which is a real shame. It seems slightly ironic that the so-called 'Cradle of Mankind' is now almost entirely unpopulated.

Today it's possible to see fossils of a giant tortoise that lived three million years ago, an ancient species of crocodile (*Euthecodon brumpti*) that grew up to 15m long, and a big-tusked behemoth (*Elephas recki*), a predecessor of today's elephant. The petrified forest south of these sites is evidence that the area was lush and forested seven million years ago. Every year rains and wind expose more fossils, so many that the most impressive are simply ringed with stones. Never remove any fossils from these sites as future research may be compromised.

The National Museums of Kenya (NMK) maintain a small museum and **Koobi Fora** (www.kfrp.com), a research base that is often home to permanent researchers, visiting scientists and students. It's usually possible to sleep in one of the base's **bandas** (per person KSh1000) or to pitch a tent in KWS' **campsites** (adult/child US$8/5).

It's best to come in July and August, when the ferocious temperatures break slightly and when activity increases at Koobi Fora. Contact both **KWS** (kws@kws.org; PO Box 219, Lodwar) and **NMK** (☎ 020-3742131; www.museums.or.ke; PO Box 40658, Nairobi) before venturing in this direction.

Getting There & Away
In the dry season it's a tricky seven-hour drive north from Loyangalani to Sibiloi. Make sure you get precise directions from locals in Loyangalani as well as from the KWS and NMK before heading north. In the wet season your only real option is to fly, which means dropping some dough and chartering a plane.

KALACHA
Huddled around a permanent watery oasis in the middle of the Chalbi Desert, the village of Kalacha is home to the fascinating Gabbra people and many a doum palm. Take shelter in the shade and watch the Gabbra at work or check out the biblical murals in the church, a prelude for those of you heading northward to Ethiopia. The changing colours in the desert at sunset are reason enough alone to stop here.

The Kalacha Women's Group are soon to open **Kalacha Oasis Lodge & Camping** (☎ 069-2296; PO Box 298, Marsabit), which will have basic accommodation and camping facilities. Funds raised flow back to the Gabbra community. You'll have to bring your own food, though.

Funded by the EU and Farm Africa, **Kalacha Camp** (☎ 062-32890; PO Box 161, Nanyuki; s/tw US$110/220, full board US$165/330) comprises four simple bandas made from doum palm trunks and leaves, each with their own toilet and cold-water showers. The camp is owned by the Gabbra community (managed by Tropic Air) and provides much-needed income for their continued survival.

Kalacha sits north of the road connecting North Horr and Maikona, which puts it 120km northeast of Loyangalani, 150km northwest of Marsabit and 65km from the Ethiopian border. **Tropic Air** (☎ 062-32890; www .tropicair-kenya.com) charter flights from Nanyuki are your only option in the wet season.

MARICH TO TURKANA'S WESTERN SHORE

Despite boasting some of northern Kenya's greatest attributes, like copious kilometres of Jade Sea shoreline, striking volcanic landscapes and vivid Turkana tribes, this remote corner of the country has seen relatively few visitors. With security on the mend there's now a unique opportunity for independent travellers to explore here, thanks to regular public transport currently covering the breadth of the region. The only downside for those of you in your own vehicle is the fact that you can't get your vehicle across the lake or into Sudan, which makes for a lot of backtracking.

MARICH TO LOKICHAR

The spectacular descent from Marich Pass through the lush, cultivated Cherangani Hills leads to arid surroundings, with saisol plants, cactus trees and acacias lining both the road and the chocolate-brown Morun River. Just north, the minuscule village of Marich, near the A1's junction with the B4 Kerio Valley road, marks your entrance into northern Kenya.

Sights & Activities

Although the northern plains may beckon, it's worth leashing the 4WD and heading into the hills for some eye-popping and leg-loving trekking action. **Mt Sekerr** (3326m) is a few kilometres northwest of Marich and can be climbed comfortably in a three-day round trip via the agricultural plots of the Pokot tribe, passing through forest and open moors. The views from the top are magnificent in clear weather.

The **Cherangani Hills**, which sit immediately south, are also ripe with trekking options. Reaching the dome of **Mt Koh** (3211m), which soars some 1524m above the adjacent plains, is a hard but rewarding one-day slog. A more horizontally endowed (13km one way) and vertically challenged (only 300m elevation gain) trek is possible up the **Weiwei Valley** from **Sigor** to **Tamkal**. See p315 for more Cherangani Hills trekking options.

The **Marich Pass Field Studies Centre** (right) offers English-speaking Pokot and Turkana guides are for half-day (KSh450), full-day (KSh550) and overnight (KSh1000) treks. The guides can also help you explore the numerous small **caves** dotted around the hills, most of which have special significance for the local Pokot.

If you'd rather explore with your vehicle, you can head southeast from Marich past Sigor and check out the **Elgeyo Escarpment**, which rises above the Kerio Valley to more than 1830m in places and offers spectacular views and waterfalls. At the foot of the escarpment (and accessible by matatu) is **Lomut** and its fascinating Saturday market, which brings together the pastoral Pokot from the northern plains and the farming Pokot from the southern hills. Much of the Pokot culture remains intact and tourists are usually blissfully ignored.

About 15km north of Marich along the A1 Hwy to Lokichar is the turn-off for **Nasolot National Reserve** (adult/child US$15/5) and **Turkwel Gorge** (admission incl with Nasolot NR). Although the reserve is home to elephants, lesser kudus, lions and leopards, you'll probably only spot the diminutive dik-diks bounding by the roadside. The main attraction is the gorge itself, with towering rock walls and plenty of pretty precipices. The imposing hydroelectric dam sits about 23km from the reserve gate, which is 6km off the A1. Those without vehicles are allowed to hike in the park with an escort (free with reserve admission). With security back under control, the KWS is hoping to soon reopen the campsites.

In the dry, rugged hills further north along the A1 is the **South Turkana National Reserve**. The reserve has yet to be developed and, like Nasolot, it's not possible to spend the night. The roads are in brutal shape (4WD only) and if you want to explore, you must take a ranger with you. Entry is free but you'll have to negotiate a fee for the ranger.

Just when you're getting to like the feel of the scrub desert en route to Lokichar, a sudden and all-too-brief burst of green and heavenly cool envelop the road and remind you of the lushness you've left behind.

Sleeping & Eating

The only reasonable accommodation between Marich and Lokichar is at **Marich Pass Field Studies Centre** (www.gg.rhul.ac.uk/MarichPass; PO Box 564, Kapenguria; camping KSh300, dm KSh350, s/tw/tr/q KSh1100/1500/2250/3000, with shared bathroom KSh700/950/1425/1900), which is well signposted just north of Marich and the A1's junction with the B4. Essentially a residential facility for visiting student groups, it's also a great place for independent travellers to base their adventures. The centre occupies a beautiful site alongside the Morun River and is surrounded by dense bush and woodland. The birdlife is prolific, monkeys and baboons have the run of the place, and warthogs, buffaloes, antelopes and elephants are occasional visitors. Facilities include a secure

NORTHERN KENYA

campsite with drinking water, toilets, showers and firewood, as well as dorm beds and simple, comfortable bandas. There's a **restaurant** (meals KSh220-350) with vegetarian options, but all meals should be ordered in advance. They also offer self-catering facilities, though there are few supplies in the area. Besides guides for trekking, they offer guided walks discussing ethnobotany (KSh500) and birds (KSh600) for groups of up to five.

Getting There & Away
The easiest way to reach Marich is from Kitale via Makutano and Marich Pass on the oh-so-scenic A1 Hwy, which is often described as 'Kenya's most scenic tarmac road'. The buses plying the A1 between Kitale and Lodwar can drop you anywhere along the route, whether at Marich, the field studies centre or at the turn-off to Nasolot National Reserve. You may be asked to pay the full fare to Lodwar (KSh700), but a smile and some patient negotiating should reduce the cost.

The other route is extremely rough (4WD only) and approaches Marich along the B4 from Lake Baringo through the Kito Pass and across the Kerio Valley to Tot; it's tough going, with little in the way of signs, but it does allow you to visit the hot waterfalls at Kapedo. From Tot, the track skirts the northern face of the Cherangani Hills and may be impassable after heavy rain.

Between Marich and Lokichar the A1 is a bumpy mess of corrugated dirt and lonely islands of tarmac. The first 40km north of Lokichar is better but you'll still spend more time on the shoulder than on the road. The opposite is true for the remaining 60km to Lodwar, where patches outnumber potholes and driving is straightforward.

If security takes a turn for the worse the police checkpoint just north of Marich may again start requiring vehicles to travel in convoy to Lodwar. Another thing to keep an eye for on this stretch are the flash floods that periodically fill the odd dry river bed with churning chocolate milk – be patient and remember that the water can drop as quickly as it rose.

LODWAR
☎ 054
Besides Lokichoggio near the Sudan border, Lodwar is the only town of any size in the northwest (although that's not saying much). Barren volcanic hills skirted by traditional Turkana dwellings sit north of town and make for impressive early morning sunrise spots. Lodwar has outgrown its days as just an isolated administrative outpost of the Northern Frontier District, and has now become the major service centre and tourist hub for the region. If you're visiting Lake Turkana, you'll find it convenient to stay here for at least one night.

Information
The Kenya Commercial Bank (it has no ATM) changes cash and charges 1% commission (minimum KSh250) for travellers cheques. The post office has Lodwar's only Internet connection.

Sights & Activities
There's little to do in the town itself, but the atmosphere is not altogether unpleasant if you can stand the heat, and just listening to the garrulous locals is entertainment in itself. The small market is a good place to watch women weaving baskets, and there's an endless stream of Turkana hawkers who wander around town selling the usual souvenirs.

You're bound to be approached by several sharp young businessmen calling themselves the Lodwar Tour Guides Association. Each will proudly unfold their photocopied piece of paper stating they are an official guide and most will also humorously claim to be the chairman. They'll offer to escort you to Lake Turkana, into the hills and local communities, or even to Central Island National Park. They try hard to please and are a useful source of information, although their prices are a bit steep for the services provided – KSh1500 just for a guide to the lake!

Sleeping
Unless you're both cold-blooded and thick-skinned, it's worth spending more for a room with a fan and mosquito net. The cheaper places are hellishly hot and the mosquitoes can be something fierce.

Nawoitorong Guest House (☎ 21208; camping KSh200, s/tw with shared bathroom KSh400/600, s/tw cottages from KSh700/900) Built entirely out of local materials and run by a local women's group, Nawoitorong is an excellent option, and the only one for campers. Thatched roofs alleviate the need for fans and all rooms have mozzie nets. There's a pleasant restaurant

HARAMBEE

The women's group guesthouse in Lodwar is just one example of the very Kenyan concept of *harambee*, a cornerstone of independence ideology drummed into the national consciousness by the first president, Jomo Kenyatta. Essentially it encapsulates the idea of a common goal, encouraging community self-help, and today few towns in Kenya are without their own local initiatives.

In practice, this can take on many forms. Numerous highly respected enterprises have sprung up around the country, from the Green Towns Partnership to the Youth Awareness and Resource Initiative (YARI), founding projects promoting everything from women's rights and community health to street kids and drug awareness, with considerable success. However, there are also plenty of organisations whose fund-raising activities are limited to fleecing tourists, and probably an equal number whose profits somehow never quite make it back to the community.

In politics, too, *harambee* has proved to be a double-edged sword. The idea of togetherness preoccupied Kenyatta to such an extent that any opposition came to resemble a dangerous strain of dissent, renewing his determination to run a one-party state. Despite increasing democratisation, this situation largely prevailed under Daniel arap Moi, and the rallying cry of 'national unity' can still overrule any number of objections. It seems that the new government, elected in 2002, is keen to put the darker side of *harambee* to rest.

and the shared-bathroom prices include breakfast. The one-bedroom Ekaato cottages are cheap but not nearly as charming as the two-bedroom Nadoua cottage, which also has a cooking area. The Napekitoi cottage is perfect for families.

Hotel Splash (☎ 21099; PO Box 297, Lodwar; s KSh450) Well signposted and west of the main crossroads, Hotel Splash has great, smallish singles with fans, mozzie nets, sitting chairs, reading lamps and decent bathrooms. The foam mattresses are pleasantly firm and there's secure parking to boot.

Turkwel Lodge (☎ 21099; s/tw KSh350/700, cottages s/d KSh800/1350; P) Turkwel offers spacious rooms containing fans and nets, but lacks the crisp, clean feel of its neighbour, Hotel Splash. Some beds are a bit of an Ikea slat experiment gone horribly wrong – not so comfy. There's secure parking and quiet, more roomy cottages at the rear.

Africana Silent Lodge (☎ 21254; s/tw with shared toilets KSh150/300; P) Small and cell-like, these rooms aren't what you'd call pleasant, but they are cheap. The shared squat toilets are equally displeasing. On the upside, there's fans throughout and safe parking inside.

Eating

Despite some impressive menus, most eateries only have one or two dishes on the go at once. If you want something specific on the menu you'll have to order a few hours in advance.

Turkwel Hotel (meals KSh60-210) Their green lentil curry is particularly good, but you have to get your order in about three hours prior! Oh, and don't forget to order the chapattis at the same time. Their local dishes require less waiting and are some of the best in town.

Nawoitorong Guest House (meals KSh160-225) Burgers and toasted sandwiches join local curries and various meaty fries on their menu.

Africana Silent Lodge (meals KSh40-110) A popular eatery with locals for cheap Kenyan fare and fried fish.

New Salama Hotel (meals KSh40-110) The best place for pre-departure breakfasts of eggs, chai and *mandazis* (Kenya's triangular version of a doughnut).

If you're self-catering, there's a well-stocked Naipa Supermarket next to the Kobil petrol station.

Drinking & Entertainment

Locals, young and old alike, love the video rooms scattered around town, where a kung fu flick or Hollywood blockbuster will cost you about KSh10. Some are more deafening than others and power failures seem painfully tied to crucial scenes – can you tell us what the heck happened in *The Crying Game*?

The large outdoor bar at the Nature Hotel is probably the best place to have a drink, although the Turkwel Hotel is still the more popular of the two.

Getting There & Away

Several companies, including Kenya Witness, have daily buses to Kitale (KSh500, 8½ hours) each night at 7.30pm (most services pick up passengers near the New Salama Hotel), while erratic matatus serve Kalokol (KSh150, one hour) and Lokichoggio (KSh500, three hours).

While UN vehicles were still travelling in armed convoys along the sublimely sealed 210km stretch of tarmac to Lokichoggio at the time of research, the security situation had improved enough that local trucks and matatus weren't travelling in convoy or taking armed escorts. Always check with locals and police to ascertain the latest security situation before travelling on this road.

Drivers will find several petrol stations here, though it's almost KSh20 more per litre than in Kitale.

ELIYE SPRINGS

Spring water percolates out of crumbling bluffs and brings life to this remote sandy shore of Lake Turkana, some 66km northeast of Lodwar by road. Growing from the moist sloping sands are oodles of doum palms, which give this usually barren environment a pronounced, albeit incongruous, tropical feel. Down on the slippery shore children play in the lake's warm waters while Central Island lurks magically on the distant horizon. These lake views are almost as spellbinding as the stars that occupy the dark night sky.

On arrival you'll encounter an instant small crowd of colourful Turkana women selling trinkets, ranging from bracelets and fish-backbone necklaces to fossilised hippo teeth. As only a few vehicles visit each week, it's a real buyer's market and prices are absurdly low. It's worth a look because the same items in Lodwar cost much more, despite most of them being made here.

Beneath the bluff, the skeleton of an old beach resort sits half eaten by its surroundings and makes for an interesting place to drop your tent. Locals now manage the leftovers and charge KSh200 for camping and KSh250 for sleeping beneath one of the remaining thatched roofs. Besides the spring water there are no facilities, so you'll have to be entirely self-sufficient. Note that more than the odd scorpion and carpet viper also call this place home, so shoes are a good idea.

Getting There & Away

The turn-off for Eliye Springs is signposted about halfway along the Lodwar–Kalokol road. The gravels are easy to follow until they suddenly peter out and you're faced with a fork in the road – stay left. The rest of the way is a mix of gravel, deep sand and dirt tracks (4WD only), which can turn into a muddy nightmare in the wet season.

If you don't have your own vehicle, you can usually arrange a 4WD in Lodwar to drop you off and pick you up at a predetermined time later for about KSh4500.

FERGUSON'S GULF

While a more accessible part of Lake Turkana than Eliye Springs, Ferguson's Gulf has none of its southern neighbour's tropical charm. Fishing boats in various states of disrepair litter its grubby western beach and a definite feeling of bleakness pervades. The gulf's eastern shore (accessible by boat only) is just as desolate, but has an inexplicably attractive air about it.

Birdlife is prolific, particularly in March and April, when thousands of European migratory birds stop here on their way north. There are also hippos and crocodiles (and bilharzia), so seek local advice before diving in.

If you're planning on visiting Central Island National Park (opposite) or Sibiloi National Park (p338), this is the best place to arrange a boat.

Set on the eastern shore, **Lake Turkana Lodge** (☎ 0722-703666; turkana@hillbarrett.com; camping US$10, s/tw US$25/40) is the only official accommodation in the area. Sixteen large timber cabins, each with their own bathroom and scenic veranda, provide sleeping quarters, but lighting is limited at best – bring a torch. The skeleton staff can provide meals (with advance warning) or for a small fee you can use the kitchen. The bar is an excellent place to absorb the scenery and is usually well stocked with beer, water and soft drink. Boat transfers across the gulf are an additional US$10.

There's no longer any accommodation in the nearby village of **Kalokol**.

Getting There & Away

Ferguson's Gulf is accessed from Kalokol, which is reachable by matatu from Lodwar along a good 75km stretch of tarmac. From Kalokol, follow the tarmac north for a few kilometres before turning left onto the dirt road next to the fading Italian fishing project sign. This leads towards a substantial building before veering to the right and dropping you in the middle of the gulf's fishing fleet. For those walking from Kalokol, you can shorten your trek from 6km to 4km by hiring a local to guide you through the sea of dead acacias.

CENTRAL ISLAND NATIONAL PARK

Rising from the depths of Lake Turkana and climbing 170m above its surface is the Central Island Volcano, which was last seen belching molten sulphur and steam just over three decades ago. Today the island is quiet, but its stormy volcanic history is told by the numerous craters scarring its weathered facade. Several craters have coalesced to form two sizeable lakes that are almost 1km wide and 80m deep.

Both a **national park** (adult/child US$15/5) and Unesco World Heritage Site, Central Island is an intriguing place to visit and the view atop the cinder cones is well worth the short scramble. But no matter how temping, stay clear of the lakes as the island is famous for its 14,000 or so Nile crocodiles, some of which are massive in proportion. Like Ferguson's Gulf, the island boasts countless numbers of migratory birds in March and April.

Camping (adult/child US$8/5) is possible and, unlike South Island NP, there are trees to tie your tent to. However, there's no water or any other facilities, so come prepared.

Hiring a boat from Ferguson's Gulf is the only real option to get here. Depending on what you drive up in, locals can ask anywhere from KSh10,000 to KSh50,000 for the trip. A fair price is KSh6000 for a motorboat – don't ever think about being cheap and taking a sailboat. The 10km trip and sudden squalls that terrorize the lake's waters aren't to be taken lightly, so ensure the craft is sound before boarding.

NORTH TO LOKICHOGGIO

Although the A1 Hwy from Lodwar to Lokichoggio via the UN refugee camps at Kakuma has been off limits to everyone but armed aid convoys for the last several years, improved security means that the odd intrepid traveller is now able to taste this remote northwest corner of Kenya. Remember that it's imperative to check with

locals, NGOs and police in Lodwar before heading off.

The perfect tarmac between Lodwar and Lokichoggio is a sight in itself – simply transcendent! As you head northwest from Lodwar, you'll wind through some rocky bluffs before dropping into a vast valley resembling a lush lawn in wet season and a white sea during drier periods. After passing through the Pelekech Range's stratified slopes, which mark the valley's western side, you'll see a dramatic and seemingly fictitious horizon of sharp mountainous peaks beyond the numerous refugee camps at Kakuma. In reality your eyes are making mountains out of mole hills, as the seemingly large peaks are only 100m- to 200m-high volcanic cinder cones.

Along the entire route you'll encounter rather marvellous Turkana people in striking tribal attire, either walking the roadside, selling sacks of charcoal or resting in the shade of lonely trees. Your steady gaze at these colourful souls will only be broken by the odd termite mound mystifyingly giving you the middle finger.

Despite being backed by the Mogila Range, Lokichoggio is rather unattractive. However, what it lacks in looks it makes up for in aid activity, with the World Food Program (WFP), UN and other NGOs basing their Sudanese operations here. Twenty WFP aircraft and six UN Hercules were based here when we were in town.

Information

There's a post office with Internet access, but no banks. High-speed Internet is available in Trackmark Camp and Africa Expeditions for KSh10 per minute.

Sleeping & Eating

The need to house NGO workers in Lokichoggio has resulted in some pretty plush accommodation options being added to the mix.

Makuti Bar (☎ 0722-257262; A1 Hwy; d with shared bathroom KSh400-500) This is the only reasonable budget option in town, with small but clean rooms. All have mozzie nets and the cheaper rooms near the bar (which is a bit loud) also have fans.

Trackmark Camp (☎ 054-32245; lokicamp@yahoo .com; full board tents s US$50, bandas s/d US$55/80; ❄ 💻 ♨) An absolute haven of peace with a gorgeous pool, sun deck and open-air TV room laden with comfy cushions. Choose between very comfortable, tastefully decorated air-conditioned *toculs* (bandas) or well-appointed semipermanent tents. You'll save US$5 if you opt for a shared bathroom. The restaurant (breakfast KSh350, buffets KSh750) offers great Western fare and the menu differs daily. Nonguests can swim and eat lunch for KSh1000.

Africa Expeditions (☎ 0721-262440; full board tents US$45, bungalows s US$50-55; 🔀 🖳 🔊) Similar in scope to Trackmark Camp, but offers none of their friendliness or laid-back vibe – it's all business here.

The town's most popular **restaurant** (meals KSh60-250) is out front of the Makuti Bar and serves *nyama choma*, roast chicken and fried fish.

Getting There & Away

The border with Sudan was closed at the time of writing – check for updates at Lodwar's military post.

Petrol in Lokichoggio is readily available and costs KSh10 less per litre than it does in Lodwar. For more information on the road conditions in the area and the transport options available between Lokichoggio and Lodwar, go to p342.

Directory

CONTENTS

Accommodation   345
Activities   348
Business Hours   350
Children   351
Climate Charts   352
Courses   353
Customs   353
Dangers & Annoyances   353
Disabled Travellers   355
Discount Cards   355
Embassies & Consulates   355
Festivals & Events   357
Food   357
Gay & Lesbian Travellers   357
Holidays   358
Insurance   358
Internet Access   359
Legal Matters   359
Maps   359
Money   360
Photography & Video   361
Post   362
Senior Travellers   363
Shopping   363
Solo Travellers   364
Telephone   365
Time   365
Toilets   365
Tourist Information   366
Visas   366
Women Travellers   367
Work   367

PRACTICALITIES

- Major newspapers and magazines in Kenya include the *Daily Nation,* the *East African Standard,* the *East African,* the *Weekly Review* and the *New African.*

- KBC and NTV, formerly KTN, are the main national TV stations; the CNN, Sky and BBC networks are also widely available on satellite or cable (DSTV).

- KBC Radio broadcasts across the country on various FM frequencies. Most major towns also have their own local music and talkback stations, and the BBC World Service is easily accessible.

- Kenyan televisual equipment uses the standard European NSTC video system.

- Kenya uses the 240V system, with square three-pin sockets as used in the UK. Bring a universal adaptor if you need to charge your phone or run other appliances.

- Kenya uses the metric system – distances are in kilometres and most weights are in kilograms.

ACCOMMODATION

Kenya has a good range of accommodation options, from basic cubicle hotels overlooking city bus stands to luxury tented camps hidden away in the national parks. There are also all kinds of campsites, budget tented camps, simple bandas (often wooden huts) and cottages scattered around the parks and rural areas.

During the low season many companies offer excellent deals on accommodation on the coast and in the main wildlife parks, often working with airlines to create packages aimed at the local and expat market. The website of **Let's Go Travel** (www.lets-go-travel .net) displays almost all the major hotels and lodges in Kenya, giving price ranges and descriptions, while www.kenyalastminute.com is a good port of call for discounted bookings at some of the more expensive camps, lodges and hotels, particularly on the coast.

Where appropriate accommodation options are split into budget, midrange and top-end categories for ease of reference. In general, a budget double room is anything under KSh1000. You can pay as little as KSh150 for four walls and a bed, with foam mattress and shared squat toilet; for KSh400 and up you'd usually get a private bathroom, and at the upper end of the scale shower heaters and breakfast may be on offer. Surprisingly, bedding, towels and soap are almost always provided however much you pay, though cleanliness varies widely and toilet seats can be rare luxuries.

In most of the country, midrange accommodation falls between KSh1000 and KSh3500 for a double room – the major exception to this is Nairobi, where you can pay anything up to KSh6000 for the same standards. In this bracket you'd usually expect breakfast, private bathroom, telephone and good-size double beds with proper mattresses; the more you pay the more facilities you get, from restaurants and bars to TVs, hot showers and the odd swimming pool.

Everything over KSh3500 (or US$80 in Nairobi) counts as top end, and what you get for your money varies enormously. Once you hit US$100 you should count on breakfast, TV, phone, air-con (on the coast), room service and toiletries as standard, and in the upper realms of the price range the extras can include anything from complimentary minibars to casinos, Jacuzzis and free activities. The most expensive places are the exclusive getaways tucked away in national parks and other remote corners of the country, which can exceed US$600 for a double but don't necessarily include all the trappings you'd expect elsewhere.

Although most midrange and top-end places quote prices in US dollars, payment can be in local currency. Note that most places have separate rates for residents, and these are often much less than the nonresident rates. All prices quoted in this book are nonresident rates.

Many midrange and (especially) top-end options also change their prices according to season, which can be confusing as very few places use exactly the same dates. In principal there are high, low and shoulder seasons, but some hotels can divide their year into five or more distinct pricing periods. For lodges in the national parks, the norm is to charge high-season prices from July to March, with low-season prices only applicable from April to June. On the coast, where things are much more seasonal, peak times tend to be July to August and December to March, and a range of lower rates can apply for the rest of the year.

Note that however high season is defined, premium rates or supplements always apply over Christmas, New Year and Easter, and can be as much as double the high-season tariffs. Conversely, hotels that are near empty in low season may be open to some negotiation on rates.

In this book, 'high season' refers to rates quoted for the longest peak period (not premium rates), and 'low season' refers to the lowest prices available out of season – any other variations should fall between these two guidelines.

African Safari Club

Although it's package tourism at its most developed, the UK-based **African Safari Club** (UK ☎ 020-84660014; www.africansafariclub.com) has some splendid properties on the coast and in several of the national parks. The company even has its own airline ferrying in guests from Europe. There are African Safari Club resorts at Watamu, Kilifi, Shanzu Beach and Kikambala on the coast, and in Tsavo East and Masai Mara National Parks. Rates are typical for up-market resorts, but are quoted as part of holiday packages so few offers are for less than a week or so.

Bandas

These are basic huts and cottages, usually with some kind of kitchen and bathroom that offer excellent value for budget travellers. There are KWS (Kenya Wildlife Service) bandas at Shimba Hills, Tsavo West, Meru and Mt Elgon, and near the marine reserves at Malindi and Shimoni. Some are wooden huts, some are thatched stone huts and some are small brick bungalows with solar-powered lights; facilities range from basic dorms and squat toilets to kitchens and hot water provided by wood-burning stoves. The cost varies from US$10 to US$20 per person. **Let's Go Travel** (☎ 020-340331; www.lets-go-travel.net) in Nairobi is the agent for an increasing number of bandas. You'll need to bring all your own food, drinking water, bedding and firewood.

Beach Resorts

Much of the coast, from Diani Beach to Malindi, is taken up by huge luxury beach resorts. Most offer a fairly similar experience, with swimming pools, water sports, bars, restaurants, mobs of souvenir vendors on the beach and 'tribal' dance shows in the evening. They aren't all bad, though especially if you want good children's facilities, and a handful of them have been very sensitively designed. Nightly rates vary from US$40 per person at the small family resorts to US$500 at top-end places. Not that the majority of these places will close in the early summer, generally from May to mid-June or July.

Camping

There are many opportunities for camping in Kenya and it is worth considering bringing a tent with you, although gear can also be hired in Nairobi and around Mt Kenya. There are KWS campsites in just about every national park or reserve, though these are usually very basic. There'll be a toilet block with a couple of pit toilets, and usually a water tap, but very little else.

As well as these permanent campsites, KWS also runs so-called 'special' campsites in most national parks; these sites move every year and have even fewer facilities than the standard camps, but cost more because of their wilder locations and set-up costs. A reservation fee of KSh5000 per week is payable on top of the relevant camping fee.

Private sites are rare but they offer more facilities and may hire out tents if you don't have your own. It's sometimes possible to camp in the grounds of some hotels in rural towns, and Nairobi has some good private campsites. Camping in the bush is possible but unless you're doing it with an organised trip or a guide, security is a major concern; don't even think about it on the coast.

All campsite prices in this book are per person unless otherwise specified.

Hostels

The only youth hostel affiliated with Hostelling International (HI) is in Nairobi. It has good basic facilities and is a pleasant enough place to stay, but there are plenty of other cheaper choices that are just as good. Other places that call themselves 'youth hostels' are not members of HI and standards are extremely variable.

Hotels & Guesthouses

Real bottom-end hotels (often known as 'board and lodgings' to distinguish them from 'hotelis', which are often only restaurants) are widely used as brothels and tend to be very run-down. Security at these places is virtually nonexistent; the better ones are set around courtyards and are clean if not exactly comfortable.

Proper hotels and guesthouses come in as many different shapes and sizes as the people who stay in them. As well as the top-end Western companies, there are a number of small Kenyan chains offering reliable standards across a handful of properties in particular towns or regions, and also plenty of private family-run establishments.

Self-catering options are common on the coast, where they're often the only mid-priced alternative to the top-end resorts, but not so much in other parts of the country. A few fancier places offer fully fitted modern kitchens, but more often than not the so-called kitchenettes will be a side room with a small fridge and a rusty portable gas hob.

Terms you will come across frequently in Kenya include 'self-contained', which just means a room with its own private bathroom, and 'all-inclusive', which differs in exact meaning from place to place, but it's generally all meals, certain drinks and possibly some activities should be included in the room rate.

Rental Houses

Renting a private house is a popular option on the coast, particularly for groups on longer stays, and many expats let out their holiday homes when they're not using them. Properties range from restored Swahili houses on the northern islands to luxurious colonial mansions inland, and while they're seldom cheap the experience will often be something pretty special.

Safari Lodges

Hidden away inside or on the edges of national parks are some fantastic safari lodges. These are usually visited as part of organised safaris, and you'll pay much more if you just turn up and ask for a room. Some of the older places trade heavily on their more glorious past, but the best places feature five-star rooms, soaring *makuti*-roofed bars (with a thatched roof of palm leaves) and restaurants overlooking waterholes full of wildlife. Staying in at least one good safari lodge is recommended, if only to see how the other half lives! Rates tend to come down a lot in the low season.

Tented Camps

As well as lodges, many parks contain some fantastic luxury tented camps. These places tend to occupy wonderfully remote settings, usually by rivers or other natural locations, and feature large, comfortable, semipermanent safari tents with beds, furniture, bathrooms (usually with hot running water) and often some kind of external roof thatch to keep the rain out. There are a few moderately priced options in Tsavo East National Park but most of the camps are very posh and the tents are pretty much hotel rooms under canvas. The really exclusive properties occupy locations so isolated that guests fly in and out on charter planes.

ACTIVITIES

If bombing around in a safari bus isn't active enough for you, Kenya has an amazing range of distractions and diversions to keep you on your toes from dusk till dawn. Trekking and snorkelling are among the most popular pursuits inland and on the coast respectively, as they require no expensive equipment and can be arranged very easily locally; more adventurous activities include a whole world of water sports and aerial adventures from balloons to gliders. For more ideas on organised trips and activities, see p59.

Ballooning

Balloon trips in the wildlife parks are an absolutely superb way of seeing the savanna plains and, of course, the animals. The almost ghostly experience of floating silently above the plains with a 360° view of everything beneath you is incomparable, and it's definitely worth saving up your shillings to take one of these trips.

The flights typically set off at dawn and go for about 1½ hours, after which you put down for a champagne breakfast. You will then be taken on a wildlife drive in a support vehicle and returned to your lodge. Flights are currently available in the Masai Mara for around US$390. Check out the following companies:

Adventures Aloft (Map pp102-3; ☎ 020-214168; Kimathi House, Kimathi St, Nairobi) This company operates out of Mara Fig Tree Lodge and you can book there, in Nairobi, or at any other lodge in the Masai Mara.

Balloon Safaris Ltd (☎ 020-605003; www.balloon safaris.com; Wilson Airport, Nairobi) This company operates out of Keekorok Lodge.

Governors' Balloon Safaris (☎ 020-2734000; www .governorscamp.com) This company operates out of Little Governors' Camp in Nairobi.

Transworld Balloon Safaris (☎ 020-2713333) Based at the Sarova Mara Lodge in the Masai Mara.

Cycling

An increasing number of companies offer cycling and mountain-biking trips in Kenya. Popular locations include the edge of the Masai Mara, Hell's Gate National Park, Central Highlands and Kerio Valley. The best specialist operator is **Bike Treks** (☎ 020-446371; www.biketreks.co.ke).

Many local companies and places to stay around the country can arrange cheap bicycle hire, allowing you to cycle through places such as Arabuko Sokoke Forest Reserve and Hell's Gate National Park. Hire is usually between KSh300 and KSh500 per day. See p376 for more information on cycling in Kenya. For details of companies which offer cycling safaris, see p70.

Diving & Snorkelling

There is a string of marine national parks spread out along the coast between Shimoni and Malindi (see p151 for further details), with plenty of opportunities for snorkelling and scuba diving. The better marine parks are those further away from Mombasa, at Wasini Island (p179), on the south coast and at Malindi (p205) and Watamu (p198), to the north. The Lamu archipelago (p212) also has some fine reefs, off the islands of Manda Toto and Kiwayu.

Just about any boat trip will include some time snorkelling or 'goggling' on one of the many local reefs, and masks are readily available wherever you go for around KSh200. However, snorkellers are discouraged from wearing flippers (fins) because of the damage they can do to the coral.

There are distinct seasons for diving in Kenya. October to March is the best time, but during June, July and August it's often impossible to dive due to the poor visibility caused by heavy silt flow from some of the rivers on the coast. This doesn't necessarily mean that no companies will take your money for trips during this period! In 1997, there was a huge coral die-off as part of a warming of the ocean attributable to El Niño and global warming. However, the coral is slowly recovering and there are thousands of colourful fish species and even marine mammals.

If you aren't certified to dive, almost every hotel and resort on the coast can arrange an open-water diving course. By international standards, they aren't cheap – a five-day

PADI certification course will cost between US$330 and US$450. Trips for certified divers including two dives go for around US$90. The cheapest way to dive is on dhow tours to Wasini, where you only pay US$50 for two dives, although you have to pay for the tour as well.

Nairobi Sailing & Sub Aqua Club (Map p126; ☎ 020-501250; Nairobi Dam, Langata Rd, Nairobi) offers British Sub Aqua Club diver training and runs diving trips to the coast between September and April.

If you're going to scuba dive on the coast, note that the only decompression chamber in the region is in Mombasa and is run by the Kenyan navy.

Fishing

The **Kenya Fisheries Department** (Map pp98-9; ☎ 020-3742320; Museum Hill Rd, Nairobi), opposite National Museums of Kenya, operates a number of fishing camps in various parts of the country. However, they're difficult to reach without your own vehicle and directions from the Fisheries Department, from whom you'll also need to get a fishing licence.

The deep-sea fishing on the coast is some of the best in the world and various private companies and resorts in Shimoni, Diani Beach, Mtwapa, Watamu and Malindi can arrange fishing trips. Boats cost from US$250 to US$500 and can usually fit four or five anglers. You'll pay the same price if it's just you in the boat. The season runs from August to April.

For freshwater fishing, there are huge Nile perch as big as a person in Lakes Victoria and Turkana, and some of the trout fishing around the Aberdares and Mt Kenya is quite exceptional. See p68 for more details on fishing safaris in Kenya.

Fishing licences for Mt Kenya, Mt Elgon and Aberdare National Parks can be obtained from the respective park gates at a cost of KSh100 per day. In addition to this fee, park visitors are required to pay the standard daily park-entry charges and KWS guide fees at KSh500 per day.

Gliding & Flying

The **Gliding Club of Kenya** (☎ 0733-760331; gliding@africaonline.co.ke; PO Box 926, Nyeri), near Nyeri in the Central Highlands, offers silent glides over the Aberdares (p254).

RESPONSIBLE DIVING

Please consider the following tips when diving:

- Never use anchors on the reef, and take care not to ground boats on coral.

- Avoid touching or standing on living marine organisms or dragging equipment across the reef. Polyps can be damaged by even the gentlest contact. If you must hold on to the reef, only touch exposed rock or dead coral.

- Practise and maintain proper buoyancy control. Major damage can be done by divers descending too fast and colliding with the reef.

- Take great care in underwater caves. Spend as little time within them as possible as your air bubbles may be caught within the roof and thereby leave organisms high and dry. Take turns to inspect the interior of small caves before leaving.

- Resist the temptation to collect coral or shells, or to loot marine archaeological sites.

- Ensure that you take home all your rubbish and any other litter you may find. Plastics in particular are a serious threat to marine life.

- Do not feed fish.

- Minimise your disturbance of marine animals. Never ride on the backs of turtles.

Flying lessons are easily arranged in Nairobi and are much cheaper than in Europe, the USA and Australasia. Contact the **Aero Club of East Africa** (☎ 020-608990) and **Ninety-Nines Flying Club** (☎ 020-500277), both at Wilson Airport.

Sailing

Kilifi, Mtwapa and Mombasa all have sailing clubs, and smaller freshwater clubs can also be found at Lake Naivasha and Lake Victoria, which both have excellent windsurfing and sailing. If you're experienced, you may pick up some crewing at the various yacht clubs, although you'll need to become a temporary member. While it isn't hands-on, a traditional dhow trip out of Lamu is an unforgettable experience.

Trekking & Climbing

For proper mountain trekking Mt Kenya (p261) is the obvious choice, but other promising and relatively unexplored walking territory includes Mt Elgon (p312) on the Ugandan border, the Cherangani Hills and Kerio Valley (p309) east of Kitale, the Matthews Range and the Ndoto Mountains (p327) north of Isiolo, the Loroghi Hills (p335) north of Maralal, the Mau Forest region (p242) near Nakuru, the upper reaches of the Aberdares (p256) and even the Ngong Hills (p130), close to Nairobi.

For more trekking information refer to the relevant chapters in this book, get hold of a copy of Lonely Planet's *Trekking in East Africa,* or contact the **Mountain Club of Kenya** (MCK; ☎ 020-602330; www.mck.or.ke) in Nairobi (for more details, see p97). Its website has good advice on Mt Kenya as well as on technical climbing and trekking throughout Kenya.

In addition to rafting trips (right), **Savage Wilderness Safaris** (☎ 020-521590; www.whitewaterkenya.com; Sarit Centre, PO Box 1000, Westlands, Nairobi) offers mountaineering trips to Mt Kenya and rock climbing at sites around the country, as well as some more unusual options like caving.

Water Sports

Conditions on Kenya's coast are ideal for windsurfing – the country's offshore reefs protect the waters, and the winds are usually reasonably strong and constant. Most resort hotels south and north of Mombasa have sailboards for hire; rates vary from KSh400 to KSh800 per hour, and instruction is also usually available. The sheltered channel between Lamu and Manda Islands (p223) is one of the best places to windsurf on the coast.

As well as the ubiquitous windsurfing, diving and snorkelling which is always on offer, some of the larger resorts have watersports centres giving visitors the opportunity to try out absolutely everything from jet skis and banana boats to bodyboarding and traditional surfing. Kitesurfing is the latest craze to catch on, with tuition available. Diani Beach (p174), south of Mombasa, is the best place to go if you want to try any (or all) of these activities.

White-Water Rafting

The Athi/Galana River has substantial rapids, chutes and waterfalls and there are also possibilities on the Tana River and Ewaso Ngiro River near Isiolo. The most exciting times for a white-water rafting trip are from late October to mid-January and from early April to late July, when water levels are highest.

The people to talk to are **Savage Wilderness Safaris** (☎ 020-521590; www.whitewaterkenya .com; Sarit Centre, PO Box 1000, Westlands, Nairobi), run by the charismatic Mark Savage. Depending on water levels, rafting trips of up to 450km and three weeks' duration can be arranged, although most trips last one to four days and cover up to 80km.

One of the most popular short trips (US$95 per person, one day) is on the Tana River, northeast of Nairobi, which covers grade two to five rapids. Overnight trips with more time spent on the river cost US$140. Also possible are three-day adventures on the Athi River, southeast of Nairobi (US$380 per person plus US$95 per extra day), and the Ewaso Ngiro River, northwest of Isiolo (US$450 per person with additional days at US$105 per day).

The above prices include transport from Nairobi, tented accommodation, good-quality food, soft drinks and beer. You are also provided with all necessary rafting equipment including life jackets and helmets. At least four people are required for the Tana trip and at least six for the other rivers.

The company also offers a wide range of other land- and water-based activities including kayaking and sailing.

BUSINESS HOURS

Most government offices are open Monday to Friday from 8am or 8.30am to 1pm and from 2pm to 5pm. Post offices, shops and services open roughly from 8am to 5pm Monday to Friday and 9am to noon on Saturday; in Nairobi and other large cities the big supermarkets are open from 8.30am to 8.30pm Monday to Saturday and 10am to 8pm Sunday. Internet cafés generally keep longer evening hours and may open on Sunday.

Banking hours are from 9am to 3pm Monday to Friday and from 9am to 11am Saturday; some smaller branches may only open on the first and last Saturday of the month.

n tourist resorts and larger cities banks may stay open until 4.30pm or 5pm Monday to Saturday. Forex bureaus are typically open from 9am to 6pm Monday to Friday and 9am to 1pm on Saturday. Barclays Bank at Nairobi's Jomo Kenyatta International Airport is open 24 hours and is the only bank in the country to open on Sunday.

Restaurant opening hours vary according to the type of establishment – as a rule cafés and cheap Kenyan canteens will open at around 6am or 7am and close in the early evening, while more expensive ethnic restaurants will be open from 11am to 10pm daily, sometimes with a break between lunch and dinner. International restaurants and those serving breakfast and/or alcohol are usually open from 8am until 11pm. Bars that don't serve food are open from around 6pm until late, while nightclubs open their doors around 9pm and can keep going until 6am or later at weekends!

In this book we have only given specific opening hours where they differ significantly from these broad guidelines.

CHILDREN

Many parents regard Africa as just too dangerous for travel with children, but it is possible, and even easy, if you're prepared to spend a little more and take comfort over adventure for the core of the trip.

Local attitudes towards children vary in Kenya just as they do in the West: screaming babies on matatus elicit all the usual sighs and tuttings, but usually kids will be welcomed anywhere that's not an exclusively male preserve, especially by women with families of their own.

For invaluable general advice on taking the family abroad, see Lonely Planet's *Travel with Children* by Cathy Lanigan.

Practicalities

Budget hotels are probably best avoided for hygiene reasons. Most midrange accommodation should be acceptable, though it's usually only top-end places that cater specifically for families. Camping can be exciting but you'll need to be extra careful that your kids aren't able to wander off unsupervised into the Kenyan countryside.

Most hotels will not charge for children under two years of age. Children between two and 12 years who share their parents'

room are usually charged at 50% of the adult rate. You'll also get a cotbed thrown in for this price. Large family rooms are often available, especially at the upper end of the price scale, and some places also have adjoining rooms with connecting doors if your kids are old enough for a bit of independence.

Be warned that some exclusive lodges, including Treetops, the Ark and Shimba Rainforest Lodge, impose a minimum age limit for children; typically they must be aged at least eight to be admitted. If camping, be alert for potential hazards such as mosquitoes, dangerous wildlife and campfires. It's particularly important to consider the risks posed to children by tropical diseases – talk to your doctor to get the best advice. Mosquito repellents with high levels of DEET may be unsuitable for young children.

Street food is also likely to be risky, as is unwashed fruit. Letting your children run around barefoot is usually fine on the beach (beware of sea urchins!), but may be risky in the bush because of thorns, bees, scorpions and snakes. Hookworm and bilharzia are also risks.

Travelling between towns in Kenya is not always easy with children. Car sickness is one problem, and young children tend to be seen as wriggling luggage, so you'll often have them on your lap. Functional seatbelts are rare even in taxis and accidents are common – a child seat brought from home is a good idea if you're hiring a car or going on safari. The journey to and from the coast by train is highly enjoyable for people of all ages.

Canned baby foods, powdered milk, disposable nappies and the like are available in most large supermarkets, but are expensive. Bring as much as possible from home, together with child-friendly insect repellent (this can't be bought in Kenya).

Sights & Activities

The coast is the obvious place to go for anyone travelling with children, as virtually all the resort hotels have pools, private beaches, playgrounds, games, entertainment and even kids' clubs to take the little darlings off your hands if you need a break. We've used the child-friendly icon (🏊) throughout this book to indicate hotels with dedicated children's facilities.

Short boat trips can be great for slightly older children. If you stay in Diani Beach

DIRECTORY

(p172) or Malindi (p205) there are also several national parks or reserves within easy reach, so you can go on safari without having to drive for too long to get there. Mwaluganje Elephant Sanctuary (p170) should capture most children's imagination and is accessible but wild enough to be exciting.

Many parents swear by Lamu (p212) as a good family destination – it's small and safe but has plenty to see and provides a taste of an exotic culture as soon as you step off the ferry. The large population of donkeys also provides a hefty dose of cuteness for young animal-lovers.

If you want to go on a full-scale safari, bear in mind that a four-hour wildlife drive with strangers can be an eternity for an uncomfortable child. It's best to choose one of the smaller, more open parks such as Nairobi National Park (p125), Amboseli (p137) or Lake Nakuru (p243), where there's plenty to see and the distances involved are relatively short. The kind of accommodation you choose will depend on the age, tolerance and curiosity of your offspring.

In Nairobi, the Langata Giraffe Centre (p128), David Sheldrick Wildlife Trust (p127), National Museum (p104) and Railway Museum (p105) are all good for children. Bomas of Kenya (p124) has a good children's playground.

CLIMATE CHARTS

Kenya's diverse geography means that temperature, rainfall and humidity vary widely, but there are effectively four distinct zones.

The hot, rainy plateau of western Kenya has rainfall throughout the year, the heaviest usually during April when as much as 200mm may be recorded, and the lowest in January with an average of 40mm. Temperatures range from a minimum of 14°C to 18°C to a maximum of 30°C to 36°C throughout the year.

The temperate Rift Valley and Central Highlands have perhaps the most agreeable climate in the country. Average temperatures vary from a minimum of 10°C to 14°C to a maximum of 22°C to 28°C. Rainfall varies from a minimum of 20mm in July to 200mm in April, falling in essentially two seasons – March to the beginning of June (the 'long rains') and October to the end of November (the 'short rains'). Mt Kenya and the Aberdare mountains are the country's

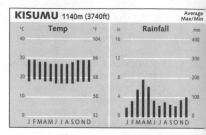

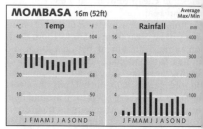

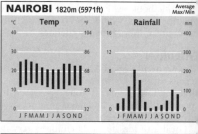

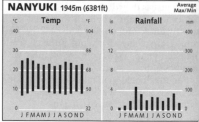

main water catchments, with falls of up to 3000mm per year recorded in these places.

In the semiarid bushlands of northern and eastern Kenya temperatures vary from highs of up to 40°C during the day to less than 20°C at night. Rainfall in this area is sparse and, when it does occur, is often in the form of violent storms. July is usually the driest month, and November the wettest. The average annual rainfall varies between 250mm and 500mm.

The consistently humid coast region has rainfall averages from 20mm in February to around 300mm in May. Rainfall is dependent on the monsoon, which blows from the northeast from October to April and from the southwest for the rest of the year. The average annual rainfall is between 1000mm and 1250mm (less in drought years). Average temperatures vary little during the year, ranging from 22°C to 30°C.

These charts illustrate the typical annual conditions in key cities around the country; see p14 for a general overview of peak visitor periods.

For the latest local weather forecasts online, visit the **Kenya Meteorological Office** (www.meteo.go.ke).

COURSES

If you intend to spend considerable time in Kenya, learning Swahili is an excellent idea. The Anglican Church of Kenya (ACK) runs the best language school. Taking a language course (or any course) also entitles you to a 'Pupils' Pass', an immigration permit allowing continuous stays of up to 12 months. You may have to battle with bureaucracy and the process may take months, but it can be worth it, epecially as you will then have resident status in Kenya during your stay.

The fee for a Pupil's Pass varies. A charge will be levied by your school for sorting out the paperwork so expect to pay around KSh3000 for a one-year pass. A deposit of KSh5000 or a letter of guarantee by an approved body registered in Kenya (your language school) is required along with two photographs and a copy of your passport (if applying from overseas). Check out the following language schools:

ACK Language & Orientation School (☎ 020-2723200; www.ackenya.org; Bishops Rd, Upper Hill, PO Box 47429, Nairobi) Full-time courses (US$450) last 14 weeks and take up five hours a day. More flexible is private tuition, which costs US$4 per hour. Study materials will cost around US$40.

Language Center Ltd (☎ 020-570610; Ndemi Close, off Ngong Rd, PO Box 40661, Nairobi) This is a good cheaper option; classes cost KSh250 per hour in a group or KSh450 for one-on-one tuition, and you can study two, three or seven days a week.

CUSTOMS

There are strict laws about taking wildlife products out of Kenya. The export of products made from elephant, rhino and sea turtle are prohibited. The collection of coral is also not allowed. Ostrich eggs will also be confiscated unless you can prove you bought them from a certified ostrich farm. Always check to see what permits are required, especially for the export of any plants, insects and shells.

Usual regulations apply to items you can bring into the country – 50 cigars, 200 cigarettes, 250g of pipe tobacco, 1L of alcohol, 250ml of perfume and other personal items such as cameras, laptop computers and binoculars. Obscene publications are banned, which may extend to some lads' magazines.

You are allowed to take up to KSh100,000 out of the country.

DANGERS & ANNOYANCES

While Kenya is a safe destination in African terms, there are still plenty of pitfalls for the unwary or inexperienced traveller, from everyday irritations to more serious threats. A little street sense goes a long way here, and getting the latest local information is essential wherever you intend to travel.

Banditry

Wars in Somalia, Sudan and Ethiopia have all had their effect on the stability and safety of northern and northeastern Kenya. AK-47s have been flowing into the country for many years and the newspapers are filled with stories of hold-ups, shoot-outs, cattle rustling and general lawlessness. Bandits and poachers infiltrating from Somalia have made the northeast of the country particularly dangerous, and with the American 'War on Terror' shutting down the funding for many warring factions within Somalia, these problems are only going to get worse.

In the northwest, the main problem is armed tribal wars and cattle rustling across the Sudanese border. There are Kenyan *shifta* (bandits) too, of course, but cross-border problems seem to account for most of the trouble in the north of the country.

Despite all the headlines, tourists are rarely targeted, as much of the violence and robberies take place far from the main tourist routes. Security has also improved considerably in previously high-risk areas such as the Isiolo–Marsabit, Marsabit–Moyale and Malindi–Lamu routes. However, you should check the situation locally before

DIRECTORY

taking these roads, or travelling between Garsen and Garissa or Thika.

The areas along the Sudanese and Ethiopian borders are very risky, although most visitors are very unlikely to have any reason to go there in the first place.

Crime

Even the staunchest Kenyan patriot will readily admit that the country's biggest problem is crime. It ranges from petty snatch theft and mugging to violent armed robbery, carjacking and of course white-collar crime and corruption. The wealthy are content to surround themselves with more and more armed guards and razor wire and little is done to address the causes of the problem. As a visitor you needn't feel paranoid, but you should always keep your wits about you, particularly at night.

Perhaps the best advice for when you're walking around cities and towns is not to carry anything valuable with you – that includes jewellery, watches, cameras, bum bags, day-packs and money. Most hotels provide a safe or secure place for valuables, although you should be cautious of the security at some budget places. Cheap digital watches and plastic sunglasses can be bought in Kenya for under KSh100 and you won't miss them if they get taken.

While pickpocketing and bag-snatching are the most common crimes, armed muggings do occur in Nairobi and on the coast (see the relevant chapters for more details). However, they usually occur at night or in remote areas, so always take taxis after dark or along lonely dirt roads. Conversely, snatch-and-run crimes happen more in crowds. If you suddenly feel there are too many people around you, or think you are being followed, dive straight into a shop and ask for help.

Luggage is an obvious signal to criminals that you've just arrived. When arriving anywhere by bus, it's sensible to take a 'ship-to-shore' approach, getting a taxi directly from the bus station to your hotel. You'll have plenty of time to explore once you've safely stowed your belongings. Also, don't read this guidebook or look at maps on the street – it attracts unwanted attention.

In the event of a crime, you should report it to the police, but this can be a real procedure. You'll need to get a police report if you intend to make an insurance claim. In the event of a snatch theft, think twice before yelling 'Thief!'. It's not unknown for people to administer summary justice on the spot, often with fatal results for the criminal.

Although crime is a fact of life in Kenya, it needn't spoil your trip. Above all, don't make the mistake of distrusting every Kenyan just because of a few bad apples – the honest souls you meet will far outweigh any crooks who cross your path.

Money

With street crime a way of life in Nairobi, you should be doubly careful with your money. The safest policy is to leave all your valuables in the hotel safe and just carry enough cash for that day. If you do need to carry larger sums around, a money belt worn under your clothes is the safest option to guard against snatch thefts. However, be aware that muggers will usually be expecting this.

More ingenious tricks include tucking money into a length of elasticised bandage on your arm or leg, or creating a hidden pocket inside your trousers. If you don't actually need your credit card, travellers cheques or cash with you, they'll almost always be safer locked away in your hotel safe. Don't overlook the obvious and leave money lying around your hotel room in plain view, though – however well you get on with the staff, they're unlikely to resist a free month's wages if they've got a family to feed.

Scams

At some point in Kenya you'll almost certainly come across people who play on the emotions and gullibility of foreigners. Nairobi is a particular hotspot, with 'friendly' approaches a daily, if not hourly, occurrence (see p104 for examples of favourite tricks). People with tales about being refugees or having sick relatives can sound very convincing, but they all end up asking for cash. It's OK to talk to these people if they're not actively hassling you, but you should always ignore any requests for money.

Be sceptical of strangers who claim to recognise you in the street, especially if they're vague about exactly where they know you from – it's unlikely that any ordinary person is going to be *this* excited by seeing you twice. Anyone who makes a big show of inviting you into the hospitality of their

---

STREET KIDS

Nairobi in particular has huge problems with street children, many of whom are AIDS orphans, who trail foreigners around asking for food or change. It's up to you whether you give, but if you do, the word will go around and you won't get a moment's peace. It's also debatable how much your donations will help as the older boys operate like a mini-mafia, extorting money from the younger kids.

If you want to help out, money might be better donated to the charity **Homeless Children International** (☎ 020-573013; www .hcikenya.org), which works to improve conditions for these children.

---

home also probably has ulterior motives. The usual trick is to bestow some kind of gift upon the delighted traveller, who is then emotionally blackmailed into reciprocating to the order of several hundred shillings.

Tourists with cars also face potential rip-offs. Don't trust people who gesticulate wildly to indicate that your front wheels are wobbling; if you stop, you'll probably be relieved of your valuables. Another trick is to splash oil on your wheels, then tell you the wheel bearings, differential or something else has failed, and direct you to a nearby garage where their friends will 'fix' the problem – for a substantial fee, of course.

Terrorism

Kenya has twice been subject to terrorist attacks: in August 1998 the US embassy in Nairobi was bombed (see p32), and in November 2002 the Paradise Hotel, north of Mombasa, was car-bombed at the same time as a rocket attack on an Israeli jet. While these events caused a brief panic in the tourist industry, it now seems they were isolated incidents and that Western travellers to Kenya can expect to have a trouble-free time in the country. Visitors to the predominantly Muslim coast region should be aware that anti-American sentiment can run high here, but actual violence against foreigners is highly unlikely.

DISABLED TRAVELLERS

Travelling in Kenya is not easy for physically disabled people, but it's not impossible.

Very few tourist companies and facilities are geared up for disabled travellers, and those that are tend to be restricted to the expensive hotels and lodges. However, if you're polite you're likely to get assistance from people wherever you need it. Visually or hearing-impaired travellers, however, will find it very hard to get by without an able-bodied companion.

In Nairobi, only the ex-London taxi cabs are spacious enough to accommodate a wheelchair, but many safari companies have experience taking disabled people out on safari. The travel agency **Travel Scene Services** (☎ 020-215404; travelscene@insightkenya.com) has lots of experience with disabled travellers.

Many of the top-end beach resorts on the coast have facilities for the disabled, whether it's a few token ramps or fully equipped rooms with handrails and bathtubs. Many of the hotels owned by **Lonrho Hotels** (Nairobi ☎ 020-216940; www.lonrhohotels.com) can make provisions for disabled people – Mount Kenya Safari Club has its own wheelchair for guests' use. In Amboseli National Park, **Ol Tukai Lodge** (Nairobi ☎ 020-4445514; oltukai@mitsuminet.com) has two disabled-friendly cottages.

For further information about disabled travel contact the following:

Access-Able Travel Source (☎ 303-2322979; www .access-able.com; PO Box 1796, Wheatridge CO, USA)

Association for the Physically Disabled of Kenya (☎ 020-224443; apdk@iconnect.co.ke; APDK House, Lagos Rd, PO Box 46747, Nairobi) This group in Kenya may also be able to help disabled visitors.

Holiday Care (☎ 0845-1249971, minicom 0845-1249976, outside the UK 208-760072; www.holidaycare.org.uk; Sunley House, 4 Bedford Park, Croydon, Surrey CR0 2AP, UK) Advice for disabled and less-mobile senior travellers.

DISCOUNT CARDS

There's no uniformly accepted discount card scheme in Kenya, but a residence permit entitles you to claim the very favourable resident rates all over the country. Students are eligible for concessionary rates at museums and some other attractions on producing suitable ID – the international ISIC card should be widely recognised. Despite Kenyans' general respect for age and wisdom, there are no concessions or discounts for seniors.

EMBASSIES & CONSULATES

Kenya has diplomatic representation in many countries. Where there is no Kenyan embassy or high commission, visas can be obtained from the British embassy or high commission.

It's important to understand what your own embassy – the embassy of the country of which you are a citizen – can and can't do to help you if you get into trouble. Generally speaking, it won't be much help in emergencies if the trouble you're in is remotely your own fault. Remember that you are bound by the laws of the country you are in. Your embassy will not be sympathetic if you end up in jail after committing a crime locally, even if such actions are legal in your own country.

In genuine emergencies you might get some assistance, but only if other channels have been exhausted. For example, if you need to get home urgently, a free ticket home is exceedingly unlikely – the embassy would expect you to have insurance. If all your money and documents are stolen, the embassy might assist with getting a new passport, but a loan for onward travel is out of the question.

Kenyan Embassies & Consulates

Australia (☎ 02-62474788; kenrep@dynamite.com.au; QBE Bldg, 33-35 Ainslie Ave, Canberra, ACT 2601)
Austria (☎ 01-7123919; kenyarep-vienna@aon.at; Neulinggasse 29/8, 1030 Vienna)
Canada (☎ 613-5631773; www.kenyahighcommission .ca; 415 Laurier Ave, East Ottawa, Ontario, KIN 6R4)
Ethiopia (☎ 01-610033; kenya.embassy@telecom.net.et; Fikre Miriam Rd, PO Box 3301, Addis Ababa)
France (☎ 01-56622525; kenparis@wanadoo.fr; 3 Rue Freycinet, 75116 Paris)
Germany (☎ 030-25922660; embassy-kenya.bn@ wwmail.de; Markgrafenstr 63, 10969 Berlin)
India (☎ 011-26146537; www.kenyamission-delhi.com; 34 Paschimi Marg, Vasant Vihar, 10057 New Delhi)
Israel (☎ 03-57546333; kenya04@ibm.net; 15 Rehov Abba Hillel Silver, Ramat Gan 52522, PO Box 52136, Tel Aviv)
Italy (☎ 396-8082714; www.embassyofkenya.it; Via Archmede 165, 00197, Rome)
Japan (☎ 03-37234006; www.embassy-avenue.jp/kenya; 3-24-3 Yakumo, Meguro-Ku, Tokyo 152)
Netherlands (☎ 070-3504215; kenre@dataweb.nl; Niewe Parklaan 21, 2597, The Hague)
South Africa (☎ 012-3622249; kenp@pta.lia.net; 302 Brooks St, Menlo Park, 0081, Pretoria)
Sudan (☎ 011-460386; Street 3 Amarat, PO Box 8242, Khartoum)
Tanzania (☎ 022-2112955; khc@raha.com; NIC Investment House, Samora Ave, PO Box 5231, Dar es Salaam)

Uganda (☎ 041-258235; Plot No 41, Nakasero Rd, PO Box 5220, Kampala)
UK (☎ 020-76362371; www.kenyahighcommission.com; 45 Portland Pl, London W1N 4AS)
USA (☎ 202-3876101; www.kenyaembassy.com; 2249 R St NW, Washington DC 20008)

Embassies & Consulates in Kenya

Many countries around the world maintain diplomatic missions in Kenya; a selection of these is listed following. Missions are located in Nairobi (area code ☎ 020) unless otherwise stated.

Australia High Commission (Map pp98-9; ☎ 445034; www.embassy.gov.au/ke.html; ICIPE House, Riverside Dr)
Austria (Map pp102-3; ☎ 319076; nairobi-ob@bmaa .gv.at; City House, Wabera St)
Canada High Commission (☎ 3663000; www.nairobi.gc.ca; Limuru Rd)
Ethiopia (Map pp98-9; ☎ 2732050; State House Ave)
France (Map pp98-9; ☎ 316363; www.ambafrance -ke.org; Barclays Plaza, Loita St)
Germany (☎ 4262100; www.nairobi.diplo.de; 113 Riverside Dr)
India (Map pp102-3; ☎ 222566; www.nairobi.indianhighcommission.com; Jeevan Bharati Bldg, Harambee Ave)
Ireland Honorary Consulate (Map pp98-9; ☎ 556647; irconsul@swiftkenya.com; Masai Rd)
Israel (Map pp98-9; ☎ 2722182; Bishops Rd)
Italy Embassy (Map pp102-3; ☎ 319198; cooperazione@ utlnairobi.org; International Life House, Mama Ngina St); Consulate (p158; ☎ 041-314705; Jubilee Bldg, Moi Ave, Mombasa)
Japan (Map pp102-3; ☎ 315850; embjap@wananchi .com; ICEA Bldg, Kenyatta Ave)
Netherlands (☎ 4447412; Riverside Lane)
South Africa High Commission (☎ 2827100; Roshanmaer Pl, Lenana Rd)
Spain (Map pp102-3; ☎ 246009; embespke@mail.mae .es; International House, Mama Ngina St)
Sudan (Map pp98-9; ☎ 2720883; sudanemb@wananchi .com; AON-Minet Bldg, Mamlaka Rd) At the time of research, this embassy did not issue visas.
Switzerland (Map pp102-3; ☎ 228735; International House, Mama Ngina St)
Tanzania High Commission (Map pp102-3; ☎ 311948; Reinsurance Plaza, Aga Khan Walk)
Uganda High Commission (☎ 4445420; www.uganda highcommission.co.ke; Riverside Paddocks); Consular section (Map pp102-3; ☎ 311814; Uganda House, Kenyatta Ave)
UK High Commission (Map pp98-9; ☎ 2844000; www .britishhighcommission.gov.uk/kenya; Upper Hill Rd)
USA (☎ 3636000; http://nairobi.usembassy.gov; United Nations Ave)

FESTIVALS & EVENTS

Major events happening around Kenya include the following:

Maulid Festival Falling in March or April for the next few years, this annual celebration of the prophet Mohammed's birthday is a huge event in Lamu town, drawing hundreds of visitors (see p218).

Rhino Charge (www.rhinoark.org) Charity cross-country rally in aid of Rhino Ark (see p258), pitting mad motorists against crazy obstacles. Held in June.

Tusker Safari Sevens (www.safarisevens.com) International rugby tournament held every June near Nairobi (see p107).

Kenya Music Festival (☎ 020-2712964) The country's longest-running music festival (see p107), held over 10 days in August.

Mombasa Carnival (zainab@africaonline.co.ke) November street festival, with music, dance and other events (see p162).

East Africa Safari Rally (www.eastafricansafarirally .com) Classic car rally now in its 50th year, covering Kenya, Tanzania and Uganda using only pre-1971 vehicles. Held in December.

FOOD

You can eat well in Kenya, though outside the major towns variety isn't always a priority – see p92 for a full rundown of the restaurant scene. In general you should be able to snack for KSh10 to KSh100 on the street and fill up for under KSh200 in any cheap Kenyan cafeteria; an Indian or standard Western meal will cost around KSh500, a Chinese meal anything up to KSh1000, and a top-flight meal in a classy restaurant with wine and all the trimmings can easily exceed KSh2000 per person.

In this book we have organised restaurants by type of food where appropriate, for ease of reference.

GAY & LESBIAN TRAVELLERS

Even today there is still a widespread perception across Africa that homosexuality is somehow an un-African phenomenon, introduced to the continent by degenerate European colonials. It goes on covertly of course, particularly on the coast, but under Kenyan law, homosexuality is still punishable by up to 14 years in prison. There are very few prosecutions under this law, but it's certainly better to be discreet; some local conmen do a good line in blackmail, picking up foreigners then threatening to expose them to the police!

Awareness is increasing in Kenya, but with the churches exerting a hardline 'moral' stance on their followers, homosexuality continues to be frowned upon: as recently as June 2005, 98% of respondents to a national survey said that same-sex marriage was against their personal and religious principles. Only a third declared themselves totally against homosexuality in itself, but 96% said it was against their beliefs, showing just how far the Kenyan gay community still has to go to achieve equality. However, polls of this kind and calls for public debate give some hope that the issue will at least cease to become such a taboo subject over the next few years.

According to the UN, sex between gay men accounts for only 5% to 10% of HIV/ AIDS cases in Kenya. Despite the best efforts of international aid organisations, condoms are still as unpopular with Kenya's gay community as they are in heterosexual circles, and due to the secret nature of most gay relationships some men will also have unprotected sex with women who are unaware of their same-sex partners, increasing the risk factor exponentially.

Although there are probably more gays and lesbians in Nairobi, the coast is more tolerant of gay relationships, at least privately. There is now a Swahili word for gay, coined here: *msenge*. Lamu has long been considered a paradise getaway for gay couples, but it's no longer as tolerant as it once was. Memories still linger from 1999, when a couple was taken into protective custody in Lamu to shield them from an angry mob of locals opposed to their plans for a gay wedding.

The closest Kenya has to a 'scene' is the tolerant Gypsy's bar (see p117) in Westlands, Nairobi, though as of September 2005 the organisation **Gay Kenya** (www.gaykenya.com) has introduced an official bi-monthly gay night, also in Westlands – call ☎ 020-4452691 for details.

The **Purple Roofs travel directory** (www.purple roofs.com/africa/kenyata.html) lists a number of gay or gay-friendly tour companies in Kenya and around the world that may be able to help you plan your trip. For luxury all-inclusive packages, the travel agencies **Atlantis Events** (www.atlantisevents.com) and **David Tours** (www.david tours.com) can arrange anything from balloon safaris to luxurious coastal hideaways, all with a gay focus. For information, **Behind the Mask** (www.mask.org.za) is an excellent website covering gay issues and news from across Africa.

HOLIDAYS

Kenya's tribal groups have their own local festivals, but they're private affairs and you probably won't get to see them. Animal sacrifices and ritual circumcision are common events so this may not be a bad thing!

All government offices and banks close on public holidays, and most shops and businesses will either close or run according to their usual Sunday opening hours. Popular events such as Madaraka Day can cause a run on accommodation at the lower end of the budget scale, and transport may run less frequently or be more crowded than usual.

Muslim festivals are significant on the coast. Many eateries there close until after sundown during the Muslim fasting month of Ramadan, which runs from 24 September 2006, 13 September 2007 and 2 September 2008. The Maulid Festival (see p357), marking the birth of the Prophet Mohammed, is also widely celebrated, especially on Lamu. This will take place on 12 April 2006, 20 March 2007 and 20 March 2008.

Public Holidays

1 January New Year's Day
March/April Good Friday and Easter Monday
1 May Labour Day
1 June Madaraka Day
10 October Moi Day
20 October Kenyatta Day
12 December Independence Day
25 December Christmas Day
26 December Boxing Day

School Holidays

Kenyan schools run on a three-term system much like the British education establishments on which they were originally modelled, though summer vacations tend to be shorter. Holidays usually fall in April (one month), August (one month) and December (five weeks). As few Kenyan families can afford to stay in tourist hotels these holidays mostly have little impact on visitors, but more people will travel during these periods and popular public areas like the coastal beaches will be that bit more crowded.

INSURANCE

Two words: get some! A travel-insurance policy to cover theft, loss and medical problems is a very sensible precaution. The policies handled by STA Travel and other student travel organisations are usually good value. Some policies offer lower and higher medical-expense options, but the higher ones are chiefly for countries such as the USA that have extremely high medical costs. Medical cover is the most vital element of any policy, but make sure you check the small print:

- Some policies specifically exclude 'dangerous activities', which can even include motorcycling, scuba diving, even trekking. If such activities are on your agenda you'll need a proper comprehensive policy, which may be more expensive. Using a locally acquired motorcycle licence may not be valid under your policy.
- You may prefer a policy that pays doctors or hospitals direct rather than you having to pay on the spot and claim later. If you have to claim later, make sure you keep all documentation.
- Some policies ask you to call back (reverse charges) to a centre in your home country where an immediate assessment of your problem is made. Be aware that reverse-charge calls are only possible to certain countries from Kenya (see p365).
- Check that the policy covers ambulances or an emergency flight home. If you have to stretch out on public transport you will need two seats and somebody has to pay for them!
- If you are travelling in remote areas, check with your insurance company that you can contact the Flying Doctors Service (see below) or AAR Health Services (see opposite) direct in the event of a serious emergency without having to confirm it with your company at home first.

If you are travelling through Africa for some time or heading to the more remote corners of Kenya, it may be worth signing up with either the Flying Doctors Service or AAR Health Services. These two organisations can come and get you should you become ill in a *lugga* (dry river bed) west of North Horr or in another remote area.

The **Flying Doctors Service** (☎ 020-602495 emergency 020-315454; www.amref.org) is part of the African Medical and Research Foundation (Amref) and operates a 24-hour air-ambulance service out of Nairobi's Wilson Airport. It will get you from wherever you are to the nearest decent hospital (often Nairobi). Tourist cover costs US$25 for two months within 500km of Nairobi and US$50 within 1000km.

The private **AAR Health Services** (Map pp98-9; ☎ 020-2715319, emergency 020-271737; www.aarhealth .com; Fourth Ngong Rd, Nairobi) is a comprehensive medical network that covers Kenya, Tanzania and Uganda and offers a road and local service as well as emergency air evacuation to any suitable medical facility in East Africa. Tourist cover starts at US$100.

INTERNET ACCESS

Email is firmly established in Kenya, although connection speeds fluctuate wildly, even in Nairobi. Most towns have at least one Internet café where you can surf freely and access Hotmail, Yahoo! and any other webmail accounts; instant messenger programmes such as Yahoo! and MSN are also very popular locally and are installed on many public machines. In Nairobi or Mombasa, you can pay as little as KSh1 per minute for access, but in rural areas and top-end hotels, the rate can be as high as KSh20 per minute.

With the increasing popularity of Internet cafés, the national Posta network has stepped in and virtually revolutionised the industry by offering Internet access at almost every main post office in the country. The real beauty of this is that every branch charges the same fixed rate of KSh1.16 per minute (KSh1 plus VAT). It's run on a pre-pay system – you pay KSh100 for a card with a PIN code, which you can then use to log in at any branch as often as you like until the money runs out. While the service can't often compete with the flashier private offices in big cities like Nairobi and Mombasa, it's well worth investigating if you're further afield.

If you're travelling with a notebook or hand-held computer, plenty of top-end hotels have ethernet connections or dataports in the rooms, and some have even embraced wi-fi. However, you should be aware that your modem may not work once you leave your home country – for more information, see www.teleadapt.com. In any case, unless

you've got important work to do carrying a laptop around can be more trouble than it's worth in Kenya, and with street crime what it is we'd generally recommend leaving expensive bits of kit like this at home.

LEGAL MATTERS

All drugs except *miraa* (a leafy shoot with amphetamine-like effects) are illegal in Kenya. Marijuana (commonly known as *bhang*) is widely available but highly illegal, and possession carries a penalty of up to 10 years in prison. Dealers are common on the beaches north and south of Mombasa and frequently set up travellers for sting operations for real or phoney cops to extort money.

African prisons are unbelievably harsh places; don't take the risk. Note that *miraa* is illegal in Tanzania, so if you do develop a taste for the stuff in Kenya you should leave it behind when heading south.

Rape laws in Kenya currently only protect women, though if the new Sexual Offences Bill being proposed at the time of writing is passed sexual assaults on both men and women will be criminal offences.

Another bill in the pipeline at the time of writing is the Tobacco Control Bill, which if passed will ban smoking in public places throughout the country – Uganda and Tanzania have both introduced similar laws. The only exception is the burning of dry tobacco leaves to scare off elephants!

MAPS

Bookshops, especially the larger ones in Nairobi, are the best places to look for maps in Kenya. The *Tourist Map of Kenya* gives good detail, as does the *Kenya Route Map;* both cost around KSh250. Marco Polo's 1:1,000,000 *Shell Euro Karte Kenya* and Geocenter's *Kenya* (1:1,000,000) are useful overview maps that are widely available in Europe. The scale and clarity are very good, but the location of some minor features are inaccurate. For those planning a longer trip in Southern and East Africa, Michelin's 1:4,000,000 map 955 (Africa Central and South) is very useful.

Macmillan publishes a series of maps to the wildlife parks and these are not bad value at around KSh250 each (three are available in Europe – *Amboseli*, *Masai Mara* and *Tsavo East & West*). Tourist Maps also publishes a national park series for roughly the same price. They might look a bit flimsy on detail, but they include the numbered junctions in the national parks.

The most detailed and thorough maps are published by the Survey of Kenya, but the majority are out of date and many are also out of print. The better bookshops in Nairobi usually have copies of the most important maps, including *Amboseli National Park* (SK 87), *Masai Mara Game Reserve* (SK 86), *Meru National Park* (SK 65), *Tsavo East National Park* (SK 82) and *Tsavo West National Park* (SK 78). It may be worth a visit to the **Kenya Institute of Surveying & Mapping** (☎ 020-8561486; http://kism.iconnect.co.ke; Thika Rd, Nairobi), but this can take all day and there's no guarantee it will have any more stock than the bookshops.

MONEY

The unit of currency is the Kenyan shilling (KSh), which is made up of 100 cents. Notes in circulation are KSh1000, 500, 200, 100, 50 and 20, and there are also new coins of KSh40, 20, 10, five and one in circulation. Old coins are much bigger and heavier, and come in denominations of KSh5 (seven-sided) and KSh1. The old 50¢, 10¢ and 5¢ coins are now pretty rare, as most prices are whole-shilling amounts. Note that most public telephones accept only new coins. Locally, the shilling is commonly known as a 'bob', after the old English term for a one-shilling coin.

The shilling has been relatively stable over the last few years, maintaining fairly constant rates against a falling US dollar and a strong British pound. Both these currencies are easy to change throughout the country, as is the euro, which is rapidly replacing the dollar as the standard currency quoted for hotel prices on the coast. Cash is easy and quick to exchange at banks and forex bureaus but carries a higher risk of theft, while travellers cheques are replaceable but not as

widely accepted and often carry high commission charges. Carrying a combination of these and a Visa ATM card will ensure you're never stuck for cash.

See p354 for information on security, p15 for information on costs, and the Quick Reference section (inside front cover) for exchange rates.

ATMs

Virtually all banks in Kenya now have ATMs at most branches, but their usefulness to travellers varies widely. Barclays Bank has easily the most reliable machines for international withdrawals, with a large network of ATMs covering most major Kenyan towns. They support MasterCard, Visa, Plus and Cirrus international networks.

Standard Chartered and Kenya Commercial Bank ATMs also accept Visa but not the other major providers, and are more likely to decline transactions. Whichever bank you use, the international data link still goes down occasionally, so don't rely on being able to withdraw money whenever you need it.

Black Market

With deregulation, the black market has almost vanished and the handful of money-changers who still wander the streets offering 'good rates' are usually involved in scams of one kind or another. The exception is at land border crossings, where moneychangers are often the only option. Most offer reasonable rates, although you should be careful not to get short-changed or scammed during any transaction.

Cash

While most major currencies are accepted in Nairobi and Mombasa, once away from these two centres you'll run into problems with currencies other than US dollars, pounds sterling and euros. Away from the coast, you may even struggle to change euros. Play it safe and carry US dollars – it makes life much simpler.

Credit Cards

Credit cards are becoming increasingly popular, with old fraud-friendly, fully manual swipe machines slowly being replaced by electronic systems that dial up for every transaction. While there's less chance of someone making extra copies of chits this way, the connections fail with tedious regularity. Visa and MasterCard are now widely accepted, but it would be prudent to stick to up-market hotels, restaurants and shopping centres to use them.

Be aware that credit-card companies will not post cards to Kenya, so you'll have to arrange a courier.

Moneychangers

The best places to change money are foreign exchange or 'forex' bureaus, which can be found everywhere and usually don't charge commission. The rates for the main bureaus in Nairobi are published in the *Daily Nation* newspaper. Watch out for differing small bill (US$10) and large bill (US$100) rates; the larger bills usually get the better rates.

Banks also change money, but they charge large commissions and there's a fee per travellers cheque, so you're better off carrying larger denominations. The rates for travellers cheques may be better than at the bureaus, and you'll have the added bonus of being able to put your money away in the secure setting of the bank foyer. American Express (AmEx) has offices in Mombasa and Nairobi, where you can buy and sell AmEx travellers cheques.

INTERNATIONAL TRANSFERS

Postbank, a branch of the Kenyan Post Office, is the regional agent for Western Union, the global money-transfer company. Using its service is an easy way (if the phones are working) of receiving money in Kenya. Handily, the sender pays all the charges and there's a Postbank in most towns, often in the post office or close by. Senders should contact **Western Union** (USA ☎ 1800-3256000; Australia ☎ 1800-501500; New Zealand ☎ 0800-270000; UK ☎ 0800-833833; www.westernunion.com) to find out the location of their nearest agency.

Tipping

Tipping is not common practice among Kenyans, but there's no harm in rounding up the bill by a few shillings if you're pleased with the service in a cheap restaurant. In tourist-oriented businesses a service charge of 10% is often added to the bill along with the 16% VAT and 2% catering levy. Most tourist guides and all safari drivers and cooks will expect some kind of gratuity at the end of your tour or trip – see p62. As fares are

negotiated in advance, taxi drivers do not need to be tipped unless they provide you with exceptional service.

Travellers Cheques

Travellers cheques are most widely accepted if they're in US dollars, British pounds or euros. High commission charges are common, and bureaus that charge no commission will often give a rate substantially below the cash rate for cheques.

PHOTOGRAPHY & VIDEO

Photographing people remains a sensitive issue in Kenya. Some tribal groups request money for you to take their photo.

You should never get your camera out at border crossings or near government or army buildings; even bridges can sometimes be classed as sensitive areas.

Film & Equipment

You'll find Kodak and Fuji 100, 200 and 400 ASA (ISO) print and slide film widely available in Nairobi, but even 100 ISO slide film is hard to find in Mombasa. If you plan to use 64 or 800 ASA film, bring it from home. As an indication of price, 36-exposure slide film in Nairobi costs about KSh400; 36-exposure colour print film is cheaper at KSh250 to KSh350 but again, only 100, 200 and (less frequently) 400 ASA are available. Watch out for out-of-date batches.

Both VHS and Hi-8 video film is available in Nairobi and Mombasa, but it's relatively expensive. You may also be able to find memory cards and other accessories for digital and DV cameras, but again prices are high and quality is not guaranteed.

If you don't have the inclination or resources to buy expensive equipment but do know a bit about photography, it is possible to hire SLR cameras and lenses in Nairobi (see p100).

Film Processing

Shops and booths offering film processing are popping up in small towns and villages all over Kenya. In addition, there are plenty of one-hour film-processing labs in Nairobi, and at least one in all other major towns. They can handle any film speeds, but results can vary. Depending on the print size, processing and printing costs about KSh480 to KSh650 for a 36-exposure film.

E6 slide processing can only be done in Nairobi and costs around KSh450 for a 36-exposure film.

Taking Pictures

As the natural light in Kenya can be extremely strong, morning and evening are the best times to take photos. A plain UV filter can also be a good idea to take the harshness out of daylight pictures.

For serious wildlife photography an SLR camera that can take long focal length lenses is necessary. Zoom lenses are best for wildlife photography as it's easier to frame your shot for the best composition. This is especially important because the animals are almost constantly on the move. The 70mm to 210mm zoom lenses are popular, and 200mm is really the absolute minimum power you'll need to get good close-up shots. The only problem with zoom lenses is that they absorb about 1.5 f-stops of light, which is where 200 and 400 ASA film starts to become useful.

Telephoto (fixed focal length) lenses give better results than zoom lenses, but you're limited by having to carry a separate lens for every focal length. A 400mm or 500mm lens brings the action right up close, but again you need fast film to make the most of it. Another option is to carry a 2x teleconverter, a small adaptor that doubles the focal length of your lens.

When using long lenses you'll find that a tripod can be extremely useful, and with any lense greater than about 300mm it's a necessity. Within the confined space of the hatch of a safari minibus, you may be better off with a folding miniature tripod, which you can then rest on the roof. Remember to ask your driver to switch off the engine to avoid vibrations affecting your photo. If you've got a large lens but no tripod, lying your camera on a small beanbag or cushion can help reduce camera shake.

A decent bag is essential to protect your gear from the elements and the rough roads – safari dust gets everywhere, particularly in parks like Samburu and Tsavo. It's also vital to make sure that your travel insurance policy covers your camera gear should it get stolen.

For more pointers on taking pictures in Africa and elsewhere, look out for Lonely Planet's *Travel Photography* book.

POST

The Kenyan postal system is run by the government Postal Corporation of Kenya, now rebranded as the dynamic-sounding **Posta** (www.posta.co.ke). Letters sent from Kenya rarely go astray but can take up to two weeks to reach Australia or the USA. Incoming letters to Kenya take anywhere from four days to a week to reach the poste-restante service in Nairobi.

Postal Rates

The airmail rates (in KSh) for items posted from Kenya are:

Item	East Africa	Europe	USA & Australia
letter	55	75	95
small postcard	30	40	55
large postcard	55	75	95
aerogram	35	45	45

Note that there are different prices for large and small postcards – if in doubt, go with the large postcard price.

Parcels

If sent by surface mail, parcels take three to six months to reach Europe, while airmail parcels take around a week. As a rough guide, a 1kg parcel sent by air/surface mail would cost KSh1160/940 to East Africa, KSh1270/1030 to Europe and KSh1330/1070 to the rest of the world.

Most things arrive eventually, although there is still a problem with theft within the system. Curios, clothes and textiles will be OK, but if your parcel contains anything of obvious value, send it by courier. Posta has its own courier service, EMS, which is considerably cheaper than the big international courier companies. The best place to send parcels from is the main post office in Nairobi (see p100).

Receiving Mail

Letters can be sent care of poste restante in any town. Make sure your correspondents write your name in block capitals and also underline the surname.

Some travellers use the **American Express Clients Mail Service** (Nairobi Map pp102-3; ☎ 020-222906; Express Kenya Ltd, PO Box 40433, Hilton Hotel, Mama Ngina St; Mombasa ☎ 041-315405; Nairobi Express

Kenya Ltd, PO Box 90631, Nkrumah Rd) and this can be a useful, and more reliable, alternative. You'll need to have an AmEx card or be using its travellers cheques to avail yourself of this service.

SENIOR TRAVELLERS

Although there are no tour companies set up specifically for senior travellers, the more expensive tours cater well to seniors' requests and requirements. Before you book, ask the operator what they can do to help make your trip possible and comfortable. The luxury-tour and safari business is well used to older travellers, and wildlife drives and other safari activities are great for older people. One company with a good reputation for catering to seniors is **Eastern & Southern Safaris** (Map pp102-3; ☎ 020-242828; www.essafari.co.ke; Finance House, Loita St, PO Box 43332, Nairobi).

You may be able to find other senior-friendly companies on the website of **Wired Seniors** (www.wiredseniors.com), which has travel links from around the world. It's also worth contacting **Holiday Care** (☎ 0845-1249971; www .holidaycare.org.uk), a UK organisation providing advice for travellers of all ages with mobility or health problems.

SHOPPING

Kenya is an excellent place for souvenirs, although much of the cheap stuff is mass-produced for the tourist trade. Look carefully at what's available before parting with your money. It is illegal to export some wildlife products (see p353).

Nairobi and Mombasa are the main souvenir centres, but many of the items come from other regions, so it's often possible to pick them up where they are made. Many top-end hotels have their own stalls or stores and there are dozens of souvenir shops at the airport, but prices are extremely high compared with the rest of the country, and it's better (and more fun) to spend some time shopping around.

It's certainly possible to buy something that will look good in your living room without spending a fortune, but, these days, something of genuine quality and artistry is going to cost real money. This particularly applies to *makonde* carvings, jewellery and paintings. In some cases, you can be talking about thousands of US dollars for a single piece.

Posting things of small value home is usually straightforward and secure (for details, see opposite).

Bargaining

Haggling is a way of life in Kenya, and prices for everything from taxi fares to hotel rooms may be negotiable. While quibbling over the price of a few bananas is probably going too far, souvenir shopping is one area where you should hold out for the best price. Do plenty of prior research, so you have a clear idea of what an item should cost and how much you're willing to pay before you set foot in the shop you want to buy from. Looking in the more expensive fixed-price outlets is a good way of checking what the real quality items should look like.

When it comes to agreeing on a price, never agree to the first amount offered, but try not to pitch your own first offer too low – this will just make you look clueless about the item's real value and force you to come up in larger increments than they come down. Once you've reached your desired price, however, stick to your guns and don't go over it unless they really don't seem to be budging. Remember, they will never sell for a loss, and you can always walk away rather than over-pay. Above all, keep it light: Kenyans bargaining among themselves may look like they're arguing, but as a visitor it's much better to stay friendly, avoid antagonism and feel good about the process whatever the outcome.

Local people are occasionally willing to swap their handicrafts for Western clothing, shoes and the like, but it's important to remember that most Kenyans need your money more than an old T-shirt – paying a fair price can make a real difference to the lives of villagers whose only income comes from selling goods to tourists. Keep this in mind when arguing over a few cents.

Baskets

Kiondos (sisal baskets) are an extremely popular Kenyan souvenir. They come in a variety of sizes, colours and configurations with many different straps and clasps. Expect to pay around US$2 for a basic basket, and up to US$10 for a large one with leather trim. Some of the finer baskets have baobab bark woven into them and this bumps up the price considerably. Reed baskets, widely used as shopping bags, cost less than KSh50.

Fabrics & Batik

Kangas and *kikois* are the local sarongs and serve many purposes. *Kangas* are colourful prints on thin cotton that are sold in pairs, one to wrap around your waist and one to carry a baby on your back. Each bears a Swahili proverb. Biashara St in Mombasa is the *kanga* centre in Kenya, and you'll pay upwards of KSh350 for a pair, depending on quality. *Kikois,* traditionally worn by men, are made with a thicker, striped cotton and are simpler and more colourful. They are originally from Lamu and this is still the best place to buy them; prices start at around KSh350 each, more for the thicker Somali fabrics.

Batik cloth is another good buy and there's a tremendous range, but the better prints are not cheap. The tradition was imported from elsewhere. You can expect to pay KSh500 and upwards for batiks on cotton, and thousands of shillings for batiks on silk.

Jewellery

Most jewellery on sale in Kenya is of tribal origin, although very little is the genuine article. The colourful Maasai beaded jewellery is the most striking and the most popular, and is very distinctive. Necklaces, bangles and wristlets are widely available and beadwork is used on all sorts of knick-knacks, from hair-slides to wallets. Prices are high, but there's lots of work involved in making them. None of the 'elephant hair' bracelets sold by hawkers in Nairobi are the real thing – most are simply plastic wire or reed grass covered in boot polish.

Soapstone

Easily carved soapstone is used to make popular chess sets, ashtrays and even abstract organic-looking sculptures. Kisumu on Lake Victoria is the best place to buy, although soapstone souvenirs are sold and produced across the country, most notably in Kisii. The only problem is that soapstone is quite fragile and heavy to carry around.

Tribal Souvenirs

Traditional tribal objects are very popular. Spears are particularly sought-after and come apart into several sections, making them easy to transport. Like the painted leather shields, most are mass-produced for the tourist market. Turkana wrist knives and Maasai knives forged from car shock absorbers are also high-kudos souvenirs.

Decorated Maasai calabashes, traditionally used to store *mursik,* a type of drink (see p93), are eye-catching but tend to pong a bit. All sorts of masks are available, although few are used in rituals today. The three-legged African stool is another very popular souvenir, and *shukas* (Maasai blankets) and shoes made from old car tyres are cheap, unusual souvenirs.

Woodcarvings

These are easily the most popular Kenyan souvenir; a painted wooden giraffe is an instant marker of a trip to East Africa. Much of the stuff on offer is of dubious taste, but there is some very fine work available. The most famous woodcarvings found here are the *makonde*-style effigies (made by the Akamba people from around the Tanzanian border), which are traditionally carved from ebony, a very black, heavy wood. They often feature wildlife, towers of thin figures and slender Maasai figurines. However, be aware that ebony is a threatened wood (see p57).

If possible, buy from one of the many nonprofit handicraft cooperatives around the country rather than souvenir shops; these people need all the help they can get. Heavy bargaining is necessary if you buy from market stalls or tourist shops. You can pay anything from KSh200 up to hundreds of US dollars for a large and intricate piece.

SOLO TRAVELLERS

The issues facing solo travellers in Kenya are essentially the same as anywhere else in the world. The biggest drawbacks are not having anyone to watch your back or your bags on the road, and the price of safaris and organised activities, which generally means you have to join a group to make any kind of trip affordable. Advantages include freedom of movement (just try flagging down a matatu when there's eight of you) and a whole different level of contact with local people.

On the whole men will find travelling alone easier than women, as the level of day-to-day harassment is generally less for males, especially on the coast. However, lone female travellers are sometimes 'adopted' by local women in a way that seldom happens to men.

TELEPHONE

The Kenyan fixed-line phone system, run by **Telkom Kenya** (www.telkom.co.ke), is more or less functional, but has been overtaken by the massive popularity of prepaid mobile phones – there are now 2.1 million mobile subscribers in the country, compared with just 127,000 in 2000!

International call rates from Kenya have come down recently, but are still relatively expensive, charged at a flat rate of US90¢ per minute in peak times and US64¢ per minute off-peak to any destination. Operator-assisted calls are charged at the standard peak rate but are subject to a three-minute minimum. You can always dial direct using a phone card. All phones should be able to receive incoming calls (the number is usually scrawled in the booth somewhere).

Calls made through a hotel operator from your room will cost an extra 25% to 50% so check before making a call.

Reverse-charge (collect) calls are possible, but only to countries that have set up free direct-dial numbers allowing you to reach the international operator in the country you are calling. Currently these countries include: the **UK** (☎ 0800-220441), the **USA** (☎ 0800-111, 0800-1112), **Canada** (☎ 0800-220114, 0800-220115), **New Zealand** (☎ 0800-220641) and **Switzerland** (☎ 0800-220411).

The minimum charge for a local call from a payphone is KSh5 for 97 seconds, while long-distance rates vary depending on the distance. When making a local call from a public phone, make sure you put a coin into the slot first. Calls to Tanzania and Uganda are priced as long-distance calls, not international.

For the international dialling code, see the inside front cover of this book.

Mobile Phones

An estimated 80% of all calls here are now made on mobile phones, and coverage is good in all but the furthest rural areas. Kenya uses the GSM 900 system, which is compatible with Europe and Australia but not with the North American GSM 1900 system. If you have a GSM phone, check with your service provider about using it in Kenya, and beware of high roaming charges. Remember that you will generally be charged for receiving calls abroad as well as for making them.

Alternatively, if your phone isn't locked into a network, you can pick up a prepaid starter pack from one of the Kenyan mobile-phone companies – the main players are **Safaricom** (www.safaricom.co.ke) and **Celtel** (www.ke.celtel.com). A SIM card costs about KSh100, and you can then buy top-up 'scratchcards' from shops and booths across the country. Cards come in denominations of KSh100 to KSh2000; an international SMS costs around KSh10, and voice charges vary according to tariff, time and destination of call.

You can easily buy a handset anywhere in Kenya, generally unlocked and with SIM card. Prices start around KSh2500 for a very basic model.

Phone cards

With the new Telkom Kenya phone cards, any phone can now be used for prepaid calls – you just have to dial the **access number** (☎ 0844) and enter in the number and passcode on the card. There are booths selling the cards all over the country. Cards come in the following denominations of KSh200, KSh500, KSh1000 and KSh2000, and call charges are slightly more expensive than for standard lines (peak/off peak US$1/70¢).

TIME

Time in Kenya is GMT/UTC plus three hours year-round. You should also be aware of the concept of 'Swahili time', which perversely is six hours out of kilter with the rest of the world. Noon and midnight are 6 o'clock *(saa sitta)* Swahili time, and 7am and 7pm are 1 o'clock *(saa moja)*. Just add or subtract six hours from whatever time you are told; Swahili doesn't distinguish between am and pm. You don't come across this often unless you speak Swahili, but you still need to be prepared for it.

TOILETS

These vary from pits (quite literally) to full-flush, luxury conveniences that can spring up in the most unlikely places. Nearly all hotels sport flushable sit-down toilets, but seats are a rare commodity – either they're a prized souvenir for trophy hunters or there's a vast stockpile of lost lids somewhere… Public toilets in towns are almost equally rare, but there are a few less-than-emetic pay conveniences in Nairobi if you've only got a penny to spend.

In the more up-market bush camps you'll be confronted with a long drop covered with some sort of seating arrangement. The best of these is in Tusk Camp high in the Aberdare National Park – you'll have a view across the forest to Mt Kenya. Things are less pleasant when camping in the wildlife parks. Squatting on crumbling concrete is common. When trekking it's good practice to take soiled toilet paper out of the park with you (consider carrying sealable bags for this purpose).

TOURIST INFORMATION
Local Tourist Offices
Considering the extent to which the country relies on tourism, it's incredible to think that, at the time of writing, there was still no tourist office in Nairobi. There are a handful of information offices elsewhere in the country, ranging from helpful private concerns to underfunded government offices; most can at least provide basic maps of the town and brochures on local businesses and attractions.

Diani Beach (Map p171; ☎ 040-3202234; Barclays Centre)

Lamu (Map p214; ☎ 042-633449; off Kenyatta Rd)

Malindi (Map p206; ☎ 042-20689; Malindi Centre, Lamu Rd)

Mombasa (Map p155; ☎ 041-225428; mcta@ikenya .com; Moi Ave)

Tourist Offices Abroad
The Ministry of Tourism maintains a number of overseas offices. Most only provide information by telephone, post or email.

Canada (☎ 905-8913909; www.kcocanada.org; 1599 Hurontario St, Suite 100, Mississauga, Ontario, L5G 4S1)

Germany (☎ 089-23662194; think@magnum.de; c/o The Magnum Group, Herzogspitalstrade 5, D-80331 Munich)

Italy (☎ 02-48102361; kenya@adams.it; c/o Adam & Partner Italia, Via Salaino 12, 20144 Milano)

Netherlands (☎ 020-4212668; kenia@travelmc.com; Leliegracht 20, 1015 DG Amsterdam)

Spain (☎ 93-2920655; kenya@ketal.com; c/o Tuset 10, 304a, 08006 Barcelona)

UK (☎ 020-78367738; kenya@iiuk.co.uk; 69 Monmouth St, London WC2H 9JW)

USA (☎ 1-866-44-53692; infousa@magicalkenya.com; Carlson Destination Marketing Services, PO Box 59159 Minneapolis, MN 55459-8257)

VISAS
Visas are now required by almost all visitors to Kenya, including Europeans, Australians, New Zealanders, Americans and Canadians, although citizens from a few smaller Commonwealth countries are exempt. Visas are valid for three months from the date of entry and can be obtained on arrival at Jomo Kenyatta International Airport in Nairobi. The visa fee is UK£35 or US$50 for a single-entry visa, and UK£70 or US$100 for multiple entries. If you have any other currencies, you'll have to change them into shillings and then back into dollars. Tourist visas can be extended for a further three-month period – see below – but seven-day transit visas (US$20) cannot.

It's also possible to get visas from Kenyan diplomatic missions overseas, but you should apply well in advance, especially if you're doing it by mail. Visas are usually valid for entry within three months of the date of issue. Applications for Kenyan visas are simple and straightforward in Tanzania and Uganda, and payment is accepted in local currency. Visas can also be issued on arrival at the land borders with Uganda and Tanzania.

Under the East African partnership system, visiting Tanzania or Uganda and returning to Kenya does not invalidate a single-entry Kenyan visa, so there's no need to get a multiple-entry visa unless you plan to go further afield. The same applies to single-entry Tanzanian and Ugandan visas, though you do still need a separate visa for each country you plan to visit. Always check the latest entry requirements with embassies before travel.

It's always best to smarten up a bit if you're arriving by air; requests for evidence of 'sufficient funds' are usually linked to snap judgments about your appearance. If it's fairly obvious that you aren't intending to stay and work, you'll generally be given the benefit of the doubt.

For information on visas for longer-term stays, see p353 and opposite in this chapter.

Visa Extensions
Visas can be renewed at immigration offices during normal office hours, and extensions are usually issued on a same-day basis. Staff at the immigration offices are generally friendly and helpful, but the process takes a while. You'll need two passport photos and KSh2200 for a three-month extension. You also need to fill out a form registering as an alien if you're going to be staying more than

90 days. Immigration offices are only open Monday to Friday; note that the smaller offices may sometimes refer travellers back to Nairobi or Mombasa for visa extensions.

Local immigration offices include the following:

Kisumu (Map p292; Reinsurance Plaza, cnr Jomo Kenyatta Hwy & Oginga Odinga Rd)

Lamu (Map p214; ☎ 042-633032; off Kenyatta Rd)

Malindi (Map p206; ☎ 042-30876; Mama Ngina Rd)

Mombasa (Map p155; ☎ 041-311745; Uhuru ni Kari Bldg, Mama Ngina Dr)

Nairobi (Map pp102-3; ☎ 020-222022; Nyayo House, cnr Kenyatta Ave & Uhuru Hwy)

Visas for Onward Travel

Since Nairobi is a common gateway city to East Africa and the city centre is easy to get around, many travellers spend some time here picking up visas for other countries that they intend to visit. If you are going to do this you need to plan ahead of time and call the embassy to confirm the hours that visa applications are received (these change frequently in Nairobi). Most embassies will want you to pay visa fees in US dollars (see p356 for contact details).

Just because a country has an embassy or consulate here, it doesn't necessarily mean you can get that country's visa. The borders with Somalia and Sudan are both closed, so you'll have to go to Addis Ababa in Ethiopia if you want a Sudanese visa, and Somali visas are unlikely to be available for the foreseeable future.

For Ethiopia, Tanzania and Uganda, three-month visas are readily available in Nairobi and cost US$50 for most nationalities. Two passport photos are required for applications and visas can usually be issued the same day.

WOMEN TRAVELLERS

Within Kenyan society, women are poorly represented in positions of power, and the few high-profile women in politics run the same risks of violence as their male counterparts. However, in their day-to-day lives, Kenyans are generally respectful towards women, although white women in bars will attract a lot of interest from would-be suitors. Most are just having a go and will give up if you tell them you aren't interested. The only place you are likely to have problems is at the beach resorts on the coast, where women may be approached by male prostitutes as well as local romeos. It's always best to cover your legs and shoulders when away from the beach so as not to offend local sensibilities.

With the upsurge in crime in Nairobi and along the coast, women should avoid walking around at night. The ugly fact is that while men are likely just to be robbed without violence, rape is a real risk for women. Lone night walks along the beach or through quiet city streets are a recipe for disaster, and criminals usually work in gangs, so take a cab, even if you're in a group.

Regrettably, black women in the company of white men are often assumed to be prostitutes, and can face all kinds of discrimination from hotels and security guards as well as approaches from Kenyan hustlers offering to help rip off the white 'customer'. Again, the worst of this can be avoided by taking taxis between hotels and restaurants etc.

WORK

It's difficult, although by no means impossible, for foreigners to find jobs. The most likely areas in which employment might be found are in the safari business, teaching, advertising and journalism. Except for teaching, it's unlikely you'll see jobs advertised, and the only way you'll find out about them is to spend a lot of time with resident expats. As in most countries, the rule is that if an African can be found to do the job, there's no need to hire a foreigner.

The most fruitful area in which to look for work, assuming that you have the relevant skills, is the 'disaster industry'. Nairobi is awash with UN and other aid agencies servicing the famines in Somalia and southern Sudan and the refugee camps along the Kenyan border with those countries. Keep in mind that the work is tough and often dangerous, and pay is usually very low.

Work permits and resident visas are not easy to arrange. A prospective employer may be able to sort the necessary paperwork for you, but otherwise you'll find yourself spending a lot of time and money at the **immigration office** (Map pp102-3; ☎ 020-222022; Nyayo House, cnr Kenyatta Ave & Uhuru Hwy, Nairobi) in Nairobi.

Voluntary Conservation & Development Work

Taita Discovery Centre (☎ 020-331191; www.savannah camps.com) in Nairobi is a conservation-based offshoot of Savannah Camps & Lodges. This purpose-built conservation research centre covers 68,000 hectares of the Taita and Rukinga ranches near Tsavo West National Park and forms a vital migration corridor for elephants and other animals between Tsavo and Mt Kilimanjaro.

Courses on a huge range of conservation topics are run here along with hands-on projects in conservation and the local community. However, doing good work doesn't come cheap. The cost is US$207 per week for a minimum of four weeks, and you'll have to make your own arrangements for getting to the sanctuary, or take a package from Nairobi or Mombasa that includes flying doctor membership (US$148 return).

Another good organisation is **Kenya Youth Voluntary Development Projects** (☎ 020-225379; kvdakenya@yahoo.com; Gilfillan House, Kenyatta Ave, PO Box 48902, Nairobi). A variety of three- to four-week projects are available, including road building, health education and clinic construction. There's a US$200 registration fee and camping accommodation is provided.

Inter-Community Development Involvement (ICODEI; ☎ 0337-30017; www.volunteerkenya.org; Reverend Reuben Lubanga, PO Box 459, Bungoma), run in conjunction with the University of Indiana in the USA, offers a number of longer community projects focusing on health issues such as AIDS awareness, agriculture and conservation. The cost is US$1300 for the first month and US$120 per extra week. This includes a three-day Masai Mara safari.

The Colobus Trust (p173), at Diani Beach, and the Elsamere Conservation Centre (p234), on Lake Naivasha, also take paying volunteers.

Foreign organisations can also assist with volunteer work. Reliable bodies include the following:

Coordinating Committee for International Voluntary Service (www.unesco.org/ccivs)
Global Volunteers (www.globalvolunteers.org)
Voluntary Service Overseas (VSO; ☎ 020-8780 2266; www.vso.org.uk; 317 Putney Bridge Rd, London SW15 2PN) Placements for professionals.
Volunteer Work Information Service (www.working abroad.com)

Transport

CONTENTS

Getting There & Away	**369**
Entering the Country	369
Air	369
Land	373
Sea & Lake	375
Tours	375
Getting Around	**376**
Air	376
Bicycle	376
Boat	377
Bus	377
Car & Motorcycle	378
Hitching	382
Local Transport	382
Safaris	384
Train	384

GETTING THERE & AWAY

Unless you are travelling overland from Southern Africa or Egypt, flying is by far the most convenient way to get to Kenya. Nairobi is a major African hub and flights between Kenya and the rest of Africa are common and relatively cheap. It's important to note that flight availability and prices are highly seasonal. Conveniently for Europeans, the cheapest fares usually coincide with the European summer holidays, from June to September. An economy return ticket from London can be about UK£400, but during December and January prices soar and availability plummets.

It's also worth checking out cheap charter flights to Mombasa from Europe, although these will probably be part of a package deal to a hotel resort on the coast. Prices are often absurdly cheap and there's no obligation to stay at the resort you're booked into.

A few adventurous and resourceful souls with their own vehicles still travel overland to Kenya from Europe, but most routes pass through several war zones and should only be considered after some serious planning and preparation.

THINGS CHANGE...

The information in this chapter is particularly vulnerable to change. Check directly with the airline or a travel agent to make sure you understand how a fare (and ticket you may buy) works and be aware of the security requirements for international travel. Shop carefully. The details given in this chapter should be regarded as pointers and are not a substitute for your own careful, up-to-date research.

ENTERING THE COUNTRY

Entering Kenya is generally pleasingly straightforward, particularly at the international airports, which are no different from most Western terminals. Visas are typically available on arrival for most nationalities (passport photos required), but you should contact your nearest Kenyan diplomatic office to get the most up-to-date information. Exchange offices or moneychangers are always present and visa fees can be paid in local currency or US dollars.

Passport

There are no restrictions on which nationalities can enter Kenya. Citizens of Tanzania, Uganda, Scandinavia, the Republic of Ireland, Rwanda, Sudan and certain Commonwealth countries did not require visas at time of writing – see p366 and check the latest situation before travelling.

AIR
Airports & Airlines

Most international flights to and from Nairobi are handled by **Jomo Kenyatta International Airport** (NBO; ☎ 020-825400; www.kenyaairports .co.ke), 15km southeast of the city. By African standards it's a pretty well-organised place, with two international terminals, a smaller domestic terminal and an incredible number of shops offering duty free and expensive souvenirs, snacks and Internet access. You can walk easily between the terminals.

Some flights between Nairobi and Kilimanjaro International Airport or Mwanza in Tanzania, as well as many domestic flights, use **Wilson Airport** (WIL; ☎ 020-603260), which is about 6km south of the city centre on Langata Rd. The other arrival point in the country is **Moi International Airport** (MBA; ☎ 041-433211) in Mombasa, 9km west of the centre, but apart from flights to Zanzibar this is mainly used by charter airlines and domestic flights.

Kenya Airways is the main national carrier and has a generally good safety record, with just one fatal incident since 1977.

The following are airlines flying to and from Kenya, with offices in Nairobi except where otherwise indicated:

African Express Airways (3P; ☎ 020-824333; hub Wilson Airport, Nairobi)

Air India (AI; Map pp102-3; ☎ 020-340925; www.airindia .com; hub Mumbai)

Air Madagascar (MD; ☎ 020-225286; www.airmada gascar.mg; hub Antananarivo)

Air Malawi (QM; ☎ 020-240965; www.airmalawi.net; hub Lilongwe)

Air Mauritius (MK; ☎ 020-229166; www.airmauritius .com; hub Mauritius)

Air Zimbabwe (UM; ☎ 020-339522; www.airzim.co.zw; hub Harare)

Airkenya (QP; ☎ 020-605745; www.airkenya.com; hub Wilson Airport, Nairobi) Kilimanjaro only.

British Airways (BA; Map pp102-3; ☎ 020-244430; www.british-airways.com; hub Heathrow Airport, London)

Daallo Airlines (D3; ☎ 020-317318; www.daallo.com; hub Hargeisa)

Egypt Air (MS; Map pp102-3; ☎ 020-226821; www .egyptair.com.eg; hub Cairo)

Emirates (EK; Map pp98-9; ☎ 020-211187; www .emirates.com; hub Dubai)

Ethiopian Airlines (ET; Map pp102-3; ☎ 020-330837; www.ethiopianairlines.com; hub Addis Ababa)

Gulf Air (GF; ☎ 020-241123; www.gulfairco.com; hub Abu Dhabi)

Jetlink Express (J0; ☎ 020-244285; www.jetlink.co.ke; hub Jomo Kenyatta International Airport, Nairobi)

Kenya Airways (KQ; Map pp98-9; ☎ 020-3274100; www.kenya-airways.com; hub Jomo Kenyatta International Airport, Nairobi)

KLM (KL; Map pp98-9; ☎ 020-32074100; www.klm.com; hub Amsterdam)

Oman Air (WY; Map p158; ☎ 041-221444; www.oman -air.com; hub Muscat)

Precision Air (PW; ☎ 020-602561; www.precisionairtz .com; hub Dar es Salaam)

Qatar Airways (QR; www.qatarairways.com; hub Doha)

Rwandair (WB; ☎ 0733-740703; www.rwandair.com; hub Kigali)

Safarilink Aviation (☎ 020-600777; www.safarilink .co.ke; hub Wilson Airport, Nairobi) Kilimanjaro only.

SN Brussels Airlines (SN; ☎ 020-4443070; www.flysn .com; hub Brussels)

South African Airways (SA; ☎ 020-229663; www .saakenya.com; hub Johannesburg)

Swiss International Airlines (SR; ☎ 020-3744045; www.swiss.com; hub Zurich)

Tickets

If you enter Nairobi with no onward or return ticket you may run foul of immigration and be forced to buy one on the spot – an expensive exercise. Note that you can't get a standby flight to Kenya unless you're an airline employee.

The airport departure tax for international flights is included in the cost of your plane ticket.

INTERCONTINENTAL (RTW) TICKETS

Discount round-the-world (RTW) tickets are a tempting option if you want to include Kenya on a longer journey, but the most common African stop is Johannesburg – if you're coming from Europe any ticket that includes Nairobi is usually much more expensive. If you're coming from Australia or New Zealand the difference may not be so great, but it's still often cheaper to buy an RTW or Australia–Europe ticket, stop over in Johannesburg and then buy a ticket on to Nairobi from there. Either way you may have to go through several travel agents before you find someone who can put a good deal together.

The following are online agents for RTW tickets:

- www.airtreks.com
- www.bootsnall.com
- www.roundtheworldflights.com
- www.travelbag.com
- www.thetravelleruk.com

Africa

Nairobi is a major African hub and there are good connections to most regions of Africa – Kenya Airways and the relevant national airlines serve everywhere from Abidjan to Yaoundé at least a few times a week, with the most frequent routes serving East and West Africa.

TANZANIA & UGANDA

Kenya Airways and Precision Air offer frequent flights from Dar es Salaam and Zanzibar to Nairobi and Mombasa, and have been so successful that Air Tanzania suspended its competing flights on the Dar–Nairobi route in 2005. If you book in advance it can be cheaper to fly to Mombasa with Precision Air then connect with a domestic KA flight to Nairobi, rather than taking a direct flight to the capital.

Several airlines fly to Nairobi daily from the Kilimanjaro International Airport near Moshi, including Airkenya, Ethiopian Airlines and Precision Air, which also has flights from Mwanza on Lake Victoria.

Kenya Airways is also the principal carrier flying between Nairobi and Entebbe (34km south of Kampala).

SOUTHERN AFRICA

Kenya Airways has regular flights from Malawi, Zambia and Zimbabwe. The only direct flights between Kenya and South Africa come from Johannesburg; Kenya Airways and South African Airways (SAA) both have daily flights on this route.

Rennies Travel (www.renniestravel.com) and **STA Travel** (www.statravel.co.za) have offices throughout South Africa. Check their websites for branch locations.

Flight Centres (☎ 021-3851530; www.africatravelco .com) in Cape Town and **Worldwide Adventure Travel** (☎ 013-40172; vfa@africatravelco.com) in Victoria Falls are partners of Flight Centres in Nairobi, and have years of experience in the budget travel business.

Asia

Kenya Airways serves Hong Kong, Bangkok and Shanghai a few times a week.

STA Travel (Bangkok ☎ 0 2236 0262; www.statravel .co.th; Hong Kong ☎ 2736 1618; www.statravel.com.hk; Japan ☎ 03-5391 2922; www.statravel.co.jp; Singapore ☎ 6737 7188; www.statravel.com.sg) proliferates in Asia. In Hong Kong you can also try **Four Seas Tours** (☎ 2200 7760; www.fourseastravel.com /english).

Australia & New Zealand

Getting to Kenya from Australia or New Zealand is harder than you might expect, as none of the trans-Asian airlines fly to Nairobi (and that includes Qantas and Air New Zealand). The most direct route from Australia to Kenya is via Mauritius with Air Mauritius, but the cheapest tickets are usually via the Persian Gulf with Gulf Airlines or Emirates, or with SAA via Johannesburg.

Return fares typically cost A$2250 to A$2600 from Sydney or Melbourne, around A$2300 from Perth and NZ$2750 to NZ$3000 from Auckland.

STA Travel (☎ 1300 733 035; www.statravel.com.au) and **Flight Centre** (☎ 133133; www.flightcentre.com .au) both have offices throughout Australia. For online bookings, try www.travel.com .au. Cheap air fares are also advertised in the travel sections of weekend newspapers, such as the *Age* in Melbourne and the *Sydney Morning Herald*.

In New Zealand, the *New Zealand Herald* has a good travel section with plenty of advertised fares. Both **Flight Centre** (☎ 0800 243544; www.flightcentre.co.nz) and **STA Travel** (☎ 0508 782872; www.statravel.co.nz) have branches throughout the country. For online bookings www.travel .co.nz is recommended.

Continental Europe

Kenya Airways' link with KLM means that you can fly to Nairobi via Amsterdam from regional airports across Europe. From Amsterdam, as from most European cities, return fares range from €600 to €800, depending on the season.

SN Brussels Airlines also has regular connections to Nairobi with cheap return fares available. Because of the Swiss Airlines connection, Switzerland is another good place to buy discount air tickets to Nairobi. The new Jetlink Express company runs regular direct flights to Italy.

STA Travel (Austria www.oekista.at; Denmark www .statravel.dk; Finland www.statravel.fi; Germany www.sta travel.de; Norway www.statravel.no; Sweden www.statravel .se), the international student and young person's travel giant, has branches in many European nations. There are also many **STA-affiliated travel agencies** (www.statravelgroup.com) across Europe. Visit the website to find an STA partner close to you.

Other recommended travel agencies across Europe include the following:

Belgium

Acotra Student Travel Agency (☎ 02 51 286 07)
WATS Reizen (☎ 03 22 616 26)

France

Anyway (☎ 0892 893892; www.anyway.fr)
Lastminute (☎ 0892 705000; www.lastminute.fr)
Nouvelles Frontières (☎ 0825 000747; www.nouvelles -frontieres.fr)

TRANSPORT

TRANSPORT

OTU Voyages (www.otu.fr) Specializes in student and youth travellers.
Voyageurs du Monde (☎ 01 40 15 11 15; www.vdm.com)

Germany
Expedia (www.expedia.de)
Just Travel (☎ 089-747 33 30; www.justtravel.de)
Lastminute (☎ 01805 284 366; www.lastminute.de)

Italy
CTS Viaggi (☎ 064 62 04 31; www.cts.it)

Netherlands
Airfair (☎ 020-620 51 21; www.airfair.nl)
NBBS Reizen (☎ 020-624 09 89)

Spain
Barcelo Viajes (☎ 902 11 62 26; www.barceloviajes.com)
Nouvelles Frontières (☎ 902 17 09 79; www.nouvelles-frontieres.es)

Switzerland
SSR Voyages (☎ 01 297 11 11; www.ssr.ch)

Indian Subcontinent
Flights between East Africa and Mumbai (Bombay) are common, due to the large Indian population in East Africa; Kenya Airways and Air India are the major carriers. Typical fares to Nairobi are about US$350.

Although most of India's discount travel agents are in Delhi, there are also some reliable agents in Mumbai. **STIC Travels** (www.stictravel.com; Delhi ☎ 11-2335 7468; Mumbai ☎ 22-2218 1431) has offices in dozens of Indian cities. Another agency is **Transway International** (www.transwayinternational.com).

Middle East
Coming from the Middle East, Kenya Airways and Egypt Airways serve the Cairo–Nairobi route several times a week. Kenya Airways also flies regularly to Istanbul and Dubai. Emirates and Gulf Air both have numerous flights to Nairobi from airports throughout the Middle East. Oman Air has twice-weekly flights from Dubai and Muscat to Mombasa, and African Air Express flies an unusual route between Nairobi and Dubai via Eldoret and Mogadishu.

The following are recommended agencies:
Al-Rais Travels (www.alrais.com) In Dubai.
Egypt Panorama Tours (☎ 02-359 0200; www.eptours.com) In Cairo.

Israel Student Travel Association (ISTA; ☎ 02-625 7257) In Jerusalem.
Orion-Tour (www.oriontour.com) In Istanbul.

North America
All flights from North America to Nairobi go via Europe. Through tickets are easy to get from travel agents, but it's often cheaper to buy a discounted ticket to London, Amsterdam or Brussels and then connect to Kenya from there.

From the USA, North West Airlines is affiliated with KLM and Kenya Airways and offers speedy connections through London or Amsterdam to East Africa. Return tickets to Nairobi from New York can cost as little as US$1300 in the low season; from Los Angeles, a return ticket costs about US$1500. Fares from Canada are about 10% more; KLM and British Airways offer flights from Toronto to Nairobi.

Discount travel agents in the USA are known as consolidators. San Francisco is the ticket consolidator capital of America, although some good deals can be found in Los Angeles, New York and some other big cities. **Travel Cuts** (☎ 800-667-2887; www.travelcuts.com) is Canada's national student travel agency.

The following agencies are recommended for online bookings:
- www.cheaptickets.com
- www.expedia.ca (Canada)
- www.expedia.com
- www.itn.net
- www.lowestfare.com
- www.orbitz.com
- www.sta.com
- www.travelocity.ca (Canada)
- www.travelocity.com

UK & Ireland
Discount air travel is big business in London. Advertisements for many travel agencies appear in the travel pages of the weekend broadsheet newspapers, in *Time Out* and the *Evening Standard,* and in the free *TNT* magazine (www.tntmagazine.com).

Charter flights can work out as a cheaper alternative to scheduled flights and the package may also include accommodation, which you aren't obliged to use if you want to travel around the country. **Somak** (☎ 020-8903 8526; www.somak.co.uk) is probably your best bet for good deals.

Recommended travel agencies include the following:

Bridge the World (☎ 0870 444 7474; www.b-t-w.co.uk)
Flight Centre (☎ 0870 890 8099; flightcentre.co.uk)
Flightbookers (☎ 0870 814 4001; www.ebookers.com)
North-South Travel (☎ 01245-608291; www.north
southtravel.co.uk) Donates part of its profit to projects in the developing world.
Quest Travel (☎ 0870 442 3542; www.questtravel.com)
STA Travel (☎ 0870 160 0599; www.statravel.co.uk)
Trailfinders (www.trailfinders.co.uk)
Travel Bag (☎ 0870 890 1456; www.travelbag.co.uk)

LAND
Bus
Entering Kenya by bus is possible on several major routes, and it's generally a breeze; while you need to get off the bus to sort out any necessary visa formalities, you'll rarely be held up for too long at the border. That said, arranging your visa in advance can save you quite a bit of time and a few angry glares from your fellow passengers.

Car & Motorcycle
Crossing land borders with your own vehicle is generally straightforward as long as you have the necessary paperwork – see p378 for more details on requirements and general road rules. Petrol, spare parts and repair shops are readily available at all border towns, though if you're coming from Ethiopia you should plan your supplies carefully, as stops are few and far between on the rough northern roads.

If you're planning to ship your vehicle to Kenya, be aware that port charges in the country are very high. For example, a Land Rover shipped from the Middle East to Mombasa is likely to cost US$1000 just to get off the ship and out of the port. This is almost as much as the cost of the shipping itself! Putting a vehicle onto a ship in the Mombasa port costs about US$600 on top of this. There are numerous shipping agents in Nairobi and Mombasa willing to arrange everything for you, but check all the costs in advance.

Ethiopia
With ongoing problems in Sudan and Somalia, Ethiopia offers the only viable overland route into Kenya from the north. The security situation around the main entry point at Moyale is changeable; the border

is usually open, but security problems often force its closure. Cattle- and goat-rustling are rife, triggering frequent cross-border tribal wars, so check the security situation carefully before attempting this crossing.

From immigration on the Ethiopian side of town it's a 2km walk to the Ethiopian and Kenyan customs posts. Be aware that a yellow fever vaccination is required to cross either border at Moyale. Unless you fancy being vaccinated at the border, get your jabs in advance and remember to keep the yellow fever certificate with your passport. A cholera vaccination may also be required. If you're travelling in the other direction, through Ethiopia to Sudan, you'll have to go to Addis Ababa to get your Sudanese visa.

If you don't have your own transport from Moyale, lifts can be arranged with the trucks from the border to Isiolo for around KSh1000 (or KSh500 to Marsabit).

Those coming to Kenya with their own vehicle could also enter at Fort Banya, on the northeastern tip of Lake Turkana. However, it's a risky route and fuel stops are rare. There is no border post, so you must already possess a Kenyan visa and get it stamped on arrival in Nairobi – immigration officials are quite used to this, although not having an Ethiopian exit stamp can be a problem if you want to re-enter Ethiopia.

Somalia
There's no way you can pass overland between Kenya and war-ravaged Somalia at present unless you're part of a refugee aid convoy, as the Kenyan government has closed the border to try and stop the flow of poachers, bandits and weapons into Kenya.

Sudan
Recent progress in the Sudanese peace process has raised many people's hopes for the future, but Kenya's neighbour to the north is still far from untroubled. If things continue to improve, the Kenya–Sudan border may reopen, but at time of writing it was still only possible to travel between the two countries either by air or via Metema on the Ethiopian border (see left for more details on the route from Ethiopia).

Tanzania
The main land borders between Kenya and Tanzania are at Namanga, Taveta, Isebania

and Lunga Lunga (for Tanzania), and can be reached by public transport. There is also a crossing from the Serengeti to the Masai Mara, which can only be undertaken with your own vehicle, and one at Loitokitok, which is closed to tourists, although you may be able to temporarily cross on a tour (see p140 for more information). Train services between the two countries have been suspended.

Following are the main bus companies serving Tanzania:

Akamba (Map pp102-3; ☎ 020-340430; akamba_prs@skyweb.co.ke)

Davanu Shuttle Nairobi (Map pp102-3; ☎ 020-316929) Arusha (☎ 057-8142) Arusha/Moshi shuttle buses.

Easy Coach (Map pp102-3; ☎ 020-210711; easycoach@wananchi.com)

Riverside Shuttle Nairobi (Map pp102-3; ☎ 020-229618) Arusha (☎ 057-2639) Arusha/Moshi shuttle buses.

Scandinavia Express (Map pp102-3; ☎ 020-247131)

MOMBASA TO TANGA/DAR ES SALAAM

Numerous buses run along the coast road from Mombasa to Tanga and Dar es Salaam, and they cross the border at Lunga Lunga/Horohoro. Most people travel on through buses from Mombasa, but it's easy enough to do the journey in stages by local bus or matatu (minibus) if you'd rather make a few stops along the way.

In Mombasa, buses to Dar es Salaam leave from around Jomo Kenyatta Ave, near the junction with Mwembe Tayari Rd. The average cost is around KSh1000 to Dar (eight hours) and KSh500 to Tanga (two hours), depending on the company you travel with and the standard of the buses.

In Dar es Salaam, buses leave from the Mnazi Mmoja bus stand on Bibi Titi Mohamed Rd, near Uhuru and Lindi Sts, along the southeast side of Mnazi Mmoja Park.

If you want to do the journey in stages, there are frequent matatus to Lunga Lunga from the Mombasa ferry jetty at Likoni. A matatu can then take you the 6.5km between the two border posts. On the Tanzanian side, there are regular matatus from Horohoro to Tanga (see p181 for more details).

MOMBASA TO ARUSHA/MOSHI

A number of rickety local buses leave Mombasa every evening for Moshi and Arusha in Tanzania. There are occasional morning services, but most buses leave around 7pm from Mombasa or Arusha. Fares are around KSh500 to Moshi (six hours) and KSh800 to Arusha (7½ hours). In Mombasa, buses leave from in front of the Mwembe Tayari Health Centre on Jomo Kenyatta Ave.

Buses cross the border at Taveta, which can also be reached by matatu from Voi (see p150 for more details).

NAIROBI TO ARUSHA/MOSHI

You have the choice of an ordinary bus or a much more comfortable minibus shuttle service between Nairobi and Arusha. Each takes about four hours and neither requires a change of service at the border at Namanga.

Riverside Shuttle and Davanu Shuttle both offer convenient shuttle services from central Nairobi, costing roughly US$30 to Arusha and US$35 to Moshi. The big advantage of both these services is being able to board the bus in the comparative sanity of downtown Nairobi. There are often touts at Jomo Kenyatta International Airport in Nairobi advertising a direct shuttle bus service from the airport to Arusha for about US$30, but they just bring you into Nairobi where you join one of the regular shuttles.

Full-sized buses are much cheaper, but most leave from the hectic River Rd area in Nairobi; thefts are common there so watch your baggage. Easy Coach is a good option, as services leave from its office compound near Nairobi railway station. Buses from Nairobi to Dar es Salaam (see below) also travel via Arusha, and small local buses leave from Accra Rd every morning. The average cost of these services is between KSh700 and KSh1000 to Arusha, and between KSh1000 and KSh1200 to Moshi, more for the real luxury liners.

It's also easy, though less convenient, to do this journey in stages, since the Kenyan and Tanzanian border posts at Namanga are right next to each other and regularly served by public transport. There are a couple of nice places to stay in Namanga if you want to break the journey, for example to visit Amboseli National Park, before heading to Nairobi or Arusha.

NAIROBI TO DAR ES SALAAM

Several Kenyan companies have buses from Nairobi to Dar es Salaam. Scandinavia Express and Akamba both have reliable daily services from their offices in the River Rd area, with prices ranging from KSh1600 to real luxury coaches at KSh3000. Journey time is around 16 to 18 hours with stops.

SERENGETI TO MASAI MARA
Theoretically it's possible to cross between Serengeti National Park and Masai Mara National Reserve with your own vehicle, but you'll need all the appropriate vehicle documentation (including insurance and entry permit).

NAIROBI/KISUMU TO MWANZA
The road is sealed all the way from Kisumu to just short of Mwanza in Tanzania, offering a convenient route to the Tanzanian shore of Lake Victoria. From Nairobi, probably the most comfortable way to go is with Scandinavia Express or Akamba; prices range from around KSh1000 to KSh2000, and the journey should take roughly 12 hours.

From Kisumu, regular matatus serve the Tanzanian border at Isebania/Sirari (KSh350, four hours); local services head to Mwanza from the Tanzanian side. Buses going direct to Mwanza (KSh500, four hours) leave frequently from Kisii.

Uganda
The main border post for overland travellers is Malaba, with Busia an alternative if you are travelling via Kisumu. Numerous bus companies run between Nairobi and Kampala, or you can do the journey in stages via either of the border towns.

Several of the main bus companies serve Uganda:

Akamba (Map pp102-3; ☎ 020-340430; akamba_prs@skyweb.co.ke)
Falcon (Map pp102-3; ☎ 020-229692)
Scandinavia Express (Map pp102-3; ☎ 020-247131)

NAIROBI TO KAMPALA
Various companies cover the Nairobi to Kampala route. From Nairobi – and at the top end of the market – Scandinavia Express and Akamba have buses at least once daily, ranging from ordinary buses at around KSh1000 to full-blown luxury services with drinks and movies, hovering around the KSh2000 mark. All buses take about 10 to 12 hours and prices include a meal at the halfway point. Akamba also has a service to Mbale in Uganda (KSh800, 10 hours).

Various other companies have cheaper basic services which depart from the Accra Rd area in Nairobi. Prices start at around KSh800 and journey times are more or less the same as the bigger companies, with a few extra allowances for delays and general tardiness.

If you want to do the journey in stages, Akamba has morning and evening buses from Nairobi to Malaba and a daily direct bus from there to Kampala. There are also regular matatus to Malaba (KSh650) from Cross Rd.

The Ugandan and Kenyan border posts at Malaba are about 1km apart, so you can walk or take a *boda-boda* (bicycle taxi). Once you get across the border, there are frequent matatus until the late afternoon to Kampala, Jinja and Tororo.

Buses and matatus also run from Nairobi or Kisumu to Busia, from where there are regular connections to Kampala and Jinja.

SEA & LAKE
At the time of writing there were no ferries operating on Lake Victoria, although there's been talk for years of services restarting.

Tanzania
It's theoretically possible to travel by dhow between Mombasa and the Tanzanian islands of Pemba and Zanzibar, but first of all you'll have to find a captain who's making the journey and then you'll have to bargain hard to pay a reasonable amount for the trip. Perhaps the best place to ask about sailings is at Shimoni (p181). There is a tiny immigration post here, but there's no guarantee they'll stamp your passport so you might have to go back to Mombasa for an exit stamp.

Dhows do sail between small Kenyan and Tanzanian ports along Lake Victoria, but many are involved in smuggling (fruit mostly) and are best avoided.

TOURS
It's possible to get to Kenya as part of an overland truck tour originating in Europe or other parts of Africa (many also start in Nairobi bound for other places in Africa). See p70 for details of safaris that are specific to Kenya.

Most companies are based in the UK or South Africa, but Flight Centres is a good local operator with offices in Nairobi, Cape Town and Victoria Falls, Zimbabwe. Trips can last from just a few days to epic grand tours of up to 13 weeks.

Acacia Expeditions (UK ☎ 020-77064700; www.acacia-africa.com)

African Routes (South Africa ☎ 031-5693911; www.africanroutes.co.za)

Dragoman (UK ☎ 01728-861133; www.dragoman.co.uk)

Explore Worldwide (UK ☎ 01252-760000; www.explore worldwide.com)

Flight Centres Nairobi (Map pp102-3; ☎ 020-210024; www.flightcentres-kenya.com); Cape Town (☎ 021-3851530; cpt@africatravelco.com); Victoria Falls (☎ 013-40172; vfa@africatravelco.com)

Gametrackers Ltd (Map pp102-3; ☎ 020-338927; www.gametrackersafaris.com)

Guerba Expeditions (UK ☎ 01373-826611; www.guerba.co.uk)

GETTING AROUND

AIR
Airlines in Kenya

Including the national carrier, Kenya Airways, four domestic operators of varying sizes now run scheduled flights within Kenya. All appear to have a virtually clean slate safety-wise (Kenya Airways have suffered just one fatal incident since 1977). Destinations served are predominantly around the coast and the popular southern national parks, where the highest density of tourist activity takes place.

With all these airlines, be sure to book well in advance (this is essential during the tourist high season). You should also remember to reconfirm your return flights 72 hours before departure, especially those that connect with an international flight. Otherwise, you may find that your seat has been reallocated.

The following airlines fly domestically:

Airkenya (☎ 020-605745; www.airkenya.com) Amboseli, Kiwayu, Lamu, Lewa Downs, Masai Mara, Malindi, Meru, Nanyuki, Samburu.

Kenya Airways (Map pp98-9; ☎ 020-3274100; www.kenya-airways.com) Kisumu, Lamu, Malindi, Mombasa.

Mombasa Air Safari (☎ 041-433061; www.mombasa airsafari.com) Amboseli, Ukunda, Lamu, Masai Mara, Malindi, Mombasa, Tsavo.

Safarilink (☎ 020-600777; www.safarilink.co.ke) Amboseli, Chyulu Hills, Kiwayu, Lamu, Lewa Downs, Masai Mara, Naivasha, Nanyuki, Samburu, Tsavo West.

CHARTER AIRLINES

Chartering a small plane saves you time and is the only realistic way to get to some parts of Kenya, but it's an expensive business. It may be worth considering if you can get a group together. For a three-day trip from Nairobi to Sibiloi National Park on the west of Lake Turkana, you can expect to pay around US$350 to US$400 each, if five people are sharing.

There are dozens of charter companies operating out of Nairobi's Wilson Airport – **Excel Aviation** (☎ 020-601764), **Z-Boskovic Air Charters** (☎ 020-501210) and **Blue Bird Aviation** (☎ 020-602338) are worth a look.

A couple of small charter-type airlines run occasional scheduled flights from Diani Beach, Lamu, Mombasa and Eldoret – see the relevant Getting There & Away sections for details.

BICYCLE

Loads of Kenyans get around by bicycle, and while it can be tough for those who are not used to the roads or the climate, plenty of hardy visiting cyclists do tour the country every year. But whatever you do, if you intend to cycle here, do as the locals do and get off the road whenever you hear a car coming. No matter how experienced you are, it would be tantamount to suicide to attempt the road from Nairobi to Mombasa on a bicycle.

Cycling is easier in rural areas, and you'll usually receive a warm welcome in any villages you pass through. Many local people operate *boda-bodas*, so repair shops are becoming increasingly common along the roadside. Be wary of cycling on dirt roads as punctures from thorn trees are a major problem.

The hills of Kenya are not particularly steep but can be long and hard. You can expect to cover around 80km per day in the hills of the western highlands, somewhat more where the country is flatter. Hell's Gate National Park, near Naivasha, is particularly popular for mountain biking.

It's possible to hire road and mountain bikes in an increasing number of places, usually for less than KSh500 per day. Few places require a deposit, unless their machines are particularly new or sophisticated. Several tour operators now offer cycling safaris (see p70 for details).

BOAT
Lake Victoria
There has been speculation for years that ferry transport will start again on Lake Victoria, but for the foreseeable future the only regular services operating are motorised canoes to Mfangano Island from Mbita Point, near Homa Bay. An occasional ferry service runs between Kisumu and Homa Bay.

Dhow
Sailing on a traditional Swahili dhow along the East African coast is one of Kenya's most memorable experiences and, unlike on Lake Victoria, certain traditional routes are very much still in use.

Dhows are commonly used to get around the islands in the Lamu archipelago (p212) and the mangrove islands south of Mombasa (p179). For the most part, these operate more like dhow safaris than public transport. Although some trips are luxurious, the trips out of Lamu are more basic. When night comes you simply bed down wherever there is space. Seafood is freshly caught and cooked on board on charcoal burners, or else barbecued on the beach on the surrounding islands.

Most of the smaller boats rely on the wind to get around, so it's quite common to end up becalmed until the wind picks up again. The more commercial boats, however, have been fitted with outboard motors so that progress can be made even when there's no wind. Larger dhows are all motorised and some of them don't even have sails.

BUS
Kenya has an extensive network of long- and short-haul bus routes, with particularly good coverage of the areas around Nairobi, the coast and the western regions. Services thin out the further away from the capital you get, particularly in the north, and there are still plenty of places where you'll be reliant on matatus.

Buses are operated by a variety of private and state-owned companies that offer varying levels of comfort, convenience and roadworthiness. They're considerably cheaper than taking the train or flying, and as a rule services are frequent, fast and often quite comfortable. However, many travellers are put off taking buses altogether by the diabolical state of Kenyan roads.

In general, if you travel during daylight hours, buses are a fairly safe way to get around and you'll certainly be safer in a bus than in a matatu, simply due to its size. The best coaches are saved for long-haul and international routes and offer DVD movies, drinks, toilets and reclining airline-style seats. On the shorter local routes, however, you may find yourself on something resembling a battered school bus.

Whatever kind of conveyance you find yourself in, don't sit at the back (you'll be thrown around like a rag doll on Kenyan roads), or right at the front (you'll be the first to die in a head-on collision, plus you'll be able to see the oncoming traffic, which is usually a terrifying experience). You should also be aware that a Kenyan bus trip is not always the most restful experience – unlike matatus, hawkers can actually board most services to thrust their wares in your face, and it's not unknown for roving preachers, herbalists and just about anyone else to spend entire journeys shouting the odds for the benefit of their fellow passengers. On certain coastal buses you'll even hear the regular Muslim call to prayer.

Kenya Bus Services (KBS), the government bus line, runs the local buses in Nairobi and also offers long-haul services to most major towns around the country. Its buses tend to be slower than those of the private companies, but are probably safer for this reason. Of the private companies, Akamba has the most comprehensive network, and has a good, but not perfect, safety record. Easy Coach is another private firm quickly establishing a solid reputation for efficiency and comfort.

There are a few security considerations to think about when taking a bus in Kenya. Some routes, most notably the roads from Malindi to Lamu and Isiolo to Marsabit, have been prone to attacks by *shiftas* (bandits) in the past – check things out locally before you travel. Another possible risk is drugged food and drink: if you want to reach your destination with all your belongings, politely refuse any offers of drinks or snacks from strangers.

The following are the main bus companies operating in Kenya:

Akamba (Map pp102-3; ☎ 020-340430; akamba_prs@ skyweb.co.ke) Eldoret, Kakamega, Kericho, Kisii, Kisumu, Kitale, Machakos, Mombasa, Nairobi, Namanga.

Busscar (☎ 020-227650) Kilifi, Kisumu, Malindi, Mombasa, Nairobi.

Coastline Safaris (Map pp102–3; ☎ 020-217592; coastpekee@ikenya.com) Kakamega, Kisumu, Mombasa, Nairobi, Voi.

Easy Coach (Map pp102–3; ☎ 020-210711; easycoach@ wananchi.com) Eldoret, Kakamega, Kisumu, Kitale, Nairobi.

Eldoret Express (☎ 020-6766886) Busia, Eldoret, Kakamega, Kisii, Kisumu, Kitale, Malaba, Nairobi.

Falcon (Map pp102–3; ☎ 020-229662) Kilifi, Lamu, Malindi, Mombasa, Nairobi.

Kenya Bus Services (KBS; Map pp102–3; ☎ 020-229707) Busia, Eldoret, Kakamega, Kisii, Kisumu, Kitale, Malaba, Mombasa, Nairobi.

Mombasa Metropolitan Bus Services (Metro Mombasa; ☎ 041-2496008) Kilifi, Kwale, Malindi, Mombasa, Mtwapa.

Costs

Kenyan buses are pretty economical, with fares starting around KSh80 for an hour-long journey between nearby towns. At the other end of the scale, you'll seldom pay more than KSh500 for a standard journey, but so-called 'executive' services on the overnight Nairobi–Mombasa route can command prices of up to KSh1500, almost as much as the equivalent international services.

Reservations

Most bus companies have offices or ticket agents at important stops along their routes, where you can book a seat. For short trips between towns reservations aren't generally necessary, but for popular longer routes, especially the Nairobi–Kisumu, Nairobi–Mombasa and Mombasa–Lamu routes, buying your ticket at least a day in advance is highly recommended.

CAR & MOTORCYCLE

Many travellers bring their own vehicles into Kenya as part of overland trips and, expense notwithstanding, it's a great way to see the country at your own pace. Otherwise, there are numerous car-hire companies who can rent you anything from a small hatchback to Toyota Landcruiser 4WDs, although hire rates are some of the highest in the world.

A few expats have off-road (trail) motorcycles, but they aren't seen as a serious means

Road Distances (km)

	Busia	Embu	Isiolo	Kakamega	Kericho	Kisumu	Kitale	Lodwar	Malindi	Meru	Mombasa	Nairobi	Nakuru	Namanga	Nanyuki	Nyeri	Voi
Busia	---																
Embu	610	---															
Isiolo	569	184	---														
Kakamega	95	525	481	---													
Kericho	218	395	351	130	---												
Kisumu	138	475	431	50	80	---											
Kitale	154	511	467	109	230	158	---										
Lodwar	440	691	735	395	522	443	285	---									
Malindi	1087	657	877	999	869	949	985	1141	---								
Meru	565	154	56	477	347	427	463	729	864	---							
Mombasa	969	618	759	881	751	831	867	1120	118	746	---						
Nairobi	482	131	272	394	264	368	380	599	605	259	521	---					
Nakuru	325	288	244	237	107	211	223	442	762	240	644	157	---				
Namanga	661	314	524	596	469	548	563	779	430	468	409	180	337	---			
Nanyuki	487	131	84	399	269	349	385	651	795	78	677	190	175	380	---		
Nyeri	508	88	140	420	290	370	406	601	752	136	634	150	151	330	58	---	
Voi	811	460	601	723	593	673	709	960	281	588	160	329	486	249	519	476	---

of transport, which is a blessing considering the lethal nature of the roads.

Automobile Associations
Automobile Association of Kenya (Map pp98-9; ☎ 020-723195; Hurlingham shopping centre, Nairobi)

Bringing Your Own Vehicle
Drivers of cars and riders of motorbikes will need the vehicle's registration papers, liability insurance and an international drivers' permit in addition to their domestic licence. You will also need a *Carnet de passage en douane,* which is effectively a passport for the vehicle and acts as a temporary waiver of import duty. The *carnet* may also need to specify any expensive spare parts that you're planning to carry with you, such as a gearbox. Contact your local automobile association for details about all documentation.

Driving Licence
An international driving licence is not necessary in Kenya, but can be useful. If you have a British photocard licence, be sure to bring the counterfoil, as the date you passed your driving test – something car-hire companies here may want to know – isn't printed on the card itself.

Fuel & Spare Parts
At the time of research, in Nairobi regular petrol was KSh70 per litre, super KSh75 and diesel KSh65. Rates are generally lower outside the capital, but can creep up in remote areas, where petrol stations are often scarce and you may end up buying supplies out of barrels from roadside vendors.

Anyone who is planning to bring their own vehicle with them needs to check in advance what spare parts are likely to be available. Even if it's an older model, local suppliers in Kenya are very unlikely to have every little part you might need.

Hire
Hiring a vehicle to tour Kenya (or at least the national parks) is an expensive way of seeing the country, but it does give you freedom of movement and is sometimes the only way of getting to the more remote parts of the country. However, unless you're sharing with a sufficient number of people, it's likely to cost more than you'd pay for an organised camping safari with all meals.

Unless you're just planning on travelling on the main routes between towns, you'll need a 4WD vehicle. None of the car-hire companies will let you drive 2WD vehicles on dirt roads, including those in the national parks, and if you ignore this proscription and have an accident you will be personally liable for any damage to the vehicle.

A minimum age of between 23 and 25 years usually applies for hirers. Some companies prefer a licence with no endorsements or criminal convictions, and most require you to have been driving for at least two years. You will also need acceptable ID such as a passport.

It's generally true to say that the more you pay for a vehicle, the better condition it will be in. The larger companies are usually in a better financial position to keep their fleet in good order. Whoever you hire from, be sure to check the brakes, the tyres (including the spare), the windscreen wipers and the lights before you set off.

The other factor to consider is what the company will do for you (if anything) if you have a serious breakdown. The major rental companies *may* deliver a replacement vehicle and make arrangements for recovery of the other vehicle at their expense, but with most companies you'll have to get the vehicle fixed and back on the road yourself, and then try to claim a refund.

COSTS
Starting rates for rental almost always sound very reasonable, but once you factor in mileage and the various types of insurance you'll be lucky to pay less than KSh6000 per day for a saloon car, or KSh8000 per day for a small 4WD. As elsewhere in the world, rates come down rapidly if you take the car for more than a few days.

Vehicles are usually rented with either an allowance of 100km to 200km per day (in which case you'll pay an extra fee for every kilometre over), or with unlimited kilometres, which is often the best way to go. Rates are usually quoted without insurance, and you'll be given the option of paying around KSh900 to KSh1500 per day for insurance against collision damage and theft. It would be financial suicide to hire a car in Kenya without both kinds of insurance. Otherwise, you'll be responsible for the full value of the vehicle if it's stolen or damaged.

Even if you have collision and theft insurance, you'll still be liable for an excess of KSh2000 to KSh150,000 (depending on the company) if something happens to the vehicle; always check this before signing. You can usually reduce the excess to zero by paying another KSh900 per day for an Excess Loss Waiver. Note that tyres, damaged windscreens and loss of the tool kit are always the hirer's responsibility.

As a final sting in the tail, you'll be charged 16% value added tax (VAT) on top of the total cost of hiring the vehicle. Any repairs that you end up paying for will also have VAT on top. And a final warning: always return the vehicle with a full tank of petrol; if you don't, the company will charge you twice the going rate to fill up.

Deposits

There's a wide variation in the deposit required on hired vehicles. It can be as much as the total estimated hire charges plus whatever the excess is on the collision damage waiver. You can cover this with cash, signed travellers cheques (returnable) or credit card.

Drop-Off Rates

If you want to hire a vehicle in one place and drop it off in another there will be additional charges. These vary depending on the vehicle, the company and the pick-up and drop-off locations. In most cases, count on paying KSh10,000 between Nairobi and Mombasa and about KSh5000 between Mombasa and Malindi.

Driver Rates

While hiring a 'chauffeur' may sound like a luxury, it's actually a very good idea in Kenya for both financial and safety reasons. Most companies will provide a driver for around KSh1000 per day – the big advantage of this is that the car is then covered by the company's own insurance, so you don't have to pay any of the various waivers and will not be liable for any excess in the case of an accident (though tyres, windows etc remain your responsibility).

In addition, having someone in the car who speaks Swahili, knows the roads and is used to Kenyan driving conditions can be absolutely priceless, especially in remote areas. Most drivers will also look after the car at night so you don't have to worry about it, and they'll often go massively out of their way to help you fulfil your travel plans. On the other hand, it will leave one less seat free in the car, reducing the number of people you can have sharing the cost in the first place.

DRIVING TO TANZANIA & UGANDA

Only the bigger (and more expensive) companies cater for this, and there are large additional charges. With Budget, Hertz or Avis, expect to pay around US$150 for them to sort out all the documentation, insurance, permits etc.

RENTAL AGENCIES

At the top end of the market are some international companies. All have airport and town offices in Nairobi and Mombasa. Of these, Budget is the best value, though it's well worth paying for the Excess Loss Waiver.

Central Rent-a-Car is probably the best of the local firms, with a well-maintained fleet of fairly new vehicles and a good back-up service. Its excess liability is also the lowest (KSh2000), but vehicles are self-drive only, with no drivers available. Apart from Central, all of these companies have steep excesses. Glory levies a staggering KSh150,000 excess – enough to bankrupt even the most well-heeled traveller!

Most safari companies will also rent out their vehicles, though you'll have few of the guarantees that you would with the companies listed here. **Let's Go Travel** (☎ 020-340331; www.letsgosafari.com) organises reliable car hire at favourable rates through partner firms. At the very bottom of the scale, local pick-ups hang around the City Market in Nairobi with 'Ask for Transport' signs, a cheap option if you just want to get from A to B but not to be recommended for more intensive trips.

On the coast, it is possible to hire motorcycles, scooters and quads at Diani Beach and Bamburi Beach, although most people just use them to zip up and down the beach road. **Fredlink Co Ltd** (☎ 040-3202647; www.motorbike-safari .com; Diani Plaza, Diani Beach) rents out 350cc trail bikes and Yamaha scooters, and also arranges motorcycle safaris. See p178 for information about Fredlink Tours and p70 for information about motorcycle safaris.

The following are local and international hire companies:

Avenue Car Hire (Map pp102-3; ☎ 020-313207; www .avenuecarhire.com)

Avis (Map pp98-9; ☎ 020-316061; www.avis.co.ke)

Budget (Map pp102-3; ☎ 020-223581; www.budget -kenya.com)

Central Rent-a-Car (☎ 020-222888; www.carhirekenya .com)

Glory Car Hire (Map pp102-3; ☎ 020-225024; www .glorycarhire.com)

Hertz (☎ 020-248777; www.hertz.co.ke)

Insurance

Driving in Kenya without insurance would be a mind-numbingly idiotic thing to do. It's best to arrange cover before you leave. Liability insurance is not always available in advance for Kenya; you may be required to purchase some at certain borders if you enter overland, otherwise you will effectively be travelling uninsured.

Car rental agencies in Kenya always offer some kind of insurance – see p379 for full details.

Parking

In small towns and villages parking is usually free, but there's a pay-parking system in Nairobi, Mombasa and other main towns. Attendants issue one-day parking permits for around KSh70, valid anywhere in town. If you don't get a permit you're liable to be wheel-clamped, and getting your vehicle back will cost you at least KSh2000. It's always worth staying in a hotel with secure parking if possible.

Purchase

It's certainly possible to buy a car when you're in Kenya – just look at public notice-boards in expat-rich areas such as the Nairobi suburbs and the coast resorts. However, the practicalities of registering, taxing and keeping your vehicle generally road-legal are quite another matter, and would require a fair bit of ground research if you seriously intended to keep the car running for a decent length of time.

Road Conditions

Road conditions vary widely in Kenya, from flat smooth highways to dirt tracks and steep rocky pathways. Many roads are severely eroded at the edges, reducing the carriageway to a single lane, which is usually occupied by whichever vehicle is bigger in any given situation. The roads in the north and east of the country are particularly poor. The main Mombasa–Nairobi–Malaba road (A104) is badly worn due to the constant flow of traffic.

Roads in national parks are all made of *murram* (dirt) and have eroded into bone-shaking corrugations through overuse by safari vehicles. Keep your speed down and be careful when driving after rain. Although some dirt roads can be negotiated in a 2WD vehicle, you're much safer in a 4WD.

Road Hazards

The biggest hazard on Kenyan roads is simply the other vehicles on them, and driving defensively is essential. Ironically, the most dangerous roads in Kenya are probably the well-maintained ones, which allow drivers to go fast enough to do really serious damage in a crash. On the worse roads, potholes are a dual problem: driving into them can damage your vehicle or cause you to lose control, and sudden avoidance manoeuvres from other vehicles are a constant threat.

On all roads, be very careful of pedestrians and cyclists – you don't want to contribute any more to the death toll on Kenya's roads. Animals are another major hazard in rural areas, be it monkeys, herds of goats and cattle or lone chickens with a death wish.

Acacia thorns are a common problem if you're driving in remote areas, as they'll pierce even the toughest tires. The slightest breakdown can leave you stranded for hours in the bush, so always carry drinking water, emergency food and, if possible, spare fuel.

Certain routes have a reputation for banditry, particularly the Garsen–Garissa–Thika road, which is still essentially off limits to travellers, and the dirt track from Amboseli National Park to Tsavo West National Park, where you're usually required to join a convoy. The roads from Isiolo to Marsabit and Moyale and from Malindi to Lamu have improved considerably security-wise in the last few years, but you're still advised to seek local advice before using any of these routes.

Road Rules

You'll need your wits about you if you're going to tackle driving in Kenya. Driving practices here are some of the worst in the world and all are carried out at breakneck speed. Indicators, lights, horns and hand signals can mean anything from 'I'm about to overtake' to 'Hello *mzungu* (white person)!' or 'Let's play chicken with that elephant', and should never be taken at face value.

Kenyans habitually drive on the wrong side of the road whenever they see a pothole, an animal or simply a break in the traffic – flashing your lights at the vehicle hurtling towards you should be enough to persuade the driver to get back into their own lane. Never drive at night unless you absolutely have to, as few cars have adequate headlights and the roads are full of pedestrians and cyclists. Drunk driving is also very common, among expats as much as locals.

Note that foreign-registered vehicles with a seating capacity of more than six people are not allowed into Kenyan national parks and reserves; Jeeps should be fine, but VW Kombis and other camper vans may have problems.

HITCHING

Hitchhiking is never entirely safe in any country, and we don't recommend it. Travellers who hitch should understand that they are taking a small but potentially serious risk; it's safer to travel in pairs and let someone know where you are planning to go. Also, beware of drunken drivers.

Although it's risky, many locals have no choice but to hitch, so people will know what you're doing if you try to flag down cars. The traditional thumb signal will probably be understood, but locals use a palm-downwards wave to get cars to stop. Many Kenyan drivers expect a contribution towards petrol or some kind of gift from foreign passengers, so make it clear from the outset if you are expecting a free ride.

If you're hoping to hitch into the national parks, dream on! Your chances of coming across tourists with a spare seat who don't mind taking a freeloading stranger along on their expensive safari are slimmer than a starving stick insect, and quite frankly it seems pretty rude to ask. You'll get further asking around for travel companions in Nairobi or any of the gateway towns.

On the other side of the wheel, foreign drivers will be approached all the time by Kenyan hitchers demanding free rides, and giving a lift to a carload of Maasai is certainly a memorable cultural experience.

LOCAL TRANSPORT

Boat

The only local boat service in regular use is the Likoni ferry between the mainland and Mombasa island, which runs throughout the day and night and is free for foot passengers (vehicles pay a small toll).

Boda-boda

Boda-bodas (bicycle taxis) are common in areas where standard taxis are harder to find and also operate in smaller towns and cities such as Kisumu. There is a particular proliferation on the coast, where the bicycle boys also double as touts, guides and drug dealers in tourist areas. A short ride should never cost more than KSh20.

Bus

Nairobi is the only city with an effective municipal bus service, run by KBS. Routes cover the suburbs and outlying areas during daylight hours and generally cost no more than KSh40. Metro Shuttle and private City Hopper services also run to areas such as Kenyatta Airport and Karen. Due to traffic density, safety is rarely a serious concern.

Matatu

Local matatus are the main means of getting around for local people, and any reasonably sized city or town will have plenty of services covering every major road and suburb. Fares start at KSh10 and may reach KSh40 for longer routes in Nairobi. As with buses, roads are usually busy enough for a slight shunt to be the most likely accident, though of course congestion never stops drivers jockeying for position like it's the Kenya Derby.

Minibus transport is not unique to Kenya but the matatu has raised it into a cultural phenomenon, and most Kenyans use them regularly for both local and intercity journeys. The vehicles themselves can be anything from dilapidated Peugeot 504 pick-ups with a cab on the back to big 20-seater minibuses. The most common are white Nissan minibuses (many local people prefer the name 'Nissans' to matatus).

In the bad old days matatus were notorious for dangerous driving, overcrowding and general shady business, but anyone revisiting Kenya will be stunned at the difference. In 2003 then Transport Minister John Michuki banned all matatus from the roads until they complied with a new set of laws, ensuring amazingly speedy results. Matatus must now be fitted with seatbelts and 80km/h speed governors, conductors and drivers must wear clearly identifiable red shirts, route numbers must be clearly displayed and a 14-person capacity applies to vehicles which used to cram in as many as 30 people. Frequent police checks have also been brought in to enforce the rules.

The changes are immediately noticeable and represent an improvement of sorts, but it hasn't taken operators long to find loopholes: most drivers have worked out how to gain extra speed on downhill stretches, conductors memorise the locations of police checkpoints and will scramble extra bodies in and out between them, and passengers seem quite happy only to buckle up when approaching a roadblock. Many drivers still also chew *miraa* leaves to stay awake beyond what is a reasonable or safe time.

Apart from in the remote northern areas, where you'll rely on occasional buses or paid lifts on trucks, you can almost always find a matatu going to the next town or further afield, so long as it's not too late in the day. Simply ask around among the drivers at the local matatu stand or 'stage'. Matatus leave when full and the fares are fixed. It's unlikely you will be charged more money than other passengers.

Wherever you go, remember that most matatu crashes are head-on collisions – under no circumstances should you sit in the 'death seat' next to the matatu driver. Play it safe and sit in the middle seats away from the window.

Shared Taxi (Peugeot)

Shared Peugeot taxis are a good alternative to matatus, though they're not subject to the same speed and safety regulations. The vehicles are usually Peugeot 505 station wagons (hence the local name) that take seven to nine passengers and leave when full.

Peugeots take less time to reach their destinations than matatus as they fill quicker and go from point to point without stopping, and so are slightly more expensive. Many companies have offices around the Accra, Cross and River Rds area in Nairobi, and serve destinations mostly in the north and west of the country.

Taxi

Even the smallest Kenyan towns generally have at least one banged-up old taxi for easy access to outlying areas or even remoter villages, and you'll find cabs on virtually every corner in the larger cities, especially in Nairobi and Mombasa, where taking a taxi at night is virtually mandatory. Fares

---

HAKUNA MATATU?

The new traffic laws were not just designed to impact on safety in matatus – they've also had a profound effect on their aesthetic qualities, the very thing that makes them such unique charabancs in the first place.

Matatus, particularly the big 20-seater ones on local Nairobi routes, frequently used to be moving works of street art, daubed with colourful graffiti reflecting whatever was currently hip in Kenya and blasting out appropriate tuneage on mega-decibel stereos. As part of the new regulations, however, strict noise limits are enforced, and every public conveyance must have a yellow stripe down the side displaying the route, vehicle number and capacity, requiring many matatus to be repainted.

Nairobi matatus have taken the change to heart, and most Nissans are now plain white with a few token stickers or paintings in the rear window. Even the names reflect the toned-down image of the 'new' transport industry: while there are still plenty of Beyoncés and Homeboyz, you're now just as likely to travel in a bus called Safety Bars, God Never Fails or Rise'n'Shine.

In Mombasa, however, hardcore is alive and well, and while the decorations are kept relatively small, the matatu names are, if anything, more provocative. Look out for Saddam, Blood Fist, Jihad and You Are Lonely When You Are Dead… Our favourite, though, has to be the delightful if slightly baffling 'U Kick My Cat – I Kill Ur Dog'. What better sentiment to keep the spirit of the matatu alive and well?

are invariably negotiable and start around KSh200 for short journeys. Most people pick up cabs from taxi ranks on the street, but some companies will take phone bookings and most hotels can order you a ride.

Tuk-Tuk

They are an incongruous sight outside South-East Asia, but several Kenyan towns and cities have these distinctive motorised mini-taxis. The highest concentration is in Malindi, but they're also in Nairobi, Mombasa, Machakos and Diani Beach; Watamu has a handful of less sophisticated motorised rickshaws. Fares are negotiable, but should be at least KSh100 less than the equivalent taxi rate for a short journey (you wouldn't want to take them on a long one!).

SAFARIS

While public transport provides ample options for moving between towns and cities, an organised safari is the best way of getting into and around Kenya's national parks and remote areas like Lake Turkana, and they can sidestep many of the day-to-day hassles of travelling independently. See p59 for a full rundown of the many options.

TRAIN

The Uganda Railway was once the main trade artery in East Africa, but these days the network has dwindled to two main routes, Nairobi–Kisumu and Nairobi–Mombasa. Both are night services of around 13 hours, much slower and less frequent than going by air or road but considerably more safe and comfortable. The Nairobi–Mombasa trip is considered one of the great rail journeys in Africa, providing an opportunity to meet other travellers, and splashing out the extra for full dining-car privileges is worth it just for the experience. As an added bonus cold beer is available on the journey – not something you'll get on a coach.

There are also a handful of weekday evening commuter services from Nairobi, but these are of little help to travellers as road transport is far more efficient.

Classes

There are three classes on Kenyan trains, but only 1st and 2nd class can be recommended. Note that passengers are divided up by gender.

First class consists of two-berth compartments with a washbasin, wardrobe, drinking water and a drinks service. Second class consists of plainer, four-berth compartments with a washbasin and drinking water. No compartment can be locked from the outside, so remember not to leave any valuables lying around if you leave it for any reason. You might want to padlock your rucksack to something during dinner and breakfast. Always lock your compartment from the inside before you go to sleep. Third class is seats only and security can be a real problem.

Passengers in 1st and 2nd class on the Mombasa line are treated to the full colonial experience, including a silver-service dinner in an old-fashioned dining car. Meals typically consist of stews, curries or roast chicken served with rice and vegetables, all dished up by uniformed waiters. There's always a vegetarian option. Tea and coffee is included; sodas (soft drinks), bottled water and alcoholic drinks are not, so ask the price before accepting that KSh1500 bottle of wine. Cold beer is available at all times in the dining car and can be delivered to your compartment.

Costs

The only downside to the train is the price of tickets, over KSh3000 for 1st class on the Nairobi–Mombasa route, including meals (dinner and breakfast) and bedding. You can reduce this considerably by just paying for the seat and bringing your own food and sleeping bag, though you're missing out on the fun half of the experience that way. The Kisumu route is much less fancy, and 1st-class tickets cost around KSh1500. Reduced rates apply for children aged three to 11.

Reservations

You must book in advance for 1st and 2nd class, otherwise there'll probably be no berths available. Two to three days is usually sufficient, but remember that these services run just three times weekly in either direction. Visa credit cards are accepted for railway bookings. If you book by phone, arrive early to pay for your ticket and make sure you're actually on the passenger list. Compartment and berth numbers are posted up about 30 minutes prior to departure.

There are **booking offices** (Nairobi ☎ 020-221211; Mombasa ☎ 041-312220) in major cities and Kisumu railway stations.

Health Dr Caroline Evans

CONTENTS

Before You Go	**385**
Insurance	385
Recommended Vaccinations	386
Medical Checklist	386
Internet Resources	386
Further Reading	386
In Transit	**387**
Deep Vein Thrombosis (DVT)	387
Jet Lag & Motion Sickness	387
In Africa	**387**
Availability & Cost of Health Care	387
Infectious Diseases	388
Traveller's Diarrhoea	392
Environmental Hazards	393
Traditional Medicine	393

If you stay up to date with your vaccinations and take some basic preventive measures, you'd be pretty unlucky to succumb to most of the health hazards covered in this chapter. Africa certainly has an impressive selection of tropical and other diseases, but you're much more likely to get a bout of diarrhoea (in fact, you should bank on it), a cold or an infected mosquito bite than an exotic disease. When it comes to injuries (as opposed to illness), the most likely reason for needing medical help in Africa is as a result of road accidents – vehicles are rarely well maintained, the roads are potholed and poorly lit, and drink driving is common.

BEFORE YOU GO

A little planning before departure, particularly for pre-existing illnesses, will save you a lot of trouble later. Before a long trip, get a check-up from your dentist, and from your doctor if you have any chronic illness, eg high blood pressure or asthma, or use regular medication. You should also organise spare contact lenses and glasses (and take your optical prescription with you); get a first aid and medical kit together (see p386); and arrange necessary vaccinations (p386).

It's tempting to leave all the preparations to the last minute – don't! Many vaccines don't take effect until two weeks after you've been immunised, so visit a doctor four to eight weeks before departure. Ask your doctor for an International Certificate of Vaccination (known in some countries as the yellow booklet), which will list all the vaccinations you've received. This is mandatory for the African countries that require proof of yellow fever vaccination upon entry, but it's a good idea to carry it anyway wherever you travel.

Travellers can register with the **International Association for Medical Advice to Travellers** (Iamat; www.iamat.org). Its website can help travellers find a doctor who has completed recognised training. Those heading off to very remote areas might like to do a first-aid course (contact the Red Cross or St John's Ambulance) or attend a remote medicine first-aid course, such as that offered by the **Royal Geographical Society** (www.wildernessmedicaltraining.co.uk).

If you are bringing medications with you, carry them in their original containers, clearly labelled. A signed and dated letter from your physician describing all medical conditions and medications, including generic names, is also a good idea. If carrying syringes or needles be sure to have a physician's letter documenting their medical necessity.

How do you go about getting the best possible medical help? It's difficult to say – it really depends on the severity of your illness or injury and the availability of local help. If malaria (p389) or another potentially serious disease is suspected, seek medical help as soon as possible or begin self-medicating if you are off the beaten track.

INSURANCE

Find out in advance whether your insurance plan will make payments directly to providers or will reimburse you later for overseas health expenditures (in many African countries doctors expect payment in cash). It's vital to ensure that your travel insurance will cover the emergency transport required to get you to a hospital in a major city, to better medical facilities elsewhere in Africa, or all the way home, by air and with a medical attendant if necessary. Not all insurance covers this, so check the contract carefully. If you need medical help, your insurance company might be able to help locate the nearest hospital or clinic, or you can ask at your hotel. In an emergency, contact your embassy or consulate.

Membership of the **African Medical and Research Foundation** (Amref; www.amref.org) provides an air evacuation service in medical emergencies in some African countries, as well as air ambulance transfers between medical facilities. Money paid by members for this service goes into providing grass-roots medical assistance for local people.

RECOMMENDED VACCINATIONS

The **World Health Organization** (www.who.int/en/) recommends that all travellers be covered for diphtheria, tetanus, measles, mumps, rubella and polio, as well as for hepatitis B, regardless of their destination. A great time to ensure that all routine vaccination cover is complete is when you are planning your travel. The consequences of these diseases can be severe, and outbreaks of them do occur.

According to the **Centers for Disease Control and Prevention** (www.cdc.gov), the following vaccinations are recommended for all parts of Africa: hepatitis A, hepatitis B, meningococcal meningitis, rabies and typhoid, and boosters for tetanus, diphtheria and measles. Vaccination against yellow fever is not necessarily recommended for all parts of Africa, although the certificate is an entry requirement for many countries (see p392). For Kenya, it is advisable to be vaccinated.

MEDICAL CHECKLIST

It is a very good idea to carry a medical and first-aid kit with you, to help yourself in the case of minor illness or injury. Following is a list of items you should consider bringing with you:

- Acetaminophen (paracetamol) or aspirin
- Acetazolamide (Diamox) for altitude sickness (prescription only)
- Adhesive or paper tape
- Antibacterial ointment (eg Bactroban) for cuts and abrasions (prescription only)
- Antibiotics (prescription only), eg ciprofloxacin (Ciproxin) or norfloxacin (Utinor)
- Antidiarrhoeal drugs (eg loperamide)

- Antihistamines (for hay fever and allergic reactions)
- Anti-inflammatory drugs (eg ibuprofen)
- Antimalaria pills
- Bandages, gauze, gauze rolls
- Insect repellent containing DEET, for the skin
- Iodine tablets (for water purification)
- Oral rehydration salts
- Permethrin-containing insect spray for clothing, tents, and bed nets
- Pocket knife
- Scissors, safety pins, tweezers
- Steroid cream or hydrocortisone cream (for allergic rashes)
- Sun block
- Syringes, sterile needles and fluids if travelling to remote areas
- Thermometer

If you are travelling through an area where malaria is a problem – particularly an area where falciparum malaria predominates – consider taking a self-diagnostic kit that can identify malaria in the blood from a finger prick.

INTERNET RESOURCES

There is a wealth of travel health advice on the Internet. For further information, the Lonely Planet website at www.lonelyplanet.com is a good place to start. The World Health Organization publishes a superb book called *International Travel and Health,* which is revised annually and is available online at no cost at www.who.int/ith/. Other websites of general interest are: **MD Travel Health** (www.mdtravelhealth.com), which provides complete travel health recommendations for every country, updated daily, also at no cost; the **Centers for Disease Control and Prevention** (www.cdc.gov); and **Fit for Travel** (www.fitfortravel.scot.nhs.uk), which has up-to-date information about outbreaks and is very user-friendly.

It's also a good idea to consult your government's travel health website before departure, if one is available:

Australia www.smartraveller.gov.au
Canada www.hc-sc.gc.ca/english/index.html
UK www.doh.gov.uk/traveladvice/index.htm
USA www.cdc.gov/travel/

FURTHER READING

Two publications produced by Lonely Planet are useful: *Healthy Travel Africa,* by

Isabelle Young, and *Travel with Children,* by Cathy Lanigan. Other useful books:

- *A Comprehensive Guide to Wilderness and Travel Medicine,* by Eric A Weiss
- *Healthy Travel,* by Jane Wilson-Howarth
- *How to Stay Healthy Abroad,* by Richard Dawood
- *Travel in Health,* by Graham Fry

IN TRANSIT

DEEP VEIN THROMBOSIS (DVT)

Blood clots can form in the legs during flights, chiefly because of prolonged immobility. This formation of clots is known as deep vein thrombosis (DVT), and the longer the flight, the greater the risk. Although most blood clots are reabsorbed uneventfully, some might break off and travel through the blood vessels to the lungs, where they could cause life-threatening complications.

The chief symptom of DVT is swelling or pain of the foot, ankle or calf, usually but not always on just one side. When a blood clot travels to the lungs, it could cause chest pain and breathing difficulty. Travellers with any of these symptoms should immediately seek medical attention.

To help prevent the development of DVT on long flights you should regularly walk about the cabin, perform isometric compressions of the leg muscles (ie contract the leg muscles while sitting), drink plenty of fluids and avoid alcohol.

JET LAG & MOTION SICKNESS

If you're crossing more than five time zones you could well suffer jet lag, which results in insomnia, fatigue, malaise or nausea. To minimise the effect of jet lag try drinking plenty of fluids (of the nonalcoholic variety) and eating light meals. Upon arrival, get exposure to natural sunlight and readjust your schedule (for meals, sleep etc) as soon as possible.

Antihistamines such as dimenhydrinate (Dramamine) and meclizine (Antivert, Bonine) are usually the first choice for treating motion sickness. The main side effect of these drugs is drowsiness. If you're concerned about taking medication, a herbal alternative is ginger (in the form of ginger tea, biscuits or crystallized ginger), which works like a charm for some people.

IN AFRICA

AVAILABILITY & COST OF HEALTH CARE

Health care in Africa is varied: it can be excellent in the major cities, which generally have well-trained doctors and nurses, but it is often patchy off the beaten track. Medicine and even sterile dressings and intravenous fluids might need to be purchased from a local pharmacy. The standard of dental care is equally variable, and there is an increased risk of hepatitis B and HIV transmission from poorly sterilised equipment.

By and large, public hospitals in Africa offer the cheapest service, but will have the least up-to-date equipment and medications; mission hospitals (where donations are the usual form of payment) often have more reasonable facilities; and private hospitals and clinics are more expensive but tend to have more advanced drugs and equipment and better trained medical staff.

Most drugs can be purchased over the counter in Africa, without a prescription. Many drugs for sale in Africa might be ineffective; they might be counterfeit or might not have been stored under the right conditions. The most common examples of counterfeit drugs are malaria tablets and expensive antibiotics, such as ciprofloxacin. Most drugs are available in capital cities, but remote villages will be lucky to have a couple of paracetamol tablets. It is strongly recommended that you bring all medication from home. Also, the availability and efficacy of condoms cannot be relied upon – bring all the contraception you'll need. Condoms bought in Africa might not be of the same quality as in Europe, North America or Australia, and they might have been incorrectly stored.

There is a high risk of contracting HIV from infected blood if you receive a blood transfusion in Africa. The **BloodCare Foundation** (www.bloodcare.org.uk) is a useful source of safe, screened blood, which can be transported to any part of the world within 24 hours.

The cost of health care might seem very cheap compared to that in first-world countries, but good care and drugs might be not be available. Evacuation to good medical care (within Africa or to your own country)

HEALTH

can be very expensive indeed. Unfortunately, adequate – let alone good – health care is available only to very few Africans.

INFECTIOUS DISEASES

It's a formidable list but, as we say, a few precautions go a long way…

Bilharzia (Schistosomiasis)

This disease is spread by flukes (minute worms) that are carried by a species of freshwater snail. The flukes are carried inside the snail, which then sheds them into slow-moving or still water. The parasites penetrate human skin as people paddle or swim and then migrate to the bladder or bowel. They are passed out via stool or urine and could contaminate fresh water, where the cycle starts again. Paddling or swimming in suspect freshwater lakes or slow-running rivers should be avoided. There may be no symptoms. However, there may be a transient fever and rash, and advanced cases may have blood in the stool or in the urine. A blood test can detect antibodies if you might have been exposed, and treatment is then possible in specialist travel or infectious disease clinics. If not treated the infection can cause kidney failure or permanent bowel damage. It is not possible for you to infect others directly.

Cholera

Cholera is usually only a problem during natural or artificial disasters, eg war, floods or earthquakes, although small outbreaks can also occur at other times. Travellers are rarely affected. The disease is caused by a bacteria and spread via contaminated drinking water. The main symptom is profuse watery diarrhoea, which causes debilitation if fluids are not replaced quickly. An oral cholera vaccine is available in the USA, but it is not particularly effective. Most cases of cholera can be avoided by drinking only clean water and by avoiding potentially contaminated food. Treatment is by fluid replacement (orally or via a drip), but sometimes antibiotics are needed. Self-treatment is not advised.

Diphtheria

Found in all of Africa, diphtheria is spread through close respiratory contact. It usually causes a high temperature and a severe sore throat. A membrane can form across the throat, requiring a tracheostomy to prevent suffocation. Vaccination is recommended for those likely to be in close contact with the locals in infected areas. This is more important for long stays than for short-term trips. The vaccine is given as an injection alone or with tetanus, and lasts 10 years.

Filariasis

Tiny worms migrating in the lymphatic system cause filariasis. The bite from an infected mosquito spreads the infection. Symptoms include localised itching and swelling of the legs and/or genitalia. Treatment is available.

Hepatitis A

Hepatitis A is spread through contaminated food (particularly shellfish) and water. It causes jaundice and, although it is rarely fatal, it can cause prolonged lethargy. If you're recovering from hepatitis A, you shouldn't drink alcohol for up to six months afterwards, but once you've recovered, there won't be any long-term problems. The first symptoms include dark urine and a yellow colour to the whites of the eyes. Sometimes a fever and abdominal pain might be present. Hepatitis A vaccine (Avaxim, Vaqta, Havrix) is given as an injection: a single dose will give protection for up to a year, and a booster after a year gives 10-year protection. Hepatitis A and typhoid vaccines can also be given as a single-dose vaccine, with hepatyrix or viatim.

Hepatitis B

Hepatitis B is spread through infected blood, contaminated needles and sexual intercourse. It can also be spread from an infected mother to the baby during childbirth. Hepatitis B affects the liver, which causes jaundice and occasionally liver failure. Most people recover completely, but some people might be chronic carriers of the virus, which could lead eventually to cirrhosis or liver cancer. Those visiting high-risk areas for long periods or those with increased social or occupational risk should be immunised. Many countries now routinely give hepatitis B as part of routine childhood vaccination. It is given singly or can be given at the same time as hepatitis A (hepatyrix).

A course will give protection for at least five years. It can be given over four weeks or six months.

HEALTH

HIV

Human immunodeficiency virus (HIV), the virus that causes acquired immune deficiency syndrome (AIDS), is an enormous problem throughout Africa, but is most acutely felt in sub-Saharan Africa. The virus is spread through infected blood and blood products, by sexual intercourse with an infected partner and from an infected mother to her baby during childbirth or breastfeeding. It can be spread through 'blood to blood' contacts, such as with contaminated instruments during medical, dental, acupuncture and other body-piercing procedures, and through sharing intravenous needles. At present there is no cure; medication that might keep the disease under control is available, but these drugs are too expensive for the overwhelming majority of Africans, and are not readily available for travellers either. If you think you might have been exposed to HIV, a blood test is necessary; a three-month gap after exposure and before testing is required to allow antibodies to appear in the blood.

Malaria

One million children die annually from malaria in Africa. The disease is caused by a parasite in the bloodstream spread by the bite of the female Anopheles mosquito. There are several types of malaria, falciparum malaria being the most dangerous type and the predominant form in Africa. Infection rates vary with season and climate, so check out the situation before departure.

The incidence of malarial transmission at altitudes higher than 2000m is rare.

Unlike most other diseases regularly encountered by travellers, there is no vaccination against malaria (yet). However, several different drugs are used to prevent malaria, and new ones are in the pipeline. Up-to-date advice from a travel health clinic is essential as different medications are more suitable for some travellers than others. Also, the pattern of drug-resistant malaria is changing rapidly, so what was advised years ago might no longer be the case.

Malaria can affect people in several ways. The early stages include headaches, fevers, generalised aches and pains, and malaise, often mistaken for flu. Other symptoms can include abdominal pain, diarrhoea and a cough. Anyone who develops a fever while in a malarial area should assume malarial infection until a blood test proves negative, even if you've been taking antimalarial medication. If not treated, the next stage can develop within 24 hours, particularly if falciparum malaria is the parasite: jaundice, reduced consciousness and coma (known as cerebral malaria) followed by death. Treatment in hospital is essential, and if patients enter this late stage of the disease the death rate may still be as high as 10%, even in the best intensive-care facilities.

TRAVEL PREPARATION

Many travellers are under the impression that malaria is a mild illness, that treatment

---

AIDS IN KENYA

Like most of its neighbours, Kenya is in the grip of a devastating AIDS epidemic. There are 2.5 million Kenyans with full-blown AIDS and nearly 700 people die from the disease every day. AIDS is predominately a heterosexual disease in Kenya and now strikes all classes of people. At least 890,000 children have been orphaned and many others are infected while in the womb.

Teachers have been badly affected – at least 18 die daily – because they are predominantly in the 20 to 29 age group that's most affected by HIV/AIDS, and Kenya is facing an education crisis as a result, leaving even fewer people to spread the AIDS-awareness message. Around 85% of prostitutes are affected, and young girls in general are especially vulnerable, due to the widespread belief that AIDS can be cured by sleeping with girls who are virgins.

Drug treatments that are available in the West to increase the lifespan of AIDS sufferers and reduce the risk of infection passing to the foetus in HIV-infected women remain well beyond the financial reach of most Kenyans, few of whom have access to even basic health care. The problem is unlikely to improve as long as Western drug companies refuse to allow developing countries to produce much cheaper generic versions of their products. Currently the cost of treating a single AIDS victim for a year is US$34,000, while the annual wage of most people in Kenya is under US$500.

is always easy and successful, and that taking antimalarial drugs causes more illness through side effects than actually getting malaria. In Africa, this is unfortunately not true. Side effects of the medication depend on the drug being taken. Doxycycline can cause heartburn and indigestion; mefloquine (Larium) can cause anxiety attacks, insomnia and nightmares, and (rarely) severe psychiatric disorders; chloroquine can cause nausea and hair loss; and proguanil can cause mouth ulcers. These side effects are not universal, and can be minimized by taking medication correctly, such as with food.

If you decide that you really do not wish to take antimalarial drugs, you must understand the risks, and be obsessive about avoiding mosquito bites. Use nets and insect repellent, and report any fever or flu-like symptoms to a doctor as soon as possible. Some people advocate homeopathic preparations against malaria, such as Demal200, but as yet there is no conclusive evidence that this is effective, and many homeopaths do not recommend their use. Some people should not take a particular antimalarial drug, eg people with epilepsy should avoid mefloquine, and doxycycline should not be taken by pregnant women or children younger than 12.

The risks from malaria to both mother and foetus during pregnancy are considerable. Malaria in pregnancy frequently results in miscarriage or premature labour. Unless good medical care can be guaranteed, travel throughout Africa when pregnant – particularly to malarial areas – should be discouraged unless essential. See Stand-By Treatment (below) if you are more than 24 hours away from medical help.

Adults who have survived childhood malaria develop a resistance and usually only develop mild cases of malaria if it recurs; most Western travellers have no resistance at all. Resistance wanes after 18 months of nonexposure, so even if you have had malaria in the past, you might no longer be resistant.

STAND-BY TREATMENT

If you are planning a journey through an area where malaria exists, particularly where falciparum malaria predominates, consider taking a stand-by treatment. Emergency stand-by treatments should be seen as emergency treatment aimed at saving the patient's life and not as routine way of self-medicating. It should be used only if you will be far from medical facilities and have been advised about the symptoms of malaria and how to use the medication. Medical advice should be sought as soon as possible to confirm whether the treatment has been successful. The type of stand-by treatment used will depend on local conditions, such as drug resistance, and on what antimalarial drugs were being used before stand-by treatment. This is worthwhile because you want to avoid contracting a particularly serious form such as cerebral malaria, which affects the brain and central nervous system and can be fatal within 24 hours. As mentioned on p386, self-diagnostic kits, which can identify malaria in the blood from a finger prick, are also available in the West.

Meningococcal Meningitis

Meningococcal infection is spread through close respiratory contact and is more likely to be contracted in crowded situations, such as dormitories, buses and clubs. Infection is uncommon in travellers. Vaccination is recommended for long stays and is especially important towards the end of the dry season, which varies across the continent. Symptoms include a fever, severe headache, neck stiffness and a red rash. Immediate medical treatment is necessary.

The ACWY vaccine is recommended for all travellers in sub-Saharan Africa. This vaccine is different from the meningococcal meningitis C vaccine given to children and adolescents in some countries; it is safe to be given both types of vaccine.

Poliomyelitis

Polio is generally spread through contaminated food and water. It is one of the vaccines given in childhood in the West and should be boosted every 10 years, either orally (a drop on the tongue) or as an injection. Polio can be carried asymptomatically (ie showing no symptoms) and could cause a transient fever. In rare cases it causes weakness or paralysis of one or more muscles, which might be permanent.

Rabies

Rabies is spread by the bites or licks of an infected animal on broken skin. It is always fatal once the clinical symptoms start (which might be up to several months after an infected bite), so post-bite vaccination should be taken as soon as possible. Post-bite vaccination (whether or not you've been vaccinated before the bite) prevents the virus from spreading to the central nervous system. Animal handlers should be vaccinated, as should those travelling to remote areas where a reliable source of post-bite vaccine is not available within 24 hours. To prevent the disease, three injections are needed over a month. If you have not been vaccinated and receive a bite, you will need a course of five injections starting 24 hours or as soon as possible after the injury. If you have been vaccinated, you will need fewer post-bite injections, and have more time to seek medical help.

Rift Valley Fever

This fever is spread occasionally via mosquito bites. The symptoms are of a fever and flu-like illness, and is rarely fatal.

River Blindness (Onchocerciasis)

This is caused by the larvae of a tiny worm, which is spread by the bite of a small fly. The earliest sign of infection is intensely itchy, red, sore eyes. Travellers are rarely severely affected. Treatment should be sought in a specialised clinic.

Sleeping Sickness (Trypanosomiasis)

Sleeping sickness is spread via the bite of the tsetse fly and causes a headache, fever and eventually coma. There is an effective treatment.

Tuberculosis (TB)

TB is spread through close respiratory contact and occasionally through infected milk or milk products. BCG vaccination is recommended for anyone who is likely to be mixing closely with the local population, although the vaccination gives only moderate protection against TB. It is more important to be vaccinated for long-term stays than for short stays. The BCG vaccine is not available in all countries, but is given routinely to many children in developing countries. The vaccination is usually given in a specialised chest clinic and causes a small permanent scar at the site of injection. It is a live vaccine and should not be given to pregnant women or immunocompromised individuals.

TB can be asymptomatic, only being picked up by a routine chest X-ray. Alternatively, it can cause a cough, weight loss or fever, sometimes months or even years after exposure.

Typhoid

This illness is spread through handling food or drinking water that has been contaminated by infected human faeces. The first symptom of infection is usually a fever or a pink rash on the abdomen. Sometimes septicaemia (blood poisoning) can also occur. A typhoid vaccine (typhim Vi, typherix) will give protection for three years. In some countries, the oral vaccine Vivotif is also available. Antibiotics are usually given as treatment, and death is rare unless septicaemia occurs.

THE ANTIMALARIAL A TO D

- A – Awareness of the risk. No medication is totally effective, but protection of up to 95% is achievable with most drugs, as long as other measures have been taken.

- B – Bites. Avoid at all costs. Sleep in a screened room, use a mosquito spray or coils, sleep under a permethrin-impregnated net at night. Cover up at night with long trousers and long sleeves, preferably with permethrin-treated clothing. Apply appropriate repellent to all areas of exposed skin in the evenings.

- C – Chemical prevention (ie antimalarial drugs) is usually needed in malaria-infected areas. Expert advice is needed as the resistance patterns of the parasite can change, and new drugs are in development. Not all antimalarial drugs are suitable for everyone. Most antimalarial drugs need to be started at least a week in advance and continued for four weeks after the last possible exposure to malaria.

- D – Diagnosis. If you have a fever or flu-like illness within a year of travel to a malaria-infected area, malaria is a possibility, and immediate medical attention is necessary.

Yellow Fever

You should carry a certificate as evidence of vaccination against yellow fever if you've recently been in an infected country, to avoid immigration problems. For a full list of countries where yellow fever is endemic visit the websites of the **World Health Organization** (www.who.int/wer/) or the **Centers for Disease Control and Prevention** (www.cdc.gov/travel/blusheet.htm). A traveller without a legally required up-to-date certificate could possibly be vaccinated and detained in isolation at the port of arrival for up to 10 days, or even repatriated.

Yellow fever is spread by infected mosquitoes. Symptoms range from a flu-like illness to severe hepatitis (liver inflammation), jaundice and death. Vaccination must be given at a designated clinic and is valid for 10 years. It's a live vaccine and must not be given to immunocompromised or pregnant women.

TRAVELLER'S DIARRHOEA

Although it's not inevitable that you will get diarrhoea while travelling in Africa, it's certainly likely. Diarrhoea is the most common travel-related illness – figures suggest that at least half of all travellers to Africa will get diarrhoea. Sometimes dietary changes, such as increased spices or oils, are the cause. To help prevent diarrhoea, avoid tap water unless you're sure it's safe to drink (see opposite). You should also only eat fresh fruits or vegetables if cooked or peeled, and be wary of dairy products that might contain unpasteurised milk. Although freshly cooked food can often be safe, plates or serving utensils might be dirty, so be highly selective when eating food from street vendors (ensure that cooked food is piping hot right through). If you develop diarrhoea, drink plenty of fluids, preferably an oral rehydration solution containing water (lots), and some salt and sugar. A few loose stools don't require treatment but, if you start having more than four or five stools a day, you should start taking an antibiotic (usually a quinoline drug, such as ciprofloxacin or norfloxacin) and an antidiarrhoeal agent (eg loperamide) if you are not within easy reach of a toilet. If diarrhoea is bloody, persists for more than 72 hours or is accompanied by fever, shaking chills or abdominal pain, seek medical attention.

Amoebic Dysentery

Contracted by eating contaminated food and water, amoebic dysentery causes blood and mucus in the faeces. It can be relatively mild and tends to come on gradually, but seek medical advice if you think you have the illness as it won't clear up without treatment (which is with specific antibiotics).

Giardiasis

This, like amoebic dysentery, is caused by contaminated food or water. The illness usually appears a week or more after exposure to the parasite. Giardiasis might cause only a short-lived bout of typical travellers' diarrhoea, but may cause persistent diarrhoea. Ideally, seek medical advice if you suspect you have giardiasis, but if you are in a remote area you could start a course of antibiotics.

MANDATORY YELLOW FEVER VACCINATION

- North Africa – Not mandatory for any areas of North Africa, but Algeria, Libya and Tunisia require evidence of yellow fever vaccination if entering from an infected country. It is recommended for travellers to Sudan, and might be given to unvaccinated travellers leaving that country.

- Central Africa – Mandatory in Central African Republic (CAR), Congo, Congo (Zaïre), Equatorial Guinea and Gabon, and recommended in Chad.

- West Africa – Mandatory in Benin, Burkina Faso, Cameroon, Côte d'Ivoire, Ghana, Liberia, Mali, Niger, Sao Tome & Principe and Togo, and recommended for The Gambia, Guinea, Guinea-Bissau, Mauritania, Nigeria, Senegal and Sierra Leone.

- East Africa – Mandatory in Rwanda; it is recommended for Burundi, Ethiopia, Kenya, Somalia, Tanzania and Uganda.

- Southern Africa – Not mandatory for entry into any countries of Southern Africa, although it is necessary if entering from an infected country.

ENVIRONMENTAL HAZARDS
Heat Exhaustion

This condition occurs following heavy sweating and excessive fluid loss with inadequate replacement of fluids and salt, and is particularly common in hot climates when taking unaccustomed exercise before full acclimatisation. Symptoms include headache, dizziness and tiredness. Dehydration is already happening by the time you feel thirsty – aim to drink sufficient water to produce pale, diluted urine. Self-treatment: fluid replacement with water and/or fruit juice, and cooling by cold water and fans. The treatment of the salt-loss component consists of consuming salty fluids such as soup, and adding a little more salt to foods than usual.

Heatstroke

Heat exhaustion is a precursor to the much more serious condition of heatstroke. In this case there is damage to the sweating mechanism, with an excessive rise in body temperature; irrational and hyperactive behaviour; and eventually loss of consciousness and death. Rapid cooling by spraying the body with water and fanning is ideal. Emergency fluid and electrolyte replacement is usually also required by intravenous drip.

Insect Bites & Stings

Mosquitoes might not always carry malaria or dengue fever, but they (and other insects) can cause irritation and infected bites. To avoid these, take the same precautions as you would for avoiding malaria (see p391). Use DEET-based insect repellents. Excellent clothing treatments are also available; mosquitos that land on treated clothing will die.

Bee and wasp stings cause real problems only to those who have a severe allergy to the stings (anaphylaxis.) If you are one of these people, carry an 'epipen' – an adrenaline (epinephrine) injection, which you can give yourself. This could save your life.

Sandflies are found near many African beaches. They usually only cause a nasty itchy bite but can carry a rare skin disorder, cutaneous leishmaniasis. Prevention of bites with DEET-based repellents is sensible.

Scorpions are frequently found in arid or dry climates. They can cause a painful bite that is sometimes life-threatening. If you are bitten by a scorpion, take a painkiller. Medi-

cal treatment should be sought if collapse occurs.

Bed bugs are often found in hostels and cheap hotels. Bites lead to very itchy, lumpy skin. Spraying the mattress with crawling-insect killer then changing the bedding will get rid of them.

Scabies is also frequently found in cheap accommodation. These tiny mites live in the skin, particularly between the fingers. They cause an intensely itchy rash. The itch is easily treated with malathion and permethrin lotion from a pharmacy; other members of the household also need treatment to avoid spreading scabies, even if they do not show any symptoms.

Snake Bites

Basically, avoid getting bitten! Do not walk barefoot, and don't stick your hand into holes or cracks. However, 50% of those bitten by venomous snakes are not actually injected with poison (envenomed). If bitten by a snake, do not panic. Immobilise the bitten limb with a splint (such as a stick) and apply a bandage over the site, with firm pressure – similar to bandaging a sprain. Do not apply a tourniquet, or cut or suck the bite. Get medical help as soon as possible so antivenom can be given if needed.

Water

Never drink tap water unless it has been boiled, filtered or chemically disinfected (such as with iodine tablets), except in South Africa. Never drink from streams, rivers and lakes. It's also best to avoid drinking from pumps and wells – some do bring pure water to the surface, but the presence of animals can still contaminate supplies.

TRADITIONAL MEDICINE

At least 80% of the African population relies on traditional medicine, often either because conventional Western-style medicine is too expensive, because of prevailing cultural attitudes and beliefs, or simply because in some cases it works. It might also be because there's no other choice: a World Health Organization survey found that although there was only one medical doctor for every 50,000 people in Mozambique, there was a traditional healer for every 200 people.

Although some traditional African remedies seem to work on illnesses such as malaria, sickle cell anaemia, high blood pressure and some AIDS symptoms, most African healers tend to learn their art by apprenticeship, so education (and consequently the application of knowledge) is inconsistent and unregulated. Conventionally trained physicians in South Africa, for example, angrily describe how their AIDS patients die of kidney failure because a *sangoma* (traditional healer) has given them an enema containing an essence made from powerful roots. Likewise, when traditional healers administer 'injections' with porcupine quills, knives or dirty razor blades, diseases are often spread or created rather than cured.

Rather than attempting to stamp out traditional practices, or simply pretend they aren't happening, a positive first step taken by some African countries is the regulation of traditional medicine by creating healers' associations and offering courses on such topics as sanitary practices. It remains unlikely in the short term that even a basic level of conventional Western-style medicine will be made available to all the people of Africa (even though the cost of doing so is less than the annual military budget of some Western countries). Traditional medicine, on the other hand, will almost certainly continue to be practised widely throughout the continent.

HEALTH

Language

CONTENTS

Swahili	**395**
Pronunciation	395
Accommodation	396
Emergencies	396
Conversation & Essentials	396
Directions	396
Health	397
Language Difficulties	397
Numbers	397
On Safari	397
Question Words	397
Shopping & Services	398
Time & Dates	398
Transport	398
Travel with Children	399

English and Swahili (called Kiswahili in the language itself) are the official languages of Kenya and are taught in schools throughout the country. There are also many major indigenous languages (including Kikuyu, Luo, Kikamba, Maasai and Samburu) and a plethora of minor tribal languages. Hindi and Urdu are still spoken by residents of Indian subcontinent origin.

Most urban Kenyans and even tribal people who deal with tourists speak English, so you shouldn't experience too many problems making yourself understood. Italian is almost the second language on the coast, and Kenyans working in the tourist industry may also speak German. Most tourists to the coast also visit the national parks, so safari operators almost always speak some Italian and German.

Swahili is widely spoken in Kenya, but the language becomes more basic the further you get away from the coast, with a lot more English words creeping in. You'll also find that there are more books and newspapers available in English than there are in Swahili. Nonetheless, a working knowledge of Swahili, especially outside urban areas, is very useful. It will enrich your travel experience and open doors, often enabling you to communicate with people who don't speak English, particularly speakers of different tribal languages.

Another language you may come across in Kenya is Sheng, which is spoken almost exclusively by the young people. Essentially a patois, it's a mixture of Swahili and English, with a fair sprinkling of Hindi, Gujarati, Kikuyu and other tribal languages. Unless you can speak reasonable Swahili, you probably won't realise Sheng is being spoken – listen out for the distinctive greeting between friends – *Sassa!*. The response can be *Besht*, *Mambo* or *Fit* (pronounced almost like 'feet').

SWAHILI

The Yale website at www.yale.edu/swahili/ is an excellent general online reference to the language and contains a useful audio pronunciation guide. Get a copy of Lonely Planet's *Swahili Phrasebook* for a handy, pocket-sized language guide chock full of useful Swahili.

PRONUNCIATION

Perhaps the easiest part of learning Swahili is the pronunciation. Every letter is pronounced, unless it's part of the consonant combinations discussed in the 'Consonants' section below. If a letter is written twice, it is pronounced twice – *mzee* (respected elder) has three syllables: m-ze-e. Note that the 'm' is a separate syllable, and that the double 'e' indicates a lengthened vowel sound. Word stress is almost always falls on the second-last syllable.

Vowels

Correct pronunciation of vowels is the key to making yourself understood in Swahili. If the following guidelines don't work for you, listen closely to how Swahili speakers pronounce their words and spend some time practising.

Remember that if two vowels appear next to each other, each must be pronounced in turn. For example, *kawaida* (usual) is pronounced ka-wa-*ee*-da.

LANGUAGE

a	as in 'calm'
e	as the 'ey' in 'they'
i	as the 'ee' in 'keep'
o	as in 'go'
u	as the 'oo' in 'moon'

Consonants

Most consonants in Swahili have equivalents in English. The sounds **th** and **dh** occur only in words borrowed from Arabic. The **ng** combination is tricky at first but gets easier with practice.

r	Swahili speakers make only a slight distinction between **r** and **l**; use a light 'd' for **r** and you'll be pretty close.
dh	as 'th' in 'this'
th	as in 'thing'
ny	as in 'canyon'
ng	as in 'singer'
gh	like the 'ch' in Scottish *loch*
g	as in 'get'
ch	as in 'church'

ACCOMMODATION

Where's a ...?	... iko wapi?
camping ground	uwanja wa kambi
guesthouse	gesti
hotel	hoteli
youth hostel	hosteli ya vijana

Can you recommend cheap lodging?
Unaweza kunipendekezea malazi rahisi?
What's the address?
Anwani ni nini?

Do you have a ... room?	Kuna chumba kwa ...?
single	mtu mmoja
double	watu wawili, kitanda kimoja
twin	watu wawili, vitanda viwili

How much is it per day/person?
Ni bei gani kwa siku/mtu?
Can I see the room?
Naomba nione chumba?
Where's the bathroom?
Choo iko wapi?
Where are the toilets?
Vyoo viko wapi?
I'll take it.
Nataka.
I'm leaving now.
Naondoka sasa.

EMERGENCIES

Help!	Saidia!
There's been an accident!	Ajali imetokea!
Call the police!	Waite polisi!
Call a doctor!	Mwite daktari!
I'm lost.	Nimejipotea.
Leave me alone!	Niache!

CONVERSATION & ESSENTIALS

It's considered rude to speak to someone without first greeting them, so even if you only want directions, greet the person first. *Jambo* and *salama* can be used as the Swahili equivalents of 'excuse me'. *Shikamoo* is also a respectful greeting used for elders: the reply is *marahaba*.

Hello.	Jambo or Salama.
Welcome.	Karibu.
Goodbye.	Kwa heri.
(Until) tomorrow.	Kesho.
Goodnight.	Lala salama.
See you later.	Tutaonana.
Yes.	Ndiyo.
No.	Hapana.
Please. (if asking a big favour)	Tafadhali.
Thanks (very much).	Asante (sana).
You're welcome.	Karibu.
Excuse me.	Samahani.
Sorry.	Pole.
How are you?	Habari?
I'm fine, thanks.	Nzuri.
What's your name?	Unaitwa nani?
My name is ...	Jina langu ni ...
Where are you from?	Unatoka wapi?
I'm from ...	Mimi ninatoka ...
Where do you live?	Unakaa wapi?
I live in ...	Ninakaa ...
May I take a picture?	Naomba kupiga picha.
Just a minute.	Subiri kidogo.

DIRECTIONS

Where's ...?	... iko wapi?
It's straight ahead.	Iko moja kwa moja.
near	karibu na
next to	jirani ya
opposite	ng'ambo ya

Turn ...	Geuza ...
at the corner	kwenye kona
at the traffic lights	kwenye taa za barabarani

| left | kushoto |
| right | kulia |

HEALTH

| I'm sick. | Mimi ni mgonjwa. |
| It hurts here. | Inauma hapa. |

I'm allergic to ...	Nina mzio wa ...
antibiotics	viuavijasumu
aspirin	aspirini
bees	nyuki
nuts	kokwa
peanuts	karanga

antiseptic	dawa ya kusafisha jeraha
condoms	kondom
contraceptives	kingamimba
insect repellent	dawa la kufukuza wadudu
iodine	iodini
painkillers	viondoa maumivu
thermometer	pimajoto
water purification tablets	vidonge vya kusafisha maji

LANGUAGE DIFFICULTIES

Do you speak (English)?
    Unasema (Kiingereza)?
Does anyone speak (English)?
    Kuna mtu yeyote kusema (Kiingereza)?
What does (asante) mean?
    Neno (asante) lina maana gani?
Yes, I understand.
    Ndiyo, naelewa.
No, I don't understand.
    Hapana, sielewi.
Could you please write ... down?
    Tafadhali ... andika?
Can you show me (on the map)?
    Unaweza kunionyesha (katika ramani)?

NUMBERS

0	sifuri
1	moja
2	mbili
3	tatu
4	nne
5	tano
6	sita
7	saba
8	nane
9	tisa
10	kumi
11	kumi na moja
12	kumi na mbili
13	kumi na tatu
14	kumi na nne
15	kumi na tano
16	kumi na sita
17	kumi na saba
18	kumi na nane
19	kumi na tisa
20	ishirini
21	ishirini na moja
22	ishirini na mbili
30	thelathini
40	arobaini
50	hamsini
60	sitini
70	sabini
80	themanini
90	tisini
100	mia moja
1000	elfu

ON SAFARI

Look there.	Tazama pale.
What is there?	Iko nini pale?
What animal is that?	Huyo ni mnyama gani?
electric fence	usiguse sengeni
Watch out!	Angalia!/Chunga!
Danger (on signs)	Hatari

African buffalo	mbogo
antelope	pofu/kulungu
baboon	nyani
bird	ndege
bushbaby	komba
cheetah	duma
crocodile	mamba
elephant	ndovu/tembo
gazelle	swala/swara/paa
giraffe	twiga
hippopotamus	kiboko
impala	swala pala
jackal	mbweha
leopard	chui
lion	simba
mongoose	nguchiro
rhinoceros	kifaru
snake	nyoka
spotted hyena	fisi
water buffalo	nyati
zebra	punda milia

QUESTION WORDS

Who?	Nani?
What?	Nini?
When?	Lini?

LANGUAGE

Where?	Wapi?
Which?	Gani?
Why?	Kwa nini?
How?	Namna?

SHOPPING & SERVICES

department store	duka lenye vitu vingi
general store	duka lenye vitu mbalimbali

I'd like to buy ...	Nataka kununua ...
I'm just looking.	Naangalia tu.
How much is it?	Ni bei gani?
Can I look at it?	Naomba nione.
I don't like it.	Sipendi.
That's too expensive.	Ni ghali mno.
Please lower the price.	Punguza bei, tafadhali.
I'll take it.	Nataka.

Do you accept ...?	Mnakubali ...?
credit cards	kadi ya benki
travellers cheques	hundi ya msafiri

more	zaidi
less	chache zaidi

Where's (a/the) ...?	... iko wapi?
bank	benki
market	soko
tourist office	maarifa kwa watalii
... embassy	ubalozi ...
hospital	hospitali
post office	posta
public phone	simu ya mtaani
public toilet	choo cha hadhara
telecom centre	telekom

TIME & DATES

What time is it?	Ni saa ngapi?
It's (ten) o'clock.	Ni saa (nne).
morning	asubuhi
afternoon	mchana
evening	jioni
today	leo
tomorrow	kesho
yesterday	jana

Monday	Jumatatu
Tuesday	Jumanne
Wednesday	Jumatano
Thursday	Alhamisi
Friday	Ijumaa
Saturday	Jumamosi
Sunday	Jumapili

January	mwezi wa kwanza
February	mwezi wa pili
March	mwezi wa tatu
April	mwezi wa nne
May	mwezi wa tano
June	mwezi wa sita
July	mwezi wa saba
August	mwezi wa nane
September	mwezi wa tisa
October	mwezi wa kumi
November	mwezi wa kumi na moja
December	mwezi wa kumi na mbili

TRANSPORT
Public Transport

What time is the ... leaving?
... inaondoka saa ngapi?
Which ... goes to (...)?
... ipi huenda (...)?

bus	basi
minibus	matatu
plane	ndege
train	treni

When's the ... (bus)?
(Basi) ... itaondoka lini?

first	ya kwanza
last	ya mwisho
next	ijayo

A ... ticket to (...).
Tiketi moja ya ... kwenda (...).

1st-class	daraja la kwanza
2nd-class	daraja la pili
one-way	kwenda tu
return	kwenda na kurudi

cancelled	imefutwa
delayed	imeche leweshwa
platform	stendi
ticket window	dirisha la tiketi
timetable	ratiba

Private Transport

I'd like to hire a/an ...	Nataka kukodi ...
bicycle	baisikeli
car	gar i
4WD	forbaifor
motorbike	pikipiki

Are you willing to hire out your car/motorbike?
Unaweza kunikodisha gari/pikipiki yako?
(How long) Can I park here?
Naweza kuegesha hapa (kwa muda gani)?

Is this the road to (Embu)?
  Hii ni barabara kwenda (Embu)?
Where's a petrol station?
  Kituo cha mafuta kiko wapi?
Please fill it up.
  Jaza tangi/tanki.
I'd like ... litres.
  Nataka lita ...

diesel	*dizeli*
leaded/unleaded	*risasi/isiyo na risasi*
I need a mechanic.	*Nahitaji fundi.*
I've had an accident.	*Nimepata ajali.*
I have a flat tyre.	*Nina pancha.*
I've run out of petrol.	*Mafuta yamekwisha.*

The car/motorbike has broken down (at Chalinze).
  Gari/pikipiki ime haribika (Chalinze).
The car/motorbike won't start.
  Gari/pikipiki haiwaki.

Could I pay for a ride in your truck?
  Naweza kulipa kwa lifti katika lori lako?
Could I contribute to the petrol cost?
  Naweza kuchangia sehemu ya bei ya mafuta?
Thanks for the ride.
  Asante kwa lifti.

TRAVEL WITH CHILDREN

I need a/an ...	*Nahitaji ...*
Is there a/an ...?	*Kuna ...?*
baby seat	*kiti cha kitoto*
child-minding service	*anayeweza kumlea mtoto*
disposable nappies/ diapers	*nepi*
(English-speaking) babysitter	*yaya (anayesema Kiingereza)*
highchair	*kiti juu cha mtoto*
potty	*choo cha mtoto*
stroller	*kigari cha mtoto*

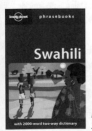

Also available from Lonely Planet:
Swahili Phrasebook

Glossary

The following are some common words that you are likely to come across when in Kenya. For a more complete glossary of food terms, see p94.

abanyamorigo – medicine man
askari – security guard, watchman

banda – thatched-roof hut with wooden or earthen walls or simple wood-and-stone accommodation
bao – traditional African board game
beach boys – self-appointed guides, touts, hustlers and dealers on the coast
boda-boda – bicycle taxi
boma – village
bui-bui – black cover-all garment worn by Islamic women outside the home

chai – tea, but also a bribe
chai masala – sweet tea with spices
chakula – food
chang'a – dangerous homemade alcoholic brew containing methyl alcohol
choo – toilet; pronounced 'cho'
Cites – UN Convention on International Trade in Endangered Species

dhow – traditional Arabic sailing vessel
dudu – a small insect or bug; a creepy-crawly
duka – small shop or kiosk selling household basics

fundi – repair man or woman who fixes clothing or cars, or is in the building trades; also an expert

gof – volcanic crater

hakuna matata – no problem; watch out – this often means there is a problem!
harambee – the concept of community self-help; voluntary fundraising; a cornerstone of Kenyatta's ideology
hatari – danger
hoteli – basic local eatery

idli – south Indian rice dumpling
ito – wooden 'eyes' to allow a dhow to see obstacles in the water

jinga! – crazy!; also used as an adjective
jua kali – literally 'fierce sun'; usually an outdoor vehicle-repair shop or market

kali – fierce or ferocious; eg *hatari mbwa kali* – 'danger fierce dog'
kanga – printed cotton wraparound incorporating a Swahili proverb; worn by many women both inside and outside the home
KANU – Kenya African National Union
KC – Kenya Cowboy, a young white male Kenyan
kikoi – striped cotton sarong traditionally worn by men
kiondo – woven basket
kitu kidogo – 'a little something'; a bribe
kofia – cap worn by Muslim men
KWS – Kenya Wildlife Service

Laibon – chief or spiritual leader of the Maasai; known as Olonana earlier, and Lenana today
lugga – dry river bed, mainly in northern Kenya

makonde – woodcarving style, originally from southern Tanzania
makuti – thatch made with palm leaves used for roofing buildings, mainly on the coast
malaya – prostitute
mandazi – semisweet, flat donut
manyatta – Maasai or Samburu livestock camp often surrounded by a circle of thorn bushes
mataha – mashed beans, potatoes, maize and green vegetables
matatu – once-feared public minibuses used throughout the country, now 'tamed' by new safety regulations
matoke – mashed plantains (green bananas)
mboga – vegetables
miraa – bundles of leafy twigs and shoots that are chewed as a stimulant and appetite suppressant
mkate mayai – fried, wheat pancake filled with minced meat and raw egg; literally 'bread eggs'
moran – Maasai or Samburu warrior (plural morani)
murram – dirt or part-gravel road
mursik – milk drink fermented with cow's urine and ashes
mwananchi – worker of any kind but usually agricultural (plural *wananchi*, which is also used to refer to 'the people')
mwizi – a thief
mzee – an old man or respected elder
mzee kipara – bald man; literally means 'mosquito airport'
mzungu – white person (plural *wazungu*)

Narc – National Rainbow Coalition
Ng'oroko – Turkana bandits
Nissan – see *matatu*

nyama choma – barbecued meat, often goat
Nyayo – a cornerstone of Moi's political ideology, literally meaning 'footsteps'; to follow in the footsteps of Jomo Kenyatta

panga – machete, carried by most people in the country-side and often by thieves in the cities
parking boys – unemployed youths or young men who will assist in parking a vehicle and guard it while the owner is absent
pesa – money
Peugeot – shared taxi
pombe – Kenyan beer, usually made with millet and sugar

rafiki – friend; as in 'my friend, you want safari?'
rondavel – circular hut, usually a thatched building with a conical roof

safari – 'journey' in Swahili
sambusa – deep-fried pastry triangles stuffed with spiced mince meat; similar to Indian samosa

shamba – small farm or plot of land
shifta – bandit
shilingi – money
shuka – Maasai blanket
sigana – traditional African performance form containing narration, song, music, dance, chant, ritual, mask, movement, banter and poetry
sis – white Kenyan slang for 'yuck'
siwa – ornately carved ivory wind instrument, unique to the coastal region and often used as a fanfare at weddings

Tusker – Kenyan beer

ugali – maize meal set hard and served in brick-shaped pieces
uhuru – freedom or independence

wa benzi – someone driving a Mercedes-Benz car bought with, it's implied, the proceeds of corruption
wananchi – workers or 'the people' (singular *mwananchi*)
wazungu – white people (singular *mzungu*)

Behind the Scenes

THIS BOOK

Hugh Finlay and Geoff Crowther researched and wrote the first three editions of Kenya and the fourth was updated by Matt Fletcher. The fifth edition was revised and updated by Joseph Bindloss and Tom Parkinson, with Sean Pywell contributing the Wildlife Guide. For this edition Tom Parkinson revisited Kenya, taking the helm and contributing front and end chapters as well as covering Nairobi, Around Nairobi, Southern Kenya and the Coast, while Matt Phillips covered countless kilometres in researching the Rift Valley, the Central Highlands, Western Kenya and Northern Kenya. Will Gourlay wrote the Snapshot chapter and updated the Culture, Tribes of Kenya and Food & Drink chapters.

This guidebook was commissioned in Lonely Planet's Melbourne office and was produced by the following:

Commissioning Editor Will Gourlay, Alan Murphy
Coordinating Editor Brooke Clark
Coordinating Cartographer Julie Dodkins
Coordinating Layout Designer Steven Cann
Managing Editor Melanie Dankel
Managing Cartographer Shahara Ahmed
Assisting Editors Helen Christinis, Bruce Evans, Justin Flynn, Carly Hall, Martin Heng, Evan Jones, Pat Kinsella, Danielle North, Stephanie Pearson, Simon Williamson
Assisting Cartographers Jack Gavran, Malisa Plesa, Amanda Sierp, Natasha Velleley, Jody Whiteoak
Assisting Layout Designers Jacqui Saunders
Cover Designer Jim Hsu
Colour Designer Vicki Beale

Project Manager Glenn van der Knijff, Rachel Imeson
Language Content Coordinator Quentin Frayne

Thanks to Carol Chandler, Sally Darmody, Jennifer Garrett, Adriana Mammarella, Kate McDonald, Raphael Richards, Celia Wood

THANKS
Tom Parkinson

A traditional *asanteni sana* to everyone who helped out and made this trip more pleasure than chore: Will G; Matt P; Nicholas; Sammy; Helen, Chelsea, Dex, Ian and Steve; everyone at New Florida; Line and Sara; Judy, Milan, Bree, Nadia, David, Monique, Penny, Crystal and Barry; Steven the lingala dancing man; Debbi, Lionel and friends; Paul (thanks for driving and black tie!), James, Daryl, Phil, Adele, Tessa and Carlos Rock Spider; Pop and Grev; Linzi, Boris and the Twits; Chris and Rowena; Daniel and Natasha; the Colobus volunteers; Ben at KMC; Erik, Kate, Sam, Caleb, Rachid, Patrick, Kamau, Swaleh and all at Casuarina; Isa, Djemba and the Shela boys; Malaria Boy and Blondie; and everyone at ZIFF. Tuskers all round next time we meet.

Special thanks to Rachel Fraser, Cleo, Patra and the Muffin Man for the inside dope on KCs, and *hej älskling* to Cecilia 'Pirate Queen' Ohlsson (Balsameringsfläder) for the lowdown on Lamu.

Matt Phillips

Thanks to: Georgina for your devotion, support, understanding and love; Will Gourlay for sending my butt back to Kenya; Tom Parkinson for your hard work on this title; Shahara Ahmed for your

---

THE LONELY PLANET STORY

The story begins with a classic travel adventure: Tony and Maureen Wheeler's 1972 journey across Europe and Asia to Australia. There was no useful information about the overland trail then, so Tony and Maureen published the first Lonely Planet guidebook to meet a growing need.

From a kitchen table, Lonely Planet has grown to become the largest independent travel publisher in the world, with offices in Melbourne (Australia), Oakland (USA) and London (UK). Today Lonely Planet guidebooks cover the globe. There is an ever-growing list of books and information in a variety of media. Some things haven't changed. The main aim is still to make it possible for adventurous travellers to get out there – to explore and better understand the world.

At Lonely Planet we believe travellers can make a positive contribution to the countries they visit – if they respect their host communities and spend their money wisely. Every year 5% of company profit is donated to charities around the world.

mapping support; everyone at Lonely Planet who worked behind the scenes to put out such a good book; Onesmus Kassim Katili for being the best driver and desert companion I could have hoped for; the Kenyan government for installing seatbelts and speed governors in matatus!; my mum and Bernie for their smiles and laughter; Dad and Vikki for teaching me to dream big; Pam for being my most ardent supporter; Margaret, Eunice, Alex, Bonnie, Lizzy and Rose for keeping me in their thoughts; my wonderful friends in Vancouver and London for always looking out for me; Kenya for opening her arms and always showing me her best side; and the wonderfully generous Kenyans who helped along the way.

OUR READERS

Many thanks to the hundreds of travellers who used the last edition and wrote to us with helpful hints, useful advice and interesting anecdotes:

A Husain Akbar, Marlene Anderson, Jesper Andersson, Ghislaine Annez, Jim Archer, Sharon Ashley **B** Helen Backlund, Helen Ball, Penny Barten, Rosanna Batista, Glenn Bewes, Sebastien Bigand, Katja Bloigu, Frederic Bonnet, Esther Bonrath, Danette Borg, Nathalie Brauns, Cristina Brecciaroli, Anja Brinch Jensen, Sue Britton, Vanessa Broes, Sarah Brown, Alberto Brusacà, Tina Buckley, Marleen Buis, Kelly Buja **C** Bruno Cassiers, Lynn Chen, Lisa Chothia, Ivar Christensen, Bharti Chudasama, Karolina Claesson, Bram Claeys, David Connell, Andy Cooper, Corrine Couto, Benedict Cox, Tom Craven, Pam Cunneyworth **D** Hans Daalen, Ruth & Ruben Dahm, Jane Davies, Alison Davis, Emma Davis, Chloe Day, Hugh de la Bedoyere, Bram de Rooij, Dixie Dean, Jan den Hollander, Tamsin Dewé, Gauri Divan, Terry Diver, Eveline Driessen, Caroline D'Souza, Mike Ducker, Natasha Duncan **E** Sean Earle, Reinier Ellenkamp, Tina Emmerich, Robert Eppinga **F** Grahame Finnigan, Ilya Fischhoff, Diodato Francesco **G** Paul & Ann Gates, Christophe Gimmler, Amy Givler, Ulf Goebel, Richard Goodwin **H** Simon Harby, Jon & Felicity Hart, Jane Hawes, Krissie Hayes, Jonathan Hayssen, Chris Heege, Peter & Koen Hendrix, Pippa & Jonathan Higgins, Paul Hill, Simon Hill, Booke Hixson, Marloes Hoebe, Ida Hogstedt, Cynthia Holmes, Florian Hugenberg, Carolien Hulshof, John Hutson, Jonathan Hyatt **I** Anna Ireland **J** Ben Jansen, Vicky Johnson, Glenn Jolly, Whitney Justin **K** Hanne Kaergaard, Jen Kayes, Caroline Kilga, Numbere Kingbo, Mathew Kipturgo, Christel Koehler, Linda Koeppel **L** Howard Lambert, Kylie Laxton-Blinkhorn, Vanesa Lee, Rosemary Leffelaar, Ashley Leigh, Yvette Lievens, Gideon Liniger **M** Geralyn Macfadyen, Jim Macfarlane, Z Maler, Jessica Mantooth, Dan Mark, Perry Martin, Tom Martin, Sylvia Massy, Melinda McCann, Stephen McElhinney, Dick Meijer, Mark Meulenbroeks, Akhil Monappa, Chris & Sandy Morgan, Dave Moser, Sukumar Mukherji, Allen Murphy, Jonathan Mwangi **N** Hilary Newmark, Helen Nowak, Dominic Nurre **O** Ingmar Ohrn, Charlotte Birk Olsen, Lise Ørskov, Owen Ozier **P** Meryl Pannaci, Tapan Parekh, Fabienne Passerini, Penny Piddock **R** Mary Ralston, Benjamin Randell, Peter Rawcliffe, Cliff Richards, Pamela Riley, Christy Robinson, Mandy Romanowski, Paul Roos, Darren Rose, Richard Russell **S** Beth Schaeffer, Hedwig Seidl, Douglas Selinger, Nixsha Shaw, Xia Shen, Nick Silver, Johannes Starostzik, Robert L & Donna Starr, Simon Stevens, Claudia Straessle, John Strong **T** Jackie Taylor, Darla Tenold, Lisa Thacker, Richard Thimbleby, Marc Timmins, Nadia Tjong Ayong, Shauna Todd, Andrew Towne, Ran Trilessky **V** Lauretta Vaassen, Marsha van Bladeren, Bart van den Eijnden, Natasja van Dulmen, Janneke van Eldonk, Russ van Horn, Henny van Lanen, Tamara van Leeuwarden, Brigitta van Niel, Evert Vandenbergh, Sharon Vincin, Nanda Visser, Michi Vojta, Godela Von Döhren, Holger & Steffi von und zu Harms **W** Dave Wall, Andy Ward, Hannah Ward, Karen Ward-Kavita, Stephen Waterbrook, Leann Webb, Valerie Werkhoven, Lotte Wevers, Lorna Whitfield, David & Rayna Wigglesworth, Martin Willoughby-Thomas, Jan Wirix, Ben Wisdom, Orawan Wongcharoen, Hayley Wood, Chris & Denise Wright **Y** Amy Yates **Z** Kelly Zabes

ACKNOWLEDGEMENTS

Many thanks to the following for the use of their content:
Globe on back cover ©Mountain High Maps 1993 Digital Wisdom, Inc.

SEND US YOUR FEEDBACK

We love to hear from travellers – your comments keep us on our toes and help make our books better. Our well-travelled team reads every word on what you loved or loathed about this book. Although we cannot reply individually to postal submissions, we always guarantee that your feedback goes straight to the appropriate authors, in time for the next edition. Each person who sends us information is thanked in the next edition – and the most useful submissions are rewarded with a free book. See the Behind the Scenes section.

To send us your updates – and find out about Lonely Planet events, newsletters and travel news – visit our award-winning website: **www.lonelyplanet.com/feedback**.

Note: We may edit, reproduce and incorporate your comments in Lonely Planet products· such as guidebooks, websites and digital products, so let us know if you don't want your comments reproduced or your name acknowledged. For a copy of our privacy policy, go to www.lonelyplanet.com/privacy.

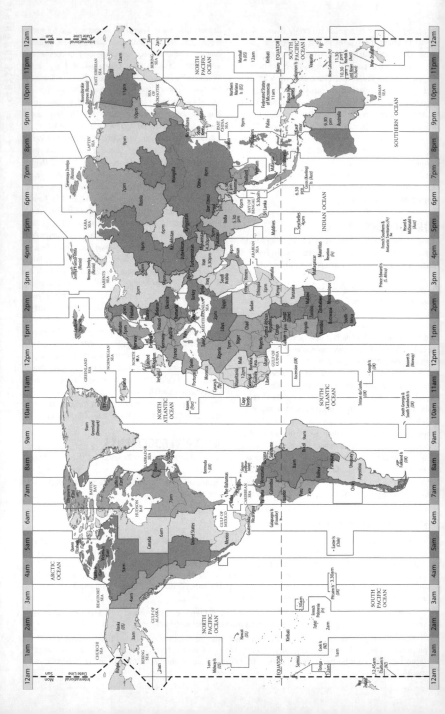

Index

A

aardwolf 78, *78*
Aberdare National Park 256-9, **257**, *186*
Aberdares 253-61
accommodation 345-8
    African Safari Club 346
    bandas 346
    beach resorts 346-7
    camping 347
    hostels 347
    hotels & guesthouses 347-8
    rental houses 347
    safari lodges 347-8
    tented camps 347-8
activities 348-50, *see also individual activities*
Adamson, Joy & George 104, 234-5
African Heritage House 128-30
Africans 37, *see also tribes*
air travel 369-73, 376
    airlines 370, 376
    airports 369
    tickets 370
    to/from Kenya 369-73
    within Kenya 376
Akamba people 37, 43
altitude sickness 261
Amboseli National Park 137-9, **138**, *190*
American Embassy Memorial Garden 106
animals 52, 73-88, *see also individual animals*
antelope
    roan 85, *85*
    sable 85, 169, *85*
Arabuko Sokoke Forest Reserve 201-2
archaeological sites
    Gede ruins 202-5, **204**
    history 25
    Hyrax Hill Prehistoric Site 243
    Jumba la Mtwana 195
    Kariandusi Prehistoric Site 239
    Mnarani 196-7
    Nabahani ruins 226
    Olorgasailie Prehistoric Site 141

    Sibiloi National Park 338
    Takwa ruins 226
    Thimlich Ohinga 297
Archer's Post 323-4
art galleries 105, 106-7
arts 40-2, *see also individual arts*
Athi River 131-2
ATMs 360

B

baboon 75, 138, 243, 286, 312, *75*
Baden-Powell Museum 254
ballooning 288, 348
Bamburi Beach
    accommodation 193
    nightclubs 194
    restaurants 193
banditry 353-4
Baragoi 335
bat-eared fox 76, *76*
beaches
    Bamburi Beach 184-94
    Diani Beach 172-8, **171**
    Kikambala 195-6
    Kilifi 196-8, **197**
    Manda Beach 226, **206**
    Mtwapa 195
    north of Mombasa 181-212, **183**
    Nyali Beach 182-4
    Shanzu Beach 194-5
    Shela 222-5
    Shelly Beach 169
    Tiwi Beach 170-2, **171**
    Vipingo 195-6
    Watamu 198-201, **199**, **202**, *7*, *188*
bird-watching 143
    Central Highlands 256, 274, 279, 281
    coast, the 169, 199, 202
    northern Kenya 342
    Rift Valley 234, 243, 246, 248
    western Kenya 296, 297, 310, 312, 315
Bissel 136-7
black market 360
Blixen, Karen 127
boat travel
    to/from Kenya 375
    within Kenya 377, 382

boda-bodas 382
Bomas of Kenya 124-5
books 16, *see also* literature
    animals 145
    culture 38
    environmental 51
    history 28, 30
    photographic 16
    travel 15
    trekking 261
    wildlife 52
Borana people 43
border crossings 373-5
buffalo 84, *84*
    around Nairobi 125
    Central Highlands 253, 256, 275, 279, 281
    northern Kenya 321
    Rift Valley 237, 239, 243, 246
    southern Kenya 138, 140, 143
    western Kenya 286, 312, 327
Buffalo Springs National Reserve 324-7, **325**, *190*, *192*
bus travel
    costs 378
    reservations 378
    to/from Kenya 373
    within Kenya 377-8, 382
bushbaby 74, *74*
bushbuck 83, *83*
Busia 309
business hours 350-1
Butterfly Africa 127

C

cape clawless otter 77, *77*
car travel 378-82
    driving licence 379
    insurance 381
    road rules 381-2
    safety 381
    to/from Kenya 373
    within Kenya 378-82
caracal 79, *79*
carving 57, 140, 299
cash, *see* money
Central Highlands 251-82, **252**, *185*
Central Island National Park 343
chang'a 91

cheetah 80, 125, 138, 237, 279, 286, 4, 80
Cherangani Hills 315, 339
children, travel with 351-2
Chogoria 279-82
Christian churches 159
Christianity 38
Chyulu Hills National Park 140-2, 186
cinema 42, 118, see also film
circumcision, male 303
climate 352-3
climbing 350, see also trekking
coast, the 151-228, **153**
coffee 90-1
  production 254
conservation 233
consulates 355-6
costs 15, 62
courses 353
credit cards 360-1
crime 354, see also safe travel
crocodiles 279
culture 35-42, 43-50
  dress 35
  family 36
  Swahili 26, 152, 202-5, 213-15
  women in Kenya 324
customs regulations 353
cycling 184, 246, 348, 376

D
da Gama, Vasco 26, 207
dance 42
dangers, see safe travel
David Sheldrick Wildlife Trust 127-8
dhow trips 377
  coast, the 161, 174, 179, 180, 216-17, 225, 228
Diani Beach 172-8, **171**
  accommodation 175-7
  activities 174
  attractions 173-4
  entertainment 178
  organised tours 174
  restaurants 177-8
  safe travel 173
  special events 175
dik-dik 88, 145, **88**
disabled travellers 355
diving 348-9
  coast, the 174, 180, 208, 223
dolphin spotting 179, 180
drinks 90-2
driving licence 379

dudu 145
duiker 84, **84**

E
East African Safari Rally 37, 357
economy 36
education 35, 306
El Karama Ranch 275
eland 83, 140, 234, 237, 239, 274, 279, **83**
Eldoret 306-8, **307**
electricity 345
elephant 80, **80**
  Central Highlands 256, 275, 279, 281
  coast, the 169, 170
  northern Kenya 324, 326, 327
  southern Kenya 138, 140, 143, 145
  western Kenya 286
Eliye Springs 342
El-Molo people 37, 44, 336, **44**
Elsamere Conservation Centre 234-5
embassies 355-6
Embu 37, 280-1, **280**
environmental issues 55-8, 290
  conservation 233
  deforestation 239, 246
  education 304, 310
  endangered species 52
  farming 247
  private conservation 56-7
  tsunami 51
  vegetation 138
  wildlife conservation 55-7, 272, 278, 322, 323, 326, 327
equator 272
Ethiopia 330, 331-6
exchange rates, see inside front cover

F
falconry 174, 208
Faza 227
female genital mutilation 39
Ferguson's Gulf 342-3
festivals 218-19, 357,
  see also special events
  Kenya Fashion Week 107
  Kenya Music Festival 107
  Lamu Cultural Festival 219
  Maulid Festival 357
  Mombasa Carnival 162
film 16, 29, 31, 42, 145,
  see also cinema
fishing 180, 199, 200, 208, 223, 258, 312, 349

flying lessons 349
food 89-90, 94, 163-6
  glossary 94
  vegetarian 93
Fort Jesus 26
Forum for the Restoration of Democracy (FORD) 31-2

G
Gabbra people 44-5, 338
Galla 37
gay travellers 357-8
  Lamu 215
gazelle 88, **88**
  Central Highlands 253, 279
  Nairobi 125
  Rift Valley 234, 237, 239, 243, 246
  southern Kenya 138
  western Kenya 286
Gede ruins 202-5, **204**
genet 77
geography 51, 230
giraffe 82, **82**
  around Nairobi 125
  Central Highlands 253, 275, 279
  northern Kenya 324
  Rift Valley 234, 237
  southern Kenya 138, 140
  western Kenya 286, 297
gliding 254, 349-50
glossary 400-1
golf 174
Gusii people 37, 45, 299

H
haggling 363
Harambee 341
hartebeest 86, 253, 286, **86**
health 385-94
  books 386-7
  HIV/AIDS 36, 357, 389
  insurance 385-6
  internet resources 385, 386
  malaria 157, 389-90, 391
  vaccinations 385
Hell's Gate National Park 237-8
Hindu temples 159
Hinduism 38-9
Hippo Point 235-6, 293,
  see also hippopotamus
hippopotamus 82, 143, 145, 235, 239, 243, 275, 281, 286, **82**
history 25-34, 96, 152
  ancient 25, 34, 131
  Arabs & Persians 25-6, 152, 213

history *continued*
British colonialism 27-8, 156
early settlement 25
Fort Jesus 26
independence 30
Leakey family 33, 34
Mau Mau rebellion 29-30
Moi years, the 31-3
Omani Arabs 27, 152, 158
Portuguese 26, 152, 154-6, 157-8, 227
white settlement 28
hitching 321, 382
holidays 358
Homa Bay 296-7
honey badger 77, **77**
hot springs 131, 246, 314
hyena 78, 138, 256, 286, **78**
hyrax 81, 243, **81**

I
immigration 37-8
impala 88, 239, 293, **88**
independence 30, 37, 252
insurance 358-9
Internet access 359
Internet resources 15-17, 56, 58, 90
Isiolo 319-21, **321**
Islam 38-9
islands
Funzi Island 179
Kiwayu Island 228
Lamu 213-22
Manda Island 225-6
Mfangano Island 298-9
Paté Island 226-7
Rusinga Island 297-8
Wasini Island 179-81
itineraries 18-23, 71-2
activities 23, **23**
authors' favourite trips 12, **12**
Classic Kenya 19, **19**
coast, the 18, **18**
desert 20, **20**
national parks 22, **22**
safaris 71-2
tribal tour 23, **23**
walking tour 22, **22**
western wetlands 21, **21**

000 Map pages
000 Photograph pages

J
jackals 76, 138, **76**

K
Kabarnet 309
KADU 30
Kakamega 303-4
Kakamega Forest Reserve 304-6, **305**
Kalacha 338-9, **6**
Kalenjin people 37, 45
Kampi ya Samaki 248
KANU 31-2
Karen 124-34, **125**
accommodation 128
entertainment 130
restaurants 129-30
Karen Blixen Museum 127, *see also* Blixen, Karen
kayas 160
Kendu Bay 296
Kenya African Democratic Union 30
Kenya African National Union 31-2
Kenya African Union 29
Kenya Wildlife Service 55-6, 58, 125
Kenyatta Conference Centre 106
Kenyatta, Jomo 28-34
Kericho 300-2, **302**
Kerio Valley National Reserve 309-10
Kiambu 133
Kibaki, Mwai 33
Kikuyu people 37, 45-6, 252
Kilifi 196-7, **197**
Kimana Wildlife Sanctuary 139-40
Kipepeo butterfly farm 205
Kipungani 225, **7**
Kisii 299-300, **299**, **189**
Kisite Marine National Park 180-1
Kisumu 290-6, **292**
accommodation 293-4
attractions 292-3
bars 295
internet access 291
medical services 291
safe travel 292
travel to/from 295-6
travel within 296
Kisumu Bird Sanctuary 293
Kitale 310-12, **311**, **185**
kitesurfing 174
Kiwayu Island 228
klipspringer 87, 246, **87**
kudu 83, 246, 247, **83**
KWS 55-6, 58, 125

L
Lake Baringo 247-50, **247**, **187**
Lake Bogoria National Reserve 246-7, **247**, **187**
Lake Challa 150
Lake Elmenteita 239
Lake Kamnarok National Reserve 310
Lake Magadi 131, **186**
Lake Naivasha 233-7, **234**
Lake Nakuru National Park 243-5, **244**, **6**, **190**
Lake Turkana 332-44
Lake Victoria 290-8
Lamu 213-22, **214**, **218**, **189**
accommodation 219-20
activities 216-19
attractions 215-16
entertainment 221
festivals 218-19
Internet access 215
medical services 215
restaurants 220-1
safe travel 215
travel to/from 222
travel within 222
walking tour 217-18
Lamu archipelago 212-28, **223**, **7**
Langata 124-30, **125**
Langata Giraffe Centre 128
language 395-9
food vocabulary 94
Leakey family 33, 34, 55, 239, 338
legal matters 359
Lekurruki 322-4
leopard 79, **79**
around Nairobi 125
Central Highlands 256, 275, 279
coast, the 169
northern Kenya 321, 324, 329
Rift Valley 237, 243, 246
southern Kenya 143
western Kenya 286
lesbian travellers 357-8
Lesiolo 335
Lewa Wildlife Conservancy 321-2
Limuru 133-4
lion 80, **80**
around Nairobi 125
Central Highlands 274, 275, 279
northern Kenya 327
Rift Valley 237
southern Kenya 138, 140, 143, 145
literature 41-2, *see also* books
Lodwar 340-2
Loitokitok 140

Lokichoggio 343-4
Longonot National Park 231
Loyangalani 336-8
Lumo Community Wildlife
    Sanctuary 150
Lunga Lunga 181
Luo people 37, 46-7
Luyha people 37, 46, 303

M
Maasai people 27, 28, 37, 47-8, 286,
    5, 47
Machakos 132-3, **133**
Makindu 140
Makindu Handicraft Cooperative
    Society 140
Malaba 309
Malindi 205-12, **206**
    accommodation 208-10
    attractions 207-8
    emergency services 205
    entertainment 211
    Internet access 205
    organised tours 208
    restaurants 210-11
    safe travel 207
    tourist information 207
Malindi Marine National Park 207-8,
    187
Mamba Village Crocodile Farm 182
Manda Island 225-6
maps 359-60
Marafa Depression 212
Maralal 332-5, **333**
Marich Pass 339-40
marine parks
    Kisite Marine National P
        Park 180-1
    Malindi Marine National Park
        207-8, **187**
    Mombasa Marine Park 184
    Mpunguti Marine National
        Reserve 180
    Watamu Marine National Park 199
Marsabit 327-9, **328**
Marsabit National Park 329-30, **330**
Masai Mara National Reserve 285-90,
    287, 8, 185, 187, 191, 192
matatus 382-3
Matondoni 225
Matthews Range 327
Mau Forest 246
Mau Mau rebellion 252
Maulid Festival 357
Mbita 297-8

Mboya, Tom 46, 298
Menengai Crater 242-3
Meru 275-7, **276**
Meru National Park 277-9, **278**
Meru people 37, 48
metric conversions, *see inside front*
    cover
Mfangano Island 298-9
Mijikenda people 37, 160
miraa 275, 277
Moi, Daniel arap 31-3
Mombasa 154-68, **155, 158, 189**
    accommodation 162-3
    activities 159-62
    attractions 157-60
    bars 166
    emergency services 156
    entertainment 166
    festivals 162
    Fort Jesus 157-9
    Internet resources 156
    medical services 156-7
    Old Town 154, 160-1, **161**
    safe travel 157
    shopping 166-7
    tourist offices 157
    tours 161-2
    travel to/from 167-8
    travel within 168-70
    walking tour 160-1, **161**
Mombasa Marine Park 184
money 15, 355, 360-8, *see also inside*
    front cover
    safety 354
moneychangers 361
mongoose 78, **78**
monkeys 279
    blue (samango) 74, **74**
    colobus 75, 173, 174, 235, 281,
        312, **75**
    vervet 74, **74**
mosques 106, 159, 160-1, 173, 195,
    196, 203, 207, 218, 227
motorcycle travel 378-82,
    see also car travel
    safety 381
    to/from Kenya 373
    within Kenya 378-82
Mt Elgon National Park 312-15,
    313
Mt Kenya National Park 261-9, **263,**
    266, 271, 6, 8
    accommodation 264
    Chogoria route 269
    clothing & equipment 262-3

    food 264-9
    Naro Moru route 267-8
    organised tours 264-5
    Sirimon route 268
    Summit circuit 269
Mt Kilimanjaro 137
Mt Kulal 337
Mt Susa 231
Moyale 330-2, **331**
Mpunguti Marine National
    Reserve 180
Mtwapa 195
museums
    Baden-Powell Museum 254
    German Post Office 216
    Kisumu 292-3
    Kitale 310
    Lamu 215-16
    Railway Museum 105-6
    Swahili House 216
music 40-1
    African 40
    hip-hop 41
    rap 41

N
Nairobi 95-122, **98-9, 102-3, 104,**
    124, 5, 188
    accommodation 107-11
    activities 106-7
    attractions 104-6
    bars 116-17
    cafés 116
    cinemas 118
    emergency services 97
    events 107
    festivals 107
    history 96
    live music 118
    medical services 99-100
    nightclubs 117-18
    restaurants 111-16
    safe travel 101-4, 105
    shopping 119
    theatre 118-19
    tourist information 101
    tours 107
    travel to/from 119-21
    travel within 120-2
Nairobi National Park 125-7, **126, 192**
Nairobi's southern outskirts 124-31
Naivasha 231-3
NAK 33
Nakuru 239-42, **240**
Namanga 137

Nanyuki 272-4, **273**
Narc 34
Naro Moru 270-1
Narok 285-6
Nasolot National Reserve 339
National Alliance Party of Kenya 33
National Archives 105
National Museum 104-5
national parks & reserves 53-5,
   see also marine parks, wildlife
   sanctuaries
   Aberdare National Park 256-9,
      257, 186
   Amboseli National Park 137-9,
      138, 190, 191
   Arabuko Sokoke Forest
      Reserve 201-2
   Buffalo Springs National Reserve
      324-7, **325**, 190, 192
   Central Island National Park 343
   Chyulu Hills National Park 140-2
   Hell's Gate National Park
      237-8, **238**
   Kakamega Forest Reserve
      304-6, **305**
   Kerio Valley National Reserve
      309-10
   Lake Baringo National Reserve
      247-50, **247**, 187
   Lake Bogoria National Reserve
      246-7, **247**, 187
   Lake Kamnarok National
      Reserve 310
   Lake Nakuru National Park 243-5,
      244, 6, 190
   Longonot National Park 231
   Marsabit National Park 329-30, **330**
   Masai Mara National Reserve
      285-90, **287**, 8, 185, 187,
      191, 192
   Meru National Park 277-9, **278**
   Mt Elgon National Park
      312-15, **313**
   Mt Kenya National Park 261-9,
      263, 6, 8
   Mwea National Reserve 281
   Nairobi National Park 125-7,
      126, 192
   Nasolot National Reserve 339
   Ndere Island National Park 293
   Ol Donyo Sabuk National Park 281-2

Ruma National Park 297
Saiwa Swamp National Park 315
Samburu National Reserve 324-7,
   325, 191, 192
Shaba National Reserve 324-7
Shimba Hills National Reserve
   169-70
Sibiloi National Park 338
South Island National Park 336-7
South Turkana National
   Reserve 339
Naivasha 231-3, **232**
National Rainbow Coalition 134
Ndere Island National Park 293
Ndoto Mountains 327
newspapers 345
Ngong Hills 130-1
Ngulia Rhino Sanctuary 143
northern Kenya 316-44, **318**
Nyahururu 259-61, **260**
Nyali Beach 182-4
nyama choma 89
Nyeri 253-6, **255**
   accommodation 254-5
   attractions 253-4
   bars 256
   food 255-6

O
Ol Donyo Sbauk National Park 281-2
Olaf Palme Agroforestry Centre 310
Olorgasailie Prehistoric Site 131
organised tours 161-2, 248,
   264-5, 288
oryx 86, 253, 279, **86**
ostrich 125

P
pangolin 75, **75**
parliament house 106
passports 369
Paté Island 226-7
photography 361-2
planning 14-17, 355,
   see also itineraries
   health 385
   holidays 358
   safaris 59-64
plants 53
Pokot 37
Pokot people 37, 48
politics 24
pollution 233
population 36
postal services 362-3

R
radio 345
Railway Museum 105-6
reedbuck 85, 243, **85**
religion 38-9
Rendille people 37, 48-9, 329, **48**
restaurants 294-5
rhinoceros 81, 128, 143, 243, 253,
   256, 258, 274, 278, 286, **81**
Rift Valley 229-50, **230**, 185
road distances **378**
rock-climbing 143, 248
Rukinga Wildlife Conservancy 149
Ruma National Park 297
Rusinga Island 297-8

S
safaris 59-72, 384
   animal spotting 61
   bird-watching 67
   camel 67-8
   camping 64-6
   cultural 68
   cycling 70-1
   do-it-yourself 72
   fishing 68-9
   flying 69
   itineraries 71-2
   Lake Turkana 69
   lodge & tented-camp safaris 66-7
   minimal impact 66
   motorcycle 70
   planning 59-64
   truck 70
   walking 70-1
safe travel 353-5
   coast, the 169
   Kisumu 292
   Lamu 215
   Malindi 207
   Mt Kenya 261
   Nairobi 101-4, 105
   northern Kenya 317, 343
   Rift Valley 235
Sagala Hills 149
sailing 159-60, 349-50
Saiwa Swamp National Park 315
Samburu National Reserve 324-7,
   325, 191, 192
Samburu people 37, 49, 332, **49**
scams 354-5
senior travellers 355, 363
serval 79, **79**
Shaba National Reserve 324-7
Shela 222-5

Shela Beach 222-3
Shetani lava flow & caves 142
Shimba Hills National
    Reserve 169-70
Shimoni 179-81
shopping 363-4
Sibiloi National Park 338
Sigana 41
Siyu 227
snorkelling 174, 179, 180, 199, 207,
    223, 226, 348-9
soda lakes 131
Solio Game Reserve 253-4
solo travellers 364
Somali people 37, 49, 329
South Horr 335-6
South Island National Park 336-7
South Turkana National
    Reserve 339
southern Kenya 135-50, **136**
special events 258, 322, 334, 357
    Diani Rules 175
    East Africa Safari Rally 37, 357
    Rhino Charge 258
    Tusker Safari Sevens 107
sports 36-7, 130-1, 162, see also
    individual sports
    Diani Rules 175
    East African Safari Rally 37
    Moi Stadium 37
    Tusker Safari Sevens 107
steenbok 87, **87**
Swahili people 37, 50

T
Taita Hills 149-50
Taita Hills Game Reserve 149-50
Takwa ruins 226
Tana River 212-13
Taveta 150
tea plantations 301
telephone services 194, 365
terrorism 32, 96, 355
theatre 42
Thika 282
Thimlich Ohinga 297
Thomson's Falls, see Nyahururu
Timau 275
time 365, **403**
tipping 361
Tiwi Beach 170-2, **171**
toilets 365-6
topi 86, **86**
tourist information 366
tours, see organised tours

trade 132, 154, 205
    ivory 213
    slaves 26, 27, 152, 213
    spice 26, 27, 37, 152
traditional beliefs 39-40
train travel 384
    Uganda Railway 37, 384
travellers cheques 361
trekking 350
    books 261
    Central Highlands 257, 261-9,
        280, 282
    northern Kenya 335, 337, 339
    Rift Valley 231, 242
    western Kenya 309, 314, 315
tribes 37, 43-50, see also individual
    tribes
Tsavo East National
    Park 145 -7, **141**
Tsavo National Park 142-7, **141**
Tsavo West National
    Park 143-5, **141**
tuk-tuks 384
Turkana people 37, 50, 336, 342,
    343, **5**, **50**
TV 345

U
Uganda Railway 37, 384
Utamaduni 127

V
vaccinations 386-7
vegetarian travellers 93
video systems 345, 361
visas 366-7, see also passports
Voi 147-8, **148**
volcanoes 142, 231, 237, 242, 312,
    327, 336, 343

W
walks 106, 179, see also trekking
    around Mt Kenya 270
    coast, the 169, 173, 184, 202,
        203-5, 217-18, **161**, **218**
    Nairobi safari walk 125
    northern Kenya 323, 328, 336
    western Kenya 288, 301,
        304, 310
warthog 82, 125, 138, 243, 286, **82**
Wasini Island 179-81
Watamu 198-201, **199**, **202**, **7**, **188**
Watamu Marine National Park 199
water sports 350, see also individual
    sports

waterbuck 84, 145, 234, 279, **84**
water-skiing 223
weights & measures 345
western highlands 298-315
western Kenya 283-315, **284**
white-water rafting 350
wild dog 76, **76**
wildebeests 87, 138, 140,
    286, **87**
wildlife sanctuaries
    Bio Ken Snake Farm &
        Laboratory 198
    Crater Lake Sanctuary 234
    Crescent Island 234
    David Sheldrick Wildlife Trust
        127-8
    donkey sanctuary 216
    Haller Park 184
    impala sanctuary 293
    Kigio Wildlife
        Conservancy 238-9
    Kimana Wildlife
        Sanctuary 139-40
    Kisumu Bird Sanctuary 293
    Lewa Wildlife Conservancy 321-2
    Lumo Community Wildlife
        Sanctuary 150
    Malindi Crocodile Farm
        & Snake Park 208
    Mwaluganje Elephant
        Sanctuary 170
    Ndere Island National Park 293
    Ngulia Rhino Sanctuary 143
    Nguuni Wildlife
        Sanctuary 184
    Ol Pejata Conservancy 274
    Rukinga Wildlife
        Conservancy 149
    Sanctuary 150
    Solio Game Reserve 253-4
    Tana River National Primate
        Reserve 212, 213
windsurfing 174, 223
women in kenya 39-40
women travellers 364, 367
work 367-8

Z
zebra 81, **73**, **81**
    around Nairobi 125
    Central Highlands 275, 279
    northern Kenya 324
    Rift Valley 237, 239
    southern Kenya 138, 140, 143
    western Kenya 286

INDEX

MAP LEGEND

ROUTES

Tollway	One-Way Street
Freeway	Street Mall/Steps
Primary Road	Tunnel
Secondary Road	Walking Tour
Tertiary Road	Walking Tour Detour
Lane	Walking Trail
Under Construction	Walking Path
Track	Pedestrian Overpass
Unsealed Road	

TRANSPORT

Ferry	Rail
Metro	Rail (Underground)
Bus Route	Tram

HYDROGRAPHY

River, Creek	Canal
Intermittent River	Water
Swamp	Lake (Dry)
Mangrove	Lake (Salt)
Reef	Mudflats

BOUNDARIES

State, Provincial	Regional, Suburb
Marine Park	Cliff

AREA FEATURES

Airport	Mall
Area of Interest	Market
Beach, Desert	Park
Building	Reservation
Campus	Rocks
Cemetery, Christian	Sports
Forest	Urban
Land	

POPULATION

CAPITAL (NATIONAL)	CAPITAL (STATE)
Large City	Medium City
Small City	Town, Village

SYMBOLS

Sights/Activities
Beach
Castle, Fortress
Christian
Diving, Snorkelling
Islamic
Jewish
Monument
Museum, Gallery
Point of Interest
Pool
Ruin
Skiing
Surfing, Surf Beach
Trail Head
Winery, Vineyard
Zoo, Bird Sanctuary

Eating
Eating

Drinking
Drinking
Café

Entertainment
Entertainment

Shopping
Shopping

Sleeping
Sleeping
Camping

Transport
Airport, Airfield
Bus Station
Cycling, Bicycle Path
General Transport
Parking Area
Petrol Station
Taxi Rank

Information
Bank, ATM
Embassy/Consulate
Hospital, Medical
Information
Internet Facilities
Police Station
Post Office, GPO
Telephone
Toilets

Geographic
Lighthouse
Lookout
Mountain, Volcano
National Park
Pass, Canyon
Picnic Area
River Flow
Waterfall

LONELY PLANET OFFICES

Australia
Head Office
Locked Bag 1, Footscray, Victoria 3011
☎ 03 8379 8000, fax 03 8379 8111
talk2us@lonelyplanet.com.au

USA
150 Linden St, Oakland, CA 94607
☎ 510 893 8555, toll free 800 275 8555
fax 510 893 8572
info@lonelyplanet.com

UK
72-82 Rosebery Ave,
Clerkenwell, London EC1R 4RW
☎ 020 7841 9000, fax 020 7841 9001
go@lonelyplanet.co.uk

Published by Lonely Planet Publications Pty Ltd
ABN 36 005 607 983

© Lonely Planet Publications Pty Ltd 2006

© photographers as indicated 2006

Cover photographs by Lonely Planet Images: A Samburu warrior from Maralal, Tom Crockrem (front); Safari van at sunset, Christer Fredriksson (back). Many of the images in this guide are available for licensing from Lonely Planet Images: www.lonelyplanetimages.com.

Printed through Colorcraft Ltd, Hong Kong.
Printed in China